D0773180

CAPTIVE NATION

JUSTICE, POWER, AND POLITICS

Coeditors
Heather Ann Thompson   Rhonda Y. Williams

Editorial Advisory Board
Peniel E. Joseph   Barbara Ransby
Matthew D. Lassiter   Vicki L. Ruiz
Daryl Maeda   Marc Stein

The Justice, Power, and Politics series publishes new works in history that explore the myriad struggles for justice, battles for power, and shifts in politics that have shaped the United States over time. Through the lenses of justice, power, and politics, the series seeks to broaden scholarly debates about America's past as well as to inform public discussions about its future.

More information on the series, including a complete list of books published, is available at http://justicepowerandpolitics.com/.

CAPTIVE NATION

BLACK PRISON ORGANIZING
IN THE CIVIL RIGHTS ERA

Dan Berger

The University of North Carolina Press | Chapel Hill

This book was published with the assistance of the
John Hope Franklin Fund of the University of North Carolina Press.

© 2014 THE UNIVERSITY OF NORTH CAROLINA PRESS

All rights reserved. Manufactured in the United States of America.
Set in Calluna by codeMantra. The paper in this book meets the guidelines
for permanence and durability of the Committee on Production Guidelines for Book
Longevity of the Council on Library Resources. The University of North Carolina
Press has been a member of the Green Press Initiative since 2003.

Jacket illustration: The Soledad Brothers being transported from court, 1970.
Photo by Dan O'Neil.

Complete cataloging information can be obtained online at the
Library of Congress catalog website.

ISBN 978-1-4696-1824-1 (cloth: alk. paper)
ISBN 978-1-4696-1825-8 (ebook)

18 17 16 15 14   5 4 3 2 1

Part of chapter 5 has been reprinted with permission in revised
form from "Carceral Migrations: Black Power and Slavery in 1970s
California Prison Radicalism," in *The Rising Tide of Color: Race, State
Violence, and Radical Movements across the Pacific*, ed. Moon-Ho Jung
(Seattle: University of Washington Press, 2014), 213–36.

ALSO BY DAN BERGER

Letters from Young Activists: Today's Rebels Speak Out (coeditor, 2005)

Outlaws of America: The Weather Underground and the Politics of Solidarity (2006)

The Hidden 1970s: Histories of Radicalism (editor, 2010)

*The Struggle Within: Prisons, Political Prisoners, and Mass Movements
in the United States* (2014)

IN MEMORY OF

Marilyn Buck (1947–2010),
Dara Greenwald (1971–2012), and
Stephanie M. H. Camp (1968–2014),
loving and beloved friends, dedicated dreamers, visionary artists
who gave us all a glimpse of a more perfect world.

And for those who, in their tradition,
create with purpose and passion.

So it was that, to the Negro, going to jail was no longer a disgrace
but a badge of honor. The Revolution of the Negro not only attacked
the external cause of his misery, but revealed him to himself. He was
somebody. He had a sense of *somebodiness*. He was *impatient* to be free.

—MARTIN LUTHER KING JR., *Why We Can't Wait* (1963)

At first, you were coons, darkies, colored, niggers, Negroes;
then we became crime in the streets.

—AUDLEY "QUEEN MOTHER" MOORE, interview (1972)

They tell us that the prisons are overpopulated.
But what if it were the population that were being over-imprisoned?

—MICHEL FOUCAULT, press conference (1971)

Contents

Illustrations

Preface

I first went to prison at age nineteen. It was the spring of 2001, and the United States had passed a dystopic milestone one year earlier: more than two million people were now incarcerated in prisons and jails around the country, a higher rate of incarceration and a higher number of people in prison than anywhere else on the planet. Unlike the thousands of other teenagers who went to prison that year, however, my trip was voluntary and brief. I was just a visitor. I was a sophomore in college, interested in social movement history and just beginning to get passionate about school. Ninety miles from my small-town college campus was a maximum-security federal prison that held a former member of the Black Panther Party who had been incarcerated since 1973. My first time inside, I tried to notice all the details—the gun towers surrounding the prison and the perennials cracking through the sidewalk leading up to it, the concertina wire guarding us and the vending machines feeding us. It was just another high-tech institution in our dotcom world—except it wasn't that at all.

Once inside, we had a grand time laughing, talking politics, and eating overpriced chips and popcorn. During my visit, I learned about life in the Black Panther Party and life in a federal penitentiary. I was learning, in fact, a deeper history of the intersection of black protest and state repression. It was the story not just of state violence but of alternate worldviews, a fact made plain by the letters Veronza Bower sent me, which were dated "ADJ." The first letter I received from him was dated "30 years 231 days ADJ AKA 22 March 2001." I learned that ADJ stood for "After the Death of Jonathan Jackson," the seventeen-year-old brother of radical prisoner and author George Jackson. Both Jacksons died bloody deaths at the hands of the California prison system, Jonathan in an August 1970 attempt to free three prisoners from a Marin County trial and George a year later during a takeover of San Quentin's solitary confinement unit. After Jonathan was killed, George wrote that his brother's death marked a new phase of time—a tradition that some dissident prisoners continued to honor more than thirty years later. At the time, I knew little about George Jackson, but I was beginning to learn the parallel cosmology of prison organizing. Because the prison sought to control all aspects of life, dissident prisoners rewrote the taken-for-granted elements of everyday life. They politicized things typically taken for granted, whether through marking time or through identifying as "New Afrikans" to locate their identity within the complex social, political, historical, spatial, and discursive factors that have shaped black life in the United States in, through, and despite confinement.

By the time I met Veronza Bower in person, I had been corresponding with several American political prisoners for three years. As a sixteen-year-old high school junior and naive new organizer, I wanted to have a better understanding of social movement history and practice. But no one I knew was asking those questions in the suburbs of South Florida, where I had recently moved with my family. Through reading various radical newspapers, I came across groups that described themselves as supporting U.S. political prisoners—longtime activists who had been in prison longer than I had been alive. Finally, I had found people who had committed their lives to social justice, people who had retained their political commitments despite old age and restrictive conditions. They had names and addresses. The past suddenly did not seem so remote.

I began corresponding with people who were serving lengthy or life sentences stemming from their involvement in the Black Power, New Left, and Puerto Rican independence movements of the 1960s, 1970s, and 1980s. I continued to write to them even after my parents forbade it. (I was, after all, a teenager.) I rented a post office box and continued the correspondence—my first lesson in the furtive communications that often accompany prison organizing. My relationships with these women and men, America's political prisoners, have been a vital part of my subsequent education. Over the years, I joined letters with visits and phone calls and eventually, in some cases, e-mails.

My first teachers about the complex histories of prisons, prison protest, and the long arc of the two-plus decades of protest casually referred to as "the sixties" came from Sundiata Acoli, Herman Bell, Veronza Bower, Marilyn Buck, David Gilbert, Ray Luc Levasseur, Oscar López Rivera, Claude Marks, Jalil Muntaqim, Alicia and Lucy Rodriguez, Russell Maroon Shoatz, Laura Whitehorn, Donna Willmott, and others. These current and former prisoners, their friends and family members, introduced me to the realities of imprisonment, including the ways incarceration intersects with social movements and political economies. They encouraged me to take seriously the study of history and politics, a commitment that ultimately led me to pursue graduate education and the professoriate.

I did not initiate such correspondence out of any particular concern with the prison. To that point, I had been sheltered from the criminal justice system. Rather, I was interested in broader historical lessons and ideas about contemporary politics. But I slowly learned the idioms of incarceration, the petty and picayune rules that have a shared arbitrary nature but whose details vary across institutions: the byzantine mailroom policies and limited programming available, the overpriced phone calls and vending machines, the routine medical neglect that constitutes prison health care, and the bittersweetness of the visiting room. I learned the vernacular of incarceration, the shorthand ways of describing different events and the ways in which language choices convey complex ideological loyalties. What began as an idealistic but innocent act came to dominate my personal and political life. The prison haunted my social networks, as I counted more and more prisoners, former prisoners, and supporters of people in prison among my friends, colleagues, and acquaintances. I found myself in a growing but little-discussed category: those with incarcerated loved ones. I realized that far from being a static institution, the prison connects histories, ideas, and relationships that have been largely forced on certain communities even as its impacts have been more widely felt.

The prison is also a living archive, steeped in a denial of the histories it confines. My relationships with these prisoners and their loved ones caused me to think more about the space of the prison and all the ways that it had become interwoven with my own life. After serious reflection, it seemed neither coincidental nor conspiratorial that the prison was the best place for a white suburban teenager to learn about the histories and legacies of Black Power and the radicalism it inspired in the decades after World War II. The reasons were political, social, spatial, historical. As both a historian and an organizer, I was eager to learn from the life experiences of the incarcerated. The prison houses untold histories, complex identities, and diverse associations. It is a vital node in a complex network of personal and political ties that stretch across generations. If prison walls could talk, their stories would reveal profound and largely untapped reservoirs of politics and culture.

This book is one exploration of those reserves. From the mid-1950s until the early 1980s, the prison generated, intersected with, and constituted a vital form of black protest. *Captive Nation: Black Prison Organizing in the Civil Rights Era* tells the story of the multifaceted rebellions that occurred in and through American prisons. It attempts simultaneously to tell the story from the perspective of prison organizers and to uncover the conditions that created such worldviews. The interpretive frame is of course my own, though I have been guided by the rich archival voices of the prison and its captives. For that reason, I have retained all the original spellings and emphases found in direct quotations. The grammar of prison protest, with its alternate spellings and nontraditional modes of accenting key points, is often part of its political critique. Further, except for in direct quotations, I have refrained from the medicalized language of "inmates" and its consonant association with voluntary confinement or rehabilitative care.

Finally, the prison is a massive and monstrous classificatory enterprise, cataloging its captives by narrowly defined and rigidly policed categories of race and gender. As a result, I pay particular attention to how even prisoners working against the prison are still shaped by its confines. Their thinking about gender and race animates the following pages, as I believe it does the intellectual life of the prison itself. Prisoners are institutionally separated by sex yet divided by race, a fact that has often contributed toward making race a central and explicit subject of political critique. I am interested in what imprisoned intellectuals might teach us about the great American paradox—the coexistence of the mutually exclusive categories of freedom and racism, democracy and confinement—while recognizing the limitations placed on them by their environment.

Dissident prisoners, their family members, and a large, sometimes surprising supporting cast of figures populate this story, conveying some of the counterintuitive sense of possibility that has emerged from among the world's bleakest locations. Perhaps, then, the critical reflection on this history can contribute to eliminating the ongoing tragedy of American imprisonment.

Abbreviations

The following abbreviations are used throughout the book.

AC	Adjustment Center, solitary confinement unit in California prisons
BGF	Black Guerrilla Family
BLA	Black Liberation Army
BPP	Black Panther Party
CP	Communist Party
CR	Critical Resistance
DVI	Deuel Vocational Institution, prison in Tracy, California
FALN	Fuerzas Armadas de Liberación Nacional (Armed Forces of National Liberation)
FBI	Federal Bureau of Investigation
GIP	Groupe d'Information sur les Prisons (Prison Information Group)
LAPD	Los Angeles Police Department
NAACP	National Association for the Advancement of Colored People
NAARPR	National Alliance against Racist and Political Repression
NAPO	New Afrikan Prisoners Organization, later the New Afrikan People's Organization
NCBL	National Conference of Black Lawyers
NLG	National Lawyers Guild
NOI	Nation of Islam
PFOC	Prairie Fire Organizing Committee
RNA	Republic of New Afrika
SBDC	Soledad Brothers Defense Committee
SCLC	Southern Christian Leadership Conference
SNCC	Student Nonviolent Coordinating Committee
SWAT	Special Weapons and Tactics police units
UN	United Nations
UPU	United Prisoners Union

CAPTIVE NATION

Introduction

The prison cannot be victorious because walls,
bars, and guards cannot conquer or hold down an idea.
—HUEY P. NEWTON, "Prison, Where Is Thy Victory?" (1970)

On November 3, 1970, prisoners at California's Folsom State Prison launched a work strike. For the next nineteen days, more than twenty-four hundred men—almost the entire prison population—refused to leave their cells or participate in any way in the routine functioning of the prison. At the outset, the men released a "Manifesto of Demands and Anti-Oppression Platform" that amounted to an auspicious challenge to the prison as an institution. "We the imprisoned men of Folsom Prison seek an end to the injustice suffered by all prisoners, regardless of race, creed, or color," the statement began. The platform consisted of thirty-one demands covering a wide range of issues from daily conditions to the structure of confinement itself. The manifesto's demands pertained to individual liberties (access to adequate legal representation, medical care, and reading material); political reform (fair parole policies, an end to the rampant and racist abuse of prisoners, payment and union representation for prisoner labor); the right to organize; freedom for political prisoners; and prisoners' ability to offer financial support to their family members.[1]

In challenging "the fascist concentration camps of modern America," these prisoners connected everyday life in prison to the pursuit of social justice. Seeing the strike as a dramatic step in a larger campaign against the prison as an institution that shaped the United States as a whole, the Folsom Manifesto sought to claim space for the right and ability to organize. It concluded with a nod to the prisoners' global consciousness, insisting that prisoners deserved the constitutional rights of American citizenship as well as the fundamental human rights ostensibly guaranteed by the United Nations if not a higher power. "In our peaceful efforts to assemble in dissent as provided under the nation's United States Constitution, we are in turn murdered, brutalized, and framed on various criminal charges because we seek the rights and privileges of *all American people*. In our efforts to keep abreast of the outside world, through all categories of news media, we are systematically restricted and punished by isolation when we insist on our human rights to the wisdom of awareness."[2]

The manifesto and the strike that accompanied it exposed the political radicalism that had for years been circulating inside American prisons. The document also revealed a set of tensions within the country's prison system animated by a fundamental contradiction. Prison may restrict physical mobility, but it is also based on movement: the state moves people from their home communities into the criminal justice system—a forced migration that typically runs along an urban-to-rural axis—and it moves them from prison to prison. Prisoners bring their knowledge, connections, and passions from one place to the next, and they continue to consume media despite their confinement. Further, physical movement often generates social movement as people press to better their conditions and achieve more control in the face of powerlessness. As prisoners are moved from unit to unit and facility to facility, they trade information and build or tap into networks of solidarity. The prison is not nearly as remote and impenetrable as it may seem. The strategies of state control undermine the prison's presumed stasis. As officials transfer "difficult" prisoners to other facilities as punishment, they can create the conditions for ideas to spread across the otherwise hermetic seal of confinement. Even a *forced* migration of people and ideas can make possible a global eros and ethos of rebellion.[3]

Such was the case with the Folsom strike. What became known as the Folsom Manifesto originated in the restrictive B section of San Quentin, California's oldest prison, located two hours from Folsom. Earlier in 1970, a multiracial collective of prisoners in B section—men whom prison officials had labeled troublemakers—drafted a document outlining their common grievances against the prison system. Then they went on strike and destroyed their cells. The men worked hard to craft demands that would appeal to a wide cross-section of prisoners challenging the administration. In their plea for unity, they excluded demands that did not at least potentially apply to all prisoners, including a demand for combs to use on Afros. Though black prisoners as well as Latino prisoners aligned with them bore the brunt of institutional violence and were the key strategists against it, the black radicals in B block wanted the entire prison population to strike. That meant building coalition with the many white and some Latino prisoners who were more invested in racial distinction than class struggle. They did so by creating venues for prisoners to express their collective grievances against the system as a whole.[4]

In response to their strike, a federal judge condemned B section, ordering that no prisoners could be housed in that unit until it was repaired. As officials had to move the dissident prisoners throughout the facility, their manifesto made its way to the general population. Soon, prisoners on the mainline launched their own strike against the prison. To break that strike, prison authorities transferred several of the men involved to Folsom. One of them, Steve Kumasi Simmons, brought with him a copy of the document first drafted in San Quentin's B section, and he soon found other radicals. The insights he gleaned from San Quentin combined with the political fervor that had already been developing at Folsom brought about the November 1970 strike.

Though the document originated at San Quentin, it became known as the Folsom Manifesto. It provided a rough draft for the demands that dissident prisoners would use in strikes across the country—most famously, in the statement released as part of the four-day rebellion at New York's Attica Correctional Facility in September 1971. The Attica Brothers borrowed from the Folsom rebels the form as well as the content, labeling their statement a "Manifesto of Demands and Anti-Depression Platform."[5]

The Folsom strike, its origins, and its afterlife illustrate a larger field of prison organizing. While prisoners were a central element of the civil rights and Black Power movements, their organizing was less a claim to expand rights than it was a critique of rights-based frameworks. Prisoners were dead before the law, excluded from juridical rights or public compassion. As prison rebellions informed one another, they became woven into the larger fabric of the era's radicalism. Against the backdrop of a massive outpouring of books and articles from incarcerated people, these strikes and uprisings were the product of larger circulations of radicalism that characterized the three and a half decades after World War II. In that time, diverse social movements, spearheaded domestically by the black freedom struggle, challenged a variety of American institutions and mores, including the idea of "America" itself. Their efforts, then, point less toward securing rights than toward a critique of the state. Their organizing called for reconsiderations of freedom, dignity, and empathy beyond what the U.S. state could imagine or would allow.[6]

To call this period the "civil rights era" is not to separate it from its global context but to emphasize what anchored this spirit of global revolt inside the United States. Around the world, this project of social change called itself the Third World: a political, social, and cultural assertion of independence emerging from the colonized world. As various Marxist and nationalist revolutionaries passed through the prison gates of empires and military juntas, the anticolonial project became at some level an anticarceral one. Around the world, prison organizing spoke a shared language of humanity and socialism rooted in an antiracist critique of colonialism. In the global revolutionary imagination of the postwar years, dissident prisoners were counterintuitive symbols of political possibility.

Revolutionary movements since at least the French Revolution have tended to reach a stage during which their critique of the ancien régime emphasizes the prison as a site of state repression. In the prison, they see a place where the oppressive system has incarcerated and tortured its dissidents that therefore comes to symbolize the larger corruption of such regimes. Long an aggregator of inequality, the prison comes to stand in for bigger structures of violence, and the prisoner becomes a symbol whose freedom marks a step toward larger, collective liberation. The revolutionary currents of the post–World War II years continued this historical tendency: from Cuba and Vietnam to South Africa and Northern Ireland and all points in between, the experience of colonization or military rule was bound up with that of confinement.[7]

Through the prison, activists asserted that black lives matter. Prisoner rebellions spoke the language of Black Power revolt, and several prisoners or former prisoners became leading spokespersons for black militancy through their published works and involvement in organizations such as the Black Panther Party and the Republic of New Afrika. The study of prison radicalism also reveals the broader arc of the Black Power movement: it lasted longer and affected more places than is often recognized. *Captive Nation* studies the prison as both a strategic metaphor and a structuring institution of black life. Prisoner efforts at exposure were the first to reveal an abiding truth about racism in an age of formal legal equality: antiracism has needed to overcome the relative invisibility of racial oppression after the dissolution of Jim Crow. Part of what has made the new racial landscape so challenging is the popular idea that contemporary injustices are individual or cultural rather than historical and structural. The prison's geographic remove and racial disparities made it a strategic testing ground for engaging the new racism. In their writings and actions, radical prisoners identified the paradox of postmodern racial capitalism, where racism is seen as impolite but remains constitutive. They worked to expose the workings of racism from behind steel and concrete.

Captive Nation investigates how the black freedom struggle made use of the prison. In particular, the book emphasizes how prisoners made sense of freedom from positions of confinement. Black activists thrust the prison into public view, established prisoners as symbols of racial oppression, and conceptualized confinement as a persistent feature of black life woven throughout the American racial landscape. One of the most striking things about black prison organizing was its ability to connect the prison to other sites of black activism, whether the public housing project, the struggle against police brutality, or the anticolonial revolutions around the world. Indeed, black radicals expanded the prison from a singular institution of repression to a central node in the reproduction of social struggle. This connectivity formed the scaffolding of prison radicalism. The history of the prison is simultaneously the history of postmigration black politics as it developed outside of but in relation to the U.S. South as well as the history of black politics in the final years of a political order sensitive to civil rights demands.

The United States has been a leader in carceral violence both because of its roots in settler-colonial racism and its egalitarian distrust of state power, which paradoxically upholds degrading punishment over beneficent state action for those deemed "criminals."[8] Race, especially antiblack racism, has been the primary modality through which this pairing of colonization and confinement has transpired in the United States. Forcible confinement haunted black life from capture in Africa through the Middle Passage and sale in the Americas. Chattel slavery initiated a racial regime rooted in confinement: plantation slavery was as much a carceral force as the early penitentiary.[9] Enslaved people routinely likened their condition to imprisonment, describing the slave as "a prisoner for life" and the plantation as "jus' the same as we was in jail."[10]

The abolition of chattel bondage was the birth of prison bondage: passed in 1865, the Thirteenth Amendment outlawed slavery "except as punishment for a crime."[11] The amendment provided the legal rationale establishing the prison and the wider criminal justice system as institutions central to sustaining racial oppression. Beginning with the Black Codes enacted at the end of slavery and expanding exponentially with the dismantling of Reconstruction, the primary institutions of American society—the government, the academy, the media—have largely defined blackness in and through criminality.[12] The age of Jim Crow was one of confinement, experienced as a continuation of carceral life begun under slavery. W. E. B. Du Bois opened his classic 1903 book, *The Souls of Black Folk*, by objecting to "the prison-house closed round us all." In *Black Reconstruction*, his magnum opus published thirty-two years later, Du Bois described antebellum society as an "armed camp" and decried the "caged human being" that was the black condition after the Civil War.[13] Throughout American history, the idea of criminal justice has been bound up with antiblack racism: black communities have been disproportionately harassed, policed, arrested, tried, convicted, confined, killed, and generally thought to be deserving of punishment.

The prison adds complex structures of classification that reproduce subordination through race and other social categories by means of diverse administrative and disciplinary procedures. Race has been at the core of American imprisonment. The prison's structure reproduces the forms of racial rule: race has been both an indicator and a by-product of imprisonment, as well as a weapon of control and division within sex-segregated institutions. The prison operates through classification: it officially separates people by sex and criminal offense; it divides them further, if unofficially, by race, religion, political views, and sexual orientation or gender presentation.[14] The prison catalogs people, often arbitrarily, and then decides the level of violence or isolation that corresponds to each category.

The prison is an odd institution, governed by the state yet not public in the way we normally understand the term. The prison is the place where state power is perhaps most forcefully expressed and publicly legitimized without being seen. In other words, the prison is an example of raw state power at its most violent extreme as well as an example of the ways that power cloaks itself in invisibility.[15]

Further, organizing around prisons is difficult: they tend to be far away from population centers, deeply stigmatized, and maintained through complex political processes. While resistance may be routine, organized movements in and against prisons are rare. To surpass the physical isolation of confinement, prison organizing after World War II pursued what I call a strategy of visibility. With limited mobility, prisoners relied on diverse means to reach people outside of prison. Riots, writing, and collective rituals were the building blocks of prison radicalism, and they were orchestrated to make the prison and especially its captives visible to people around the world. Antiprison activists, whether incarcerated or not, hoped that their interventions in the public sphere would render confinement ineffectual and therefore unnecessary. They challenged the prison as an incubator of violence: a place that buries alive its captives, a place that responds with overwhelming violence to the uprisings it provokes.

Alongside their experiences of literal imprisonment, black activists and artists have used the prison as a metaphor for describing their confrontations with the American state.[16] Indeed, the history of black radicalism can be thought of as a long opposition to confinement. The prison reproduces a form of race consciousness and racial identification that has, at certain historical junctures, produced radical antiracist movements. As scholar-activist Angela Davis noted in 1971 when she was a political prisoner, "The disproportionate representation of the black and brown communities, the manifest racism of parole boards, the intense brutality inherent in the relationship between prison guards and black and brown inmates—all this and more causes the prisoner to be confronted daily, hourly, with the concentrated, systematic existence of racism."[17]

To expose the cruelties occurring outside public view, dissident prisoners and their supporters developed what literary scholar Houston Baker has called the "black public sphere of incarceration."[18] This furtive public sphere exemplifies the fugitive freedom of black radicalism. Black activists have always found and forged freedom amid confinement. The struggle against the racialization of "crime" is but a more concentrated example of the continual reanimation of this freedom dream throughout time.[19]

The period between 1955 and 1980 was remarkable not only for the expanded criminalization and state punishment of black radicalism, practices that long predated this period and grew dramatically at the end of it. More notable was the way in which black activists turned prisons into, as a common refrain of the time put it, schools of liberation: training grounds and battlegrounds in larger struggles against racism in the form of state violence. While some prisoners have worked together to achieve a modicum of personal power—typically in the form of sex, supplies, or the intimidated respect of other prisoners—prison organizing during the civil rights era took on the political tone and style of black radicalism.[20] Dissident prisoners worked to understand their imprisonment in a larger historical and structural context—that is, in relation to the prevailing structures of political economy that disproportionately refused to hire but arrested, tried, imprisoned, and killed black youth. Further, they sought to make political connections between prisoners and those "outside" of both the prison and the United States. Prison radicalism displayed an internationalism that is stunning given the circumstances of its origins.

Both self-consciously and coincidentally, black prison organizing utilized strategic frameworks similar to those used by nineteenth-century slaves and their progeny. These frameworks included the central role of "kinship, labor, and circuits of communication and education."[21] Radical prisoners asserted their humanity in a myriad of ways, and in each case, their opposition to the prison was a strike against the racializing nature of confinement. While treated as narrowly self-interested by race and as the latest example of a black menace to white civilization, black prison radicalism sought broad coalitions against larger structures of domination. Indeed, the shape and structure of black prison organizing involved whites, Latinos, and others. As they challenged prison conditions, prison organizers advanced a radical critique of what might be called rightlessness, a state-sponsored deprivation of group rights and political action. Indeed, organizers defined not just the prison but racism itself as the structural reproduction of rightlessness.[22]

During a period of heightened activism, this connection facilitated a united front on prison issues. Members of this short-lived coalition did not agree on the larger political critiques, including whether prisons should be reformed or abolished, yet the demands of prisoner struggles proved elastic enough to sustain an alliance of liberals and radicals for several years. Those involved understood that people organized through the means at their disposal, which meant that prisoners had different tools for challenging authority than did those who were not incarcerated. Yet these different groups united to expose the misery of prison conditions and work for humane resolutions to the crisis of confinement.

What I am calling black prison organizing took place in prisons as well as on the streets. Much as black politics in slavery revolved around the peculiar institution even for those who were not enslaved, so, too, did the prison loom large in the popular imagination of the civil rights era. Dissident prisoners became a metaphor for freedom itself for a growing number of people frustrated by alienation and violence in postwar American society—not just in black communities but among other constituencies. In a 1972 letter written at San Quentin, prison organizer David Johnson summarized the hopeful identification that diverse radical and racialized groups then made with prisoners: "To this system we are the nightmare that won't go away. . . . Our presence marks their end and the people's beginning."[23]

During these years, a coterie of black prisoners, young men and women inspired by Third World revolutionary movements, turned the prison into a node of struggle within the wider black freedom struggle. The most prominent black political organizations of the era participated in this movement, including the Black Panther Party, the Nation of Islam, the NAACP, the Republic of New Afrika, the Southern Christian Leadership Conference, the Student Nonviolent Coordinating Committee, and the US organization. A large number of other progressive and leftist organizations representing different constituencies could be added to this list. These groups, along with a host of smaller organizations, ad hoc coalitions, and defense campaigns, served as breeding grounds for prison organizing, places where those with more political savvy served as mentors for less experienced activists both in and out of prison. Organizations provided a bridge across levels of experience and geographies of confinement. But the prison movement was larger than any one organization or set of organizations.

The racial consciousness developing in prison during the civil rights era most often took the form of revolutionary nationalism. This development owed debts both to the national liberation movements of the time and to the structure of the prison itself. Many people held in cages looked with great interest on formerly colonized countries defeating regimes only recently thought to be invincible. Nationalism helped prisoners imagine themselves as part of a collective force strong enough to challenge the totalizing authority of the prison. Specifically, revolutionary nationalism helped black prisoners contest white domination in prison—domination both by the almost all-white staff of guards and by white prisoners—by appealing to an imagined community that extended well beyond the prison and beyond the American nation-state.

Through nationalism, prisoners identified their struggle with long-standing black resistance to slavery. Black prison nationalism connected a savvy understanding of the prison structure, where nationalism often served as the framework for group identification, with a sophisticated understanding of the politics beyond the prison, where revolutionary nationalism had global currency. The development of nationalism in prison was, therefore, both organic to the prison and part of the Black Power movement on the streets. Black prison nationalism shared many of the ambiguities of other nationalist forms, and these issues were exacerbated by the structure of prison life: a propensity for violence, a rigid approach to politics, and a masculinist framework of political action. Yet nationalism also provided a useful means for prisoners to oppose white supremacy as part of a larger collective, even if they could not physically access it.[24]

Revolutionary nationalism emerged from and in response to feelings of captivity. Thus, prisoners spoke of captivity as itself constituting nationality. Prisoners used the notion of national captivity to pursue justice as both prisoners and racial subjects in the United States. They described themselves as part of a captive nation to name their relation to the country. By invoking the prison, black activists critiqued the racialization of punishment by the U.S. state. Revolutionary nationalism joined opposition to the state with calls for alternative forms of affiliation and a hybrid form of socialism. In practice, this notion of national captivity also referred to prisoners' attempts to reach the public. Their power as a social movement, through books and strikes, used captivity in both senses: they sought a captive audience to help set free the captive nation. By challenging captivity, radical prisoners spoke to widespread cultural anxieties. Those concerned with shifts in the experience of race and gender, with changes in the world political economy, or with any number of other phenomena found solace in prisoner demands for freedom. The poignancy of the prison as a metaphor for alienation and exploitation helped a generation name, if not make sense of, epochal change.

The prison exacerbated preexisting gender and class tensions. The incarceration of large numbers of working-class black men offered an alternate politics of respectability to the one traditionally advanced by the black middle class, with its emphasis on racial uplift and consumption.[25] Radical prisoners, describing their individual "guilt" as the problem of an oppressive larger system, called into question guilt itself. And to the extent that middle-class activists also found themselves imprisoned or supporting those in prison, they had support from the larger prison movement. Seeing righteousness in those defined as guilty, the prison movement identified blackness as "guilty" in all the right ways.[26] This embrace of the guilty was a stunning rebuke to upward mobility and middle-class notions of integration. It opposed the authority of the prison guard, the president, and the preacher. It was a coalition of the unruly. Yet this idea of respectability had a conservative gender politics attached to it. The prison's sex segregation indelibly shaped how opposition to imprisonment emerged. On a basic level, it meant that prisoners worked directly only with those of the same sex. This reality influenced relationships between prisoners and others, especially when some male prisoners sought the romantic affections of women supporters. The prison provided another layer of taboo to the historic American fear of sexual contact between black men and white women.

The prison—and the larger strategy of governance rooted in policing, surveillance, and incarceration that scholars have dubbed the "carceral state"—also exacerbated the conservative idea that black activism needed to restore or establish black patriarchy. Men's prisons witnessed far more violent rebellions and escape attempts than did women's prisons. The statements of male prisoners in revolt routinely insisted on their manhood. "We are men, not beasts, and we will not be driven or treated as such," the Attica Brothers famously declared in 1971.[27] The passionate declarations of masculinity that accompanied such uprisings gave the false impression that men were more resistant than women. Certainly, the dominant representatives of prison organizing were largely men. Although men were and are disproportionately incarcerated, the focus on male prisoners was not just a numbers game. The focus on men in resistance obscured women prisoner struggles outside of the feminist and gay liberation movements as well as the fact that prison organizing in general consists primarily of work that is, as historian Rebecca Hill writes, "typically gendered female." The work of prison organizing is "supportive, reproductive, and, despite its importance for the shaping of revolutionary consciousness, often defined as secondary to and diversionary from 'real' struggles over material issues."[28]

The "women's work" of prison organizing was well pronounced in struggles involving men in prison. Prison organizing is designed to protect safety, maintain networks among disparate individuals, and catalyze public action by the pain of state violence. Yet because the prisoner in these years reached public consciousness largely through dramatic actions that were more likely to be taken by men, and because the state treated men as more serious political actors, masculinity emerged as the normative basis of prisoner resistance even as women did much of the organizing work to keep prisoners in the public eye. Further, black prison organizing adopted the tropes of the antilynching movement that emphasized the violence done predominantly to black men. Such gendered divisions have a deep history in American politics and were generally exacerbated by the growing number of young black men incarcerated by the expanding carceral state during the mid-twentieth century.[29]

Captive Nation: Black Prison Organizing in the Civil Rights Era is a critical history of racial justice activism and the prison between 1955 and 1980. It identifies both the prison's influence on the postwar black freedom struggle and the movement's impact inside prison. It studies the formation of prison-based radicalism in the transition from civil rights liberalism to neoliberal multiculturalism, noting how such dissent informed popular conceptions of justice, power, and politics at this time. The prison occupied a central place in popular understandings of blackness, and as this book demonstrates, prison activists authored such conceptions as much as state institutions did. By telling a history of imprisonment from the perspective of prisoners and their allies, this book inserts the prison into the study of twentieth-century black activism, incorporates resistance into the study of incarceration, and investigates the ways social movements offer their own conceptions of race and justice. *Captive Nation* is one contribution to the growing body of literature on prison protest and imprisoned intellectuals.[30] This volume brings together a history of prisoner ideas with one of prisoner action. Coming to terms with prison organizing expands our understanding of the sites and strategies of black radicalism and of the path from civil rights legislative victories to the large-scale, racially disparate imprisonment that followed it. *Captive Nation* reveals the social context, political milieu, and intellectual interventions of prison organizing over a twenty-five-year period.

The prison is a fluid and fluctuating institution. It remains fundamental to understanding many of the large-scale transformations of the second half of the twentieth century. These connections were both tangible and idealized, lived and imagined. Rather than yield to the prison's attempt to impose stasis, radical prisoners emphasized movement and migration. *Captive Nation* follows their path: focusing on the prison without being bound by it, it follows the circulation of people and ideas as they confronted diverse institutions of confinement. The book begins in the South, with the rise of the civil rights movement (chapter 1), before moving north to explore the Black Power movement (chapter 2).

Southern black activists in the 1950s and 1960s turned the jail and the prison into a public site of community and commitment. By deliberately flouting the laws of segregation, these women and men counterintuitively imagined the jailhouse as the center of freedomland. They used their confinement to highlight the urgency of their campaign against Jim Crow, positioning the jail cell as a necessary stop on the road to freedom. In so doing, they put an end to almost a century of rule in which the prison buttressed Jim Crow through the convict leasing system. I do not embrace a uniquely southern view of the prison or see the South as the distinctive origin of the U.S. carceral state. Rather, I identify the centrality of racial politics in the South—where the specter of slavery loomed large and where black activists achieved some success in confronting white supremacy through brave, highly publicized demonstrations that dramatized racial confinement—in the circulation of prison protest as a central element of black politics. Turning incarceration from a taboo into a resource through which to promote a more radical politics of respectability, their actions demonstrated not only the prison's centrality to America's racial landscape but also the urgent need to redress its problems.[31]

Throughout post–World War II history, opposition to policing, prisons, and the larger carceral state was a particular point of black unity. The southern-based civil rights movement coexisted with a Black Power movement more rooted in the urban North, with both movements shaped by the growing carceral state. Activists in both environments showed that the prison could house contentious national debates about race, politics, and freedom. In northern and western cities, black organizers challenged the disproportionate policing and incarceration of black children and adults, especially the working-class migrants who had arrived from across the South. The dialectics of black social and political life in the mid-twentieth century were grounded in this tension between the city block and the cell block, the urban and the carceral. The prison, then, was both a material institution that disproportionately incarcerated black people and a metaphor that symbolized the endurance and enormity of white supremacy. While scholars have debated the differences between the civil rights and Black Power movements, the two came together in opposition to the carceral state.[32]

In both the North and the South, black activists identified the prison as fundamentally entangled with the creation and persecution of blackness. Figures such as Malcolm X, a formerly incarcerated man who challenged the stigma of incarceration by telling audiences that "America means prison," and organizations such as the Black Panther Party turned a long-standing critique of the racist application of the law into a poignant metaphor for the black urban condition. The metaphor of the prison also captured the imagination of the New Left, facilitating the rise of the Black Panthers as an international symbol of Black Power and enlisting the support of a range of activists and cultural workers who turned their attention to the prison. In their approach to the carceral state, we can read the northern Black Power movement as roughly analogous to the southern civil rights movement: both were elements of a larger form of black radicalism that took shape in struggles against the confining restrictions of white supremacy. Both used the prison as a poignant metaphor for the constricting experience of American racism.

Perhaps the most well-known theorist of prisons to emerge from the Black Power movement was California prisoner George Jackson, who became a bestselling author with his 1970 book of prison letters, *Soledad Brother*. The book was published while Jackson and two others were awaiting trial for the death of a prison guard in response to the killing of three black prisoners. More than others had done before or since, Jackson made visible a black condition characterized by confinement and the racialization of criminality. Jackson was central to black prison organizing and, as the subject of chapter 3, stands at the center of *Captive Nation*. His critique of the carceral logic characterizing the American state proved prophetic of the massive expansion of policing and punishment that would arise after (and in response to) Jackson's death in 1971. During his brief time in the spotlight, Jackson developed a politics that blended political radicalism, physical militancy, and cultural production in a political framework of revolutionary black nationalism that gained widespread appeal. His fame was bound up with his eloquence and his alleged violence. Both of them were highlighted by his younger brother's failed and bloody attempt to free three black prisoners from the Marin County Courthouse in August 1970. Together, George and Jonathan Jackson defined a revolutionary strategy rooted in visibility: both men used spectacular violence to undermine the "prestige" of the prison and the society it came to represent.

So powerful was his influence that prison organizing in these years might be categorized as the George Jackson generation of prison protest. Chapters 4–6 concern Jackson's posthumous influence and the ways that his ideas continued to shape black prison organizing across a variety of sites in the 1970s, an influence that continues into the twenty-first century. Jackson's death in an alleged escape attempt in August 1971 failed to blunt his influence. In death as in life, he remained a symbol for prison protest around the country and antiracist critiques of American power around the world.

Through Jackson's death we can examine the deeper logic of imprisonment as it structured the lives of activists—what I take up in chapter 4 as a pedagogy of the prison. Those navigating the political possibilities amid confinement emphasized memorialization and peer education. Activists on both sides of the prison wall paid tribute to Jackson in a variety of ways that sought to extend his critique of confinement. Even more than in life, the martyred Jackson became a symbol of radical opposition. He inspired supporters to act with urgency, to study diligently. Jackson's second book, *Blood in My Eye*, completed days before his death and published posthumously, demonstrated that even death could not erase his political legacy. At the same time, the confusing circumstances of his death generated a concern for the "real" George Jackson that ultimately bolstered law-and-order conservatism.

Yet Jackson continued to inspire action. When he wrote that as "a slave, the social phenomenon that engages my consciousness is, of course, revolution," he expressed a wider concern of black prison radicalism: the ways in which the carceral experience not only continued but also approximated slavery.[33] Slavery weighed heavily on the minds and actions of 1970s radical prisoners as they sought to characterize the racial project of twentieth-century confinement and contribute their own ideas of what blackness meant in an age of formal equality. Rebellious slaves of the nineteenth century were of great inspiration to prison radicals of the twentieth, with earlier words, images, and names shaping the iconography and strategy of prisoner dissent. The salience of slavery resulted from several factors, including the southern origins of many black prisoners and the similar technologies of incapacitation that joined slaves and prisoners. Dissident prisoners maintained that slavery was a permanent feature of black life, less as a regime of labor than as a system of injustice, a form of social alienation and political oppression. These prisoners were not concerned about forced labor, since many of the most forceful ideas about prison slavery came from people who did not work and were held in solitary confinement units. Their critique anticipated the larger shift in the American prison system away from the idea of prisons as places of "correction" or "rehabilitation" and toward a new model of imprisonment based on incapacitation.[34]

Chapter 5 tracks this notion of prisoners as slaves among California prisoners. While evaluating the currency of slavery as an analytic through which to make sense of imprisonment, I concentrate on three major trials involving prison activists in the 1970s: those of Ruchell Magee (1970–74), Angela Davis (1970–72), and the San Quentin 6 (1971–76). All of these prosecutions involved the defendants' relationship to George or Jonathan Jackson: Magee was the only surviving participant in Jonathan Jackson's raid on the Marin County Courthouse, and Davis was charged with providing the guns used in the assault. The San Quentin 6 were prisoners charged with joining George Jackson in a failed escape attempt that led to his death and the deaths of five others. In each case, the courtroom was a crucial arena through which prisoners challenged the slavery of confinement—less through judicial procedure than through the public forum that the court provided. In the context of a larger social interest in chattel slavery, these prisoners used the courtroom and the public attention their trials garnered to put the afterlife of slavery on trial.[35]

While pressing for civil and human rights in the courtroom, prisoners continued to pursue other means of self-determination. As popular support for prisoners receded, radical prisoners sounded a nationalist theme of self-reliance that joined the Black Arts movement, black religiosity, and armed self-defense. Their efforts to continue the black radical tradition inside conclude this book. By merging the metaphoric prison of race with the materiality of black prison protest, this brand of revolutionary nationalism epitomized the ways black activists of this generation viewed the prison. This approach used print culture and collective rituals to maintain prisoner connections to outside publics. Black prison nationalism in the late 1970s circulated through a variety of prisoner magazines that emerged in that time, including California's *Arm the Spirit* newspaper, Illinois's *The Fuse* newsletter, and New York's *Midnight Special* magazine. It could also be found in Black August, a prison-based holiday initiated in San Quentin by the Black Guerrilla Family in 1979 as a way to solidify nationalist sentiment among prisoners and between them and their supporters. Black August turned the history of prison protest, especially the deaths of the Jackson brothers (August 1970 and 1971), into a nationalist ritual emphasizing the power of prisoners.

Insurgent nationalism helped prisoners maintain the connections to diverse global publics that confinement threatened to sever. As a result, nationalist explanations proliferated among dissident prisoners as the conditions of their incarceration grew more severe: the more prison tried to control the worldview of its captives, the more certain activist prisoners turned to nationalism as an antidote. These prison-based expressions of nationalism anticipated the rise of the prison as a mechanism of an alternate nation-building in the 1980s. As Ronald Reagan's election seemed to consecrate the growing power of conservatism, imprisoned black radicals committed themselves to transcending the prison nation through study, exercise, and sheer will. Their determination contributed to the enduring circulation of black prison radicalism in a climate that made organizing far more difficult.

The prison needs to be thought of in the context of movement—if nothing else, the forced migration from home to prison—rather than stasis. This need is especially urgent for the civil rights era, when prison activists constituted key members of an internal migration across the United States. Further, the global imagination and influence of prison protest undermines any effort to treat it in purely state or local terms. The local, the national, the global; the rural, the suburban, the urban; the past, the present, the future: prison organizing traversed space and time. It saw the individual prison as representative of larger inequalities. It pursued transformative theories of the racial state while failing to respond adequately to the policies that produced a dramatic expansion of the American prison system.

Captive Nation tells a national story: prison organizing was as nationally dispersed as the mass incarceration that replaced it, and many of the themes traced here manifest in prisons throughout the country. I concentrate largely but not exclusively on California to place its notorious prison history within a larger scope.[36] California has been a national leader in imprisonment in the postwar period: it led the country in liberal prison reform in the 1940s and 1950s, prisoner radicalism in the 1960s and 1970s, and prison expansion in the 1980s and 1990s. California's radical prisoners, typically southern migrants or their children, influenced the shape and structure of prison protest nationally as they also nurtured a global sense of racial justice within the black diaspora.

Yet California's policies and protests were connected to other regional, national, and global developments. Particularly for prisoners, the specter of the South loomed large in prison organizing. With its explicit reference to and rigid policing of racial hierarchies, the South's political geography seemed to mirror that of the prison. And in California, many of those who led uprisings, wrote exposés, or otherwise populated what was called the "prison movement" were southern migrants or their children, shaped by southern racial hierarchies and modes of resistance. Their understandings of the violent and racially polarized world of confinement joined the southern collective memory of chattel slavery with the Western experience of police brutality and hyperincarceration to arrive at their critique of prisons as a form of slavery.

The defense industry beckoned people west during the run up to World War II. Between 1940 and 1960, Los Angeles's black population skyrocketed from 63,774 to 334,916. As historian Daniel Widener reports, "By 1960, more than one out of every eight residents of the city would be an African American."[37] Oakland experienced a similarly large wave of black migration, with its black population growing from 3 percent in 1940 to 12 percent in 1950 and more than 50 percent by 1980. Black southerners continued to head to California during the 1950s and 1960s as they sought a life outside of Jim Crow or were enticed by the Golden State's promise of reinvention. This population boom helped propel California to be the nation's most populated state by 1962. This southern diaspora, as historian James Gregory has characterized it, built the West Coast wing of the Black Power movement in Soledad and San Quentin as much as in the streets of Oakland and Los Angeles.[38]

In the years after World War II, California offered the promise of paradise and reinvention premised on the idea that, as Joan Didion put it, the state was unburdened by and perhaps even outside of history.[39] Yet for the black and Latino men and women who found themselves in prison during the civil rights era, histories of racial oppression were far too determinative of their experience. For they had experienced the kind of collective insecurity that postwar American prosperity pledged to eradicate. From substandard housing and schooling—the result of pervasive disinvestment and discrimination—to political disenfranchisement, police brutality, and then incarceration, the radical prisoners of the 1960s era came of age in a context of official neglect and state violence. They drew on their personal experience to offer a powerful and tragically prophetic indictment of the massive inequality sanctioned by racism. They offered a warning of the high human toll of criminalization and imprisonment that would soon come to make the United States a world leader in incarceration.

Their warning has become a reality. For more than forty years, the country has devoted an ever-larger amount of money and resources into policing and imprisoning its population. California has pioneered many of these strategies. As geographer Ruth Wilson Gilmore writes, California's "prisoner population grew nearly 500 percent between 1982 and 2000, even though the crime rate peaked in 1980 and declined, unevenly but decisively, thereafter." The state built twenty-three prisons, "thirteen community corrections facilities, five prison camps, and five mother-prisoner centers" between 1984 and 2007.[40] California was early to experiment with three strikes and mandatory minimum sentences that contributed to the massive spike in the number of prisoners since the 1970s. After World War II, the state was seen as a leader in rehabilitative "corrections"; since the 1980s, it has been a leader in punitive policing and imprisonment.

But the sources of carceral expansion, much like the expressions of prison protest themselves, transcend particular state boundaries. Captivity, like the gendered and classed color line it has enforced, is a problem for the country—and the world—as a whole. The United States has 5 percent of the world's population but 25 percent of its prison population. On any given day, the United States incarcerates more than 2.3 million people in prisons and jails—with tens of thousands of immigrants incarcerated and deported from separate detention centers. One in one hundred adults in the United States is now incarcerated.

These numbers are shocking in their own right but even more frightening when we consider who gets locked up. Almost everyone in prison is poor or working class, and most are black or Latino. One in nine black men between the ages of twenty and thirty-four is incarcerated. Black men are imprisoned at a rate 6.4 times greater than white men. Black women are imprisoned at almost three times the rate of white women. Latinos, especially Latinas, are a fast-growing group within the American prison system, as well as being subject to the growing archipelago of detention centers. An additional five million people are on probation, parole, or some form of supervised release, meaning that one in thirty adults in the United States is under some form of correctional control. The majority of people in prison come from and return to economically devastated cities, bonding the fate of American cities to the vast carceral landscape.[41]

The country's criminal justice system is an index of inequality; from who gets arrested to who gets sent to prison, from who gets put in solitary confinement to who maintains communal ties amid such violence, the carceral state punishes the most marginalized and the most rebellious elements of society. The United States is the only industrialized country to have the death penalty, make such widespread use of solitary confinement, or sentence so many people—including juveniles—to life without parole.

Black prisoners connect the dots, conceptually and practically, of late twentieth-century political transformations in ways few other groups can. They faced these bitter realities in the civil rights era, before they became such a generalized reality. Black radical prisoners understood the prison as a regime of institutions that constricted black lives. They understood the racialization embedded in punishment long before mass incarceration made that connection clear. Further, they anticipated the coming expansion of state punishment by place and race. Their organizing on the fine line between spectacle and surveillance revealed a broader tension that has continued to define American society. These prisoners can help us understand the meanings of justice and the dynamics of power over a period of tumultuous change. They speak not only to the conditions of their age but to subsequent generations as well. Prison organizing in the civil rights era offers insights into the contemporary racial landscape, where race remains pervasive and perplexing, publicly seen but privately suffered.

The theme that most animates the study of prison organizing is, of course, freedom. But in an age where "freedom" has been taken to mean private enterprise and high-tech warfare, the idea of freedom is hardly self-evident. Black prison organizing reveals that the question is not *whether* freedom but rather what kind of freedom will be had and who will reap its rewards. Throughout the civil rights era, black prisoners offered a series of prophetic challenges to confinement. Reviewing their tribulations from an era of security and mass incarceration reminds us that freedom is an avocation that needs to be continuously created and chosen.

CHAPTER ONE

The Jailhouse in Freedom Land

We in the nonviolent movement have been talking about jail
without bail for two years or more. The time has come for us to mean what
we say and stop posting bond. . . . This will be a Black baby born in Mississippi
and thus, wherever he is born, he will be born in prison. I believe that if I go to
jail now it may help hasten that day when my child and all children will
be free—not only on the day of their birth but for all their lives.
—DIANE NASH, public statement on her refusal to
cooperate with the court system (1961)

I t was unlike any testimony the committee had heard before. Then again, there was little typical about the August 1964 Democratic National Convention. Gathered in Atlantic City, the Democratic Party was experiencing the most profound political challenge imaginable as a group of black Mississippians, most of them tenant farmers, worked to unseat the openly white supremacist delegation of that state. The Mississippi Freedom Democratic Party formed officially on April 24 of that year, emerging from years of tireless work by civil rights activists in the Sunflower State. Four months after it began, the Freedom Democrats shook the national Democratic Party to its core. They gathered in front of the 110-person credentials committee to argue that they, not the all-white delegation of Mississippi Democrats that had also made the trek to New Jersey, should be seated as the state's voting members of the convention. The Freedom Democrats submitted to the committee between four and five thousand briefs in support of their position; for their part, the regular Democrats filed only sixty briefs and denied all claims of black disenfranchisement.

It was not the briefs that captured the nation's attention. Rather, it was the testimony of Fannie Lou Hamer, a forty-seven-year-old sharecropper. In just eight minutes, Hamer offered a vivid portrait of life in the apartheid South. She described a life of confinement and brutality. Hamer told the committee and the assembled media of the vicious violence she had encountered a year earlier in the Montgomery County Jail in Winona, Mississippi. Hamer and four others had attempted to desegregate the bathroom and café at the bus station on June 9, 1963. Police arrested them for their efforts. Police had kicked and cursed at Hamer as they arrested her and had subsequently beaten young activists June Johnson and Annell Ponder. James West and Hamer had received beatings from other prisoners, acting on orders from the police. Two black male prisoners had beaten Hamer all over her body with blackjacks, in the process attempting to remove her clothes so that their blows would land directly on her skin and so that the abuse would be amplified by the specter of sexual assault. After the beating, Hamer's skin was like "raw cowhide."[1]

Hamer testified that the five activists had survived the assaults through their faith and determination and by singing freedom songs. She concluded her short speech with a pointed indictment: "If the Freedom Democratic Party is not seated now I question America. Is this America, the land of the free and the home of the brave, where we have to sleep with our telephones off the hook because our lives be threatened daily, because we want to live as decent human beings in America?"[2]

The violence that Mississippi jailers inflicted on Hamer and her fellow activists was nothing new to the southern prison system. The county jail where the civil rights activists were beaten sits seventy miles from Parchman prison farm, which had for nearly a century been notorious for its brutality. Parchman rivaled Louisiana's Angola Prison, which sits on the grounds of a former plantation, as the harshest prison in a land of harsh prisons. Since the end of Reconstruction, southern prisons had earned a reputation as sites of extreme racial violence. The fall of abolition democracy by 1877 ushered in an era of racial retrenchment that saw increasing authority vested in institutions of policing and punishment. The criminal justice system became a vital implement through which whites tried to discipline black workers. These developments were constitutive, not coincidental. Embedded in the southern Democrats' dismantling of Reconstruction was the criminalization of black civic and political life.[3]

Beginning in the late nineteenth century and backed by the investment of northern capital, southern businesses (especially industrial but also agrarian) used black "criminals" the way they once had used black slaves. Black men and women continued to serve as a reservoir of cheap labor. Arguably even less concerned for the health of their captive workers now than under slavery, southern elites enforced a brutal regime of forced labor that violently punished even the slightest transgressions with imprisonment. Black prisoners resisted as they could, often through individual acts of sabotage or self-mutilation. The convict leasing system—dubbed by one recent chronicler the "re-enslavement of black Americans"—continued until World War II. Convict leasing was the premier element that made the southern legal apparatus—from the police to the courthouse and the prison—a formidable foundation of the Jim Crow South. Even after the practice of convict leasing subsided, the southern criminal justice system remained a bastion of white supremacy.[4]

Until the civil rights movement challenged the foundations of the Jim Crow order, the criminal justice system openly coerced black labor and enforced white supremacy. As journalist Douglas Blackmon reports, "More than 12,500 people were arrested in Alabama in 1928 for possessing or selling alcohol; 2,735 were charged with vagrancy; 2,014 with gaming; 458 for leaving the farm of an employer without permission; 154 with the age-old vehicle for stopping intimate relations between blacks and whites: adultery."[5] Throughout the first half of the twentieth century, whites freely terrorized blacks through the law—with economic reprisals, with political disenfranchisement—and then used the law to evade punishment. White extralegal violence against blacks, especially brutal throughout the southern Delta, was so pervasive as to be functionally and sometimes even technically legal. At the same time, whites could challenge any act of black civic life, no matter how constitutionally protected, without fear. The level of violence, both legal and extralegal, against black southerners was so immense that it took a great degree of support from northern black communities, whose members had fled the region during the Great Migration, for the civil rights movement to achieve success in the South.[6]

Criminalization and incarceration provided the ideological basis for white supremacy from the end of slavery forward, not just in the South but nationally. Across the country, white elites held that "segregation maintains law and order, while integration breeds crime." Indeed, as political scientist Naomi Murakawa puts it, "The U.S. did not confront a crime problem that was then racialized; it confronted a race problem that was then criminalized."[7] The management of race increasingly transpired through the language and policy of crime. The specter of interracial marriage had long been white supremacists' rationale for using carceral as well as extralegal force to maintain their way of life.[8] Yet as black activists became more emboldened in pursuit of their freedom dreams, their violations of segregationist laws "only further reinforced the idea that black civil rights activists were disrespectful agitators and deliberate lawbreakers."[9] Law and order, the rallying cry of segregation, would become the language of American politics writ large.

As the South modernized white supremacy, it made increasing use of incarceration. From Virginia and Georgia to Florida and Texas, southern states used their jail cells to aggregate racial injustice. The most spectacular abuses, however, occurred in Mississippi and neighboring Alabama—two states that would become central battlegrounds in the fight over civil rights in the mid-twentieth century. In a region becoming known globally for its gruesome spectacles of white supremacy, Alabama and Mississippi stood out with regard to the horrific histories of convict leasing and mob violence. Across the twentieth century, deep, abiding connections persisted between the police and the extrajudicial infrastructure of white supremacist violence in the form of the Ku Klux Klan. Indeed, both the police and the Klan constituted elements of the "police power," the broadly conceived capacity of state agents to punish in the name of enforcing public order.[10]

The police power entails policing, laws, and the institutions that regulate social norms. It is a question of governance in the service of state power. While this capacious notion of the police power has preoccupied a range of legal thinkers since the eighteenth century, its importance in the United States increased in the aftermath of slavery. The Thirteenth Amendment prohibited slavery "except as punishment for a crime, whereof the party shall have been duly convicted." This wording wrote slavery into law in the form of penal punishment, thereby providing the framework for replacing the era of Radical Reconstruction with the era of Jim Crow racial subjugation.[11]

The prison and the larger carceral system of which it was a part proved a central component of black life in the twentieth century. And between 1955 and 1965, the combination of black civil disobedience and white civil disorder continually converged around the jail cell.

Both black liberationists and white segregationists saw the prison as holding the key to a larger social order, though they differed about whether that order should be rooted in universal human equality or governed by white supremacy. Segregationists relied on imprisonment as a crucial element of the police power, using the law to do in practice what Cold War anticommunism did as ideology: punish, stigmatize, and divide.[12] Black activists, meanwhile, boldly endeavored to remake the prison into a site of liberation. The movement interrupted the most haunting power of imprisonment, the stigma of criminality, and instead made it synonymous with moral authority. These efforts to amplify and to interrupt the police power echoed in the years to come: as white elites experimented with mass incarceration, black activists learned the potency of dramatic action against confinement. The battles in southern cities and jail cells established some of the parameters that would later come to define the struggle in prisons around the country.

Consequently, the best place to know freedom was where it was most elusive. For the civil rights movement, jail served many purposes: it was a rite of passage, a form of community, and a tool for political mobilization. Imprisonment was so common to the civil rights movement that historians often take it for granted. Movement partisans breathed an air thick with the threat of incarceration, earning their stripes by surviving a night or more in jail.[13]

This intimacy with incarceration was part of a larger battle over the meaning of freedom in postwar America. White power brokers and black activists—North and South, pacifist and otherwise—took up the issue of legality and criminality to battle over morality. This shared investment in the legal system as a site of contestation ultimately yielded the prison movement of the late 1960s and 1970s. For the prison to emerge as a site of political struggle, the wider criminal justice system of which it was a part needed to be problematized. And the civil rights movement did just that. The emergence of revolutionary prisoners such as George Jackson and Assata Shakur owes as much to civil rights activists Martin Luther King Jr. and Fannie Lou Hamer as it does to stalwart nationalists such as Malcolm X and Audley "Queen Mother" Moore.

For all its talk of integration, the southern civil rights movement broadcast the seeds of nationalism, or at least a certain protonationalism that can be seen in its direct-action approach to prison. In their effort to fill the jails, activists put forth a face of unshakable black (and multiracial) unity in the face of white authority. King's consistent plea for unity among the civil rights organizations, including a willingness to downplay certain strategic differences, demonstrated a nationalistic willingness to sublimate difference for the sake of political and racial unity. Civil rights organizations positioned this unity as a necessary antidote to the captivities of the state. As a result, direct action united the civil rights movement with the burgeoning Black Power movement. Both shared a black nationalist notion of racial oppression and racial solidarity in the face of overwhelming state repression. For all their philosophical and political differences, then, both the Southern Christian Leadership Conference (SCLC) and the Nation of Islam (NOI), among others, defined blackness in this era as a condition of captivity.

Speaking on the first night of the Montgomery Bus Boycott in 1956—and in his first mass movement speech—King claimed to speak for all black people "tired of going through the long night of captivity. And now we are reaching out for the daybreak of freedom and justice and equality."[14] Student Nonviolent Coordinating Committee (SNCC) leader Diane Nash echoed this theme of black captivity five years later. Facing jail, the pregnant Nash said that all black children are "born in prison." Echoing the fill-the-jails ethos of the moment, Nash proclaimed that her willingness to "go to jail now . . . may help hasten that day when my child and all children will be free."[15] Nash refused the judge's patriarchal benevolence, saying she would rather serve two years in prison than pay a fine or appeal her sentence. Not wanting to contravene the bizarre algorithm of the South's gendered racism, the judge "simply declined to impose the two-year sentence. Nash ended up serving only ten days in jail for refusing to move to the side of the courtroom reserved for blacks."[16]

This notion of blackness as uninterrupted confinement is typically associated with a later phase of northern Black Power that developed a theory of "internal colonialism" that characterized black people as a nation captive within a nation, defined either as a "white nation" or simply the American nation. The NOI, the Black Panther Party, the Republic of New Afrika, and similar groups deserve credit for popularizing a notion of racial confinement. Yet southern civil rights activists also engaged this line of reasoning; SNCC leader Stokely Carmichael recalled that "'nationalism' was no exotic import from Northern ghettoes, but indigenous to the southern communities out of which [SNCC activists] came."[17] Their entanglements with the most dreaded southern institution facilitated their ideas that race and freedom were grounded in a carceral experience.

The fact that women civil rights activists could be attacked with the same vitriol and incarcerated at the same rate as their male counterparts lent credence to civil rights activists' nationalistic claims: all black people, and certainly those who challenged white supremacy, were being incarcerated. And in the South more than the North, this short-term mass incarceration meant that black women who fulfilled certain standards of respectability could emerge as symbols of black radicalism. This gendered politics of respectability was bound up with the South's sexual citizenship, where black women experienced racism in the form of sexual violence at the hands of white men. By refusing to be bullied in the streets by police or vigilantes, by exiting the domestic sphere and embracing potential assault through incarceration, black women activists such as Rosa Parks and Diane Nash demonstrated a subversive respectability. Their organizing allowed for the creation of mid-1970s defense campaigns focusing on black women who challenged sexual violence, such as Joan Little and Dessie Woods. These subsequent campaigns thrived without attempting to appeal to middle-class notions of respectability.[18]

This enthusiasm for direct action became a bedrock principle of activism for years to come. In writings from and about jail, civil rights groups contributed to an American theory of antiracist revolution that sought to polarize racial injustice. That polarization, toward which Black Power theorists of armed struggle also worked, proved central in other political struggles against white supremacy. The civil rights movement, therefore, initiated a broader spectacular politics that the Black Power movement would later take up and take in new directions. Southern pacifists and other civil rights workers, not Black Power militants, first selected bombast and spectacle as an orientation for promoting black radicalism.

Rather than seeing patient organizing as the opposite of dramatic spectacle, the civil rights movement demonstrates their coexistence. Tensions certainly existed between media-made actions and the door-knocking campaigns of traditional community organizing; the two strategies coexisted but did so unevenly, and these tensions grew as the media took greater interest in certain individuals and tactics. Yet these tensions should not distract us from the shared emphasis on direct action that united the Congress of Racial Equality, the SCLC, and SNCC along with the local people who comprised the backbone of the movement as a whole. All of them relied at some level on turning incarceration into a spectacle of freedom. Mass arrests and an attempt to repurpose the jail cell required mass attention from black and white neighbors as well as among the national media. Further, these different strands were united by circumstances beyond their control: those who cautioned against media-driven actions nonetheless worked under the constant threat of arrest as they sought to organize black communities to claim their freedom. When arrested, more patient organizers relied on the same tactics of publicity as those who voluntarily sought out incarceration through dramatic acts of conscience.[19]

Paradoxically, the ubiquity of imprisonment removes the focus from any one particular location—even a location as seemingly fixed as a prison. Because so many activists were jailed, telling the story of the jail's role within the civil rights movement transcends any specific locale but instead pushes us to see the prison as a "regime"—a form of power dispersed across multiple sites.[20] City jails, county jails, and state prisons existed as part of a singular, if dispersed, system of incarceration. The differences in management between one prison and another, between a jail and a prison, mattered far less than the fact that these repressive institutions enforced the same set of power relations throughout the region—and, indeed, throughout the country. For the civil rights movement, "jail" and "prison" were largely interchangeable words to describe both the idea and the fact of incarceration. There are, of course, significant differences between the jail and the prison: the former is used for short-term or pretrial detention, whereas the latter holds people who have been convicted. This distinction mattered in terms of the length of confinement and to some extent the treatment, with the prison usually harsher (although Hamer's experience demonstrates how dangerous jails could be). But civil rights activists approached the jail and the prison with the same alchemy, turning the horror of imprisonment into the potency of camaraderie.

Hamer's intervention at the 1964 Democratic National Convention joined her experience in jail with a demand for what historian Hasan Jeffries calls "freedom rights"—that is, the bevy of "civil and human rights that slaveholders denied" black people, a list that includes the constitutionally guaranteed rights of speech, religion, assembly, due process, and suffrage as well as the human rights to live, love, work, move, and study without restriction.[21] The pursuit of freedom rights had engaged the southern criminal justice system a generation prior to the modern civil rights movement. Earlier generations of civil rights activists, especially those associated with the Communist Party, had challenged the southern judicial system as nothing more than an extension of the lynch mob. Several World War II–era cases catalyzed national and even international attention on the peculiarities of the thing called southern justice. Once again, this dynamic played out with special intensity in Alabama and Mississippi.

A string of dramatic frame-ups involving black men and white women focused greater attention on the Jim Crow South for a two-decade period beginning with the conviction of nine young men in Scottsboro, Alabama, in March 1931 and continuing at least until the execution of Mississippi truck driver Willie McGee in May 1951. The charges in each case synthesized the race/gender nexus at the heart of Jim Crow: in each instance, black men were imprisoned on false charges of raping white women. The Scottsboro and McGee cases were atypical only in the attention they drew, the mass outcry they provoked. A vibrant Communist Left rallied around the Scottsboro Boys, as they were called, providing attorneys, protests, and publications on their behalf. The Scottsboro campaign renewed a phase of leftist organizing against political repression. These defense campaigns enlisted the support of leftists and civil libertarians around the world to challenge the wholesale persecution of black people of all political persuasions and radicals of all colors. While the defendants were typically men, the organizers were disproportionately women. Progressive and leftist women spoke, wrote, petitioned, lobbied, strategized, and organized a social movement to save persecuted men (and some women) from the killing state.[22]

These cases often came to depressing endings: the Scottsboro Boys served years in prison, and Mississippi executed McGee, while scores of other fraudulent arrests took place and several executions occurred against the continuing backdrop of the lynch mob.[23]

More than any given legal outcome, these cases laid the groundwork for the next generation of activists to challenge the southern racial order. Both the NAACP and the Communist Party provided sophisticated critiques of southern legal practice, including the use of all-white juries to produce all-but-guaranteed convictions of black defendants. Both groups also provided resources for defending several targets of southern legal violence. The NAACP in particular refined an apparatus for using the legal system to challenge the racial injustice that often expressed itself through precisely that system. The organization's resources and savvy were often little match for white supremacy's powerful grip, and the group lost many court cases, but it nevertheless provided a spirited opposition to southern mores. Further, the NAACP identified the arena of criminal justice as a vital battleground for pursuing black freedom demands.[24]

With their bold direct action campaigns of the mid-1950s and 1960s, the new civil rights activists took this history of black anticarceral activism in a new direction. For them, the jail cell was a metaphor for the extent of racist depravity—especially in the South—as well as a sign of rising militancy. Both symbolically and in fact, the jail represented the harsh realities of southern life. Yet as activists repurposed the prison into an extension of the mass meeting, it took on another, more surprising meaning: it came to be a place of freedom. If jail could not break the movement, partisans reasoned, nothing could.

By the time of Hamer's stirring testimony, the black freedom struggle had nearly a decade of experience in using the jail cell as a strategic point of departure for gaining public attention to the fight against Jim Crow. The jails of Birmingham and Selma, Greenwood and Winona, and countless other places served as key battlegrounds in a two and a half decade national struggle during which black activists used the criminal justice system as a counterintuitive site in which to spark national action at the intersection of race and freedom. Literary scholar Houston Baker argues that civil rights activists turned "the entire apparatus of white policing and surveillance . . . into a vocational site for liberation. The white-controlled space of criminality and incarceration was transformed into a public arena for black justice and freedom." Baker dubs this the creation of a "black public sphere of incarceration" that has characterized the United States, in different ways, ever since.[25]

Beginning in the mid-1950s, then, white supremacy and black resistance met at the jailhouse door with special fervor. Southern segregationists hoped that arrest and imprisonment would enforce docility, whereas civil rights activists saw the criminal justice system as the best symbolic staging ground on which to challenge white supremacy. The population of southern jails and prisons was disproportionately black, as it had been since the dismantling of Reconstruction. But this campaign was not, as it would soon become, aimed at transforming or dismantling the criminal justice system. Rather, both sides sought to use that system to advance their solutions to the crisis of a segregated South. Incarceration was literally central to the movement. It occupied a structuring place in movement tactics and was a midpoint through which activists necessarily passed on the journey from emerging consciousness to committed political activism. The jail thus served as a critical tool in movement narratives at the time, just as it remains a distinctive feature of subsequent memoirs and biographies. Incarceration was a fundamental component of black life and activism.[26]

The jail was a consequence of challenging segregation but also an ongoing front in that struggle as activists brought the public consciousness into the prison, if briefly. In doing so, they carried on a tradition initiated through black vernacular, folklore, and popular culture—especially music—that sought to make freedom out of incarceration.[27] The terms could not have been more starkly put: as the movement struggled for "Freedom Now," it passed through the jail cell, while the condition of unfreedom that it opposed extended well beyond prison walls to encompass the totality of Jim Crow America. The movement demanded, even if it did not quite define, freedom. Freedom was the destination as well as the journey, something found in fellowship, direct action, and community organizing.

Freedom was the antithesis and the antidote to law and order: they were equally capacious, equally open-ended articulations of oppositional world orders. Freedom lay at the heart of the movement's culture: its songs and pictures and naked idealism. Movement songs, sung to annoy jailers as much as uplift activists' spirits, resounded throughout and beyond the prison. The songs constituted the leading thrust of the opposition to the police power, exposing the inability of even the harshest institutions to dampen spirits. This stubborn insistence on freedom conjured and simultaneously undermined its opposite, for why would someone need to demand freedom unless it had been denied? The repetition of the freedom demand challenged the typical American notion of where freedom could and could not be located. Civil rights activists turned the institution most associated with freedom lost—the prison—into a gateway to freedom found. Imprisoned together, movement activists claimed to be freer than they were in their daily lives of apartheid America. As they did so, they challenged the prison as a private institution removed from public life, sight, or access. Their position was clear: the jail could not imprison civil rights activists, for white supremacy already did.

In retrospect, this ubiquity of imprisonment can be seen as a dispiriting prophecy of the hypercriminalization that would mark the late twentieth century and beyond, where black youth every day faced arrest for petty infractions. Indeed, the threat of jail constantly hung over the movement. Imprisonment was the possible outcome of such otherwise banal activities as trying to vote or register to vote, ride a bus, order a hamburger, or go to the bathroom. But the story has another, equally interesting element: the ways in which civil rights activists embraced the jail and sought to repurpose it show a tactical continuity, too often overlooked, between Fannie Lou Hamer and Angela Davis, between Martin Luther King Jr. and George Jackson, notwithstanding their differing commitments to nonviolence and American ideals. The civil rights movement showed that the prison could be made public and turned into a source of power where prisoners could trump their literal and figurative jailers.

The direct action campaigns that illuminated the southern wing of the freedom struggle reveal a fascinating similarity between South and North, civil rights and Black Power. This similarity is born of a shared entanglement with the carceral state. Seen from the perspective of imprisonment, the southern civil rights movement shares much with the Black Power militants who were its contemporaries as well as its successors. Both movements exhibited a nationalistic commitment to racial unity as the precondition of interracial harmony and took for granted the women's labor needed for success. Both shared a strategic orientation premised on soliciting public support or sympathy through spectacular direct actions that appealed to the media. And both subscribed to a politics of respectability that sought to demonstrate the dignity of black life amid the dehumanization of white supremacy that extended from the city bus to the city jail, from the ghetto to the prison.

"FILL THE JAILS"

When Rosa Parks refused to give up her seat on that Montgomery bus in December 1955, she did more than rest her tired body and continue her tireless activism. Parks, a veteran organizer and champion of black women's dignity and integrity, inaugurated an era of black activism that used the prison system as its staging ground. Parks had a long organizing history with the NAACP, fighting sexual violence and other forms of black disenfranchisement. Yet she did not plan to launch a yearlong boycott of the city's public transportation system at the moment she challenged segregation on that Alabama bus. The recalcitrance of Alabama officials helped stiffen the movement's resolve. The nascent Montgomery Improvement Association, formed around the boycott but with deep roots in the Women's Political Council and the local NAACP, initially offered compromise solutions that would lessen the extent but maintain the structure of segregated transit. Indeed, the association's plan called for adopting the segregation practice used on the buses of Mobile, in the southern part of the state. There, black people sat from back to front and whites from front to back, but no one using that system was denied a seat.[28]

Yet Montgomery city officials refused to compromise and instead doubled down. They pressed charges against Parks, refused all of the movement's demands, and in February 1956 indicted eighty-nine black activists. The city leaders, fresh from a pro-segregation rally, described the indictments as part of a get-tough strategy. In fact, the move was an early skirmish in a law-and-order counterrevolution. The indictments held that the activists violated a 1921 statute prohibiting boycotts "without just cause or legal excuse."[29] It was the biggest indictment in Alabama history.[30]

The Montgomery activists—respectable women and men who had rarely run afoul of even the Jim Crow legal system—seized the moment and elected to go to jail. They surprised the city's elites by voluntarily turning themselves in while dressed in their Sunday best. They laughed with each other, sitting up straight and defiant for their mug shots. They expressed no fear of jail. The photos became and remain artifacts of black courage, proof that the movement sought to remake every aspect of the prison experience, from surveillance and isolation to fear and shame.[31]

From indictments came icons. The activists' dignity and comportment, starting with Mrs. Parks's initial arrest, nurtured a collective identification with the jailed and emboldened black activists. "Overnight these leaders had become symbols of courage," legendary organizer Bayard Rustin wrote of the scene at the first mass meeting after the group was released. "Women held their babies to touch them. The people stood in ovation."[32] The dignity of the indicted protesters impressed a wide audience. Following the arrests, the boycott organizers stiffened their Gandhian resolve and found support pouring in from around the country as a result of their commitment to bear witness against injustice. Just as important, the black residents of Montgomery began to shed their fear of the state's formidable criminal justice system, regardless of their views on Gandhian nonviolence. They became determined to conquer the prison.

The indictments had another unexpected outcome: they turned King, a young preacher, into a national symbol of the burgeoning civil rights movement. King's first arrest had come just a month before his inclusion in the sweeping Montgomery indictment. The Montgomery Improvement Association had recently launched a carpool system so that people could get to and from work without use of the city buses, and on January 26, 1956, King picked up a couple of people at one of the carpool's designated locations. Police arrested King on a spurious traffic violation and hauled him to jail. As on many previous occasions, a crowd gathered outside the jail demanding that the captive be released into the hands of the mob. But this crowd was different. It was not a lynch mob. Rather, it saw the prisoner as its hero, not its enemy. Much as abolitionists and antilynching activists had done decades earlier, the crowd demanded the prisoner as a symbol of its desire for freedom rather than a symbol of its desire for racial hierarchy. Fearful at the response, the jailers released King on his own recognizance. Here was the antilynch mob in full force, coming out to rescue a man they had only begun to know.[33]

This unexpected response was the first psychic break for black activists in weakening the stigma of the jail. It turned a historically taboo location into a place of pride and principle. It also brought added international attention to the boycott, which until that moment had been largely a local affair. And it forced the realization that southern power brokers cared nothing for moderation, pushing the movement to adopt more radical demands that challenged the system at its core.[34] Global attention, a collective refusal of the stigma of incarceration, and a stiff resolve against the dampening effect of moderation— these would be crucial resources in repurposing the criminal justice system throughout the civil rights era.

Montgomery was luck; the dramatic display of dignity and widespread support for the protesters caught many people across the nation by surprise. Subsequently, however, the civil rights movement sought out situations where injustice could be exposed. And the willingness to go to jail was a crucial weapon in the developing arsenal of this new wave of the black freedom struggle. As King ultimately laid out the logic, the plan was to orchestrate confrontations that would yield "the *surfacing* of tensions already present."[35] One's commitment to risking incarceration was crucial to this process of exposing the latent but structuring political tensions of American life.

The Montgomery Bus Boycott ushered in an era of nonviolent direct action in which activists demonstrated dedication in part through a willingness to go to jail. The boycott brought with it certain class- and gender-laden notions of which prisoners deserved support. Ideas of innocence continued to reign, even when embracing the guilty. For example, Parks's color and class status made her—rather than the younger, poorer, and darker-skinned women (Mary Louise Smith, Aurelia Browder, Susan McDonald, and Claudette Colvin) who had been arrested earlier in 1955 for refusing to give up their seats—the icon around whom the Montgomery Bus Boycott was built. The boycott's organizers came from middle-class backgrounds, which for black southerners in the 1950s meant steady employment, moderate comportment, and aspirations of upward mobility. Such incarcerations were more distinctive than those of the black poor, for whom the jail cell was a more familiar—and less voluntary—site.

Middle-class activists encountered the carceral state in more limited ways, largely in pretrial detention in jails or short-term lockup in state prisons for conscious political acts. Intimidating and rife with abuse as the jail experience almost always was, the activists were not serving lengthy prison sentences. Many of them differentiated themselves from other prisoners, describing part of the injustice of their incarceration as stemming from their treatment "like a criminal."[36] This position may have prevented deeper cohesion from emerging, but many imprisoned activists expressed their solidarity with the women and men they met inside.

The boycott inaugurated a new spirit of resistance. The next wave of this kind of direct action and widespread political incarceration did not crest until the spontaneous emergence of the 1960 sit-ins and the following year's Freedom Rides. In the interim, jail remained a looming presence in the lives of civil rights activists and southern black communities more generally. Imprisonment remained the potential price of registering to vote or infringing on Jim Crow's other written and unwritten rules. The southern criminal justice system was one of several expressions of white supremacist violence. Many civil rights activists during the late 1950s focused on developing adequate responses to racist terror, and the responses ran the gamut from increased training in Gandhian methods of nonviolent resistance to the institutionalization of armed self-defense units such as the Deacons for Defense and the Monroe, North Carolina, chapter of the NAACP, headed by military veteran and militant activist Robert Williams. These semiclandestine formations existed alongside a wider belief in self-defense among many in the rural towns where the civil rights movement set up shop.[37]

Such self-defense efforts not only attempted to maintain the physical safety of activists and community members but also signaled a growing fighting spirit. And even many activists who were attracted to Gandhi were more taken with his bold leadership and creative direct actions than with his philosophy of nonviolence.[38] Their tactical differences notwithstanding, committed pacifists, pragmatic nonviolent activists, and practitioners of armed self-defense displayed similar commitments to hastening the fall of Jim Crow throughout the 1950s and into the 1960s.

The sudden growth of the sit-in movement, which began with the efforts of four Greensboro, North Carolina, college students on February 1, 1960, offered a new vision of ways to protest Jim Crow with a mixture of creativity and democratic simplicity. The men attempted to order food at a Woolworth's and stayed seated after waiters refused them service. Nothing happened to them that day, so they returned the following day with more people. Local media covered the calm uprising, and the sit-in tactic spread. By the end of the week, sit-ins had occurred in eight North Carolina cities. By the end of the month, writes historian Clayborne Carson, "Nashville, Chattanooga, Richmond, Baltimore, Montgomery, and Lexington were among over thirty communities in seven states to experience sit-ins. The protests reached the remaining southern states by mid-April. By that time, according to one study, the movement had attracted about fifty thousand participants."[39]

Although the initial Greensboro sit-in did not attract the police, subsequent sit-ins elicited both white violence and mass arrests of black activists. The sit-ins inaugurated a wave of spectacular protests in the first half of the 1960s, with activists using creative and often courageous confrontations to dramatize Jim Crow barbarism. Such protests transpired alongside and in conjunction with the patient work of grassroots community organizing that enabled such spectacles to generate long-term mobilization.

The palpable enthusiasm for direct action nurtured throughout the 1950s exploded in the early 1960s. With direct action becoming the calling card of civil rights, activists increasingly questioned the state's ability to act as an arbiter of justice. How could the state that protected segregation sit in judgment of its critics? Activists began to view their court-imposed punishments as extensions of the segregated lunch counters and bus terminals. This growing radicalization yielded two new movement strategies, summarized in the slogans "Fill the Jails" and "Jail, No Bail." The former signaled the movement's decreasing fear of incarceration and embrace of spectacular confrontations, whereas the latter emphasized a rejection of state authority. Many activists felt that paying bail or a fine stemming from an arrest for movement activity would only legitimate the segregationist system. Choosing prison over payment, supporters of civil rights struck a blow against the "plantation mentality" by seeking to repurpose the institution that had replaced the plantation in the structure of southern life.[40]

In choosing prison, activists attempted to signal that they would no longer submit to Jim Crow. The "Jail, No Bail" strategy was controversial, and it never sustained the support of every activist who was arrested. Strategic or medical reasons at times prompted certain individuals to post bail, and political differences arose because that strategy was costly and required substantial human sacrifice. Nonetheless, the call to spend time in jail rather than post bail or pay fines fueled the movement. Across the South, a critical mass of activists began to fill the jails—first through an explicit attack on segregationist niceties, second by refusing to legitimize the system through pecuniary reprisals. This one-two nonviolent punch spread rapidly. Freedom Rides brought groups of people dedicated to this strategy to twelve southern states, while SNCC and the SCLC staged confrontations in particular cities and towns. News of these dramatic confrontations circulated widely, kicking off similar eruptions elsewhere.

As the sit-in insurgency spread across the South and calls to "fill the jails" grew louder, incarceration became not just a rite of passage but a precondition for leadership. The prison experience did not just embolden activists in their opposition to segregation but also constituted a possible point of division. At SNCC's April 1960 founding conference, one participant suggested that decision-making authority be vested only in those who had been arrested: "Everybody has the right to speak, but in this organization if you haven't been to jail you can't vote."[41] That position, an ironic twist on the risk of arrest that accompanied black attempts to vote in the South, did not win out but nevertheless reflected the prized position of the jail experience in the activist imagination. A few months later, King found himself challenged when he initially balked at the invitation to join student activists in an action in downtown Atlanta. "I indicated to him that he was going to have to go to jail if he intended to maintain his position as one of the leaders in the civil rights struggle," said activist Lonnie King, who convinced the reverend that he would need to participate in such actions if he hoped to retain his esteemed status in the burgeoning movement.[42]

These struggles over who would go to jail continued to follow the older, more established, more famous, and more moderate of the civil rights figures—including Martin Luther King Jr., though he largely came to agree with his critics in this regard, as well as others from SCLC and such top NAACP brass as Roy Wilkins. The message was clear: civil rights activists needed to go to jail to be taken seriously.

"FROM DUNGEONS OF SHAME TO HAVENS OF FREEDOM"

From their experience in southern jails and prisons, along with what they knew or learned of the long history of convict leasing, civil rights activists grew sensitized to the prison experience. The conditions inside were shocking enough to ultimately capture the attention of even the most moderate civil rights organizations, as witnessed by a variety of documents, including a 1968 report by the Southern Regional Council on the endurance of convict leasing in southern prisons.[43] But neither the heroic greetings from other black prisoners nor the brutal conditions inside—including savage beatings for refusing to address the warden as "Sir"—transformed the civil rights movement as such into a prisoners' rights movement. Rather, it strengthened activists' resolve to take down the broader "prison" of white supremacy while empowering other prisoners to launch their own efforts to improve their conditions.[44]

Through these direct actions, the jail experience became an extension of the mass meeting. Overflowing jails joined overflowing church pews to sustain the movement's energy. Reverend King praised the movement's success at having "transformed jails and prisons from dungeons of shame to havens of freedom and justice." Assuming the presidency of the Mississippi NAACP chapter, Aaron Henry pledged to turn the state's jails into "Temples of Freedom."[45] Other activists expressed similar sentiments. Jail offered a chance to recruit, to demonstrate one's spiritual and political resolve, a place to debate tactics and strategy. In dark cells and dilapidated cafeterias, activists strengthened their relationships and commitments to one another and to the movement that brought them to prison.[46]

When they were not placed in isolation, these short-term political prisoners, especially the black ones, often tried to forge common cause with the other men and women they met while incarcerated. While all civil rights activists faced violence from prison guards and staff, white activists often suffered jeers or assaults from the prisoners with whom they were segregated, whereas black activists frequently established a camaraderie with the other prisoners they met inside. Whether hostile or hospitable, though, these relationships were almost always short-term. The jail remained primarily a symbol for the broader problem of racial oppression.

The time in jails and prisons also gave rise to a black literary culture that proved especially catalytic for the Black Power movement. Prior to the 1960s, black prisoners had produced a rich and largely musical folk culture that described the racial ordeal of confinement. Black activists in the civil rights era added a literary element, and prison narratives began to blossom in the mid- to late 1960s. These narratives are understandably associated with figures such as Malcolm X and George Jackson, but the southern civil rights movement also produced its own literature of confinement. The signal text in this regard was King's "Letter from Birmingham Jail." Today, King's letter is remembered as a stirring indictment of passivity as itself a form of injustice; the document stands as an artifact of the civil rights movement's higher moral purpose, a defense of its urgency against the false promise of liberal moderation. It also helped to instantiate a genre of American prison writing that takes the prison as the staging ground for antiracist critique.[47]

Over the next decade, millions of people discovered the prison through the written words of dissident prisoners—both those incarcerated for their activism, such as King, and those whose activism arose from their incarceration. As confinement limited physical access, it privileged the written word. This emphasis on the written—and more to the point, *published*—record highlighted the knowledge and eloquence of the author. At the same time, it obscured the various labors that had gone into getting the letter, essay, or book from a prisoner's cell to the public eye. King's letter was part of an emerging literary field that utilized a gendered division of labor, whereby a select few male prisoners became well-known dissident authors, while the women who transcribed, published, or distributed these writings—as well as other equally articulate political prisoners who were less inclined to write—often labored in anonymity.[48]

King wrote his open letter on scraps of paper smuggled out of jail while he was serving time for violating a city injunction against protest marches. King addressed the letter to eight white Alabama clergymen who had publicly chastised the movement for going too far, too fast. King's response, written as the confrontational campaign reached its apex, outlined the inner workings of a nonviolent campaign and offered a passionate explanation of the movement's demands. King could have easily addressed the letter to any of the more overtly hostile forces allayed against the movement. His choice of the white moderate as his intended audience highlighted the movement's urgency and anticipated the ways black revolutionaries would, within a few years, use the occasion of their imprisonment to launch their own critiques of liberalism. From prison, King (as with later prison authors such as George Jackson) challenged the cowardice of moderation. His writing anticipated the Black Power critique, leveraged by Jackson, among many others, that liberal pleas for calm and respect for established channels perpetuated injustice.

Undergoing the indignities of confinement, then, afforded a certain moral authority to demand immediate freedom. Noting that "tension" could be productive, King also sought to locate the source of conflict as the system of white supremacy. "We merely bring to the surface the hidden tension that is already alive," King wrote. "We bring it out in the open, where it can be seen and dealt with. Like a boil that can never be cured so long as it is covered up but must be opened with all its ugliness to the natural medicines of air and light, injustice must be exposed, with all the tension its exposure creates, to the light of human conscience and the air of national opinion before it can be cured."[49] Imprisonment in pursuit of such exposure, he argued, was obedience to a higher law.

Initially obscure, King's "Letter" achieved growing popularity as an urtext of the southern civil rights movement. It was gathered in his 1963 book, *Why We Can't Wait*, along with other writings about the Birmingham campaign, which was pivotal for the southern phase of the civil rights movement. In Birmingham, the Manichaean struggle orchestrated by the movement played out with the most dramatic and violent force. Not surprisingly, then, imprisonment remains a persistent trope throughout King's book, a metaphor for the black condition as well as an all-too-common reality. In "The Sword That Heals," King noted how the new mood of black activism had reconfigured the meaning of the southern jail cell. Whereas imprisonment once meant physical violence and economic insecurity for southern blacks, the movement now offered a different meaning. Because the movement had offered jail as a way to expose the cruelties of Jim Crow, King argued that "to the Negro, going to jail was no longer a disgrace but a badge of honor. The Revolution of the Negro not only attacked the external cause of his misery, but revealed him to himself. He was *somebody*. He had a sense of *somebodiness*. He was *impatient* to be free."[50]

Imprisonment was a point of pride, a crucial site in the development of black politics; Jim Crow was so barbaric a system that going to jail now revealed a deep humanity that everyday life in the South sought to deny. King praised the tactic of filling the jails, arguing that about 5 percent of the black population in Albany, Georgia, went to jail as part of the protests there in 1961. "If a people can produce from its ranks 5 per cent who will go voluntarily to jail for a just cause, surely nothing can thwart its ultimate triumph," King predicted.[51]

In addition and quite unexpectedly, jail produced a certain joy. Going to jail was not just duty or sacrifice; it produced a counterintuitive sense of pleasure at refusing the shame of being arrested, the stigma or sheer terror of being incarcerated. (It helped, of course, that most activists were incarcerated for short periods in jails rather than long periods in state or federal prisons.) Movement activists delighted in getting arrested for their beliefs, in being able to fill the jails beyond capacity, and hoped that their dedication would tumble Jim Crow. "I felt no shame or disgrace," John Lewis recounted of his first arrest, for a 1960 sit-in as part of the militant Nashville student movement. "I didn't feel fear either. As we were led out of the store single file, singing 'We Shall Overcome,' I felt exhilarated. As we passed through a cheering crowd gathered on the sidewalk outside, I felt high, almost giddy with joy. As we approached the open rear doors of a paddy wagon, I felt elated."[52]

Such sentiment, while dulled by the boredom and violence of confinement, nevertheless continued for many activists inside the jail cell. In 1963, the movement brought the city of Birmingham to a standstill and rejoiced at the success. So many people were imprisoned there—more than twenty-five hundred—that the city could not arrest anyone else. With so many adults in jail, movement leaders decided to accept the support of the city's children, declaring that anyone old enough to go to church was old enough to get arrested. The police agreed. During one march on the "Children's Crusade," people were arrested "at the rate of ten per minute for nearly two hours."[53] The movement's pledge to fill the jails had become a boast that there were more activists in the movement than there were jail cells to hold them. In the Birmingham campaign and elsewhere throughout southern civil rights campaigns, jail was not just a moral act of witnessing but an exhilarating harbinger of freedom. As they had done in church pews and meeting halls, civil rights activists in jail cells sang freedom songs and sung the praises of the courage to commit oneself to the jailer. In songs laden with religious imagery, the activists sung of captivity and liberation, of suffering and redemption, of hope and perseverance.[54] Civil rights organizer Bernice Johnson Reagon, who later founded the a cappella group Sweet Honey in the Rock, said freedom songs served as a "medium of unity and communication" within the cross-class group of incarcerated black women and men.[55]

Throughout the South, black organizers emboldened by their dramatic confrontations with southern authorities viewed the prison as another bastion to conquer. Impatient to be free, they entered jail with a spirit of determined resistance. Imprisonment was an intellectual as well as a spiritual enterprise: activists formed study groups and debated political ideas with passion and urgency, bringing some of their organizational apparatus and movement culture into the prison. They sought first to endure imprisonment and second to enjoy it, a combination that would undermine incarceration's intended purpose. Throughout the 1960s and 1970s, black organizers maintained that the prison could not hold them.

In a Georgia prison after a raucous antiwar demonstration in 1966, SNCC organizer Michael Simmons, who had refused induction into the military, brought a healthy spirit of irreverence with him. When a guard told the ten imprisoned SNCC militants to stop chanting "Black Power" while they conducted menial labor, Simmons told him off. The guard then pulled out his gun. "You motherfucker," Simmons responded. "What you going to do, shoot us?" Simmons walked toward the armed guard, holding the pick with which he had been splitting rocks. "You got six bullets," he told the guard. "There are ten of us. Four of us are going to kill you." Simmons told him to put the gun away. "And I just kept walking towards him. Man, he put it away." Simmons acknowledges that his action was pure bluster, high on the collective spirit of black radicalism. "All he had to do was to shoot one shot in the air and say, 'Well goddamnit . . . it won't be your ass killing me,' and I would've shit all over myself," Simmons concedes. But the guard balked at this unexpected display of strength.[56]

To a large extent, activists' claims that they enjoyed or did not fear imprisonment were undoubtedly bravado. To confront a terrifyingly violent order, movement activists needed to convince themselves of their own power. They needed to make themselves feel invincible. They needed to turn the prison from a dreaded end into a tolerable point on a longer journey. They needed, in short, to strip the repressive regime of one of its most potent weapons: the fear it generated among its captives. And what better way to do that than to willfully undermine that most formidable of southern institutions?

Many activists found no joy in jail, and even those who found some modicum of it—typically the most stalwart of movement activists—at times feared for their safety. Life inside certainly bored everyone. This joy did not exist separate from the other feelings elicited by forced confinement: the terror and tedium of jail, the monotony and resentment. The difficulty of staying clean, eating healthy foods, and being treated with respect were a constant source of anger and frustration in jails and prisons. To them, life in lockup was a more concentrated form of the abuse they experienced throughout society. But activists took delight in the freedom songs they sang, the discussion groups they held, and the expressions of solidarity from other prisoners and from outside supporters that enabled them to, at times, talk back to the guards, protest the racial epithets and denigration, or launch work strikes with a stunning collective unity.

These emotions coexisted in the temporary communities forged through unfreedom. Indeed, as incarceration became an ever more prevalent feature of black social life and especially black political life, civil rights activists took their growing militancy into prison. The movement had at least temporarily accomplished a major feat: the jail was no longer an abstract bogeyman. If, as the reigning penal ideology at the time put it, jail was supposed to be the punishment rather than the place where punishment was meted out, a certain feeling of invincibility circulated within the civil rights movement. Activists believed that the guards could not carry out most of the threats they wielded against other prisoners because the jails could not hold all of the movement's supporters, especially as their cause garnered increasing public attention.

Ruby Doris Smith was one of four SNCC activists who traveled to Rock Hill, South Carolina, to fill the jails in protest after nine men were arrested during a sit-in there. The publicity their protests generated made Smith's brief prison stint even lighter. "We receive letters from all over the country congratulating us for our courageous action," she wrote to a Spelman student in the Fulton County jail after another sit-in. "I feel so guilty and unworthy because we are really enjoying ourselves." She concluded, "This isn't prison, it's paradise." Fellow SNCC organizer Charles Sherrod, sentenced to thirty days hard labor in Rock Hill, agreed. "You get ideas in jail. You talk with other young people you've never seen. . . . We're up all night, sharing creativity, planning action. You learn the truth in prison, you learn wholeness. You find out the difference between being dead and alive."[57]

This counterfactual embrace of the jail was premised in part on the leniency, at least in terms of sentencing guidelines, for multiple misdemeanor arrests at the time. While the treatment people received inside of jail cells was often quite brutal, as the testimony of Hamer and others so powerfully illustrated, people arrested multiple times in cases of civil disobedience faced relatively light penalties, especially with so many lawyers offering their services to the movement. Further, the middle-class aspirations of many of those who filled the fearsome jails of the South also promoted this surprising repurposing of carceral space. Precisely because college students, who might escape the fate of black agricultural serfdom, as well as the ministers and church leaders who functioned as power brokers within the community eagerly sought out imprisonment, such willful, temporary mass incarceration threatened the prison's taboo symbolism.

Not just class but Christianity shaped this paradoxical embrace of the prison. Activists' willingness to sacrifice their freedom, risk violent assault, and suffer for a higher moral power was in keeping with the Gandhian-inspired Christian ethic that dominated the early years of the most visible elements of the southern civil rights movement. Both the tactical decisions and the spiritual ethos of these partisans fit well within the longer history of nonviolent direct action among Catholics, Quakers, and other faith-based communities during World War II.[58] These earlier activists, including those who participated in the first Freedom Ride by the pacifist organization Fellowship of Reconciliation in 1947, bequeathed a legacy of submitting to incarceration to protest war and injustice. Even the many people who did not possess a moralistic or philosophical commitment to nonviolence shared what Carmichael later called a "moral stubbornness" that allowed them to use Gandhian methods.[59] As a result, abuse by jailers generally failed to quell the movement because its participants saw suffering and sacrifice as either rites of passage or helpful tools in movement building, sources of individual and collective strength. Whatever their beliefs regarding the methods and goals of the black freedom struggle, activists shared a willingness to put their bodies on the line—through risky direct action, through the ordeal of imprisonment, and in several cases through engaging in hunger strikes while incarcerated. These actions combined to strip Jim Crow of its power by denying its impact down to the level of the individual body.

Imprisonment featured monotony and isolation punctuated by the constant threat and frequent experience of violence. Yet the prison also served as a polarizing institution, a perpetual reminder of who and what the real enemy was. Even where people disagreed about specific tactics, they joined forces for the sake of upholding unity against the prison and the society it represented.

Difficulties and differences arose in a context that clarified the underlying stakes of opposition. Denied its power of secrecy, the prison proved a unifying force within the southern civil rights movement.

People's experiences in southern jails and prisons were not easy or uniform. People were often afraid, and some had more serious mental breakdowns.[60] The prison routinely exacerbated political or strategic differences. It is no surprise that the high-pressure environment of incarceration would result in bickering or divisions among those committed to moral witnessing and those invested in political struggle. This difference often manifested in debates over escalating tactics. Carmichael, for example, recounted a jailhouse debate over whether to go on hunger strike, with the committed Gandhians viewing the strike as the logical way to protest while incarcerated and strike opponents (including Carmichael) arguing that refusing to eat was dangerous and ineffectual. Stubborn and upset at having to spend his twentieth birthday in prison—the first of several birthdays he spent incarcerated as a result of his political activities—Carmichael joined the strike and was the last one to come off of it precisely so that he could tell his comrades never again to pursue that tactic. "I'm a very young man but I intend to be fighting the rest of my life so I'll probably be in jail again," Carmichael yelled to his fellow prisoners in neighboring cells after the strike ended. "So probably will some of you. So this may not be the last time we are together in prison. That's why I want you to remember my name. Because if we are ever in jail again and any of you even mention the words *hunger* and *strike*, I'm gonna denounce you properly."[61]

Both the joy and the misery of jail were structured by the gender of southern racism. Historian Zoe Colley writes that because black men were arrested more often, white men and black women in the civil rights movement had the worst experiences in prison: they were more often isolated from their comrades by the prison's segregation by both race and sex.[62] The relatively few white men who risked arrest for civil rights work could be set up for attack by racist white prisoners. Further, as seen in the brutality Hamer and scores of other black women experienced, black women were at particular risk for sexual assault by guards or prisoners acting on the guards' behalf. And the always latent, sometimes actualized threat of sexual violence was indeed a potent weapon used against some black women in prison or in police custody. Recognizing this vulnerability, some civil rights organizers launched the Youth Emergency Fund to "assure the personal privacy and protection of girls and women in southern jails." They pledged to visit women incarcerated for their organizing and to help them with any urgent needs. This short-lived development fit within black women's organizations' larger opposition to Jim Crow's sexual violence.[63]

All encounters with the criminal justice system were fraught with danger, both because of what would happen in prison and because of the prison's place within a larger geography of white violence. During Freedom Summer, the auspicious 1964 effort to organize Mississippi black communities and focus national attention on the apartheid South, more than one thousand people were arrested. In one of the most notorious murders of the era, civil rights workers James Chaney, Andrew Goodman, and Michael Schwerner were arrested on specious charges in Neshoba County. The sheriff released them to the Ku Klux Klan, which lynched the three men. Their mutilated bodies were not found for forty-four days.[64]

Though movement activists praised Christ and Gandhi, Bayard Rustin, Miles Horton, James Lawson, and A. J. Muste provided the protesters with mentorship in direct action. The anticolonial theorists who would so inspire the Black Panther Party and its generation of black revolutionaries—Fanon and Mao and Cabral and Guevara—had not yet put pen to paper or had not yet had their works translated and widely circulated in English. Yet the movement's emphasis on dramatic "acts of conscience" to polarize public sympathies and press for change shared much with the theory of armed struggle emerging from the world's national liberation struggles.

Indeed, the call from participants in sit-ins and Freedom Riders to "fill the jails" can be seen as an American foco.[65] Most often associated with Che Guevara and the Cuban Revolution, the foco theory held that a small, disciplined, and ideologically committed group could inspire the masses to action through exemplary actions. In Cuba and among U.S. insurrectionists in the early 1970s, such exemplary actions included violent assaults on government or corporate property or on police officers. Yet the southern phase of the civil rights movement utilized a similar logic: small groups of ideologically committed activists used dramatic actions as catalysts for mass uprisings. The four students who sat in at the Greensboro lunch counter launched a massive wave of sit-ins across the South, while four hundred Freedom Riders traveling in smaller groups elevated civil rights to a regular news item for six months in 1961. Both actions motivated others to pick up the cause when death, injury, or arrest prevented the original participants from continuing. For example, when white supremacists beat Congress of Racial Equality Freedom Riders in Anniston, Alabama, and burned the bus on which they were traveling, activists from Nashville quickly stepped in to fill the void. The dedication of this "nonviolent army" yielded much in the way of financial and moral support from around the country.

The bus fire in Anniston and the urgent embrace of the legal system to quell black insurgency reveal a deeper tension in the civil rights movement. The nonviolent army, with its protonationalism, coexisted with another form of nationalism that had its own army and far more institutional power. The white nationalism of the apartheid South pulled out all the stops to maintain the region's way of life. Historians have recently offered portraits of the white South as a more nuanced, internally divided region than it seemed at the time.[66] The white South was not a monolithic entity—differences existed in politics as well as strategy throughout the region; white moderates grew tired of the excesses of vigilante violence; and even committed white supremacists differed over whether to defend their order through the law or outside of it. Yet many officeholders and everyday citizens nonetheless organized on behalf of more police and harsher sanctions against those who violated an ever-expanding litany of laws. As civil rights activists broke the law in pursuit of grand goals, southern segregationists used the law to maintain their power. Demonstrators received lengthy sentences on spurious charges. The state's carceral capacity was strengthened by mass arrests and a wide range of collective punishment, including economic reprisals.

Mass arrests of political activists provided a dry run for mass incarceration, especially when joined with the economic transformations wrought by mechanization and migration. The civil rights movement gave states an early taste of what it would mean to arrest, prosecute, and imprison large groups of people (and to do so as pure punishment rather than coerced labor). Facing sharp challenges to their order and a diminishing need for black labor, southern states turned instead to the criminal justice system. Recognizing the ways in which the movement was making the most of incarceration, Mississippi authorities during the Freedom Rides altered the state's disorderly conduct provisions so that people who failed to pay bond within forty days lost their right to appeal and had to serve their entire sentence. Jackson officials used civil rights activity to justify the purchase of new weapons—including a tank—for the city police force. Other police departments followed suit, further militarizing American police departments. In 1963, Alabama officials tried to raise the bail amount required in misdemeanors from three hundred to twenty-five hundred dollars. Though the effort failed, it was one of many ways in which governments responded to the movement by attempting to amplify the police power.[67]

Local and state governments across the South enacted punitive ordinances to at least delay if not outright ban civil rights agitation. While these changes were in some sense precipitated by the direct actions of the civil rights movement, they sought a broader political realignment whose center of gravity came to be called "law and order." That the battle against segregation would take the form of a struggle over law and order is not surprising. After all, the law was precisely what was in question. Activists willfully violated and attempted to abrogate the laws of segregation, while southern white power brokers took refuge in the law to maintain their power. The racial disparity of incarceration had already been institutionalized, and whites who physically attacked movement activists were rarely arrested and even less frequently prosecuted for their assaults; in contrast, black activists filled the jails.

At the height of the movement's march from Selma to Montgomery in 1965, Lowndes County officials moved the voting registrar's office from the courthouse to the jailhouse. According to historian Hasan Jeffries, "The old brick jail, with its blood-stained cells, was the one place in Lowndes County that evoked more fear in African Americans than the courthouse."[68] The move also reduced the transport time should officials want to incarcerate any would-be voters. And where the stick failed, officials occasionally tried the carrot. As the movement succeeded in using imprisonment as a base for organizing, some southern sheriffs wanted to keep certain activists away. Montgomery police commissioner Clyde Sellers, an open member of the White Citizens' Council, paid Martin Luther King Jr.'s fine to keep him *out* of jail in 1958. The incident, repeated in Albany in 1962, was slightly embarrassing for King, who had vowed to stay in jail rather than pay a fine and thus legitimate the arrest for violating Jim Crow. White officials hoped that keeping King out of jail would weaken public sympathy for the movement, since they realized that imprisonment gave King power. Other high-profile figures also had difficulty staying in jail as southern elites noticed the movement's ability to translate imprisonment into public sympathy.[69]

Some notable movement leaders enjoyed an occasional buffer of protection from the white elites they opposed, though rank-and-file activists never had that insulation. Mayors, police chiefs, judges, and governors throughout the South used mass arrests to intimidate and thus quell the movement or at least temporarily quiet it. As white southerners responded to the civil rights movement with a combination of legal restrictions and mob violence, the jail became a way for elites to have both order and segregation, two things they prized highly. White mob violence aroused the nation's conscience and spurred a reluctant federal government to act. But in the context of larger economic shifts, the use of the criminal justice system arguably left a larger legacy. State police and officials tried to criminalize civil rights activists through arrests, injunctions, and bans while rattling the saber of law and order to prevent greater organizing.[70]

The white South responded to the civil rights movement by expanding and modernizing its carceral capacity. Southern states relied more heavily on the jail cell than the lynch mob, embracing the lawful state as a more reliable and less controversial enforcer of political order than the lawless crowd. In the coming years, local, state, and federal authorities launched an unprecedented campaign of prison construction and expanded police powers, and this carceral power proved itself far more enduring than a civil rights movement whose object was freedom. The popularity of the civil rights movement, which saw even young children willing to submit to arrest, left in its wake a strategy of policing that was increasingly comfortable with the incarceration of youth. In the decades that followed, the United States came to rely less on extrajudicial and vigilante violence and more on modern, technology-based forms of policing and incarceration. Police in Albany, Georgia, and Jackson, Mississippi, deflated the movement's attempts to stage dramatic confrontations in those cities in 1961 through a quick burst of mass arrests. Policing and imprisonment did what white riots did not: stunted the civil rights movement's ability to reach a national audience, earn public sympathy, and press for policy changes. In Albany, police arrested more than four hundred people in less than a week; police and white bystanders were not permitted to attack the demonstrators.[71]

Police officials succeeded because of their slick carceral management, arresting people quickly and quietly carting them off to jail. The use of widespread arrests was no coincidence; after studying Gandhi and the civil rights movement's "Jail, No Bail" policy, Albany police chief Laurie Pritchett determined that he needed to use swift, mass arrests. Pritchett instructed his deputies to follow a four-point plan calculated to both silence and criminalize black activists. First, police violence would not occur in front of the media. Second, arrests would be made on color-blind pretenses, such as trespassing, rather than for violating Jim Crow laws. Third, "Incarcerate, incarcerate, incarcerate." Finally, no negotiations with the movement would take place.[72]

The civil rights movement often benefited from confrontations where the carceral regimen was much more openly brutal and visible and where the movement could elicit public support by filling the jails. As a result, the state adopted a domestic counterinsurgency. It set out to weaken the movement through a combination of expanded arrests and limited public exposure. The savvy opposition refused not only to negotiate but also to give black organizers any venue, such as the media, that would enable them to reach a wider public. For the rest of the century and into the next, the United States would not lack for carceral capacity.

"I AIN'T GOING TO JAIL NO MORE"

As the movement shifted its strategies to prioritize political struggle over public sympathy, civil rights activists ultimately tired of the jail cell as a step on the way to a grander freedom. The beatings, deprivation, and collective and arbitrary punishments inflicted in prison had long defined black working-class life across the country and became an increasingly common feature of the black condition in the decades to come. But the foot soldiers of the civil rights movement came to see the jail as an obstacle to rather than a vehicle for liberation. This shift became evident in a speech by Carmichael on June 17, 1966, in Greenwood, Mississippi. Local police had arrested the SNCC chair during a massive march in the wake of the shooting of civil rights activist James Meredith. Released from custody, Carmichael was furious about the arrest and the larger violence it represented. "Every courthouse in Mississippi ought to be burned down to get rid of the dirt," he told those assembled. "This is the twenty-seventh time I have been arrested. I ain't going to jail no more. The only way we gonna stop them white men from whupping us is to take over. We have been saying 'Freedom Now' for six years and we ain't got nothin." With the help of fellow SNCC organizer Willie Ricks, Carmichael exhorted the crowd with a new demand: "What we gonna start saying now is Black Power."[73]

Carmichael's speech attracted a great deal of press attention and consternation at the time for allegedly shattering the civil rights coalition. In reality, he was naming a parallel and long-standing political tendency. The phrase "Black Power" had already become part of the black radical lexicon. Where civil rights activists had for years celebrated their march to the jails, Carmichael's demand for Black Power was a demand that advocating civil rights no longer be considered a crime for which jail was an appropriate punishment. Calls for Black Power came from multiple sources: from Harlem street speakers and Detroit mosques, from a growing number of books and plays, from prisoner organizing, and from within the civil rights movement. As more and more organizations dedicated to Black Power began to sprout up, many observers contrasted them with traditional civil rights groups. Of central concern were tactical and philosophical matters—most notably, whether groups were committed to nonviolence. Arguably more crucial were the demographic differences. The civil rights demonstrators tended to be drawn from the black middle class, with many preachers and students participating and with women serving as prominent and unifying figures.

Black Power, especially in its embrace of the prison, was a more masculine-centered project that appealed specifically to "brothers on the block"—both the street block and the cell block. This shift in class and gender demographics accompanied the urban uprisings of the mid-1960s, which were launched largely by under- and unemployed young black men. But as much as anything else, Black Power's success resulted from the bold direct action and strategic insights of civil rights workers. Women served as key strategists and insurgents, generals and foot soldiers in the wave of civil disobedience actions across the South that sought to repurpose the prison as a site of liberation. Women's work enabled the rise of a national movement among prisoners, even if public attention and mass militancy were more concentrated among male prisoners.

The civil rights embrace of nonviolent fellowship and the Black Power elevation of revolutionary armed struggle are not as far apart as they often have been described. Both shared an emphasis on media-generated spectacle. Both counterintuitively used the prison as a place of regeneration. And both told a story of collective racial confinement. This narrative centered the prison as a site of both repression and redemption. When it came to imprisonment, southern civil rights activists articulated a racial nationalism rivaling that of any Harlem street corner or Oakland college campus. They spoke of a whole people imprisoned at birth by virtue of their race and without regard to class or gender. And they showed the prison to be a jumping-off point for a broader struggle for freedom. Rosa Parks, Diane Nash, Martin Luther King Jr., Fannie Lou Hamer, John Lewis, Stokely Carmichael, and countless others marched into southern jails and prisons in hopes of making America mean democracy for African Americans. Many Black Power activists reared in New York, Chicago, Los Angeles, and other cities had been to prison for reasons other than civil disobedience, and they took a different lesson from those experiences. To them, as Malcolm X put it and the Black Panther Party later dramatized it, "America means prison."

CHAPTER TWO

America Means Prison

Don't be shocked when I say I was in prison.
You're still in prison. That's what America means—prison.
—MALCOLM X, "Message to the Grassroots" (1963)

illie Robert Tate was like a lot of young black men in California. He was born in Alabama and had lived in Texas before migrating with his family to the Golden State in the 1950s. As a teenager, his anger at the pervasive racism he encountered, especially from police, made him headstrong. And like many men of his age, race, and class, he soon found himself on the wrong side of the law.

He was first arrested at age fourteen. He had run away from home for six months, and when he returned, his parents told the police, who locked him up for three days. Thus began almost two decades of incarceration. The day after his fifteenth birthday, Tate entered the California Youth Authority for an assault charge. He spent the next twenty-one months in three different juvenile lockups. Released in April 1961, he was back in the system eighty-eight days later. By October of that year, he was at Deuel Vocational Institution (DVI) in Tracy, the heart of California's otherwise agricultural San Joaquin Valley. A decade later, Tate was a defendant in the biggest trial in California history, but in 1961, he was just another errant black man in the eyes of the state.[1]

As in prisons across the country, racism governed DVI. White prisoners harassed black prisoners with racial epithets all day and night. "I ain't never experienced racism as when I was sent to California prisons," Tate recalled. Amid a constant stream of racist taunts, prisoners fought each other with whatever means were available. "Tracy was a gladiator school," he said. The constant barrage of racial insults, especially prevalent in the lockdown and solitary confinement units, led to a running series of fights and stabbings—a state of undeclared but permanent war between black and white prisoners that was tolerated if not encouraged by the white guards. While Soledad and San Quentin became California's most notorious prisons, the violence at DVI was persistent.[2]

Black prisoners willing to fight white racism quickly bonded. At DVI in the early 1960s, Tate met a slew of individuals who constituted a growing cadre of black militants within California's prisons: George Jackson, "Big Jake" Lewis, Jimmie Carr, W. L. Nolen, Warren Wells, Herman Brown, "Little John" Gordon, and numerous others. They held study groups, discussed world affairs, debated political theory from Plato and Aristotle to Marx and later Mao Tse-tung. For most of these men, DVI was a temporary stop on a forced tour of California's high-security prisons. Later ports of call included Folsom, Soledad, and San Quentin, often with multiple visits to each. The lives of these men intersected over and over again at their various stops as they came to exemplify an emerging class of people whose fates were fundamentally bound up with the prison.

The process of protesting white violence bonded a black community that spanned California's penal system. As these prisoners joined forces, they tapped into a growing network of nationalist-inflected black insurgence. Indeed, the specter of black nationalism haunted American officialdom by the 1960s. A generation of organizing by the Nation of Islam (NOI) after World War II led many prisoners to identify with the group, and prison guards in California as elsewhere around the country labeled any black prisoner who expressed anti-racist ideas a black nationalist.

On February 21, 1965, Tate sat in the San Joaquin County Jail awaiting trial for stabbing a white prisoner as part of the ongoing battles at DVI when a guard approached his cell. "Your leader is dead," the guard told Tate with obvious pleasure. Denied much media access and not especially interested in the NOI, Tate did not realize that the guard was referring to Malcolm X. Tate liked Malcolm's ideas but did not consider the former NOI minister his "leader." Despite his disinterest in joining the NOI, Tate had crossed paths with adherents of the NOI and been impressed: they were disciplined and focused in their daily lives, confident and self-assured in their dealings with guards. And now, the guards delighted at the death of the most well-known, if former, member of the group.

While Tate's full appreciation of Malcolm X came later, the guards were not wrong in identifying Tate's sympathies with the black social movements arising in American cities. Across the country, young black women and men adopted increasingly radical politics and tactics to combat white supremacy. Their experience was formed at the intersection of spatial segregation, economic marginality, and political disenfranchisement. Steeped in histories of black self-defense, many of these young activists resisted the nonviolent doctrine espoused by Martin Luther King Jr. Veterans of violent assaults by the police and catalyzed by global ripples of social change, more and more black people, especially men, vowed to fight back physically. Their routine encounters with police inculcated a critique of the prevailing liberal order, since the promised benefits of the New Deal never seemed to materialize in the ghettoes of Harlem, North Philadelphia, South Central Los Angeles, and other predominantly black areas. And while the Great Society programs of the mid-1960s reduced poverty overall, black families remained impoverished at far higher rates than white families.[3]

By the middle of the century, the black urban experience was entangled with the black experience of confinement. The prison and the ghetto were two locations in a larger "carceral landscape" that encompassed black life.[4] As a result, a variety of black leftists and nationalists leveraged their critique of the American racial hierarchy as a rejection of imprisonment. They described racism as a prison that confined people to ghettoes, kept them under- and unemployed, subjected them to violence on the street, and caged them in a variety of punitive state institutions. A fiery orator, Malcolm X, put this idea most succinctly when he told his audience not to be surprised by his imprisonment, since America itself was a prison.

This rhetoric was picked up by a variety of radical organizations, most centrally the Black Panther Party, and it is no coincidence that many members of the Black Panthers, like Malcolm X, had been incarcerated in their youth. Having experienced egregious forms of state violence, these activists identified the prison as emblematic of American society. The prison reproduced a more volatile version of the racial differences that governed the United States at large. Developing in big cities and prisons around the country, black revolutionary nationalism responded to the shift from an industrial manufacturing economy to a finance and information economy. Automation eliminated thousands of jobs—disproportionately those held by black workers—and the new economy required a smaller, more specialized labor force. With limited options for gainful employment, many young black men found themselves in prison.[5]

The revolving door between the ghetto and the prison cell fostered black nationalist sentiment. The absence or loss of jobs and the expansion of policing fostered a radical politics of collective self-sufficiency in communities of color. Given that these communities, especially in major cities, experienced severe forms of state punishment, often in a segregated context, they defined intraracial unity as a vital ingredient of personal and group survival.

Black Power's critique of American apartheid spoke in an anticarceral vernacular. This framework affected the broader spectrum of insurgent politics during the 1960s. Black radicalism established the context in which the New Left and others also raised critiques of imprisonment. Members of these groupings drew on their own negative experiences with the police and the prison system; they were not mimicking black radicalism but rather following its lead in crafting political opposition to the prison as a repressive force. Indigenous sovereignty, Latino radicals, antiwar activists, community organizers of all types, and assorted countercultural rebels faced truncheons and fraudulent legal charges with increasing regularity throughout this era, drawing participants in these movements more deeply into relationships with the black social movements also confronting such state violence.

During the 1960s and beyond, the prison functioned as both a metaphor for race and an example of racial management. This combination animated the radical movements of the time but was helped along by a coterie of reformist social scientists, progressive and conservative alike, who described the city as a carceral space. Academics ranging from conservative Edward Banfield to liberal Kenneth Clark shared with Elijah Muhammad and Huey P. Newton a dreary description of the city as a place in peril and on lockdown.[6] Drawing on their experiences of policing and confinement, black social movements of the era described the city in carceral terms. In developing a theory of internal colonialism, Black Power activists borrowed Lenin's characterization of Russia as a "prison house of nations" to describe the United States.[7]

Men such as Malcolm X and organizations such as the Black Panther Party turned a long-standing critique of the racist application of the law into a poignant metaphor of the black urban condition. In an age of urban revolt and massive policing of black protest, this metaphor was highly material. To call the city an "occupied territory," in the words of author James Baldwin, or a "concentration camp," as in Clark's writings, was to indict the wider system of American racial capitalism as upheld by police and the criminal justice system.[8] This viewpoint facilitated the rise of the Black Panthers as an international symbol of Black Power. It captured the imagination of the New Left and the attention of a new generation of urban studies scholars who took up the question of internal colonialism. And it enlisted the support of a range of activists and cultural workers who turned their attention to the prison.[9]

American confinement was upheld by the police as well as the prison. As in the South, the police in the North and West constituted a frontline battleground over white supremacy. Whereas the southern legal apparatus dictated segregation across social and political arenas, the formal equality of the North was undermined by pervasive racialized poverty that the police, as an institution, enforced at every step. Through violence and ritual humiliation, police departments enforced spatial boundaries of segregation and "vice" at the street level. As Detroit NAACP branch secretary Arthur Johnson noted in 1960, in encounters with the police, "Negroes are daily made openly and painfully aware of their second-class status in the community."[10] Up until the 1970s, most police forces around the country were almost entirely white, and officers—many of them southern migrants, even more of them prone to racist invective—lived far away from the black enclaves they policed. As a result, the police became a common but foreign presence in the life of black urban denizens, a presence confirmed by black expressive culture throughout the twentieth century.[11]

The pervasive police presence led to greater institutionalization of black women and men in reformatories, jails, and prisons. Indeed, the police officer and the judge joined the social worker as embodiments of the ways the American state regulated black lives in the urban North. In the years after World War II, police departments in the North and West underwent a rapid modernization that saw them centralizing their resources and expanding their capabilities for surveillance. The expansion of police departments demonstrated the growing salience that the politics and policing of "crime" held within the evolution of American governance.[12]

Throughout the twentieth century, criminalization bonded the white supremacy of the modernizing South, with its convict leasing system, to that of the urbanizing North, where urban analysts across the political spectrum defined race, especially blackness, through criminality and devoted themselves to gathering evidence of black inferiority. These scholars and putative experts agreed that while many people violated the law, certain racial groups were predisposed to commit crimes. This process of racializing crime once included Eastern and Southern European immigrants, but by the early twentieth century it had been firmly attached to blackness. Social science, the modernization of knowledge production, greatly facilitated the process by providing seemingly empirical (and therefore, presumably impeccable) metrics detailing the race of crime.[13]

With these metrics in hand, white elites sought to manage the criminalized races through diverse institutions and spatial regulations. Real estate covenants, limited job prospects, and white mob violence restricted the criminalized races to certain areas of the city. These ghettoes experienced an excess of both carrots and sticks: they were heavily policed and disproportionately the subject of middle-class reform efforts seeking to remold the urban poor in the image of patrician white America. Both private individuals and city governments utilized an array of institutions to aid in this effort. Where that failed, especially as American cities underwent deindustrialization, elites increasingly relied on prisons to manage these now unruly populations. In the shadow of restricted immigration and job competition, black communities were typically thought to be the most unruly population. The state increasingly devised structures to mitigate disorder rather than to mitigate inequality.[14]

If the civil rights movement used the jail to make southern racial oppression a national issue, black militants in the urban North and West used their prison experience to nationalize their claim that white supremacy defined America itself. They shifted the focus from the southern jail to the northern (and national) prison. As black men of working-class origin, their experiences with confinement were more typical than the experiences of the southern civil rights activists who deliberately sought out the jail cell in protest. Even more than their civil rights counterparts, Black Power activists used the prison to illustrate the ways that race and class conspired to prevent democratic access. The prison, therefore, was a critical institution in the rise of Black Power as something both connected to and separate from the civil rights movement.

The prison was central not just to the black radical *imagination* but also to its *reality*. Building on U.S. counterinsurgencies staged overseas, state governments around the country relied on police violence and imprisonment to retain control. They saw in every demonstration, planned or spontaneous, a threat to their rule; in response, they offered a mixture of concessions and reprisals. They instituted a series of reforms in the urban landscape. Along with the antipoverty programs came a greater reliance on the criminal justice system: the policeman's truncheon, the judge's ruling, the politician's laws, the prison guard's keys. Indeed, this expansion of the criminal justice system also happened through the War on Poverty, as women receiving public assistance funds began to face surveillance and a host of punitive restrictions. The reality of counterinsurgency was increasingly summarized in three simple words: law and order.[15]

Central to the failed presidential bids of Barry Goldwater in 1964 and George Wallace in 1968, "law and order" was picked up by Richard Nixon in his successful 1968 presidential campaign. But law and order was a bipartisan affair. It resulted in more police, stricter laws, and ultimately massive growth in the scale and scope of the prison system. Criminalization, the making of people and actions into criminals and of criminals into public enemies, was the center of gravity that enabled the success of law and order. Like all counterinsurgencies, law and order was a project to remake society. But the law-and-order regime named a more specific and racialized enemy in the form of black insurgency. Longtime nationalist organizer Audley "Queen Mother" Moore, a veteran of both the Garveyite movement and the Communist Party, described law and order as the latest epithet in a long history of racist violence: "At first, you were coons, darkies, colored, niggers, Negroes; then we became crime in the streets."[16]

The growth of Black Power engaged the prison experience of working-class black people (especially men, who were disproportionately imprisoned). Indeed, though the overall prison population fell during the 1960s, the rates of black and Latino incarceration relative to white incarceration rose, as did the overall numbers of black and Latino prisoners.[17] Reflecting on a series of prominent black American activists who had spent time in prison, innovative theorist and seasoned world traveler C. L. R. James wrote that the political consciousness of black prisoners in the United States resulted from "the surroundings and experiences of urban blacks."[18]

These activists became the spokespersons for and shock troops of the Black Power movement—especially in two of the most well-known militant organizations of the period, the Nation of Islam (late 1950s to 1964) and the Black Panther Party (1966 to the early 1970s). These and other organizations renewed a long-standing critique of the confining nature of white supremacy and the racist character of American punishments.

This connection was bigger than any particular organization; it belonged to the bigger "southern diaspora"—the generations of black migrants who fled the South in favor of the urban North and West.[19] Indeed, millions of African Americans left the South in the mid-twentieth century: "In 1940, 77 percent of the total black population lived in the South. . . . By 1970, more than half of the African American population settled outside the South with over 75 percent residing in cities. In less than a quarter century, urban became synonymous with 'black.'"[20] Hundreds of thousands of black migrants settled in California, especially Oakland and Los Angeles. The experience of migration was itself pedagogical, showing migrants that seemingly impermeable structures such as Jim Crow could be breached through flight. The experience of physical movement held out hope for political and social movement. This lesson proved crucial in transforming the prison into a place of activism, whereas subsequent generations would know only the carceral ghetto without the same experience of global mass movements.

While black migrants and their children between the 1950s and 1970s may have escaped convict leasing and lynch mobs, they still found themselves trapped in a system of racist state violence in the form of excessive policing and disproportionate punishment. They populated a range of Black Power organizations, took to the streets in cities big and small during the "long hot summers" of urban rebellions (1963–68), and took over prisons during the historic wave of rebellions (1968–72). Indeed, if 1963 was the year of the "Negro Revolt," then 1968 was the year Black Power shook the world. As a result, the vernacular and strategy of the Black Power movement increasingly converged on the prison.

Given the intricate interweaving of race, punishment, and death, Black Power constituted an effort to craft a transformative politics of survival—to develop its own terms for confronting the carceral state. Black Power was an attempted mass prison break, an all-out effort to disentangle blackness from the carceral landscape of the ghetto and the prison alike.

"WHITE SOCIETY'S CRIME"

The first organization to turn the prison into a mass recruiting ground was the Nation of Islam. Formed in Detroit in 1943, it grew to become a vibrant organization throughout urban and carceral America. In part because two of its founding fathers had been incarcerated—Wallace D. Fard in the 1920s and Elijah Muhammad (born in 1897 as Elijah Poole) as a war resister during World War II—the NOI recognized the disproportionate number of black men incarcerated and saw prisons as a place to generate new members and spread its ideas.

Although formally eschewing politics, the NOI proclaimed its staunch opposition to American society. In its place, the NOI offered the dream of an independent black nationhood rooted in strong patriarchal authority. It described black men as natural geniuses and born leaders, preaching a combination of strident self-respect in dealing with whites and benevolent male supremacy in dealing with women. The NOI's unorthodox definition of Islam borrowed heavily from Marcus Garvey's black nationalism—the young Poole had been a member of Marcus Garvey's Universal Negro Improvement Association in the 1920s—and diverse strands of black evangelical religion, Moorish science, and numerology. For the Nation, only total racial separation could restore the dignity stolen from black people through the metaphoric prison that whites had created; the group's heterodox ideology even saw it make alliances with the American Nazi Party in pursuit of their shared desire to remove blacks from the United States. The Nation's mixture of racial paranoia, religious doctrine, and the promise of collective redemption appealed to thousands of urban black denizens frustrated with American racism.[21]

Throughout the 1950s and early 1960s, the NOI developed a reputation inside American prisons for the personal transformation and collective racial pride of its members. Elijah Muhammad actively recruited prisoners, responding directly to those who wrote to him and sometimes sending money.[22] Based in the black metropolises (Chicago, Detroit, Los Angeles, New York, Philadelphia), facing massive police violence, and recruiting from prisons, the NOI was for a time situated on the cutting edge of black life in the postwar United States.

It is not surprising that the Nation gained such a popular following among prisoners. The prison experience was marked by a loss of autonomy as individuals became numbers, not names. Their days were highly structured, and subservience was demanded. For many black prisoners, this environment represented a continuation of their experience of being controlled by white men on the job, on the street, or in dealing with government workers.

The NOI challenged these elements of imprisonment by neatly inverting their structure. It offered a metacritique of the prison, claiming that it was but an exaggerated expression of American society overall. Adherents to the Nation of Islam took on the last name "X" in respect for the surname that had been lost during the Middle Passage. These naming rites offered an affirmative embrace of a collective if unknown identity for those reduced to a number and a criminal conviction. The organization demanded that its members carry themselves with discipline—a self-regulation rooted in self-respect amid the coercive disciplining of the prison. And the idiosyncrasies of NOI cosmology offered adherents a powerful conversion narrative: an insider account of the "true" history of race and the structure of the United States, a set of codes and mores that invited people to make themselves anew for a higher spiritual purpose, a sense of superiority in an institution that continually told them that they were inferior.

For people subject to arbitrary and capricious rules made in private, the idea of a mad scientist creating white people may not have been so far-fetched. The NOI offered hostility to the prison and a host of personal practices adherents could adopt to give them a purpose beyond immediate survival. The Nation prescribed a personal rebirth rooted in high levels of discipline and pride, offering a familiar but far more welcoming hierarchy for men well versed in the strictures of confinement.[23]

The Nation of Islam offered a political explanation for black imprisonment as well as a personal code of conduct for responding to confinement. According to Elijah Muhammad, "The black prisoner 'symbolized white society's crime of keeping black men oppressed and deprived and ignorant.'"[24] The NOI's political economy of black imprisonment argued that black men were serving time as low-level dealers for a drug trade controlled by whites. Emphasizing white control of the formal and informal drug economy, the NOI offered a provisional class analysis—unabashedly pro-capitalist but stridently opposed to the racial concentration of wealth and power—for comprehending criminality.

Angered by the NOI's popularity, police attacked members of the group on several occasions. In California, the Los Angeles Police Department staged a violent raid on Temple No. 27 and shot seven members, killing one. Especially given the NOI's encouragement of black self-defense, such conflicts added to the group's allure for California's black prisoners, many of whom came from the Los Angeles area and were well versed in LAPD violence. The harassment and violence prison guards inflicted on NOI members—including the February 1963 murder of the San Quentin NOI minister Booker X—only confirmed the NOI's insistence that the prison was merely an exaggerated microcosm of the abuse black people faced in the broader United States.[25]

The Nation also offered some material support to prosecute "white society's crime." In particular, the NOI supported efforts to advance the religious freedom of black prisoners. Throughout the 1950s and early 1960s, the Nation supported a number of lawsuits against prison officials around the country that enabled NOI members to practice their faith. These lawsuits responded to official attempts to prevent NOI members from meeting together, recruiting others, praying, and eating the diet of their choice. The lawsuits, in other words, emerged from and served as points of organization for Muslim prisoners. Incarcerated members of the Nation of Islam worked together to demand diets without pork, east-facing cells, and religious exemptions from vaccinations; at the same time, NOI study groups and prayer circles facilitated an antiracist collectivity—in the form of consciousness and group action—in an institution governed by divisive individualism.[26]

The California Supreme Court agreed with prison officials' hostility to the NOI. In 1961, a judge ruled that the Nation's belief "in the solidarity and supremacy of the dark-skinned races . . . present[s] a serious threat to the maintenance of order in a crowded prison environment."[27] Illinois officials similarly argued against the NOI's growing popularity on the grounds that "any concession [to the Black Muslims] is a step towards chaos."[28] Echoing other elite approaches to the threat of disorder, the court allowed black nationalism to justify punitive policies. Yet the lawsuits kept coming: between 1961 and 1978, more than sixty federal decisions involved NOI members.[29] While these various cases produced mixed verdicts—including some stunning victories—the bigger impact lay in the fact that they provided a judicial precedent for challenging prison conditions. Through a combination of popular pressure and judicial rulings, prisoners began to have more religious freedom, less mail censorship, and greater political power. These lawsuits initiated more than two decades of court battles for prisoners' rights and further exposed the prison to public critique as a site of black repression—and black organizing.[30]

The NOI's popularity in those years owed in large part to the talented speeches of Malcolm Little, a petty hustler turned powerful orator and organizer who became known to the world as Malcolm X. Born in Nebraska in

1925 to Earl and Louise Little, devoted members of Marcus Garvey's Universal Negro Improvement Association, Malcolm first experienced a "detention home" for boys in Michigan at the age of fourteen, six months after his mother was institutionalized in a mental hospital. By his late teenage years, Malcolm was living with an aunt in Massachusetts, where he was part of a small group that committed a series of burglaries. In a two-year period, he was arrested three times for robbery, larceny, and breaking and entering. In February 1946, three months short of his twenty-first birthday, Little was sentenced to serve between eight and ten years in prison, a harsh penalty that he attributed to the fact that he had committed robberies with a group of black men and white women.

Two years later, after receiving several letters from siblings who had converted, Little joined the Nation of Islam. He spent his remaining time in prison reading voraciously and agitating for religious freedom. With other NOI converts, he demanded a pork-free diet and an eastward-facing cell and wrote a series of protest letters to state officials and local media. He also dropped his surname and became known as Malcolm X. Released from prison in 1952, he was working full time for the Nation of Islam within a year.[31]

For the next decade, Malcolm was a dedicated disciple of the NOI and its leader, Elijah Muhammad. Muhammad preached about the evils of "white society" but rejected anything resembling formal politics. He urged his followers not to register to vote, a drastic divergence from one of the primary strategies of the southern freedom movement. Malcolm X shifted the NOI's avoidance of electoral politics as well as its self-described "nonpolitical" stance. He broadened the NOI's message with a radical anti-imperialism that took the NOI's claustrophobic nationalism in explicitly political directions. Malcolm aligned himself with the Third World, situating the black freedom struggle as part of a global struggle to "end white world supremacy."[32] He led several militant demonstrations against police departments around the country that had arrested, beaten, and detained NOI members. With the newspaper *Muhammed Speaks*, Malcolm established another medium for spreading a message of personal and political transformation.

The specter of imprisonment haunted blackness, and Malcolm tapped into a deep-seated black experience of confinement. "You let this caged-up black man start realizing, as I did [while in prison], how from the first landing of the first slave ship, the millions of black men in America have been like sheep in a den of wolves. . . . 'The white man is the devil' is a perfect echo of that black convict's lifelong experience," Malcolm wrote in his autobiography.[33] He offered a politics of metaphor, arguing that blacks needed to overcome centuries of slavery and false consciousness. He described "twenty million Black people in a political, economic, and mental prison" and connected his personal history of incarceration with the racism endemic to the United States. "If you're black, you were born in jail, in the North as well as the South," he told listeners on more than one occasion.[34] His depiction of the overarching prison that confined all black Americans connected the plantation to the modern-day ghetto. He excoriated blacks who submitted to whites (a category in which he included participants in the modern civil rights movement, whom he described as being moderated by the influence of middle-class Christian pacifism) as pitiful "house Negroes" while praising militants as "field Negroes."

Metaphors make compelling polemics but lousy history: house slaves were often central to slave resistance precisely because of their proximity to the master's family.[35] But his framing left a lasting impact on black radical politics, especially inside American prisons. Malcolm helped shatter the stigma of incarceration by speaking openly about his six-year incarceration. He encouraged commitment, discipline, and action. He provided a political reading of imprisonment as entwined with racism and dating back to enslavement, and he offered a potent example of conversion from the petty criminality fostered by inequality to a dignified masculinity fostered by spiritual devotion and revolutionary nationalism.

For more than a few prisoners, Malcolm's influence was more pervasive than a commitment to the NOI itself, and when Malcolm parted ways with the NOI, these militants followed him. "Malcolm X had a special meaning for black convicts," Eldridge Cleaver wrote from his California prison cell. "A former prisoner himself, he had risen from the lowest depths to great heights. For this reason, he was a symbol of hope, a model for thousands of black convicts who found themselves trapped in the vicious PPP cycle: prison-parole-prison."[36] To Cleaver, who was attracted to the NOI for its oppositional posture, Malcolm's censure by Muhammad exposed the limitations of the Nation's antipolitical position. Prisoner members of the NOI advocated self-defense and pressed for religious freedom, including the right to hold meetings and study collectively. The NOI continued to be a gathering ground for black men seeking an anti-Western mode of personal transformation in prison. But the Nation's support for prisoner organizing did not extend to other human rights challenges to imprisonment, and those prisoners loyal to Malcolm X's political doctrine over Elijah Muhammad's religious one looked for other means of pressing their demands.[37]

Dissident black prisoners saw in Malcolm a prophet of black radicalism who could stand up to the structures of white supremacy. His life, especially as told in the posthumously published autobiography written with Alex Haley, offered the sort of powerful conversion story that has long anchored prison narratives: the transition from hustler to principled, self-possessed man. Published in 1965, *The Autobiography of Malcolm X* appeared in the middle of a prison literary renaissance. While earlier narratives, including three popular books by California death row prisoner Caryl Chessman between 1954 and 1957, offered intimate portraits of prison life, Malcolm's autobiography joined the prison narrative to the rich tradition of black testimonials on slavery or Jim Crow. It put to paper a black critique of confinement that had previously been most widely circulated through song.[38]

The story arc of Malcolm's *Autobiography* would inform a slew of prisoner writings throughout the time period: each one chronicled upbringing amid urban poverty, experiences of racism and an explicit search for a positive racial identity in the context of an assumed framework of masculinity, and a personal/political redemption that came during the author's incarceration for criminal acts. In these narratives, the prison and the city were two sides of the same carceral coin. While none of the books described life in prison in great detail, the prison was a necessary setting in which each author transformed himself into a self-actualized, racially conscious man. The prison therefore emerged as a step on the ladder out of poverty, usually to a position of political radicalization. In a twist on the rehabilitative ideal of imprisonment, such descriptions painted the prison as a conduit of political transformation. The prison was not a static, totalizing site but a breeding ground for a radical politics of survival. The city served as the prominent setting for the author's upbringing, exposure to white supremacy, and descent into crime; politicized in prison, the author then returned to the city dedicated to fighting racism.[39]

Malcolm parted ways with the Nation of Islam just as urban revolts around the country seemed to demonstrate the black insurgency of which he spoke. Dissident black prisoners increasingly pinned their hopes to these new urban guerrillas. Between 1963 and 1968, hundreds of urban rebellions took place as a consequence of black dissatisfaction with a racial hierarchy most visibly characterized by structural unemployment and rampant police brutality. The biggest of these incidents—Watts in 1965, Detroit and Newark in 1967—caused millions of dollars of damage and resulted in dozens of deaths and hundreds of people being imprisoned. But no city was immune to the spirit of black militancy and frustration. Plainfield, a small suburban town in northern New Jersey, experienced an uprising in 1967 that saw insurgents raid the Plainfield Machine Company, a local gun manufacturer, and use the weapons to hold off police and the National Guard.[40]

Alongside legal victories against Jim Crow, notably the Civil Rights Act of 1964 and the Voting Rights Act of 1965 as well as the 1967 Supreme Court ruling that ended "miscegenation" law, black protest erupted with increasing stridence in northern cities. These legal developments offered new possibilities for black involvement in U.S. political society, but their tardiness and limited scope also illustrated what the law could not do or at least had not yet done to eliminate white supremacy. These changes incorporated some African Americans and radicalized others as well as heightened national interest in the race, racism, and racial justice activism of the urban North and West. This shift created space for other groups, among them Chicanos in the Southwest and Puerto Ricans in the Northeast and Midwest, to attract national attention. These uprisings were crucial to this burgeoning awareness of racial tensions. As one participant in the Watts uprising declared, "We won, because we made them pay attention to us."[41]

The attention was undeniable, but the response was often undesirable. As with the response to the wave of mass direct action across the South, northern elites at both the local and national levels treated the urban uprisings of the mid-1960s as an exercise in counterinsurgency. The response included an acceleration of the War on Poverty as well as a dramatic expansion of the police power. Elected officials used police and the National Guard to carry out widespread arrests and jailings amid widespread speculation that the city itself was a space of confinement and danger: a carceral space. Such responses, discursive and juridical, connected black and Latino urban residents to fears of disorder and decay. The urban rebellions of 1964–68, in other words, "eased the conflation of street crime with black frustration over equality."[42] Local governments in the North already had been enlarging their policing apparatus in response to black activism and migration, and they now sped up this process. During the 1967 Detroit rebellion, for example, more than seven thousand people were arrested. Although these arrests resulted only in brief incarcerations, they were dry runs at dedicating massive state resources to widespread imprisonment. As the economy began its postindustrial turn, elites changed these urban uprisings into experiments in detaining large numbers of people.[43]

The demographics and tactics of American policing shifted after the uprising. As black politicians increasingly assumed mayoral positions, they worked to increase the number of black police officers in hopes of decreasing police brutality.[44] At the same time, many police chiefs and white politicians beat the drums for greater police power so that policing would be as all-encompassing as the revolt. Police department Red Squads, Cold War creations dedicated to tracking and undermining erstwhile communists and their sympathizers, could not handle the job alone. Many officials pursued a police apparatus that was highly militarized and highly visible.

After the 1965 rebellion in the Watts section of Los Angeles, California took a leading role in this expanded policing apparatus. The five-day uprising resulted in thirty-four deaths and hundreds of millions of dollars in damage. The scale of the uprising made the police enhance their capacities. Sparked by an incident of police brutality, the Watts rebellion was a protest against the police as an institution at the crux of black oppression. It also catalyzed a growing action orientation among black militants that did not stop at nonviolence. After Watts, the LAPD instituted "stop-and-frisk" policing. In 1967, the department inaugurated the first Special Weapons and Tactics (SWAT) team, a hypermilitarized elite police force that has since become a standard part of American policing. SWAT teams formalized the militarization of police departments in other cities as well; after Watts, Detroit police launched a "tactical mobile unit" that extended its aggressive policing practices in poor black neighborhoods and ultimately led to the creation of an undercover paramilitary unit.[45]

At the federal level, officials conceived a sweeping overhaul of federal police practices as well. In response to the rising urban discord, including a conservative chorus in favor of greater "law and order," Lyndon Johnson declared a "war on crime" in 1965 and lobbied Congress to pass the Law Enforcement Administration Act. The Office of Law Enforcement Assistance opened its doors in 1965, "a small but significant expansion of the federal role in crime control."[46] The Law Enforcement Administration Act took effect with the Omnibus Crime Control Act of 1968. By the time the agency closed its doors in 1981, it had stewarded a sweeping overhaul of federal law enforcement. The acts strengthened connections between federal and local police as well as between police and corrections and provided millions of dollars to fund new police hardware and research on effective policing strategies.[47] The Omnibus Crime Control Act was the most sweeping measure enacted in 1968, but it was not the year's only boon to police power: on April 11, one week after Martin Luther King Jr. was assassinated in Memphis, setting off street protest around the country, Congress passed the Federal Anti-Riot Act, popularly known as the H. Rap Brown Act, after the fiery SNCC leader who allegedly inspired its passage. The act mandated harsher sentences for those who crossed state lines for the purposes of rioting.[48]

Richard Nixon rode the wave of legislation, advocated by a liberal president and passed by a Democratic-controlled Congress, to electoral victory that fall by promising to restore law and order. At the Republican National Convention, Nixon promised that "the long dark night for America is about to end."[49] The rush to pass new laws, to institute new modes of state security, gained less attention but was no less significant than the rebellions themselves. The counterinsurgency, first manifest through a massive boost to police forces, had a carceral need. As with any counterinsurgency, the target was not just the insurgents but society as a whole. Now that police had the tools and authority to arrest more people, now that prosecutors had the official mandate to try more people on more charges, now that prison officials had the authority to keep people in prison longer, where were all these newly criminalized populations going to go?

"WE WANT FREEDOM"

In politics, spontaneity is often the midwife of organization. The urban rebellions of the mid-1960s were expressions of collective frustration. Typically catalyzed by incidents of police violence, the uprisings bespoke lifetimes of frustration, marginalization, and hope. The uprisings targeted both police and property, symbolizing urban residents' lack of authority over their domain.[50] In the wake of these rebellions, a variety of groups worked to harness the explosive energy of the black, Chicano, and Puerto Rican inner city. Research at the time indicated that those who took part in the riots were largely men aged fifteen to twenty-four, disproportionately un- and underemployed, undereducated, and sympathetic to black radicalism even if they were not members of existing groups.[51] Several organizations worked to seize the initiative in response to the urban uprisings, including semicovert organizations such as the Revolutionary Action Movement.[52] But the organization best able to speak to this population, the organization best able to channel and reflect the spirit of open revolt against the racialized class system of the United States, was the Black Panther Party for Self-Defense (BPP).

Huey P. Newton and Bobby Seale formed the Black Panther Party in Oakland, California, in October 1966. Newton and Seale encapsulated the rise of black Oakland: born in the South, studying at the working-class Merritt College, well traveled in the field of black protest, and veterans of the two primary institutions that, as the old joke went, gave black men an education. Seale served in the military and Newton had been incarcerated as a juvenile in the California Youth Authority. Both men had been active in black radical study groups and organizations, the Soul Student Advisory Council and RAM, prior to forming the Panthers. From these experiences, they crafted a radical politics of self-sufficiency to confront urban inequality.[53]

The BPP began as a local organization but within two years had chapters around the globe and was seen as a standard-bearer for revolutionary politics, a reputation that remains attached to the organization's legacy. Before the Black Panther Party was exceptional, however, it was typical. Its approach, in both politics and aesthetics, reflected the contours of black youth revolt in American cities. Its response echoed that of several other organizations confronting the everyday conditions of racism. Black women and men around the country were gravitating toward a politics that combined community organizing, anti-imperialism, personal dignity, self-defense, black pride, and bold confrontation with the state. Many youth who witnessed or participated in the urban uprisings or who had other violent encounters with police were looking for more direct ways to confront the system. More than a few greeted the growing militarization of the police by seeking access to weapons and training in how to use them.[54]

The Black Panthers formalized rather than invented this radical trajectory. Two of the organization's most well-known attributes—its name and its widely influential ten-point platform—were borrowed from other black radical organizations. The group took its name from two earlier Black Panther parties: a radical electoral effort in Lowndes County, Alabama, and a Harlem-based effort to unite revolutionary nationalists beginning in the summer of 1966. Neither group lasted as long as the Oakland Black Panthers, but each contributed something to the rise of the better-known group.[55]

In addition, the Oakland BPP took its emphasis on education and self-defense from a long history of southern black struggles. The group's platform, first publicized in May 1967 under the name "What We Want, What We Believe," built on a document Malcolm X had written for the NOI in 1963. Malcolm's platform, titled "What the Muslim Wants, What the Muslim Believes," began with a bold declaration that the Panthers repeated: "We want freedom." Malcolm's platform sounded other themes that reappeared in the Panthers' version, including calls for separate national territory, education relevant to black children, equal employment, and freedom for black prisoners. Malcolm's version specified freedom for Muslims in federal prison, where Elijah Muhammad had been held as a war resister. The Panthers, all of whom were men at this point and many of whom had spent time in juvenile or adult detention, broadened Malcolm's message: "8. We want freedom for all Black men held in federal, state, county, and city prisons and jails. 9. We want all Black people when brought to trial to be tried in court by a jury of their peer group or people from their Black communities. As defined by the constitution of the United States."[56] In explaining these demands, the Panthers deployed a colloquial but learned constitutionalism to challenge the extreme racial disparities in arrests, trials, and imprisonment.

The Black Panther Party and the militant Black Power movement of which it was a central element targeted the prison as well as urban institutions, especially schools and hospitals. Unlike other institutions, however, the prison was inherently an impediment to freedom; a change in management could not fix its problems. The BPP's critique of prisons included both the brick-and-mortar institutions and the wider political order that governed them. The growing importance of the prison in black political thought can be traced through the Panthers' evolution.

If Malcolm X had taught a generation that prison could be the site of personal transformation, the Black Panthers showed that it could also be a site of collective transformation. As successive Panthers found themselves facing police harassment, serious charges, or time in prison, the party's concern extended beyond fair trials to more directly challenge the prison as an institution. Prisons influenced the daily work of what it meant to be a Black Panther, as members were expected to visit, write letters to, answer phone calls from, and generally raise awareness about the existence of its political prisoners. By 1972, the BPP program called for "the elimination of all prisons and jails in the U.S., and trial by a jury of peers for all persons charged with so-called crimes under the laws of this country." "Oppressive conditions" were labeled "the real cause" of black imprisonment, making all trials under U.S. rule inherently unfair.[57]

The platform, along with the organization's active partnership with other leftist groups, encapsulated the Black Panthers' position as a revolutionary black organization dedicated to class struggle. While the politics would gain a large following, what first made the BPP stand out was its twinned public display of the gun and the law book alongside a uniform of sunglasses, leather jacket, black beret, and a sharp-tongued response to the police. The Panthers' blunt style of organizing brought direct action and self-sufficiency to new performative heights. Noted French novelist and playwright Jean Genet, a vocal and prominent supporter of the group, argued that the Panthers' skillful use of images authored its success as well as its downfall. Genet was denied a visa to enter the United States, but his admiration for the Panthers led him to sneak into the country to lecture and raise funds on their behalf. He recognized the power of their symbols even as he maintained that symbols could not supplant more real acts. "The Black Panthers attacked first by sight," he argued.[58] Lacking a base of land to call their own, Genet wrote, black Americans needed another venue for political challenges, and they found it "in people's consciences. Wherever they went the Americans were the masters, so the Panthers would do their best to terrorize the masters by the only means available to them. Spectacle. . . . But spectacle is only spectacle and it may lead to mere figment, to no more than a colorful carnival; and that is a risk the Panthers ran."[59]

Genet's meditations on the role of spectacle in amplifying the power of the powerless endeared him to the Black Power movement and its emerging prison outposts. His interest in spectacle and in tropes of light and dark as metaphors for discovering the nuances of stark social divides made him a natural ally for the bombastic iconography of the Black Panther Party, with its uniforms and its trenchant dismissal of traditional American authority. In his public lectures, Genet implored his listeners to support the Panthers, arguing that they had the moral force to compel a wholesale abandonment of American institutions and norms. Black political prisoners, Genet said, were the lynchpin of this ethical mode of antiracist action. "And if it becomes necessary, I mean if the Black Panther Party asks it of you," Genet told American students as Seale and his fellow Panther, Ericka Huggins, awaited trial in Connecticut, "you ought to desert your universities, desert your classrooms, in order to speak out across America in favor of Bobby Seale and against racism."[60]

The Black Panther Party was made and unmade by its encounters with state repression. The Panthers faced steady police assault that, when used to spur further organizing and outreach, contributed to the BPP's quick development into a national and then global organization. Its ability to turn repression into resistance, at least initially, resulted in part from the fact that many of its early recruits had spent time in juvenile detention. The campaigns to save party leadership from prison after altercations with police gave rise to Panther chapters around the world.

The Panthers spread across California in 1967 and across the world the following year, largely in response to the arrest and prosecution of cofounder Huey P. Newton and the assassination of Martin Luther King Jr. For many young people, King's death and Newton's incarceration demonstrated the need for militant responses to the virulence of American racism. Newton was arrested on October 28, 1967, following an encounter with Oakland police that left officer John Frey dead and another officer and Newton wounded. One year after the Panthers' founding, then, its key theorist and leader was in jail facing the death penalty.

Newton's arrest came weeks after Bay Area antiwar activists held a weeklong series of militant demonstrations to shut down the U.S. Army induction center. The activists' street battles with police and mass arrests further aligned antiwar activists with the Panthers' radical critique of police and prisons. Many of those involved had already developed a critique of the prison system through long histories of civil rights and antiwar activism, and the Panthers asked participants in Stop the Draft Week to help build the Free Huey campaign. The subsequent conspiracy trial of seven leaders of the Stop the Draft Week action also brought antiwar activists closer to the Panthers, especially since Panther attorney Charles Garry was part of the defense team for the Oakland 7. As growing numbers of draft resisters confronted exile or imprisonment, the prison occupied a growing place in the work of a variety of New Left activists, sparking further identification with the Black Panthers.[61]

Alongside their work against police brutality, the Panthers now focused on freeing Newton. The campaign to spare Newton from prison and possibly the death penalty was perhaps the largest such effort since the Rosenberg case of the early 1950s. The turn to defense campaigns, which became increasingly important as the FBI and local police sought to destroy the organization, brought the Panthers into ever-larger coalitions with diverse groups of activists and civil libertarians. The campaign for Newton, which resembled earlier leftist defense campaigns in emphasizing simultaneously the legal innocence and revolutionary mettle of the accused, also brought greater numbers of people to focus on exposing the cruelties of imprisonment.[62]

Indeed, as historian Rebecca Hill writes, such political defense campaigns historically "have worked primarily through appeals to public opinion in the media, used stories of terror and heroism to build alliances across lines of class and race, and have been formative in the creation of radical political identities. They are united in proposing an alternative argument about power in contrast to the predominant liberal theories of the relationships between minorities and majorities or the interests of the individual in relation to the prerogatives of a state, assumed to represent the community as a whole." The Panthers extended these traditions with a Black Power vernacular that drew "white radicals into solidarity with carnivalesque attacks on the 'pig' in support of a Black 'lumpen' revolution."[63]

As Newton issued edicts from his jail cell, he showed that prison walls could not blunt the message of black liberation. The centerpiece of Newton's campaign was not his innocence but the system's guilt. The impossibility of black revolutionaries receiving fair trials in white America would become a familiar theme over the next decade, repeated in other high-profile trials of black activists. This viewpoint, with deep roots in centuries of criminal justice racism, had its immediate origins in the political worldview of currently and formerly incarcerated black activists. Malcolm's metaphor of America as a prison for black people had empowered the black poor, in and out of prison, to speak out against the larger system of confinement.

Much of the public campaign for Newton was organized by former prisoner turned author, journalist, and Black Panther minister of information Eldridge Cleaver. Cleaver had been in and out of prison since the age of twelve on various charges that included burglary, drug possession, and assault with intent to kill, a 1957 charge that stemmed from a rape. Convicted of that offense, Cleaver became a leader of the Nation of Islam while at San Quentin and at Folsom, California's oldest, largest and most notorious prisons. Malcolm X provided the greatest boost to Cleaver's recruitment efforts inside; Cleaver distanced himself from the Nation after Malcolm's censure and eventual departure and left the Nation around the time of Malcolm's assassination.

In an effort to find at least spiritual redemption if not physical release, Cleaver turned to writing while in prison. He began communicating with Beverly Axelrod, a radical Bay Area attorney. Impressed with Cleaver's literary talent, Axelrod smuggled some of his writings out of prison as legal materials and showed them, along with Cleaver's letters, to editors at *Ramparts*, a weekly magazine that had Catholic origins but a growing influence in the New Left. In 1966, *Ramparts* published some of his letters and articles, and its editors joined a list of other well-known critics and writers, including Maxwell Geismar (who later wrote the introduction to Cleaver's book of prison writings) and Norman Mailer, in calling for Cleaver's release. Axelrod argued that Cleaver's literary acumen alone merited his release.[64]

Cleaver left prison in December 1966 and immediately joined the staff of *Ramparts*. He also became a member of the Black Panther Party, although he initially kept this association secret for fear of being sent back to prison. Brash, charismatic, macho, and aggressive, Cleaver's influence in the Panthers grew as authorities jailed other leaders. Through his job at *Ramparts*, Cleaver built a campaign for Newton's freedom that could spread the BPP's politics. "Free Huey" became not just a demand bearing on a legal case but an extension of the Panthers' ten-point program for socialism and an end to white supremacy.[65]

The "Free Huey" campaign preoccupied the Panthers and garnered a significant amount of media throughout 1968, helped by Newton's commitment to serving as a visible party leader by issuing decrees and giving interviews despite and even because of his incarceration. Thousands of people attended an Oakland rally on February 17, 1968 (Newton's twenty-sixth birthday), and a Los Angeles rally on the following day. In addition to raising money and garnering significant press coverage, the rallies brought together high-profile black militant activists, including SNCC leaders Stokely Carmichael, H. Rap Brown, and James Forman. At the Oakland rally, however, the civil rights organizers were introduced as "honorary" members of the Black Panthers. In addition to aggrandizing the Panthers' stature as the vanguard black political organization in the country, these titles conveyed the message that the struggle to free a black prisoner could unite all black people, along with progressive whites and other people of color. And if this coalition could not free its prisoners, it would at least bring down the system responsible for their incarceration.

The SNCC leaders repeated the slogan that Panther leaders had used, saying that Newton must be freed or "the sky's the limit." In defending this slogan, which took the martyrdom of male leaders as cause for dramatic action, Forman offered a formula for calculating how political status connected with retaliatory violence. Forman said that if he were "assassinated," the response should be "ten war factories destroyed, fifteen blown-up police stations, thirty power plants destroyed, . . . one Southern Governor, two mayors, five hundred racist cops dead." Declaring that such reprisals were "no theatrics," Forman argued that the price for Brown and Carmichael should be even higher because of the threats already made against them. As the Black Panther minister of defense and as a black man facing the death penalty, Newton's death would merit the highest level of retaliation—"The sky's the limit."[66]

Although Newton was already a BPP leader, the campaign to free him elevated his status to almost mythic proportions. Cleaver's writings and speeches proclaimed "the genius of Huey P. Newton," suggesting that the government wanted to kill him because of his intellectual prowess.[67] Cleaver's fealty to Newton at this time extended nearly to the realm of self-sacrifice. Facing a return to prison for violating his parole, Cleaver declared that his priority remained sparing Newton the death penalty: "Helping Huey stay out of the gas chamber was more important than my staying out of San Quentin, so I went for broke. TV, radio, newspapers, magazines, the works."[68] Cleaver used the attention focused on his possible return to prison to build support for his defense, Newton's defense, and the promotion of the Black Panther Party. The "Free Huey" campaign was one of several events that kept the Panthers in the American media and political spotlight between 1968 and 1972.[69] Panther posters and signs featured Newton, Seale, and other imprisoned leaders and declared them political prisoners. A picture of Newton's face, stern and determined under a black beret, adorned the front cover of each issue of the *Black Panther* newspaper during his incarceration; calls to "Free Huey" and other political prisoners appeared regularly as well.

Eleven days after the birthday rally in support of Newton, Cleaver's book of prison writings hit bookstores. *Soul on Ice* ranges from literary criticism and foreign policy analysis to love letters to his lawyer. The book's cultural analysis is a raw and angry display of black masculinity. In it, Cleaver problematically

A February 11, 1970, rally for imprisoned Black Panther leaders at the Federal Building in San Francisco. Supporters hold pictures of Black Panther Party minister of defense Huey P. Newton and minister of information Eldridge Cleaver. Newton had been in prison since October 1967. Cleaver was arrested following a shootout with police after Martin Luther King Jr.'s assassination. Both men had been imprisoned as juveniles or young adults, with Cleaver having served many years on a variety of charges. Photo © 2014 Ilka Hartmann.

defined the black freedom struggle as an effort to reclaim manhood: Cleaver challenged gay author James Baldwin for displaying "self-hatred" by being insufficiently masculine, and he described his use of rape as a form of revenge, with black women serving as practice for his real target, white women.[70] Cleaver continued the objectification of black women popularized in Senator Daniel Moynihan's report for the Department of Labor that attributed the poverty of black communities to the predominance of female-headed households. In titling the report "The Negro Family: The Case for National Action," Moynihan argued for state and federal intervention to address the allegedly matriarchal structure of black families.[71]

Soul on Ice chronicles a shift in its author's view of black women. In the opening essay, Cleaver describes black women as so powerless as to constitute sexual target practice. The last essay, an open letter addressed "To All Black Women, from All Black Men," describes women as queens—of a past African glory and a future black urban triumph. Indeed, Cleaver ends the book by urging black women to "put on your crown . . . and build a New City" on the "ruins" of the United States.[72] Both the letter and the book, however, explicitly seek to restore black masculinity from the damage done by a white supremacy that castrates them literally and psychologically. Extending a line of black patriarchal nationalism, Cleaver uses masculinity as his challenge to the gendered pathology of racism.

At the same time, Cleaver extends Malcolm X's description of blackness as a site of incarceration: "It is only a matter of time until the question of the prisoner's debt to society versus society's debt to the prisoner is injected forcefully into national and state politics, into the civil and human rights struggle, and into the consciousness of the body politic. It is an explosive issue which goes to the very root of America's system of justice, the structure of criminal law, the prevailing beliefs and attitudes toward the convicted felon."[73] Critics praised the book for its honesty and literary skill, and it had sold more than a million copies by 1970.[74] The book's success made the brusque Cleaver a national spokesperson for Black Power and black (male) rage. He used that attention to build support for Newton's release, the Black Panther Party, and his 1968 presidential candidacy through the Peace and Freedom Party. Through newspapers and television, he sparred with California governor Ronald Reagan, especially when Reagan tried to prevent Cleaver from teaching a class at the University of California at Berkeley. With characteristic bluster, Cleaver challenged Reagan to a duel and threatened to "beat him to death with a marshmallow."[75]

When Newton's trial began on July 15, 1968, more than two thousand people staged a rally outside the Alameda County Superior Court demanding his release. However, the following September, Newton was convicted of manslaughter and sentenced to serve between two and fifteen years. In what would become a common refrain, the Panthers described Newton as primarily guilty of being black.[76] Newton continued to issue Panther decrees and grant media interviews until he was released on appeal in August 1970. His ongoing prominence and eventual release showed his supporters that prison was not the totalizing institution many had thought it to be: the campaign for his freedom kept Newton in the public consciousness while he continued his (symbolic) leadership of the BPP.[77]

Newton's statements from prison were militant and uncompromising. On March 1, 1968, for example, after an armed police raid on the house of Eldridge and Kathleen Cleaver, Newton issued "executive mandate number 3," which required all members of the Black Panther Party to acquire the skills and equipment necessary to "defend" their households and families from police

Black Panther Party cofounder Huey P. Newton is swarmed by supporters and journalists at a press conference following his release from prison in August 1970. Attorney Charles Garry, who represented many members of the Black Panthers during several trials, is to Newton's immediate right. To Newton's left is attorney Fay Stender. Photo © 2014 Ilka Hartmann.

incursion; those who failed to comply were threatened with expulsion from the party.[78] This call to arms showed not only that prison walls could not prevent him from hearing news of fellow radicals but also that the Panthers were willing to resort to armed defense to protect their leading representatives. That several of Newton's public statements, including an interview with the left-wing documentary collective Newsreel, openly dealt with issues of violence and self-defense, implied that the prison could not restrain a militant spirit or forestall what some now viewed as an inevitable people's war. Prison, of course, limited Newton's access to media or other public outlets, leading some supporters to claim that the prison's "close scrutiny" made it "not possible for him to communicate his political thoughts."[79]

Organizing against repression required some sense of empowerment. If the state was massive and violent, activists needed to believe that their movements were strong enough to overcome it. Many found such empowerment in a heroic masculinity that could turn the space of confinement into one of liberation. Well versed in this practice of projecting great strength since his days in the NOI at Folsom and San Quentin, the ever-brash Cleaver described the U.S. government as nearly helpless. "I would never allow anyone to place restrictions on my freedom of opinion or expression," he said in a press conference following his release on bail after two months in prison for an April 1968 shootout with police.[80] The incident had occurred following the murder of Martin Luther King Jr. and was part of Cleaver's agitation for violent revenge; during the shootout, police had killed seventeen-year-old Black Panther Bobby Hutton.

Cleaver, one of the main architects of the defense campaign that made the Black Panthers into an international organization, now needed his own defense campaign. Supporting Cleaver, *Ramparts* editor Robert Scheer wrote that even if Cleaver were to be reimprisoned, he had attained a freedom that transcended captivity. He noted also that Cleaver troubled "white America" because he had been such a public figure. As Cleaver had said of the jailed Newton, Scheer argued that Cleaver faced persecution for so publicly and passionately articulating the grievances of black people everywhere.[81]

"PROJECTION OF SOVEREIGNTY"

Cleaver summarized the Panthers' approach as a "projection of sovereignty, an embryonic sovereignty."[82] This embryonic sovereignty made the whole of the Panthers greater than the sum of its parts: strident rhetoric, bold physical presence in the face of police, and programs to serve black communities. The community programs were co-constitutive of the BPP's antagonism to the state, two sides of the same anticarceral coin. For the Panthers, revolution was a combination of fighting the state and supplanting its power.[83] The Panthers ran a variety of community programs, from monitoring the police to providing free breakfast to schoolchildren, free clothing giveaways and medical care, and a bus to prisons that allowed community members to visit their incarcerated loved ones.

The BPP's two most enduring counterinstitutions were the weekly *Black Panther* newspaper (formed in 1967) and the Oakland Community School (formed in 1971 as the Intercommunal Youth Service). Both entities lasted until the Panthers folded as an organization in 1982. While many critics looked on the Panthers' weapons and black leather jackets as signs of unbridled masculinity, its community programs signaled a more feminized if not explicitly feminist current to the party's work. Its community efforts, which Newton dubbed programs for "survival pending revolution," emphasized collective nurturing and mutual aid, health care, and education. Such a focus on providing for the community offered a holistic rather than purely militarist notion of self-defense. Self-defense was about collective survival, about providing sustenance for communities facing violence through a combination of attack and abandonment.

The Panthers' experiments in sovereignty challenged the hegemony of the American state with a direct and unparalleled power. The Panthers' work catalyzed similar responses by organizations and individuals around the country. The BPP's boldness inspired others to confront systems of authority. For that reason, law enforcement worked to crush the Panthers, while other institutions—chiefly American universities—tried to blunt the inspiration that the BPP and other Black Power groups offered. Both efforts utilized the expanding carceral state. Black organizers experienced a cavalcade of petty police harassment punctuated by routine and sometimes murderous attacks by police and a series of major trials on often-fraudulent charges. Police regularly arrested Panthers, raided the party's offices, and beat its members.[84] Through police Red Squads and the FBI's counterintelligence program (COINTELPRO), law enforcement infiltrated the party to an extent that only became clear in retrospect (and much of that activity still remains secret). Government agents not only gathered information but sowed distrust internally and with organizations that might otherwise have been Panther allies.[85]

The carceral and extralegal violence targeted not just Newton, Cleaver, and the other leaders of the Oakland chapter. After more than a decade of left-wing repurposing of prison, Panther cadre were quick to turn their experiences of confinement into opportunities to expand their work. Panther members and sympathizers wrote articles for the *Black Panther* newspaper about (and from) prison. Bobby Seale's memoir of the Black Panthers, *Seize the Time*, was based largely on tape recordings he made while in the San Francisco County Jail. Members of the New York Panthers awaiting trial on serious but specious charges drafted a collective autobiography and took their title, *We Will Return in the Whirlwind*, from a 1925 letter that Marcus Garvey had written from prison.[86]

Police bore direct responsibility for the deaths of dozens of Black Panthers and created the conditions in which others were killed. The year 1969 was bookended by the murders of four leading members of the organization. In January, Los Angeles Panthers Alprentice Bunchy Carter and John Huggins were shot and killed on the UCLA campus, while in December police killed Illinois Panthers Fred Hampton and Mark Clark. Along with the New York branch, the Los Angeles and Chicago BPP chapters were the organization's largest, most dynamic, and fastest growing. These deaths, combined with other attacks, devastated the party.

Los Angeles in the mid-twentieth century was a city of migrants, and many young blacks from the South joined radical organizations while some of their white counterparts became police officers. The Los Angeles chapter of the Black Panthers was one of the first outside of Oakland, and under Carter's leadership, it became one of the biggest and most militant. Carter was a veteran of the California prison system, having spent time in Youth Authority custody as well as in Soledad. He was inspired by Malcolm X to join the Nation of Islam, where he befriended Cleaver. Carter left prison a revolutionary and became a Panther after meeting Newton in 1967. Carter had previously been a member of the Slausons gang, a five-thousand-member street organization that had branches scattered throughout Los Angeles. Membership in the Slausons gave young black men a sense of ownership over their neighborhoods and offered an early example of collective self-defense. The Slausons and other street organizations contributed to the militancy of the Watts rebellion. After leaving Soledad, Carter politicized the Slausons: he brought most of his branch into the Panthers, trading criminal activity for community organizing.[87]

Terrified by Carter's charismatic leadership, FBI and police worked hard to eradicate the chapter. The LAPD frequently raided the homes of party members and arrested them as they tried to sell the *Black Panther*, and in August 1968, police killed three Panthers. The FBI supported these measures while undertaking more covert means of devastation. The bureau seized on political differences between the Panthers and the US organization, a rival nationalist group whose offices were in the same Black Congress building as the Los Angeles Panthers. The US organization criticized the Panthers' socialism and multiracial coalitions, and some US members had been previously associated with one of the Slausons' gang rivals. The FBI sent threatening, mocking letters purported to be from one organization to the other and increased tensions between the two groups to the point of violence. On January 17, 1969, US members shot and killed Carter and Huggins during a meeting about the UCLA Black Student Union. Following the murders, police and FBI raided the chapter's primary household and arrested everyone present—including Huggins's widow, Ericka, and their month-old daughter, Mai.[88]

Local police hounded chapters of the organization around the country, and the body count—of leaders, of rank-and-file members—started to rise. The most dramatic episode came in Chicago. Early on the morning of December 4, the city's police killed twenty-one-year-old Fred Hampton and twenty-two-year-old Mark Clark as they slept in Hampton's Chicago apartment. Police fired nearly one hundred shots into the apartment during an unannounced predawn raid. Hampton, a dynamic leader of the Chicago Panthers with a growing national reputation, had been drugged by an FBI informant working in the party, so he was asleep when police shot him at point-blank range. Officers then arrested everyone in the apartment, including Hampton's pregnant wife.[89]

Four days later, Los Angeles police launched a predawn armed assault on the Panther office there. But that chapter always retained a spirit of militancy that was connected both to the southern self-defense traditions with which most members had grown up and to the gangs to which several members had previously belonged. The murders of Carter and Huggins early that year also left the chapter on edge. The presence of military veterans such as Louisiana native Elmer Geronimo Pratt added to the group's technical proficiency. Pratt had ensured that the party's office was well fortified, and the Panthers held off the police assault for several hours. When the Panthers ultimately surrendered, they did so in full view of the media and the surrounding community as a protection against being slaughtered in the streets.[90]

Other black radical organizations fared little better. The Republic of New Africa (later changed to "Afrika," in keeping with Swahili linguistic practices for the hard "c" sound) formed in March 1968, signing its own declaration of independence from the United States. The RNA advocated the creation of a separate nation for black people—New Afrika—by carving territory out of the five Black Belt states of the Deep South: Alabama, Georgia, Louisiana, Mississippi, and South Carolina. Slavery had been most strongly concentrated in these states, and many black folks still lived in the region in the 1960s, even though black people had been continuously migrating north and westward since the end of World War II. In March 1969, RNA members gathered in Detroit's New Bethel Baptist Church, pastored by the Reverend C. L. Franklin, an SCLC member and the father of soul singer Aretha Franklin, to celebrate their one-year anniversary. When a shooting occurred outside the church, police surrounded the building and opened fire. Some RNA members were armed and returned fire; one officer was killed, and police arrested 140 people inside the church.[91] From the urban rebellions to the organizations that sprung up in their wake, police around the country experimented with massive albeit more temporary incarceration of young black men.

Universities, for their part, greeted the growing campus unrest by calling in the police, who used ever more violent tactics. Indeed, much of the tumult in communities of color intersected with campus struggles that cohered during the last two years of the 1960s in the form of mass arrests and conspiracy trials.[92] While black activists experienced the most extreme forms of this repression, it was generalized across the multiracial Left. Between 1968 and 1970, student strikes at San Francisco State University, the University of California at Berkeley, Columbia University, South Carolina State University, Howard University, Cornell University, Voorhees College, Kent State University, Jackson State College, and numerous other institutions resulted in hundreds of arrests and the deaths of at least nine students (a total of five black students in South Carolina and Mississippi, plus four white students at Kent State).

The prevalence of conspiracy trials generated its own idiom. In labeling cases by the city where the charges originated and the number of those tried—the Chicago 8, Camden 28, Harrisburg 8, LA 13, New York (or Panther) 21, Oakland 7, Seattle 7, and others—activists provided a geography of conflict with the carceral state. Eight here, seven there, twenty-one elsewhere: the numbers were almost interchangeable as symbols of repression and resistance. The fact that so many social movements were experiencing such trials, alongside the threat of incarceration facing those who resisted the draft, generalized an incipient critique of imprisonment within the American Left.

These collectives were increasingly described in racial terms, as in Los Siete de la Raza, seven Chicanos charged with the 1969 murder of a San Francisco police officer in a case that served as a catalyst for pan-Latino and black-brown coalitions in the Bay Area, complete with a BPP-style political platform. This process grew as attention increasingly focused on activist prisoners and not just those facing prison.[93] Defendants in these political trials were said to be representatives of the movements and causes from which they came, encouraging supporters to see their fates as bound up with those standing trial. Such conspiracies emerged from diverse sectors of society—Catholic pacifists and hippie students and Black Panthers—demonstrating the representative as well as the exceptional status of those facing legal charges. Repression was a badge of honor and a sign of commitment.

Many of the trials became potent political theater; as Chicago 8 defendant Abbie Hoffman put it, "Our role in the court is to destroy its authority, and the next generation will come along and destroy its power."[94] The courtroom was a staging ground in which activists could continue to articulate a critique of the American state. The extreme nature of these political trials invited an exaggerated response from the defense table. Not to be outdone, the enforcement of anticonspiracy laws turned the courtroom into a place to discipline defendants even before it could punish them. The Chicago 8 case was the most elaborate version of this spectacle. In addition to helping codify a vernacular of political conspiracy, the Chicago 8 identified a political stance in relation to the hallowed halls of American justice. The trial lasted from September 1969 to February 1970 and often parodied the generational and cultural clash between young leftists and the Establishment. The defense placed a picture of Che Guevara and the flag of the National Liberation Front of Vietnam on its table to create "a 'liberated zone' right in front of the jury's eyes."[95]

At the same time, conservative Judge Julius Hoffman cited the defendants and their attorneys for contempt of court, imposing extra prison time and thousands of dollars in fines by the time Abbie Hoffman and the other members of his group were convicted. (The appeals court overturned the convictions and dropped the fines in November 1972.) Most dramatically, in October 1969, Judge Hoffman had Bobby Seale, chair of the Black Panther Party and the only nonwhite defendant, bound and gagged when he demanded to act as his own attorney and called the judge a racist. Seale's case was severed from the rest of the Chicago 8 shortly thereafter.[96]

The image of Seale handcuffed to a chair with a cotton cloth stuffed in his mouth became a potent symbol of the government's escalating attacks against black radicalism and the Left more generally. Supporters routinely used variations on the image to drum up support for Seale when he was on trial in 1970 with eight other Black Panthers for the murder of a suspected police informer in New Haven, Connecticut.[97] The image of Seale silenced by the state conveyed a deeper political message about government repression: the carceral state was attempting to prevent political activists, especially militant black ones, from having a voice. The struggle, then, concerned more than the issues involved, more than being seen or heard. The shackled or subservient black body has long been visible in American history. Rather, the struggle concerned the terms on which visibility transpired. Black radicals fought for public visibility as a form of self-determination. They identified the state's repressive capacity, evident through policing, prosecution, and imprisonment, as threatening to render black life invisible or obsolete.

Activists feared being silenced, and as Seale's treatment in a Chicago courtroom demonstrated, they had good reason to do so. Thus, BPP members worked to place in public view those facing state repression. They played with images of light and dark, sight and blindness, positioning the strength of their persecuted leaders against the cowardice of a bullying state. While Newton awaited trial, Cleaver organized a rally not far from the county jail cell where Newton was confined. "Held in the shadow of the Alameda County jail . . . the theme of the rally was 'Come See About Huey,'" explained the Panthers' minister of information.[98]

This insurgent form of seeing had two goals. It might save the lives of those immediately facing prison or death. It could also, organizers hoped, prevent such repression from becoming normalized and permanent. Radicals hoped they could provide parallel and counter forms of surveillance, keeping tabs on and alerting the public about the ways the government kept tabs on and attacked them. Prior to his death, Hampton defined working for Seale's release as of the utmost importance: "So we're going to see about Bobby regardless of what these people think we should do, because school is not important and work is not important. Nothing's more important than stopping fascism, because fascism will stop us all."[99]

Black Power activists and others defined the fight against state repression, embodied in those social movement leaders facing criminal trials, as instrumental to the national future. According to the 1970 Black Student Revolution Conference, "In the wake of this racist repression it becomes clear that black people are engaged in a life and death struggle of national salvation. It is only natural for black people to be concerned and motivated by what is happening to Bobby Seale and the New Haven Panthers and other black political prisoners, here in dying racist Amerikkka. Black students have always felt the importance of working with the Black Panther Party and understood that the outcome of our struggle lies in the ability to free all of our political prisoners."[100]

Black students were not alone in challenging the political persecution of the Black Panther Party. The Panthers as well as personal experiences with police violence moved large sections of the New Left to come out against the carceral state. The May 1970 National Student Strike, ostensibly sparked by the invasion of Cambodia and the killing of four students at Kent State by the National Guard, demanded first and foremost that "the U.S. Government end its systematic repression of political dissidents and release all political prisoners, such as Bobby Seale and other members of the Black Panther Party." Only then did the strikers demand troop withdrawal from Southeast Asia, an end to the war, and an end to university complicity with the war. By May 22, the National Strike Information Center reported that students at one hundred schools were on strike for the three demands.[101]

"THE PRISONS OF THE STREET"

Challenges to the criminal justice apparatus—a fundamental part of American power—made the prison both a discursive field of struggle and a material one. In writings and speeches, the black freedom struggle and allied urban movements challenged the prison as a place and a symbol. Materially, Newton wrote that prisons would not squelch revolutionary energy: "The prison cannot be victorious because walls, bars and guards cannot conquer or hold down an idea."[102] Symbolically, the prison represented all forms of oppression and confinement, especially in the deepening structures of urban inequality.

In a widely used phrasing, the minister of information for the New York–based Young Lords Organization, which was renovating Puerto Rican revolutionary nationalism in the model of the Black Power movement, called people to action against "the prisons of the street."[103]

The prison was not just a place; it was a strategy of governance that sought to confine ideas and people that challenged the status quo. Its power, activists insisted, was multifaceted. Simultaneously, this approach defined structural inequity as itself a form of confinement: the prison was the defining feature of an unjust regime, encompassing black alienation from private property and the means of production in an economy shifting away from the aspiration of full employment in manufacturing-based production to a smaller and more specialized workforce based in finance, insurance, information technology, and real estate. Historically concentrated in and restricted to agricultural and industrial labor, black workers were increasingly superfluous in this new economic order.[104]

The popularity of the prison as a metaphor for injustice enabled people in prison to be seen as organizers, activists, intellectuals, and artists. Prison organizing—not, as some observers have claimed, leftist dogma—made prisoners into political subjects needing popular support. Radical social movements formed amid the growing carceral punishment of unruly populations. Those pursuing abstract ideals of freedom and justice increasingly articulated a critique of repression as constitutive of the United States itself. Such views, alongside regular encounters with police, brought radical movements into more contact with prisoners, who were catalyzed by such movements into action. The prison movement developed organically through such connections, a mixture of prisoner organizing and leftist movements developing a shared analysis involving prisons' role in enforcing structures of American inequality. While the BPP's initial critique of the criminal justice system focused on trial rather than imprisonment, the group always viewed "criminals" and prisoners as a vital political subject.

The Panthers were inspired by psychiatrist and revolutionary Frantz Fanon's discussion of colonization and resistance. Fanon documented the psychological impacts of colonization and upheld violence as a necessary aspect of removing it. He saw the "lumpen-proletariat" as the cutting edge of political struggle among colonized people. According to Fanon, although the lumpen had been dismissed by orthodox Marxists as a parasitic class isolated from the means of production, they now stood at the forefront of resistance in colonized cities. "For the lumpen-proletariat, that horde of starving men, uprooted from their tribe and from their clan, constitutes one of the most spontaneous and the most radically revolutionary forces of a colonized people. . . . So the pimps, the hooligans, the unemployed and the petty criminals, urged on from behind, throw themselves into the struggle for liberation like stout working men. These classless idlers will by militant and decisive action discover the path that leads to nationhood."[105] Denigrated in traditional liberal and Marxist thought, the lumpen emerged as a special, hypermasculine category for Third World revolutionaries—even Fanon and others who did not think such a class alone could make revolution or lead a government. The same people whom urban policymakers had dismissed as being trapped in a pathological "culture of poverty" were, to radicals in the Black Power movement, people whose distance from the political establishment and isolation from the means of production made them potential recruits for the revolution. Reinvesting these "classless idlers" with political subjectivity, radicals in the late 1960s identified constituencies liberal and Left groups had written off or never considered.

Alienation, exploitation, marginalization—all were watchwords of 1960s counterculture and idioms of dissent.[106] As a result, prisoners were more than recruits; they became international symbols of radicalism. Prisoners lay at the heart of the BPP's internationalism, including its foreign policy approaches to Third World movements and governments. Algeria and Cuba, both newly independent, became vital refuges for political exiles escaping either the threat or the actuality of prison. From 1970 until at least 1981, several former Panthers and others fled to those countries for safety, sometimes on hijacked planes.[107] Vietnam offered to trade captured American GIs for imprisoned black radicals and did release groups of POWs to prominent representatives of the American antiwar movement, and the Chinese communist government offered moral support for the black freedom struggle, including black prisoners.[108]

Indeed, the Black Power movement made opposition to state repression in the form of policing and imprisonment a fundamental ingredient of political struggle. The Panthers and related groups characterized radicalism as opposition to state violence in the form of the military, the various policing agencies, and the many forms of confinement. Building on the southern civil rights movement, the Black Power movement looked on jails and prisons as incubators of radical ideas. Located primarily in urban areas and noting the concentration of black people in urban environments, the Black Power movement defined the city as its battleground. Black Marxist autoworker and author James Boggs, for example, offered an urban-centered notion of struggle. The Detroit-based activist wrote that "the city is the black man's land."[109]

This urban movement recast the value of the most marginalized city dwellers. The Panthers looked to the lumpen as their favored recruits, including people whom white elites and the black middle class had long castigated as the dregs of society. To the Panthers, such people were some of the party's most valuable members. With BPP members and especially leaders in jail and facing lengthy prison sentences, the Black Panther dictum to organize those "brothers on the block" increasingly included those in the cell block as well as on the city block. The *Black Panther* newspaper claimed that most Panthers "were street and prison educated."[110] The ghetto, the prison, and the university—though removed from one another geographically—were each central nodes of black protest.

Many Panthers viewed the constant stream of political trials as evidence of the confinement at the heart of the American experience. In New York City, the setting for so many experiments in policing and spatial segregation, Panther Zayd Shakur wrote that "America is the prison." "Prisons are really an extensions of our communities," he said, because people "live at gun point" in both places.[111] A pamphlet by the Bay Area Prison Solidarity Committee extended this metaphor by defining prison as "a ghetto in itself where people's everyday problems are magnified and aggravated by hired guns and hired wardens who hold immediate power over life and death."[112] Many Panthers and other radicals began to speak of prisons as "maximum security" and designated the rest of the United States as "minimum security." In an effort to describe the possible solidarities between male prisoners and the rest of society, California prison activists wrote that the "brothers inside the prisons (maximum security) are struggling just as courageously as the brothers and sisters in minimum security (outside the prisons)."[113]

Black Power disrupted the dichotomy between prison and freedom. Rather than see the two as mutually exclusive, Black Power described them as co-constitutive. Prisons were everywhere, and freedom needed to be found or made in practice—whether in a cage or on the street. In the eyes of New Left journalist Robert Scheer, Cleaver's prison writings had been composed in the "leisure of Cleaver's forced confinement," whereas his postprison essays and speeches were prepared "on the run" in the fugitive stance of black political struggle.[114] Cleaver also declared the prison to be more a condition than a place—saying, for example, that "one continues to go back to prison until he gets his shit together, and then he refuses to go back."[115] The prison was a part of the urban environment and central to any conceptual map of black life.

Nonetheless, Cleaver distinguished more carefully between prison and the streets when he faced a return to San Quentin in 1968.[116] Cleaver fled the country in November 1968 after a judge ordered him to return to prison for his part in the April shootout with Oakland police. He took up residence first in Cuba and then in Algeria, establishing the International Section of the Black Panther Party until his split with Newton in 1971.[117] Cleaver's escape from the country led him to pursue increasingly dramatic tactics in the effort to break out of what he dubbed the prison of "Babylon" America. Confinement structured black life in the United States, so fleeing the country was in fact an epic prison break. While Cleaver fled prison America in pursuit of freedom, others worked to turn American prisons into sites through which freedom might emerge.

"BLUE DENIM UNITY"

Narratives by former prisoners published in the mid- to late 1960s contributed to introducing the prison as an institution vital to contemporary experiences of race. Even if imprisonment was not their central concern, these publications helped enable the activism that had been building inside prisons to break into the broader public landscape. Word of prisoner activism passed through a few sympathetic outsiders who worked in the prison, media reports (which first appeared in the underground press and ultimately were picked up by traditional media), and popular culture. These forces coalesced in northern California and were then projected onto the country overall.

San Quentin in particular became an iconic image of prison and its possibilities, one of a handful of prisons across the country whose visibility helped the public begin to understand prisons. Particularly after the 1963 closure of Alcatraz, once the nation's highest-security prison, San Quentin was one of the country's most well-known prisons, located in a state praised as a national leader in corrections policy since World War II. Both Alcatraz and San Quentin were located near San Francisco, a regional media hub and center of leftist activity. Tension had long permeated San Quentin, both racially (between black and white prisoners) and politically (between prisoners and guards, almost all of whom were white). In 1968, six months after guards killed a prisoner to end a fight in the yard, prisoners initiated a newsletter, *The Outlaw*. Issues of the stenciled newsletter ranged between one and four pages and included prisoner grievances and mocking criticism of the prison administration. When prison officials tried to shut down the publication, prisoners sent the text to outside supporters who "had it mimeographed and mailed back into the prison." Prisoner clerks in the mailroom received the contraband and distributed it to "key cells in each cell block."[118] *The Outlaw* called for a "Convict Unity Holiday" (a strike) in February 1968, demanding parole reform, better food and living conditions, and increased wages. Mostly focused on the conditions of confinement and release, the prisoners offered a provisional public health approach to certain criminal acts that also reflected status hierarchies among prisoners: organizers demanded that prisoners convicted of sexual offenses against children be sent to mental institutions.[119]

A University of California at Berkeley graduate student doing interviews at San Quentin saw the proposal and informed several Bay Area newspapers. Only the *Berkeley Barb*, one of the most well-known and widely read underground newspapers of the era, was interested. A counterculture publication that reported on various Bay Area political movements, the *Barb* promoted the strike on the front page, printing the prisoners' list of grievances alongside news of the strike, and reprinting *The Outlaw* as a special insert. The *Barb* touted its "exclusive" story, writing that the incident constituted the first time prisoners could "tell their plans and purposes to the public in advance of their action, before the official version is spoon-fed to the mass media."[120] As a result, prison authorities gave *Barb* readers in their custody twenty-nine days in solitary confinement. (According to the *Barb*, a similar punishment awaited those caught with copies of *The Outlaw*.)[121] The *Barb* described its coverage of the strike as vital to the prisoners' success: "Their only weapon is to make their story known, hoping that public opinion will pressure honest state legislators to make a thorough investigation of the California prison system, without favoritism to the entrenched bureaucracy."[122] A *Barb* reporter also challenged the prison's censorship of radical literature during a public lecture by San Quentin warden Louis "Red" Nelson the night before the strike.[123]

The *Barb*'s large readership and consistent coverage of the protest helped bring more than four hundred people to the gates of San Quentin for the February 15 strike. The members of the Grateful Dead brought their instruments, amplifiers, and a generator. Along with the Phoenix and members of Country Joe and the Fish, the Dead performed a free concert on a flatbed truck for the strikers inside and the protesters outside. Twenty percent of the San Quentin prison population—about seven hundred people—went on strike, going to their cells rather than to their jobs. Hearing the makeshift concert awakened prisoners to the possibility of inside-outside collaboration and to the idea that their concerns mattered to activists who were not incarcerated: for the rest of the week, 75 percent of San Quentin's prisoners—more than twenty-six hundred people—struck. The Peace and Freedom Party provided a bus to transport musicians and demonstrators to the gates of San Quentin on February 15, and members held sympathy protests every day at noon for the duration of the strike.[124] As protests at prison gates became more routine and linked the growing New Left with this burgeoning prisoner radicalism, authorities worried that leftists would launch a military attack on the prison. San Quentin officials devised an emergency plan to shut down the roads leading to the prison if necessary to prevent a "storming of the Bastille."[125]

Both the prisoners and the prison administration saw the strike's visibility as its greatest asset. As a result, *The Outlaw*, the most identifiable voice of prisoner dissidence, became the source of a power struggle: the warden tried to shut it down, while prisoners used it to agitate further. It continued publishing after the strike, lampooning Nelson, who had transferred to Folsom prison several people whom he suspected of involvement in the publication. That summer, the anonymous editor/writer called for another "unity day" in August. This time, prisoners stayed in their cells on a weekend, effectively boycotting voluntary activities rather than withholding their labor. This tactic made it harder for prison officials to discipline the dissidents and gave the strikers a symbolic victory. It showed a certain tactical sophistication, allowing prisoners to flex a collective muscle while circumventing reprisals. In calling for the August strike, *The Outlaw* argued that unity could usurp the prison's power of division:

> We permit them to keep us at each others['] throats. A handful of us are calling for UNITY. This is for a purpose. We want to crush this empire that has been erected on our suffering. . . . The time has once again come to speak of UNITY. Not partial UNITY. Not meaningless nor simless [*sic*] UNITY, but whole and purposeful UNITY. A UNITY that includes every man wearing blue denim, a UNITY that includes every man that is aware of the need to overthrow the [California Department of Corrections] if we are to ever again be dealt with as man and not as chattle [*sic*].

Such unity across difference, the author argued, would ensure that outside supporters would take up the prisoners' message and embarrass the prison regime. It was a demand for a united front across prison walls.[126]

The two strikes frightened the prison administration, which responded by calling for greater surveillance of various Left organizations and periodicals and specifying black people, Chicanos, and students as the greatest threats. Associate warden James Park reasoned that officials could curtail prison activism by monitoring those who supported it and that these efforts would provide insight into the political thought that was inspiring rebellious prisoners and thus enable the elimination of support for prisoner demands. Looking to the 1968 strikes, Park identified "the underground press and radio" as initiating the publicity that other media outlets then picked up. He encouraged prison administrators to monitor the underground press, study the revolutionary thinkers prisoners were reading (specifically, Frantz Fanon, Che Guevara, Malcolm X, and Mao Tse-tung), and keep tabs on Black Power and Chicano organizing.[127]

Irate and impressed by prisoners' organizing, Park argued that the two strikes at San Quentin "demonstrated, perhaps for the first time in American penal history, that outsiders could conspire with prisoners to cripple the normal operation of a prison."[128] Park called for a new administrative strategy to combat the dissension spreading through California's prison system and blunt the Left's influence. He correctly predicted that people on both sides of prison walls would see disturbances in prison as "but one tactical event in a larger strategy of social revolution."[129] This revolutionary impulse in prisons, he said, was heavily influenced by "racial and ethnic consciousness" among black and Chicano political movements and by the "youth revolt . . . in all industrialized nations." Park was particularly concerned about the role of publicity in what he called "the new prison rebellion."[130]

While prison officials encouraged greater surveillance, radicals practiced greater spectacle. Throughout 1968, both prisoner organizing and campaigns supporting radicals facing charges characterized racism and confinement as mutually constitutive. The following year, a different kind of occupation in California showed that prison walls could not keep determined activists out even if they kept prisoners in. An ad hoc group, Indians of All Tribes, occupied Alcatraz Island on November 20, 1969, and remained there until June 11, 1971. The occupiers charged that only by seizing a physical prison, even a closed one, could the daily imprisonment of Indian life be made visible. Liberated Alcatraz was home to a motley crew of militants and hippies, a gathering of the disaffected from among many Indian tribes, and several veterans, who kept the Coast Guard from docking at the island.[131]

The occupation generated international media attention. Berkeley's KPFA radio station launched *Radio Free Alcatraz*, a half-hour show that aired five days a week and featured a spokesperson for Indians of All Tribes; other Pacifica stations across the country rebroadcast the program.[132] A steady stream of donated food and supplies sustained the rock-dwellers. Richard Oakes, one of the spokespersons for the occupiers, called the prison a symbol of hope. Once again, the metaphor was the message: according to scholars Paul Chaat Smith and Robert Warrior, "Indians held a brilliant, astonishing metaphor—a defiant, isolated Rock surrounded by foreboding seas, a reservationlike piece of real estate with stark conditions, and a prison that represented the incarcerated spirit of Indian people everywhere."[133] A flyer in support declared "Alcatraz is not an island . . . Alcatraz is an idea."[134]

The Alcatraz occupation extended what was becoming a familiar connection: the young Indians challenged settler colonialism by dramatizing the space of confinement. Emphasizing spaces of constraint invited greater attention to those who occupied them—voluntarily in the case of Alcatraz, involuntarily in the case of residents of ghettoes, barrios, reservations, and actual prisons. At the same time, the Alcatraz occupiers attempted to turn the space of confinement, represented by a prison still notorious after its closure, into a space of freedom by creating a commune in an unexpected location. This effort initially appeared successful but grow harder to sustain as it continued: resources and patience diminished on the island, and support among outsiders, including the media, decreased as the months wore on. But the audacity of the action inspired other militants. The occupation of prison territory led some activists to conclude that prisoners themselves could be liberated from the shackles of the state.

Others picked up on the prison metaphor to describe their feelings of alienation, separate from a racial or colonial context. The 1960s counterculture celebrated criminality in the form of a romanticized "outlaw" image, cultivated in popular films of the era such as *Bonnie and Clyde* (1967), *Cool Hand Luke* (1967), *Butch Cassidy and the Sundance Kid* (1969), and *Easy Rider* (1969). These movies featured young, attractive actors whose characters robbed banks, sold drugs, and otherwise disrespected traditional authority. They did not always succeed—the often tragic ending was a consistent theme in the masculine outlaw antihero trope—but at least they had a good time.[135]

These movies were matched by a spirit of antiauthoritarianism in the music of popular young artists such as Bob Dylan and Aretha Franklin. Perhaps one of the most enduring antiheroes of this moment came from a surprising source: country music. In 1968, singer Johnny Cash fulfilled his long-standing dream by recording a live concert at California's Folsom prison. At the time, prison concerts were routine—Cash, for example, had performed thirty times at various prisons over the preceding decade—but his album, *At Folsom Prison*, featured the first recording of a prison concert.[136] The album appeared in May 1968, just as students at Columbia University were fighting with police in an attempt to shut down the university; nine antiwar activists from the Catholic Left were arrested for burning draft records with napalm in Catonsville, Maryland; and Eldridge Cleaver was challenging Ronald Reagan to a marshmallow duel while getting ready to leave the country.[137] Cash's songs expressed yearning, heartbreak, and gallows humor as he tried to show his listeners that he was one of them. Cash identified with the prisoners, trading on his working-class roots while falsely implying in his banter with the crowd and in the liner notes that he, too, had been in prison. He performed a song, "Greystone Chapel," written by Folsom prisoner Glen Sherley.[138]

At Folsom became a best seller and rocketed the singer to mass popularity. It led Cash to return to the California prison system the following year and to release an album and a documentary, At San Quentin. The singer was far more brash at San Quentin. He cursed and courted the prisoners' applause and jeers by taunting the guards, and he stuck up his middle finger at the video cameras.[139] In "Wanted Man," cowritten with Bob Dylan, Cash sang of an elusive outlaw whose ego grew with the expanding list of cities where he was wanted for unspecified crimes. In "San Quentin," Cash dismissed the institution itself.

> San Quentin, may you rot and burn in hell
> May your walls fall and may I live to tell
> May all the world forget you ever stood
> And the whole world will regret you did no good
> San Quentin, you've been living hell to me.

Prisoners instantly demanded that he play the song again. The video shows an almost all-white audience cheering and jeering alongside Cash throughout, suggesting a widening audience for the anticarceral imagination popularized by the Black Power movement but with roots in the experience of Appalachian poor whites and others. Cash's performance was equally successful on the outside: At San Quentin sold even more copies on release than At Folsom and topped the Billboard charts for four weeks.[140]

The success of these two albums transformed Cash briefly into a critic of prisons. In 1969, he donated ten thousand dollars to the Inmate Welfare Fund at Folsom and another ten thousand to the San Quentin fund, although journalist Jessica Mitford later revealed that prison administrators siphoned off the funds.[141] Cash also helped Sherley record an album and get out of prison (in that order), and the two men testified before the U.S. Senate in 1972 in support of prison reform.[142] Swept up by the metaphoric connection that black radicals had established between prisons and the wider structures of domination and alienation, Cash told one writer, "I just don't think prisons do any good. . . . Nothing good ever came out of a prison."[143] In a subdued version of Malcolm X's claims of American captivity, Cash hypothesized that the popular interest in his albums bespoke a larger cultural phenomenon. "I think prison songs are popular because most of us are living in one kind of prison or another," Cash told a reporter, "and whether we know it or not the words of a song about someone who is actually in prison speak for a lot of us who might appear not to be, but really are."[144]

Such messages of American confinement revealed deep-seated and widespread feelings of alienation, whether as a consequence of racial oppression or metaphysical detachment. These messages emerged organically from different communities and were made popular in a context established by black radicalism. The circulation of these ideas brought the prison to life for millions of people who had not directly experienced confinement, much as the rising tide of radicalism in the streets convinced many prisoners that they could change the conditions around them. The hundreds of urban rebellions in the mid-1960s gave way to scores of prison rebellions in the late 1960s and early 1970s.[145]

As urban rebellions put the spotlight on cities while politicians discussed the Great Society programs to facilitate urban uplift, so, too, did prison rebellions draw attention to confinement while Richard Nixon and others demanded "law and order" as the solution to the nation's ills. Much as people pushed out of the dominant American political economy took to the city streets to protest liberal inequality over the long hot summers of 1964–68, so, too, did they work to transform their places of confinement into schools of liberation amid a sharp right turn in American politics. The same spirit of revolt in American streets now wound its way throughout American prisons. The locus of black protest was forcibly moved from the city streets to the prison cell block, sparking unprecedented forms of opposition to the carceral state.

Political protest and public displays of militancy, combined with the countercultural embrace of the outlaw and the accused, meant that the prison was no longer a far-off place that could only be fearfully imagined. For countless numbers of people, the prison was at the center of life, especially urban life, in the United States. All roads were converging on the prison, especially in California. Birthplace of the Black Panthers, ground zero for the culture industries, and home to a popular mythology that imagined itself free of the institutional racism that nonetheless structured the state, California was quickly becoming the capital of the captive nation.

CHAPTER THREE

George Jackson and the
Black Condition Made Visible

> Being born a slave in a captive society and never experiencing any
> objective basis for expectation had the effect of preparing me for the progressively
> traumatic misfortunes that lead so many blackmen to the prison gate. I was
> prepared for prison. It required only minor psychic adjustments.
> —GEORGE JACKSON, *Soledad Brother* (1970)

There was plenty of champagne and good cheer at the book party held outside the gates of San Quentin on October 15, 1970. Friends and colleagues from Berkeley, Oakland, and San Francisco extolled the author. So did the book's editor, Gregory Armstrong of Bantam Books, who flew out to Marin County from New York City to speak at the celebration. The event organizers gave everyone in attendance a free copy of the book, which soon became a best seller. The only person missing was the author. From his cell, George Jackson, prisoner A63837, could not see the crowd that had gathered to celebrate the publication of his first book, *Soledad Brother*. Capturing the mood of the event, one of the attendees yelled at the prison gates, "Like Johnny Cash said, 'San Quentin, I hope you rot; you never did no good.'"[1]

Soledad Brother: The Prison Letters of George Jackson was and remains the most famous literary expression of black prison radicalism in this period. The book gathered dozens of letters that Jackson had written between 1964 and 1970. Most of the letters were addressed to his parents, while some were to his sisters or his brother, who was only seven years old when George went to prison in 1960 and was dead by the time the book appeared. Except for five introductory letters written in 1970 expressly for the book, the letters were arranged in chronological order beginning in 1964. As Jackson became a known force among leftists, first in California and then across the country and around the world, his list of correspondents grew. Many of the later letters were addressed to his attorney, to his editor, and to a small but growing coterie of female supporters. Because California prisons at the time did not allow prisoner letters to cover more than the front and back of one sheet of paper, most of them were brief, though some were grouped because they had been written within days of each other and to the same person.

Jackson was eighteen when he was sent to prison to serve between one year and life for a petty robbery. Now he was about to turn twenty-nine and a published author. To read *Soledad Brother* was to track the development of the author's increasingly radical politics. Indeed, Jackson's attorney and publisher had arranged the book's contents to emphasize a political evolution that used prison conditions as an allegory for the black condition overall. They wanted to expose the conditions of confinement in hopes of generating wider antiracist mobilization, echoing the strategy pursued by abolitionists during slavery and antilynching activists after the defeat of Reconstruction. They hoped that exposing the cruelest forms of racism, the most violent and constricting experiences, would motivate people to act against a larger system of racial oppression. As in those earlier movements, prison organizers focused on the wounded yet dignified black, usually male, body, hoping that if people identified with the aggrieved, if they could see that the prison was not a static or impenetrable site, they would realize that the political order itself was simultaneously more brutal and more vulnerable than it was believed to be.

Jackson issued a powerful call to arms: "When we attack the problem with intellectualism [alone] we give away the advantage we have in numbers." But he also served as a liaison from the prison, informing the world of the political conversations happening in cages and cell blocks. "Growing numbers of blacks are openly passed over when paroles are considered," Jackson explained. "They have become aware that their only hope lies in resistence [*sic*]. They have learned that resistence [*sic*] is actually possible. The holds are beginning to slip away."[2] Jackson offered a stunning rebuke of imprisonment from within. That the book's title appropriated the name of a prison where Jackson stood accused of killing a prison guard showed an irreverent challenge to the prison system itself, a refusal of the prison's power to determine social solidarities.

Part of the book's appeal undoubtedly came from Jackson's ability to turn the barest conditions of survival into a site of deep personal transformation. In fact, *Soledad Brother* is perhaps most eloquent in its defense of the life of the mind. Jackson's letters express the dialectic of imprisoned radical intellectuals, proclaiming a freedom of and through the mind while simultaneously challenging the oppressive weight of racism and confinement as "the closest to being dead that one is likely to experience in this life."[3] To Jackson, the life of the mind was essential to the body's survival. The allure of George Jackson as both author and organizer lay in his stubborn insistence that the prison was not all-powerful. He trounced the guards and the entire system they represented while providing an existential meditation on freedom. Indeed, Jackson offered his evolving political consciousness as the dividing line between life and death. "I must follow my mind. There is no turning back from awareness. If I were to alter my step now I would always hate myself. I would grow old feeling that I had failed in the obligatory duty that is ours once we become aware. I would die as most of us blacks have died over the last few centuries, without having lived."[4]

The book was just one side of making visible the prison as a site of black racial and political formation. Indeed, the book release party's large crowd and media interest arose from more than the novelty of the location at the front of the prison, the strength of the marketing campaign, and the prepublication buzz around an eloquent book that had been serialized in the *New York Review of Books*. It arose from years of organizing by prisoners, complemented by greater attention from outside radical groups to the prison and punctuated by a stunning act of violence. On August 7, 1970, five weeks before the *Soledad Brother* release party, George Jackson's younger brother, Jonathan, stormed the Marin County Courthouse with a satchel full of guns during a trial of a San Quentin prisoner. The seventeen-year-old Jackson armed three prisoners, and the group took five hostages, among them the judge and district attorney. San Quentin guards and area police opened fire on the group, killing Jackson and two of the prisoners along with the judge. It was a tragic and gruesome incident, and it foreshadowed George Jackson's death at the hands of prison guards one year and two weeks later.

The Jackson brothers' actions, literary and military alike, took place in the middle of a massive wave of prison riots, with a reported fifteen such incidents in 1968 and at least forty-eight in 1972, the most of any year in U.S. history up to that point (and the actual number of disturbances was likely quite higher).[5] These riots were joined by a spike in prisoner assaults on guards as well as guard attacks on prisoners.

The culture of American prisons was changing. While prison is an inherently tumultuous place, rebellions and attacks had a more explicitly political character in the late 1960s and early 1970s than at most other moments in American history. This political character could be found both in the intent of such disturbances as well as in their reception: prison-based rebellion captured the radical imagination during these years. The Black Power and New Left movements gathered energy from news of prison unrest, and prisoners imbibed the ideas and culture of the political movements outside—and now inside—the prison walls. Influencing many activists and artists on the street, prisoner radicalism was most inspirational to other prisoners, who responded most frequently and most militantly to prisoner writings or uprisings with more writings and more uprisings. Dissident prisoners at varying institutions recognized a common project in the tumult facing 1970s prisons: the struggle for survival was embedded in a makeshift campaign against the brutality of confinement and criminalization.

Jackson emerged as a translator of the discontent that had been growing inside prisons. He was part of a generation of black prisoners who challenged racism in prison and whose politics were shaped by the extrajudicial killing of black prisoners by white guards or white prisoners, often acting with the collusion of guards. Jackson exposed the contentious and violent struggles behind prison walls. His words provided a coherent narrative through which people could understand rising prison protest. In Jackson's urgent telling, prisons were schools, rapidly graduating dedicated revolutionaries who transformed themselves behind bars: "There are still some blacks here who consider themselves criminals—but not many. Believe me, my friend, with the time and incentive that these brothers have to read, study, and think, you will find no class or category more aware, more embittered, desperate, or dedicated to the ultimate remedy—revolution. The most dedicated, the best of our kind—you'll find them in the Folsoms, San Quentins, and Soledads. They live like there was no tomorrow. And for most of them there isn't."[6]

Jackson's description of the polarized prison environment was also an argument about the broader constrictions that structure black life. To be black, Jackson claimed in a prescient analysis of the carceral state, was to live in and struggle against confinement. Black politics required "improvising on reality" from within what Jackson elsewhere called "the Black contingencies of Amerika."[7]

The prison's social significance emerged from this combination of eloquence and violence, vision and action. Prison organizing utilized what could be called a strategy of visibility. Prisoners and their allies reasoned that if the prison's power lay in its invisibility, its ability to remove people from view and access, thereby subjecting them to untold and untellable forms of violence, then exposure constituted a means of resistance. Visibility ran counter to the prison's mission and, they hoped, ability to function on a daily level. Their tactics, ranging from the pen to the sword, were designed to spread dissident views and nurture popular revolt against the status quo. This strategy generated a series of political linkages, connecting the inside to the outside while creating space for alliances among revolutionaries, progressives, and moderates. The stark conditions of confinement, in other words, drew the attention of a wide cross-section of society interested in the human rights demands coming from American prisons.

Prisoners' struggle over basic conditions of life called into question the system that sustained such massive vulnerabilities. Liberal reformers and militant revolutionists thus met at the prison walls, with a shared motivation to expose the horrors transpiring within—horrors that tarnished the veneer of racial innocence outside the South, especially in California. Making the racism of imprisonment visible undermined the assumption that northern states generally and California in particular were somehow immune to such violence.[8]

This emphasis on visibility was, for revolutionaries such as George Jackson, articulated through prevailing Marxist ideologies developed especially through the Third World revolutions of China, Algeria, and Cuba. In each, persistent armed struggle served as a rallying cry through which colonized populations garnered popular support. For many who grew up poor and subject to routine state violence in this age of revolution, these countries provided powerful examples of Goliath's long-awaited defeat. Viewing the rigidly hierarchical and racially violent world of the prison as an extension of the colonial world, prison organizers deployed a similar combination of intensive action and active iconicity. These prisoners made visible a black condition shaped by their highly masculinist surroundings; they operated within the sex-segregated world of the prison and defined their success through the scale of disruption.

George Jackson became the symbolic and global figurehead of a political and intellectual movement located in American prisons. He was charismatic and intelligent, strong and soft-spoken. He had a way with words, bestowing nicknames on his friends and romantic sobriquets on his love interests—and more important, situating imprisonment within a sharp political economic critique that was self-consciously steeped in black intellectual life. He had a keen ability to distill complex ideas into relatable, accessible terms. He was, according to many who knew him, easy to talk to and quick with a smile, at least among friends. To them, he was generous with his time, knowledge, and what little resources he had available to him. He delighted in sharing his prodigious knowledge with anyone who would listen as well as in using it to advance his ideas about prisons, economics, and military strategy. He taught interested fellow prisoners Marxism and martial arts: how to fight back intellectually as well as physically.[9] He retained a hard edge among competitors and antagonists, and like anyone, he could be vicious when he wanted to be. But his eloquence, intellect, and political commitments propelled his popularity within and beyond the California prison system.

A wide-ranging thinker steeped in the black radical tradition, he patterned himself after a series of heroic warriors—from slave rebels such as Nat Turner to anticolonial theorist Frantz Fanon to folk heroes like Stagolee, "the lawbreaking, woman-chasing, gambling man" who had long populated black outlaw ballads and had been revived as an icon among 1960s black nationalists.[10] Jackson's hypermasculinity overemphasized his authoritarianism, overshadowing some of the traits that made him the most radical: his collectivity, his mentorship, his fierce intellect and passion for change. Indeed, one unfortunate by-product of Jackson's macho posturing—an example of prison's exaggerated masculinity—is the way that it obscured the cooperative, nurturing elements of his praxis, including giving the proceeds of his writings to his comrades in prison and in the Black Panther Party. He viewed his notoriety as bound up with a collective politics; in turn, he sought to give back to that collective.

The frenzied period that saw Jackson move from dissident prisoner to celebrated author and from global revolutionary icon to one of six people killed on San Quentin's bloodiest day resulted from competing claims about who he was. As historian Rebecca Hill notes, Jackson tested "the left's ability to trust Black men, to believe in imperfect heroes, and to define itself without the long-standing and comfortable logic of white rebellion and Black victimization."[11] Indeed, Jackson's life and death in the partial spotlight, as well as his death's continuing reverberations in prison politics throughout the decade and beyond, tested not just the Left but American society at large. The story of George Jackson is a story of cross-cutting narratives in which both Jackson the person and *Soledad Brother* the book were distinct figures among a large cast of characters. Jackson was caught between the story he wished to tell about himself not just in books but in actions and the stories that publishers, journalists, activists—and a long list of antagonists—wished to tell about him. For all of these actors, Jackson's story was a microcosm of the black condition itself.

Only by situating Jackson within these different narratives and their wider historical context can we make sense of who he was and what he did. At a different moment, Jackson would never have gotten a book contract, and his ideas never would have caught the attention of millions of people worldwide. He never would have been seen as a beacon of revolutionary humanity or emerged as a global icon of black radicalism without fifteen consistent years of black activism passing through prison gates. But in 1970, the Black Panthers were Public Enemy No. 1, Richard Nixon was expanding the war in Southeast Asia he had promised to end, and the prison became a powerful site in which to make sense of America's enduring racial hierarchies in the early years of formal equality before the law.

George Lester Jackson was the second oldest of five children and the oldest son of Lester Jackson, a postal employee, and Georgia Jackson, a homemaker. His parents were from southern Illinois, although like many black people who moved to Chicago in the interwar years, they traced their roots to the South. Lester and Georgia married in Chicago's West Side ghetto. Georgia gave birth to their first child, Delora, in 1940. George came fifteen months later, on September 23, 1941. Over the next twelve years, three more children followed: Frances, Penelope, and Jonathan. The Jacksons were like many black families during World War II and its aftermath: hardworking and nominally race conscious but not politically involved. Georgia introduced her children to the writings of black scholars and novelists but does not appear to have belonged to any political organizations.[12]

Their experience was typical in another way: like many teenage boys, George—or George Lester, as the family liked to call him—began to get in trouble.[13] Indeed, the Jackson family had moved from Chicago to Los Angeles in 1956 in the hopes that the new environment would put young George on a different path. But he continued to run afoul of the law, and police arrested him three times in 1957 for attempted petty burglary. On one of those occasions, officers shot the sixteen-year-old Jackson in the forearm and leg. He spent eighteen months in a reform school for boys before being paroled at the end of 1958. He completed his sophomore year of high school under the tutelage of the California Youth Authority, the state's juvenile justice system, which loomed large over the lives of poor black migrants to the Golden State. Upon his release from the reform school, Jackson continued to court danger amid the hyperpolicing of the ghetto. Four more arrests for fighting and robbery followed, and he served another few months under the authority's auspices.

On September 18, 1960, five days before his nineteenth birthday, Jackson was on his way back to Pasadena from Tijuana with a friend when they held up a gas station, netting seventy-one dollars. Jackson was the getaway driver, but in light of his prior offenses, his court-appointed attorney convinced him to plead guilty in exchange for leniency. The judge, taken more with Jackson's record than with his plea, sentenced him to serve between one year and life in prison. The vagueness of Jackson's prison term, his "indeterminate sentence" of one year to life, was a hallmark of California's ostensibly liberal penal policy. It became the most controversial aspect of Jackson's eleven years in prison. Rather than assigning a fixed range of years as punishment, indeterminate sentencing meant that the parole board, the Adult Authority (or, for those in juvenile detention, the Juvenile Authority), would examine each prisoner's application on a case-by-case basis to see if the person met the standards for release. California's indeterminate sentencing law was passed in 1917 but gained steam as a model of social engineering during World War II. The law effectively made the parole board, not the judge or jury, the sentencing body; it alone decided when and under what criteria people had proven themselves sufficiently "reformed" to be released.

What made California's prison system liberal was its architects' belief that the state would remove wayward individuals from society in order to remake them into proper citizen-subjects. Rightlessness was supposed to be temporary and transformative. Critics charged that the Adult Authority used prison time as a bludgeon to ensure compliance with the prison rules and a self-discipline modeled on a bourgeois Western work ethic. Prisoners critiqued the idea of "rehabilitation" as meaning little more than being obsequious to the prison's authority—and with it, the injustices that continued to characterize the American state.[14]

Jackson entered a California prison system in the wake of transition, with the contradictions of its liberal prison governance producing more turmoil within the institutions. Four months before Jackson's imprisonment in 1960, the state had executed Caryl Chessman, a man serving time for rape and robbery who had written four best-selling books while incarcerated.

That year also saw the state open a solitary confinement unit at San Quentin known as the "Adjustment Center" (AC). The name bespoke the coercive model of rehabilitation touted by California prison officials in the postwar years, involving medicalized attempts to "correct" deviant individuals.[15] Life inside the AC was a mixture of routine violence and structural boredom. Prisoners spent twenty-three or twenty-four hours a day locked in their dimly lit cells, with limited human contact, time outside, or access to programming and showers. San Quentin's AC consisted of three tiers, with seventeen cells on either side of the floor separated by an alley that was not accessible to foot traffic. The top floor was reserved for death row prisoners, while the second floor held prisoners who were in protective custody. The bottom floor of this prison within a prison held up to thirty-four prisoners whom the guards deemed the most incorrigible. Almost all of the men in the cells on the ground floor of the AC were black and Latino, and several of them knew each other from other prisons or from other units of the prison. The men could yell to the people in adjoining cells but could not see or visit with them. Within the AC, prisoners were largely hidden even from other prisoners.[16]

Jackson began his sentence at Soledad Correctional Training Facility, a prison twenty-five miles southeast of Salinas in California's Central Valley. The

Soledad prison had opened in 1951, surrounded by the vineyards of the Salinas Valley. Jackson spent eleven years going back and forth largely between Soledad and San Quentin, disaffectedly called "the Q" and located in Marin County, less than twenty miles from Berkeley, Oakland, and San Francisco. Unlike Soledad, the modern prison in rural farmland, San Quentin was an archaic dungeon near San Rafael Bay. It had been built by convict labor in 1852, two years after California became a state and the U.S. Congress passed the Fugitive Slave Act, which committed national resources to maintaining slavery through policing black mobility. It was the oldest prison in California and soon became one of the most famous prisons in the world.[17]

Upon entering prison in 1960, Jackson inhabited a world even more sharply polarized by race than the neighborhoods he had once called home. The few sanctioned social spaces inside the prison were segregated, and white prisoners and guards regularly attacked black prisoners. Jackson's response became one of collective self-defense. In 1962, he gathered a few other black prisoners to avenge the racially motivated stabbing of another black prisoner; guards foiled the plot with guns and gas and then shipped Jackson and his coconspirators to San Quentin. It was the first of several write-ups Jackson received, and each reprimand took him further from the possibility of parole.

Journalist Min Yee reported that between "1962 and 1970, Jackson was cited forty-seven times for disciplinary infractions. He was denied parole ten times, even though his crime partner in the gas station robbery had been released years before." Most of his infractions "were for minor matters—playing poker, grabbing more food from the chow line when he was hungry," having more cigarettes in his possession than were allowed, failing to line up at the bars during count or to clean his cell. While some of these infractions resulted only in reprimands, he was often placed in solitary as punishment. Between 1965 and 1969, he received three citations for fighting and two for possessing weapons; all of the other incidents involved nonviolent activities that constituted small acts of protest against the picayune protocols of prison life.[18]

Jackson displayed a strong political consciousness throughout his incarceration, emphasizing self-defense and self-determination. His involvement in the prison's illicit economy, where food and cigarettes were currency, was rooted in an ethic of solidarity that took an increasingly radical political tone. He dreamed of autonomy, telling friends as early as 1962 that he wanted to create his own forms of governance on an island somewhere. He organized a food strike at the Deuel Vocational Institution in 1962 and continued to explore a wide variety of tactics, strategies, theories, and philosophies. The year he went to prison, seventeen countries in Africa won their independence, and he saw the work of revolutionary movements there as having a direct bearing on the issues he personally faced.

Conditions in California prisons were atrocious: rancid food, limited programming, segregated facilities, limited access to basic hygienic measures, arbitrary and extended solitary confinement. Black and politically active prisoners suffered even more than others, aware that they faced constant threats of violence from white prisoners and guards in addition to the restrictions that racial segregation already placed on them. Many prison officials not only nurtured racism but demanded absolute obedience to their authority, no matter how capricious their demands.

As Jackson's politics grew more radical, he participated in clandestine study groups reading Marxist classics and contemporary works, from Lenin and Trotsky to Fanon and Mao. He introduced many prisoners to these and other thinkers and led political education sessions in the San Quentin yard about racism and political economy. Jackson began to discuss socialism, constantly referring to people as "comrades" and earning himself the nickname "the Comrade." (Even that moniker was educational, since some prisoners unfamiliar with the word initially thought Jackson wanted to be called "Conrad.") Jackson convinced skeptical black and Latino prisoners that socialism was relevant to their lives.[19]

Jackson was part of a wider circle of mostly black radicals looking to end structural violence and the ways it manifested through interpersonal racist attacks. In this context, prison organizing was a matter of urgency and delicacy. On the one hand, black (and many Latino) prisoners needed to defend themselves against racist assault. On the other hand, as long as prisoners of different racial groups remained antagonistic, institutional conditions would not change. Jackson took the lead among a group of black prisoners in attempting to break the stalemate: he emphasized the importance of prisoner unity against guards. He imagined this united front in successive waves, allowing black prisoners to defend themselves against white prisoners' attacks while working toward greater unity among all prisoners premised on a shared rejection of the prison state. He preached the same message to activists on the outside: "I know I am black. I know that no one can better represent his blackness than I. I can and have always represented mine. . . . If a man wants to relate to my blackness, fine, but I would prefer he relate to me on the basis of my status as a soldier in the WORLD revolution."[20]

Part of developing such multiracial unity in prison required breaking the guards' monopoly on the use of force. Only they had arms, and they had complete license to beat or kill prisoners. Jackson was one of many prisoners who

thought that prisoners should defend themselves by striking back, by responding in kind when guards killed prisoners.[21]

By the mid-1960s, with California's overall prison population declining, Jackson had gained notoriety throughout the California penal system.[22] His reputation spread by word of mouth and the transfers of friends and associates to
other prisons. A network of black radicalism existed across the state penal system as people were transferred from the California Youth Authority to prison
and from prison to prison, with organizations such as the Nation of Islam, the
Black Panthers, and US facilitating its spread.

When Black Panther cofounder and minister of defense Huey P. Newton
went to prison in 1968 for the manslaughter of police officer John Frey, he recognized Jackson's influence in the actions of other black prisoners. Although
Newton and Jackson never met face-to-face, they communicated through a
growing network of supporters and mutual friends (including Los Angeles
Black Panther Geronimo Pratt). Jackson, after all, was to the prison environment what Newton was to the urban one: a minister of defense, a self-taught
theoretician, a strident black revolutionary nationalist and Marxist. The two
men had a lot to offer each other in helping circulate the message of black revolution between the cell block and the city block. Newton connected Jackson to
Fay Stender, a young attorney who was working for Black Panther lead counsel
Charles Garry at the time and who went on to found the Prison Law Project.
Newton asked Garry and Stender to look into Jackson's case in 1969 after the
Panther leader heard from other prisoners about this man they considered a
living legend.

Stuck in a prison cell, Jackson corresponded with his growing list of supporters. He wrote periodically for the *Black Panther* newspaper and joined
the Black Panther Party, receiving the military rank of field marshal. He was
charged with expanding the party's paramilitary apparatus by recruiting members from the prison's ranks. Many Panthers celebrated the move as extending
the party's reach more formally inside of prisons, since Jackson's involvement
would increase the organization's profile among those it considered prime recruits. In practice, this designation institutionalized what Jackson was already
doing and continued to do; indeed, he routinely boasted that his primary political role was of a military nature.[23]

Jackson's deepening connections with the party emerged in tandem with his
growing commitment to Third World revolutionary struggles. His membership, as much symbolic as substantive, extended the BPP's emphasis on prisons
beyond the arrests and trials of its Free World members. A series of deadly
incidents inside the California prison system in early 1970, part of a simmering

war between prisoners and guards, pushed Jackson beyond the pages of the *Black Panther* newspaper and made him into a global icon of black militancy.

"NO ONE ELSE COULD HAVE DONE IT"

At Soledad, 1970 began with a series of killings. Tensions between black prisoners and white prisoners and white guards had been rising for some time. In early January, W. L. Nolen warned his parents that he felt that the guards were trying to kill him. Arrested for robbery in 1963, Nolen was a prison boxing champ and proto–black nationalist who had tutored several prisoners at Soledad as he had earlier at San Quentin and Folsom. He and Jackson met in 1966 and became fast friends. Nolen filed several lawsuits protesting the threats against his life by white prisoners and the guards' manipulation of racial tensions at Soledad, but the situation had worsened by the beginning of 1970. Nolen was in a wing of Soledad that had been locked down since the 1968 killing of two black prisoners. Because one of the men, Clarence Causey, had been stabbed on the prison yard, guards closed the integrated exercise yard. Yet they also continued to stoke tensions between black and white prisoners.

On January 13, Soledad guards reopened the exercise yard and let fifteen prisoners access it for the first time in more than a year. The group included eight white prisoners, among them Billie "Buzzard" Harris, leader of the Aryan Brotherhood, and seven black prisoners, including Nolen. When the prisoners, pent up for so long, began a fistfight, Soledad guard Opie G. Miller began firing without warning from the gun tower overlooking the yard. Miller was a twenty-year army veteran and expert marksman; he shot Nolen first, then Cleveland Edwards, who went to help the injured Nolen, and finally Alvin "Jug" Miller. The three men, all of them black and all of them outspoken militants, were shot in the chest and left lying in the yard for twenty minutes before being removed. All three died that night. Only one of the white prisoners involved in the fight was injured, hit by a ricocheting bullet. Many prisoners and subsequent outside observers (including a 1975 jury in a wrongful death suit brought by the families of the dead) viewed the killings as a set-up.[24]

Black prisoners responded with action, going "on hunger strikes, burn[ing] prison furniture and dispatch[ing] a voluminous amount of mail to their families and attorneys and to state officials, demanding an investigation." The prison was in an open state of rebellion. "Fistfights erupted in numerous housing wings," journalist Min Yee reported not long afterward. "White and black cons alike walked around with magazines stuffed in their shirts to blunt knife attacks." Three days later, in an interview that prisoners heard on the radio, the district attorney said that he believed that the deaths constituted "justifiable homicide." Some prisoners concluded that the law would offer them no recourse. That night, twenty-six-year-old guard John Mills, a new member of the Soledad staff, was beaten and thrown to his death off the third tier. Several prisoners initially clapped and cheered, but after about ninety seconds, they became stone quiet, fearing what was to come.[25]

The investigation into Mills's death quickly focused on Jackson, leading many observers to believe that the authorities had focused on him because of his political beliefs and organizing efforts. While some later accounts claim that Jackson privately admitted to killing Mills, the investigation was so sloppy that one analyst contended that Jackson was framed for a crime he actually committed.[26] The Soledad warden summarized the official view of the twenty-eight-year-old Jackson. Without pointing to any evidence, the warden prejudged Jackson's guilt by saying that "no one else could have done it."[27]

All prisoners on the Y wing of Soledad were held incommunicado for two weeks following Mills's death as guards repeatedly questioned 138 people. Guards plied some prisoners with good food and promises of early release in exchange for their testimony. Others were less fortunate. Captain Charles Moody, feared and hated by many prisoners, put his personal pistol to the heads of some prisoners to elicit statements. There was no independent investigation, save what the prisoners' attorneys did subsequent to the indictment.

Prison officials focused on Jackson and two others known by their Afro hairstyles and the posters they displayed in their cells to be sympathetic to Black Power. Twenty-four-year-old John Clutchette; Fleeta Drumgo, age twenty-three; and Jackson were held in isolation without contact with the outside world, for another twenty-one days. Clutchette had been in prison for four years at that point, Drumgo for five. Both men were serving time for burglary and expected to get out soon; Clutchette was just forty-five days away from parole. Prison authorities never alerted the men's families of the charges they faced, and when the mothers of Clutchette and Drumgo called the prison, officials told them that they had nothing to worry about and that their sons did not need legal representation.[28]

Like Jackson and thousands of other young black men at this time, Clutchette and Drumgo had long records filled with minor crimes—fighting, petty theft, parole violations—that dated back to when they were fourteen and eight, respectively. The three men, who barely knew each other, were formally charged with the murder on February 23, 1970. Three days later, in an incident that demonstrated Jackson's point about the impunity with which guards committed violence, San Quentin guards beat a mentally unstable black prisoner,

The Soledad Brothers, ca. 1971. John Clutchette, Fleeta Drumgo, and George Jackson were charged in the January 1970 death of a Soledad prison guard. At twenty-eight, Jackson was the oldest of the group and became the most famous. Clutchette was twenty-four and Drumgo was twenty-three when the three were charged in the case. Photo © 2014 Stephen Shames/Polaris Images.

Fred Billingslea, and left him in a tear-gas-filled cell until he died.[29] Neither youth nor mental illness offered protection from the racism of the American criminal justice system.[30]

The case attracted local media attention as well as the interest of the Bay Area Left. Stender and the Black Panthers quickly dubbed the three defendants the Soledad Brothers, and the case became paradigmatic of prison militancy throughout the decade, with George Jackson at the center. Jackson emerged as the pivotal figure for multiple reasons. Most immediately, the stakes were highest for him. The California Penal Code mandated an automatic death sentence for a prisoner who was convicted of assault while serving a life sentence. Because Jackson's open-ended sentence included the possibility of life in prison, he now faced death. Just as important to his fame, however, were his charisma, his extensive knowledge, and his commanding vocabulary. Camera-shy and less well read than Jackson, Clutchette and Drumgo were happy to have him represent the group. A veteran of the system with the eloquence to describe the injustices to which he had been subjected, Jackson was a natural spokesperson for the growing critique of American prisons as a bulwark of racial and class domination.[31]

Stender became Jackson's attorney shortly after the three men were charged with Mills's death. Stender was a hardworking, dedicated, and tenacious radical approaching age forty when she met Jackson. A Berkeley native, Stender had worked for several years with Black Panthers and other Bay Area activists. She

Fay Stender at a protest for George Jackson at the gates of San Quentin, October 1970. Stender was Jackson's attorney and had previously worked on Huey P. Newton's case. It was her idea to turn Jackson's letters into a book, and she later founded the Prison Law Project. Photo © 2014 Ilka Hartmann.

took up the case with urgency and discipline, as much a political organizer as a legal professional. She and her associates spent months interviewing more than one hundred prisoners to challenge the government's version of Mills's death. She recruited law students to help her with the research and solicited money from the Black Panthers' growing political defense funds.[32]

Stender's legal thoroughness was matched by her knack for publicity. Working alongside Charles Garry on Panther cases, Stender had learned that successful defense campaigns marshaled public attention. She needed her clients to be in the public eye and to have sympathetic narratives. She asked KPFA journalist Elsa Knight Thompson to interview the Soledad warden, helping cement an interest in prison conditions and prisoner cases at the progressive radio station that would last for several years.[33] Stender organized her friends and associates to pay attention to the case, incorporating it into the daily rhythm of Bay Area radical communities. In April 1970, she visited Soledad prison with a small delegation that included Senator Mervyn Dymally, California's first black state senator, in hopes of getting elected officials to support prisoner grievances. She had already pulled together a coalition of black activists, white leftists, and celebrities to launch the first Soledad Brothers Defense

Committee (SBDC). Stender fashioned a long list of endorsers for the committee. Carleton Goodlett, a physician and publisher of San Francisco's black newspaper, the *Sun Reporter*, who had a storied career in civil rights politics, was among the defense committee's initial endorsers and later chaired the legal committee.

Other early sponsors included a wide range of figures from the liberal to radical Left, including progressive politicians (Julian Bond, George Brown, Ron Dellums), intellectuals (Noam Chomsky, St. Clair Drake, Martin Duberman), artists (Lawrence Ferlinghetti, Jane Fonda, Maxwell Geismar, Allen Ginsberg, Pete Seeger), attorneys (Arthur Kinoy, William Kunstler, Gerry Lefcourt, Leonard Weinglass), professionals (the Reverend George Baber, Dr. Benjamin Spock, the Reverend Cecil Williams), and activists (Angela Davis, Corky Gonzales, Tom Hayden, Huey P. Newton, Mario Savio).[34] The California legislature's five-member Black Caucus was also instrumental in building early support for the Soledad Brothers. Several prisoners and their family members had contacted members of the caucus to request they investigate conditions at Soledad prison, prompting the legislators, led by Dymally and assemblyman John J. Miller, to visit the prison and meet with the warden in the summer of 1970. While the tour had broader goals, the Soledad Brothers case cast a shadow over the facility. Indeed, seven prisoners were disciplined in June 1970 for trying to raise money for the Soledad Brothers Defense Fund.[35]

As with other U.S. political defense campaigns, the support for the Soledad Brothers united public figures, who could lend their celebrity to the cause, with family members of the accused, who provided credibility.[36] Although George Jackson had a strained relationship with his parents—his father had written a summer 1965 letter to the prison warden opposing his son's release, and George often blamed his mother for his predicament—his mother and siblings played key roles in the defense campaign. The committee hoped to do more than free the Soledad Brothers; it sought to put the California prison system itself on trial. Writing to Spock as part of her efforts initiating what would become the SBDC, journalist Jessica Mitford argued that "because of what will be exposed about this [case], and what it says about prisons in general (Calif. prisons are, as you know, considered the most 'advanced' and 'reformed' in the country) I believe the case has national importance."[37] News of the case spread, and other chapters of the defense committee formed, fueled in part by personal connections to the men on trial. The mothers of Clutchette and Drumgo joined Jackson's family in the defense effort.

So did black members of the Communist Party (CP) chapter in Los Angeles. One of them, Kendra Alexander, had known John Clutchette and his brother,

The Reverend Cecil Williams speaks at a rally to support the Soledad Brothers, ca. 1970. Williams was the pastor at Glide Memorial Church in San Francisco. He was a strong supporter of the Black Panther Party and other progressive organizations at the time. Photo © 2014 Stephen Shames/Polaris Images.

Gregory, who was also imprisoned at Soledad, since junior high school.[38] The city now had a substantial and activist black population, and it became an important base of support for the Soledad Brothers. The Los Angeles chapter of the Black Panthers had brought together several formerly incarcerated people and former gang members, making it one of the truest examples of the Panthers' plan to "organize the brothers on the block." The chapter had also been plagued by police informants and devastated by tragedy, including the murders of chapter leaders Alprentice Bunchy Carter and John Huggins in January 1969 and the police assault on the party headquarters the following December, as well as running feuds with police and members of the US organization, a cultural nationalist group hostile to the BPP. Los Angeles was also home to the Che-Lumumba Club, an all-black chapter of the Communist Party. Established in 1967, the club was one expression of how the party's long but checkered history of support for black radicalism joined with the autonomous militancy of the newly pronounced Black Power movement.[39]

The club's members included not only Kendra Alexander and her husband, Franklin, but also a young graduate student, Angela Davis. Born and raised in Birmingham, Alabama, and educated in New York City, Boston, and Frankfurt,

Davis was seasoned beyond her years. She had attended a leftist high school and pursued graduate studies with Marxist theorist Herbert Marcuse, leaving Davis well acquainted with Marxism generally and the CP specifically. She joined the party through the Che-Lumumba Club in 1968, when she was an assistant professor at UCLA, teaching classes on philosophy and liberation there and at a Los Angeles freedom school established by the local SNCC chapter. In July 1969, FBI agent William Divale, who had infiltrated the CP, revealed to the UCLA student newspaper that there was a Communist Party member on the faculty. The article set off a firestorm once Ed Montgomery of the conservative *San Francisco Examiner* revealed Davis to be the person in question. Montgomery led the ranks of those demanding that UCLA fire her. The newspaper article, printed as Republican governor Ronald Reagan bullied many of the state's social movements, sparked a fierce battle over Davis's future in the University of California system. With a daily barrage of hate mail, much of it threatening violence, Davis purchased several guns for self-defense.[40]

In the winter of 1970, as she fought to preserve her academic career and protect her personal safety, she also began corresponding with George Jackson after reading newspaper coverage of the case. The pair quickly established a rapport, and their correspondence took on a more intimate tone. "My memory fails me when I search in the past for an encounter w/ a human being as strong as beautiful as you," she closed a June 1970 letter to him. "Something in you has managed to smash thru the fortress I long ago erected around my soul. I wonder what it is. I'm very glad. I love you."[41] Davis became one of the leading members of the SBDC, setting up the Los Angeles chapter in April. She also became close with Jonathan Jackson, George's younger brother, who looked up to Davis as his teacher and ultimately looked out for her as her bodyguard.

The Soledad Brothers case, with its Manichaean combination of official brutality and attractive, articulate dissidents, encapsulated the prison's growing centrality in American society. The effort to free Jackson, Drumgo, and Clutchette joined long-standing critiques of legal bias with Black Power militancy.[42] The case launched a new wave of prisoner defense campaigns; in the coming years, several prison riots captured national attention and catalyzed a variety of organizations dedicated to reforming or abolishing the prison. For several years after the Soledad Brothers case, writes historian Regina Kunzel, "leftist credibility seemed to depend on radical prison activism"; radical sectors of the feminist and lesbian and gay movements as well as other social movements of the 1970s turned their attention to the prison following the lead of the Black Panthers and New Leftists who made the Soledad Brothers into a cause célèbre.[43]

The Soledad Brothers case also became a valuable prism through which to make sense of the growing connection between race and incarceration. In 1970, the rate of imprisonment nationally was the lowest it had been in twenty years, with 96 of every 100,000 people in prison. At the same time, however, racial disparities among those incarcerated were becoming entrenched. By 1970, black people were being sent to prison at seven times the rate for whites. In 1944, California's prison population was 17 percent black, a figure that increased to 28 percent by 1969; the state's incarceration rate jumped a dramatic 505 percent over the same span. In 1971, the state imprisoned just under 23,000 people.[44] After a massive prison-building boom that began ten years later and would ultimately see 1 in 100 Americans incarcerated, California's prison population topped 150,000 people in prison by 2011.[45]

When Father Earl Neil eulogized George Jackson in August 1971 as an apostle of "the black condition," the Episcopal priest was more prophetic than perhaps he realized.[46] Writing shortly before the hyperincarceration of poor black men from the inner city became a defining feature of American urban policy, Jackson was both an eloquent writer whose books contributed to making the prison visible and a militant revolutionist whose politics were forged through the racialized brutalities of confinement. He was the primary strategist and tactician of a national prison movement. Jackson advocated violent struggle against any and all manifestations of American power; such a course, he maintained, would cleanse the black soul of the confinement of white supremacy. An American Frantz Fanon, Jackson claimed that violence would vindicate a wounded black manhood and hobble the prison system. Instead, the state increased its capacity for violence. Jackson provided a glimpse of what was to come: an upside-down world where the prison would serve as a palimpsest of the ghetto, an institution that cast a long and indelible shadow over black urban life for the rest of the twentieth century and beyond.[47]

"A BLACK REVOLUTIONARY MENTALITY"

The idea to turn Jackson's letters into a book came from Stender, Jackson's attorney of record, who was inspired by the success of Eldridge Cleaver's *Soul on Ice* and aware of attorney Beverly Axelrod's role in it. Stender saw in Jackson's eloquence an opportunity to both challenge the prison system and build support for her client. She drew on a wider circle of Panther supporters to develop the project from an idea into a publishable manuscript.

Stender contacted her friend Mitford, an enigmatic former communist from a British aristocratic family who had become a celebrated author and muckraking journalist. Mitford, who had been involved through the Communist Party in several efforts to support black prisoners in the 1930s and 1940s, was more than just politically sympathetic; she was also well connected. Mitford introduced Stender to Gregory Armstrong of Bantam Books, securing the support of a major publisher.[48] Stender also seized every opportunity to show Jackson's letters to friends and fellow activists to enlist their support in the nascent SBDC. She gave people the hard sell as well as the soft, casually sharing Jackson's letters with people over dinner to get them involved by showcasing his passionate writings, at once sophisticated and alluring.[49]

As the book neared publication, Stender asked for help from French author and Black Panther supporter Jean Genet. (She also sent his play, *The Blacks*, to the Soledad Brothers.) Genet had built a close relationship with the Black Panthers through two trips to the United States—first in 1968 to cover the Democratic National Convention, when he entered the country illegally through Canada after being denied a visa, and then in 1970 to give lectures and raise funds for the Panthers. Genet wrote the introduction to *Soledad Brother*, praising the book for displaying "the miracle of truth itself, the naked truth completely exposed."[50] Working with Ellen Wright, Richard Wright's widow and a literary agent in Paris, Genet helped arrange for the French release of *Soledad Brother* by his publisher, Gallimard. Genet also solicited the support of several prominent French authors and intellectuals, among them Jean-Paul Sartre, Michel Foucault, and Jacques Derrida, who called for Jackson's release and were influenced by his work.[51]

Genet's contribution to *Soledad Brother* gave the book an instant, international literary imprimatur. As a world-renowned playwright, reclusive yet extroverted, a former prisoner and a sophisticated analyst of identity, outlawry, and the vicissitudes of publicity, Genet exhibited many of the same characteristics that made Jackson so compelling. Having deserted the army and served time in prison for petty thievery before winning his freedom through his powerful writings, Genet embodied the outlaw image that had captivated the American imagination. Capturing the sexual ethos of outlawry, Genet described being gay as an outlaw sexuality, quieting many homophobic fears among the Left, notwithstanding Jackson's derision of prison homosexuality in *Soledad Brother*.

Extrapolating from Jackson's writings, Genet described prison and death as two sites of black redemption.[52] Like Jackson, Genet argued that prisons concentrated the racism of the American state. "One might say that racism is in its pure state [in prison], gathering its forces, pulsing with power, ready to spring."[53] As with many positive appraisals of *Soledad Brother*, Genet found the book striking for its ability to develop a structural critique through unique and emotionally revealing language. Genet described language as the first and last recourse available to black radicalism, enabling dissent to corrupt the "enemy's language . . . so skillfully that the white men are caught in his trap. To accept it in all its richness, to increase that richness still further, and to suffuse it with all his obsessions and all his hatred of the white man."[54]

Soledad Brother offered a compelling if fractured portrait of life in prison. The book's fragmentary conversations—only Jackson's letters appear—offer an atypical glimpse of black masculine common sense in the second half of the 1960s. Indeed, part of the book's appeal was in its ability for readers to see Jackson as a kind of everyman: a victim of his circumstance, working to make the best of a bad situation. His letters displayed an increasingly militant consciousness that paralleled the radicalization of black urban youth. In the words of New York Black Panther Sundiata Acoli, Jackson was "the epitome of any black person" who elected activism over apathy.[55] His letters narrate the major events of the era—the Watts uprising, the assassinations of Martin Luther King Jr. and Robert Kennedy, the constant rhythms of war and police violence—while subtly displaying the shift from a Nation of Islam–style nationalism to the growing influence of Third World–nationalist Marxism.

Restrictions on the length of prisoners' letters imposed a unique structure on Jackson's book. Political arguments come largely in staccato bursts that are bookended by lengthy letters (likely snuck out through mail to his lawyers). In *Soledad Brother*, Jackson becomes educated in Marxist economics and black radicalism and seeks to share his newfound knowledge with the members of his family. Short letters describing his repeated parole denials testify to the crushing weight of prison. Jackson writes to his younger brother as if for a large audience, projecting an image of mental and physical strength. "You're supposed to be representing me, meaning that you are to be strong, intellectual, watchful, serious, unapproachable," he tells Jonathan, then a junior at Blair High School in Pasadena, California.[56] (Jonathan, however, objected to George's frequent discussions of his young age: "It is very hard for me to command authority from anyone if he knows that I am 17," he complained to George.)[57]

Jackson intimated that the prison had hardened him and prepared him for battle. His enduring message was one of action against the forces of injustice. "I've been patient," Jackson wrote to his parents in 1965, "but where I'm concerned patience has its limits. Take it too far, and it's cowardice."[58] Jackson's sweeping, emotive language reveals an all-or-nothing revolutionary will that prides itself on being both raw and detached. "I can still smile now, after ten years of blocking knife thrusts and pick handles, of anticipating and [*sic*] faceless sadistic pigs, reacting for ten years, seven of them in Solitary. I can still smile sometimes, but by the time this thing is over I may not be a nice person. And I just lit my seventy-seventh cigarette of this 21-hour day. I'm going to lay down for two or three hours, perhaps I'll sleep."[59]

Jackson almost celebrates the perfection of emotional control that prison has inculcated in him. "So, if they would reach me now, across my many barricades, it must be with a bullet and it must be final."[60] This theme of survival through a mixture of emotional detachment and passionate engagement as a survival mechanism appears in several of Jackson's letters, both published and not. In an unpublished letter to Mitford, he wrote, "I make my appeal to arms, and the people who have escaped the mindless, yankee autonaton [sic] syndrome. . . . Dispassionately I face the men who hate us—and the real revolution will start here."[61] This emotional discipline went alongside Jackson's call for guerrilla warfare. He juxtaposed a harsh notion of revolution against anything he saw as sentimental methods for effecting social change. He privately described both sex and armed struggle as "the end-game," his missions in life.[62]

Soledad Brother merged memoir and Marxism to develop a theory of imprisonment as an extension of slavery. He often wrote of the deep memory of enslavement and the Middle Passage as foundations of the contemporary world system. "I recall the day I was born, the first day of my generation," he wrote in one such passage. "It was during the second (and most destructive) capitalist world war for colonial privilege, early on a rainy Wednesday morning, late September, Chicago."[63] The blend of systemic critique with personal detail, the cross-currents of world historical and autobiographical knowledge, has become a standard of prison literature owing in part to Jackson. It suggests the prison was a gestational site of long black memory.[64] Jackson's move between slavery and incarceration provided a racial framework through which to understand both the history and future of disproportionate black incarceration. "Blackmen born in the U.S. and fortunate enough to live past the age of eighteen are conditioned to accept the inevitability of prison. For most of us, it simply looms as the next phase in a sequence of humiliations," Jackson wrote by way of introduction to the book.[65]

Jackson's commentary on black America offered both a retrospective on the recent past and a window into an emerging racial future. That Jackson launched his critique of American society from prison was especially meaningful, for *Soledad Brother*—and the wider genre of prisoner literature that exploded in the mid-1960s—constituted a metacommentary on the growth and racialized expansion of the carceral state from the viewpoint of its victims. Writing from the shadows of society, in the wake of civil rights legislative victories, George Jackson was a voice of protest for a new generation. He spoke for those who were disenfranchised more by the globalizing corporate capitalism of racial liberalism—increasingly deterritorialized and speaking the language of color-blind inclusion—than by the white-sheeted terrorists of Jim Crow's fading regime.

In describing the intense violence of prison racism, *Soledad Brother* stubbornly insisted on the ongoing significance of race to American society. By documenting the persistence of racial hierarchies, Jackson also presaged their changing shape. Anticipating the nuanced investigations of critical race theory, Jackson showed that race persisted in and through otherwise invisible institutions. Indeed, he contended that race and racism remained central to the idea and routine functioning of the United States, regardless of whether they appeared on the public agenda. That he wrote from California's isolation cells offered a sneak peak inside what was fast becoming a premier technology of racial violence—the prison—while simultaneously illuminating a wider, enduring truth about racialization: racism persists as a material force despite and because of attempts to manage racial difference through a mixture of incorporation and repression.

At the same time, Jackson's antiracist critique revealed the increasing significance of the gendered fault lines accompanying this seismic shift in the American racial landscape. Simply put, he was the product not only of a Cold War patriarchal culture but of the sex-segregated institution in which he came of age. His masculinist appeals revealed the carceral future awaiting millions of black men while appealing to the notion of restorative patriarchy common to black nationalist groups that recruited inside prisons during the early 1960s, most centrally the Nation of Islam. His radical critique of American political economy did not obfuscate his own allegiance to a conservative, patriarchal notion of respectability.

Jackson's letters mirror the national moral panic over the state of the black family that had accompanied the 1965 Moynihan Report's claims that the allegedly matriarchal structure of black families was responsible for black poverty. Jackson's perspective, while evolving throughout the book, remains fundamentally conservative on gender. "I must be the first to admit that I see that the black family unit is in ruins. It is our first and basic weakness," he wrote, suggesting that black communities needed to restore the heteronormative family structure that chattel slavery had interrupted. Mimicking the worst elements of the pathological descriptions of black life, common both to the NOI and to wider popular culture, Jackson lambasts the "matriarchal subsociety" that has "always" characterized black America and that has its roots in the sexual violence of slave society.[66]

Jackson personalized this critique for his own family. In several passages, he argues for the restoration of black patriarchy as key to progress, both for black people in general and for his parents in particular. Indeed, the bulk of Jackson's letters in the book were written to either his mother or his father (though never to both at once). He laments their individual weaknesses, sometimes blaming them for his predicament, at other moments seeing them as exemplars of larger black failings that could only be corrected through a return to manliness and its authority. He challenges both his parents for allowing Georgia Jackson to dominate the household but also tries to protect them from one another and from his predicament. "Comfort Mom as well as you can and tell her I'm all right, healthy, happy, content," he told his father on March 26, 1967. "Of course, this is a lie, but she likes to be lied to."[67] In later letters, however, Jackson described his father as the more egregious example of false consciousness, unwittingly believing in the ideologies that repressed him. Indeed, the letters reveal that Jackson clearly saw his race-conscious mother as a sharper political thinker than his father.[68]

Though directed to his family, Jackson's concerns seemed universal. Jackson's eloquence reflected his wide reading in the sciences, economics, languages, philosophy, and anthropology.[69] His literary talents expressed an abiding internationalism that he introduced to others as much through subtle word choices as through explicit arguments about the Third World. Jackson's signature sign-off, "from Dachau with love," as well as his deliberate use of "U.S.A." to refer interchangeably to the United States of America and the Union of South Africa as white supremacist states, expressed a global critique of the violence inherent in racial states across time and space, whether the United States, Nazi Germany, or apartheid South Africa. Further, his comparative genocide approach emphasized a radical internationalism. That Jackson introduced many of his readers to the historical existence of the Nazi concentration camps or the brutal policies oppressing black South Africans demonstrated the prison's inability to contain his intellect or empathy.[70] This global vision influenced other prisoners, too. Jackson looked to the national liberation struggles in continental Africa as his greatest inspiration and encouraged others to look to the Third World for examples.[71]

His charisma blended romance and politics into a life-or-death struggle against all manner of violence and alienation. "If we can reach each other through all of this, fences, fear, concrete, steel, barbed wire, guns, then history will commend us for a great victory won. If so—it will be your generosity and my good fortune."[72] Such language prompted one reviewer to celebrate that *Soledad Brother* "breathes you in," showcasing the despair of isolation alongside the redemptive hope of human connection.[73] Jackson's growing ability to channel an existential angst through a communist analysis popularized an antiracist critique of capitalism. "I don't want to die and leave a few sad songs and a hump in the ground as my only monument," he wrote of his vision. "I want to leave a world that is liberated from trash, pollution, racism, poverty, nation-states, nation-state wars and armies, from bigotry, parochialism, a thousand different brands of untruth, and licentious usurious economics. . . . If there is any basis for a belief in the universality of man then we will find it in this struggle against the enemy of all mankind."[74]

Jackson wrote in his own voice but was steeped in the classics of black literature. He self-consciously followed the tradition of black radical authorship. In a *New York Times* interview with Mitford, Jackson spoke of reading Richard Wright and W. E. B. Du Bois as a child at his mother's urging.[75] When Jackson wrote, "I'm part of a righteous people who anger slowly, but rage undamned," he echoed the protagonist of Ralph Ellison's *Invisible Man*—one of the books Jackson had in his cell. (In Ellison's version, the invisible man exhorts a crowd protesting an eviction in Harlem by describing blacks as a "law-abiding people and a slow-to-anger people.") And Jackson's repeated refrain that "we die too easily" recalls a Du Boisian race consciousness first displayed in his classic *Souls of Black Folk*.[76]

Soledad Brother sounded similar themes to traditional uplift narratives: it valorized self-education as a necessary ingredient for racial progress, defining progress in terms of both individual responsibility and social change. In Jackson's hands, the redemptive power of education took a decidedly revolutionary (if sometimes dystopian) turn. The book shattered the idea, embedded in rehabilitative penology, that complacency accrues with time spent in a cage. Instead of making Jackson more docile and palatable, prolonged punishment made him more radical and militant. Paradoxically, the evolution chronicled in *Soledad Brother* validated the idea that prisons could transform "the criminal mentality," albeit into a revolutionary rather than an acquiescent citizen.[77] (His distaste for neat conversion stories and uplift narratives may be part of what Jackson objected to about the book's arrangement of his letters and the exclusion of his more military-oriented tracts.)[78] Yet the personal transformation Jackson demonstrated fundamentally opposed the prison regime. Jackson described the goal of his political community of prisoners as "attempt[ing] to transform the black criminal mentality into a black revolutionary mentality. As a result each of us has been subjected to years of the most vicious reactionary violence by the state. Our mortality rate is almost what you would expect to find in a history of Dachau."[79]

By the time *Soledad Brother* appeared, Jackson had been in prison for ten years, seven of them in solitary confinement, mostly at San Quentin. By November 1970, with his new book getting rave reviews, Jackson was assigned permanently to the San Quentin isolation unit after an altercation with an officer. Jackson adopted an intensive regimen to train his body and mind, all the more important once he was relegated to permanent solitary confinement. He exercised for hours a day, ultimately boasting of doing one thousand finger push-ups, and spent forty-five minutes a day studying vocabulary. His public statements demonstrated both his erudition and his physical agility. Indeed, his frequent references to physical activity revealed a thinly veiled sexual energy. Jackson's writings contained a flirtatious streak, and his sexual appeal became part of his political appeal.[80]

His prominence as a leading figure of not just prison organizing but radicalism more generally made him, in his day and ever since, the litmus test for politicized black male prisoners in an era of expanded carceral capacity. Jackson's political work, captured in writing and expressed through his collaborations with others in various prisons, encouraged prisoners to see themselves as political actors despite and because of their confinement. He nurtured a collective self-confidence, rooted in a masculine sense of racial pride. His ideas and his orientation nurtured a generation of prison protest. Jackson was both a product of the era's black militancy and a catalyst for its continued circulation. He synthesized ideas, debates, and strategies circulating widely among a growing coterie of black radicals confined in American prisons. Jackson was a partisan of armed struggle who believed that only retaliatory attacks on guards would stop them from killing prisoners, yet he also advocated both prisoner unity and larger prisoner-focused unity among the Left. As a result, he united people of diverse ideologies around the figure of the prisoner. The cohort congregating around Jackson reversed the defeatist sentiment of imprisonment. Instead of minimal conditions suited to barely sustain life, they developed express political purpose at the margins; out of near-death came political life.

As a result, prison officials treated Jackson's literary success with the same hostility with which they greeted the publication of Caryl Chessman and Eldridge Cleaver's respective books. The Golden State proved disinterested in following the bibliotherapy model, an idea dating back to 1947 that reading and writing would prove rehabilitative if prisoners turned that therapy into political critique. "Treatment-era bibliotherapy and the free reading and writing policies accompanying it had produced an ungovernable monster in the opinion of the prison administration," writes historian Eric Cummins.[81] The state's

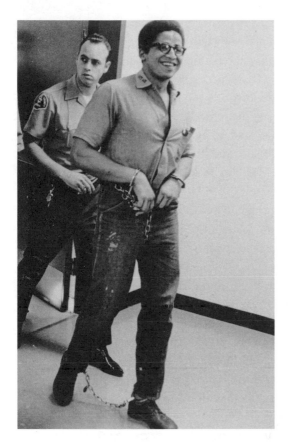

George Jackson being led to court, ca. 1971. The cuffs around his wrists are shackled to his waist and connected to the cuffs at his ankles. Jackson had been known throughout the California prison system as a theorist and a militant years before he became known to the larger public. As he became famous, many supporters celebrated his humor and charm alongside his revolutionary politics. Photo by Dan O'Neil; courtesy of It's about Time Black Panther Archive.

unwillingness to see prison authors as anything but political threats opened the prison system to critique that it was as brutal and repressive as these authors maintained. As an author, Jackson displayed a maturity of thought that demonstrated his intellectual development since his teenage days of petty criminality. That he continued to be denied parole and face constant threats from prison authorities seemed to prove the system's ideological basis. To Jackson's growing base of supporters, his ongoing incarceration betrayed the injustice of the prison system and the larger political order that sustained it.

Soledad Brother became an instant classic of black protest literature. The success and popularity of *Soledad Brother* put Jackson's work on par with the other urtexts and masculine antiheroes that had characterized the Black Power days: he was the literary heir apparent to Malcolm X and Eldridge Cleaver. He saw himself in that political tradition, while journalists and other observers saw him in that literary tradition. The parallels are not hard to spot. For all three men, the prison served as a point of politicization. Incarceration marked their point of conversion from petty criminal to political radical. Their respective books—*The Autobiography of Malcolm X*, *Soul on Ice*, and *Soledad Brother*—narrated this conversion, establishing the prison as a pivotal institution of black radical self-making. Each successive text emphasized the prison more than the last. For Malcolm, prison is the turning point. Cleaver's book anthologizes essays written during his incarceration but not published until he had been paroled and become a leading figure in the Black Panther Party.[82] Jackson, however, remained in prison, and his redemption did not lead to his release, as it did for Cleaver and Malcolm. Jackson's redemption lay in the fact that he was, as several reviewers put it, "free" behind bars: he retained his ideas and his convictions and through them his voice. Whereas Cleaver and Malcolm showed that radical politics could come out of prison, Jackson demonstrated that radical politics could develop and sustain themselves behind bars.

Even more than these earlier books, *Soledad Brother* revealed that political critique, indeed political thought itself, could travel from inside prison to the outside world, not just the other way around. Coming alongside growing interest in the plight of prisoners from the New Left, this capacity for intellectual critique was, in fact, the source of the prison establishment's anxiety about prison authors. "To San Quentin administrators, local citizen involvement in prison issues seemed so potentially violent in the early 1970s that the prison prepared for a 'storming of the Bastille' and drew up plans to close access roads to the prison and even to direct prison tower gunfire outward, for the first time in history, onto any group attempting to break *into* the prison."[83] Beating a hasty retreat from bibliotherapy, officials also worked to ban *Soledad Brother* from entering California prisons (a practice that continues in the early twenty-first century). Several California prisons refused to accept copies of the book that the publisher donated to their libraries. Word of the book still spread, and individual prisoners received copies. Jackson told the *New York Times* that prisoners "seem to be gratified that one of us had the opportunity to express himself" and appreciated that he was "getting ideas across, speaking for them, speaking for us."[84]

While they did not want other prisoners to read the book, prison officials viewed the text as a chance to conduct surveillance on prison militants and thereby undercut their efforts to mobilize. *Soledad Brother* provided the rationale for officials to curtail prisoner efforts to communicate with the outside world. L. H. Fudge, the superintendent of a northern California prison, released a memo to state prison officials suggesting that "every employee in the Department of Corrections" read *Soledad Brother* to help them understand "the personality makeup of a highly dangerous sociopath."[85] San Quentin warden

Louis Nelson justified closing or restructuring several educational organizations in the prison by pointing to media coverage describing the prison as "the best breeding and/or recruiting ground for neo-revolutionaries."[86]

Critics, however, celebrated Jackson as the latest prophet of black rage. The *New York Times*'s "Selected Books of the Year in Nonfiction" awkwardly praised *Soledad Brother* as "a document of revolutionary rage, 'the most important single volume from a black since *The Autobiography of Malcolm X*.'"[87] In a review titled "Beyond Cleaver," the *Washington Monthly* said that Jackson "picks up where Cleaver left off." But, the reviewer argued, *Soledad Brother* did more than that: it was more "inclusive" and universal than *Soul on Ice*. "Where Cleaver throws you back on yourself because you are not black, not oppressed—and that has its value—Jackson draws you in through your shared humanity."[88]

This shared humanity became part of the marketing campaign, with Bantam Books inviting readers to identify with Jackson and his family. The paperback edition of the book carried a quotation from Huey P. Newton proclaiming Jackson the "greatest writer of us all" and praising the letters as a message to a larger national "family": "Because of his burning need to communicate with his family, Jackson finally communicates with everyone." The book received the Black Academy of the Arts's nonfiction award and was named one of the American Library Association's Notable Books of 1970.[89] Reviews in British periodicals described Jackson as a "free black man in white America," attempting to obliterate "ghettos of the mind." Jackson had "lost his freedom—and found himself."[90] *Soledad Brother* was so popular that Mitford joked that "literary agents are scouting prisons for convict talent."[91] With great repression came great wisdom. Pointing to Malcolm X and George Jackson, one prison activist argued that "contemporary prison rebels have provided some of the best insights into American society."[92] For another decade, prisoners authored widely received books, poems, magazine articles, plays, and more as Black Power influences seeped into American television and cinema.[93]

These reviews of *Soledad Brother* fit with Stender's hope that the book would help build support for Jackson and the other Soledad Brothers. She and Armstrong attempted to manage Jackson's image as an icon around whom black protest might cohere. At the release party for *Soledad Brother* at the gates of San Quentin, Armstrong called Jackson "a medium, a voice for all oppressed people."[94] Armstrong and Stender sought to portray Jackson as the symbol for an individual and collective search for justice, even as Jackson himself seemed to prefer an image more heroic and less sentimental. When Julius Lester wrote at the end of his favorable *New York Times* review of the book that Jackson "makes Eldridge Cleaver look like a song and dance man on the Ed Sullivan

Show,"[95] Armstrong wrote several letters chastising the *Times* for possibly damaging Jackson's relationship with the Black Panthers. Armstrong argued that the newspaper had an obligation to print a rejoinder from Jackson for the benefit of the Soledad Brothers defense campaign and its relationship with the Black Panthers.[96] The public narrative of Jackson rested on presenting black militants as a united force; the cocreators of his image objected to reviews that undermined this presentation. Jackson's response to the *Times* called Cleaver a "master" political theorist and demanded that "any comparison between myself and Comrade Cleaver must be respectful, or it doesn't represent my feelings of fraternity and love for him."[97]

What most rankled Jackson, however, was the distance between his self-representation and the way many of his supporters described him. As his base of support grew following the book's success, Jackson criticized Stender's approach to the book. Stender wrote to Armstrong that Jackson was "angry with me for the book for cutting out the blood and guts part." Indeed, Jackson did not control which letters were included. Even before the book was published, Jackson began objecting to being presented as an innocent victim rather than an open antagonist of a corrupt system. The widespread circulation of prisoner writing required outside help, and Jackson's black revolutionary mission did not always align with the goals of white supporters interested in describing his victimization.[98]

These differences later caused some observers to wonder who the "real" George Jackson was. Yet Jackson himself remained consistent in his message of black solidarity and class struggle. "There is very little that I could say at present to make people think that I am merely an ox in a bind, an 18 yr. old candy store bandit. That hasn't worked, I knew it wouldn't. And really it wasn't my idea to try it. . . . Noone [*sic*] is going to sympathize but the others of my kind anyway."[99] Jackson saw his political authority as bound up not with innocence but rather with revolution. Surprised to capture popular attention and increasingly under threat of retaliation from prison officials who despised his existence, George Jackson entered the last year of his life stuck in an eight-by-six cell in the San Quentin Adjustment Center yet nevertheless intent on accelerating the global anti-imperialist revolution.

"WE ARE THE REVOLUTIONARIES"

The long-term and indefinite incarceration of George Jackson weighed heavily on his younger brother. Jonathan Peter Jackson stopped playing music and became intimately involved with the SBDC and the various groups connected

Angela Davis and Jonathan Jackson at a rally for the Soledad Brothers, 1970. Jonathan, the younger brother of Soledad Brother George Jackson, had become a bodyguard for Davis in response to the barrage of death threats she received after her membership in the Communist Party was revealed by an undercover FBI agent. Photo by Corbis.

to it, especially the Black Panthers and the Communist Party. He became a bodyguard for Angela Davis, George's comrade and love interest. Like George, Jonathan was convinced that violent assaults on the state could serve catalytic ends. Unlike George, Jonathan had ready access to guns: Davis owned several, as did other radicals with whom he worked.[100]

By the summer of 1970, though he was just seventeen, Jonathan had consigned himself to an early death in the service of revolution. In June he told his mother, "Mama, if I die—or if I die in any way that makes you sad—I want you to know that I died the way I wanted to die."[101] The same month, he published a letter in an underground student newspaper responding to classmates and teachers who found the motivated and intelligent student too intense: "People have said that I am obsessed with my brother's case and the Movement in general. A person that was close to me once said that my life was too wrapped up in my brother's case and that I wasn't cheerful enough for her. It's true. I have but one question to ask all of you people and people that think like you: 'What would you do if it was your brother?'"[102]

On August 7, two days after Newton was released from prison after serving his sentence for the manslaughter death of police officer John Frey, Jonathan Jackson entered a Marin County courtroom with a satchel full of guns. The Marin Civic Center, which housed the courthouse and several other municipal offices, had been designed by noted architect Frank Lloyd Wright. The courtroom had recently been renovated with a series of passageways and elevators installed specifically to keep prisoners from interacting with the public.[103] Yet Jackson, wiry and with a large Afro, created a scene in which prisoners would encounter the public in a dramatic way. "All right, gentlemen, I'm taking over now," he said as he pulled a rifle from his long black coat and distributed guns to James McClain, William Christmas, and Ruchell Magee, San Quentin prisoners who were in court that day.

The thirty-seven-year-old McClain, in prison after an attempted armed robbery at an Oakland supermarket, was standing trial on charges that he had stabbed a guard in the aftermath of Fred Billingslea's death the preceding February. Serving as his own attorney, McClain was questioning the thirty-one-year-old Magee on the witness stand when Jackson entered.[104] The group armed another San Quentin prisoner, William Christmas, a twenty-seven-year-old who had been in prison since 1964 and was waiting in the hallway to be called as a witness. Two other prisoners also in the holding cell and waiting to be called as witnesses refused to join the group.

Although they were relatively unknown even within the Left, the prisoner participants in the August 7 rebellion were longtime dissidents. McClain and Magee, like Jackson, were imprisoned in the San Quentin Adjustment Center, and authorities considered them troublemakers. They and others had tried to get a public investigation into Billingslea's death. Magee helped file writs in protest and tried to contact Angela Davis's mother for support.[105]

The members of the group tied up Judge Harold Haley and affixed a shotgun to his neck with tape and wire that Jackson had brought. They also tied up the district attorney, Gary Thomas (Haley's son-in-law), and took him, Haley, and five female jurors hostage. They released several bystanders and other court officials from the room. They spent fifteen minutes explaining to the terrified jurors turned hostages that they did not intend to hurt anyone.[106]

The group then took their hostages out of the courtroom and headed toward the elevator. A photojournalist happened on the group and began snapping pictures. One of the assailants declared, "We are the revolutionaries. Take all the pictures you want." The men wanted their actions to be seen. In fact, the camera was as much a part of August 7 as the gun. Magee later said that the group intended to take over a local radio station and broadcast news of the "torturous

Jonathan Jackson at the Marin County Courthouse on August 7, 1970. The seventeen-year-old high school student brought several guns into the courtroom and gave them to San Quentin prisoners William Christmas, Ruchell Magee, and James McClain. McClain was standing trial on charges of having assaulted a guard, and Christmas and Magee were two of his witnesses. Courtesy of the *Marin Independent Journal*.

prison conditions" and described the incident as "an effort to reach the people and dramatically awaken them to the plight of all prisoners, particularly Blacks."[107]

Jackson, the prisoners, and their hostages climbed into a van that Jackson had rented and driven to the courthouse. San Quentin guards—among them John Matthews, who had been involved in Billingslea's death—had been called in to assist local police in establishing an armed barricade to prevent the van's departure. Unbeknownst to most people, however, including the participants in the courthouse raid, San Quentin had a policy of preventing prisoner escapes at all costs, even if it meant killing hostages. The guards opened fire on the van just as Thomas wrested a gun away from one of the prisoners and began shooting inside the van. When the smoke cleared, Jackson, McClain, Christmas, and Haley had been killed. Magee, Thomas, and one of the jurors were wounded by shots fired from outside the van. Thomas was the most seriously injured; a bullet had shattered his spine, paralyzing him from the waist down. Haley, too, had been hit by bullets from outside the van, and his face had been blown off by the shotgun the assailants had tied around his neck. Thirty-four minutes had passed since Jonathan Jackson took over the courtroom.[108]

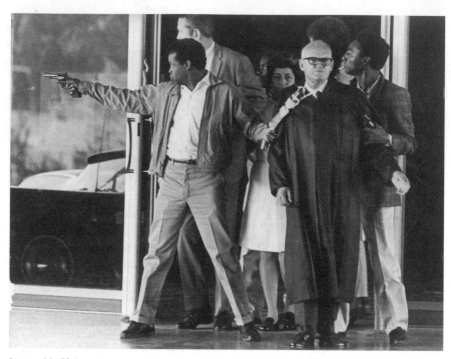

James McClain points a revolver at police while holding a shotgun taped around the neck of Judge Harold Haley on August 7, 1970. Ruchell Magee is to the right of the judge, and district attorney Gary Thomas is behind McClain. The group had also taken several jurors hostage. Moments later, San Quentin guards opened fire on the group, killing McClain, Christmas, Jackson, and Haley; Thomas was paralyzed. Courtesy of the *Marin Independent Journal*.

With the publication of *Soledad Brother* about six weeks away and excerpts from it being serialized in the *New York Review of Books*, the August 7 raid made the tumult inside and surrounding California prisons a national news story. The dramatic setting, the bloody end, and the alleged involvement of the well-known Angela Davis—to whom several of the guns used by Jackson were registered and who could not be found for six weeks afterward—all made the story a topic of interest. Because one of the prisoners shouted "Free the Soledad Brothers" as the group was leaving the courtroom, the district attorney declared the incident a conspiracy to free the three accused men, increasing attention to the fledgling SBDC and its critiques of the California prison system. Searching for the rationale for Jackson's actions, the *New York Times* pointed to the January 13 killing of three black prisoners and declared them the origins of a radical prison movement.[109]

The Marin events also became part of the publicity used to promote *Soledad Brother*.[110] Jonathan Jackson's actions provided a vivid example of the life-and-death struggle described in George Jackson's letters. *Soledad Brother* closed with a letter mournfully celebrating Jonathan. "Man-child, black man-child with submachine gun in hand, he was free for awhile," Jackson wrote of his baby brother. "I guess that's more than most of us can expect." Jackson dated the letter "August 9, 1970. Real Date, 2 days A.D.": society would have to "reckon all time in the future from the day of the man-child's death."[111] George praised his younger brother but said he would have stopped Jonathan from going alone against police and prison guards. In a letter to Mitford, Jackson said that the "Battle of Marin" would have transpired without violence were it not for the San Quentin guards, "men so automatized to kill that no logical combinations of forces or logic can contain them. [They are the] most callous and vicious men . . . in all the enemy state."[112]

Jackson's raid illustrated a hypermasculine vision of prison struggle. Such displays of masculinity had greeted Newton's release from prison two days earlier. More than a few people thought that with Newton no longer incarcerated, a wave of revolutionary action would crest in widespread armed struggle. That Newton took off his shirt at a rally celebrating his release from prison, revealing the strong physique he had maintained, encouraged this process: photos of the bare-chested Newton appeared in the *Black Panther* newspaper, on television, and elsewhere. Many radicals saw in his toned muscles a physical embodiment of the coming insurrection.[113] In fact, however, it seemed that Newton had called off plans for Black Panthers to support Jonathan Jackson's attack, part of the growing split in the BPP over questions of armed struggle.[114]

In New York, the minister of information for the Young Lords Organization, which had imported some of the Panthers' practice of political defense for its work in the city's Puerto Rican barrios, penned an article in the organization's newspaper on Newton's freedom. "Want to celebrate Huey's release into the prisons of the street? Let's get ourselves together here. . . . Say 'Hi, brother,' to the music of pigs' bodies kissing the pavement as they drop dead from double-o buckshot in the back."[115] Angela Davis's case, so intimately connected to Jackson's raid and the wider antiprison movement, never attracted such a militarist response, but a November 1970 *Black Scholar* editorial declared that "Angela Davis is campus, is community, is vanguard." Davis maintained that "the most beautiful Black revolutionaries, men and women—are prisoners of war."[116]

The Marin incident was a polarizing one. Stender, many members of the new (and at that point largely white) SBDC, and most of the Communist Party (which had been involved in the campaign through the efforts of the Che-Lumumba Club) claimed that Jonathan's actions were a tragic act of desperation from a sincere but misguided youth.[117] Jackson's raid seemed to signal that the black freedom

A mural depicting Jonathan Jackson's raid on the Marin County Civic Center. Graffiti on the wall references the Republic of New Afrika, a Black Power organization that later had substantial influence in U.S. prisons. Photo © 2014 Stephen Shames/Polaris Images.

struggle was indeed moving toward more overtly martial tactics. Indeed, several people viewed the raid as proof that spectacles of masculine militarism marked a growing revolutionary fervor. Photographs from and paintings of August 7, of the armed group and their hostages or of the young Jackson facing the camera with a rifle in each hand, were reprinted in various underground newspapers and flyers urging support for Magee and extolling the coming black revolution. Elaine Brown, future chair of the Black Panthers, recorded a song that became popular in BPP circles proclaiming "believe it, my friends / that this silence can end / we'll just have to get guns / and be men." In another song, "Jonathan," Brown praised his violent masculinity: "Jonathan / he was so young / picked up a gun / Jonathan / but a man / was he."[118]

Two days before the raid, the *Black Panther* newspaper featured a cartoon showing a group of armed black men freeing a handful of black men from behind prison bars while holding at gunpoint anthropomorphic pigs wearing police uniforms (a hallmark of Emory Douglas's stunningly bombastic artwork in the newspaper). The caption predicted the news of a few days later: "The walls must come down. The time is now for prison walls all across decadent Babylon to crumble, for prison gates to be blown to pieces, and for the prison hallways to vibrate with sounds of gunfire, hand grenades and shouts of liberation!" Asked about the image after the fact, Newton said it was "not only a prediction of the event in Marin, but of the clash of social forces that we witness in a very regular way."[119] Kathleen Cleaver wrote that the "phase of legal defense is over. . . . Jonathan Jackson ended all that. . . . Now we got to break them all out."[120] In a talk at the National Student Association meeting in Minnesota, Chicago 8 defendant Tom Hayden predicted that more kidnappings should be expected. Hayden called the courthouse raid "a very, very important thing. It changes the entire relationship between the courts and political prisoners, between the oppressors and oppressed people."[121] Other former members of Students for a Democratic Society shared in this praise. Eric Mann was imprisoned in Massachusetts for a violent antiwar demonstration that took place on the same day. In a 1974 book about George Jackson, Mann praised the raid as "brilliantly conceived and executed—more in its audacity than in its complexity."[122]

Jonathan Jackson's audacity inspired black prisoners, who saw it as making visible the challenge to prisons they had been waging largely in silence. Six prisoners charged with a riot in Auburn, New York, praised Jonathan as their role model. "He lives in the heart of the revolution, the soul of the revolutionary people, the mind of the revolutionary, the body of liberation! . . . Right on to the baddest mothafucker that ever lived and died!" The prisoners connected Jackson's raid with their legal predicament, arguing that because of such militancy, the "specter of complete freedom is haunting Racist Babylon."[123] Magee, the only surviving participant, described Jonathan Jackson as a savior and a role model, epitomizing what blackness should be: in open and visible conflict with the state. "The only Jesus for a black man today is a man like Jonnie Jackson. He's a hard driving black man with plenty of soul to recognize the time of day. He wasn't talking black, he was acting black—just like I am going to do from now on."[124]

Held at St. Augustine's Episcopal Church in Oakland on August 15, eight days after the raid, the funeral for Jonathan Jackson and William Christmas was as much a political rally as a somber burial. More than three thousand people attended. Newton praised the men as martyrs who "intensified the struggle and placed it on a higher level. A picture is worth a thousand words, but action is supreme."[125] Newton juxtaposed their martyrdom against those who remained "slaves" as a result of passivity. Several Black Panthers were listed as honorary pallbearers, and eulogies written by prisoners were read.[126] In what was likely hyperbole, Newton later said that Jonathan Jackson "should have been and would have been my successor" at the BPP's helm.[127]

Believing that the secrecy of confinement facilitated a propensity for abuse, activists in and outside of prison had for several years been pressing for greater access to the prisons. Because San Quentin had previously held prisoners in-communicado after violent incidents, activists demanded and received access to the facility after the Marin County incident. Following an August 1970 tour of San Quentin, the *San Francisco Chronicle* initiated a novel three-week series of articles on prisons that saw two of its journalists go inside San Quentin to see what life was like for both staff and prisoners. The *Sacramento Bee* provided similar coverage. Prison conditions were big news.[128]

For their part, officials blamed the August 7 raid on the prisoners' ability to access the public through the media and through open court. Consequently, administrators moved to eliminate such encounters by managing media access to the prison and temporarily relocating all trials involving prisoners to a makeshift courtroom within San Quentin's walls, a strategy that renewed questions about whether the lack of public access facilitated abuse. With the prison now doubling as the courtroom, critics alleged that the principle of in-nocent until proven guilty was a farce: the prison presumes guilt; it is a site of punishment rather than arbitration. Radical prisoners responded by attempting to turn the prison-courtroom into a political critique. They demanded that proceedings be open to the public, with activists insisting that they receive access to the prison-court. The judge pointed out that the makeshift courtroom at San Quentin (built by prisoners, for prisoners) fit as many people as did any courtroom at the Marin Civic Center, that regular courts also limit the number of spectators allowed, and that people in both places were allowed access on a first-come basis. Journalists were also allowed to cover the trials; the *San Rafael Independent Journal* did so regularly as part of its follow-up coverage of the August 7 raid.

Magee and his supporters challenged the move to host trials in prison as an attempt to silence him. During his first appearance at the San Quentin court, he cursed the judge, saying that the prison setting by definition negated any legal impact of the proceedings. He asked to be removed from the "Ku Klux Klan trial" and said that "such proceedings are what caused the Marin County incident."[129] A number of leftist groups claimed that the in-prison trials would have a chilling effect on the public. The SBDC, the Black Panther Party, and the Bay Area chapter of the National Lawyers Guild initiated a protest at the San Quentin gates on August 24, with demonstrators arguing that hiding the court behind prison walls would further isolate prisoners from public contact or civic standing.[130] Speaking to a rally of 125 people outside the court, Hayden warned of incipient fascism: "People outside the prison walls have no rights and people inside the walls have less than no rights."[131] The lawyers involved in some of the hearings tried to use the media attention devoted to the conflict over space to describe prisoners as a unified and more impartial group. At a press conference, George Jackson's attorney, John Thorne, said that he would support moving the Soledad Brothers trial to San Quentin if the men could be tried by a jury of their peers—other black prisoners. Since the prisoners "live in a unique culture," Thorne said, they "must be judged by inhabitants of the same culture."[132]

Activists agreed with officials that the makeshift courtroom resembled a traditional one only in that both were innately unfair. They challenged the secret tribunals, and a court ultimately ruled in their favor. The symbolic weight of a prison-based courtroom was too much for the liberal judges of the day, who saw it as a violation of the constitutional right to a public trial.[133] By October, all trials, regardless of where the crime in question occurred, were again conducted in courthouses.

The tension inside California prisons was increasing. "In the nineteen months following the January 13 incident, at least forty persons were killed as a result of events and circumstances in the California prison system." The casualties between January 1970 and August 1971 included seven guards, two prison staff members, and Judge Haley, with twenty-three prisoners charged in those deaths. No guard or staff member was ever charged with the deaths of the twenty-four prisoners killed in that same time span.[134] The situation, however, was bigger than tit-for-tat killings, bigger than the hundreds of nonfatal assaults between prisoners and guards, and far bigger than California. Prisoners were fighting for control of their lives. In the same period, prisoners went on strike, took over segments of the facility, or tried to escape from prisons or jails in California, Minnesota, Kentucky, Nevada, Pennsylvania, Kansas, Florida, Maryland, Idaho, Louisiana, and New York. Several institutions, especially in New York, saw repeated attempts. And while men's prisons were more prone to riots, several of these strikes took place at women's jails or prisons. Across the country, prisons were experiencing low-intensity warfare.[135]

"WAR WITHOUT TERMS"

Straddling a fine line between fame and infamy, George Jackson owed his celebrity both to literary brilliance and to revolutionary violence. Jonathan's daring, doomed act demonstrated George's revolutionary vision and sparked an urgency in him to further elaborate and encourage what he saw as a strategy of armed struggle. Of all the organic intellectuals who populated American social movements at this time, Jackson emerged as the one most interested in a political theory of military strategy. He synthesized a variety of Third World revolutionary methods. From Che Guevara and the Cuban Revolution, Jackson embraced the foco theory, which held that the disciplined armed actions of a small, focused group could catalyze mass uprisings. Turning to Algeria and revolutionary psychiatrist Frantz Fanon, Jackson argued that violence by the colonized against their oppressors had a redemptive power necessary to end the colonial relationship. And Jackson hoped that the small-scale guerrilla warfare in the present would ultimately lead to the kind of all-out "people's war" that Chinese military leaders Mao Tse-tung and Lin Biao implemented and later analyzed. In writings, interviews, and his daily practice in the San Quentin Adjustment Center, Jackson sought to implement these approaches. Especially in the prison context, Jackson maintained that a combination of broad coalitions ("united front") and direct action could ease brutality in the short term and undermine state power in the long term.

In a March 24, 1970, letter that Jackson conceded was written while in a "foul mood," he expressed his desire for revenge. "I'm going to charge them for this, twenty-eight years without gratification. I'm going to charge them reparations in blood. . . . This is one nigger who is positively displeased. I'll never forgive. I'll never forget, and if I'm guilty of anything at all it's of not leaning on them hard enough. War without terms."[136] His tone mixed the common desire of the dispossessed for revenge with the open, permanent state of conflict that characterized the California prison system.

Jackson had elaborate plans for armed struggle on both sides of the prison walls. He wanted to contribute on both levels; in true revolutionary fashion, he wanted not only to be free from prison but to escape. The death of his brother and friends, the success of his book despite his objections to some of its content, an impending trial, and the continued example of national liberation movements the world over all increased the urgency and rigidity Jackson felt. By August 1971, Jackson wrote to a supporter that "no *man* can match me for fighting dirty—no one, no group. I've worked very hard at arriving."[137]

Jackson quietly worked to advance his military aspirations from prison until he could escape and lead a guerrilla push from underground or exile. By the start of 1971, he had begun planning for a second book that would synthesize his lessons on urban guerrilla warfare. In a January 11 letter to his legal team and close supporters, he argued that "clinical, retaliatory, organized revolutionary violence" constituted the only justified approach. He challenged the recipients of the memo for questioning this position and with it the vanguard role of black prisoners in radical struggle. "Being a slave and living in the shadow of the gas chamber for years and under the knout all my life leaves me in a position above you and I'm laughing. At you."[138] He replaced Fay Stender as his counsel when she demurred at his request to have royalties from *Soledad Brother* and legal funds pay for guerrilla training. (Stender surely knew that diverting funds for legal fees to armed insurrection would destroy the prisoner support efforts; she remained committed to legal aid and opened the Prison Law Project in early 1971.)

As the summer of 1971 approached, Jackson affected a shakeup of his support committee to have his family members at the helm and the Black Panthers as beneficiaries, believing them to be more loyal to his program than the defense committee organized under Stender's direction. This move exacerbated tensions with other organizations involved and with the mothers of Clutchette and Drumgo.[139] The tension between prisoners and guards also increased. During a hearing in early April, Jackson attacked a guard who tried to remove some of his papers, including the *Black Panther* newspaper, setting off a courtroom brawl in which several antiprison activists who had been supporting the Soledad Brothers joined the fray. Two were arrested and stood trial.

Jackson did not want to go to trial in the Soledad Brothers case. He did not want to legitimize the system by going through formal, sanctioned channels, and he did not want to plead innocent in regard to an action—the retaliatory killing of Officer Mills—he supported.[140] Yet his far-fetched militarism coexisted with a shrewd political pragmatism, and on January 14 his attorneys filed a federal lawsuit to challenge the provision of the penal code that made prisoners serving life sentences subject to the death penalty. To maximize its collective weight, the suit was filed on behalf of Jackson, Luis Talamantez, and the Soledad 7, who were collectively standing trial in the July 1970 death of a Soledad guard.[141] He received a parade of visitors and requests for interviews. People sought out his opinions on a variety of topics, including women's liberation—in part a response to the macho posturing of *Soledad Brother*, in part a response to the growing feminist movement, in part a response to Jackson's stature within the Left.[142] And he continued to have an oversized impact on the prison: meeting with Jackson about the federal lawsuit against the state of California, attorney Larry Weiss saw every black prisoner in the visiting room raise a clenched fist in support as Jackson walked through, while the guards' tension became palpable.[143]

Jackson also continued to write. He composed articles for the *Black Panther* newspaper and was instrumental in getting several prisoners to join the Black Panther Party and start prison-based chapters of the group, though his feelings about the Panthers vacillated over the year.[144] He updated his will in March, naming as beneficiaries seven California prisoners (including Hugo Pinell) whose defense committees he wanted to support, as well as the SBDC. He left his "political funds and valuables" to the Black Panther Party, specifically Huey Newton and his sister, Penny, with instructions that they should "see to it that these funds are used to help smash totalitarian capitalism and all men who would defend Amerikanism."[145] He had been in contact with a London-based television crew interested in making a documentary about prison conditions.[146] In a sign of the growing support for the American prison struggle, the London chapter of the SBDC formed at the start of the year and held a three-thousand-person rally at Westminster Hall on April 20, 1971.

While support for the Soledad Brothers grew, Jackson's military plans unraveled. Jackson's trusted comrade and confidante James Carr was released from prison and he vowed to advance Jackson's ideas by working with other militants to establish a military training camp for radicals in the Santa Cruz Mountains. Carr had first been institutionalized at age eleven and had been in and out of prison ever since. He learned to read and write in prison, ultimately landing a job as a math instructor at the University of California at Santa Cruz upon release. Both his wife, Betsy, and her mother, Joan Hammer, were members of the SBDC. Joan, in fact, had been friends with George for some time and was a key figure in the SBDC. Loyal to his friends but ruthless to others, Carr was widely believed to have killed beloved Panther and SBDC organizer Fred Bennett in that training camp. Police raided the camp in January and February 1971, seizing weapons on the first raid and finding Bennett's charred remains on the second.[147]

Bennett's death illustrated the internal dysfunction dividing the Black Panthers, especially between the East and West Coasts. The split might not have happened without years of intensive police pressure and violence—in the form of infiltrators, provocateurs, surveillance, harassment, arrests, killings, and a host of FBI dirty tricks through its COINTELPRO operations. But dramatic internal differences also existed: between those favoring a more immediate turn to armed struggle (concentrated around the New York chapter), which gave rise to the Black Liberation Army, and those favoring a community organizing approach that included work in the electoral realm. Differences of personality and ego also arose, especially as Newton's postprison leadership grew more authoritarian and Cleaver's behavior became more insurrectionary. Both men were erratic and volatile, Newton living in a penthouse apartment and Cleaver trapped in exile.

The role of police infiltration, across multiple branches of law enforcement, makes it difficult to discern the full truth of what happened in 1971. The difficulty is compounded by the ways law enforcement, seizing on opposition to police repression within the Left, spread false rumors that sincere activists were in fact FBI informants. Such allegations swirled in the wake of Bennett's death and ultimately that of Carr. After Carr's 1972 murder, some people (including Newton) claimed that he was either working with police or sabotaging the Bay Area prison movement for his own ends.[148]

The mystery around Carr began early in 1971. Police claimed to find correspondence between Carr and Jackson tucked in the pocket of a pair of pants his wife brought to the dry cleaner on January 8 that detailed plans to attack San Quentin and enable Jackson's escape.[149] As with much of the police intelligence about Jackson's ostensible escape plans, however, this letter did not surface until after Jackson's death. Prison guards certainly made no discernible changes to their routine. At best, then, if Jackson was planning to escape, authorities watched it happen without intervening. At worst, they facilitated it in a plot to kill him. Prison officials unquestionably wanted him dead. On March 19, 1971, Allan Mancino, a white prisoner with Aryan Brotherhood sympathies, filed an affidavit alleging that prison officials had asked him to kill George Jackson.[150] Hugo Pinell also reported that authorities had asked him to testify against Jackson despite the close friendship between the two men.[151] Like Nolen, Jackson had long predicted his death at the hands of guards; indeed, part of his allure—in *Soledad Brother* and in person—came from the elegance with which he described his intimacy with death and the fragility of imprisoned life.[152]

George Jackson's long brush with death in prison came to swift end on August 21, 1971, two days before the Soledad Brothers were set to go to trial. It was the bloodiest day in San Quentin's history. The details of the day remain shrouded in confusion: the various theories and countertheories offered at the time and since then inevitably produce a "Rashomon effect," in which observers draw mutually contradictory conclusions from the same evidence.[153] The truth was elusive enough to generate support for a variety of claims, different versions of the events that led to the deaths of six people.

August had proceeded at the frenetic pace that had become normal at San Quentin: the *New York Times* published an interview with Jackson in which, possibly to grouse a reporter he found obnoxious, Jackson reiterated with added boldness his desire to escape rather than see the Soledad Brothers trial to completion.[154] Jackson's sisters, Penny and Delora, were banned from visiting after guards found that their young children had toy guns hidden on them, including one taped to the leg of a five-year-old. In response to the high profiles of Jackson, Magee, and other politically active prisoners, the associate warden instituted a new form of collective punishment on August 20: prisoners in lockup units such as the Adjustment Center could receive visits from reporters only once every three months.[155] The prison had already curtailed visits with legal investigators, prohibiting them from visiting someone twice in any seven-day period. As with the censorious response to August 7, officials were trying to limit prisoners' ability to communicate with the outside.

Inside the AC, Jackson was finishing what would be his final book. *Blood in My Eye* was everything *Soledad Brother* was not: a short manual on politics, economics, and military strategy. The book emerged from a collective study that Jackson had been doing with several men in the AC, and he invited some of them to contribute essays to the volume, though none did.[156] The list of books in his cell at the time resembles a reading list for an interdisciplinary graduate program, albeit one focused on great men: philosophy (Aristotle, Plato, Nietzsche, Camus, Sartre); economics (Marx, Engels, Paul Baran, Harry Magdoff); literature (June Jordan, Ralph Ellison, André Malraux, George Orwell, John Oliver Killens); history (W. E. B. Du Bois, C. L. R. James, Herbert Aptheker, Philip Foner); and political thought (Frantz Fanon, Martin Luther King Jr., Kwame Nkrumah, H. Rap Brown, Antonio Gramsci). Jackson had books about Gandhi and Rockefeller, about oil and the origins of human civilization. He had an almanac, a dictionary, and the Pentagon Papers.[157]

Jackson shared drafts of the manuscript with several of the men in the AC who had been reading some of the books along with him. The twenty-six other men on the ground floor of the AC at that point included several stalwart prison radicals, steeped in the politics of prisoner solidarity that Jackson had come to exemplify. They were a testament to the racial disparity not just of who went to prison but who was punished and abused within the prison: the group included seventeen black people, five Latinos, and four whites. On the same side of the tier as Jackson were Black Panther Johnny Larry Spain and Soledad Brothers John Clutchette and Fleeta Drumgo; as well as Louie Lopez, Hugo Yogi Pinell, and Luis Bato Talamantez, Latino prisoners who identified with the black revolutionaries inside. Pinell was the most recent arrival, having been transferred to San Quentin in June and sent to the AC in early August for assaulting an officer. Talamantez found himself in the AC after being charged with assault for breaking up a fight among prisoners.[158]

On the other side of the tier were Magee; Earl Gibson and Larry Justice, who were awaiting trial for the stabbing death of a San Quentin guard a month previously; and veteran radicals Willie Sundiata Tate and David Johnson.[159] Tate had known Jackson since 1962 and had recently joined the Panthers at Jackson's request. Johnson, who had been sent to the AC a month earlier, had been part of the US organization in San Diego but had become close to the Panthers since his incarceration; he had ties to the New York BPP chapter and Black

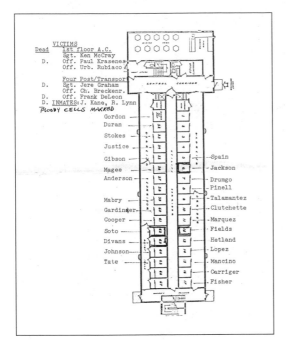

The San Quentin Adjustment Center on August 21, 1971, with the cell assignments marked. The shaded cells are where six guards and two prisoners were attacked. Both prisoners and three of the guards were killed, mostly with handmade knives. The alley between the two rows of cells does not allow movement; it marks the back of the cells. George Jackson and Johnny Spain ran out of the door by the control corridor at the front of the unit, indicated with a small arrow at the top right of the map. Courtesy of the *People of California v. Bingham et al.* trial records.

Liberation Army supporters. The white prisoners in the AC included Mancino as well as Ray Carriger and Gary Hetland, who were acquainted with some of the radicals and at times were baited by other whites as "nigger lovers."[160]

Some of the men in the AC had strong bonds; others had a grudging familiarity born of shared time across different California institutions, from youth authority to the state prisons; others were strangers. All hated the guards, and all had a history of refusing to accept their place in the institution. Sometimes that could provide enough to foster a sense of shared purpose.

On August 21, Jackson had a visit from a young radical attorney, Stephen Bingham. Bingham had other plans that day but postponed them after receiving a call that morning from the Berkeley Black Panther office asking him to help legal investigator Vanita Anderson gain access to the prison. She had visited earlier that week and was barred by the new regulations from going again so soon.[161] Bingham had met Jackson a few times over the preceding months after Thorne had asked the National Lawyers Guild to help Jackson explore the possibility of a civil suit about conditions inside the Adjustment Center. Bingham was a young tenant rights lawyer who had gone south during Freedom Summer and was an active guild member. Though not directly involved in the prison movement, Bingham knew of Jackson through *Soledad Brother* and legal circles and was excited to help with Jackson's lawsuit. On

August 21, Bingham picked up Anderson at the Berkeley Panther office and headed to San Quentin.

The two arrived at the prison around 10:15 A.M. and went through the metal detector. After three hours of waiting and pressing the guards for access, Anderson was denied entrance and Bingham was approved. He was on his way in when a guard encouraged him to take Anderson's tape recorder with him. Bingham and Jackson met for about an hour so that Jackson could go over the page proofs of his new book. They did not talk much; at one point, Jackson wrote a question for Anderson about the book, so Bingham left to give her Jackson's note and returned to give him her written response. During Bingham's brief absence, Jackson was locked out of the room and under watch by guards. The visit ended around 2:15, and Bingham left to have a late lunch with his uncle, as he had originally planned. Jackson was again strip-searched before being escorted the seventy-five yards back to the Adjustment Center. From the time Bingham left, Jackson remained under guard by between one and three correctional officers.[162]

By 2:30, Jackson had a gun and control of the AC. Exactly how he got the gun remains the subject of a variety of unproven theories, some more outlandish than others. Officials claimed that, in an effort to escape, Jackson somehow took a gun and one or two magazines of ammunition out of a wig covering his Afro— all items he was alleged to have received from Anderson's tape recorder during his visit with Bingham—and then slammed the ammunition into the gun and took two guards hostage before they could stop him. Other analysts claimed either that a guard pulled a gun on Jackson but was overpowered or that both men had guns and Jackson was the more powerful figure.[163] AC guards were supposed to be unarmed for the purpose of overall prison security, but they often carried weapons—indeed, four of the AC guards present that day had knives on them, against protocol but standard practice, and San Quentin guards routinely passed guns from the prison armory through the AC to the main facility.[164]

Jackson—like many other prisoners—certainly wanted to escape, and ample evidence (especially a series of cryptic notes Jackson had sent over the preceding few months) suggests that he was pursuing supplies and support. But ample evidence also shows that the prison system wanted him dead and that his plans did not include a spontaneous attempt to escape from the claustrophobic confines of the Adjustment Center on August 21, 1971.[165] His escape plans would not have included the impossible prospect of scaling the San Quentin wall. So did authorities interrupt the transmission of escape supplies that he was gathering for later use, perhaps at the start of the Soledad Brothers trial, when he was likely to have been transported to and from court via helicopter? Did authorities let him gather certain supplies to establish a pretext for killing him? Or did they seize an opportunity to kill him and come up with a rationale only after the fact?

Beyond dispute are the facts that at least one gun was inside the Adjustment Center that afternoon and that a gun came into George Jackson's possession. Jackson then held the officers at gunpoint and forced them to open the first-floor cells. The first prisoner out was Johnny Spain, who was housed in the cell closest to the control corridor (and next to Jackson's cell). Spain rushed to Jackson's aid as other prisoners decided what to make of their cell doors suddenly and simultaneously opening. Most ambled out, cautious and confused, for they were never allowed out of their cells more than one at a time and without reason. For some the sudden change was too frightening. Luis Bato Talamantez counseled two intimidated white prisoners to tie their cell doors shut.[166]

And then began the "chaotic" "half-hour revolution."[167] Jackson moved guards Kenneth McCray, Paul Krasenes, and Frank DeLeon down the tier to his cell, 1AC6, where he and a few other prisoners hogtied and beat the officers before slashing their throats with a makeshift knife. Krasenes died of that wound; Jackson shot and killed DeLeon; McCray ultimately survived. Later, when another guard, Jere Graham, came down to the AC, Jackson placed him in the cell and shot him, too. After opening the cells, Jackson took another guard, Urbano Rubiaco, hostage, along with Charles Breckenridge, an officer who had entered the AC close to 3:00 P.M. after escorting Clutchette back from a visit with his mother.

Some prisoners hoped that holding the guards hostage would spare their lives, but others became impatient. They took Rubiaco and Breckenridge down the other side of the tier, where they were tied up, placed in cell 1AC62, and had their throats slashed, though both survived. Prisoners Ronald Kane, twenty-eight, and Johnny Lynn, twenty-nine, who were being held in protective custody on the second floor of the AC and kept their distance from the radicals below, came down to deliver meals in the midst of the rebellion. They were assaulted, placed in a cell, and killed with a handmade knife.

By that point, other guards knew that Jackson had seized control of the prison. Likely recognizing that men with guns were coming to kill him and anyone with him, Jackson ran out the door and into the prison yard. He did not want to die in the enclosure of solitary confinement, and he might have hoped for a fairer fight in the yard. He certainly knew that the guards despised him and may well have hoped that his departure from the AC would protect the other men there. Only Spain followed Jackson, holding a vial taken from his cell that he mistakenly believed contained an explosive liquid. (A subsequent search of Jackson's cell revealed a similar vial of harmless liquid that likely had been smuggled in by a visitor. The mysterious yet harmless vials provide evidence to support the theory that Jackson was set up by prison officials, informants, or agents provocateurs within the Black Panther Party.)

Jackson ran in the direction of the prison hospital, while Spain ran toward the chapel. From the gun rail overhead, two guards fired down at Jackson. One shot ricocheted off the sidewalk and hit Jackson in the ankle. He fell, quickly pushed himself up, and was shot again with a bullet that medical examiners said entered his lower back and exited his brain.[168] Spain, out of options and with no leader, dove into the bushes to await capture. Guards quickly entered the yard, led by Lieutenant Eugene Ziemer, who had suffered four ruptured discs after being kicked in the back by Jackson during an altercation years earlier. Ziemer discovered Jackson splayed out face down on the concrete in a pool of blood and turned him on his back. George Jackson, the best-selling author and world-renowned revolutionary, was dead, one month shy of his thirtieth birthday. The guards handcuffed him and left his body there for four hours.

CHAPTER FOUR

The Pedagogy of the Prison

This monster—the monster they've engendered in me will
return to torment its maker, from the grave, the pit, the profoundest pit.
Hurl me into the next existence, the descent into hell won't turn me.
I'll crawl back to dog his trail forever.
—GEORGE JACKSON, *Soledad Brother* (1970)

His parents named him Luis Talamantez, but everyone called him Bato, a Mexican Spanish colloquialism for a respected man, a comrade. He had been in and out of California state institutions since the age of twelve. In 1965, Los Angeles Superior Court judge Joseph Wapner (the same Judge Wapner who later became famous on the television show *The People's Court*) sentenced the twenty-three-year-old Talamantez to two five-year-to-life sentences stemming from two robberies that netted him $130. No one was hurt in either incident, but Wapner appeared to want to make an example out of Talamantez, much as an earlier judge had given George Jackson a similarly lengthy sentence after a similarly petty robbery. During his years inside, Talamantez earned a reputation for being principled and creative. He wrote poetry and read books about ancient history. Talamantez was one of a few Latinos who associated with black prisoners at San Quentin, working to end hostilities between the two groups. That and other efforts earned him the enmity of several guards and a few prisoners, and on several occasions, he had to fend off attacks. So it was that he found himself in the Adjustment Center on August 21, 1971.[1]

Like most of the men in the AC that day, Talamantez left his cell when Jackson forced the guards to open the doors. Curious and cocky—Jackson had nicknamed him "Machismo"—Talamantez joined the majority of AC prisoners in wandering the tier for the chaotic half hour during which they were out of their cells. He was in the foyer of the unit, near the door leading out to the yard, when Jackson went outside. There had been an "eerie quiet" before Jackson exited the building. Though Jackson said nothing, Talamantez thought he had a look that asked, "Is anyone coming with me?"[2] Sundiata Tate seemed to want to follow Jackson, but Talamantez held him back. The only thing waiting for them in the yard was a giant wall.

Just one prisoner, Johnny Spain, followed Jackson into the yard. The other men assembled in the foyer—Talamantez, Tate, Louie Lopez, Hugo Pinell—did not move. They were disoriented and in shock. Then they saw the guards set up on the balcony rail gun post above them and heard the gunshots above the blaring escape siren. Through the open doorway, Tate saw Jackson go down.[3] At that point, knowing that many more officers were on their way down to the tier, the twenty-odd prisoners who had been out of their cells since Jackson took over the AC ran to the other end of the floor and barricaded themselves inside four of the strip cells. These cells were Spartan, even for the AC: they had no toilet, just a hole in the floor. Talamantez was in a cell with at least four other men, gripping the iron door to hold it closed against the impending rush of the guards. In the cell next to them, David Johnson sat with Pinell, Tate, and Ruchell Magee, convinced they were all about to be killed. Though he did not smoke, Johnson asked Tate for a final cigarette.[4]

The guards came into the unit and fired a burst from a machine gun. Then they called out the names of the guards who had gone missing. They first called out for "Ruby," AC officer Urbano Rubiaco, who, still bleeding from cuts to his throat, ran into his coworkers' arms. Removed from the unit, Rubiaco demanded a gun so that he could go kill the prisoners in the AC.[5] Once the guards had custody of Rubiaco and the other two surviving officers, Charles Breckenridge and Kenneth McCray, they called out for the best known of the remaining prisoners in the AC. "Magee! Come on out with your hands up! Walk backwards naked," they yelled to Ruchell Magee, the only surviving participant from Jonathan Jackson's August 7 raid and a prodigious writ writer well versed in protesting prison conditions. The guards repeated that instruction for each prisoner by name, one by one.

Walking to the guards in the foyer gave the prisoners a chilling feeling: they knew they would be beaten and chained, but they also knew they had no other choice. "One at a time, they did us like that," Talamantez recalled. "They grabbed us. Made us all come out naked. Walk backwards, too. It was very traumatic at the time. We were all scared to death. And you could just see, these guards wanted to kill us so bad."[6] As each prisoner reached the row of guards at the end of the tier, he was hit and thrown into the courtyard outside the AC to be handcuffed.

The guards left twenty-six men, naked and handcuffed, many of them hogtied, with their wrists cuffed to their ankles, on the San Quentin green for several hours. A photograph taken from a helicopter overhead showed the naked and prone men; the first public knowledge of the day's events at San Quentin would be visually associated with prisoners prostrate and humiliated. At one point, prisoner Allan Mancino claimed that his handcuffs were too tight, and a guard shot him in the buttocks. Lying near Mancino, Johnson dug his face into the grass and prepared to die.[7]

The guards uncuffed the prisoners only long enough to make them crawl on their elbows back to the building. That evening, they questioned the men, still naked and cuffed, about the events of the day. Then the guards beat them again and placed most of them in B section, the toughest unit within general population, now temporarily converted into an isolation unit. The rest were moved to the second floor of the Adjustment Center.[8]

San Quentin guards had physically overpowered the men that afternoon and spent the evening taunting them, reminding them of their powerlessness. They called all the prisoners "niggers" and turned the classic antiracist Civil War song about iconic abolitionist John Brown into racist ridicule: "George Jackson's body lies a-mouldering in the grave," they sang. "George Jackson's body is rotting in the grave / The revolutionary soldiers are rotting in their cells."[9]

In the weeks and months that followed, prisoners across the country went on hunger strikes or engaged in other forms of nonviolent protest to mark his death. The most famous reaction occurred at Attica, a medieval-looking prison in western New York, where a silent memorial for Jackson demonstrated prisoner unity and led to a massive four-day rebellion in mid-September. On the outside, a variety of radicals taken with Jackson's message of retaliatory violence attacked institutions of state authority, bombing Department of Corrections offices and shooting at police officers to protest the loss of an articulate symbol of revolutionary hope. The Weather Underground blew up the offices of the California Department of Corrections, and a unit of the Black Liberation Army killed a police officer in San Francisco.[10] Others marked the occasion more solemnly. The two years following Jackson's death saw the creation of the George Jackson Health Clinic in Oakland, run by the Black Panthers, and the George Jackson Prisoner Contact Program in Scandinavia. The Black Panther Party's survey for potential recruits after 1971 included questions about Jackson and other black political prisoners.[11] Countless memorials, sung and spoken and visualized, paid tribute to Jackson for having inspired the better selves of oppressed people, especially men. Jackson himself participated in a certain memorialization through his book, *Blood in My Eye*, which was published in early 1972.

The response to Jackson's death provides a useful staging ground for examining the larger field of political action made possible through the limitations imposed by the prison. Premised on repression, the prison does not eliminate

George Jackson lies dead in the San Quentin courtyard on August 21, 1971. Jackson was shot by guards as he ran out of the Adjustment Center after leading prisoners in a brief takeover of the unit. Courtesy of the *People of California v. Bingham et al.* trial records.

San Quentin Adjustment Center cell 1AC-6 on August 21, 1971. This is the cell where George Jackson spent most of the last year of his life. Several guards were brought to the cell and had their throats slit after Jackson temporarily took control of the unit. Courtesy of the *People of California v. Bingham et al.* trial records.

politics but rather seeks to control its emergence and shape its form. Jackson's death offered an extreme lesson in the social dynamics inherent to the prison. In death as in life, the figure of George Jackson—or, more precisely, the ways in which some groups laid claim to the figure of George Jackson—was enmeshed in bigger struggles over the form and function, the race and gender, of power in the United States.

In their confrontations with confinement, opponents of the prison learned a political style that sought to make death into a generative force. For systems where death is an overdetermined outcome, death is not just the ending of life. It is the condition of life.[12] In the prison, as on the plantation, the battlefield, and other sites so structured by the loss of life, death defines the meaning of being alive. The immediate fear or threat of death characterizes the communities that people form in these circumstances. Prison, as scholar Dylan Rodríguez argues, is the closest approximation to death a living person is likely to experience.[13]

Prison organizers on both sides of the wall formed social bonds through confrontations with death. Three forms of death animated prison organizing: social, spatial, and physical. Socially, the law exempted prisoners from moral value; their criminal record suggested that they deserved punishment, and they became objects rather than subjects of the law. The prison adds the invisibility and isolation of spatial distance to the open-ended exclusion of being denied access to society's institutions and rights. Finally, as Jackson's killing makes clear, the physical death of dissident prisoners exemplified the absent presence at the heart of prison radicalism.[14]

With death comes memory. Because of the prison's geographic remove, maintained through extreme force and a prevailing ideology that disregards criminalized populations, prisoners are forcibly exiled to areas that geographer Ruth Wilson Gilmore calls "forgotten places."[15] To organize in and against the prison, then, is an act of memory. It requires remembering, across the divide of space more than time, the existence, the humanity, of those in prison.

The memorial work at the heart of prison radicalism generally takes many forms, from attacks on the prison system to a variety of efforts geared at prisoner empowerment. At the center of each of these efforts is a struggle over knowledge: the particular ways of knowing generated by secretive and punishing institutions. Rigid, confining, and aggressive, the prison invites the pursuit of knowledge as one way to escape the strictures of isolation, to maintain connections to a life outside. By its structure, the prison lends itself to oppositional forms of organizing that revolve around producing and sharing knowledge. Prisoner study groups and memoirs, investigations into prison conditions, communication between prisoners and those outside of prison—all engage the access and transmission of knowledge. Even attacks on the prison system or other symbolic representatives of the criminal justice apparatus constituted knowledge struggles because insurgents in the 1970s hoped that such violence would provide teachable moments revealing the "true" nature of the system.

Although it may be a school of a sort, the prison has a pedagogy different from those found in other sites of education. Jackson's death and the responses it generated reveal the ways that prison always structured political expression.

The pedagogy of the prison is a multifaceted struggle over knowledge, identity, and statecraft. These facets manifest in the interplay between the structure of the prison and the agency of the prisoners. In foreclosing many traditional means of political expression, the prison created new opportunities for mobilization that prisoners and their supporters worked to seize. Indeed, the pursuit of knowledge and transparency was a centerpiece of prison organizing. These activists worked to make the prison knowable to those outside its walls. The acquisition of knowledge was critical to their efforts. From basic literacy to theories of revolutionary change to the origins of humanity, prison organizing was characterized by prisoner efforts to learn and study. Because Jackson's erudition was so central to his appeal, many prisoners accelerated their study after his death.

The response to Jackson's killing illustrated what anthropologist John L. Jackson Jr. has described as the "racial paranoia" that emerged after civil rights legislative victories. It is characterized by "extremist thinking, general social distrust, the nonfalsifiable embrace of intuition, and an unflinching commitment to contradictory thinking."[16] The unanswered questions of Jackson's death—How did he get a gun? What role did authorities play? Who knew what and when?—sparked a larger battle over what knowledge the prison either made possible or foreclosed. The lack of a clear, agreed-on story of how he died made George Jackson an even more potent figure: the symbol leftists needed to believe that the prison was not a totalizing force and that law and order advocates needed to justify an expansion of precisely the system that had created him. As different factions battled over Jackson's memory and legacy, they engaged troublesome claims to political authenticity that were steeped in the prison's gendered conservatism. His spirit continued to haunt the prison, greeting newly politicized prisoners and terrifying their ostensible captors. The haunting presence of death, the problematic allure of authenticity, and the enduring power of education as a response to confinement all constituted the prison's pedagogy.

"A BAD EXAMPLE FOR THE OTHER SLAVES"

The mourners filed into St. Augustine's Episcopal Church in Oakland to a recording of Nina Simone's "I Wish I Knew How It Would Feel to Be Free." Simone's soulful and aspirational melody captured the spirit of Jackson's work. When she sang, "I wish you knew what it was like to be me / then you would see that every man should be free," she gave voice to what supporters most appreciated about Jackson—his ability to speak of universal freedom from the particular place of prison. The song suggested that the United States under-stood neither the subjection nor the aspirations of the black condition. As the first eulogy of the day, the song suggested that black prisoners represented the dialectic between hope and despair, oppression and liberation.

Although fewer people attended this funeral than the one for Jonathan Jack-son, the church was filled beyond capacity. Many of the two thousand people present could not squeeze inside; they listened to the proceedings over loud-speakers. Father Earl Neil, who worked closely with the Black Panther Party, presided over the funeral. In his eulogy, Neil described Jackson as a martyr in the biblical sense. "To us, George was a fire that never went out," Neil said, after thanking Georgia Jackson for giving the world her two sons as an offer-ing "to the liberation of our people." The Jackson brothers, Neil said, were the latest heroic figures to contest black confinement. "The black condition is our imprisonment," he said, arguing that this condition made black unity essential in the face of white supremacy. "George has brought us together today. . . . We have been brought together by his spirit, by his passion," across differences of race, age, and gender. "But we are going to stay together when we leave here," Neil cautioned. That unity in action marked Jackson's presence. "George is with us today. He is telling us to rise up, to take steps toward freedom, to not lay around begging for freedom."[17]

In his remarks, Panther leader Huey P. Newton described Jackson as part victim, part Superman. Newton found Jackson's superheroism both in his mili-tary approach to the prison and in his far-reaching analysis of confinement as a problem of the racial state itself. Newton used this second point to argue against the government's claim that Jackson was trying to escape, saying that his assessment of American society was too sophisticated for him to attempt an escape from the Adjustment Center. He was too good a writer to be so bra-vura an actor. According to Newton, Jackson realized that "you don't break out of prison into freedom. It's just an extended wall. . . . George realized the wall was very large. He realized that those prison victims were inside the wall and outside the wall, and this is why he began to write."[18] Jackson's connection to the victims inside the wall was reflected in the choice of honorary pallbear-ers: John Clutchette, Fleeta Drumgo, Jonathan Jackson, Ruchell Magee, Hugo Pinell, and "all revolutionary brothers in the prison camps across America."[19]

After the Bay Area funeral, Jackson's body was flown to Mt. Vernon, in southern Illinois, to be buried in the family plot next to his brother. Several members of the United Front, a Black Power group in Cairo, Illinois, attended the funeral, alongside the Jackson family and close friends. Uninvited, the FBI and area police also attended the burial, as they did the Oakland funeral

Pallbearers load George Jackson's casket, draped in a Black Panther flag, into the funeral car as thousands of attendees raise clenched fists, August 28, 1971. Georgia Jackson, who had lost both of her sons in a twelve-month period, is in the background (partially obscured), wearing sunglasses and with her fist raised. Photo © 2014 Stephen Shames /Polaris Images.

service. In addition to their long-standing interests in monitoring black radicalism, officials wanted to see whether Jackson's death would spark violent retaliations. Distrustful of the media as well as the government, Georgia Jackson barred the news media from photographing her son's burial. A few mourners punched two photographers and tried to destroy their film after they took pictures against the family's wishes.[20]

As they mourned, Jackson's supporters raised questions about the circumstances of his death. The immediate response seemed quite in line with Jackson's desire that his death would serve pedagogic ends. Jackson was fond of Che Guevara's exhortation of a revolutionary death: "Whenever death may surprise us, it will be welcome, provided that this, our battle cry, reaches some receptive ear, that another hand reach out to take up weapons and that other men come forward to intone our funeral dirge with the staccato of machine guns and new cries of battle and victory."[21] In and out of prison, followers of Jackson and Guevara tried to heed their call. Bay Area activists demonstrated at the prison gates, while supporters abroad protested outside U.S. embassies.[22] His mother called for a UN investigation, and others continued to call

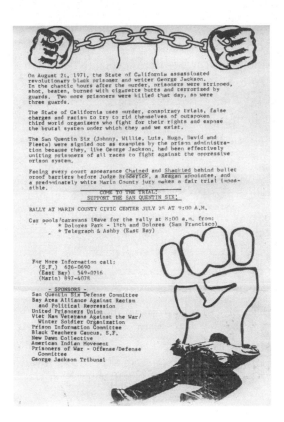

On August 21, 1971, the State of California assassinated revolutionary black prisoner and writer George Jackson. In the chaotic hours after the murder, prisoners were stripped, shot, beaten, burned with cigarette butts and terrorized by guards. Two more prisoners were killed that day, so were three guards.

The State of California uses murder, conspiracy trials, false charges and racism to try to rid themselves of outspoken third world organizers who fight for their rights and expose the brutal system under which they and we exist.

The San Quentin Six (Johnny, Willie, Luis, Hugo, David and Fleeta) were singled out as examples by the prison administration because they, like George Jackson, had been effectively uniting prisoners of all races to fight against the oppressive prison system.

Facing every court appearance Chained and Shackled behind bullet proof barriers before Judge Broderick, a Reagan appointee, and a predominately white Marin County jury makes a fair trial impossible.

COME TO THE TRIAL!
SUPPORT THE SAN QUENTIN SIX!

RALLY AT MARIN COUNTY CIVIC CENTER JULY 28 AT 9:00 A.M.

Car pools/caravans leave for the rally at 8:00 a.m. from:
* Dolores Park - 18th and Dolores (San Francisco)
* Telegraph & Ashby (East Bay)

For More Information call:
(S.F.) 626-0690
(East Bay) 549-0216
(Marin) 897-4075

- SPONSORS -
San Quentin Six Defense Committee
Bay Area Alliance Against Racism
and Political Repression
United Prisoners Union
Viet Nam Veterans Against the War/
Winter Soldier Organization
Prison Information Committee
Black Teachers Caucus, S.F.
New Dawn Collective
American Indian Movement
Prisoners of War - Offense/Defense
Committee
George Jackson Tribunal

A flyer distributed by Bay Area activists encouraging people to attend the trial of the San Quentin 6, ca. 1975; the image of Jackson's prone body flowing into the clenched fist was used throughout the mid-1970s. Among the distributors of this leaflet was the George Jackson Tribunal, which was an effort to establish an independent investigation into Jackson's death. Courtesy of It's about Time Black Panther Archive.

for independent tribunals to investigate his death. (As late as 1975, some Bay Area activists continued to call for such an investigation.)[23]

Inside the AC, prisoners tried to circumvent their now incommunicado status. They wrote an affidavit detailing the beatings they received and the constant threats they faced. Ruchell Magee wrote most of it, and prisoners circulated hand-copied drafts to one another for comment. All twenty-six men remaining in the AC signed onto it. Drumgo smuggled it out of the prison and into a court hearing the week after Jackson's death. The collective statement was a small sign of multiracial political unity among the prisoners against what officials, relying on the standard canard of carceral divisions, were already describing as a race war.[24] The family members of those incarcerated at the Adjustment Center and other activists pressed for public access to investigate claims of prisoner abuse. San Quentin authorities permitted two delegations to tour the prison: one group of three conservative journalists and another group of four liberal black politicians and professionals. Both delegations found evidence of abuse and isolation but disputed the prisoners' claims of torture.[25]

The most dramatic responses, however, came from male prisoners around the country. To them, Jackson had exposed a vulnerability of the prison system. In death even more than in life, he was the figure they needed to believe in a power greater than the system that caged them. His influence was clearly visible at Attica, in Upstate New York, where prisoners responded to the news of Jackson's death by launching a silent protest and fast. For several months, they had been pressing administrators for a variety of improvements to their living conditions, but the one-day silent hunger strike demonstrated a dramatic unity among prisoners that buoyed their spirits and terrified the guards.[26]

Two and half weeks later, on September 9, a scuffle between a small group of prisoners and guards spilled over into a full-blown rebellion as prisoners seized control of Attica's D yard. For the next four days, prisoners created a minicommune while surrounded by police and observed by national media. Their negotiating power rested on the guards they had taken as hostage, but the revolt's political aims were evident in the passionate declarations emerging from the prison. "We are men, not beasts, and we will not be treated or beaten as such," they declared in a collective statement that accompanied a set of demands. The men selected a negotiating committee that included representatives of the Black Panther Party, the Nation of Islam, and the Young Lords as well as attorney William Kunstler, journalist Tom Wicker, and politician Herman Badillo. The rebellion seemed a living testament to Jackson's political project of prisoner unity against the prison system, since the uprising seemed to provide the conditions under which the prison's notorious racial divides faded in light of united prisoner action. "The racial harmony that prevailed among the prisoners—it was absolutely astonishing, that prison yard was the first place I have ever seen where there was no racism," Wicker recalled.[27]

New York governor Nelson Rockefeller refused to meet with the rebels, however, and on September 13, he ordered state troopers—some of them armed with their personal rifles—to retake the prison. The troopers gassed the prisoners from a helicopter and then opened fire, killing twenty-nine prisoners and ten of the hostages.[28] State troopers forced the survivors to strip naked and crawl through mud as state photographers captured their humiliation from helicopters above. Guards beat the naked captives with clubs, burned them with cigarettes, and hurled racial epithets at them along with threats of castration, torture, and murder.[29]

The violent retaking of Attica replayed the events at the San Quentin Adjustment Center three weeks earlier but on a grander scale. Indeed, the two incidents became joined in the radical imagination for years to come. In both cases, the state response targeted the symbolic as well as the physical power prisoners had demonstrated. Attica was even more spectacular than San Quentin, unfolding over several days in a heavily televised (though still largely circumscribed—the government barred news media from flying overhead during the retaking of the prison) manner involving thousands of prisoners and an utterly avoidable tragic ending. Prisoners had forced authorities to carry out their brutality in public, and though the incident failed to incite popular rebellion, it did cement Attica in the public consciousness and cultural imagination. The Attica rebellion was a fixture of the 1970s: the prisoners faced trials for their dissent, a special committee investigated the rebellion and the state response, and Rockefeller faced questions about his military response when he ascended to the vice presidency in 1974. "Attica" became a rallying cry, an example of state violence and a plea for justice. It was rendered most powerfully so in the 1975 film *Dog Day Afternoon*, based on a 1972 incident, when a bank robber (played by Al Pacino) leads the crowd gathered around the bank in chanting "Attica, Attica" in a rebuke of police authority.

The state's response at Attica demonstrated that while arguments for political spectacle might have come from the Left, their execution was always more potent and dramatic when carried out by the state. Initial news reports falsely claimed that the dead hostages had been killed by prisoners. Further, officials initially made the specious claim that some of the hostages had been castrated, suggesting that such emasculation necessitated the state's overwhelming show of force in response. For all the public concern over prisoner actions, the state proved far more determined to use swift, brutal violence and to do so in ways calculated to torment the spirit of resistance as well as the bodies of resisters.[30]

To destroy the Attica rebellion and erase the memory of George Jackson required an ideological assault on the popular idea that prisoners could be intellectuals. In keeping with that spirit, writers from *Time* described a "crude but touching" poem that Attica prisoners had scrawled onto the wall during the rebellion. However, the journalists did not realize that the poem was Claude McKay's classic ode to black resistance, "If We Must Die."[31] Written in 1919, during an earlier generation of racial terrorism, McKay's poem insisted on the honor of a dignified death amid a militarily superior force.

> Though far outnumbered, let us show us brave,
> And for their thousand blows deal one deathblow!
> What though before us lies the open grave?
> Like men we'll face the murderous, cowardly pack,
> Pressed to the wall, dying, but fighting back![32]

The poem was a fitting epitaph for the Attica uprising.

Denying the intellectual capacities of people in prison only strengthened their resolve to see Jackson as a hero, proof that the black male prisoner could fulfill a revolutionary purpose. Part of Jackson's appeal lay in his pedagogy of black masculinity as an insurgent force. For other men in prison, Jackson's blackness was defined through his masculinity. An Illinois prisoner described Jackson as "everything and some of what all twenty-some-odd million Blacks in this *strange* land of North America should be: A Real Bad Nigger." In keeping with the various descriptions of Jackson's physical capabilities, this prisoner described the other killings of August 21 as proof of Jackson's heroic victory: Jackson, he said, killed five people before they killed him. Oppositional to the end, Jackson was the ideal prisoner. "Therefore, we—in these prisons—must spend long hours studying, to live up to that image."[33] Echoing Ossie Davis's famous eulogy of Malcolm X as a "shining black prince," a San Quentin prisoner called Jackson "the epitome of manhood." To him, Jackson's manhood was measured by his pedagogical impact: he had taught prisoners political and physical literacy.[34]

Several prisoners in the San Quentin Adjustment Center released a statement proclaiming that they would "vindicate" Jackson "because we are the ones who knew him best and loved him the most." The statement, like the AC prisoners' affidavit, described the severe physical reprisals the men had experienced.[35] In her memoir, Angela Davis called Jackson "a symbol of the will of all of us behind bars, and of that strength which oppressed people always seem to be able to pull together."[36] Gregory Armstrong, the editor of *Soledad Brother* and *Blood in My Eye*, wrote that Jackson had been killed near the prison walls because he was attempting to draw guard fire away from the other prisoners housed in the Adjustment Center: "He sacrificed his own life to save them from an official massacre. This would only have been in keeping with the character of his entire life."[37] Like other martyrs, then, Jackson was said to have chosen his death in order to give others life.[38]

Jackson gave voice to a broader political impulse that characterized radical movements of the early 1970s, whereby the existence of political prisoners signified a reason to pick up arms. Political prisoners became symbols of struggle in Germany, Ireland, Palestine, South Africa, and elsewhere. Their images adorned street murals, their statements were read at rallies, their freedom was demanded through a variety of demonstrations, their continued incarceration was used as justification for a series of plane hijackings, shootings and bombings. George Jackson was the American representative in a global iconography of prison dissidents that included figures Ulrike Meinhof, Bobby Sands, Leila Khaled, Nelson Mandela, and numerous others.[39] In each case, the prisoner served as a call to arms, a figure whose disappearance by the state convinced others to adopt a voluntary disappearance into the ranks of guerrilla war. Political prisoners signaled a paradox of state power, showing at once a top-down cruelty to the individual and a bottom-up inspiration in the collective of which they were a part. Internationally, however, political prisoners tended to be figures imprisoned for their actions as part of political movements. Because Jackson joined radical movements only after being incarcerated, his inclusion in the pantheon of political prisoners opened the door to a wider critique, a larger rejection of the prison system itself.

Beginning shortly after his death and continuing throughout the 1970s, Jackson's image gave rise to a variety of spectacular assaults on police authority. This approach came straight from Jackson's political playbook. In marking Jackson's death with two bomb attacks against buildings housing offices of the California prison system, detonated hours before Jackson's funeral, the Weather Underground commemorated Jackson "for what he had become [at the time of his death]: Soledad Brother, soldier of his people, rising up through torment and torture, tyranny and injustice, unwilling to bow or bend to his oppressors."[40] The "George L. Jackson Assault Squad" of the Black Liberation Army, a splinter group of the Black Panther Party, announced that it had killed a San Francisco police officer in revenge for the "intolerable political assassination of Comrade George Jackson in particular, and the inhumane torture of P.O.W. (Prisoner of War) Camps in general."[41] In the Pacific Northwest, a clandestine group calling itself the George Jackson Brigade carried out a series of bombings and attempted prisoner escapes in the late 1970s. Its first action was to bomb Washington's State Department of Corrections to draw attention to abuse of prisoners in the Walla Walla prison. Because Jackson had promised to torment his oppressors from beyond the grave, his name seemed a fitting title for this small group's actions—a way to remind the rulers that Jackson would forever haunt them. In 1972, an unrelated group of San Quentin prisoners also called itself the George Jackson Brigade.[42]

Revolutionaries around the country used Jackson's name as inspiration to mark their antagonism to the prison system. In the Northeast and in the Bay Area, separate groups used Jonathan Jackson's name (and that of slain Attica prisoner Sam Melville) when carrying out other bombings of government buildings.[43] In the Bay Area, the "August 7 Guerrilla Movement" claimed responsibility for several attacks, including a 1973 shooting of a police helicopter that killed two officers and a communiqué threatening to kidnap the director of prisons unless certain prisoners were released (a threat never actualized).[44] The Bay Area prison movement continued to produce other attempts at armed struggle, among them the New World Liberation Front, the Symbionese Liberation Army, and Venceremos. And to the extent that these efforts produced more prisoners, they added experienced organizers to the prison population as well as inadvertently providing public support for harsher sanctions as part of the domestic war on crime that undermined revolutionary groups.[45]

The climate of anger and revenge surrounding Jackson's death was worsened by the state's failure to adequately explain the circumstances. While crucial elements of the state's version of events were discredited, no suitable alternative theory supplanted it. The full extent of infiltrators and agents provocateurs among the Black Panther Party and other organizations connected to the prison movement remains a mystery decades later.[46]

Officials could not even reach a consensus on basic details such as what kind of gun Jackson had. In the week following Jackson's death, prison officials posited six different guns of varying sizes before ultimately settling on an Astra 9mm. But such a heavy pistol would not have fit in Anderson's tape recorder (the way officials said the gun had entered the prison) or under the wig where Jackson supposedly hid it. The last known sighting of the particular Astra that Jackson allegedly used occurred when police arrested its owner, Black Panther Louis Randy Williams: How did a gun in state custody make its way to San Quentin prison?[47] Officials failed to explore alternative theories for how Jackson got the gun and neglected to interview several potential suspects, including Anderson and other people in the visiting room that day.

The official story of Jackson's death did not make sense, and the confusion seemed only to confirm what Jackson had been saying about the prison as a site of black death premised on open warfare between guards and prisoners. James Baldwin poignantly described Jackson's death as an extension of his imprisonment, itself an extension of a longer black imprisonment. Writing in the *Black Panther* newspaper, Baldwin said that "George remained in prison because something in him refused to accept his condition of slavery. This made him a bad example for the other slaves, because the Americans still believe that they are running a plantation, and that this plantation is now the world. In the eyes of America all of us are Black today, and if you think I am exaggerating take a look at the results. . . . [F]rom this point on, every corpse will be put on the bill that this civilization can never hope to pay."[48] The prison, with its constant reminders of extreme state control, generated a distinctly racial paranoia that Jackson's death epitomized. Baldwin summarized this feeling succinctly when he said that "no black person will ever believe George Jackson died the way they say he did."[49]

Jackson was the latest in a string of slain black male revolutionaries who had defined the 1960s era—Medgar Evers and Malcolm X, Martin Luther King Jr.

and Fred Hampton, as well as the larger number of men and women killed by police or vigilantes. To many observers, Jackson's demise in an enclosed prison yard made his killing even more emotional. Whether it was the physical death of black men through murder or their social death through confinement, activists were increasingly using the word "genocide" to explain American racism.[50]

Four members of the East Palo Alto municipal council passed a resolution calling for an investigation into Jackson's death and declared their "disgust and dismay at this atrocious act of genocide."[51] Actor-activist Ossie Davis argued as much in his 1970 foreword to the reprint of *We Charge Genocide*, black communist William Patterson's 1951 petition to the United Nations detailing American racism. In a passionate introduction dated ten days after Jonathan Jackson's raid on the Marin County Civic Center, Davis argued that "genocide" was the only label adequate for the combination of expendable labor and brute force to which the United States subjected black people. "History has taught us prudence—we do not need to wait until the Dachaus and Belsens and the Buchenwalds are built to know that we are dying," Davis wrote. "We live with death and it is ours; death not so obvious as Hitler's ovens—not yet. But who can tell?"[52]

The fear of black genocide was not just a polemic. Several analysts in the early 1970s argued that black labor was being eviscerated by a combination of automation and white supremacy. With no more need for black labor, they argued, the U.S. elite no longer had any need for black people—hence their abuse by police and incarceration. Charting the economic health of black communities after World War II, sociologist Sidney Willhelm argued that "white racism and elimination from sustained employment bring the American Negro to the identical, ultimate fate of the American Indian"—that is, spatially confined and at risk of annihilation. Willhelm's was a prescient analysis of black fates at the onset of what has been called the neoliberal era.[53]

Jackson's death taught the world about American racism. His writings and the prison conditions that produced them facilitated the increasing significance of race in the emerging postcolonial world. Cultural theorist Manthia Diawara remembers Jackson and Davis, along with Eldridge Cleaver, Malcolm X, and Muhammad Ali, among others, introducing an American blackness into Mali, then recently independent of French colonialism. These figures of black American defiance, most of whom were or had previously been in prison, taught Africans a certain practice and ideology of blackness. Diawara and his high school classmates in Mali began to imitate "our black American heroes" in dress, nicknames, and linguistic style and "began to see racism where others before us would have seen [only] colonialism and class exploitation."[54] Knowledge of these figures, down to particular legal updates and other current events, became a cultural marker of independence. Through such knowledge, "African youth . . . were creating within us new structures of feeling, which enabled us to subvert the hegemony of *Francité* [French ways of speaking and thinking] after independence."[55]

Jackson's death confirmed to these black activists the genuine threat black prisoners represented to the U.S. status quo. In a eulogy written three months later, Guyanese scholar-activist Walter Rodney praised Jackson "because he discovered that blackness need not be a badge of servility but rather could be a banner for uncompromising revolutionary struggle." Yet Jackson's killing also exposed the depth of the American racial order: as Rodney wrote, "Ever since the days of slavery the U.S.A. is nothing but a vast prison as far as African descendants are concerned. Within this prison, black life is cheap."[56]

One of the most enduring influences Jackson had was in France. Thanks to Jean Genet's support, Jackson's work circulated widely among the French intelligentsia, and his ideas informed the development of what ultimately became known as poststructuralist French critical theory. Historian Rebecca Hill argues that *Soledad Brother* "inspired the young Michel Foucault to think about the relationship of the reform of the soul to the maintenance of power."[57] Working with philosophers Jean-Paul Sartre and Gilles Deleuze, among other prominent intellectuals, Foucault was one of the spokespersons for the Groupe d'Information sur les Prisons (GIP), which investigated and reported on French prisons, borrowing from the American prison movement an approach that joined the public's right to know with prisoners' right to dignity. GIP released several reports about American prisons, including one about Jackson's death.[58]

What most survives this encounter between black American prisoners and white French intellectuals is Foucault's classic, *Discipline and Punish*. First published in 1975, the book makes no acknowledgment of Jackson's influence, GIP, or the broader radical milieu in which Foucault traveled. Rather, the book offered a historical and theoretical examination of modern state power. Foucault argued that the prison colonized the souls of the condemned, with power relations encoded in the daily functioning of the institution rather than in sweeping spectacles of brute force. In particular, Foucault argued that the architecture of the classic prison worked through a "panopticon," with prisoners becoming more docile because they might be under direct surveillance at all times by guards sitting in a central tower. His analysis was far more applicable to Europe than to the United States, where brute force remained a critical ingredient of race-making and state power, especially in the figure of the prison.[59] Still, Foucault's insights into the subtle applications of power through individual bodies have been taken up widely by scholars and others. While Foucault emphasized the eighteenth-century European prisoner as the normative carceral subject, his arguments about the constrictions of regulatory power could be found in Black Panther writings generally and *Soledad Brother* particularly.[60]

Jackson routinely described how the prison had dulled his emotional sensibility so that he remained affectively closed off as well as well as physically self-regulating. Jackson alternated between pride and lament in describing the ways imprisonment had forced emotional self-control on him. His frequent references to his rigid exercise regimen and the need to "repress the sex urge," alongside the barely concealed sexual tension of his descriptions of his physical strength, show how the prison's discipline worked its way through the body of the condemned. These elements of life in prison, the daily characteristics of living inside such extremely controlled and repressive institutions, formed the backbone of Foucault's interest in the disciplinary elements of imprisonment as played out on both the individual prisoner and society at large.

These French critics reserved a special critique for the American media, so central to the circulation of Jackson's image yet now so dependent on the state for its sources and credibility. Foucault and the GIP published a pamphlet, with an introduction by Genet, describing Jackson's death as a "masked assassination." They concluded that the prison was a state of war, a new front in revolutionary struggle, and that "the entire black avant-garde lives under the threat of prison."[61] The pamphlet indicted the media for colluding with the prison system in the "manipulation of public opinion" and the destruction of "the public image (so that Jackson would not survive) and the function (so that no one would take his place)."[62] These missions were accomplished through descriptions of prisoner violence and guard beneficence as well as a campaign of deliberate misinformation about the source and caliber of Jackson's gun. The GIP's analysis of media coverage was neither incorrect nor complete. Because journalists lacked steady accounts of what happened inside San Quentin, the GIP argued that this confusion was part of tarnishing Jackson's reputation; it obscured the truth but reveled in Jackson's death as an armed killer.

Yet some journalists also did valuable research that exposed the contradictions in the state's case. Reporters at the *San Francisco Chronicle* used a black model wearing an Afro wig to test the state's theory that Jackson had hidden the gun under such a wig and walked, with the gun undetected, more than fifty yards accompanied by armed guards who did not notice the weapon. The *Chronicle* found that the gun did not fit under the wig and wobbled as the

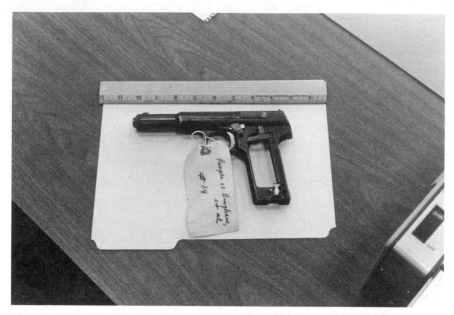

The gun that authorities alleged was smuggled to George Jackson. Officials claimed that Jackson received this nine-inch gun during a legal visit and that he hid it under a wig and walked seventy-five yards without the guards noticing the weapon. The *San Francisco Chronicle* tried to verify this story and found that the gun visibly wobbled with every step the model took. Courtesy of the *People of California v. Bingham et al.* trial records.

model walked just a few feet. In response, the government announced that the gun was of a different caliber, though in subsequent trials, officials again reversed themselves on the point. Likewise, a second autopsy, conducted a month after his death, revealed that Jackson had been killed by a shot in the back—not, as had been initially reported, in the head. Several prisoners in the Adjustment Center and other skeptics had alleged as much from the start, though some insisted that Jackson had also been shot point-blank in the head after being wounded.[63]

Journalists questioned some of the facts presented by government sources but did not, as many activists and artists did, reject outright the story of Jackson's alleged escape. Instead, journalists attempted to re-create the details of the escape and fill in the missing pieces. In doing so, they were especially reliant on prison officials for access to the crime scene. They also recounted the gory details of the five other murders that occurred in San Quentin on August 21. According to the GIP, the blood-and-guts details of the events in the Adjustment Center served an ideological function, presenting the incident as a "savage massacre" committed by prisoners run amok.[64]

Because journalists knew little of what happened inside the San Quentin Adjustment Center, they emphasized lurid details of violence—who had their throat slashed and in what order, how the victims spent their terrifying final moments, what words they uttered last. Even progressive journalists, lacking a viable counternarrative, were trapped by the constraints on access to information and resorted to the grim, knowable details. The mystery of George Jackson continued to haunt and confound, with the confusion enabling the prison to regain its symbolic authority.[65]

Dissident prisoners responded by challenging the media's reliance on government sources. They identified the government and the media as twinned forces responsible for the prisoners' confinement and most Americans' negative views of the incarcerated. Prison officials, wrote Ruchell Magee, "will tell (not Pay) those foolish news media dogs to lie publicly. . . . [A] lot of people would hear where the pigs have charged people with a lot of verbal shit written on paper, and hear the news media lies and convict innocent people before they are tried."[66] Other prisoners accused the mainstream media of helping "fabricate a non-existent world" and of using "publicity tricks" to shape public consciousness against black demands. Against this enemy of a corporate media reliant on state power, some black prisoners encouraged self-reliance in pursuit of an anti-Establishment truth. They declared that all writers, amateur and professional, had a "sacred obligation" to make sure that "our people" know the "*real things*."[67]

By critiquing the media for enforcing state violence, these prisoners maintained that the harshest elements of racism functioned through invisibility. The shroud of secrecy surrounding the prison pointed to the emerging racial landscape in which covert forms of racial categorization and the violence they enable have become increasingly central. As public policy formally embraced "color-blind" equality, the structures of racial inequality grew further entrenched. This seeming paradox, whereby the state has been "forced to exercise racial rule covertly," gave credence to paranoid suspicions of official power and its machinations.[68] In other words, the new racism would be characterized by what was unknown and unspoken, by what was hidden from view, where it had previously seemed to be defined by explicit references.

Black radical prisoners, then, worked to expose the new racial apartheid, in which physical isolation through heavily policed ghettoes and prisons would hide the extreme violence to which poor black and Latino communities were subjected. As a prisoner in Auburn, New York, wrote in a 1973 poem, "I am a political prisoner, charged with the unwritten / law of race."[69] Prisoners described blackness as the cause of both confinement and rebellion. In an interview with a journalist, Robert Blake, a black prisoner on the team negotiating an end to the 1970 uprising in the New York City jail system, described blackness in America as a form of natal alienation that prompted radical politics. "Q. What is your name? A. I am a revolutionary Q. What are you charged with? A. I was born black. Q. How long have you been in? A. I've had troubles since the day I was born."[70]

If official racism now took cover in opaque institutions governed by administrative rather than explicitly racial segregation, its opponents needed to be vigilant regarding its origins. With an air of proselytization, prison activists cast their message as a signal flare against black genocide. As a result, they spoke with a great urgency. "A warning: BLACK PEOPLE: what is happening in San quentin maximum security concentration camp is only a small example of what is to come in the minimum security concentration camp" of society, declared a statement by an Oakland prisoner support group. "Your reactions will indicate how fast or slow they will go with their program of genocide. WE SEEM TO THRIVE ON DECEIT: AWARE BLACK PEOPLE LET THIS BE AWARNING [sic] ESPECIALLY TO YOU."[71] And because genocide is as much about the past as it is the future, prison activists appealed to a parallel sense of history. "Brothers and Sisters we care nothing about our Brother going down in White History," wrote supporters of Ruchell Magee, "but we care very much that he goes down in Black History. *You can only see to that.* In the meantime, a lot of Black people's hopes are pinned up in [Magee's] moves."[72]

"THEY'LL NEVER COUNT ME AMONG THE BROKEN MEN"

George Jackson was writing from the grave long before he was killed. In early 1972, his militant will and testament appeared publicly in the form of his second book, *Blood in My Eye*. The book's dedication marked its militarist ambitions in an eerie testimonial to the author's death: "To the black Communist youth / To their fathers / We will now criticize the unjust with the weapon."

Jackson had completed the book in early August, less than two weeks before he was killed. The most important part, for Jackson, was that he completed the book without the same meddlesome interventions of attorneys and editors. It was not, like *Soledad Brother*, a heartfelt if selective description of his conditions or his political maturation. It was a manual for guerrilla war. "I'm not a writer but all of its [sic] me the way I want it, the way I see it," Jackson said of the manuscript on August 11.[73]

Blood in My Eye emphasized revolutionary violence, especially from within the "principal reservoir" that "lies in wait inside the Black Colony" of ghettoes and prisons, against capitalism and the incipient fascist threat.[74] A manual on the theoretical and practical underpinnings of guerrilla war, the book combined essays with theoretically driven (rather than emotionally expressive) letters. Unlike the largely chronological order of his first book, *Blood in My Eye* is arranged into thematic chapters to emphasize the political interventions Jackson wanted to advance. It is difficult to evaluate the extent to which *Blood in My Eye* reflects a change in Jackson's thinking or whether the ideas he expressed were beliefs that editorial interventions had prevented him from expressing in his first book. Even with the goal of positioning Jackson as an innocent victim, *Soledad Brother* contained several passages about armed struggle and revolutionary violence, the central themes of his posthumous tome and a preoccupation in his conception of social change.

Blood in My Eye synthesized Jackson's views on political violence and revolutionary symbolism. Jackson argued that revolutionary action could expose the criminal justice system by demonstrating the brutality of the American state. He saw prison radicalism as the natural conduit for the use of violence as a revolutionary strategy. "Only the prison movement has shown any promise of cutting across the ideological, racial and cultural barricades that have blocked the natural coalition of left-wing forces at all times in the past. . . . The issues involved and the dialectic which flows from an understanding of the clear objective existence of overt oppression could be the springboard for our entry into the tide of increasing world-wide socialist consciousness."[75]

The book argued for symbolic politics of violence to destroy the prison's prestige. In Jackson's conception, such attacks would undermine popular support for the institutions of governance. He saw violence as a spectacular force to shift collective consciousness and break the "isolation" of repression.[76] Even where this politics of violence invited greater state violence, Jackson held that "repression exposes" the state's monopoly of force. He saw violence as a rupture in the hegemonic order: "Prestige must be destroyed. People must see the venerated institutions and the 'omnipotent administrator' actually under physical attack."[77] Institutions maintained their authority by popular acquiescence in their permanence; thus, they needed to be violently uprooted so that people could understand that institutions of control were not all-powerful. Jackson had learned that lesson by observing the toppling of colonial rule in the Third World as well as by seeing the prison movement emerge from a series of small skirmishes with guards and other officials. According to Jackson, the visible destruction of elite prestige, accomplished only through violence, was necessary to build a "revolutionary culture." State violence in the form of police brutality was an effort to extend that prestige by using spectacular displays of force to coerce submission.[78] Jackson hoped that revolutionaries could use that algorithm for their own ends.

Blood in My Eye was a manual for the urban guerrilla more than the imprisoned one, though both groupings revered the book. Jackson wanted to turn America's black colonies, the carceral cities, into sites of revolutionary war. Jackson dramatically overestimated the potential for revolution that existed in 1971, but his description of the macabre metropolis proved prophetic. As the wars on crime and drugs expanded beginning in the 1970s, Jackson's prophecy seemed to materialize. Everything but the black revolution came to pass, as one observer put it: the "armored personnel carriers, military helicopters, military style raids cordoning off entire sections of the ghetto . . . are a reality in urban America as a result of the War on Drugs and the militarization of law enforcement."[79] In short, Jackson's critique proved far more salient and incisive than his proposed violent solutions.

Jackson had intended the volume to be a how-to book for the black urban guerrilla, but its ideas were indelibly shaped by the brutal mixture of constant racial violence and limited human contact that is the American prison. Not withstanding its singular emphasis on violence, *Blood in My Eye* can be read as a manifesto on the importance of symbolism. Jonathan Jackson was crucial to George's attempt to theorize prestige as a locus of power. If *Soledad Brother* uses George Jackson's letters to construct an image of a transformed prisoner, *Blood in My Eye* uses Jonathan Jackson's letters to construct an image of a martyred revolutionary. *Blood in My Eye* describes Jonathan as a tragic example of this effort to destroy prestige as well as a theorist of this approach to violent exposure. The first part of the book consists of a running dialogue between the Jackson brothers in which the elder brother casts his fallen sibling as a hero. While George had been saying as much since Jonathan's death, *Blood in My Eye* gave Jonathan more of a voice by reprinting some of his letters to George. Jonathan Jackson, like his brother, was imperiled for his actions, remembered through his words. George reprinted Jonathan's letters as part of a dialogue so that people would know as well as wonder "what forces created him, terrible, vindictive, cold, calm man-child, courage in one hand, the machine gun in the other, scourge of the unrighteous."[80]

Between Jonathan's death and the publication of *Blood in My Eye*, however, Jonathan's only written words that circulated publicly, as if to give insight into his motivations for attacking the Marin courthouse, were contained in an article published in his high school newspaper in which he acknowledged that he was "obsessed" with his brother's case.[81] *Blood in My Eye* revealed him to be less focused on George in isolation and more concerned with guerrilla war as a strategy of black revolution. In a November 1969 letter, for example, the younger Jackson argued that the ubiquity of police power was an illusion: "Their present show of strength is actually their weakness—show—they're too visible."[82] Jonathan argued that the covert attacks of guerrilla war could demobilize elites and provide a potent source of power for the oppressed. George mythologized Jonathan as an alter ego: "He has to be the baddest and strongest of our kind: calm, sure, self-possessed, completely familiar with the fact that the only things that stand between black men and violent death are the fast break, quick draw, and snap shot."[83]

The bleak urgency of *Blood in My Eye* revealed something about the conditions of its creation. As Jackson articulated the simmering state of war between prisoners and guards, he imbibed the symbolic uses of violence central to imprisonment. Violence is never just about hurting bodies; rather, it is about portraying an image of power, reinforced where possible by an architecture of domination. As the response to Jackson's death and the Attica revolt made clear, Jackson's emphasis on the symbolic dimensions of warfare proved a prescient analysis of how those in power utilized violence.

"HE WAS JUST TOO REAL"

Jackson's attention to the subtleties of language and politics helped make *Soledad Brother* influential beyond the black literary canon. A student of the rigidly hierarchical disciplinary world of the prison, Jackson made profound observations of the ways institutions disenfranchise social as well as individual bodies. Such insights spoke to the zeitgeist of New Left critical theory and its offshoots around the world. Where authenticity was defined through alienation, the prisoner's voice earned a measure of popular support.[84]

After reading an article about Jackson's death in the fall of 1971, Bob Dylan, who had largely abandoned political songwriting by this time, immediately wrote a song, "George Jackson," and recorded it the following day. Eight days later, the single hit stores. To ensure that radio stations would play the song, the record only featured two different versions of the song.[85] A commercial flop that never made it to a full-length album, "George Jackson" was a musical elegy for slain authenticity, emphasizing Jackson's impact and character: "Authorities, they hated him / Because he was just too real." Through Jackson, Dylan performed the popular perspective that prisoners were too real, too truthful and potent, for American society to handle. Echoing black radicals, Dylan sang that America itself was a prison, with walls and barbed wire merely separating those in maximum security from those in minimum security. As Dylan put it,

"Sometimes I think this whole world / Is one big prison yard / Some of us are prisoners / The rest of us are guards."[86]

A number of analysts and partisans from a variety of perspectives used the trope of authenticity to debate Jackson's significance. But authenticity emphasized the individual over the systemic, the hero or the villain over the collective. Even worse, the concern with authenticity naturalized a connection between black masculinity and confinement. The search for the "real" George Jackson, like the elaboration of prisoners as standard-bearers of revolutionary mettle, also trafficked in troublesome stereotypes about sexuality and aggression. People not only pursued the real George Jackson but interrogated those around him. His death provided an occasion to test his political worldview and his peers. Understood through authenticity, the pursuit of truth amid the prison's secrets ceded victory to the conservative push for law and order. The metaphoric prisoner was easily incorporated into the revanchist imagination of punishment.

Throughout the 1970s, black music and cinema took the prison as their setting for exploring freedom and its opposites. James Brown's 1971 live album, *Revolution of the Mind*, did not mention Jackson specifically but imagined imprisonment as an authentic feature of black life. The album cover featured a picture of Brown behind bars. "Revolution" was the most visible word in the title, and underneath it, Brown, with an Afro and a black leather jacket, resembled a Black Panther. The album title and imagery presented the prison as a natural site of black revolution. Also in 1971, B. B. King released a live album recorded in Chicago's Cook County Jail, and the following year, jazz artist Archie Shepp commemorated the prisoner rebellion with *Attica Blues*. The bloody retaking of Attica alongside critiques of police brutality and American imperialism informed a series of pieces in which poet-musician Gil Scott-Heron connected the deaths at Attica to the wider cruelties of racial rule.[87] Even at the end of the decade, Jackson remained a salient image of black resistance: the black British reggae band Steel Pulse called for "three cheers for Uncle George" in "Uncle George," included on the 1979 album *Tribute to the Martyrs*.[88]

These tributes to black prisoners often displayed conservative gender politics. Songs about Jackson typically celebrated his masculine heroism. Only the a cappella group Sweet Honey in the Rock, founded by civil rights movement veteran Bernice Johnson Reagon, took seriously the political significance of black women prisoners, releasing a 1976 song, "Joanne Little," that chronicled the story of a black woman prisoner in North Carolina who killed a guard who sexually assaulted her. "Joanne is you and Joanne is me / Our prison is the whole society," they sang. More often, however, the cultural symbol of black women in relation to the prison system was often understood through heterosexual romance. Between Angela Davis's arrest in 1970 and her 1972 trial, for instance, some of her supporters bought into the prosecution's argument that Davis's love for Jackson knew no bounds, when they claimed that the case was illegitimate because the two were really in love. Even some of Davis's supporters, then, promoted a conservative view of black women's activism. Whether victim or villain, these depictions of Davis as motivated by love minimized her political work. Davis did indeed express love for Jackson; such loyalty was not invented. But when described in romantic or sexual terms, this love depicted a hyperemotional irrationality more than political agency or legal innocence.

Two songs released in 1972 in support of Davis pursued this theme of criminal love. On their album *Sometime in New York City*, John Lennon and Yoko Ono open "Angela" with the suggestion that Davis was put in prison because "They shot down your man." A picture of Davis, with an Afro and mouth wide open, appeared on the album cover, which was designed to look like the front page of a newspaper.[89] The Rolling Stones also honored Davis with a stripped-down blues song, "Sweet Black Angel," that is one of the group's few explicitly political songs. In contrast to Lennon and Ono's tribute, which critics regarded as banal and a softly sung protest anthem, "Sweet Black Angel" became an interesting artifact in the Stones's repertoire. It is also a prime example of the patronizing ways in which white men have represented the sexuality of black women.[90] Using an affected slave dialect, Mick Jagger sings about Davis as "a sweet black angel / woh / not a sweet black slave." The song upholds her sexual symbolism, calling her a "pin up girl." But with "her brothers . . . a fallin'," now "de gal in chains." The song ends with a call to "free de sweet black slave."[91] Such depictions neatly inverted the case against her: rather than challenging the idea that her legal predicament resulted from her unbridled passion, they gave this passion a positive sheen.

This passive, patriarchal view of Davis informed 1970s cinema as well. The low-budget blaxploitation genre produced a series of films that represented a cheap knockoff of Jackson's image through a variety of violent, macho men and buxom women carrying out simplistic revenge fantasies against symbolic representatives of a white power structure. Davis often served as the caricatured and unacknowledged inspiration for the hypersexualized, Afro-wearing, weapon-wielding black woman fighting the (white) man, often to save her imperiled black male lover or avenge his martyrdom.[92]

Jackson's death, Davis's trial, and the violent end to the Attica rebellion became the vehicles through which people across the political spectrum tried to come to terms with life's desperations. For some, the lesson involved the severity of incarceration combined with the shocking display of state violence. Prison activists and leftist attorneys described radical prisoners as bearers of civilization. Fay Stender, Jackson's attorney and the architect of the Soledad Brothers defense campaign, felt that "person for person, prisoners are better human beings than you would find in any random group of people." Reflecting on her work with men in California prisons, she said, "They are more loving. They have more concern for each other. They have more creative human potential."[93] William Kunstler, perhaps the preeminent leftist attorney of the era and a negotiator for the Attica Brothers, hyperbolically described prisoners as the basis for modern civilization. "If it was not for the difficult roads that these Brothers and Sisters chose, we would still be living in a jungle," he said in a 1972 interview.[94] Writing less than a month after Jackson was killed, Mel Watkins suggested that Jackson had the last word. His death put the spotlight on prison in ways that other challenges to black confinement had not. "The idea that all black Americans are symbolically imprisoned is, of course, a cliché," Watkins wrote in the *New York Times*. "But it may be realistically said that prison is an exaggerated facsimile of society for those who suffer from racism, violence and bureaucratic insensitivity."[95]

Black prison narratives helped popularize an idea that prison was both a metaphor for and the epitome of the hidden constraints in American society. Many radical feminists made similar arguments about the confining limits of patriarchy. Pat Halloran of the Free Our Sisters Collective defined the prison as a ubiquitous component of patriarchal power. "For women, to be outside the walls of a jail is in some sense an allusion [*sic*]. . . . We must work not only to break down the stone walls that enclose some of our sisters, but to break down the barriers of written and unwritten laws that would call us criminal if we refuse to be slaves."[96] Others, however, took a more philosophical approach. "We all live in a prison of some kind, don't we," author Thomas Gaddis asked in his introduction to a 1975 anthology of prison writings, poems, and songs.[97]

Yet most people ultimately seemed more interested in the metaphoric prisoner, stuck in a job or a frustrating home life, than the one locked in a cage. In fact, several conservatives leveraged the fear of abstract confinement to push for more prisons and tougher sanctions. Demonstrating a destroy-the-village-to-save-it mentality, several prominent commentators justified punitive policies on the premise that they were necessary to prevent a larger, metaphorical confinement of homeowners scared to leave their property or upstanding white citizens imprisoned by fear of street crime. Such themes could be found in the growing popularity of vigilante films of the era, including the *Dirty Harry* (five films between 1971 and 1988) and *Death Wish* (four films between 1974 and 1994) franchises, among others. But it also animated public policy debates. Paradoxically, the confounding circumstances of Jackson's death created space for critics to raise questions about his life and the way supporters had allegedly misrepresented it. Equally invested in Jackson's symbolism, these critics attached that symbolism to a negative view of the prisoner. They objected that Jackson's fame relegated to the shadows the other five people killed on August 21, 1971. These subsequent narratives of George Jackson increasingly described black people, prisoners, and black prisoners as threats.

The national perception of the George Jackson story was evolving from victimhood to villainy. This shift in Jackson's significance utilized some newly revealed information but depended as much on a shift in the salience of facts that had been well known: his physical strength, for example, was now said to signal not an ability to endure confinement but his capacity for violence. Such depictions of Jackson appeared in initial reports of his death and increased in severity throughout the 1970s.

Conservatives treated Jackson's death as a strange validation of the prison system's harshness and the reason why it needed to become even more punishing. To do so, they appealed to well-worn tropes of black men as hypersexualized, violent brutes. Such efforts worked to reconcile an image of Jackson with the counterinsurgent aims of a rightward refashioning of the United States. California governor Ronald Reagan penned a *New York Times* opinion piece that used Jackson's death to call for greater law and order. In "We Will All Become Prisoners," Reagan argued that support for Jackson illustrated that society risked being imprisoned by "the falsehood that violence, terror and contempt for the moral values of our society are acceptable methods of seeking the redress of grievances."[98] Other prominent conservatives sounded a similar note. William F. Buckley Jr. praised the *Los Angeles Times* for posthumously emphasizing Jackson's prior run-ins with the law rather than his victimization. Whereas liberals and leftists described Jackson's incarceration in terms of his indeterminate sentence, Buckley, following the *Los Angeles Times*, noted that Jackson had been denied parole ten times in eight years and had racked up forty-seven disciplinary violations in that time. Buckley quoted several people, interviewed for the original news story, who described Jackson as having a violent temperament before and during his incarceration.[99]

Even without using Jackson as a symbol of the need for greater law and order, journalistic investigations into Jackson made him visible as the hypersexualized by-product of white imagination—the black projection of white fantasy. In a lengthy 1972 *Esquire* article about the relationship between Davis and Jackson, Ron Rosenbaum talked with an anonymous supporter of Jackson about his significance. Rosenbaum opens the article by describing a "pale yellowish stain" on the front of a flirtatious letter that Jackson had sent the woman—a letter she quickly removed from view. The move encapsulates Rosenbaum's argument that the woman does not want to expose for public scrutiny troublesome aspects of Jackson's personality, including his sexual advances. She later expresses this protective urge by telling Rosenbaum not to write about the semen-stained letter or Jackson's note calling the document his "'physical evidence of love.'" Rosenbaum, however, was more concerned with detailing what the woman says is *not* important about Jackson (his sexual exploits and aggressively flirtatious letters) than what she claims as his importance (his emphasis on multiracial class struggle).[100] Like Buckley and Reagan, Rosenbaum charged that radicals had falsely represented George Jackson.

Buckley, Reagan, and Rosenbaum were among the first responders in a larger right-wing shift that described Jackson and other men of his station as dangerous criminals. For several years beginning in the mid-1970s, a series of books about Jackson described the radical Left more generally as imprisoned by a paranoid and violent fantasy. These texts included memoirs by Jackson's editor, Gregory Armstrong (*The Dragon Has Come*, 1974), and his friend, James Carr (*Bad*, 1975), as well as Jo Durden-Smith's investigative account *Who Killed George Jackson?* (1975) and novelist Clark Howard's true-crime story about August 21 (*American Saturday*, 1981). Also in 1981, former New Leftist David Horowitz marked his hard-right turn by criticizing the prison movement in a magazine article about Fay Stender.[101]

Like American politics more generally, these narratives grew more conservative with time, and the more conservative the narrative, the greater closure it provided to the George Jackson story. The brief, popular romance with the radical prisoner as representative of broader social conditions was coming to an end in mainstream American intellectual life.[102] A far more conservative set of ideas would gained traction, viewing prisoners as part of an intellectually inferior, preternaturally violent substratum of society that deserved nothing but force from the American state. From this perspective, prisoners neither needed nor deserved rehabilitation; they needed to be entirely removed from society.

Such ideas have ebbed and flowed throughout American history, and they did not go unchallenged in the 1970s. Indeed, these years featured the most self-consciously radical versions of criminology the American academy had yet known. But the revanchist mind-set increasingly converged with a wide range of official interests. Here was the intellectual culture that produced an unprecedented boom in prison construction and a public policy approach rooted in the idea of an undeserving "underclass."[103]

A PRISON EDUCATION

The focus on authenticity obscured the ongoing work inside prisons, where George Jackson's influence continued to inspire some male prisoners to better themselves through education and expanded political horizons. The pedagogy of the prison was an ongoing enterprise in California and around the country. As an institution rooted in classificatory regulations, administered by force and physical separation, the prison taught certain lessons to those who encountered it—whether as prisoners, guards, family members, or community activists. Those seeking to undermine the prison, whether from within or from without, had perhaps the sharpest instruction in carceral power since they crafted their own education alongside and against the messages delivered through confinement.

The pedagogy of the prison was a highly gendered education, facilitated by the rigid sex segregation of confinement. The focus on heroes—the *need* for heroes to demonstrate that the prison was not all-powerful—drew attention to individual prisoners or collective prison riots in ways that overemphasized physical confrontation (primarily in men's prisons). Such an emphasis overlooked a variety of work by and on behalf of prisoners in both men's and women's facilities. It also overlooked the collective spirit that characterizes all forms of prisoner resistance.

More than anything else, the social life of prison organizing required creativity. Like the plantation and the slave ship, the prison combined quotidian and spectacular forms of punishment. Attorney Larry Weiss described San Quentin in the 1970s as comprising "90 percent boredom and 10 percent explosive danger."[104] To survive that combination required a great deal of ingenuity, which is how David Johnson and Hugo Yogi Pinell, denied reading material, found themselves playing game after game of chess on chessboards they made with stubby golf pencils and scraps of paper taken from the sacks in which their lunches were delivered. The men shouted out their moves from their individual cells, separated by thick sheets of steel and slabs of concrete. Sometimes other prisoners played, too.[105]

The prison provided the necessity out of which a variety of inventions sprung. Prisoners turned gelatin, toilet paper, and pen caps into devices that could publish clandestine newspapers, circulate banned literature, or turn off televisions when guards refused to do so. Creativity motivated prisoners to seek a variety of means of engaging people on the outside about prison conditions, global politics, and popular culture. Without a life of the mind, however it could be expressed, the social death of confinement would prove far more totalizing, far more destructive. That was the legacy they took from George Jackson.

Care work, in the form of building and sustaining human relationships through a variety of affective ties, lies at the heart of prison organizing. In institutions premised on isolation, collectivity itself was a vital tool of resistance that prisoners employed to preserve their physical safety, increase their collective capacities, and expand their social and intellectual horizons. Even those who agitated for violent conflict counseled looking out for one's comrades at every step. Such solidarity was an article of faith for them. This emphasis on collectivity and care revealed a fundamental paradox of the prison, where cooperative struggle emerged through conditions of spatial death.[106]

As with any organizing project, prisoner organizing is possible only through relationship building, a process made more difficult and in some cases more enticing by the distance and danger of confinement. Prison activism requires the active labor of people who are not incarcerated to attract broader recognition and support for those who lack the physical mobility necessary to publicly state their case. Key to initiating and maintaining these relationships are family members and loved ones of the incarcerated, social justice activists, and activist or sympathetic professionals whose work brings them into contact with prisoners. In the 1970s, professionals—primarily attorneys, but also nurses and journalists—played a central role. Such relationships between prisoners and outside supporters had a distinctively gendered hue. Women, especially mothers but also partners, children, and friends, did much of the work to support both male and female prisoners.[107]

The physical presence of the prisoner in the community and the community in the prison was critical. Inez Williams spoke of visiting her son, Fleeta Drumgo, weekly in hopes that her presence would convince the guards that people were aware of their behavior: "Maybe they won't beat him because they know I'm there. But I do go and they still beat him. . . . I think if enough black and brown people got together and started bitching loud enough, they would have to stop and listen."[108] This physical presence in the prison visiting room—and later in the courtroom—provided prisoners with a lifeline to the outside world. It offered the promise of interrupting the invisibility in which the violence of incarceration transpired. Ruchell Magee defined public support as critical to the success of his stance and the broader political campaigns for justice. "The courts won't open the prison until the people open the courts," he wrote in a 1971 letter to journalist Jessica Mitford and her husband, attorney Robert Treuhaft.[109]

Efforts to challenge the stigma of incarceration produced several sexual relationships, especially between imprisoned black men and white women on the outside. With the legal prohibition on interracial romance so recently lifted, black-white sexual intimacy added another level of danger and political intrigue to supporting certain prisoners. Several high-profile black and Latino prisoners struck up relationships with white women who wrote to express their support and concern. "We were famous, so we were all trying to get girl-friends," Talamantez recalled. Most of these connections were fleeting dalli-ances transpiring through flirtatious letters, photographs, and visiting room make-out sessions. Fleeta Drumgo had a collection of photographs sent to him, often at his request, by female admirers. These flirtations were laden with the prisoners' loneliness and longing and were rendered even more complex by the difficulty establishing genuine human connection across prison walls and generations of the gendered color line. The prevailing racial nationalism, with its separatist leanings, added a further layer of difficulty.[110]

Some relationships became serious long-term partnerships. Without the prison movement, Ernest Shujaa Graham and Phyllis Prentice would likely not have met. Graham had been born in Louisiana, raised in Watts, and educated in the California prison system—first in a variety of juvenile detention camps and then at Chino, the Deuel Vocational Institution (DVI), Soledad, and San Quen-tin. During his time in the state's many Adjustment Centers, Graham met a va-riety of longtime prison organizers. Being told to "Remember George Jackson, Remember Attica," helped Graham discover a sense of his own humanity that overrode his criminal conviction. It was the "spirit of the Panther Party" and the "spirit of George Jackson" that motivated Graham. "We had many George Jacksons, but they had different names."[111]

Those names included Graham and Eugene Allen. The two men were charged with the November 1973 stabbing death of a guard at DVI. They went through four trials, facing the death penalty under the same statute under which Jackson had been prosecuted during the Soledad Brothers case. During his third trial, Graham was in the San Francisco County Jail when he met Phyl-lis Prentice, a New Left activist from a conservative Iowa family. As a nurse in New York City, she worked on the collective that published the prison news-paper *Midnight Special*. She first read about Graham and Allen in its pages but knew little about them. She met them during the trial, and she and Graham slowly struck up a relationship that continued after Graham was finally acquit-ted and freed from prison in 1982.[112]

Prison organizing took shape through a series of inside-out connections rooted in a shared emphasis on education in different sites. As Graham put it, prison activists on both sides of the walls saw in Jackson's death a "responsibility . . . to educate and organize and mobilize" wherever they were, whether in solitary confinement or the general population, the college campus, the workplace, or an underground organization.[113] For those not incarcerated, this tripartite mission emphasized the need to educate the public about the horrors of confinement. Activists held a series of conferences aimed at educating the public about and coordinating opposition to prisons as institutions of social and political control. Through such forums and a myriad of publications, these activists sought to hold in tension the pragmatic challenge to the everyday indignities of incarceration with the visionary embrace of a world without the violence of state punishment.

Among the first and most significant gatherings at the time was the January 1972 "Tear Down the Walls" Prison Action Conference at the University of California at Berkeley. The conference was organized by an ad hoc coalition of supporters of political prisoners, including Huey P. Newton and the Soledad Brothers, as well as people involved in the burgeoning field of critical criminology, which was briefly centered at the university until administrators purged the program of its radical voices. As with other prison-related conferences during and since that time, "Tear Down the Walls" sought to advance short-term changes that would improve prison conditions or the possibilities for release while working toward a broader critique of the prison system as such. "Tear Down the Walls" was the organizers' slogan for their ultimate goals of abolishing both the prison and "the walls in the outside society that keep men and women chained to a meaningless life in an inequitable social system. The most basic question in the long run isn't how good or bad the prisons are, but the social and economic factors which force thousands of people into those prisons every month. Prisons will be abolished only when we have collectively built a new society and can collectively maintain a culture which places human needs over property rights."[114]

The conference workshops identified what would become strategic elements of prison organizing on the outside: behavior modification and medical testing in prison; sentencing policy; the connections among economics, racism, and incarceration; the imprisonment of juveniles, women, and dissident soldiers; and relationships between prisoner organizations and community groups.[115] Conferences and correspondence over the next three years sounded similar themes, together with the need to confront new prison growth and increasingly severe sanctions.[116] The radical criminologists then at Berkeley went on to found the journal *Crime and Social Justice* (now *Social Justice*) and to publish a variety of studies about policing, prisons, and the dangerous power of criminalization.[117]

Other prison organizing on the outside also emphasized education. In Los Angeles, the Harriet Tubman Prison Movement began in the early 1970s. Although never a large organization, the movement nonetheless claimed chapters in seven cities and operated a bookstore in South Central Los Angeles. The group's three stated purposes included providing free reading materials for prisoners, supplying free transportation so that families could visit their incarcerated loved ones, and supporting a minimum wage law for working prisoners. They saw these issues as overarching ones for black people from the ghettoes to the prisons. "These are the same demands of all our people, whether on the 'inside' or on the 'outside,' whether you live in Watts or San Quentin, Harlem or Attica, these demands are the demands of Black and other minority oppressed peoples inside the United States."[118] In focusing on literacy (in the form of access) and mobility (in the form of prison visits), the Harriet Tubman Prison Movement, like other prison activists who pursued similar approaches, utilized some of the same tools for black empowerment against slavery: prisoners and prison activists confronted the same state practices that denied slaves education and itinerancy. These groups picked up the tools of slave resistance in hopes that they could once again serve as instruments of liberation.

Literacy and mobility remained essential to the self-education of people in prison. Nineteen-year-old Dorsey Nunn was sent to prison in February 1972, six months after Jackson's death. In prison, Nunn met most of his former Little League teammates—all except the one white player, he says. The demographics of prison were the first part of his political education. "It was like damn, 'where'd all these Black people come from? Where'd all these Latinos come from?'" At that point, the "question stopped being a person question, and started being a political question." Answering that question was the basis of Nunn's wide-ranging education. Imprisoned in Tracy, California, Nunn summarized the experiences of many prisoners when he said, "The state may have tested me and given me a GED, but the people who actually educated me were political organizers on the yard at DVI."[119] There, literacy was a far more central battleground. The low levels of literacy among many prisoners, the product of disinvested school systems and the increasing abandonment of inner-city black communities, typified the ways in which prison constitutes what former political prisoner Ashanti Alston called "social death at its extreme."[120]

Many prisoners became politically active by first admitting their illiteracy to well-read prisoners. Radical prisoners created a culture inside that enabled others to make themselves vulnerable—to admit their illiteracy, to ask for help, to learn how to read and write from fellow prisoners and to then teach other prisoners. Literacy was a form of power, not only in the immediate sense of being able to read and write but also because the process of learning involved asking questions, doing research, and participating in collective discussions.

Literacy fueled a feeling of hopefulness inside and a push toward greater connection to the outside. "Everyone I encountered, even the ones that had a whole lot of time—the vision was that 'I'm going to get out of here, and we need to prepare ourselves for when we get out,'" recalled Hakim Ali, who spent more than thirty years in prison, mostly in the federal system, starting in 1971. Before televisions became a staple of institutional life, while revolutions continued to unfold throughout the Third World, literacy gave prisoners a certain sense of empowerment. Because dissident prisoners developed an intellectual component to survival, even those with life sentences talked about what they would do once they got out of prison. Study allowed them to aspire to bigger things, for themselves and for the world, while producing a knowledge of freedom. In covert study groups, prisoners discussed issues and reported back on their research. "And we would have dialogue. . . . As a result of a lot of that study, we started giving leadership from the inside to the outside," Ali said. "Informing our families about what was going on. Informing some of the young people in our neighborhoods where we lived what was going on."[121]

The prison movement was, among other things, an intellectual and literary phenomenon. Part of George Jackson's fame relative to other revolutionary prisoners of the era, and the reason his legacy continued to educate prisoners in a radical politics after his death, was not just his palpable intellect but the fact that he was a published author.[122] Physical isolation elevated the power of the written word; to be able to write was to be able to access the world beyond the walls in the form of books, magazines, poetry, and letters. Literacy and more specifically authorship established a certain intellectual hierarchy of prison activism. Jackson's eloquence and the passionate declarations of the Attica Brothers bequeathed to prison activists a literary tradition that they hoped would spark a broader public critique of the carceral state. A series of early 1970s books focused attention on the people and places that had already captured a mass audience: the California and New York prison systems, in particular articulate individual or rebellious groups of black prisoners describing the traumas of confinement. Letters, poems, and investigative reports promoted individual experience, hoping—as a variety of reform movements have hoped throughout American history—that personal narratives would shift public consciousness and promote political change.[123]

Such dependency on politicizing personal narratives shared the women's liberation movement's slogan that "the personal is political." And for feminist activists organizing with women incarcerated in prisons and psychiatric institutions, this overlap led to a great synthesis of feminist opposition to prisons. As part of a larger systemic critique of the prison's reproduction of gender violence, these women worked to support women standing trial for killing men who raped or otherwise abused them. This critique failed to produce a synthesis between the multigendered "prison movement," focused on men in prison, and the emerging prison movement among multiracial feminist and gay and lesbian activists. Organizing around prisons in these years often mirrored the institution's atomization by sex and celebrity: support for women prisoners was largely limited to antiracist sectors of the feminist movement, and only a few individual women prisoners became well known to broader masses of people.[124]

While uprisings at women's prisons briefly received some attention, they did not generally capture long-term interest the way uprisings at men's prisons did. Though women's prison organizing had a vibrant print culture, its texts did not get taken up in the same way as did writings by Jackson or the Attica Brothers. The focus on charismatic individuals, especially in the context of default adherence to male spokespersons, not only maintained public attention on the disproportionate incarceration of men but also obscured the ways in which prisoner organizing, including literacy efforts, was always a collective enterprise.

Violent and nonconsensual as it was, prison offered time and space for intellectual life. As with any cultivation of the life of the mind, prisoners balanced individual and collective study. Prisoners faced a growing and often arbitrary set of administrative restrictions on the kinds of materials they could receive. They lived under the constant threat of losing their property when they were moved to different facilities or when guards seized their materials during a cell search. As a result, dissident prisoners acted collectively and creatively to access reading materials. They shared books, whether in their printed forms or transcribed. Indeed, they copied texts—news articles, legal briefs, and whole books—by hand or typewriter onto legal tablets and passed them from one cell to another every few days. The topics varied but included works of black history and politics; Kalima Aswad, then imprisoned at San Quentin, remembers transcribing and sharing an *Ebony* article about Frederick Douglass.[125]

Of particular interest, however, were banned books of political theory and strategy, including George Jackson's *Blood in My Eye* and Robert Taber's *War of the Flea*, a journalistic account of guerrilla movements around the world.

Other popular texts at the time included books of quotations (by Mao Tse-tung, Kwame Nkrumah) and letters (by George Jackson, Eldridge Cleaver) or autobiographies of famous revolutionaries (Malcolm X). These books had formats that made them ideal for those with lower literacy levels and contents that introduced people to revolutionary ideas and ethics. In the context of collective study and discussion on the yard or in the tier, radical prisoners moved quickly from these texts to more trenchant works: Karl Marx and Adam Smith on political economy, Plato and Machiavelli on the connection between knowledge and institutional power, Erich Fromm and Wilhelm Reich on the social psychology of domination.[126]

Dissident prisoners were drawn to modes of analysis that offered rubrics of self-discipline. This interest took them from ancient Greece to revolutionary China. Prison imposed one version of self-regulation—limiting bodily movement, restricting the prisoner's conceptual as well as physical access. At the time, authorities justified such restrictions on the basis of protecting society until the prison could "retrain" its captives to be proper citizens. As black prison radicals charged that American citizenship never had room for their kind, they sought theories of selfhood that provided alternate explanations for how individuals could exist within broader social and political collectives. They rejected liberal notions of selfhood, which saw the individual as a rational being with rights from and responsibilities to the polity. Instead, they were attracted to more austere ideologies of the self: philosophies that emphasized conflict, contradiction, and questioning perceptions of reality; ideas about ascetic modes of survival, discipline, and conduct.

Such an interest dovetailed nicely with Third World Marxism, which emphasized the personal transformation of revolutionaries, often as a result of austere conditions. The directives of Mao Tse-tung were especially powerful here, since the Chinese communist leader had written pithy instructions about how revolutionaries ought to conduct themselves (emphasizing obeying orders, speaking politely, not harming captives, and the like). Experienced in the shadow of the Cultural Revolution, the polarizing world of confinement lent credence to the hallmarks of Maoist thought: national liberation, dogmatic fidelity to a fine-tuned intellectual position, and a belief in the political expedience of armed struggle.[127]

Literacy helped expand the prisoner's horizons, rescuing the imagination from the dreary banality of isolation. Literacy was a vital element of attempts to build collectivity inside prisons. Prisoners turned literacy into communal enterprises, guided as much by a desire to break the isolation of confinement as by the incipient knowledge that good educational practice is collaborative.

Where possible, more well-read prisoners would convene study groups around the weights in the yard, reading aloud from the one copy of a book that dissident prisoners shared.[128] Literacy, especially political literacy about antiracist or anticolonial struggles, went hand in hand with social relationships with activists not in prison. Identifying with struggles in Africa and knowing that people on the outside cared about prisoners' cases and circumstances helped situate prisoners within a larger field of affective ties that disrupted the prison's ability to isolate them physically and socially. Internationalism and outside support counteracted the prison's attempt to narrow the prisoner's perspective and contact.

Such a learning community was one of several ways in which prisoners attempted to transform and transcend their conditions. The forms of struggle inside reflected the limited space in which prisoners could operate. Prisoners established their personal power by exerting control over what they had at their disposal: their bodies, minds, and worldviews. Such were the terrains on which prisoners could best challenge their confinement. As a result, prisoners demonstrated their commitment and self-discipline through physical and mental exercise and showed their collectivity by supporting other prisoners and looking for opportunities to challenge or exist outside the prison's grasp. Prisoners derived small doses of power from study and from working collectively.

These efforts at collectivizing life against the atomization of imprisonment challenged some of the gendered logics reproduced in prison. While a staple of women's resistance, such an emphasis on collectivity in men's facilities belied some of the hypermasculinity of the constant calls to arms that celebrated the power of a heroic individual. Radical prisoners felt a responsibility to each other and often to any prisoner who stood up against the system. Living up to this responsibility entailed a commitment to contact the family members of individuals being harassed by guards, since experience showed that the prison system would not alert families to the troubles prisoners faced. A stubborn commitment to that responsibility often trumped strategic efficacy, since effectively demonstrating resolve of character was far more possible than displacing the power of prison authorities.[129]

In the balance of urgency and duration that constituted political organizing in the violent context of confinement, living by one's principles was more important than winning, for winning was so hard to imagine. In the daily work of challenging the prison regime, prisoners had only their bodies and their reputations. Prison activists on the outside also learned the lesson of the beautiful struggle, as summarized in a pamphlet authored by the Prison Action Project shortly after Jackson's death. In a rebuke of the indeterminate sentencing policy that had caused Jackson to be incarcerated for eleven years for a petty robbery, the Bay Area activists wrote, "There will be no democracy, no justice, no freedom until we have a new language and a new reality where criminal is not equated with being poor and law is not equated with the protection of capital. Until then, freedom will only be found in the struggle."[130]

From beyond the grave, George Jackson continued to inspire prisoners to write, study, and organize. His image informed prisoner activism around the country throughout the 1970s and beyond. The continued circulation of his memory was just one way that prisoners used the past. As his death helped others make sense of their own lives, the specter of slavery haunted the carceral landscape, and dissident prisoners took to the court to attack the peculiar institution of incarceration.

CHAPTER FIVE

Slavery and Race-Making on Trial

To some degree, slavery has always been outlawed and
condemned on the outside by the hypocritical mockery of chattering lips.
But on the inside of people and prisons, where slavery is embedded and
proudly displayed as a Western way of life and a privilege of god
himself, slavery is condoned on all of its numerous levels.
—RUCHELL MAGEE, open letter (1972)

Ruchell Magee was angry but focused as he rose to denounce the court-room proceedings. It was June 1971, and Magee was on trial for his role in the Marin County Courthouse escape attempt the previous August, when Jonathan Jackson armed three prisoners. Jackson and two of the prisoners were felled by San Quentin guards before they could escape, and now Magee, the only surviving participant, stood trial for the death of Judge Harold Haley, the one hostage killed in the incident.

Magee was resolute and intractable. He demanded that the court hold a hearing on the "illegal slavery" in which he had been held since 1963. For Magee, any resolution to the Marin County Courthouse incident of August 1970 would first require a court hearing on his original conviction. Magee offered to plead guilty to Haley's death if he did not satisfactorily prove his "enslavement." He then called all the attorneys involved, including his own, "buzzards" and said that the presiding judge was in "direct conspiracy with a bunch of insane, sorry, sick racist dogs." He challenged the structure of the court, rejecting the judge's presumed authority from on high and the attorneys' ability to do anything but shill for state authority. Angela Davis and Magee were still codefendants at this point, and her lawyers supported his claim for a hearing if not his means of pursuing it.[1]

The thirty-two-year-old prisoner had disrupted more than a few court hearings since his first encounter with the law eleven years earlier. Magee had been in and out of—mostly in—prison since 1960. His years of squaring off against the criminal justice system had convinced Magee that only through such full-throated harangues of the court could he hope to get his point across. For Magee and an increasing number of radical prisoners in the early 1970s, the courtroom held significance as one of the rare public venues available to people who otherwise spent their days confined in cages and behind walls. For these women and men, the courtroom was more a site of public intervention than of legal wrangling. This distinction mattered a great deal to Magee.[2]

While Magee had no respect for the law, he was not ignorant of it. He had become a sophisticated legal analyst over the years of his incarceration. He had studied dozens of law books, teaching himself case law and writ writing in an effort to overturn his 1963 conviction. Other prisoners saw him as a legal resource, and he helped several prisoners have their day in court.

He also used his knowledge of the law to bring attention to the harshest cruelties of prison life: the beatings and extrajudicial killings by guards. Magee and a few other prisoners tried to elicit public intervention in response to the February 26, 1970, death of San Quentin prisoner Fred Billingslea. Viewed as mentally unstable, Billingslea had set fire to the mattress in his cell. Guards shot tear gas into the unventilated cell and closed the door, hoping to quiet Billingslea. He was pronounced dead the next morning. Magee joined with other prisoners in writing letters and petitions about the incident and even tried to contact Angela Davis's mother, Sallye, for support, though he had no prior contact with either woman. Magee later maintained that his attempt to secure justice for Billingslea led the guards to open fire on him on August 7, 1970. While San Quentin's severe no-hostage policy makes it likely that guards would have fired regardless of who was involved in the escape attempt, one of the officers involved in Billingslea's death testified in court that he fired the shots that killed Jonathan Jackson, James McClain, and William Christmas.

Magee's knowledge of the law placed him in an odd situation: years of frustration with the efforts of incompetent attorneys made him suspicious of the government's intentions and prone to lash out at any attempt to quiet him, while the hours spent memorizing legal statutes made him something of a strict constructionist when it came to legal process. One moment he would cite legal precedent, the next he would denounce the judge as a Klansman and the prosecutor as a pig in a profanity-laced tirade. Magee often referred to himself in the third person when speaking in court, as if quoting from a writ. Yet his persistence ultimately caused six judges to recuse themselves from his trials for prejudice (including their unwillingness to hear his condemnations). He filed hundreds of writs and motions in a few months' time. San Quentin warden Louis Nelson described him as "the most miserable person I have had to deal with in 30 years in prison work."[3]

Magee's critique of slavery was instructive. Since the fall of Reconstruction, black activists have identified the enduring power of slavery, its afterlives. While a foundational metaphor of black intellectual life, however, its use by prisoners expressed added urgency as a result of their stringent conditions. Prison organizers castigated the justice system as the new "peculiar institution" of black enslavement.[4] By framing their confinement as enslavement, dissident prisoners positioned themselves as the latest links in an unbroken chain of white supremacy that stretched back hundreds of years. New civil rights laws and the rise of black elected officials led some in the mainstream to voice a cautious optimism regarding America's racial future, but these prisoners and their allies tried to refocus attention on the persistence of racial injustice, arguing that the prisoners' plight illuminated the historical continuity of antiblack racism at the heart of American society. The use of chains, the constricted mobility, the condition of social death, and the ubiquity of physical punishment were routine facets of imprisonment to which prisoners pointed as proof of their enslavement. And like nineteenth-century slaves, twentieth-century prisoners turned to diverse publics, nationally and internationally, for support.

Prisoners were not off base in drawing on the history of slavery to challenge their imprisonment. The prison coexisted with the plantation and incorporated a certain plantation logic in becoming a site of racial discipline. Colonial elites used the prison to teach docility, to show men and women their place in a racially stratified society. Officials made no pretense at rehabilitation, at molding prisoners in the image of elites. Rather, they wished that the lower classes would accept their station.[5] So when George Jackson, Ruchell Magee, and other prisoners spoke of their enslavement, they intuitively tapped into deep histories of carceral management. They endeavored a total critique of the prison system and its place in maintaining inequality along lines of race and class. Their challenge reveals a nuance that should not go overlooked, for in challenging the slavery of confinement, they identified the contradictions of a system that classified people as legally dead—rightless in the eyes of the law—yet confined to a site ostensibly for their rehabilitation.

Armed with such arguments, designed as much to advance an analysis as win a case, radical prisoners turned the court system from an arbiter of the law into a venue through which to critique it as well as the broader apparatus of state power that maintained it. Backed up by the attention their actions generated from both mainstream and alternative media, prisoner attempts to repurpose the court did more than raise legal issues. They sought to reinterpret the public meanings attached to prisons and punishment. That is, prisoners viewed the courtroom as a site for consolidating a radical black politics that could intervene in broader efforts to delineate the ongoing significance of race.

Radical prisoners saw the court as a vital arena for "exposing" racism, including but not limited to their imprisonment. In the heavily policed courts, prisoners could—at least within certain limits—demonstrate black dignity. So prisoners took the courtroom as a rare, vital public arena while vociferously objecting to the court's decorum: its routines, conventions, and authority as the state-sanctioned arbiter of truth. Prisoners sought to publicize their concerns in court and therefore objected to any person or practice that tried to prevent them from doing so. Incarcerated prison organizers attempted to use the court as a space for public education. The lesson, as former California prisoner Shujaa Graham summarized it, was one of intervention: "Don't worry about what they charge you with. Use that case as an opportunity to educate the jury, even if you get convicted."[6]

A critique of slavery informed both the narratives and strategies of prison radicalism. Black prisoners were now arguing that they, like slaves, were engaged in a battle against the state. Moreover, in this perspective, slavery described both prisoners' material reality (to be imprisoned was to be enslaved) and their ideological position (the prison ought to be understood as a form of slavery). They maintained that the prison drew its power from being neither seen nor understood as an institution of slavery, and only by making public such enslavement could prisoners hope to be free from it.

Especially through their dramatic stances in court, prisoners joined political formulations from slavery and its aftermath with Black Power displays of cultural pride and Marxist rebellion. They anticipated scholar Saidiya Hartman's characterization of slavery as a question of personhood against an objectifying state: "Slaves are not consensual and willful actors, the state is not a vehicle for advancing their claims, they are not citizens, and their status as persons is contested."[7] Black radical prisoners arranged their actions according to a similar logic—they sought to demonstrate that the state was holding them against their will, excluding them from meaningful social and political life. Subjection, not forced labor, provided the basis for the comparison.

Activist prisoners described the state's capacity to punish as a form of white terrorism against black bodies that had continued since the days of chattel slavery and had become directed at other poor and racialized populations. They were interested in what Angela Davis called the transition "from the prison of slavery to the slavery of prison."[8] As a state of unceasing bondage, slavery provided the most readily available terminology to describe the prison as an explicitly racialized system of repression.[9] For example, Davis described how she became involved in the Soledad Brothers case after seeing a picture of the three men that accompanied a February 1970 *Los Angeles Times* story about the case. The sight of the chained men impressed on Davis the continuation of black bondage. A few months later, when Davis herself was facing trial, she, too, described herself and was described by supporters as a slave.[10]

The idioms used by antiprison organizers were not limited to the chattel slave experience. Rather, they drew from a range of black experiences of white terror: trials of black revolutionaries were frequently described as modern-day "lynchings"; in an allusion to the Middle Passage, incarcerated individuals were declared to have been "kidnapped" by the state; and U.S. prisons were often compared to Nazi "concentration camps." Still, slavery provided the most enduring framework, and many black prisoners made self-conscious references to its history.

The issue of slavery pervaded 1970s prison organizing, structuring the ways that many black people in prison understood both their particular imprisonment and the general place of black people in the American political economy. At the same time, the description of prison as a form of slavery sparked divisions among prison activists. Those who embraced that characterization did not appeal to prisoners as unwaged workers but instead argued that qualitative differences existed in the conditions experienced by workers and by slaves. Though activists agreed on many things, they disagreed about whether prisoners should form unions and press for remuneration or seek to negate the prison system as a weapon of state violence. These political schisms reproduced some of the nineteenth-century divisions between "wage slaves" and chattel slaves.[11]

Both prisons and slavery are conditions of captivity, of incapacitation.[12] Several recent scholars have argued that the slave ship rather than the plantation is the closest analogue to the prison. After all, prisons are more like warehouses than factories; most prisoners do not work in any traditional sense. Further, the constant captivity and proximity to death more closely resembles the cramped quarters of the Middle Passage than the slightly more open world of the plantation.[13] Of course prisoners in the 1970s experienced neither the slave ship nor the slave plantation, though many had worked on brutal Jim Crow plantations. Still, the comparison, especially when launched from California prisons, was allegorical at best.

Yet this interest in the history of slavery stood at the forefront of popular debates about blackness. The 1970s witnessed a new historiography of slave politics that emphasized slave agency on the plantation and began a fuller accounting of slave resistance. The publication and television broadcast of *Roots* between 1974 and 1977 introduced slavery to a national audience. Prisoners did not, by and large, keep up with this new scholarship on slavery. But in focusing their critique on the prison as a form of slavery, they appealed to a general sense of slave militancy, drawing on books by left-wing historian Herbert Aptheker and the metaphoric invocation of slavery popularized by Malcolm X. The 1970s witnessed a new narrative about slavery emerging in popular culture and the academy alike, and prisoner evocations of their own enslavement were a highly charged element of this widespread interest in slavery.[14]

Black prison organizers saw themselves as rebellious slaves and defined imprisonment as an extension of slavery. They sought to upend the prison as both an institution and an idea. Central to that effort was challenging the apathy that, according to these dissident prisoners, allowed chattel and carceral slavery to continue. Slavery became a narrative tool in the development of black nationalism within American prisons. It followed, therefore, that not only the prison but slavery itself could be undermined by sharp declarations of black militancy and individual confrontation with the state. Activists defined blackness as both the source and scourge of imprisonment and held that race both explained incarceration and could serve as a potential basis for undermining the prison's control. Blackness was a source of resistance, representing persistent confrontation with the slave state.

The American South heavily informed prisoners' constructions of race and conceptions of representation, in part because so many of them traced their origins to that region. The two Black Panthers whose fate and notoriety became synonymous with imprisonment were southern transplants. Eldridge Cleaver made his way to Watts and then Folsom Prison by way of Little Rock, Arkansas. Huey P. Newton was born in Louisiana, the youngest of seven children born to sharecropper parents.[15] Soledad Brothers John Clutchette (born in Texas) and Fleeta Drumgo (Louisiana) were from the Deep South and as children moved to Watts with their families.[16] Johnny Larry Spain, who left the Adjustment Center with George Jackson on August 21, 1971, was born of a white mother and a black father in segregated Mississippi. The target of physical abuse at school and verbal abuse from his white stepfather, Spain was sent to live with a black family in California. Willie Sundiata Tate, who was also in the Adjustment Center that day, was born in Alabama and lived as a child in Texas before coming to California.[17] Angela Davis was born and raised in Birmingham, Alabama, home to many of the pitched battles and acts of white terrorism that targeted the southern wing of the civil rights movement. And Ruchell Magee moved to Los Angeles shortly after being released from prison in his native Louisiana. These activists, with the exception of Newton, moved from the South not only to the West but to Los Angeles specifically, contributing to the massive spike in southern California's black population during the mid-twentieth century.

The locus of black prison radicalism, then, traveled in one generation from the rural and urban South to urban Los Angeles and then again—involuntarily—from the industrial metropolis to the rural small towns where California's prisons were (and are) located. Black migration structured prison activism, first in the form of those who left the South for cities in the North and West and subsequently as young men in particular found themselves ensnared in the prison system. They brought with them an understanding of slavery as the origin of the American state and its racial hierarchies.

But their critique of prisons as slavery did not stop at the prison walls. Rather, as historians of slavery have suggested of the nineteenth-century United States, these activists claimed that all black people, if not also all non-elites, were enslaved by white supremacy. Imprisoned intellectuals argued that the racially disproportionate nature of confinement made the prison a vanguard of state racism. They maintained that the prison, like slavery, was a race-making institution central to maintaining the U.S. state. As it developed in prison, the critique of slavery was by and large a nationalist trope. By challenging prisons as slavery, nationalist prisoners upheld racial solidarity as an ideological counterpoint to the prison of racism.

As with so much else relating to prisons at this time, Soledad Brother George Jackson was a foundational figure in developing this position. Alive he was a spokesperson for the prisoner as slave. His death immortalized this connection and his association with it. Jackson wrote of a persistent connection between imprisonment and enslavement, describing the prison as the latest expression of black slavery and claiming that "time has faded nothing. I recall the very first kidnap."[18] He argued that the contemporary American state was merely a more sophisticated slave plantation. "Blacks are still doing the work of the greatest slave state in history. The terms of our servitude are all that have been altered," he wrote in a posthumously published letter.[19] Throughout *Soledad Brother*, Jackson used slavery both to designate the material existence of black people in the United States and to deride the mentality of those who failed to challenge the system. "If they kill me, Mama, I'll just be dead, but I'll not be any man's slave," Jackson wrote in a passage widely reprinted by prison activists as a testament to self-respect as an element of prisoner dissent.[20] Georgia Jackson expressed a similar, albeit far less referenced, sentiment in March 1970, before her son became a celebrity: "That's the way I raised him. . . . They might kill my boy but he'll never be any man's slave."[21]

Jackson wrote that the height of political consciousness was to recognize oneself as trapped in a system of slavery yet to reject being a slave. "I have, I hope, trained all of the slave out of me," he wrote to attorney Fay Stender.[22] According to Drumgo, the prison was a "slave plantation" that breeds passivity and attempts to indoctrinate its racialized subjects "like we've been indoctrinated for four hundred years." Drumgo declared that such a scheme would fail because those inside "recognize our blackness."[23]

At San Quentin, Magee described slavery as a system of power and a feeling of entitlement for whites. "To some degree, slavery has always been outlawed and condemned on the outside by the hypocritical mockery of chattering lips. But on the inside of people and prisons, where slavery is embedded and proudly displayed as a Western way of life and a privilege of god himself, slavery is condoned on all of its numerous levels."[24] Magee used the image of slavery to explain the prison much in the same way that French theorist Michel Foucault used the image of the panopticon in his 1977 book, *Discipline and Punish*. Foucault argued that the panopticon, an architecture of permanent surveillance, encouraged consent to the status quo. Magee made a similar claim, though his formulation paid more attention to race. For Magee, slavery was so central to official governance that it became stamped on people's hearts. Slavery, like the panopticon, was both a diffuse and a centralized form of power. By pointing to a subterranean slavery inside of people and prisons, Magee argued that the prison extended far beyond any particular institution.

Black prison organizers were among the first to challenge the otherwise widely accepted racial project of color blindness. They understood in real time what Foucault later became famous for demonstrating historically—that the prison constitutes a form of discipline that works away at both the body and soul of the condemned. By arguing that slavery was "condoned" in private, Magee identified the paradox of race after the civil rights legislative victories, where racism was seen as impolite but remained constitutive. The inside/outside of racism of which Magee spoke was not the division between personal prejudice and structural neutrality. Rather it was an argument about the ways state institutions increasingly buried white supremacy in out-of-sight institutions or convoluted policies while remaining formally color-blind.

Dissident prisoners challenged the prison as a mechanism of social control that tried to coerce submission to the prevailing rules of society. They theorized incarceration as a form of psychological and social control. In keeping with a rich history of black protest, these prisoners defined slavery as an uninterrupted fact of black life in the United States. The prison turned its subjects into slaves, they reasoned, so their job was to turn prisoners into rebellious slaves. This analysis was the basis for the formation of a community among black prisoners.[25] Although many activists acknowledged that white prisoners were disproportionately poor and working-class people, few black prisoners characterized white prisoners as slaves. For black nationalist prisoners, slavery was a condition of black life that reached its zenith in the prison. To the extent that they offered slavery as an analytic to be taken up by other people of color and white people, they did so within the framework of expanding a black radical notion of freedom.[26]

Activists who were not incarcerated also embraced the analysis of the prison as a form of slavery. And like the prisoners they supported, these outside agitators looked to the legacy of slave resistance as models of action. This inspiration ranged from small acts of subversion, much as feigned illness or work slowdowns provided slaves a subtle way to contest power, to the symbolic terrain informing prison activism. Journalist Reginald Major argued that he and other black people who attended the Angela Davis trial were "constitutionally incapable of making the line up [to be let into court] on police time. The tardiness was not so much a protest as the beginnings of resistance, a quiet ideological tensing up in rejection of absolute police authority."[27] He implied that rejecting the temporal niceties of court was a small-scale act of resistance inherited from slaves, a small way to contest the space of the courtroom.

ABOLITION AND THE "CONVICT CLASS"

If prisoners were slaves, did that make them workers? In describing their enslavement, radical prisoners such as Magee pointed more to a system of racial bondage than to one of compulsory labor. But many other prisoners spoke about their role as captive workers. Militant rank-and-file unionism swept the country in the first half of the 1970s: workers in auto factories, in coal mines, on farms, in steel mills, and in other sectors launched wildcat strikes, took over their workplaces, and fought to democratize their unions.[28] Prisons were not immune to this labor upsurge. Prisoner unions emerged with a nineteen-day strike at California's Folsom Prison in November 1970. The strikers' demands included a combination of labor, economic, and general human rights, from wages and the right to unionize to the abolition of indeterminate sentencing and the Adjustment Center.[29]

Hundreds of prisoners across the country began working to form unions. They garnered a good deal of attention through campaigns to organize the "convict class," as they called it, on the basis of their position as laborers.[30] In some parts of the country, including Walpole, Massachusetts, and Walla Walla,

Washington, prisoner unions joined forces with Black Power expressions of prison militancy to create forms of prisoner self-governance. In Walpole, prisoners ran the prison for four months, while in Washington they agreed to a power-sharing agreement with authorities that lasted for three years.[31] In California, where the analysis of prison as slavery was perhaps most forcefully articulated and where prison unionism enjoyed a strong following, the union activists and black nationalist prisoners had a rockier relationship. Militant unionists and revolutionary nationalists often collaborated on work strikes and other protests against the prison system but otherwise remained at odds over politics, tactics, and strategies.

Prison uprisings in this era bridged claims of class and nation, including demands for greater human and civil rights for prisoners and an overhaul of sentencing and parole decisions.[32] But the two positions—at least as they played out in California, with its union history and revanchist prison guard union—differed in their views of crime and punishment: Were prisons tools of racial domination or economic exploitation? Had prisoners been pushed out of the labor force, or were they workers laboring in a factory? Was prison protest aligned with the Third World colony or the domestic shop floor? And fundamentally, was the prison a legitimate institution for dealing with social problems? The polarized world of the early 1970s posed sharp questions about tactics and analysis, making lasting alliances difficult. Though each position attracted multiracial groups of prisoners and former prisoners, unionists held greater attraction for white prisoners, while the antislavery position especially appealed to black prisoners with protonationalist sensibilities.[33]

Activists with the Prisoners Union and its associated groups argued that prisoners were laborers who ought to receive protection and remuneration for their work inside. Organizers waged semitraditional union campaigns to win prisoners the right to bargain collectively as well as several other rights advocated by the Black Panthers and similar groups. Yet divisions over race and class—often played out as race *versus* class—increasingly separated the two forms of organizing. By 1973, Prisoners Union organizer Willie Holder identified four principles of prisoner unionism: "1. accepting labor issues as primary 2. presenting a 'non-political' overt posture 3. establishing viable locals which represent every ethnic-racial segment of a particular prison and 4. maintaining an intensive sensitivity to the threat of opportunism."[34] The first two principles ran in direct opposition to the organizing of black nationalist prisoners, who did not accept labor issues as *primary* elements of incarceration and who adopted an overtly political posture; the fourth point can be seen as a challenge to the persistence of criminal activities among some ostensible prison radicals. These principles were also an indirect rebuke of Wilbert "Popeye" Jackson, a former prisoner with black nationalist politics who had recently been kicked out of the Prisoners Union for allegedly stealing money from the organization and who headed a splinter group, the United Prisoners Union (UPU).[35]

Lurking behind these schisms were larger divisions about the function of the prison. Unionists saw prisoners as slaves only to the extent that they were workers denied wages and collective bargaining rights. They defined slavery along an economic axis and said little about the civic status of prisoners. One UPU broadside urged unionization in a Marxist idiom against slavery: "Prisoners UNITE, or what have you to lose but your chains!!! Slaves of the state, RISE UP!"[36] Prison unionists saw themselves organizing a workforce like any other union except that the people in their sector of the labor market were imprisoned. These organizers demanded "power to the convicted class," and the UPU's newspaper printed "poetry of the convicted class."[37]

The UPU sought to develop a shared class identity among the incarcerated and to improve the terms of employment for those behind the walls. They did not challenge the prison's inherent legitimacy as much as its conditions. With their labor focus primary, unionists accepted some of the terms of incarceration. The Prisoners Union, in fact, declared "that society has a right to punish persons for law violations, but we submit that this punishment should be spread evenly among the largest number of law violators as possible and not heaped upon a few. Moreover we accept incarceration for reasonable periods as punishment, but only after conviction."[38]

Among prisoners who viewed their condition as one of slavery, usually through the lens of black nationalism, the word "convict" was anathema—a sign of acceding to the hegemonic and racist construction of criminality. That the prison constituted slavery was a question of political subjectivity, of access to social resources and civic life, *before as well as during incarceration*. They did not see the issue as primarily involving labor. Underpinning the nationalist invocation of the prison as slavery was a critique of the state's legitimacy to punish as well as its ability to control the terms of labor, not just its surplus value. Indeed, the main labor issue to these prisoners was the absence of labor for young black and Latino men. That so many people in their prime working years were incarcerated for long periods of time and often for property crimes spoke to an official disregard for black life.

For them, calling the prison "slavery" constituted a rejection of the idea of prison reform by appealing to a transhistorical form of black confinement.[39] Chattel slavery was not just a system of compulsory and uncompensated labor. Confinement was inherently punitive, a condition of "soul murder" characterized by rightlessness that could quickly become corporal punishment and physical death. Like the slave, the prisoner lacked basic human rights of mobility, bodily integrity, and civic standing.[40]

Although rarely argued in such terms at the time, there was another reason the split between "slaves" and "workers" was so dramatic. Many prisoners did not labor, save for a remedial job such as tier tender or kitchen worker. The issue of productive work, much less paid work, did not apply to them. The most forceful advocates of the "slavery" position, black nationalists and established agitators, were often housed in isolation units that further removed them from the general population. Laboring in prison was a privilege rather than an economic necessity. The differences between these expressions of prison radicalism resulted in part from the explanatory power of organizing on the basis of one's political relationship to the state as opposed to on the basis of one's economic relationship to the means of production. As scholar Frank Wilderson rhetorically posits, "The worker demands that productivity be fair and democratic. . . . In contrast, the slave demands that production stop, without recourse to its ultimate democratization."[41] Historian Steven Hahn notes that unlike labor disputes, which are regulated principally by the market, slave rebellion "challenges the fictions of domination and submission around which slavery was constructed, and is thereby imbued with a political resonance that would not necessarily be true for the worker's defiance."[42]

Prisoner-slaves consequently cast their demands as part of the revolutionary effort to escape slavery and overturn the slave system—from prisons to the racist state that needs prisons. Just as slavery followed black bodies, even formally free ones, off the plantation and onto southern chain gangs or segregated factories nationwide, so, too, did black prison organizers in the 1970s find the prison to be a ubiquitous field of control, a condition more than a place.[43]

For some prisoners, describing themselves as slaves coincided with declaring themselves "political prisoners." At the federal prison in Marion, Illinois, prisoner Akinshiju Chinua Ola sounded a familiar theme when he wrote that "*all* Blkpeople are political prisoners," regardless of their incarceration—even if "unfortunately, *all* of us don't *act* like political prisoners." For him, to be a political prisoner meant being a victim of racial oppression regardless of whether one was engaged in explicitly political struggle.[44] But other analysts distinguished between "slaves" and "political prisoners," for reasons pragmatic and political. In honor of those grassroots campaigns appealing to international law on the treatment of political prisoners, these observers wanted to reserve the sanctity of that label for people incarcerated as a result of their political beliefs or actions.

The bigger, if related, reason was that slavery described the condition of captivity itself, regardless of the political motivations of those incarcerated. Richard X. Clark said in 1972 that he saw himself and the other Attica Brothers not as political prisoners but as slaves. "The political prisoner is subjected to reprisals by the system because of his views but a slave is subjected to reprisals because of his situation." Clark noted that the Attica prison population had grown disproportionately black (and Puerto Rican) "because blacks are subjected to atrocities from birth—education-wise, job-wise, and economically." Only in prison, when he took the time to study and analyze, did Clark identify the enslavement black people faced from birth. Only when he became a prisoner did Clark realize that he had always been a slave.[45]

For the prisoner-slave, the watchword was less abolition than revolution. George Jackson defined the terms as such in *Blood in My Eye*: "As a slave, the social phenomenon that engages my whole consciousness is, of course, revolution."[46] However, the call to abolish prisons was growing and was often coming from outside prison and from people who did not necessarily see prisoners as slaves. Prison abolition was a strong but inconsistent and often ill-defined feature of early 1970s U.S. prison radicalism; such calls also circulated among intellectuals in France and Scandinavia.[47]

Some leading American abolitionists came from predominantly white, faith-based communities that wanted to eradicate prisons as immoral institutions. Perhaps the most sustained effort at theorizing prison abolition in the U.S. context and at developing the community responses to social problems necessary to supplant imprisonment as an institution was undertaken by the Prison Research Education Action Project in New York state. This ecumenical and predominantly pacifist group was best known for its self-published 1976 book, *Instead of Prisons: A Handbook for Abolitionists*. Using a mixture of analysis and worksheets, the volume described the prison's inability to solve crime or social problems and outlined potential community-based responses (that is, alternatives to incarceration) for rape, theft, and other acts that violated social mores.[48]

Although *Instead of Prisons* offered perhaps the most sustained theorization, it was not alone in calling for prison abolition. In fact, abolition was a topic of popular debate in the early 1970s. Significant members of the Establishment, including those who worked in the criminal justice sphere as well as some academics and journalists, spoke of a gradual phasing out of imprisonment. These observers called for or optimistically resigned themselves to the withering away of prisons. Some did so because they believed prisons to be a relic of slavery or otherwise proof of modern barbarism. Others did so out of a belief that society must develop better means of rehabilitating and regulating behavior.

The death of George Jackson and the violent retaking of Attica by New York state troopers, along with the revelation of a mass grave at the Cummins State Prison Farm in Arkansas and other atrocities, sparked an abolitionist spirit among a disparate grouping of penologists, journalists, clergy, politicians, and others around the country.[49] Some faith-based groups attempted to halt the construction of new prisons. Former attorney general Ramsey Clark gestured toward abolition in his book *Crime in America* (1970), and the following year, Institute for Policy Studies resident fellow Arthur Waskow circulated and then published in the *Saturday Review* a call for a campaign to abolish prisons and jails by the Bicentennial. John Boone, the Massachusetts commissioner of corrections in 1972–73, tried to reform the state's prison system in hopes that it would wither away; instead, he was forced out after he sided with prisoners at Walpole when they struck over the issue of the guards' behavior. In 1976, Boone founded the National Coalition to Abolish Prisons. Such critics had different answers to the question of what would replace prisons, yet they agreed that prisons would or should be abolished.[50]

Some figures shied away from calling for abolition but still called for fundamental overhauls of American prisons, sometimes in ways that were consonant with abolition. Herman Badillo, a member of the U.S. Congress and part of the negotiation team at Attica, wrote that the lesson of that revolt was "not that we reform our prisons, but that we drastically transform them."[51] Senator Charles Goodell, a moderate Republican from New York, published *Political Prisoners in America* in 1973 to grapple with "the darker side of American history."[52] Academics Ronald L. Goldfarb and Bruce Jackson penned articles in *Look* magazine and the *New York Times*, respectively, calling the American prison system an exercise in failure. Criminologist Norval Morris suggested that his field begin "conscious planning" for "the decline and likely fall of the 'prison' as that term is now understood."[53]

Not just the province of isolated individuals, this view reflected a distinct and growing current of thought. In 1973, with the incarceration rate at a thirty-year low, the National Advisory Commission on Criminal Justice Standards and Goals, a regulatory body, "submitted a report to President Nixon that recommended closing down juvenile detention centers and freezing prison construction for a decade."[54] According to this panel of experts, the United States had more than enough prisons. Such people were not so much unaware of the revanchist sentiment growing in Washington, in Hollywood, and on Main Street as overwhelmed by it. In the context of economic recession and the many-pronged assault of counterinsurgency, this tide proved more powerful than these critics realized.

Law-and-order politics had a clear simplicity: more police, more prisons, and longer sentences. Proto-abolitionists, on the other hand, often lacked clear policy prescriptions. As journalist Jessica Mitford noted in a criticism of Clark's and Waskow's takes on the subject, calls for abolition were marred by inconsistencies. Both Clark and Waskow offered nonconsensual confinement—for example, on rural farms—as an option, thereby compromising their calls for prison abolition by re-creating forms of physical restraint as punishment and by suggesting that it occur in the same geographic areas where prisons were already located. As important, they did not emphasize alternative models of dealing with harm, such as restorative justice.[55]

Without a clear alternative, the call to dismantle prisons was no match for the call to get tough on crime and abandon penal rehabilitation in favor of pure punishment. In addition to resonating with the American racial order, these harsh sentiments had political and financial support that the abolitionists could not rival. Further, the spatial realignment of American politics concentrated black populations in ever-poorer cities, resulting in increased urban violence—and calls for additional policing—while mostly white suburbs became bastions of the New Right law-and-order conservatism.[56] The growing political power of the suburbs drowned out the supporters of radical change with a combination of austerity and retrenchment.

Would-be abolitionists and law-and-order enthusiasts shared a hostility to liberalism. Both the Far Right and the Far Left looked on the modern prison as a failure, claiming that the goal of rehabilitation was a diversion from what prisons did or were supposed to do. Both sides advocated an antiliberal approach to the existing criminal justice system and in that sense opposed traditional prison reform. In the ensuing battle of ideas, retrenchment held greater sway than abolition. The Right was better organized, better funded, and better able to draw on core American beliefs of harsh and degrading punishment for violators of the Protestant moral order. Radicals saw "prison reform" as a ruse through which to expand state power and instead encouraged people to, as the 1972 Prison Action Conference put it, "tear down the walls." Despite the Right's advantages in resources and organizations, radicals continued to voice their critique, though they had far less success in implementing their visions.

Abolitionism could be spotted in George Jackson's claim, echoed by other imprisoned intellectuals, that reforming the system would merely bolster its capacity to repress. Jackson went so far as to say that "if one were forced for the sake of clarity to define [fascism] in a word simple enough for all to understand, that word would be 'reform.'"[57] Clutchette similarly described reform as obfuscation, writing that "prison reform obstructs, falsifies, mis-leads, attacks and oppresses the call for abolishing U.S. neo-concentration camps."[58] Writing in a law review journal, a Pennsylvania prisoner, Samuel Jordan, contended that prison reform amounted to a domestic version of the "strategic hamlet" program that the U.S. military used to displace and re-create villages in Vietnam as a method of anticommunist counterinsurgency. Prison reform was, in this analysis, domestic imperialism—or worse. "The prison reformer—wittingly or unwittingly—is an agent of capitalism, a used-car salesman."[59]

Much as nineteenth-century radical abolitionists objected to gradual or electoral emancipation schemes, black radical prisoners insisted on revolutionary empowerment instead of reform. They sought to eradicate not just prisons but the social, political, and economic systems that created them. This hard-line position created fissures among prison reformists much as it had among abolitionists a century earlier. Describing the prison as a form of slavery represented an attempt to foster a shared racial identity and political stance. Slavery could only be overturned, not reformed. Abolitionism, therefore, was at the heart of 1970s prison radical discourse but was marginal to its organizing strategies. More common among those who saw the prison as a form of slavery were calls for revolution: campaigns to free prisoners as a step toward undermining the authority of state power. This strategy underpinned the trials of Ruchell Magee, Angela Davis, and the San Quentin 6.

"SLAVES HAVE THE RIGHT TO REBEL"

Ruchell Magee was arguably the most vocal prisoner of the period to define the prison as a form of slavery. Like Jackson, Magee only became a public figure after having been incarcerated for much of his life. He had previously served time at Angola State Penitentiary, a prison located on a former slave plantation in northwest Louisiana. (The prison, whose most famous captive was blues singer Huddie "Leadbelly" Ledbetter in the 1930s, was named after the African country where most of its nineteenth-century enslaved laborers originated.) Magee was released from Angola and traveled to an aunt's house in Compton, California, before being arrested again in 1963 after getting into a fight, ostensibly over a woman's affection and some marijuana. Because the fight occurred in a moving car, Magee was charged with "kidnapping for the purpose of robbery" and sentenced to life in prison.

During his first trial, the judge had him gagged with bath towels for interrupting proceedings to voice his innocence. At a retrial two years later, the same judge had Magee silenced with a dog muzzle. His court-appointed attorney entered a plea of not guilty by reason of insanity, a plea to which Magee objected as an insult to his integrity and intelligence. In addition to these personal grievances, Magee argued for his release on the legal grounds that the judge had improperly instructed the jury and that the stenographer had altered or erased large sections of the trial transcript.[60]

Such experiences left Magee convinced that the court system viewed the Constitution as optional. A seventh-grade dropout who had arrived in prison functionally illiterate, Magee became an accomplished jailhouse lawyer in an effort to overturn his 1963 conviction. His mastery of the Constitution and formidable legal skills helped several prisoners successfully litigate their own cases, even if he remained unsuccessful in reversing his conviction. His trial and his efforts to win his release convinced Magee that he was being held captive by the state, that the criminal justice system was an inherently racist institution that had reinstituted slavery under the shadows of its walls and laws, and that only he could adequately represent his interests in exposing the slavery of imprisonment.

Magee was charged with conspiracy, murder, and kidnapping for the death of Judge Harold Haley during the escape attempt orchestrated by Jonathan Jackson.[61] As a prisoner accused of murder, he faced the death penalty under the same penal code under which George Jackson was being prosecuted for the death of the Soledad guard. Angela Davis, then an instructor at UCLA, was also charged in the courthouse incident because several of the guns Jonathan Jackson used were registered in her name. Davis disappeared following the day's events and was not found until October 13, when she was arrested in New York City. Two months later, she was extradited back to California, where she met her codefendant for the first time. Like Magee, she faced the death penalty if convicted.

Davis and Magee entered their joint legal predicament from vastly different places. Davis was a young, promising professor known for her involvement in the Soledad Brothers Defense Committee and her highly publicized fight to remain on the UCLA faculty despite calls to fire her because of her membership in the Communist Party. Magee, however, was known to few people outside of prison. While both Davis and Magee faced the death penalty, a world of difference existed between trying to get out of prison and trying to stay out of prison. This difference followed them throughout their legal ordeals, which first proceeded in tandem before the two cases were severed in July 1971. These differences partially explain why their trials yielded such contrasting results. Before and after their cases were severed, however, Davis stressed her solidarity with Magee and objected to media depictions of them as fundamentally at odds.[62]

Angela Davis and Ruchell Magee at a preliminary hearing at the Marin County Civic Center, ca. 1971. Magee was the lone surviving participant in the August 7, 1970, raid; Davis was accused of providing the guns used. Popular attention focused on Davis, the professor and antiprison activist, especially once her case was severed from Magee's. However, Davis pledged solidarity with Magee and other dissident prisoners. Courtesy of the *Marin Independent Journal*.

Still, Davis and Magee had much in common in addition to their shared charges. Both believed that the prison was enmeshed with slavery, viewed the events of August 7 as a slave rebellion, and fought to serve as their own attorneys (known as going pro se). Self-defense in court was fundamental to their strategy. It flouted the expected standards of the court and equipped the prisoner with greater agency in articulating a political position, turning the court from an instrument of elite rule into a vehicle for the spread of insurgent politics. Whereas in Western legal practice, lawyers represent clients, Magee and Davis maintained that in their legal self-defense, their "clients" were oppressed people as a group. Their presence in the court was based on political rather than legal authority. By rejecting traditional legal representation, Magee and Davis suggested that black people in general and black prisoners in particular needed to be heard in court because they could not be seen in prison.

The act of going pro se was about visibly resisting the slavery of imprisonment. It was an argument that the legal system itself was too corrupt, too invested in white supremacy, to abide by its own strictures. The courts could be useful sites of public intervention—a vehicle for prisoners to assert their humanity in the face of dehumanizing incarceration. Reginald Major, a black journalist who covered the trial for the *San Francisco Sun Reporter*, argued that legal self-defense was a blow against slavery. "In the final analysis, a man stripped of the right to defend himself is a man being prepared for slavery. Every person who goes to prison as the result of incompetent or indifferent legal representation, in a situation where he had no wish for the attorney representing him to conduct the case, has been reduced to a slave."[63] For Magee, representing himself constituted a rejection of slavery's attempt to deny the slave political agency or legal standing before the court—the legal version of physical self-defense. Magee defined both his actions on August 7 and his self-representation in court as forms of self-defense against slavery. His supporters saw his case as evidence of the need for armed self-defense against a slave state. The Ruchell Magee Defense Committee at Stanford University saw the August 7 "slave revolt" as a blow against slavery since "an unarmed people are subject to slavery at any given time."[64]

Magee's playbook—armed self-defense, the pursuit of mass publicity, strident declarations of freedom from oppression—blended histories of southern black resistance stretching back more than a century with the bravado of contemporary Black Power masculinity. He rejected legal representation altogether. Based on his previous experience with attorneys, he argued that the only way he would get out of prison was by his own efforts. He refused to accept the attorneys appointed for him by the court, lashing out at them verbally and sometimes physically. He accused them of being part of a broader attempt to silence him. He described the court system as criminally disempowering and the attempts to impose attorneys on him as but another in a string of violent acts by the state. The state's refusal to let him be his own attorney was evidence of its prejudice: "What dreadful crimes the oligarchy has committed that they fear the voice of one man," he noted.[65]

According to Magee and his small but vocal collection of supporters, he was a rebellious slave who was being persecuted for resisting the structures of domination that held all slaves in bondage. "His fight is our fight—slaves have the right to Rebel," proclaimed a flyer in support of Magee. From this viewpoint, open rebellion offered the best hope for slaves to escape their bondage. When that approach failed, publicly describing his conditions and motives was the next-best means of indicting and exposing white supremacist state power. Asserting a mixture of masculine dignity, antiracist critique, and legal strategy, Magee argued that justice could be secured only by "having the right to control your own defense so that the Courts must deal with the truth."[66] His voice, therefore, carried the added imperative of exposing what his supporters described as "the racism and repression of the legal system" and of showing that "he had the right to rebel Aug. 7, 1970[,] because he is being

Ruchell Magee raises a shackled, clenched fist during his trial, while a guard tries to seat him, ca. 1971. Magee had been imprisoned since 1963 and was the only surviving participant in Jonathan Jackson's 1970 raid on the Marin County Courthouse. Frustrated and distrustful of the legal system, Magee represented himself as his own attorney. Photo by UPI.

held illegally as a slave of the judicial system."[67] Yet the effort to have his voice heard often resulted in confrontation. As was increasingly common in cases involving black revolutionaries, Magee routinely disrupted court proceedings and was removed several times for disrespecting the judge, the prosecutor, or his own court-appointed attorney.

In an attempt to underscore his enslavement and make visible the case law he used as precedent, Magee renamed himself Cinque. Many black nationalists, in and out of prison, adopted Swahili, Yoruba, or Arabic names in the 1970s. But Magee had an even more specific reason for choosing this name. The original Cinque had led the 1839 rebellion aboard the slave schooner *Amistad* during which a small group of Africans killed the captain and seized control of the boat. Hoping to return to Africa, the insurgents were captured by the U.S. Navy and held for trial. In 1841, and for reasons altogether different from those Magee argued in his own case, the U.S. Supreme Court declared the uprising to be a "justified rebellion."[68] The *Amistad* case was one of the only instances in which slaves received a hearing—and even more notably, a positive ruling—from an American court, and Magee sought a similar outcome. He saw that ruling as justification for his own situation: "Having no other recourse," he had "rebelled [against] slavery attempting to reach the people to expose his flagrant racist slave case." Presenting himself as a modern-day Cinque, Magee argued that he had both a moral obligation and a legal right to resist the slavery of imprisonment.[69]

In describing his situation as enslavement, Magee undermined the widely accepted narrative of the state of California's racial innocence. His case demonstrated the national reach and ongoing influence of chattel slavery through the criminal justice system—even in states where slavery had never been legal. He argued for removing the case to federal courts, appealing to statutes utilized by the civil rights movement to advocate federal intervention against states that refused to desegregate. Blending an understanding of slavery's history with his experience of Jim Crow, Magee argued that California was a slave state and therefore biased against him. Davis's legal advisers disagreed, at least regarding their client; they believed that she stood a much better chance in the California courts on trial and preferred to reserve the federal option for appeal if need be. Yet Magee continued to file his own motions on this matter and many others, including his effort to impeach President Nixon. For a man who had been locked down so long, even the limited hearing provided by the courtroom was a rare chance to be heard by a larger public. He was not going to miss the opportunity.[70]

Magee's defense hinged on defining the events of August 7 as a slave revolt, the only step available in his personal fight for freedom as well as a decisive element of the black freedom struggle. He had some allies in taking this position. While he never enjoyed the widespread support that Davis did, Magee received some short-term critical aid from a few well-placed individuals. Nicholas von Hoffman, a protégé of community organizer Saul Alinsky and a columnist at the *Washington Post*, penned several feisty columns in support of Magee. Von Hoffman described Magee as a rebellious slave in search of respect. "He was born forgotten 32 years ago," von Hoffman wrote of Magee, "and he's stayed forgotten even now." The journalist saw the prisoner as a noble lost cause. Society had stacked the deck against Magee. "He is the unwanted, lower-class black male, an object too dangerous and of too little value even for the uses of political martyrdom."[71]

Perhaps most dramatically, Dr. Kenneth Clark testified for Magee. Clark was one of the most well-known psychologists in the country at the time. He had graduated from Columbia and was part of the research team for sociologist Gunnar Myrdal's famous 1944 study on racism, *An American Dilemma*. Clark and his wife, Mamie, studied the impact of racism on childhood self-esteem; the Supreme Court cited their findings in ruling against "separate but equal" educational facilities in *Brown v. Board of Education*. The former head of the American Psychological Association, Clark was also a community activist in Harlem: he was the president of the Metropolitan Applied Research Center, he and his wife had opened the Northside Center for Child Development, and he served on the New York Board of Regents for two decades, during which he advocated for greater educational equity. Clark was the consummate urban race man. His widely cited work contributed to understanding the city as a carceral space, and his 1965 book, *Dark Ghetto*, quickly became a classic social psychology explanation of black urban life in America. Journalists, politicians, liberal activists, and others subsequently sought him out as a spokesperson or expert witness in issues dealing with race and the city. Clark had long demonstrated, through both scholarship and public intellectual engagement, his fealty to those he saw as representatives of the black freedom struggle.[72]

Though Clark's involvement in Magee's defense was limited to testimony, his presence reveals the broad base of support, at least in black America, for dissident prisoners. Clark was a staunch integrationist, a liberal whose primary emphasis was on school reform and housing equality. He was an outspoken critic of Black Power, which he saw as mirroring the exclusion of white supremacist groups. But by the early 1970s, he was increasingly, if briefly, concerned with policing and prisons. He chaired a committee investigating the Chicago police's 1969 murders of Black Panthers Fred Hampton and Mark Clark (with results published in 1973), spoke out against police brutality, and testified at Magee's trial. His support for Magee, like the high-level support from a string of black celebrities that Davis enjoyed, suggested that the prison was at the frontlines of American racism in the new age of formal equality. Clark's testimony also gave Magee's actions the imprimatur of psychological reasoning. In court, Clark testified that Magee "had absolutely no other choice" but to rebel because his actions constituted a manifestation of "everything his life literally stood for. [It was] an actual, concrete, behavioral approach to the goal of freedom," embodied through "a black man with a gun, a black man giving orders. . . . And that is freedom, you know. That is a rejection of the racist insistence that you are not worthy." Clark also praised Magee's intelligence as "indomitable in many ways unbelievable."[73]

Magee epitomized a larger black nationalist response to the criminal justice system. His verbal and at times physical sparring with officers of the court and his attempts to be his own attorney despite reprimand or restraint echoed Panther leader Bobby Seale's battles with Judge Julius Hoffman in Illinois in 1969 and 1970. Black prison organizers interpreted any interference in the routine functioning of white supremacy as a political good in its own right. Disruption was a strategy, not just a tactic, because such contrarian actions might penetrate the seeming invincibility of such control. Prisoners such as Magee hoped to negate a system of racial rule by undermining its basis in legal conventions. Eldridge Cleaver summarized this approach as "a projection of sovereignty, an embryonic sovereignty that black people can focus on and through which they can make distinctions between themselves and others, between themselves and their enemies—in short, between the white mother country of America and the black colony dispersed throughout the continent on absentee-owned land."[74] The rejection of the law through the courtroom was part of a broader effort among black liberationists to demonstrate their own forms of control despite and even because of the circumscriptions of the criminal justice system.

Magee's fight to serve as his own attorney, then, was the latest in a string of black radical attempts to remake the court system that dated back to at least Marcus Garvey if not to the original Cinque.[75] Magee was simultaneously engaged in a struggle for freedom from prison and a struggle for dignity, demanding to be respected as a competent, capable black man. He objected to a court-imposed gag order preventing him from accessing the media as akin to the physical gag placed in his mouth at his earlier trials. His courtroom stance blurred the boundaries between literal and figurative silencing, seeing any attempt to block him from speaking as a form of state violence that affronted his personal dignity. He attempted to circumvent this ruling by publishing pamphlets and open letters through supporters. A small group of independent leftist journalists took up this challenge by producing a fact sheet to improve the accuracy of news coverage, while prison activists associated with the Venceremos Study Group published and distributed Magee's writings.[76]

Throughout various legal proceedings, Magee continued to directly confront what he saw as the efforts to gag him and strip him of his dignity. He objected when prosecutors in the 1971 trial used the results of IQ tests administered in 1956 and 1963, when he was functionally illiterate, to disqualify him from serving as his own attorney. Magee filed a 1972 libel suit against the company that published the *San Francisco Chronicle* and the *San Francisco Herald-Tribune* for printing this IQ score as well as against the district attorney and prison records officer for releasing the score, which he said biased the public against him. He said the gag order prevented him from filing the suit or speaking to the media when reports first appeared. The suit was dismissed.[77]

The IQ test, like the attorney who entered an insanity plea on his behalf but against his wishes, was another affront to his dignity. Magee described the IQ test as further proof of the ways slavery continued to place black people outside the bounds of American citizenship. Magee's protests encapsulated a long history of black diasporic radicalism. Representing and restoring black dignity necessitated a fundamental break from American nationalism and its replacement by racial solidarity. Magee proposed a metaphysical, even surrealist, rejection of the American nation-state, offering in its place a long history of global black revolt. "Further, if one reviews history, it is one of the basic principles of racism, and an integral part of the fascist government, that Black people have always been labeled illiterate, ill-mannered and the like," he wrote in a prisoner newspaper. "This relates to something that I said before . . . that while Blacks are *in* Amerika, they are not *of* Amerika."[78]

His brash, profanity-laced style competed for attention with his layered political and legal arguments. In late 1972, Magee was cited for obscenity after telling a judge, "Kiss my ass and suck my dick, your honor." Attorney Thomas Siporin of the National Lawyers Guild defended Magee's approach, writing that the outburst did not constitute obscenity but rather had the "socially redeeming purpose of waking up the oppressed masses to see the true obscenity of [the judge's] denial of self-representation and/or choice of counsel." Magee's attempt to serve as his own attorney was, by extension, an attempt to enable oppressed people to achieve adequate representation: "So while Nobody may represent Ruchell; Ruchell truly represents them."[79]

Prison activists cast the efforts of insurgent prisoners, these rebellious slaves, to represent themselves in and out of courtrooms as a literal effort to speak truth to power. According to Siporin, prisoners' attempts at self-representation actually constituted a collective representation of revolutionary politics by all oppressed people. The act of struggling to represent himself, to remove the barriers separating him from narratives about himself, paradoxically cast Magee as a collective symbol. As Major observed in covering the trial for the *Sun Reporter*, this repurposing of juridical spaces made the courtroom into a theater of black politics. Black activists welcomed black defendants with "Right on." While judges and prosecutors objected to this greeting, Major argued that this exchange served a similar function as an "Amen" in church: it expressed an affirmation with the master of ceremonies. In Major's analogy, the prisoner assumed the role of spiritual leader, transcending the earthly limitations of the court system.[80]

Magee's defense in court and in public opinion rested on a combination of dignity and militancy, masculinity and constitutionality.[81] It was a potent, at times confounding, combination that characterized many of the prisoner legal battles of the era. The worse the outcome looked, especially after Magee's case was severed from Davis's, the more hypermasculine the definition of Magee's enslavement became. Black Mothers United for Action, a small Oakland group involved in Magee's defense efforts, objected that Davis received most of the popular attention that the case attracted. In a flyer, the group charged that the media emphasis on her was a legacy of slavery's attack on black masculinity and upheld black folk wisdom as the antidote to "the devil's policy to use the Black woman in the efforts to try and fender [sic] our BLACKMEN ineffectual in their fights for our liberation."[82] They urged others to support Magee's defiant, masculinist assertion of dignity. However, it yielded mixed results, drawing short-lived attention to his predicament but failing to win his case. Angela Davis pursued a similar course, stripped of its masculinist stance, with greater success.

Angela Davis maintained that her "life is at stake in this case—not simply the life of a lone individual, but a life which has been given over to the struggles of my people, a life which belongs to Black people who are tired of poverty and racism, of the unjust imprisonment of tens of thousands of our brothers and sisters."[83] While the stakes were large, her approach to the court was more measured than Magee. For Davis, legal self-representation meant acting as cocounsel in her defense, alongside an accomplished legal team that included Howard Moore, Leo Branton, Margaret Burnham, and Doris Brin Walker. The four had three decades of experience defending persecuted activists (unionists, communists, and civil rights workers), often with great success, and all were active members of the National Conference of Black Lawyers (NCBL), the National Lawyers Guild (NLG), or both. And all supported Davis's role as cocounsel.

Burnham noted that in demanding legal self-defense, "Ruchell and Angela join a growing number of Black prisoners who are dispensing with a lawyer-spokesman in the courtroom . . . in their constant search to find new forms of forcefully and effectively defending themselves and [for politically motivated defendants] their movement."[84] Unlike Magee, however, Davis wanted assistance in defending herself. Her actions reflected a mixture of principle and expediency, a recognition of her legal inexperience as well as an affirmation of the prisoner as a political subject.

While both Davis and her attorneys insisted on her representative status— one of many revolutionaries, one of many victims of state repression, and above all one of many black women—her uniqueness explained the popularity

Angela Davis leaving court with attorneys Haywood Burns, far left, and Howard Moore, middle, with arm raised, June 1972. Davis's case sparked a major international movement in support of her freedom. Moore and Burns were part of a legal team that also included accomplished lawyers Leo Branton and Doris Brin Walker. Moore had represented the Student Nonviolent Coordinating Committee, and Burns cofounded the National Conference of Black Lawyers. Photo © 2014 Stephen Shames/Polaris Images.

of her case. Magee called his case an instance of "flagrant racist slavery" and sought to reverse his conviction. Davis, aware of her notoriety, often downplayed the particulars of her case in favor of expressing solidarity with other imprisoned women and political activists. The result was paradoxical: supporters extracted a collective political position from Magee's bold declaration of his selfhood, whereas Davis's insistence on collectivity was overshadowed by the attention focused on her person and the particulars of her case. Indeed, Sol Stern wrote in the *New York Times* that most local journalists knew Magee only as "the other defendant" in the Davis case.[85] Journalists emphasized the distinctive nature of the Davis case with lurid speculation: a young attractive female professor, a rising academic star hounded by her ostensibly controversial affiliations, accused of arming an escape by male prisoners, possibly to free her incarcerated lover. Supporters also described her as an exceptional figure, dynamic and captivating. Thus, even while Davis downplayed certain aspects of her biography, minimizing her middle-class status for the sake of larger solidarity, many people characterized her as unique.[86]

It is unlikely that anyone else could have united the diverse figures who came together in support of Angela Davis. As a well-known activist, professor, and member of the Communist Party, a black Marxist cultural critic and proto-feminist, her case garnered support from leftists around the world, including a wide cross-section of the U.S. Left. Magee's active support base, such as it was, was concentrated in the Bay Area and lacked a national network on which to draw. Not so for Davis.

Other black women activists who became high-profile defendants later in the 1970s—Safiya Bukhari, Joan Little, Assata Shakur, and Dessie Woods, all of whom had active defense campaigns—did not have the kind of support that Davis did. By 1970, the Communist Party of the United States had four decades of experience with political defense cases at both the local and national levels and a vast array of global connections and practical skills. Indeed, her case was among the last major defense efforts involving an American prisoner that the U.S. party and its international affiliates organized. Though many CP members privately had reservations about Jonathan Jackson's actions and Davis's case, it initiated the defense campaign, the National United Committee to Free Angela Davis and All Political Prisoners (NUCFAD), upon Davis's arrest on October 14, 1970, at a Howard Johnson hotel in Manhattan.[87]

The fight to free the twenty-six-year-old Davis began immediately, with attempts to prevent her extradition to California and noisy demonstrations outside the Manhattan Women's House of Detention in Greenwich Village. Prominent party members, including veteran organizer Louise Thompson Patterson as well as younger communists Charlene Mitchell and Bettina Aptheker, headed up local and national branches of the committee. While NUCFAD devised the strategy for building public support for Davis, a wide variety of individuals and organizations joined in the effort. Actor Ossie Davis headed the Angela Davis Defense Fund, one of many celebrities who offered their support, and local committees emerged around the world. All were united in pursuit first of Davis's release on bail, which was denied until California overturned the death penalty in February 1972 (meaning that she no longer faced capital charges), and ultimately of her acquittal in court.[88]

When it comes to the law, silence means death. Prisoner defense has always involved visibility, keeping people in the public eye in hopes of raising issues, influencing public opinion, and pressing for a positive outcome in court. Such was certainly the case with Davis. The preexisting media attention on Davis combined with the broad coalition of financial and political support that lined up behind her—both of which were products of the early 1970s, when high-profile political trials were routine—boosted her defense campaign. It was always easier to organize on behalf of a well-known person who was not in prison than one who was.

To that end, Branton's first court motion was to have the entire trial televised. He argued that the public interest would be served by opening up the closed circuit television surveillance of the trial so that the proceedings could be broadcast. Barring that, Davis's attorneys asked for a larger courtroom that would accommodate more spectators.[89] Their motion was denied. Nevertheless, NUCFAD released trial bulletins, local and regional newsletters, pamphlets containing statements of support (and later the defense's opening and closing statements in court), and a December 1971 book, *If They Come in the Morning*, edited by Bettina Aptheker, Davis, and members of NUCFAD. The book was part of the group's campaign to build support for Davis and to a lesser extent Magee. The volume included several essays that Davis had written from the Marin County Jail, including updates about other political prisoners across the country. Her advanced education notwithstanding, Davis's prolific writing behind bars, much of it gathered in this anthology, was an extension of the black prisoner emphasis on the free mind in captivity.

The book's title was taken from a November 19, 1970, open letter that author James Baldwin had sent to Davis via the *New York Review of Books* and that was reprinted in the anthology. Alluding to Martin Niemöller's famous poem about the cost of remaining silent amid genocidal regimes such as the Nazis, Baldwin wrote, "If they take you in the morning, they will be coming for us that night." Baldwin cast the Davis trial as a clear manifestation of enduring black slavery. "One might have hoped that, by this hour, the very sight of chains on Black flesh, or the very sight of chains, would be so intolerable a sight for the American people, and so unbearable a memory, that they would themselves spontaneously rise up and strike off the manacles," Baldwin wrote. "But, no, they appear to glory in their chains; now, more than ever, they appear to measure their safety in chains and corpses."[90]

Baldwin's letter was the clearest contemporary example of the ways in which black prison activism prophesized the rise of mass incarceration. Alive to contemporary forms of repression as current manifestations of the long history of black struggle against confinement, Baldwin's poignant words pointed to the centrality of punishment in American society. He described a frightening American future in which the black experience of confinement would be broadened into a national security state marked by "chains and corpses."

Davis's arrest, extradition, and trial generated a global debate about race, racism, judicial impartiality, and imprisonment. The debate was often expressed through troublesome claims regarding black sexuality that hearkened back to slavery. Davis's supporters invoked slavery to make sense of her flight, capture, incarceration, and prosecution. Bettina Aptheker, an activist whose father, Herbert, was a renowned communist and historian of slave revolts, likened the FBI's intensive national search for Davis to the "response of slave owners to slave rebellions"—a modern-day reenactment of the Fugitive Slave Act.[91]

That Davis was extradited from a Manhattan jail to a California one against her wishes in the middle of the night with legal action against her transfer pending suggested a continued state investment in controlling the place, terms, and conditions of black mobility. Police took Davis from her Manhattan jail cell at 3:05 A.M. on December 22, 1970, eleven hours after her stay of extradition had expired, though her extradition remained under appeal. Under heavily armed guard, she was transferred to the Marin County Jail.[92] One of Davis's attorneys declared that the government was proceeding as if it was "prosecuting a fugitive slave case." Magee described the "indeterminate sentence law of California [as] the *Fugitive Slave* law warmed over. . . . The '*Judicial and Prison Systems*' are '*Practicing Slavery under color of law.*'"[93]

Davis contributed to this association between prisons and slavery in several writings from her jail cell, including articles about slavery and sexuality and about race and contemporary political repression. In interviews from jail, she described herself above all as "a Black woman [who has] dedicated my life to the struggle for the liberation of Black people—my enslaved, imprisoned people."[94] She likened her flight from California after August 7 to that of a fugitive slave. "Let me ask this question," Davis said. "When a slave who managed to escape from the whips and wheels of the white slave master fled to another state, was this evidence of his guilt? . . . I fled because I was convinced that there was little likelihood that I would get justice in California."[95] Slavery continued to animate Davis's description of repression even after her acquittal. She began her 1974 autobiography, *With My Mind Set on Freedom* (subsequently republished as *Angela Davis: An Autobiography*), by describing her flight, time underground, and arrest, a narrative tool that "cannot help but echo slave narratives. In both cases, the goal is physical freedom, escape from impending captivity."[96]

The context of black prison organizing, to which Davis herself had already contributed, provided the foundation for her arrest itself to be read as an extension of slavery. The massive attention to her flight and capture, supporters argued, offered proof that slavery continued to define the terms of black life in the United States. The obsession with Davis's whereabouts during her two months underground reached the highest level of American power, as she was placed on the FBI's Ten Most Wanted list. Two days after she was arrested in New York City in October 1970, Richard Nixon publicly congratulated J. Edgar

Hoover and the FBI while signing the Organized Crime Control Act of 1970. In a prejudicial assumption of her guilt, Nixon called Davis's arrest "a warning to those who engage in these acts."[97] Her supporters claimed that her case could signal a larger form of antiblack state violence. The Reverend Jesse Jackson said that even though there "are few like Angela Davis," her conviction would mean that "concentration camps are next."[98]

If her case signaled the imperiled state of black activism, it also reflected black solidarity. Even before Davis had chosen legal representation, the NCBL convened a panel of twelve law professors from eleven colleges to provide her with advice and counsel. The Presbyterian Church, through its Emergency Fund for Legal Aid (a rainy-day fund for social justice causes run by its Council on Church and Race), gave ten thousand dollars to the Davis defense campaign in hopes of promoting a fair trial for a person whom one Presbyterian minister called "beloved angel": "Angela Davis has become a Symbol of every black who has ever been slapped down by the power of white government when he stood up and challenged it."[99]

Davis was a popular symbol for a range of figures. Singer Aretha Franklin offered to raise bail money, reasoning that because she earned her money from black people, she wanted to spend it in a way that would benefit them. "Jail is hell to be in," the singer said. "I'm going to see her free if there is any justice in our courts . . . because she's a Black woman and she wants freedom for Black people." Franklin saw Davis as an exemplar of a larger freedom struggle. "Black people will be free. I've been locked up, and I know you got to disturb the peace when you can get no peace."[100] At the Marin County Jail, Davis received a parade of well-known visitors that included Maya Angelou, Nina Simone, Toni Morrison, and Ralph Abernathy. Singer, comedian, and actor Sammy Davis Jr., a Republican, spoke at a benefit rally for Davis, saying, "I share her blackness, man, and that's where it's at." Seeing such widespread support, Moore pledged that Davis would be freed through a "black defense" that put racism on trial, an approach that he predicted would succeed on account of its honesty. "White people know they are racists," he claimed, but only a smart and straightforward acknowledgment of this racism would compel "white people [to] respect their own law."[101]

Davis's body and her sexuality were crucial sites of evidence for supporters and detractors alike. Much of the hate mail that Davis received in the wake of the revelation of her membership in the Communist Party contained openly racist threats of sexual violence. Further, as was common in journalistic depictions of women at the time, news stories about her emphasized her physical description—"slender," "tall," and "beautiful." Journalists writing for black newspapers as well as other public supporters also used the term "beautiful," using it to describe both her physique and her oppositional stance.[102]

This constant obsession with her body became a feedback loop that structured the trial itself. The prosecution used Davis's skin complexion, conventionally attractive looks, hairstyle, and height as well as the gap between her front teeth in asking witnesses to identify her. "The general description of Angela that [the witnesses] all had heard [from the district attorney] was that she was a tall, light-complected black woman, wearing an afro, and that she had a space between her two front teeth," Aptheker wrote. "They chanted this like a mantra on the witness stand, and the very monotony of it cast doubt on whom, if anyone, they had seen. One witness even said that he 'couldn't remember about the teeth.'"[103] This focus on Davis's body exposed a larger pattern of casual racism. A gas station owner who claimed to have seen Davis with Jonathan Jackson the day before the courthouse raid testified that he served enough black customers to "notice individual differences" among them. He claimed to remember Davis because she was "more good looking than most black people."[104]

Most significantly, Davis became known for her Afro. She and many other black people decided to wear their hair natural at this time, and the Afro became Davis's trademark in popular culture. During her time underground, the Afro was both an identifying characteristic that police used in their search and an expression of solidarity adopted by other black women. Davis estimates that "hundreds, perhaps even thousands, of Afro-wearing black women were accosted, harassed, and arrested by police, FBI, and immigration agents during the two months I spent underground." Other women proudly wore Afros in hopes of serving as decoys and providing extra cover for Davis.[105]

The photographic documentation of Davis became its own trope of black womanhood. Decades later, Davis noted two primary purposes that photographs of her served during the 1970s: journalists and the government depicted her as a foreboding anti-American and antiwhite terrorist. Supporters, meanwhile, often depicted her with her mouth wide open as if speaking, "a charismatic and raucous revolutionary ready to lead the masses into battle. Since I considered myself neither monstrous nor charismatic, I felt fundamentally betrayed on both accounts: violated on the first account, and deficient on the second."[106]

The popular focus on her body included specific, troublesome attention to her sexuality. The prosecution claimed that Davis had conspired with Jonathan Jackson because of her passion for his imprisoned brother. As proof, district attorney Albert Harris pointed to the vivid expressions of love Davis wrote in eighteen pages of letters found in George Jackson's cell after his death. The letters were written between July 6 and August 5, 1971, weeks before Jackson was killed but nearly a year after the Marin incident for which she now stood trial. The letters contain several expressions of love for Jackson—politically and emotionally, but also romantically and erotically. In them, Davis routinely refers to herself as Jackson's "wife" and lover. She reminisced about two brief trysts during her legal visits to him and found it "inconceiveable [*sic*] that any Black man or woman who's half-way sane can avoid, after the slightest contact, falling madly in love with you." The stream-of-consciousness letters offer information on matters serious (details of the support campaign) and mundane (whether women's legs are more attractive when shaven or unshaven), but never germane to the charges she was facing.

The later letters express her confusion and pain as a result of a letter in which Jackson accused her and other communist members of the SBDC of undermining his leadership and his plans. He expressed this sort of paranoia and frustration during his final few months as he pushed supporters to accelerate preparations for armed struggle. The final three letters are short and express her frustration that Jackson had not yet responded to her repeated efforts to sort through an apparent miscommunication. Mostly, however, the letters chronicle a love affair that transpired more through mail and conversation than through physical consummation. The letters display a complicated romantic bond built across prison walls and through a shared commitment to revolution.[107]

By using these letters as evidence, the prosecution charged that Davis was captive to lust. She was not capable of love in a full human sense. Her love was violent and criminal. By using her love letters to Jackson to demonstrate a criminal conspiracy, the prosecution foreclosed the possibility of black romantic intimacy. Because the letters were written while Davis was in jail, nearly a year after the crime for which she stood accused, her attorneys argued that they were irrelevant to her state of mind prior to or on August 7. After much legal wrangling, the judge allowed a two-and-a-half-page excerpt to be introduced into the trial, and the prosecution read that excerpt as its last piece of evidence before resting its case. Davis and her attorneys and supporters argued that the letters should be excluded from evidence on the basis of their deeply personal contents. They not only called the prosecutor's strategy insensitive and unconvincing but argued that turning love letters into legal evidence reproduced the slave-system logic of rendering black women's sexuality illegitimate. Slavery had defined its female captives as sexual objects who lacked rational capacities. Here, in the denial of black love, was the gendered racism of the larger criminal justice system hearkening back to the plantation logic of black women's licentious sexuality.[108]

The prosecutor's argument revolved around the idea that Davis's unchecked sexual passion led her to conspire to free Jackson, "sacrificing" his brother and other prisoners in the process.[109] The defense responded by asserting black sexual humanity. The first and most eloquent voice to do so was Davis herself. She analyzed the historical origins and continuing salience of such discourse even prior to the prosecutor's attempt to use her letters in court. In a 1971 article written in the Marin County Jail, Davis offered an indirect response to this focus on black women's bodies such as hers. "Reflections on the Black Woman's Role in the Community of Slaves," one of several intellectual efforts Davis made during this period to theorize slavery and freedom, was an attempt to counter the "black matriarch" thesis, popular since the 1965 Moynihan Report and echoed in a variety of putatively leftist organizations, that blamed black women for black poverty. Davis called that position "an open weapon of ideological warfare" developed by the southern elite.[110] A towering intellectual contribution made all the more significant given the conditions of its creation, the essay shifted the focus away from armed revolt as the only form of challenging slavery, whether in the nineteenth century or the twentieth. Davis argued that "survival-oriented activities were themselves a form of resistance. Survival, moreover, was the prerequisite of all higher levels of struggle."[111] Further, in describing the plantation's gendered division of labor, in which women and men worked in the fields but only women did domestic labor for both white masters and black slaves, Davis offered a much-needed feminist rendering of traditional accounts of slave life.

While the essay influenced the study of slavery for decades to come, its immediate impact was to redirect the conversation about black women's activism. For a Left concerned about black women's role, Davis depicted them as an ever-present revolutionary force that, as scholar Alys Weinbaum put it, "routinely *provoked* and *countered* counterinsurgency." Davis showed reproduction to be as important as production in the ecology of racism. Reproduction, understood as a range of survival strategies from childbirth to emotional support and beyond, must therefore be central to antiracist opposition.[112]

Davis's essay was a response to the conservative gender politics of mainstream and leftist common sense about black women and specifically to George Jackson's depictions. Davis asserted in a preface that at the time of his death, "George was uniquely aware of the need to extricate himself and other black men from the remnants of divisive and destructive myths purporting to represent the black woman as a revolutionary duty, but also, and equally important, as an expression of his boundless love for all black women."[113] Jackson's death makes evaluating this claim impossible. Jackson's posthumously published volume, *Blood in My Eye*, continues a universal masculine subject and makes no strong reference to women's liberation. Davis subsequently remarked on how much she "did not know" about gender and feminism at the time.[114]

As an institution that often racially segregated its already sex-segregated subjects, the prison was (and is) intensely gendered. Sensitivity to sexism or to women's liberation within men's prisons was a challenging enterprise. That women comprised the base of emotional support for individual male prisoners and organized outside political support for prisoners interrupted the total masculinity of these prisons and motivated a few male prisoners to express concern for women's labor. Yet for most, their definition of slavery was one shaped heavily by the sex-segregated world of the prison.

The most dramatic articulation of slavery in the Davis case came from Branton's closing argument to the court. Branton used slavery to make sense of Davis's predicament and to show how race structured views of the criminal justice system. In Branton's exquisite telling, blackness developed through a rejection of prisons, much as carceral frameworks produced whiteness. The prison contributed to fashioning political identities, whether reparative or punitive. He likened Davis's case to that of Frederick Douglass, who fled to Canada after being charged with conspiracy in the wake of John Brown's 1859 raid on Harpers Ferry as part of a war against slavery. Branton argued that Douglass, like Davis, was charged only for "having spoken so eloquently on the right of all men to be free." According to Branton, "no black person in this world" would wonder why Davis fled, "only why she allowed herself to be caught."[115] And, Branton argued, he shared in this experience of slavery: "As a black person, you realize that the chains of slavery, visible or invisible, are still there in your everyday life." To ensure that jurors would judge the case fairly and understand "what it is about the history of this country which has made an Angela Davis," Branton asked the jury to "think black with me, to be black." Branton concluded by relieving jurors of "that responsibility" but admonished them that he did "not relieve you of your responsibility to be fair and just human beings in spite of the fact that you are not black."[116]

Before ending his statement, Branton made a move to restore the humanity to black sexuality that the prosecution sought to criminalize. He had Dalton Trumbo, a Hollywood screenwriter and member of the blacklisted Hollywood 10 whom Branton had defended against the House Un-American Activities

Committee in 1947, turn the excerpt of Davis's letter to Jackson that the prosecution had entered into evidence into a poem. He read the poem to the jury, arguing that it showed only Davis's ability to express emotion. Branton's playful rhetoric, temporarily impaneling an all-black jury, defined blackness as a conceptual orientation to social justice. Through his use of poetry and the licensing of black identity, he depicted Davis as a brilliant scholar, a dedicated activist, and a slave with a loving heart.[117]

The trial had begun on February 28, 1972, the same day that the two remaining Soledad Brothers, John Clutchette and Fleeta Drumgo, were acquitted in the death of Soledad guard John Mills. On June 4, Davis, too, was found innocent. Several news stories pointed to Branton's powerful closing statement as articulating the racial drama embedded in the case. Some jurors were moved to tears, though others maintained that the statement had no impact. Harris told journalists that Davis's acquittal, which he attributed in part to Branton's closing statement, represented an expression of "white guilt."[118]

Whereas her supporters had defined the case as an instance of persecution and enslavement, some critics opined that her acquittal vindicated America's judiciary. Within mainstream political discourse, the exonerated prisoner showed that the system worked, that claims of repression—much less slavery—were hyperbolic protestations from people who, in the words of California governor Ronald Reagan, "ought to sit down and think a little bit about whether they want to run around and stage any more demonstrations again."[119] The conservative *Los Angeles Times* editorialized that the "meticulous fairness of the court proceedings [including an all-white jury in a mostly white town] refuted the claims of the propagandists, here and abroad, who so monotonously asserted that it is not possible for a black militant to receive a fair trial in the United States."[120] Reagan, long a foe of Davis, also said that the verdict "vindicated" the criminal justice system against critics who "have found the United States and our system of justice guilty without a trial."[121] In London, one writer responded to the acquittal by writing a cynical and shortsighted eulogy for Davis: had she been convicted, she would have become a martyr, but, he argued, in legal innocence her political symbolism had died.[122]

"SYMBOLS OF SLAVERY"

With journalists and critics debating her symbolism, Angela Davis continued her organizing. Immediately after her acquittal, Davis expressed her commitment to keep fighting against the prison system and for the freedom of political prisoners.[123] As she had done during her trial, Davis attempted to redirect the attention focused on her to support other prisoners. Eleven months after her acquittal, she participated in the founding of the National Alliance against Racist and Political Repression (NAARPR). Built on the foundation laid by NU-CFAD, which had grown to almost one hundred chapters in the United States and a few dozen internationally by the time the case concluded, the NAARPR was a coalition of organizations from across the country. The NAARPR revived the Communist Party's earlier efforts to build mass defense campaigns. Many top alliance leaders were members of the party, but it did not control the NAARPR's work.[124]

The NAARPR was dedicated to a broad range of efforts in support of prisoners, and it fought against numerous policies attached to the burgeoning law-and-order ideology. The NAARPR especially emphasized the South: it organized support for the Wilmington 10, ten men and women, nine of them black, who were charged with firebombing a North Carolina grocery store during a 1971 riot. (The most well-known of the group was the Reverend Ben Chavis, who was a fellow traveler.) The NAARPR was also active in the campaign to support Joan Little, a black woman accused of murder in the self-defense slaying of a prison guard who sexually assaulted her. After a massive campaign involving dozens of antiracist, feminist, and other leftist organizations, Little became the first woman acquitted of murder on the grounds that she had been defending herself against rape. Her case provided a black feminist framework for defense campaigns in a series of similar cases.[125]

A multiracial, multi-issue coalition of progressive and radical organizations, the NAARPR did not view its efforts as primarily a battle against slavery. Rather, in the blend of radical antiracism and civil libertarianism that has characterized much of the party's history in confronting political repression, it emphasized broad opposition to state and, in the wake of a resurgent Ku Klux Klan, vigilante violence.[126] Emerging at a time of widespread political uncertainty, the NAARPR was one of several attempts to engage with the role of police and imprisonment in American society. Major trials involving Native Americans, antiwar activists, feminists, black liberationists, and others continued through the first half of the 1970s. Together with revelations about the massive corruption inside the Nixon White House, these cases contributed to ongoing public debates about state repression.

Black opponents of imprisonment continued to define slavery as their enemy. Magee again protested his "enslavement" when his trial resumed in late 1972 after Davis's acquittal. Without Davis to anchor public attention, Magee's small support base attracted much less notice than had previously been the case. Magee continued to frustrate the attorneys and judges with

Angela Davis speaks at a rally after her release, ca. 1972. After Davis was acquitted, her defense campaign became the National Alliance against Racist and Political Repression. For another decade, with Davis as a leading member, the group worked for the freedom of political prisoners and against the expanded U.S. carceral state. Photo © 2014 Stephen Shames/Polaris Images.

his intransigence and his outbursts in court; on one occasion, he overturned the defense table and spit on the presiding judge after one of his motions was denied.[127] Fearing another acquittal, prosecutors dropped the conspiracy charge against Magee and refrained from discussing the Soledad Brothers case. Magee served as his own attorney yet again, this time with former U.S. attorney general Ramsey Clark as cocounsel. After a six-month trial, the jury voted 11–1 to acquit Magee on the murder charge and 11–1 to one to convict on the kidnapping charge. Juror Moses Shepard, a black man, said, "I don't think Magee was guilty of anything."[128] Hopelessly deadlocked, the judge declared a mistrial. Prosecutors subsequently dropped the murder charge, and when the retrial on the kidnapping charge began on May 11, 1974, Magee pleaded guilty. He tried to withdraw the plea three days later, but the judge refused the request, and Magee received another life sentence.[129]

So why was Ruchell Magee convicted (again) and sentenced to life in prison (again), while Angela Davis walked free? Magee was an active participant in the day's events, whereas Davis's connection was at best obscure and indirect: Magee was photographed holding guns against hostages, and he was found at the scene next to a judge whose face had been blown off by a shotgun blast. Magee owned his participation as a badge of honor, whereas the Davis legal team cast their client as a victim of state repression whose connection to the event in question was merely circumstantial. Further, Magee's resistance to counsel may have been understandable in light of his previous experiences, but it put him in a difficult situation. His brash style earned him few friends, especially in court, and his erratic behavior cast doubt on his earlier pleas. His lengthy rap sheet, the fact that he was already serving a life sentence, and his frequent disruptions of the proceedings counted against him. In short, she cut a more sympathetic figure than he did. A proud partisan in the war between prisoners and their keepers, Magee stood little chance of earning the sympathy of the court. That he escaped the death penalty, defeated the more serious charges against him, and wore down the prosecution during multiple trials was as close to victory as Magee would come. With another life sentence added to his record, the erratic Magee had lost many of the supporters who had rallied to his defense after George Jackson's death.

However, Magee remained a legal resource for some prisoners at San Quentin. In fact, the six prisoners charged for the violence accompanying Jackson's death had initially requested Magee as their attorney.[130] In October 1971, a grand jury indicted seven men on a total of forty-six charges of murder, assault, and conspiracy related to the deaths of the three guards and two prisoners. Six of those charged—Hugo Pinell, Johnny Larry Spain, Luis Talamantez, Fleeta Drumgo, David Johnson, and Willie Sundiata Tate—were black and Latino men in their twenties who were imprisoned at the San Quentin Adjustment Center.

The seventh, Stephen Bingham, was also in his twenties but was a white attorney from a well-to-do family. Bingham maintained his innocence, and like Angela Davis, went underground when he learned what happened to Jackson. He ultimately fled the country, living in France until 1984, when he returned to the United States and turned himself in to stand trial. In 1986, Bingham, again like Davis, was acquitted of all charges.

The rest of the San Quentin 6, as the group was known, vowed to fight the case collectively. Though some of the men had not known each other before Jackson's death, all were friendly with Jackson, and all were well-known dissidents in the California prison system. Drumgo had been one of the Soledad Brothers. Johnson and Tate, along with Magee and others, had worked to expose and protest the February 1970 killing of Fred Billingslea by San Quentin guards. All three had long histories of activism inside of prisons. Johnson, the only one of the six who had a history of organized political activism prior to his incarceration, had been a member of the US organization in the mid-1960s. While in prison, Johnson found that his sympathies lay more with the Black Panthers and their supporters; when the Panthers split, he turned his loyalties to the Black Liberation Army.

Spain had participated in work strikes in prison and had joined the Black Panthers shortly before Jackson was killed. Pinell, imprisoned since 1964 when he was nineteen, was a comrade of W. L. Nolen, who had been killed at Soledad in January 1970. Pinell's frequent altercations with prison guards led California attorney general Evelle Younger to call him "one of the most dangerous prisoners in the entire penal system."[131] Talamantez was a poet and peacemaker inside, with a special interest in world history. As Latinos—Pinell is Nicaraguan and Talamantez is Chicano—in what was seen as largely a black movement, the pair were also crucial in fostering some sense of racial unity among black and Latino prisoners against Aryan prison gangs and white guards.[132]

The grand jury split about whether to indict the men. Seven of the nineteen jurors voted against the indictment; in protest, three left the session and one of them resigned. "What this grand jury does isn't justice but vengeance," one of the jurors charged. "This grand jury reflects society, which it represents, which is suffering from racism, paranoia and economic bias."[133] These jurors' reactions seemed to confirm the prisoners' claims that the state was interested not in finding the guilty parties but in eliminating political organizing by targeting George Jackson's comrades and associates. The six men argued that the grand jury did not constitute a jury of their peers or a fair cross-section of the community since it lacked blacks or Latinos, members of the "low wage blue collar class," and San Quentin prisoners, formerly incarcerated people, or those with criminal backgrounds. But the prosecutors got the twelve votes they needed to secure an indictment. In response, the San Quentin Six Defense Committee published a pamphlet describing the twelve jurors who had voted yes, with the pointed title "Whose Peers?" The pamphlet featured a drawing of a black man gagged and shackled.[134]

The San Quentin 6 case was one of the most significant episodes in the 1970s to place the prison at the heart of multiracial struggles for justice. It ranked alongside prison riots, which typically resulted in temporary truces among nearly all prisoners, regardless of race, as a source of antiracist mobilization against the divisive domination of imprisonment. As the incarceration rate began its steady climb in the early 1970s—from 161 U.S. residents in prisons and jails per 100,000 people in 1972 to 767 per 100,000 people by 2007, representing a growth of 500 percent—prisons continued to be perceived as bastions of interracial violence. But the racial makeup of the San Quentin 6, along with the fact that they had earned the respect of several white prisoners, undermined the district attorney's attempt to paint the events of August 21 as a race war.[135]

Their unity also challenged the racial animosities that were becoming increasingly important elements of prison governance. The case came to trial at a time of rising tensions between black and Chicano prisoners at San Quentin and throughout the California penal system. These rifts included gang warfare between black, Chicano, and white prisoners, with the two main Chicano gangs—Nuestra Familia and the Mexican Mafia—falling on opposite sides of the divide between the Aryan Brotherhood and black militants.[136] Pinell and Talamantez, friends of Jackson and defendants in a case involving his legacy, offered the possibility for black-brown unity in the context of antiracist mobilization against state violence. Because the case included two Latinos, various Latino organizations took an interest. Support for the San Quentin 6 appeared in an array of Chicano papers as well as in leftist media and prison-based publications.[137]

Once indicted, the men struggled to be represented by the attorneys of their choice. A judge initially appointed attorneys to represent them, against the wishes of both the attorneys and their clients. A 1973 letter signed by Father Daniel Berrigan, Congressman Ronald Dellums, and journalist Jessica Mitford and sponsored by a number of other notable individuals, among them Maya Angelou, Howard Zinn, and two members of the Marin County grand jury, solicited contributions to help the men secure their own attorneys.[138] The case also attracted several veteran political lawyers, including Black Panther attorney Charles Garry, who represented Spain, as well as competent public defenders. Talamantez was briefly represented by Oscar Acosta, a flashy attorney who had worked with the civil rights movement while in law school, had represented several activists in the Chicano movement, and was immortalized as Hunter S. Thompson's sidekick, "Dr. Gonzo," in the drug-infused *Fear and Loathing in Las Vegas*. Talamantez ultimately settled on Robert Carrow, a former mayor of Novato and onetime lawyer for Ruchell Magee who was a calm and thorough litigator. Only Pinell represented himself, with the help of a legal adviser. Several of the lawyers later said that their involvement provided them with an invaluable political education.[139]

Though each defendant was free to pursue his own line of inquiry in the case, the men agreed to fight the case together. Initially, they declined to enter any kind of plea, trying to stall or stop the trial through intransigence. They wanted to stand trial together, to support one another's motions and positions in court and in dealing with the prison system. Among their strategies, the San

San Quentin 6 defendants (front to back) Fleeta Drumgo, Hugo Pinell, and David Johnson stage an impromptu sit-in at San Quentin in July 1975. San Quentin 6 trial jurors toured the prison, accompanied by a photographer. Upon seeing the group approach, the three shackled men sat down in protest. Photographer unknown.

Quentin 6 endeavored to put the prison system on trial. Mobilizing a critique of prison slavery, they sought to vacate their indictment on the grounds that the grand jury's composition had been biased. They also went on the offensive with an ambitious lawsuit that challenged the abusive conditions at the San Quentin AC. This approach enabled them to survive five years of trial, during which time they were routinely subjected to tear-gas assaults by guards and constant shackling. It also allowed them to make a case against prison slavery.[140]

In 1974, Judge Vernon Stoll dismissed the indictment because of the all-white composition of the grand jury. The case was held up for almost a year before an appeals court overturned Stoll's ruling, and the trial of the San Quentin 6 finally began on March 25, 1975, at the Marin County Courthouse. The jurors included eight women and four men, eleven of them white and one black. The specter of slavery loomed large over the case, especially through the state's techniques of control. The men hoped, like their predecessors, to use the courtroom to bring prison conditions to light: the long-term isolation, the repression of political activity, the constant humiliation and threat of death. These routine functions of life in disciplinary custody, they said, amounted to slavery.

The accoutrements of slavery were everywhere visible and modernized in the San Quentin 6 case. Judge Henry Broderick authorized that the men be shackled for the length of the trial after jurors said that the sight of men in chains would not be prejudicial. At various points, the defendants were chained not just at the hands and feet but also at the hips and neck. Spain, a Black Panther and the only one of the defendants who had left the Adjustment Center with Jackson, was at times chained more heavily than the others. Police also shaved the heads of the five imprisoned defendants (Tate had been released on bail two months earlier), further displaying them as wards of the state. In Tate's view, the trial was dominated by the "symbols of slavery."[141] After fighting for their right to legal self-representation, the men fought for their physical self-representation—their bodily integrity in court. All of the defendants except Tate "appeared in court chained and shackled to their chairs," which were bolted to the floor. The five men "were transported together from San Quentin to the Hall of Justice in a specially constructed bus in which each was enclosed in a separate compartment. In the courtroom they sat behind a bulletproof screen." The divider was thick enough that spectators needed a public address system to hear the proceedings.[142]

The judge required all spectators to pass through metal detectors, submit to body searches, and present valid identification. In addition to such visible surveillance, the San Francisco FBI office covertly monitored attendees to make sure that the "political overtones" of the case did not stoke violent responses.[143] Authorities claimed that the additional security was necessary because of the defendants, their charges, and the fact that the trial was taking place in the same courtroom where Jonathan Jackson had staged his 1970 raid. (For security reasons, Ruchell Magee was initially transported to his trial by helicopter.) Nonetheless, supporters of the six men argued, in now familiar terms, that public witnessing comprised a collective battle against slavery. "Whether they are treated as men rather than animals or slaves depends on us . . . It is a fight for all of us," urged a pamphlet on their behalf.[144] Several attorneys and civil liberties groups said that the conditions violated the sentiment of the constitutional guarantee of speedy public trials.[145]

This treatment continued outside of court: lawyers for the men protested that their clients were chained and separated from their attorneys by an acrylic plastic barrier during meetings to discuss the case, forcing participants to yell to be heard. This arrangement, according to the attorneys, violated

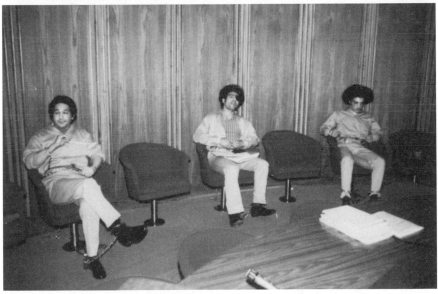

The San Quentin 6 on trial, ca. 1976. In the top photo, *left to right*, David Johnson and Fleeta Drùmgo sit and Willie Sundiata Tate stands in front of the hard plastic barrier that authorities erected to separate the defendants from spectators. Tate had been released on bail and so is not shackled, though Johnson and Drumgo are. In the bottom photo, *left to right*, Bato Talamantez, Hugo Pinell, and Johnny Larry Spain sit shackled during the trial. Drumgo, Talamantez, and Tate were acquitted of all charges. Johnson and Pinell were convicted of assault. Spain was convicted of murder. From the defense files of the *People of California v. Bingham, Pinell, et al.* trial records; courtesy of Larry Weiss.

attorney-client privilege by making the content of their meetings known to the guards stationed directly outside the room.[146]

Moreover, the prisoners were routinely beaten, and tear gas canisters similar to the ones soldiers used in Vietnam were fired into their cells. To dilute the gas and prevent it from burning their eyes so intensely, the men would shove their heads into their toilets. On one occasion, the men were gassed so heavily that when they reached the courtroom, the judge and attorneys turned red and began coughing. The judge refused to acknowledge that gas had been used but nevertheless adjourned a recess.[147]

The San Quentin 6 and their lawyers called witnesses to talk about the psychological effects of long-term solitary confinement, physical abuse, and white supremacy. Among those witnesses was University of California at Berkeley sociologist Robert Blauner, author of an influential 1969 article that described urban uprisings as a response to the "internal colonialism" black people faced. Another was Philip Zimbardo, a Stanford University social psychologist who had conducted a 1971 experiment that found that prison guards were prone to abuse and prisoners to depression.[148] During an often boisterous trial, the six men and their attorneys sought to expose a government plot against George Jackson and the dissident prisoners of the AC. The crux of the argument was that abominable prison conditions had caused the August 21 violence, regardless of who was individually responsible for the deaths of the three guards and two prisoners. More specifically, they argued that the government had conspired to kill Jackson, sacrificing the lives of the six men on trial and the other five men killed on August 21 in pursuit of this end. Testifying under oath in his own defense, Pinell claimed that the melee started after San Quentin guards pulled a gun on Jackson as he returned from his visit with Bingham.[149]

One defense witness, put on the stand by Garry on behalf of Spain, seemed to confirm the existence of a government plot. Louis Tackwood, a self-proclaimed informant for the Los Angeles Police Department, testified that he worked for a special section of the LAPD dedicated to destroying black radicalism, especially the prison movement. He revealed his role as a police informant in October 1971. Tackwood wanted to tell the truth about the prison system the way Daniel Ellsberg had done about the Vietnam War by releasing the Pentagon Papers. His revelations came seven months after antiwar activists had broken into a Pennsylvania FBI office, stolen documents related to its secret counterintelligence program (COINTELPRO), and leaked them to the media. Tackwood told his story to journalists at the radical *Los Angeles Free Press*, who joined with others to form the Citizen Research and Investigation Committee, which first verified his claims and then publicized them. Avon Books, publisher of 1970s best sellers *Jonathan Livingston Seagull* and *I'm Okay, You're Okay*, released Tackwood's book. *The Glass House Tapes* (1973), was part of a wave of popular books in which lawyers, journalists, scholars, and activists detailed the enormity of covert police intervention against social movements.[150]

In that climate, Tackwood's allegations were riveting, revealing, and bizarre. He said he had begun working for the Los Angeles Police Department in 1962 to avoid going to jail for stealing cars. Police evidently thought him a natural choice to bring down the prison movement: he was married to the sister of James Carr, one of George Jackson's best friends. The events Tackwood described explain some of the paranoia, violence, and bad luck that befell the prison movement. Tackwood was a confusing character, though, and it was hard to know what to make of some of his claims, including the most explosive one: his final assignment was smuggling a gun into San Quentin so that guards would have a reason to kill George Jackson.[151]

Tackwood claimed to have been present in early August when two officers from a covert LAPD unit smuggled a broken gun into San Quentin with the help of a guard. The gun was to be given to Jackson, thereby enabling guards to kill him in what would be described as an escape attempt. While some of Tackwood's claims were compelling, he was a confusing and contradictory witness. Jurors—and, privately, several members of the defense team—had mixed views about whether to trust any of his testimony.[152]

During the criminal trial, the San Quentin 6 scored a victory in federal court when Judge Alfonso Zirpoli ruled in December 1975 that the San Quentin AC was "cruel and unusual punishment in violation of the Eighth and Fourteenth amendments."[153] At the end of 1973, Spain had filed a writ protesting the AC's solitary confinement, shackling, and abuse. That writ found its way to attorneys Mark Merin and Fred Hiestand, who took the case and launched a major investigation into the San Quentin Adjustment Center. The resulting case, *Spain v. Procunier*, provided the testing ground for a challenge to the tools of slavery. The case centered on the physical restraints routinely used against the six: tear gas, shackling when they were out of their cells, and other restrictions on their mobility, including the denial of outdoor exercise. The case relied on the six men's testimony as well as a barrage of medical evaluations and expert testimony about the intersections of racism, physical abuse, and psychological torture. The court found in the plaintiffs' favor, providing a stunning if relatively short-lived victory for prisoner rights.[154]

The San Quentin 6 criminal trial concluded just months after their victory in federal court. The criminal trial had lasted seventeen months; the jury deliberated for another four months, making it the longest trial in California history. At two million dollars, it was also the most expensive trial up to that time.[155] The verdict came on August 13, 1976, almost exactly five years after the incident that had sparked the case. The verdict failed to vindicate either side in full. Drumgo, Talamantez, and Tate were acquitted on all charges, so Tate immediately became a free man. Talamantez was paroled one week later, having spent eleven years in prison, and Drumgo was released on August 25 after nine years behind bars.[156] Spain was found guilty of conspiracy and two counts of murder, while Pinell was convicted of two counts of felony assault, and Johnson was convicted of felony assault on a guard. Johnson received a suspended sentence and three years probation, and he was released from prison shortly after Drumgo. Had it not been for this case, Johnson, Drumgo, and Talamantez would likely have been paroled years earlier. Both Spain, the youngest of the defendants at twenty-six, and Pinell, thirty, were sentenced to life in prison. Prison activist and journalist Karen Wald hypothesized that the mixed verdict was a product of a mid-1970s political culture in which people doubted both the powerful and the powerless. Spain was released on appeal in 1988 after Bingham's 1986 acquittal undermined his conspiracy conviction. Pinell remains in prison.[157]

The responses of Ruchell Magee and the San Quentin 6 to their respective cases were examples of a well-worn global tradition of radical attempts to repurpose the courtroom for political protest. These cases coincided with an increase in prisoner use of the court system to litigate the conditions of confinement. In 1974, the U.S. Supreme Court declared, "There is no iron curtain drawn between the Constitution and the prisons of this country."[158] In 1980, prisoners had filed 12,718 civil rights claims in court, compared to 218 such suits filed in 1966. As with the plethora of legal actions that the NAACP and others filed in the fight against segregation two decades earlier, these suits attempted to use the courts to improve conditions. Civil rights litigation on behalf of prisoners, launched partly in response to the lessons of Attica and the Soledad Brothers, created vital protections for incarcerated people and moved the struggle for prisoner rights firmly into the judicial realm as grassroots prison organizing receded.[159] For a time, these cases turned the courts into a viable and oft-utilized mechanism to safeguard certain rights of people in prison.

However, the rising tide of law and order and the murky waters of economic recession soon washed away much of the popular support for prison organizing as a frontline struggle against the American racial state. As prisoners achieved their hearing in the nation's highest courts, often by drawing connections between carceral confinement and enslavement, they lost their footing in the larger public imagination. Instead, radical prisoners had to find other means of engaging the public, other ways of retaining their connections to worlds outside the walls.

CHAPTER SIX

Prison Nation

The fate of the black prisoner has always been intrically [*sic*] tied
up with the fate of the imprisoned black nation and vice versa. In each
instance, "gaining our freedom" remains the primary concern.
—SUNDIATA ACOLI, "The Black Prisoner" (1979)

George Jackson's death gave many people imprisoned in the early 1970s a new life. Jackson had been the most effective spokesperson for prisoner grievances, and his death meant that new voices of discontent would need to emerge. One person who took up this challenge was Robert Lee Duren, who had been in prison since 1968. Prior to his incarceration, he had not expressed any interest in politics. His story was an increasingly familiar one: reared in poverty, he came of age amid gangs and widespread violence and ultimately got involved in increasingly antisocial behavior. In 1969, he was convicted of killing five people in the course of robberies in Los Angeles and sentenced to death.[1]

On August 21, 1971, he was confined at San Quentin's death row, two floors above the Adjustment Center. Like everyone else there, he knew of the famous prisoners who were confined below him: Bato Talamantez, Ruchell Magee, Fleeta Drumgo, John Clutchette, and of course George Jackson. After police had regained control of the Adjustment Center, they were in a fury about the dead and wounded guards. According to Duren, guards slammed the cell doors of the Adjustment Center so hard that the vibrations reached the third floor.

Three days later, Duren saw Fleeta Drumgo on the afternoon news removing his shirt in court to show the judge the cigarette burns he had received from vengeful guards over the previous seventy-two hours. A half hour later, Drumgo and Clutchette were back at San Quentin and the guards turned up the exhaust fans as loud as possible—possibly to hide Drumgo's screams. "We could hear it anyway," Duren recalls. Duren flushed the toilet to create a vacuum, enabling him to communicate with Talamantez in the Adjustment Center below him. "Are Fleeta and John back from court?" he asked. "Yes,"

Talamantez replied. "Was that Fleeta they're beating?" Duren shouted down the toilet. Again the response came in the affirmative. "I got off the line then," Duren says, ceasing his questions so as to avoid drawing attention to their surreptitious communication.

After a sympathetic guard told them how to reach federal judge Alfonso Zirpoli, Duren joined with other prisoners to draft a letter of protest about the violence at San Quentin. They sent it on August 26 but received no response. Duren felt helpless, defeated. He cried because "there was nothing to do." Then he looked at a collage in his cell: it showed Frederick Douglass, Martin Luther King Jr., and another black radical, probably Malcolm X. And Duren had a vision. "Angela Davis on the left, Malcolm X on the right, and Martin Luther King Jr. in the middle. Reverend King pointed his finger at me and said, 'Get up, nigga. Nigga, get up!' I felt this powerful surge of strength well up in me. I got off the bunk, faced the direction I thought his office was located, and said, 'Warden, you might be god of this prison, but I will never bow down to you.'" Then he wrote another letter to the judge, solidifying a life of oppositional writing. He had joined the prison movement.

With the death penalty temporarily abrogated in 1972, Duren was moved from death row to the main line. In the coming years, he came to know many of San Quentin's radicals, including former Black Panthers Geronimo ji Jaga Pratt and Jalil Muntaqim. Duren was a member of the prison chapter of the Panthers until fallout from the party's 1971–72 split made the Panther label largely irrelevant to those outside of Oakland. Tensions within the party looked different to those in prison. Many of the incarcerated Panthers were sympathetic to or members of the Black Liberation Army (BLA), the party's military offshoot. They opposed Huey P. Newton's growing authoritarianism, drug use, and consolidation of party resources into the Oakland chapter. They especially opposed Newton's lavish apartment and the Panthers' involvement in local electoral politics, which included running Bobby Seale and Elaine Brown as candidates for office. The Panthers turned BLA members shared with Jackson's imprisoned contemporaries a revolutionary analysis but often differed about strategies and tactics, and several of Jackson's associates and students, most of whom had found politics after entering prison, organized themselves under the mantle of the Black Guerrilla Family (BGF).

Duren followed the lead of the Panthers he knew. He began to communicate with organizers outside of prison, too. Some of his letters and articles were read on Berkeley's KPFA radio by sympathetic left-wing journalists. Duren's life changed thoroughly as a result of his newfound political passions. Around 1975, Robert Duren converted to Islam and renamed himself Kalima ("one with the word") Aswad ("the word"). Islam was reemerging as both a political and spiritual path for black prisoners. The Nation of Islam had fallen out of favor among many black militants in the early 1960s as a result of its antipolitical stance and its split with Malcolm X, but it experienced a resurgence with the death of Elijah Muhammad in 1975 and the conversion of the organization to traditional Sunni practice by Muhammad's son and successor, Warith Deen. In prison, the NOI remained more politically passive, but Sunni Islam was gaining ground among politically conscious black prisoners. Islam, like other spiritual or political cosmologies, provided prisoners with a connection to communities beyond confinement. As prisoners learned to read Arabic and to care about the Arab world, Islam also facilitated a growing consciousness much in the same way Third World Marxism did. Several prisoners worked to join the two philosophies.[2]

Aswad's turn to Islam followed on the heels of the conversions of several other well-known black radicals, including Black Panther Anthony Bottom (now Jalil Muntaqim), former SNCC chair H. Rap Brown (now Jamil Al-Amin), and Revolutionary Action Movement cofounder Max Stanford (now Muhammad Ahmad).[3] Aswad's conversion signified his growing political involvement. His story shows the ongoing power of conversion, political and religious, for black prisoners during the end of the civil rights era in the mid- to late 1970s. As a writer, Aswad contributed to the ongoing preservation of prison-based print culture. He furtively distributed reports on prison conditions via handwritten notes. Then, with the help of black nationalists and white anti-imperialists in the Bay Area, Aswad and a small team of prisoners launched a newspaper, *Arm the Spirit*, that was one of several prison-based revolutionary nationalist publications that connected black prisoners to supporters and struggles on the outside. His role at the helm of one of the era's most significant prisoner newspapers shows the innovative use of self-reliance strategies among dissident prisoners.

The prison had ceased to capture public attention as it had a few years earlier. Mainstream newspapers generally no longer had beat reporters for prison issues, and undercover journalists no longer got jobs in prisons to report on conditions inside. Those newspapers that had not lost interest in prison issues in the face of growing cries for law and order found that wardens increasingly blocked access to prisoners in hopes of avoiding publicity and eliminating opportunities for prisoners to communicate with the outside world. Journalist Jessica Mitford joined a lawsuit against Washington State's McNeil Island prison after the warden there refused to allow her to interview prisoners involved in a February 1971 strike. The suit was settled in June 1973, when the Ninth Circuit Court of Appeals upheld the prison's right to deny journalists access. Having confirmed their power to control access, officials held an open house for journalists in early 1974.[4] The message was clear: if prisoners were to remain connected to any outside public, they would need their own media.

The story of the radical prisoner print culture of the late 1970s is only just beginning to be told. The existence of this vibrant print culture challenges the received wisdom of the prison movement, which holds that prisons became politically barren by mid-decade.[5] But prison radicalism did not disappear in a fit of self-destructive violence in the wake of George Jackson's death or the bloody defeat of the Attica rebellion. It continued, smaller and more divided but persistent. The acquisition of literacy, self-education, and knowledge production remain a vital legacy of black prison organizing. In struggling to access and promote literacy, dissident prisoners affirmed that knowledge—as an active, living process of engagement—gives life meaning. Indeed, prisoner literacy in this context included both basic skills and political sophistication.[6]

Print culture was the backbone of prison organizing in the second half of the 1970s. These publications marked a new era in prison politics, enabling prisoners to continue functioning as political actors—to read the news, write their opinions, and debate political theory—after the high tide of prison organizing had ebbed. They provided prisoners with a means to define the issues on their terms. With less public backing and little in the way of a mass movement to support them, prisoners used media to sustain connections with other prisoners and with sympathetic outsiders. As collective action became more difficult, writing and editing provided an opportunity for politically conscious prisoners to continue working collaboratively with others on both sides of the prison walls. While publications provided the most consistent outlet for these alliances, they also manifested in several prisoner-initiated petitions to the United Nations.

This turn to media production coincided with dissident prisoners' increased emphasis on revolutionary nationalism. With growing isolation inside prison and growing conservatism outside, revolutionary nationalism was one vital lifeline for intractable militants. Through appeals to unite the "black nation," prisoners, especially black men, proposed large-scale solutions that positioned themselves as the best spokespeople for black people generally. Through newspapers and other writings, prisoners hoped to demonstrate the existence of a captive nation, consolidate political opinion among their rank, bolster a flagging black protest movement, and solidify alliances with a wide array of groups and communities. In short, dissident prisoners used print culture in the same way that nationalist movements historically have.[7]

Nationalism provided the framework for prisoners to connect with one another, to forge alliances outside of prison, and to identify with popular struggles across the world. A subset of a larger prison movement, black prison nationalism was part and parcel of the Third World liberation struggles of the 1970s. In Ireland and South Africa, Palestine and Puerto Rico, the battle lines of anticolonialism were more sharply drawn in the 1970s. Both colonial powers and their antagonists grew more determined, resulting in increased violent conflict on all sides. The prisoner remained a global symbol of national struggle under these conditions, an icon of the desire for freedom from oppressive external rule.

Within the United States, the consolidation of black prison nationalism, largely in men's prisons, coincided with a rising tide of interest in prisoners among other social justice movements. Like earlier social movements, these movements worked to free those it considered political prisoners—whether defined as people incarcerated for their activism or as a result of the oppression they faced. Indeed, while prisoners faded from general public sympathy, many social movements—including those among indigenous and Puerto Rican communities as well as multiracial gay and feminist movements—challenged imprisonment in some fashion. The feminist and gay liberation critique of the prison built upon the analysis developed by the largely heterosexual, largely male prisoner writings of people such as George Jackson: the prison was a metaphor for the state and interpersonal violence that marginalized groups experienced as well as the physical place where such violence reached its logical conclusion. Yet out of that framework, these movements offered a more synthetic—later called "intersectional"—challenge to the prison. That is, they described oppression on a multidimensional axis that included gender and sexuality as well as class and race. And because women, gays, and lesbians often found themselves facing state violence through a wider range of institutions that included mental health hospitals, these movements developed a critique of what they called the "prison/psychiatric state."[8]

The prison was the precondition for antiracist feminist coalitions. Several prominent cases of the era—including women who defended themselves from physical abuse, such as Joan Little (North Carolina), Yvonne Wanrow (Washington), Inez Garcia (California), and Dessie Woods (Georgia)—joined lesser-known but still significant struggles over prison conditions stretching from the California Institution for Women in Chino to the federal penitentiary at Alderson, West Virginia, and beyond.[9] At the prison in Walla Walla, Washington, a group of prisoners, most of them gay, banded together and armed themselves to stop prison rape, calling themselves Men against Sexism. One of the founders of the group was Ed Mead, an avowed communist and revolutionary who was imprisoned for taking part in the George Jackson Brigade. A

Former San Quentin 6 defendants, *left to right*, Bato Talamantez, David Johnson, and Willie Sundiata Tate speak at a rally with Inez Garcia at the San Francisco Civic Center, November 1976. Garcia was charged with murder for killing one of two men who sexually assaulted her in 1974. She spent two years in prison before her conviction was overturned on appeal. Hers was one of several mid-1970s incidents that brought together a large coalition of activists challenging the prison as a site of racial and sexual oppression. From the Collection of the Freedom Archives.

small clandestine collective comprising several former prisoners, the George Jackson Brigade carried out a string of bombings, funded by bank robberies, in Seattle in the mid-1970s in support of unions, prisoners, and revolutionary movements around the world.[10]

Its influence on a larger field of prison organizing notwithstanding, black prison nationalism by the late 1970s no longer enjoyed primacy of place among many progressives. But it was not for lack of trying. Black prison nationalism synthesized long histories of black anti-imperialism, the dynamics of prison protest, and the currency of national liberation. Like other forms of anticolonialism, black prison nationalism was both a worldview and a code of behavior. It offered an explanation of imprisonment and a personal praxis for resisting it, each one rooted in an internationalist sensibility that saw the United Nations as a possible ally.

The typical nationalist theme of self-reliance gained added power in the repressive condition of imprisonment. Prison nationalism allowed its adherents to experience a measure of power and self-control in an environment structurally engineered to deny them both. This nationalism expressed itself primarily, though not exclusively, through the media. As the decade came to a close, nationalist prisoners in California initiated a holiday, Black August, that would allow them to build a collectivity emphasizing the prison as the breeding ground for white racism and black resistance. Together with the Black August holiday, newspapers such as *Arm the Spirit*, *Midnight Special*, and *The Fuse* defined the prison as the root of the black nation.

Black prison nationalism expressed itself through a mix of connectivity and self-reliance. This combination is not the paradox it might at first seem. Black communities survived segregation on the southern plantation and in the northern ghetto with a similar balance of autonomous self-help organizations (both religious and political) and networked associations. The prison thrives on segregation: it segregates prisoners from the outside world, and then segregates prisoners from one another based on assorted administrative protocols. Segregation is a mode of discipline that prison officials around the country used with increasing impunity to isolate prisoner organizing. Through media and ritual, prisoners sought to demonstrate their sovereignty in a place that sought to incapacitate them altogether.

Black prison nationalism developed alongside another nationalism focused on imprisonment—a conservative law-and-order nationalism that increasingly relied on prisons as the response to crime and other social problems. In markedly different ways, both forms of nationalism naturalized connections among blackness, imprisonment, and nation building. During the 1980s, these connections were legislated through the war on drugs and a massive spike in prison construction, the likes of which the world had never before seen. Yet before mass incarceration existed, before a variety of state concerns and economic interests converged on cages as their panacea, incarcerated black radicals located the prison as the premier institution of the American racial state. For them, the prison was the centerpiece of the nationalist imagination. It structured white nationalism and sustained black nationalism.

"FOUNDATIONS OF THE BLACK NATION"

The concept that black people were a colony domestic to the United States, "a nation within a nation," was a well-worn idea of the 1960s Black Power movement. This idea held that the pervasive history and ongoing structure of racism had bonded black people into a nationality. Black organizations, intellectuals, and politicians who disagreed on much else shared an analysis of their "national oppression." In 1962, poet Amiri Baraka proclaimed, "Black is a country." Ten years later, the Black Political Convention, held in Gary, Indiana, with the blessing of the city's first black mayor, declared that it was "Nation Time!" If white supremacy imprisoned black people, it was no surprise that some would see black prisoners—the most literal embodiment of this oppression—as spokespeople for the black nation.

The blossoming of a distinctly prison-based black nationalism owes a great deal to Republic of New Afrika (RNA). Formed in Detroit in 1968, the RNA had always looked south, seeing a black national homeland in five former slave states of the Deep South: Alabama, Georgia, Louisiana, Mississippi, and South Carolina. This position revived one held by the Communist Party in the 1930s and echoed by many of the small communist parties emerging in the 1970s, which held that the history of racial slavery and its afterlives had created a colonized people in the Cotton Belt South.[11] Unlike some of the communists, the RNA held that white supremacy colonized all black people everywhere. To them, the five states were not a base of oppression but the territory of a solution. At a time when popular attention to black politics focused on the urban North, the RNA turned its attention back to the Black Belt South. New Afrikans upheld the South as a more strategically defensible and historically authentic location of black politics than the city.[12]

The RNA consolidated several prominent themes of black radicalism in the twentieth century: cultural pride, anti-imperialism, spirituality, self-defense, self-governance, and economic uplift. The group attached these issues to its pursuit of reparations and a territorial homeland in the U.S. South. Its founders, Milton and Richard Henry (who renamed themselves Gaidi and Imari Obadele), had deep roots in Detroit and were leading figures in the rise of a national Black Power movement.

One of the group's principal advisers was Audley "Queen Mother" Moore, who had a long and storied career with the Black Left. Born in 1898, Moore joined Marcus Garvey's Universal Negro Improvement Association in New Orleans during the 1920s, and Garveyism influenced the rest of her life. Impressed with the Communist Party's defense of the Scottsboro Boys, Moore joined the CP in Harlem in the 1930s. She was a prominent fixture at party meetings, tenant campaigns, and street-corner speeches until she resigned from the party in 1950. She was also a lifelong member of the National Council of Negro Women, an intractable advocate for reparations, and a longtime supporter of black prisoners. In 1955, Moore, whose grandmother had been a slave, founded the Committee for Reparations for Descendants of U.S. Slaves. She mentored Malcolm X and members of the New York Black Panther Party. In 1968, four months shy of her seventieth birthday, Moore was one of the signers of the Republic of New Afrika's Declaration of Independence.[13]

Self-defense advocate Robert F. Williams was the group's first president, albeit more in name than function. Williams became director of the Monroe, North Carolina, branch of the NAACP in 1956. A military veteran, he advocated armed self-defense against white terrorism and offered weapons training to his chapter members. As a result of his militancy, the national NAACP leadership suspended him in 1959, and local white officials ran him out of town two years later. Framed on the typically ludicrous charges that characterized Jim Crow legality, Williams first fled to Michigan and then left the country, taking up residence in Cuba, Vietnam, and then China and Tanzania. From exile, he remained involved in and worked to internationalize the black American freedom struggle through writings and radio. The RNA helped coordinate his return to the United States in 1969, and he resigned his post with the group shortly thereafter.[14]

New Afrikan politics appealed to a broad cross-section of the black liberation movement. In addition to Williams and Moore, RNA founders Milton and Richard Henry could count as friends or mentors Malcolm X, militant activist-intellectuals James and Grace Lee Boggs, black nationalist minister Albert Cleage, and Kwame Nkrumah, the first president of an independent Ghana, who had attended Lincoln University with Milton Henry. At its founding, RNA officials included Muhammad Ahmad and Herman Ferguson of the Revolutionary Action Movement; Maulana Karenga of US (before he was expelled in 1969 after members of US killed two Black Panthers at UCLA); Amiri Baraka, then of the Committee for a Unified NewArk; H. Rap Brown of SNCC; and Malcolm X's widow, Betty Shabazz.

As an organization, the RNA joined the Black Arts cultural renaissance with the militancy of the Black Panther Party and a spiritual cosmology informed by different expressions of black Islam. Like the Black Arts movement, the RNA professed a connection with Africa yet remained firmly rooted in the United States.[15] The RNA shared the linguistic practices of many Black Arts figures, inspired by Garveyism and Rastafarianism. All of these groupings emphasized collectivity by capitalizing "We" and lowercasing "i" and spelled "Afrika" with a "k," in keeping with Swahili's use of the letter for the hard-"c" sound in English.[16] Like other black nationalists, New Afrikans often changed their names to demonstrate a reconnection to their African ancestry and a rejection of the "slave names" they had received at birth. New Afrikans described the United States as "Babylon," characterizing black liberation as a biblical struggle. And like the Nation of Islam, the RNA's "New Afrikan creed" maintained the "genius of black people," regulated personal behavior such as dress and hygiene, and upheld the heteronormative family as the natural unit of political community. The RNA's commitment to black liberation as at least partly a spiritual enterprise mirrored the Black Arts cultural pride with elements of NOI doctrine likely inherited from Malcolm X's tenure with the organization.

"New Afrikans" centered slavery as the origin of a new nation; only land and reparations could compensate for the oppression that originated with slavery. The idea of New Afrika attracted far more adherents than did the group that initiated it. The self-proclaimed New Afrikan Independence Movement emphasized not just "freedom" but "independence." From its founding, the RNA constituted itself as a government in exile, complete with elected officials and consulates throughout the United States. RNA officials met with representatives from several foreign governments, including those of China and Tanzania. Like the Black Panthers, New Afrikans demanded a UN-supervised plebiscite for black people to determine whether they desired U.S. control. Even more than the Panthers, New Afrikans hoped that the rhetoric of international law would demonstrate the existence of the black nation. New Afrikans framed their politics in the language (if not always the form) of international law. New Afrikan prisoners labeled prisons "detention centers," "death camps," and "koncentration kamps," categories governed by United Nations protocols on genocide and the treatment of prisoners of war.[17] At Illinois's Stateville prison, New Afrikan prisoner Atiba Shanna opined that talking of "P.O.W.'s, and in particular of Afrikan P.O.W.'s [in the United States] is a way of building revolutionary nationalist consciousness, and of realizing the liberation of the nation."[18]

New Afrikan politics was part of a resurgent Pan-Africanism among black Americans in the 1970s. By the middle of the decade, Amiri Baraka had launched the Maoist-influenced Congress of Afrikan People in New Jersey; Revolutionary Action Movement cofounder Muhammad Ahmad formed the Afrikan People's Party in Philadelphia; Owusu Sadaukai, an adviser to North Carolina's Malcolm X Liberation University, had helped organize African Liberation Day and the African Liberation Support Committee in solidarity with continental national liberation movements; and several former SNCC organizers built organizations such as the All-African People's Revolutionary Party or gatherings such as the Sixth Pan-African Congress.[19] New Afrikan politics existed within an orbit of political identifications that sought connection to Africa while acknowledging that the experience of slavery made impossible any simple notions of return or reclamation. Adherents therefore argued that the New Afrikan nation formed in the seventeenth century, with the first arrival of African slaves on the shores of what had not yet become the United States.[20]

More than that of any other black political entity at the time, the RNA's growth was facilitated rather than destroyed by the prison. While the RNA was one of several black nationalist groups, it exerted the greatest political influence over black prisoners after the split in the Black Panthers and the death of George Jackson. RNA politics spread rapidly through American prisons, leading many black prisoners to proclaim themselves New Afrikans. Many Black Panthers in the 1970s, especially in California and New York, declared themselves New Afrikans when they were incarcerated. Other black prisoners, politicized by the conditions of their confinement, also turned to New Afrika.[21]

Indeed, the RNA's framework proved popular with dissident black prisoners. Small groups of prisoners in several midwestern and southern states, sympathetic to New Afrikan politics, organized collectives called Black On Vanguards. The name was chosen to connote racial pride as the antithesis of "backing off."[22] The group urged black men, especially in prison, to display greater diligence in challenging white supremacy. Members of the group in Ohio and North Carolina endorsed a poem, "I Have Seen America," that captured the New Afrikan position when it declared, "I do not qualify for justice. I was kidnapped from my / Native land, I saw Brother George and Malcolm killed / I have seen America." Black On members also coauthored a letter urging prisoners and others to offer special support to captured black revolutionaries. "It is asked in Blackness[,] to progress materially as well as spiritually, that each of our brothers and sisters, comrades in the struggle[,] . . . start supporting our own."[23]

The popularity of New Afrikan politics resulted from two factors. First, eleven members of the RNA, including cofounder Imari Obadele, were arrested in predawn raids on two of the group's Jackson, Mississippi, headquarters on August 18, 1971, three days before George Jackson was killed.[24] They spent most of the rest of the decade in various federal prisons, part of the expanding prison-made internal diaspora. Once in prison, Obadele and the other RNA activists continued their organizing. They used the strict conditions of their confinement as further proof of their political arguments. Obadele participated in the formation of a multiracial coalition of radical prisoners at the federal prison in Marion, Illinois, and wrote for *Black Pride*, a black nationalist prisoner magazine based there.[25] In 1972, with its leaders in prison, the RNA released a legislative "Anti-Depression Program." The title was similar to the manifesto of demands released during the previous year's rebellion at Attica. Both writings demanded legislative changes while upholding self-reliance as a necessary practice on the way to self-determination.

The RNA program was included in *Foundations of the Black Nation*, a book of Obadele's prison writings that the RNA published in 1975. Together with the location of its author, the book's title suggested that the experience of forced confinement was fundamental to bonding African descendants in the Americas as a national group.[26]

The RNA also grew quickly because it took up and extended an argument that resonated with prisoners. The notion of New Afrika as a nation formed by slavery extended the position that black prisoners were imprisoned by white supremacy long before they were incarcerated. The RNA's ongoing work in prison and with prisoners gave this concept greater materiality than had been present when Malcolm X first popularized the metaphoric prison of racism. New Afrikans claimed that prisoners were on the front lines within the prison that held all black people. Staking their authority "by the grace of Malcolm," New Afrikans extended his message that the black condition involved perpetual imprisonment. They spoke of the United States as imprisoning the New Afrikan nation, urged adherents to support prisoners' struggles, and promoted prisoners as strategists for the developing black revolution.[27]

New Afrikan prisoners decried the Thirteenth and Fourteenth Amendments as hypocritical. Central to New Afrikan political thought was the idea that the Fourteenth Amendment of the U.S. Constitution, said to allow for due process, imposed the duties of American citizenship on former slaves without guaranteeing the rights that were supposed to accompany such civic status. The amendment, according to New Afrikans, offered but did not grant American citizenship. A study group of New Afrikan prisoners in Illinois determined that the Thirteenth Amendment, which outlawed slavery except as punishment for a crime, was part of an elite strategy to ensure the continuation of black bondage, now through prisons rather than plantations.[28] New Afrikans argued that black people had never been given a chance to choose whether they wanted the citizenship that had been forced on them yet had never truly been granted. In opposing the constitutional basis of black incorporation into the American nation-state, New Afrikans identified the prison and slavery as mutually supportive elements of the United States.

The prison was central to the New Afrikan political imagination. From their cells, black prisoners became spokesmen (and, in a few instances, spokeswomen) in a struggle to "free the land!" New Afrikan prisoners argued that their incarceration reflected the ways that "U.S. imperialism" had denied the existence and thwarted the independence of New Afrika. Prisoners were therefore the black nation's ambassadors to the Third World; their existence would certify the existence of a colony internal to the United States.

This line of reasoning was voiced most clearly from a prison cell in north-ern Illinois. Atiba Shanna (born James Sayles and later known as Owusu Yaki Yakubu) was, like many Illinois prisoners, from Chicago's South Side. He went to prison in 1972, sentenced to two hundred years for the deaths of a North Side white couple.[29] Shanna was already a politically conscious writer and a nationalist and was involved in the local Black Arts group, the Organization of Black American Culture. Other members of the group included poet Haki Mad-hubuti and novelist Sam Greenlee, author of *The Spook Who Sat by the Door*, a cult classic novel that told of a black nationalist who infiltrated the CIA to gain skills needed to teach guerrilla war to ghetto residents. In prison, Shanna became the most prolific and insightful New Afrikan theorist. He served for a time as the RNA minister of information. But his investment in New Afrikan politics extended beyond the governmental apparatus of the RNA.

From the mid-1970s until his release from prison in 2004, Shanna worked to popularize New Afrikan ideas. With Bradley Abdul Greene, a former member of the Chicago Black Panther Party then incarcerated at Stateville, Shanna was the ideological force behind the Stateville Prisoners Organization and the New Afrikan Prisoners Organization (NAPO), which attempted to unite prisoner groups at several different Illinois facilities. NAPO formed in 1977 as a way to sharpen collectivity among prisoners and between prisoners and the urban communities from which they came. Within the Illinois prison system, NAPO led study groups, wrote articles, tried to foster unity among disaffected black prisoners, and worked to maintain connections to black organizing in Chicago and other big cities. Ultimately NAPO ceased being a prisoner group and became the New Afrikan Peoples Organization.[30] According to Shanna, "Prisoners will play a significant role in the formation of a national, *revolutionary*, black political party and in the formation of a national, *revolutionary*, black united front."[31] That united front never materialized, but hints of it were visible through the rise of prison-based publications. Indeed, prisoner journalism and print culture were the central building blocks of black prison nationalism and the larger prison movement of which it was a part.

"REMOVE THE BARRIERS BETWEEN THE OUTSIDE AND INSIDE"

There is nothing inherently subversive about prisoner writings. Believing reading and writing to be therapeutic and educational—that is, rehabilitative—some prison administrators had allowed prisoners to produce newsletters as early as the 1950s. This "bibliotherapy," as it was called, originated in the postwar spirit of prison reform that California symbolized nationally. These media, timid and apolitical products that reported mostly on prison happenings, were printed in-house and read predominantly by prisoners and staff.

As prisoners began to challenge their confinement in the late 1960s, their writings became more subversive in tone and method of distribution. Prisoners produced a number of covert publications, such as *The Outlaw* (1968, San Quentin), *The Iced Pig* (1971, Attica), and *Aztlán* (1970–72, Leavenworth). Radical prisoners worked alone or in small groups to create these publications, often acting surreptitiously and with minimal access to the tools of design. Radical newspapers on the outside occasionally reprinted some or all of these texts, but they were intended primarily to rally prisoners against guards.[32]

Prison-based black nationalist publications of the 1970s had a different magnitude and purpose. These publications spoke the language of Third World anticolonialism and used their own nationalist idiom. They provided a chance for prisoners to circumvent the prison by working with outside activists on writing and editing. They did not, as some had earlier, suggest that the revolution would come solely from within prisons. But they posited that as a result of their incarceration, prisoners were and ought to be providing some intellectual leadership for the black nation. These newspapers joined books by Malcolm X, George Jackson, and others as tools of literacy and political education. The publications sought to connect dissident prisoners amid the growing atomization caused by the increasing use of lockdowns and the declining significance of the written word after prison officials began installing televisions.[33]

These prisoner newspapers emerged on the coattails of the 1960s underground media and shared similar goals of education and agitation.[34] They attempted to establish a united front among black prisoners while making alliances with Latinos and where possible white antiracist prisoners. Their primary purpose, however, was to establish connections between prisoners and outside supporters under the mantle of revolutionary nationalism. Overt dissent in the form of riots and strikes had become substantially harder, so prisoners turned to media as a way to foster unity and facilitate communication.

Publications were the lifeblood of black nationalist prison organizing, promoting a shared political understanding of the problems of confinement and the potentials of nationalism. California, Illinois, and New York remained central to the development of black prison nationalism, even though self-proclaimed New Afrikans could be found in prisons across the country. Prisons in those three states hosted at least eight regularly published newspapers and magazines steeped in New Afrikan politics and with an ongoing connection to prison issues: *Arm the Spirit*, *Awakening of the Dragon*, and *Seize the*

Time (California); *Black Pride, The Fuse* (originally *Stateville Raps*), and *Notes from an Afrikan P.O.W.* (later *Viva wa Watu*) (Illinois); and *Take the Land* and *Midnight Special* (New York).

In politics as in real estate, location is everything. The three states where black prison nationalism most thrived were, not coincidentally, pivotal fronts in the war between the radical Left and the Far Right. Oakland, Los Angeles, New York City, and Chicago were home to the biggest chapters of the Black Panther Party as well as to a myriad of other progressive and revolutionary organizations. Each city was also a model laboratory for the shifting urban policies of a postindustrial age. Police brutality had been a perennial problem for radical groups and black communities in these and other big cities, but developments in these four cities in particular presaged the massive state investment in policing, imprisonment, surveillance, and privatization that has largely governed the United States since the early 1970s.[35] Indeed, significant changes in Sacramento, Albany, and Springfield coincided with developments in Washington, D.C., and on Wall Street to tighten the interlocking connections among police, prosecutors, and prisons.

California gave the world Richard Nixon and Ronald Reagan, the high priests of punishment, along with a grassroots tax revolt that pitted white suburbs against increasingly black and brown cities through deeply racialized yet formally color-blind discourses.[36] The Golden State garnered praise after World War II for its rehabilitative penology, but by the mid-1970s it was better known for an anti-Left backlash, heavy-handed policing, and indeterminate sentences. Los Angeles stood at the forefront of the increasing militarization of American police departments. The Special Weapons and Tactics (SWAT) team began there in 1966, partially in response to the rioting in Watts a year earlier. As a style of policing, SWAT teams combined the latest in military technology with good old-fashioned spectacle.

In 1974, the LAPD's SWAT team staged a heavily armed and highly choreographed assault on the Compton house where members of the Symbionese Liberation Army, wanted for the murder of an Oakland school superintendent in November 1973 and the kidnapping of heiress Patty Hearst three months later, were hiding. After a shootout, police set fire to the house, burning to death the six people inside. All of it was televised. These dramatic killings were the most extreme spectacle of this heightened policing that saw members of California's black and Latino populations stopped, frisked, harassed, and arrested in ever-larger numbers. By the early 1980s, these policing strategies buttressed a political economy of punishment that helped launch the biggest wave of prison construction in world history.[37]

Other states also ramped up their police powers and prison capacity. Nelson Rockefeller may have been the last liberal Republican of his day on certain issues, but he was a pioneer of mass incarceration and its racialized consequences. The New York governor refused to negotiate with the prisoners at Attica, preferring to end the rebellion with a disproportionate display of force. The deaths at Attica showed the government to be more invested in spectacular violence than prisoner militants ever were—and with much greater capacity to carry it out. Two years later, Rockefeller advanced Nixon's war on drugs perhaps more than any other single figure through a panoply of laws (popularly known as the Rockefeller drug laws) that criminalized drug use, sale, or possession with steep prison sentences. New York's war on drugs became a model for the national drug war, sweeping state legislatures with the allure of federal dollars to launch a new era of Prohibition backed by a strong carceral state.[38]

For its part, Illinois foretold the shape of prisons to come. As University of Chicago economist Milton Friedman and others found larger audiences receptive to an antistate free-market fundamentalism, a federal penitentiary in southern Illinois demonstrated that the state's power was in fact growing rather than shrinking, at least with regard to punishment. The federal prison at Marion was built for ten million dollars in 1963. In 1972, the facility opened the first control unit prison with more than one hundred "problem inmates" (most of them black and Latino political prisoners) transferred from prisons around the country. Marion prison was a high-tech experiment in isolation and behavior modification, the most intense federal prison between the closure of Alcatraz in 1963 and the opening of the super-maximum security prison at Florence, Colorado, in 1994. Prisoners at Marion were subject to a battery of psychological abuses, including arbitrary punishment, complete isolation, and sensory deprivation. Prison officials hoped that this approach, which historian Alan Eladio Gómez has said "muddled commonplace distinctions between what constituted punishment, rehabilitation and torture," would eliminate dissent.[39] Though the experiment failed abysmally, resulting in lawsuits and a riot amid persistent lockdown, it became the basis for the control units and supermax prisons that began to comprise the new normal of American punishment.

As devised by Nixon, Rockefeller, and Reagan in accordance with proposals from conservative public intellectuals such as James Q. Wilson and Ernest van den Haag, "law and order" was a color-blind Trojan horse delivered to suburban whites in hopes that the trope of public safety in an era of white flight would promote a reactionary political agenda that, as Nixon said when discussing welfare reform, targeted black people without seeming to do so.[40] Still, the call for more police and fewer drugs garnered support from many liberals and civil rights moderates, among others. It resonated with many moderates in the decaying urban landscape, including some long-standing civil rights advocates as well as a new urban elite moving into the city at a time when many who could do so were leaving. Both sets of individuals wanted a "cleaner" city. With the mainstream media increasingly emphasizing crime news, legitimate desires for public health and safety were easily subsumed into the bogeymen animating law-and-order discourse.[41]

As mainstream news outlets failed to report the consolidation of new forms of high-tech punishment, New Afrikan publications were among the only ways such information could reach the outside world. Most but not all of these papers were edited by prisoners and produced by outside supporters. Several other publications only printed one or two issues, were locally or regionally based, and/or were prison-related media not steeped in New Afrikan thinking. These publications include *NEPA News* (published by the New England Prisoners Association), *CPSB Newsletter* (put out by the Coalition for Prisoner Support in Birmingham, Alabama), and *The Real Deal* (produced by a collective of prisoners and nonprisoners in Indiana). Left-wing bookstores such as the Red Star North Bookstore in Portland, Maine, run by the Statewide Correctional Alliance for Reform, often served as clearinghouses for this information. Among the black publications that printed news and analysis of prison protest at this time were California's *Black Scholar* and New York's *Black News* (a publication of Queen Mother Moore's organization, the East) as well as *Jet* magazine. Many of these periodicals covered ongoing cases involving well-known prisoners.[42]

What distinguished New Afrikan media, by and large, was their commitment to identifying the prisoner as ambassador of the captive black nation. The prison was so central to these publications that individual articles did not need to address imprisonment to conjure the prison. Whether calling for armed revolt or printing prisoner poetry, these periodicals documented the specter of prison in black life. Fiercely and often didactically political, they allowed prisoners to analyze society in public. The publications' broad interests included Third World movements, the rise of black elected officials, law-and-order politics, jazz, theater, affirmative action, poetry, and the emergent blaxploitation genre.

Prisoners often affirmed their ethnic pride to legitimate their arguments. In 1973, for example, *Midnight Special* printed two letters from prisoners about blaxploitation. Under the headline "Black Movies and Twentieth Century Slaves," both authors criticized the genre for perpetuating negative, propagandistic, and derogatory stereotypes about black men and women. One of the authors, imprisoned at Soledad, began the letter by establishing his good intentions: "I am writing to you, In Sincerity and Blackness, concerning my feelings of Miss Pamela Grier as an actress."[43] At Marion, prisoners writing for *Black Pride* critiqued black women's beauty standards, printed poems in honor of Angela Davis, and reviewed Amiri Baraka's plays.[44]

The nine members of the Black Cultural Society Awareness Program at Marion constituted the editorial group that produced *Black Pride*. Its motto was "Everything is political." The short-lived journal lived up to its name and motto: four of the editors had adopted Swahili names, and its articles addressed topics ranging from "pitfalls to avoid in dealing with the South Africa question" to the "beauty of the black woman."[45] *Black Pride* featured trivia about black nationalist history—people, laws, organizations—along with Swahili vocabulary lessons. Its pages carried hopeful articles about building "BlkUnity" in Marion between prisoners who were in the Nation of Islam and those who were not; analyses of the mainstream media as institutions of racial capitalism; reviews of records and plays; and calls to action on behalf of the Republic of New Afrika or Angela Davis.[46] The editors of *Black Pride*, as well as its contributors, brought Talmudic discipline to their attempts to interpret the words of Malcolm X and George Jackson.[47]

Black Pride exemplified the way that New Afrikan politics sprouted through the cracks of a federal penitentiary. The mimeographed periodical showed that the divisions between revolutionary nationalism and cultural nationalism, blurry on the street, could collapse entirely in prison. The erasure of these distinctions moved traditional cultural nationalism to the left (as seen from the journal's overtly political disposition) and revolutionary nationalism to the right (as seen from its discussions of black women).

The gender politics of *Black Pride* were more retrograde than most prisoner publications of the time, which either expressed support for women's liberation or ignored women altogether. *Black Pride*, however, revived the virgin/whore dyad that dominated Eldridge Cleaver's still-popular *Soul on Ice*, which opened with the rape of black women and closed with a love letter to the "Queen-Mother-Daughter of Africa."[48] In the pages of *Black Pride*, Angela Davis received widespread praise as the princess of the black revolution. Poems encouraged her to "keep your faith in the Black race, for we'll be doing all / we can to see that you win this case" and worried about her fate in an era where several black revolutionaries had been assassinated.[49] Yet discussions of black women in the abstract often struck a different note, as authors proclaimed the need to protect black women from the violence of white hands and ideas. This theme could appear as reflexive self-criticism: "couldn't really love you blk / woman / didn't realize your nearest oppressor—me / projecting wite values from a blk

/ perspective." But it could also go the other way, as in a review of Baraka's *Madheart* that parroted the play's misogynistic claims about the need for black men to reconquer black women from white standards.[50]

To have staying power, prisoner publications would need the coordinated support of outside organizations. In New York, such support came in the form of a monthly newsmagazine, *Midnight Special*, named after a southern black work song popularized by legendary blues musician Huddie "Leadbelly" Ledbetter, who had been incarcerated himself. The train of the title carried prisoners to freedom. The idea for the paper emerged among the members of the New York chapter of the National Lawyers Guild after the Attica rebellion. Attorneys who had been doing prisoner rights work wanted to start a newspaper to address routine legal and health care matters. The NLG persuaded New Left activist Russell Neufeld, who had been aligned with the Weathermen's faction of Students for a Democratic Society, to serve as the new publication's managing editor. Neufeld then recruited help from assorted leftists, many of whom had been involved in Black Panther defense campaigns or supporting the Attica Brothers. As with most New Left and Black Power publications, no one involved had any professional journalism training; creating the periodical was a labor of love and political commitment.[51]

The magazine was based in the basement of the New York NLG's office in the West Village. The first issue appeared in the fall of 1971. Within a few months, the publication was being produced by a collective of eight people, including two men who had recently been released after serving a combined total of twenty years at Attica. The other members of the collective, however, had only limited personal experience with the criminal justice system. Neufeld had served ninety days in the Cook County Jail after being arrested as part of an antiwar protest. Another member, Phyllis Prentice, worked at Rikers Island as a nurse and carried messages back and forth between imprisoned Black Panthers and activists outside. (She performed a similar role when she moved to San Francisco in the mid-1970s and worked at the jail there.)[52]

When *Midnight Special* began, the editors or other NLG members wrote all of the articles, but the number of prisoner contributions increased in each issue. Within a year, nearly all of the articles were written by prisoners, and circulation had topped three thousand. The editorial collective sent the paper directly to jails and prisons or distributed to groups and bookstores that supplied prisoners with reading material. While the paper made its way into many outside hands, it was based in prison. The editors mailed it to facilities that would accept it, while prisoners' lawyers and friends smuggled it into facilities that would not.

The paper was a prisoner resource: NLG lawyers answered legal questions, and workers from the Health Revolutionary Unity Movement answered medical questions. But more than any particular legal or medical question, *Midnight Special* was a communication resource, helping prisoners retain connections to their families, friends, and supporters as well as prisoners at other institutions. The magazine provided both political sustenance and personal edification. Neufeld took part in a panel discussion in the mid-1970s with a recently released prisoner who had learned to read under the guidance of a fellow prisoner who was an avid reader of *Midnight Special* and used the paper to teach reading and critical thinking skills.[53]

With its authors scattered in prisons throughout the country, *Midnight Special* had a long reach. Attica remained a symbolic touchstone of prison radicalism for the paper, whose editors and publishers were involved in various defense efforts for the prisoners there. But the paper had a national scope. It regularly printed articles by or about prisoners in Virginia, North Carolina, Maryland, Georgia, Massachusetts, California, and Washington, D.C., and organizations as diverse as the NAACP, the Black Guerrilla Family, the Black On Vanguards, and the prison chapters of the Black Panthers and the Young Lords. *Midnight Special* also featured prison struggles anywhere on the U.S. eastern seaboard and political prisoners worldwide. Of particular interest was the case of five members of the Puerto Rican Nationalist Party who were imprisoned for their dramatic attacks on U.S. authority in the 1950s and who became a lodestar for the rebirth of Puerto Rican revolutionary nationalism in the 1970s.[54]

In *Midnight Special*, prisoners wrote not only about their own prisons but also about their comrades in other prisons and about the metaphoric prisons that held captive the United States and the larger black world. Each issue featured a combination of essays, news, poems, graphics, and rants as well as reprints of petitions that prisoners had filed against their institutions or reprints from other prisoner publications. *Midnight Special* showcased the theoretical, strategic, and creative writings of hundreds of prisoners as well as drawings and other artwork.[55]

The paper sought to facilitate coalitions among prisoners at different facilities and between prisoners and social movements. While *Midnight Special* was oriented toward prisoners themselves, its editors saw a special role in securing public attention for prison struggles. "Outside support of inmate struggles is indispensable if the type of repression that occurred at Attica is not to be repeated," the editors declared, affirming their intention to "remove some of the barriers that exist between the outside and inside."[56] The paper walked a fine line between publicity and anonymity: to avoid diverting attention from the writings of imprisoned intellectuals who at times had to remain anonymous to avoid repercussions, the editors, too, remained anonymous. Anonymity allowed the paper to print prisoners' honest appraisals in which they described their confinement and the painful divisions, generational as much as spatial and emotional, it caused.

An anonymous prisoner at Soledad penned a poignant poem, "Only the Blues Is Authorized," in which he expressed his fears that those who had previously known him would no longer recognize him: "I would look strange to them / their soldier son / for I would look like the concrete / I've had so long next to my skin."[57] This poem appeared next to a Pennsylvania prisoner's ode to the songs of Billie Holiday and lamented the prisoner's invisibility to the society that produced him. Imprisonment now produced a sense of loss and a passion for justice. The blues signified the possible coexistence of love and hate, passion and detachment—the prison and a world beyond it. Other contributions to *Midnight Special* were less nuanced. A poem by a prisoner in Lorton, Virginia, declared prisoners to be the most ethical sector of society: "Wake-up Amerika if you expect to remain. / You see Amerika the solutions are under / George Jackson names."[58]

Like so much of the radical Left by the mid-1970s, *Midnight Special* joined innovation and isolation. It was a powerful catalog of prisoner activism during a time of growing public disinterest in the far Left. The paper presciently foretold the rise of mass incarceration as a weapon of class stratification that all but erased young black people from society as workers, organizers, and voters. It shined a light on organizing endeavors by unionists and nationalists, communists and anarchists, and the unaffiliated. *Midnight Special* provided prisoners with a venue in which to discuss political strategy while affording them a chance to engage in dialogue with one another. The paper recognized that struggle occurred among women and gay prisoners, denaturalizing the heterosexual black male prisoner as the sole politically active force in prison—even if black men remained the dominant focal point of the paper as well as of the prison.

Midnight Special became more rhetorically overburdened as American prisons became more racially overdetermined. According to sociologist James Jacobs, "By 1974, a nationwide census of penal facilities revealed that 47 percent of prisoners were black. In many state prisons blacks were in the majority."[59] *Midnight Special* described prisons as a staging ground for radical protest, effectively putting the prison on the same plane as struggles against British colonialism, Israeli settlement, or South African Bantustans in the production of racial consciousness. The editors described the prison as an institution that "touches us all" yet does so in unequal ways.[60] Even with the stodgy Marxist rhetoric or calls for armed struggle that increasingly characterized the paper after 1974, when several founding editors departed, the paper's voice came from the future, warning of the social costs of locking up more and more people in cages.

The connections prisoners established through *Midnight Special* and similar endeavors were useful in other ventures, campaigns that would bring prisoner ideas to the global arena. Alongside a host of stateless nations at the time, black prison nationalists turned to the United Nations as a possible avenue of redress—both for their specific imprisonment and for their broader confinement in the United States. Following from the strategy Malcolm X advocated toward the end of his life, black nationalists viewed international law, represented by the United Nations, as the best possibility for a neutral or perhaps even supportive (in light of the era's embrace of decolonization) hearing for their grievances. Appealing to the UN revealed that this black nationalist vision was global. It rejected the American state in favor of identification with the Third World and its dreams of a future autonomous government. These prisoners hoped that embarrassment in the international arena would force the United States to change. Even more than the UN as a body, these campaigns were addressed to the UN as a symbol: the biggest international institution concerned with human rights, the UN meant a rejection of U.S. authority and the possibility for alternate alliances. For that reason, Georgia Jackson petitioned the United Nations in 1972 for an investigation into the circumstances of her son's death, Marion prisoners appealed to the UN for relief, and poet-musician Gil Scott-Heron sang of appealing to the UN for reparations.[61]

Black radicals had focused on the United Nations as a venue almost since the institution formed. In 1951, the Civil Rights Congress authored and delivered a petition, "We Charge Genocide," to the UN. The text was written by black communist William Patterson and aided by the participation of performer-activist Paul Robeson. The United Nations never responded to the original petition, but it was reprinted in its entirety in 1970. In an introduction to the new edition, Patterson wrote that the petition sought "to expose the nature and depth of racism in the United States; and to arouse the moral conscience of progressive mankind against the inhuman treatment of black nationals by those in high political places."[62] Patterson and his wife, Louise Thompson Patterson, continued to organize at the intersections of communism and black liberation. As with Queen Mother Moore and other black communists involved in the Scottsboro Boys defense campaign, the Pattersons served as mentors for the New York Black Panther Party and other black militants from the city. Unlike Moore, the Pattersons were party leaders; William had headed the International Labor Defense, the Communist Party's mid-twentieth-century apparatus for supporting those facing political repression. The Pattersons' party leadership roles left them well equipped to tutor young militants in political strategy. Rooted in an internationalist perspective, the Pattersons helped circulate the idea of genocide as a conceptual framework for black antiracist struggles. They also identified the United Nations as a potentially receptive means of bringing these concerns to a global audience.[63]

In the late 1970s, the UN became the focus of several prisoner appeals. Black prisoners submitted petitions criticizing black imprisonment from slavery to the present; all of these documents identified George Jackson as an iconic figurehead. As with the New Afrikan newspapers, these prisoner appeals to the United Nations were less about prison conditions than about establishing the legitimacy and international standing of the black nation. Located behind bars, the authors of these petitions used their status to demonstrate the carceral framework of black resistance to American racism. Owing to what one prisoner described as "the extreme concentration of oppression" in prisons, people held there were the most obvious choice to launch a campaign oriented toward what one prisoner called "the 'politics of anti-oppression' . . . presented within the context of the class and national liberation struggle."[64]

The New Afrikan Prisoners Organization initiated one such effort in 1977. The petition, "We Still Charge Genocide," clearly alluded to its 1951 predecessor. Less an appraisal of contemporary racism, the new petition was a challenge to the moral and juridical basis of American power based on a study group at the Stateville prison that reexamined the Thirteenth, Fourteenth, and Fifteenth Amendments. In each of the three amendments held up as harbingers of racial progress, prisoners found proof of white supremacy's retrenchment. With the ink having dried on landmark civil rights legislation, these prisoners looked to an earlier period of legislating antiracism. And if the laws to end slavery only reinscribed white supremacy, what hope was there for laws designed to end Jim Crow? The fact that the Stateville prison population by this point was 75 percent black showed that the emerging carceral regime continued a long history of black disenfranchisement.[65]

As prisons became more severe, New Afrikan prisoners became more globally minded. From a prison in Atlanta, RNA president Imari Obadele released a letter to Fidel Castro and the United Nations Special Committee on Decolonization to request a prisoner exchange whereby the United States would release seventeen New Afrikans to Cuba in return for an equal number of "counter-revolutionaries now in Cuban jails."[66] This request situated New Afrika as a Third World nation akin to Cuba. Inspired by these prisoner efforts, outside organizations also took it upon themselves to contact the United Nations about the question of prisons in the United States. The National Conference of Black Lawyers, the National Alliance against Racist and Political Repression, and the Commission for Racial Justice for the United Church of Christ filed a petition on December 11, 1978, the twenty-fifth anniversary of the signing of the Declaration of Human Rights. The petition, given to the UN Commission on Human Rights and the Sub-Commission on Prevention of Discrimination and Protection of Minorities, detailed human rights violations in the incarceration of dozens of black, Puerto Rican, Chicano, and indigenous political dissidents. It also detailed government misconduct against these social movements as recently reported through the Church Committee hearings. As a result of that petition, the International Commission of Jurists sent a representative to visit select U.S. political prisoners.[67]

The petition submitted by the National Conference of Black Lawyers developed out of petitions attempting to resurrect political protest through a strategic focus on black prisoners. Beginning in 1976, Jalil Muntaqim initiated a prisoner petition to the UN from San Quentin. Muntaqim (originally known as Anthony Bottom) had been arrested in San Francisco in 1971, when he was a headstrong nineteen-year-old member of the Black Panthers accused of participating in a shootout with police in retaliation for George Jackson's death. In 1972, he was transferred to New York City to stand trial with four other former Black Panthers in the death of two police officers in a BLA-related shooting there. While awaiting trial, Muntaqim was confined in a special area of the Queens House of Detention whose residents also included longtime political activists Jamil Al-Amin and Muhammad Ahmad. The two elder black revolutionaries had already converted to Islam; after more than four months, they had persuaded Muntaqim, then a communist, to adopt a monotheistic faith. Muntaqim's first trial ended in mistrial, and prosecutors dropped charges against two of the defendants. In 1975, Muntaqim, Herman Bell, and Albert Nuh Washington were convicted in a second trial, and Muntaqim was sent back to San Quentin to complete his California sentence.

Back in the Adjustment Center, Muntaqim was "locked in a cell between Brother Ruchell Magee and Charles Manson."[68] Not far from him were the San Quentin 6, Black Panther Geronimo Pratt, and Symbionese Liberation Army members Bill Harris and Russell Little. Supporters had encouraged him and other AC prisoners to write articles and statements as a way to dialogue with movements outside. Muntaqim drafted the UN petition in response to a letter in which the National Committee for the Defence of Political Prisoners proposed an international campaign to free activists imprisoned with lengthy sentences. The New York–based committee was an outgrowth of the Panther 21 defense committee. Its most well-known member was Yuri Kochiyama, a friend of Malcolm X and the only nonblack citizen of New Afrika. Muntaqim wrote his proposal and shared it first with Magee. After that, Muntaqim sent it to the second floor to be reviewed by Pratt. With his approval, Muntaqim sent the petition draft to the committee. But the organization was too bound up in supporting various prisoners to launch any campaign.[69]

As he waited for a response, Muntaqim was transferred out of the Adjustment Center into general population. A prisoner there—Muntaqim knew him only as Commie Mike—introduced him to the United Prisoners Union, a small, more nationalist offshoot of the Prisoners Union. With connections to prisoners in two dozen states, the UPU took on Muntaqim's petition campaign and facilitated communication among the prisoners involved. Muntaqim's effort gathered twenty-five hundred signatures from prisoners across the country. The final version called for an international investigation into American prisons as sites of discrimination and genocide. Attorney Kathleen Burke, who had worked with Amnesty International, filed the petition as a UN document in Geneva.[70]

This support, while impressive, meant little more than verbal or written affirmation by prisoners. They were not actively involved in conceiving the campaign, although some mobilized to help it succeed. In New Jersey, for example, a group of prisoners established themselves as the August 21 Prisoners Human Rights Coalition. The petition campaign connected prisoners with one another, through organizations such as the Prairie Fire Organizing Committee (PFOC), the United Prisoners Union, and, briefly, the African People's Socialist Party. The PFOC, a public organization of antiracist whites that was formed by the clandestine Weather Underground in 1975, was critical in facilitating prisoner communication in California, Illinois, and New York. The African People's Socialist Party was a black nationalist group whose tenure with *Arm the Spirit* was marked by divisiveness and hostility that ultimately led to the paper's demise when party members tried to incorporate it into their own newspaper, the *Burning Spear*.[71]

Networks of communication also provided the basis for some international attention to the issues motivating the petition, even if the petition itself did not attract notice. According to Muntaqim, in the summer of 1978, a reporter for the French socialist newspaper *Le Matin* asked U.S. prison organizers how he could help their campaign. Via intermediaries, Muntaqim suggested that the reporter ask the U.S. ambassador to the UN, Andrew Young, whether the United States had any political prisoners.[72] Young, a veteran of the Southern Christian Leadership Conference and the first African American to represent the country before the world body, answered that "there are hundreds, perhaps even thousands of people I would call political prisoners." Although he did not name any particular individuals, Young's comments, delivered in France in the context of a discussion about the jailing of Soviet dissidents, provoked fierce opposition back home from politicians who insisted that the United States had no political prisoners. U.S. representative Larry McDonald, a Georgia Democrat, introduced a resolution in the House calling for Young's impeachment. Though his resolution was soundly defeated (293–82), Young was widely criticized, and he apologized for his remark. He was eventually forced to resign after a succession of public relations blunders.[73]

Muntaqim welcomed the Paris publicity. He asked Sundiata Acoli, another former Panther turned New Afrikan, who was imprisoned in New Jersey, to call for a protest in New York. Acoli, a former employee of the National Aeronautics and Space Administration who had tutored astronaut Neil Armstrong in math, was by this time serving life in prison. Acoli had been one of the defendants in the Panther 21 trial (1969–71), in which the government prosecuted the party's New York leaders on a series of spurious charges designed to break the chapter and separate it from the national office. Thirteen of the defendants coauthored *Look for Me in the Whirlwind*, a collective autobiography, while in jail and awaiting trial. Like many of the Panther 21, Acoli went underground after the acquittal. In 1973, he was arrested after a shootout on the New Jersey Turnpike in which fellow BLA member Zayd Shakur and a New Jersey state trooper were killed. Assata Shakur was shot and arrested; Acoli initially got away but was caught two days later.

Acoli's participation in Muntaqim's plan made the effort bicoastal. Through a coalition of nationalist-oriented groups, Acoli called for a protest at the Harlem State Office Building. The groups tried to coalesce as the National Prison Organization to do community organizing regarding prison issues and prisoner organizing regarding dynamics in outside communities. This effort, however, quickly shattered. A demonstration at the UN as part of the prisoner petition was moved to the State Office Building, and no further organization materialized.[74]

This bicoastal protest, launched by two prisoners with limited outside contact, flowed from the Black Liberation Army's attempt to turn prisons into what Acoli called strategic "instruments of liberation."[75] The BLA was a clandestine and largely decentralized military grouping whose members were accused of participating in a series of attacks on police officers and drug dealers that were allegedly financed with bank robberies. By the time Acoli called for the Harlem demonstration, the BLA was suspected in dozens of shootings of police officers nationwide. The BLA is often described as comprising those Panthers who were loyal to Cleaver after his split with Newton. While many who built the black underground shared Cleaver's insurrectionary predilections, the group was more loyal to traditions of revolutionary nationalism (including its emphasis on self-defense) common throughout the rural South and in New York City's black political history. Not surprisingly, then, many acknowledged or alleged BLA members were either southern-born or members of the New York chapter of the BPP or both. As the RNA supplanted the Panthers as the dominant expression of black revolutionary nationalism in the 1970s, several New Afrikans also counted themselves among the BLA's ranks.[76]

In the mid-1970s, with many of its members incarcerated, the BLA endeavored to use the prison as a cadre training school. Convicted BLA members tried to subvert the prison by any means necessary, including escape attempts and intellectual study. Both approaches expressed an audacious commitment to freedom. Their pedagogy and their marronage fit within a black radical tradition of living within but beyond American society. Inspired by contemporary international prisoner struggles—especially the September 1971 escape of more than one hundred Uruguayan Tupamaro guerrillas who tunneled their way out of prison and back into the armed underground—BLA members made several daring attempts at escape. Most failed, and in a couple of cases, the escapees died, but a few succeeded, at least temporarily.

Safiya Bukhari was a middle-class black woman who joined the New York City Panthers to support their community programs. She worked on the *Black Panther* newspaper and later the Cleaverite offshoot, *Right On!* She was arrested in December 1973, accused of plotting to break accused BLA members out of the city's Tombs detention facility. Cleared of the Tombs conspiracy but subpoenaed to testify in a grand jury investigating clandestine black radicalism, Bukhari went underground until she was arrested after a grocery store shootout in Virginia in 1975. She was sentenced to forty years in prison but escaped in 1976. When she was apprehended and tried for the escape, she used her trial to challenge the abysmal medical treatment in prison. Bukhari had fibroid tumors in her uterus that prison officials refused to remove until after her escape.[77]

Others followed her example. Philadelphia Black Panther Russell Shoatz was arrested for the death of a police officer in 1972. He escaped from a Pennsylvania prison in September 1977 and remained at large for a month, earning the sobriquet "Maroon," in honor of nineteenth-century escaped slave rebels. Several other escape attempts in the mid-1970s by people connected to the BLA or related groups were aborted or failed, and at least two people died in their bids for freedom. The most successful BLA escape came on November 2, 1979, when Assata Shakur escaped from a New Jersey prison with the help of a BLA unit. She lived underground in the United States for several years before taking up residence in Cuba as a political exile, where she remains.[78]

Alongside and outlasting the escape attempts, BLA members also turned to political education. BLA members led political education classes in prisons around the country. In 1975, members of the heretofore decentralized guerrilla group established a coordinating committee with members both in and out of prison and began publishing a newsletter. Two years later, the coordinating committee distributed a 150-page study guide to imprisoned supporters with the goal of solidifying BLA politics among new recruits and existing members alike. It was a primer on revolutionary nationalist thought, with sections on the black nation, dialectical materialism, democratic centralism, political economy, and other Marxist-Leninist precepts. In addition to theoretical essays on these subjects, the guide included a "political dictionary" that introduced neophytes to the revolutionary nationalist lexicon. Drawing on the experience of BLA members in court and the media, the study guide objected to elite attempts "to make the words *terrorism and revolutionary* synonymous."[79] The study guide distanced the BLA from the "indiscriminate violence and murder" of terrorism. It was part of a larger critique of the ways that terrorism was becoming an increasingly significant keyword of Western governance—a sign of a dawning age of violent extremes.[80]

The guide and the coordinating committee as a body represented the BLA's greatest centralization of structure and ideology; some members found it to be overreaching. Yet even members who distanced themselves from these developments participated in diverse political education projects inside.[81] The circulation of the study guide and the UN petition and the landscape of prisoner peer mentorship demonstrate the existence of a network for distributing information, with nodes both in and out of prison. This network proved critical to establishing the distribution networks for prisoner media, such as *Arm the Spirit*. The paper began as *Voices from within San Quentin*, a mimeographed newsletter that reported on prison conditions.[82]

Voices offered a way to foster communication among prisoners in the increasingly isolated world of San Quentin—compartmentalization was one of the defining features of the newly emerging penal environment—while continuing to provide first-person commentary on prison conditions for Bay Area prison activists. *Voices* began in the San Quentin Adjustment Center in the fall of 1977, with contributions from several of the unit's political prisoners. Funding problems precluded its printing until that winter, and six months later, it made the transition from a monthly newsletter on prison conditions to a quarterly newspaper of prisoner reporting on anticolonial movements around the world. The change was ambitious, turning a local newsletter into a national publication.

Both iterations analyzed the prison as a tool of empire. Muntaqim worked on the paper until he was transferred from San Quentin, helping to oversee the change from *Voices* to *Arm the Spirit*, at which point Aswad became the editor. The title was taken from a 1971 speech by Fidel Castro that was popular among radicals. Aswad wrote and selected articles for publication. Members of the Prairie Fire Organizing Committee got articles to Aswad and produced and distributed the paper around the country. It was free to prisoners, while others paid fifty cents an issue (three dollars for a one-year subscription). The first issue appeared in June 1978; the San Quentin warden refused to allow it into the prison until an attorney retained by PFOC threatened to sue.

Arm the Spirit took George Jackson as its inspiration even more than *Voices* did. A quotation from Jackson encouraging unity in the face of an already present fascism appeared as the paper's tag line, identifying *Arm the Spirit*'s mission: "Do what must be done, discover your humanity and your love in revolution. Pass on the torch. Join us, give up your life for the people." The editors listed the paper's three goals as providing a medium for the transmission of information about American prison radicalism, providing prisoners with an outlet for their political writings, and connecting the "various struggles" on which the paper reported.[83]

Prisoners around the country contributed articles to *Arm the Spirit*. The paper devoted most of its coverage to three areas: prison protest, black radicalism, and anticolonial campaigns among Puerto Ricans, Native Americans, and continental Africans. The paper was a catalog of revolutionary nationalism at the end of the 1970s, when Puerto Rican militancy was on the rise and when the BLA experienced a brief resurgence of activity. *Arm the Spirit* was especially taken with the bombings by the Fuerzas Armadas de Liberación Nacional (the Armed Forces of National Liberation), a clandestine Puerto Rican group that claimed responsibility for more than one hundred bombing attacks between 1974 and 1983.[84] It printed several articles about the FALN, including when one of its members, Guillermo Morales, escaped from New York's Bellevue Hospital in May 1979 despite having lost most of his fingers when a bomb he was making prematurely exploded in his hands.[85] *Arm the Spirit* also offered extensive coverage of the trial of eleven suspected FALN members who were arrested outside of Chicago in April 1980.[86]

The FALN trial marked a new display of nationalist self-assertion in keeping with the transformations of New Afrikan politics. The women and men arrested in 1980 proclaimed themselves prisoners of war and refused to recognize the legitimacy of the U.S. court system or participate in any of its hearings, instead demanding to be tried by an international tribunal. Morales had taken a similar position in court appearances prior to his escape, and other black, white, and Puerto Rican revolutionaries took the same tack at their trials over the next few years. While these militants still saw the court as a forum in which to raise issues for public (rather than legal) consideration, they now saw legal procedure as totally irrelevant. They wanted to put the government on trial, but not with a trial overseen by the government. The liberal order was crumbling, the prison regime was expanding, and these revolutionaries thought the only honest thing to do was reject the system wholesale.

This stance brought the nationalism of the U.S. Third World Left to a new level: a total rejection of U.S. authority. By proclaiming themselves prisoners of war, these women and men argued that permanent war—through colonialism, policing, and counterinsurgency—was the norm for the United States. They acknowledged their role as participants in that war, either unwittingly as members of racialized groups born on the battlefield or consciously as armed combatants or political participants. This approach confounded and infuriated judges, often leading to legal irregularities at trial but usually securing easy convictions and lengthy sentences for the accused.[87]

Arm the Spirit provides a glimpse of prisons and political movements in transition. Its pages used a combination of first-person testimony and political and economic analysis to diagnose the growth of control units within existing prisons as well as the construction of new prisons as constituting the government's war plan.[88] Articles detailed incidents in which prisoners were given lengthy sentences, placed in isolation, or beaten to death. The articles still championed the BLA, which had freed Assata Shakur in 1979 but bungled a $1.6 million robbery in Nyack, New York, two years later, leading to four deaths and several arrests. Other articles reported the "capture" of leftists living underground or jailed for refusing to cooperate with grand juries. The era of leftist guerrilla war was coming to an end. At the same time, prisoners experienced tightening conditions: less mobility, more violence, ongoing struggles with censorship, the continuation of unduly harsh sanctions, and the return of the death penalty. *Arm the Spirit* held onto its feisty, fighting tone until its demise in the early 1980s, but times were clearly changing.

Arm the Spirit newspaper, edited largely by San Quentin prisoner Kalima Aswad and distributed by a coalition that included the Prairie Fire Organizing Committee and the United Prisoners Union. The publication of *Arm the Spirit* was one of several ways in which print culture sustained prisoner organizing in the mid- and late 1970s. From the Collection of the Freedom Archives.

One of the most prominent and ultimately positive areas of coverage in *Arm the Spirit* was the case of the Pontiac Brothers, a group of seventeen black prisoners facing the death penalty following a deadly riot at an Illinois prison on July 22, 1978. The paper's attention to this case is a clear way in which prison publications went hand in hand with more traditional forms of organizing. The campaign for these prisoners was perhaps the most ambitious defensive effort of the late 1970s. Atiba Shanna and the New Afrikan Prisoners Organization at Stateville prison, about thirty miles southwest of Chicago, initiated the effort. Shanna spread information through *The Fuse*, the newsletter of the New Afrikan Prisoners Organization, of which he was the primary author.

The Fuse, like *Arm the Spirit*, was edited in prison and published by activists in a nearby city—in this case, Chicago. Its general format mirrored other prisoner publications of the time: articles discussed anticolonial movements on the African continent, connected racism in prison to the black condition, and reported on trials involving black revolutionaries and militant prisoners. The paper contained two regular historical features: a "black liberation calendar" listing important dates and historical events and excerpts from speeches

THE FUSE

No.9 Aug. 1979 / 14-ADM

NEW AFRIKAN PRISONER ORGANIZATION

UPDATE ON THE PONTIAC 31

The 17 Pontiac Brothers charged with murder and facing the death penalty were transferred to the Cook County Jail in Chicago on Aug. 1, 1979, where their trials will be held.

All 31 Pontiac Brothers urged their attorneys and supporters to fight to have all the trials held in Chicago. But the colonial state has divided the Brothers in an attempt to weaken the effectiveness of their in-court battles and the strength of their families and supporters.

Fighting to have all the trials in Chicago was based on the reality that a *"fair trial"* is totally impossible anywhere in amerikkka for black people, but that in Chicago, with its large black population, the Brothers would have a better chance of obtaining a *"jury of their peers"*, the assistance of trusted counsel and of

an organized black community. But, this is possible only if the appropriate trial strategy is employed, and if the black community can be rallied behind the slogan of *"Free The Pontiac Brothers–Put the Colonial State on Trial!"*.

* * * * *

'Il. Gov. James Thompson' is, in reality, a Colonial Administrator......

* * * * *

Pre-trial motions for the 17 are scheduled to be filed in September, and the state is trying to rush it through before the support for the Brothers builds on a national and international scale.

continued

The Fuse magazine, edited by James Yaki Sayles, also known as Atiba Shanna. The publication was produced by the New Afrikan Prisoners Organization in Illinois and was used to connect prison issues to the changing urban landscape of the 1970s. Author's collection.

or books by black radicals that *Fuse* editors felt were, as the section was titled, "worth repeating." But more than its contemporaries, *The Fuse* was preoccupied with the worsening urban condition and how it corresponded to the growing prison population. In a three-part series, "War for the Cities," Shanna described in real time the changing political geography of black America: because urban capitalists now had less use for black labor, black families were being pushed out of the city center and into working-class enclaves structured and surveilled like prisons, while the black youth who populated the freedom struggle were being herded into prison. These transformations tethered prisoners' fates to those of city residents. Stuck between the brutal prison and the decrepit ghetto, Shanna argued, the black nation was on the edge of a precipice.[89]

Seven months before the riot, NAPO described worsening conditions at Pontiac: inadequate medical care and insufficient staff to coordinate prisoner programs and requests. Pontiac prisoners made all the road signs for the state of Illinois, for which they were paid between thirty-five and fifty-five cents an hour. Readers of *The Fuse*, therefore, may not have been surprised the following summer when the "great deal of frustration and feelings of helplessness among the prisoners here at Pontiac K[oncentration] K[amp]" produced Illinois's largest prison riot, during which three white guards were stabbed to death.[90] Built in

1871, Pontiac is the second-oldest prison in Illinois. At the time of the one-day riot, the maximum-security prison housed about two thousand people—well over its capacity—and half of them participated in the spontaneous uprising. With poor medical care, contaminated food, no air-conditioning, and long-term lockdowns, Pontiac was especially harsh in the summer.[91]

The day after the riot, authorities blamed it on overcrowding and heat; five months later, in a sign of the new racial battlefield animating the carceral state, the official position attributed the violence to gangs. The State of Illinois initially charged thirty-one men, twenty-eight black and three Latino, in the three deaths. Seventeen black men ultimately stood trial on charges of conspiracy and murder. It was the largest capital case involving black men since the Scottsboro Boys case in the 1930s. During the riot and trial, Bradley Greene, now known as Abdul Shanna, was a prisoner at Stateville, a member of NAPO, and contributor to *The Fuse*. He saw the Pontiac Brothers case as a turning point in the prison movement.[92] Prosecutors sounded a familiar fear of black hordes, now conjured in the form of gangs, run amok. Supporters saw that tactic as another red herring.

The Pontiac Brothers ultimately attracted the support of Louis Farrakhan and Dick Gregory, among others, while their support coalition included the RNA, the PFOC, and the Sojourner Truth Organization. The men had a high-profile legal team, including the People's Law Office, a Chicago-based consortium of leftist attorneys well practiced in prison cases (ultimately including several related to the FALN). The attorneys won a change of venue to Cook County, where Chicago is located, on the grounds that it was the only county in the state where the men could be tried by a jury of their peers. The court spent five months selecting the jury. By that point, the case had been split into two, one involving ten defendants and another involving seven. The larger group went on trial first, endeavoring, as in the San Quentin 6 trial and similar cases, to put prison conditions on trial. The prisoners and their attorneys argued that abysmal conditions at Pontiac created the conditions for the riot.

On May 9, 1981—Mother's Day—a jury of seven blacks and five whites proclaimed all ten men not guilty on all fifty-seven charges. After five months of jury selection and four months of trial, the jury had deliberated for less than an hour. Charges were then dropped against the remaining seven men.[93] Prison organizers had won the battle, but they were losing the war.

"WE BEGIN WITH OURSELVES"

The late 1970s was a hard time for black prison organizing. What were once perceived as extreme forms of imprisonment—punishment and isolation without end—were becoming the norm of confinement. Even the limited physical movement that had been possible a decade earlier was becoming more difficult, while the conflict between guards and dissident prisoners had not subsided. In short, conditions inside had become increasingly volatile. On the outside, many organizations that had been focused on prisoner issues had splintered or disappeared. Although there was no shortage of either outrage or organizing, fewer people were paying attention to what was happening in prisons. Several organizations that had worked to improve prison conditions during much of the preceding two decades had folded or moved on to other areas of activism. The remaining organizations were smaller and often governed by a sense of scarcity that prevented coalitions from forming or lasting.[94]

Further, many organizations lacked the capacity to deal with the traumas faced by currently and formerly incarcerated people. Years of witnessing, experiencing, and fearing violence took a toll on people. After spending most of their adult—and in some cases their juvenile—lives incarcerated, some people faced steep challenges in life on the other side of prison walls. They saw cities declining and a Left ill equipped to handle people in crisis. Economic recession, urban redevelopment, and a growing ideology of privatization meant that the government offered fewer resources to help people in need.

The combination of these factors made the late 1970s a time of bloody transition for prison organizing. In California, a series of violent episodes resulted in the deaths of several leading figures and severely weakened the prison movement. Wounded and with a shrinking sense of possibility, black prison organizing survived by prioritizing survival strategies. The use of nationalism increased as a way of maintaining a larger worldview as the immediate surroundings became more constricted.

Black prison organizing always referred simultaneously to conditions in prison and conditions in the world outside of prison. The prison defined their efforts, and this dialectic solidified the nationalist mantra of self-reliance: prisoners needed to look out for one another because American institutions had proven themselves hostile to black survival. Prisoners needed to use whatever resources were at their disposal, especially education and physical self-discipline, to bolster their political resolve. "We begin with ourselves, with study and practice," Atiba Shanna wrote in his outline for rebuilding the prison movement.[95] Similar sentiments appeared in New Afrikan prison papers: as prisoners grappled with an expanding and increasingly repressive prison system, they argued that any hope for change lay in perfecting themselves—their physical care, intellectual acumen, and cultural proficiency—while simultaneously confronting the government. Such sentiments provided a left-wing gloss on the emerging conservative rhetoric of "personal responsibility" rather than government stewardship, even if such personal discipline was offered as a necessary step to rebuild a radical challenge to the state.[96]

Prison organizing continued to experiment with this outward-looking form of self-reliance in the form of Black August, a solemn holiday invented by California prisoners inspired by George Jackson. Black August emerged at a moment of transition, and prisoners hoped it would be the start of a new era of activism. Though it did not catalyze a new mass movement, it ushered in a new era of prison organizing during which a culture of prison radicalism continued despite an increasingly repressive environment.

Prisoners had attempted similar endeavors, among them the Black Solidarity Day protest held by prisoners in Auburn, New York, on November 2, 1970.[97] Black August was a new effort, merging historical memory with the prison realities of the late 1970s. Isolation and containment were the watchwords of late 1970s penal discipline as prison authorities tried to limit prisoners' contact with each other in hopes of eliminating their organizing. But violence against prisoners sparked their organizing, and such violence continued, both from guards and between rival prison gangs. An economic downturn and the growing law-and-order climate led to overcrowding in many prisons. In addition, the elimination of educational programs, the use of prison-wide lockdowns, and the spread of isolation units further atomized and frustrated prisoners.[98] The conflagrations that emerged from these conditions displayed less political overtones than earlier protests and therefore tended to be less threatening to the institution itself. In both California and New York, black prisoners faced growing violence from neo-Nazi gangs. At Eastern New York Correctional Facility in Napanoch, several guards were active members of the Ku Klux Klan.[99] The entrenchment of the racist Right inside American prisons contributed to the growing violence: at San Quentin, scores of attacks during the 1970s had led the prison system to experiment with institution-wide lockdowns.[100]

In tandem with Muntaqim's appeal to the United Nations, prison activists held demonstrations at the gates of San Quentin starting in 1977. The organizers chose August to commemorate Jackson's heroism and death. In 1977 and 1978, the protests were held on or around August 21, and the organization sponsoring the march called itself the August 21 Coalition. The prisoners' demands on behalf of which the demonstrators petitioned included access to media through which prison conditions could be exposed.[101] The coalition staged numerous large demonstrations at the gates of San Quentin, bringing together a range of groups—including, on at least one occasion, members of the Peoples Temple prior to their move to (and subsequent mass suicide in) Guyana.[102]

The August 21 demonstrations and what became Black August constituted attempts by prison activists to rebuild the political thrust of antiprison protest in the context of bleak internecine battles. Between 1977 and 1979, the California prison population increased, while a series of shootings wounded or felled a handful of noteworthy activists. On April 27, 1977, San Quentin 6 member Willie Sundiata Tate was severely wounded and Earl Satcher was killed in a shootout outside a San Francisco food co-op. Satcher, a veteran of the California prison system, had founded an ostensibly radical group called Tribal Thumb after his release. While several sincere activists were attracted to the group, Satcher used it to advance his own interests with a certain cruelty. A member of Tribal Thumb had been convicted for shooting and killing progressive schoolteacher Sally Voye and UPU organizer Popeye Jackson while the pair sat in a parked car in San Francisco in the early morning hours of June 2, 1975. Satcher apparently wanted to kill Tate as part of a forced takeover of the co-op board for personal financial gain.[103]

On May 28, 1979, in a shocking act of violence, three people entered attorney Fay Stender's house in the middle of the night. They forced her at gunpoint to write a confession proclaiming that she had "abandoned George Jackson in his time of need" and then shot her six times. She survived, paralyzed and in considerable pain. She took her own life a year later. Several attorneys who had been close to the prison movement, many of them members of the NLG, distanced themselves from certain prisoner cases after the attack on Stender, and some completely severed their ties to the prison movement.[104]

In November 1979, Fleeta Drumgo was gunned down on an Oakland street. Drumgo had been exonerated in two of the biggest cases of the era, the Soledad Brothers and the San Quentin 6, but had difficulty returning to life outside of prison. After his release, he sabotaged many of his friendships through manipulative behavior, and his death apparently resulted from a drug deal gone wrong, although some observers allege that he was killed deliberately.[105] Together, these shootings had a chilling effect on the California prison movement precisely when it was most needed to confront the rising tide of mass incarceration.

By 1979, then, dissident prisoners were isolated in prison and at greater remove from outsiders. As a result, they turned inward to maintain a political trajectory that seemed to be slipping away. Black August was said to commemorate the martyrs of the California prison movement, all of whom died in August: George and Jonathan Jackson, William Christmas, James McClain, and

Jeffrey Khatari Gaulden, who died at San Quentin on August 1, 1978. Gaulden was a comrade of Jackson's and a leading figure in the prison military formation Jackson started, the Black Guerrilla Family (BGF).

Gaulden had been imprisoned since 1967, part of the generation of prisoners who became revolutionaries during their confinement. The records of California's prison movement contain few references to him before his death, though he was well known among Bay Area prison activists and well respected among other men of color in the California prison system. Gaulden, like George Jackson and Hugo Pinell, was a student and friend of W. L. Nolen; also like them, he mentored younger prisoners in developing a political worldview. Like Nolen but unlike Jackson, he was charismatic in a behind-the-scenes way that allowed him to establish a base of organizing inside prisons and become a thorn in the sides of administrators without receiving substantial public notoriety. In May 1972, he was convicted of killing a civilian laundry worker at Folsom the previous September, allegedly in response to Jackson's death. The incident occurred just after Gaulden had been released from the Adjustment Center, and he was returned there after his conviction. Gaulden's letters appeared in a pamphlet published by Inez Williams, Fleeta Drumgo's mother, in an attempt to raise support for men imprisoned in the San Quentin AC.[106]

At the beginning of August 1978, the thirty-two-year-old Gaulden was playing football on the cramped Adjustment Center yard with nine other prisoners. According to Shujaa Graham, a friend of Gaulden's who was on the yard that day, someone pushed Gaulden too hard, and he hit his head and fell to the ground. As the other prisoners clamored for medical attention for him, guards cleared the yard one person at a time, searching everyone individually, leaving Gaulden bleeding from the head. By the time the other prisoners were cleared and taken back to their cells, Gaulden was dead.[107]

Gaulden had helped initiate the holiday that later honored him. Several prisoners had discussed trying to launch something that would combine radical politics and spiritual sustenance—something more permanent, if less tangible, than campaigns regarding individual cases that could keep the horrors of incarceration front and center on the outside. These prisoners wanted to unite the different threads of black radicalism circulating in prison—those coming from revolutionary political organizations such as the Black Panthers and Black Liberation Army as well as those developed through other sanctioned or illicit organizations.

The development of Black August is inseparable from the Black Guerrilla Family. With its direct connection to George Jackson, the BGF took up the mantle of the prison movement in the 1970s, and for many people, the BGF became synonymous with the prison movement happening inside. The BGF's roots lie in loose affiliations of black prisoners dating back to the 1960s. Nolen called this network the Black Mafia; it later went by the names of the Capone Gang and the Wolf Pack, although some within this network of prisoners claim never to have heard or used such names.[108]

Around 1967 and at the urging of George Jackson and William Christmas, among others, these associations became far more political. After his brother's bloody death, Jackson changed the name to the August 7th Guerrilla Movement and reemphasized his goal of uniting the militant prisoners within the California prison system through Marxist theory and urban guerrilla warfare. Jackson had also used the term "Black Guerrilla Family," and after his death, the name stuck. As with so much of prison politics, the BGF was as much an idea, a way to categorize a certain orientation of black prisoners, as a functional organization. It combined revolutionary nationalist politics with the do-or-die mentality found in many unsanctioned prison organizations.[109]

The decline of socialist organizations such as the Black Panther Party left an absence that was filled by heterodox groupings that combined politics and predatory behavior. More than groups such as the Aryan Brotherhood, Crips, or Mexican Mafia, the BGF began in prison and never had a large corollary structure outside of prison. The California prison system facilitated such entities by dividing prisoners by race and stoking racial hostilities inside its facilities. The BGF saw itself as the heir to a legacy of black liberationist dissent. Dorsey Nunn went to prison at nineteen and was incarcerated throughout much of the 1970s. Functionally illiterate at the time, he "learned to read from the BGF. . . . And if you didn't know a word you ask your homeboy, your comrade, and say 'Hey man! What is this word, what does it mean?' And it was rewarding to have a homeboy who started out after you come and ask you and be blessed and privileged enough to teach him." According to Nunn, the BGF was one of several organized political entities in the California prison system that held largely covert political education classes.[110]

Gangs often combined some measure of political critique with their involvement in the illicit economy. The BGF's political orientation was more pronounced than that of other prisoner groups, although its political foundations always competed with the criminal elements that provided its material foundations. Here again, the prison was not so far removed from what was happening on the streets. The circumstances that gave rise to the Crips in the streets of South Central Los Angeles in the mid-1970s—a toxic combination of limited jobs and growing police and interpersonal violence in the decaying metropolitan center—gave rise to the BGF in the cells of San Quentin.[111] Geographer

Mike Davis called the Los Angeles gangs the "bastard offspring of the Panthers' former charisma, filling the void left by the LAPD SWAT teams."[112] To the extent that the BGF's origins can be traced back to Jackson and Nolen, however, its emergence signaled an earlier, parallel origin to the "organized abandonment" of black communities that made such informal associations a central mode of organization in urban ghettoes.[113] These conditions of extreme confinement increasingly became the political reference points for a new generation of prisoners without the hopeful energy of decolonization and a political order openly responsive to popular demands.

The BGF joined the nationalist-inflected politics of early 1970s black prisoners with the emerging dominance of prison gangs, both facilitating and following the changing prison environment. This uneasy balance between political education and criminal activity was a constant source of tension within the BGF, ultimately leading to a split in the organization. The BGF demonstrated some continuity in prison politics from Jackson's time and was led in the 1970s by his contemporaries.[114] Unlike either prison gangs or street gangs that brought their organizations into the cell block, the BGF began in prison and moved only somewhat onto the street. It was an organization based in the culture of confinement. In the context of institutions that disallowed all organized political activity and fostered divisions among prisoners, groups that retained some capacity for self-defense and physical attack and that combined individual advancement with collective protection stood a better chance of survival than those that did not.

Black August began as a way to commemorate the relatively recent history of prison radicalism alongside the long history of slave rebellions. As the tradition continued, though, it came to reflect a longer black freedom struggle. Subsequent generations of Black August participants have pointed to the many historically significant incidents that have taken place in August. The Haitian Revolution began on August 21, 1791; Gabriel Prosser's slave rebellion was originally scheduled for August 30, 1800; Nat Turner launched his rebellion on August 21, 1831; and Henry Highland Garnet called for an uprising on August 22, 1843. W. E. B. Du Bois died on August 27, 1963, while Marcus Garvey was born on August 17, 1887, and he formed the Universal Negro Improvement Association in August 1914. Garvey's group held a monthlong international convention that attracted twenty-five thousand people to Madison Square Garden in August 1920. During the civil rights era, the 1963 March on Washington, as well as the 1965 Watts rebellion and the 1978 standoff between Philadelphia police and the black naturalist MOVE organization, all occurred in August.[115] Now an international hip-hop festival as well as a holiday celebrated by multiracial groups of dissident prisoners, Black August has become a celebration of black diasporic radicalism.[116] It is a holiday of pride and of protest against prisons. The freedom of black political prisoners, the memory of George and Jonathan Jackson, still looms large in these celebrations.

When it began in 1979, however, the holiday was principally concerned with honoring the slain prison activists. Because many of those involved either claimed or were thought to be members of the BGF, the creation of Black August renewed interest in the BGF by prison activists and law enforcement alike. The BGF political statement, which was designated for members' eyes only but wound its way to the FBI, proclaimed a militant anticapitalism and a hostile, patriarchal distrust of white people, whom the document described as "devious by nature" and willing to "give their daughters to put a cease to our endeavors."[117] BGF members swore an oath to the organization and the other members until death.

The BGF had long been an enigma to authorities, who considered it the worst of all possible scenarios: a combination of revolutionary politics and criminal activity, especially drugs and the violence accompanying the illegal drug trade. Law enforcement from the California Department of Corrections to the FBI took a great deal of interest in the BGF, in large part because of its association with George Jackson. This high level of interest signaled an emerging police strategy of targeting "gangs." In the years to come, alleged gang affiliation would serve as a dominant mode of policing both the inner city and the prison. In the name of stopping gangs, police departments initiated a variety of preemptive policing strategies, such as "stop and frisk." In prison, antigang policies justified widespread lockdowns and targeted isolation that made it far more difficult for people to work together. Stopping "gangs," therefore, became a key ingredient in prison growth and management; it was also an ostensibly color-blind way of punishing black and Latino youth, dissidents, and others.[118]

Policing the BGF helped define gangs as a racial threat inextricably bound to the prison. The FBI actively investigated the BGF from 1974 to 1976, during which time there were at least 268 stabbings and 56 deaths in California prisons as conflicts among gangs and between gangs and guards intensified.[119] The bureau was not merely interested in curbing prison violence but also explored possible connections between the BGF and other radical groups. The FBI sought to connect the BGF to the Black Liberation Army, the Symbionese Liberation Army, the Weather Underground, and street gangs in Boston, Chicago, and Philadelphia. The FBI took this threat seriously, sharing its files with law enforcement agencies and the U.S. Secret Service. All evidence indicated that the BGF was limited to California, however, and the bureau followed suspected members to Los Angeles and San Francisco after their release from prison. In the mid-1970s, the FBI estimated that the BGF had between two hundred and one thousand members.[120]

The FBI interest in the BGF had waned by 1976, and the Bureau closed its files on the group. In 1979, however, a series of events culminating in Black August caught the bureau's attention and returned prison protest to national law enforcement's list of concerns. First came Stender's shooting and the outraged grief it generated. Ten days later, an alleged BGF member was arrested for the shooting and for two bank robberies in Berkeley. Coming on the heels of these acts, the announcement of Black August made the FBI and the California Department of Corrections fear the second coming of George Jackson. A memo from the San Francisco FBI field office sounded the alarm: "With the announcement of 'Black August,' [officials at the California Department of Corrections] believe that the BGF is preparing to launch an all out assault within the prison system with substantial outside support in the form of revolutionary expropriations, arms collection and the establishment of 'safe houses' for the purpose of taking hostages to cause the release of BGF leaders" from the Deuel Vocational Institution, Folsom, San Quentin, and Soledad.[121]

No such attack materialized, and not just because authorities placed those facilities on lockdown. Rather, notwithstanding the BGF's commitment to armed struggle, officials' fears of violent assault masked the holiday's purpose. For militant prisoners, Black August served more of a reflective role than a combative one. It was an attempt to demonstrate the unity of black prisoners, a display of power through solemnity, not force. Tactically, Black August represented a return to some of the actions that marked the visible rise of prison protest within California—specifically, the August 1968 strike at San Quentin, in which prisoners boycotted voluntary weekend activities to demonstrate their collectivity without generating violent retaliation from the guards. As with the earlier demonstration, Black August was designed to be a protest that could be expressive and pedagogical without violating prison rules. It aimed to demonstrate collective discontent without risking harsh sanctions and was a way for individuals to participate in collective action despite the barriers to meeting as a group. Black August turned the tables of normative prison practices, whereby officials discipline prisoners through the denial of privileges. Black August organizers used asceticism as a resource, a way to withdraw from the prison's disciplinary arm. Organized as a period of commemoration, Black August was not just a protest but a nationalist ritual.

To honor Black August was to abide by a series of practices that had long defined prison organizing. During the month of August, dozens of black prisoners refused food and water before sundown, did not use the prison canteen, eschewed drugs and conceited behavior, boycotted radio and television, and engaged in rigorous physical exercise and political study. Through Black August, prisoners sought to demonstrate the personal power they maintained despite incarceration. The holiday deliberately joined the meditative emphasis of Ramadan and the influence of Islam on black prison protest with the nationalist display of self-reliance and racial pride that emphasized the most militant elements of black history. "We figured that the people we wanted to remember wouldn't be remembered during black history month, so we started Black August," recalled Shujaa Graham, a co-founder of the holiday.[122]

This historical remembrance came alongside a silent protest. The abstention from food and mainstream media constituted an effort to show prisoners' autonomy from the amenities offered by the prison and the society it represented. The rejection of television was especially significant, since TV's introduction into California prisons in the early 1970s overlapped with and helped facilitate a decline in prisoner organizing and interest in reading. Some prisoners saw access to television as a deliberate counterinsurgency by prison officials.[123] Prisoners framed their actions as a rejection of materialism in prison. In the context of an institution that sought to control their every move, Black August represented a chance to steal their lives back from the normal prison routine. They wore black armbands, either over or under their shirts, to mark their participation in the protest. Prisoners used their self-sacrifice to gain additional attention to their standing demands for the abolition of the death penalty and a moratorium on prison construction as well as to support prisoners facing charges for riots.[124]

Black August began at San Quentin but spread throughout California prisons and ultimately throughout the prison system nationally. Prisoners celebrated Black August to demonstrate their political will. As one participant put it, "Black August is the conscious effort to institutionalize standards of revolutionary thought and deeds" and "a mechanism of identity" rooted in "the dungeons of Kalifornia prison Kamps."[125]

Black August continued to connect prison dissidents with supporters outside, with the solidarity activists again following the prisoners' lead. The August 21 Coalition organized a protest and rally at the gates of San Quentin on August 25, 1979, in solidarity with the contemplative protest happening inside. The outside editors of *Arm the Spirit*, part of the coalition, used their newspaper to support the men inside and to encourage others to join the protest.[126] Some coalition members on the outside also participated in the ritual by fasting during the day, avoiding media except for "news and education programs," and abstaining from drugs and alcohol. They held daily study groups at the homes of supporters, rotating locations nightly to further collectivize their endeavors. This somber display of discipline sought to join their fate to that of the men behind bars. "Those of us struggling in the minimum security section of this vast concentration camp called Amerika wish to express our solidarity with those of you who are confined behind the walls of San Quentin and all other maximum security strongholds," announced a Black August Solidarity Statement read on Berkeley's progressive KPFA radio, which remained popular among politically conscious prisoners.[127]

Prisoners hoped that the holiday would generate greater unity between themselves and black and white activists on the outside. It is not surprising, then, that the solidarity prisoners received expressed itself in communal terms. "Prisons, for our people, represent, though sometimes difficult to view and accept, an unpleasant but real extension of the community," declared a flyer distributed at the gates of San Quentin during Black August in 1979. "And as prisons represent a real part of our community, it is *criminal* for anyone to attempt to separate us from our loved ones in prison, and it is also *unforgivable* for us to allow ourselves to be separated."[128]

More than the work strikes of prisoner unionism, the closest approximation of collective withdrawal from the prison, Black August maintained that prisoners had an inner power that could be channeled into both their survival in prison and their status outside prison. The holiday represented an effort to rebuild prison radicalism through political study, ascetic regimen, and collective discipline. The ritual sought to reject the colonizing elements of prison life by eschewing even the mundane privileges of media usage and the prison canteen. Black prison radicals attempted to gain control of their bodies in pursuit of revolutionary nationalist ends. They wanted to show that they were more powerful than the prisons that held them because they could survive without its perks or programs. Self-reliance was an attempt to reclaim the initiative, if on a small scale, amid growing conservatism.

Had Black August simply been a protest of prison conditions alone, the holiday likely would not have endured. Its longevity as an ongoing ritual connecting prisoners to one another and to communities of struggle outside results from the way it solidified the prison as an institution central to black life and politics. Prisoners turned to black history as a way of demonstrating the continuity of black protest throughout the ages. Nations rise and fall with the telling of histories, and Black August was a historical narrative to bolster the black nation. Frantz Fanon argued that "colonialism is not simply content to impose its rule upon the present and the future of a dominated country. . . . By a kind of perverted logic, it turns to the past of the oppressed people, and distorts, disfigures and destroys it."[129] Following this logic, prisoners returned to the past as a way of surviving their present and in hopes of shaping their future. Black August celebrates the history of black resistance as a national trait, often taking root against confinement. As the culmination of a generation of protest behind the walls, Black August solidified the prison as both a metaphor for racism and a site in which to combat it.

As Ronald Reagan readied to run the country, a host of conservatives anticipated the changes he would bring. Here was a politician who favored counterinsurgency, who could put an end to what conservative political scientist Samuel Huntington and others had called in 1975 the "excess of democracy" that had caused such tumult among racialized groups, women, and students. Reagan's well-established resentment of the Left enabled him to join law-and-order politics with laissez-faire economics. This combination unfolded with increasing intensity in the late 1970s and early 1980s. As the United States began to lock up more and more people, critics began to label the country a prison nation: a country defined by its maximized use of the prison and the gallows.[130]

Black August, along with the prisoner print culture of the 1970s, illuminated a different prison nation. Black prison nationalism attempted to showcase the leadership of black prisoners in the shifting political climate of neoliberalism. A new structure of black superunemployment helped to legitimize the growing prison system. Over the decade, the rate of nonemployed men in low-income black neighborhoods rose from 25.9 percent to 40.7 percent.[131]

Black August also arose from the ashes of the rehabilitative ideal. In 1977, California passed the Uniform Determinate Sentencing Act, which ended the unpopular indeterminate sentencing policy that had kept George Jackson and countless others in prisons for long periods of time on vague sentences. The new policy, however, replaced uncertainty with long, harsh sentences, a forerunner of the mandatory minimum sentencing policies that contributed so much to the prison buildup of the following decades. Also in 1977, people of color became a majority in California's prisons, with a population that was 34 percent black and 21 percent Latino. The number of incarcerated people in the state dropped to an all-time low of 19,600 that year, and a boom in prison construction soon began; by the start of the twenty-first century, California's prison population reached 160,000.[132] While California may have been advanced in embracing punishment as its own good, the rest of the country was not far behind.

Black August depicted black prisoners as exhibiting an inner strength that could withstand the prison's attempt to destroy the mind and enslave the body. This inner strength was the basis for connecting prisoners to organizations and events beyond the prison. Participants may have hoped, as the FBI feared, that Black August would jump-start a revolutionary assault on the prison system or the government more generally. At least in retrospect, though, the creation of Black August at the dawn of mass incarceration sent a different message. Prisoners had initiated a ritual to demonstrate their persistence despite the law-and-order echo chamber. Black August and black prison print culture showed the growing dominance of culture as the staging ground for black politics.[133] They affirmed the centrality of both individual and collective dignity and self-determination. They demonstrated that prisons would continue to generate collective memories of repression and resistance that would place imprisoned intellectuals as pivotal figures in the unending struggle for social justice. Much as black southerners maintained a history of black nationalism as they migrated across the country, so, too, would their offspring nurture these politics inside American prisons—a nation captive but not contained.

Epilogue
Choosing Freedom

What artists and prisoners have in common is that both know what it means to be free.
—JAMES BALDWIN, "A Letter to Prisoners" (1982)

F reedom, as an idea and as a practice, has been an enduring paradox of the United States from its origins to the present. Freedom and the various principles it is said to encompass have been encoded into the national origin story of the United States through genocide and enslavement. Violence does not just undermine the goal of American freedom; it is one of its central tenets. As a result, violence and freedom have together constituted the American experience.[1] The history of prison organizing tells us that this sad reality is not inevitable, however, for the diverse institutions, ideologies, and infrastructures that accompany a freedom expressed through domination can be redeployed to more expansive forms of freedom. The precious contingency of freedom is in fact a central legacy of black prison organizing in the civil rights era.

Throughout American history, starkly contrasting versions of freedom are evident. Since the late 1960s, the conjuncture of freedom and violence has entered a new phase of expanded freedom and expanded violence. Critical ethnic studies scholar Chandan Reddy describes the organization of the modern U.S. state as "freedom with violence," "a unique structure of state violence and social emancipation."[2] This experience of freedom is necessarily bound up with and expressed through diverse forms of violence. The U.S. state seeks legitimation for itself as an arbiter of freedom, constantly expanding its ranks by insisting on its own monopoly on violence. This insistence is both institutional and ideological and manifests in a number of violent forms, especially the permanent local-global wars on abstract concepts of communism, crime, drugs, and terrorism that have defined the United States since World War II. At the same time, the government monopoly on violence informs everyday common sense, knowledge production, and public policy. This type of freedom, steeped in "complex racial and racialized gendered inequalities," has taken shape at the limit point of citizenship.[3]

Violence has structured the fight for civic inclusion by race and sexuality, forcing communities to disavow the criminalized construction of blackness and immigrants or to join the nation by serving in the world's largest and most technologically sophisticated military. As the U.S. state has disavowed official racism and now homophobia, it has reinforced racial and sexual difference through expansive systems of policing, punishment, and predatory capitalism as well as through deportations, national security, and warfare. The United States has become more free by becoming more violent, domestically and internationally. The first black president oversaw dramatic steps toward legalizing gay marriage while deporting millions of immigrants, embracing drone warfare, and expanding state surveillance.

Freedom with violence has been the organizing principle of American neoliberalism. Since 1970, the United States has helped lead a global shift in political economy toward greater power for corporations and all manner of private industry. Neoliberalism defines unbridled capitalism as itself a form of freedom. It is a libertarian economic freedom, with free markets, free trade, and the overall free flow of capital wherever elites wish. Because it seeks to dislodge structures of social solidarity, the neoliberal freedom dream has been possible only through nightmarish violence. The ascendance of neoliberalism globally has come through a variety of wars, direct and by proxy, that have killed or displaced millions of people while bolstering a handful of Western companies and eroding different forms of local and national sovereignty. The reconfigured political order of neoliberalism has empowered a host of mercenary forces and warlords, yet this violence has been the overwhelming province of militarily strong states. Voicing a desire to remove the government, neoliberalism has needed the state's iron fist to pursue its agenda. Neoliberal freedom within the United States achieved power through a violent reordering of place and policy that have renovated racial oppression through frameworks of multiculturalism and color blindness.[4]

Freedom with violence, in other words, is the reason that a black person is killed every twenty-eight hours by police or a vigilante. It is the reason that the killers in these cases rarely face any criminal sanction for their actions—and further evidence that more prisons mean less safety. The prison and the attendant changes in criminal laws and sentencing policy that facilitated the 500 percent increase in the U.S. incarceration rate between 1980 and the early twenty-first century have nurtured this freedom with violence.[5]

In response to the political crises caused by postwar revolutionary movements, including the prison movement, and dramatic economic shifts, the U.S. state instituted a set of policies that produced a system of mass incarceration preying on the most oppressed sectors of society by race, class, geography, and sexuality. Millions of people—almost exclusively poor people of color from inner cities, a majority of them black and Latino, with strong overrepresentation of queer and trans people—have experienced freedom with violence through stop-and-frisk policing, an expanded criminal code, limited parole, and an unprecedented boom in prison construction. As a result, the United States has developed the world's largest prison system and one of its most severe: it is the only industrialized nation that imposes the death penalty and life sentences without possibility of parole, and eighty thousand people live in solitary confinement in U.S. prisons. George Jackson's fear of dying without having lived has been institutionalized through a battery of austere conditions that suspend life through incarceration and its afterlives.[6]

Indeed, the prison rebellions of the 1960s and 1970s left officials believing that prisoners had too much freedom. As prisons modernized their technology, they limited their capacities for collective action, seeking ever more ways to separate prisoners from each other and the outside world. The prison construction binge that began in the 1980s included new experiments in isolation—including whole units and facilities devoted to isolation. By the 1990s, whole prisons were structured around solitary confinement, which has been used to punish the thoughts and actions of dissident prisoners, to break people's spirits, and to reinscribe racial distinctions as political divisions among the prison population.

Solitary confinement has featured prominently in official efforts to police and control "gangs," especially but not exclusively in California. The widespread use of solitary confinement in the context of "antigang" measures in prison, "gang injunctions," and other policing of informal associations among youth of color on the outside have contributed to undermining the reach and success of prison organizing as a part of antiracist social movements. Racial distinction blunted the unity message of prison organizers as solitary raised the stakes for challenging institutional violence. In California, "gang membership" has been a key mechanism of racialization; several people have been placed in solitary confinement as gang members for their possession of literature by or about George Jackson. In other places, possession of literature about the Black Panthers or other black radical associations has justified similar punitive measures.[7]

For its victims, freedom with violence is a bleak and enveloping experience that has at times captured the imagination of subjugated populations. It has fostered an idea that oppressed people might achieve freedom *through* violence. Some have taken the ubiquity of violence to mean that violence itself can be redemptive, cathartic. Anticolonial thinker, fighter, and psychiatrist Frantz Fanon famously suggested the idea that violence not only could eradicate colonization but was necessary to cleanse the colonized world of the disempowerment naturalized by foreign rule. A generation of guerrilla fighters believed that their actions would be transformative in this manner; violent struggle had a metaphysical imperative. In the early 1970s, George Jackson was perhaps the leading American proponent of and contributor to such theories, and a smattering of revolutionaries catalyzed by their opposition to imprisonment attempted to put these ideas into practice.[8]

Practitioners of freedom through violence have described their efforts as attempting to interrupt the greater violence of state-enforced invisibility and abuse. As an insurgent philosophy, such violence has always paled in comparison to that of the state. The ability of the oppressed to exact the kind of retributive violence such a freedom dream mandates has been limited to small-scale expressions. Its violence has always been more performative, rhetorical, and even philosophical than it has been physical.

As freedom with violence has become more all-encompassing, some anti-statists of the Left and Right still hold out hope that freedom might yet be experienced through violence. Yet, precisely because its physicality cannot compete with that of the state, attempts to enact this kind of freedom have been easily countered by the larger system of freedom with violence. Freedom with violence anticipates, requires, and incorporates such violent irruptions as part of justifying its own monopoly on force and rationality. Freedom with violence finds its legitimacy in the (real or imagined) outbursts of its subjects. Each violent act by the oppressed is characterized as further need for the violent, excessive, and increasingly preemptive protection of the state.[9]

Against and beyond these options is another constellation of freedom: freedom from violence.[10] The black freedom struggle, from the plantation to the prison and beyond, has been rooted in this notion of freedom. The black radical tradition, as Cedric Robinson notes, has been characterized by an "absence of mass violence."[11] Instead, it has been grounded in something far more powerful: a vision of human emancipation and global citizenship, a politics of mass self-defense rooted in the idea that black life is worth defending because all human life matters. Freedom from violence is the freedom of mobility and thought, the freedom of bodily integrity and communal action, the freedom of creativity and communication. It is a counterfactual freedom because it is forged in conflict with opponents far more powerful and violent, because it is found in furtive spaces of struggle, because it is both a process and a destination.

Freedom from violence is the freedom dream of prison radicalism. In her poem, "Affirmation," former Black Liberation Army political prisoner turned exile in Cuba Assata Shakur summarizes this freedom as a belief in living.[12] This belief in living propelled black prisoners in the three and a half decades after World War II to boldly declaim that the American state could not crush their spirit. A belief in living as a collective goal united prisoner rebellions throughout the country, animated defense campaigns for political prisoners, and led prisoners to conduct study groups and start their own media. It inspired them to keep reaching beyond the confines of the prison.

It is difficult to reconcile the militarism of George Jackson and many people he inspired with the idea of freedom from violence. To be sure, Jackson and many other prison organizers in the civil rights era were a product of the anticolonial era. Looking to Fanon, Mao, Che, and other guerrilla practitioners, they saw armed struggle and people's wars as necessary paths to liberation. Their strategy was freedom through violence. One can still read into Jackson and other dissident prisoners, however, a desire to escape the institutional violence that structured their lives. Indeed, this desire motivated their political theories and activism. Freedom through violence held that the oppressed needed to use violence to escape greater violence. But freedom remains a question of praxis, and desiring freedom through violence meant that violence itself became a central preoccupation at the expense of pursuing the larger freedom *from* violence that informed their social commentary. In a post–Cold War, post-9/11 period, left-wing movements have largely and appropriately distanced themselves from such military ambitions.

Freedom from violence is an active, enacted set of practices. In challenging the diverse sources and structures of violence, this freedom strives for unity across difference. Prison organizing in the twenty-first century has made central the question of freedom from violence. It is the reason that many prison rebellions since the 1970s—including the labor and hunger strikes that transpired in dozens of prisons around the United States between 2010 and 2013— have been both rooted in black nationalist (principally New Afrikan) politics and multiracial in expression. New Afrikan nationalism, with its reference to ubiquitous confinement, continues to circulate, albeit in muted ways, throughout the American prison system. It provides a ready-made ideology in which dissident prisoners can identify their total rejection of the prison system and make common cause with anyone who insists on the primacy of the dignity of the incarcerated. Through a pastiche of New Afrikan nationalism and general human rights concerns, prisoners have raised demands that connect the particular conditions of confinement to the general structures of austerity.[13]

Prison protest stages a critical debate between what is and what could be. Poet and antiprison activist Emily Abendroth describes this debate as "the anticipated commons versus the currently inhabited one."[14] As gestated in campaigns against imprisonment, freedom from violence begins from shared experiences of abuse, alienation, criminalization, disenfranchisement, and marginalization—that is, from the common experiences of violence, even if one's proximity to violence differs as a result of social status. From and against this currently inhabited commons emerges the anticipated one, the aspirational vision of life and safety governed by commonly held institutions, practices, and values in the affirmative rather than by the common exposure to violence. This aspired-to commons is one of collective safety and abundance. It is, in Abendroth's words, a "frictive gasp for air" that serves as "a critical co-movement" of opposition to state violence.[15]

This attempt to reconcile these alternate notions of what we do and might have in common challenges the idea, popular among many scholars and pundits, that the United States since the 1960s can be best described as a series of increasingly fractured identities.[16] Freedom from violence offers new forms of coalition and synergy: an aspiration of freedom at levels both interpersonal and social. And in fact, a variety of social movements have adopted the frameworks of black prison organizing. Some, like the reparations movement, have done so directly as a result of individuals having been involved in both movements.[17]

Other influences have been less direct but no less powerful. The reliance on exposure and spectacle to dramatize the urgency of a political crisis afflicting socially invisible populations, the subterranean circulation of political critique through diverse cultural forms that appeal to racialized groups, and the centrality of connectivity in social struggle—the key elements of prison organizing—appeared in hip-hop and the direct-action movement to end HIV/AIDS, among other recent movements. These two movements have been key arenas where the language of prison organizing continues to be spoken and reanimated by challenging the racial logic of criminalization. Both movements emerged from and in response to the "organized abandonment" of neoliberal urban restructuring. Both movements have framed their systemic critiques in terms of a battle over life against institutions of death—whether through police brutality, the death penalty, and the prison system or through pharmaceutical profits, government neglect, and biocapitalism. As direct products of the neoliberal urban condition, both hip-hop and AIDS have been criminalized in racial terms—by the "bad blood," nonnormative genders and sexualities, delinquent style, or direct action of its adherents—and the prison remains a critical gestational site for a radical politics related to fighting AIDS, while hip-hop's "ghettocentric" style dominates prison argot and aesthetics. Both movements have passed through and been shaped by the prison.[18]

Collective rebellions are episodic. Expanded technologies of control and limited leftist movements on the outside have made such rebellions even rarer in prisons. But the long-standing black critique of American criminal justice as a system of racial dominance continues, aided and abetted by the existence of resurgent opposition to prisons beginning in the late 1990s and with added ferocity since the economic collapse of 2008. In 1998, two organizations formed with direct connections to the previous generation of prison protest. Bo Brown, who spent seven years in prison for her involvement with the Seattle-based clandestine George Jackson Brigade, and Angela Davis were part of the intergenerational founding collective of Critical Resistance (CR). CR helped popularize a systemic analysis of prisons as part of a wider organization of the political economy—a prison-industrial complex. Alongside feminist antiviolence organizations such as Incite! Women of Color against Violence, CR has worked to reengage a politics of (prison) abolition that updates 1970s innovations.[19]

The same year that CR began, former Black Panther and longtime political prisoner Jalil Muntaqim initiated the Jericho Amnesty Movement, an organization dedicated to freeing U.S. political prisoners, especially the dozens of women and men still incarcerated for political actions and associations of the civil rights era. One of Jericho's stalwart organizers on the outside was Safiya Bukhari, a former Black Panther who served nine years as a political prisoner. Prior to her death in 2003, Bukhari also worked with the Malcolm X Grassroots Movement, formed by people close to the Republic of New Afrika. The Malcolm X Grassroots Movement has organized against stop-and-frisk policing and for the freedom of black political prisoners. They turned Black August into an international hip-hop celebration of black resistance to confinement throughout history. CR began with a large conference, Jericho with a large march, and the Malcolm X Grassroots Movement circulates prison struggle through hip-hop: the response to captivity continues to be a combination of knowledge production, direct action, and cultural work.

To this list could be added a variety of local and regional organizations and campaigns that have worked to end the war on drugs; lift the barriers to the civil and human rights of formerly incarcerated people; support current and former prisoners in circulating their ideas or gaining their freedom; stop the construction of prisons, jails, and detention centers; abolish solitary confinement and the death penalty; and shift budgetary resources back to community institutions, among other priorities. Other veterans from the civil rights era's prison organizing have contributed to these developments on both sides of the walls though organizations such as All of Us or None and various prison moratorium projects. Current prisoners, from veterans of the 1960s-era social movements to more recent internees, have worked to confront the AIDS crisis and medical neglect in prisons, protest solitary confinement, and challenge the global reach of the U.S. carceral state. They have confronted mass incarceration through creative proposals for mass *decarceration* that link the reduction of imprisonment to the expansion of social justice.[20]

As prison organizing demonstrates, the pursuit of freedom from violence is rooted in care and creativity. Throughout the civil rights era, black prisoners and their allies devised a series of ways to forge freedom from violence that were most dramatically located in exposure. Through writing, uprisings, and court cases, they worked to reveal the horrors of confinement. In exposing prison abuses, they worked to expose the larger brutalities of racism. Civil rights workers rushed to fill southern jails, and Black Power organizers leveraged their experiences with incarceration for the same reason: to eradicate the many ways in which black communities have faced oppression and premature death.

As that struggle moved more firmly into prison systems over more than a decade beginning in the late 1960s, the urgency of exposing racial injustice accelerated. The Soledad Brothers case launched a new wave of prisoner-initiated efforts to reveal state violence with the hope that exposure would incite popular outrage to end such violence. Though dissident prisoners continued to press for exposure by appealing to the United Nations and filing lawsuits, they moved on to other forms of self-reliance to survive and escape such violence when it became clear that public intervention would not save them. They enacted their own rituals of sovereignty through religion and culture to experience a modicum of freedom from violence.

The daily work of prison organizing relies on labor typically gendered as female, a broadly defined notion of support that includes participating in and facilitating communication and person-to-person social networks, expanding communal ties, organizing coalitions, and providing services to those in need. In addition, standing up to the carceral state has required a great deal of ingenuity to overcome the many factors that make prisons difficult institutions around which to organize: their geographic remove from population centers, the stigma of criminalization, the oblique ways in which prisons are funded and governed. Artists, musicians, writers, and other cultural workers have been at the forefront of prison organizing precisely because such creativity has kept the prison in public memory and consciousness. This need for creative forms of resistance against such violence helps explain why prison activism, especially its abolitionist incarnations, has appealed to so many queer and trans people; the ability to imagine, in practical, daily terms, something beyond the seemingly naturalized gender binary lends itself well to the capacity to imagine a world without walls and cages. Such imagination has been instrumental in the ranks of contemporary antiprison movements, where organizers experiment with a series of alternative institutions, including modes of addressing interpersonal (especially sexual) harm outside the criminal justice system.[21]

Black prison organizing is a complex, contradictory, and robust example of the wider black freedom struggle. The tactics and strategies of that larger freedom struggle, continually revised since slavery, inform the shape and substance of black prison organizing. Because it takes shape amid extreme deprivation and violence, prison organizing is by nature contingent and disparate. Yet its impacts have been enormous. In the civil rights era, black prison organizing informed popular conceptions of race, alienation, and freedom. While the neoliberal era has witnessed an unprecedented expansion of the carceral state, prison organizing has not disappeared. The prominence of the phrase "prison-industrial complex" in scholarship, hip-hop music, and even popular journalism testifies to the ways in which terminology developed through political struggle has become part of a larger common sense that names the centrality of the criminal justice system—prisons, policing, surveillance—as it connects with schools, media, private industry, and American governance.

Contemporary opponents of the carceral state might take three major and interrelated actions from black prison organizing in the civil rights era: to care, to chronicle, and to coalesce.

Care: What social scientists at the time called "the convict code" was a robust network of communal care established outside the frameworks of liberalism. Prisoners pledged loyalty to one another, at least temporarily overlooking differences in the service of a larger unity that was, in moments of uprising, leveraged in a fight for prisoner rights. Further, the work of prison organizers on the outside—lawyer Fay Stender, journalist Jessica Mitford, nurse Phyllis Prentice, scholar Angela Davis, activist Karen Wald, and thousands of others—was premised on caring for people facing extreme state violence. Prison organizing, then and now, is about expanding a circle of care. Prison organizing lost sight of that directive at several key moments, facilitated partly by state infiltration. The long list of casualties in California from internecine battles in the movement's later years—Fay Stender, Fleeta Drumgo, Huey Newton, Fred Bennett, James Carr, Popeye Jackson, and several others, on top of the many who had been killed by the state—scared many committed activists and would-be activists away from prison organizing there and facilitated an expanded push for "law and order." Care in and of itself did not win much, but its absence contributed to heavy losses. Further, this care ought to be understood through vulnerability rather than deservingness. As contemporary critiques of mass incarceration focus on "nonviolent drug offenders," there is a danger of asking or being asked to limit our care only to those who meet some preordained moral standard akin to "innocence." But genuine care extends to those facing harm, those who have harmed, and those who do the work of maintaining communal ties. The deservingness of care ought to be premised on a recognition of shared humanity rather than jurisprudent categories.

Chronicle: All organizing is, at root, about telling stories. Whatever the issue, political success belongs to the most believable (though sadly not always the most true) story. These stories are crafted collectively and dialogically: they are the work not of one storyteller but rather of a convergence of tellers speaking through a variety of media. "Law and order" was a story about safety for certain people premised on incapacitating "those people" deemed threatening. Black prison organizing was a story about generational captivity and fugitive freedom. It was also a story about brutal conditions and better treatment. Many people—most centrally, prisoners themselves—participated in crafting this story. They told this story through uprisings, letters, poetry, newspapers, and manifestos. It was reiterated by others through conferences, books, bombs, protests, and other means. What united these various efforts was a visionary critique of the world as it was. George Jackson's *Soledad Brother* remains a poignant text because it so eloquently captures both the horrors of the prison environment and the refusal to be reduced to those horrors. Throughout, he expressed a palpable belief in transformative social change. He invited readers to be horrified by what was and inspired by what could be. As his conditions worsened in the context of political upheaval worldwide, he hoped that immediate revolutionary assault would create change. With a tunnel vision shaped by years in isolation, he drastically overestimated how many people agreed with his story and saw no need to keep breathing life into an alternate story of fugitive freedom. Some of his supporters abnegated dialogue for devotion, failing to disabuse him of his militarism or keep intervening in what stories were told about crime, justice, and prisons. They stopped telling their own stories. Amid an aggressive counterrevolution, they lost the balance of chronicling what is and what could be.

Coalesce: At its height, the prison movement had a large and surprising coalition. It consisted of activists from different communities and movements, a wide variety of sympathetic professionals and politicians, musicians and artists of all stripes, friends and family members of the currently and formerly incarcerated, with all of them gathered around the symbol and message of dissident prisoners. The movement's success lay in a constant expansion of the coalition. Uprisings, interviews, and poetry helped raise awareness and enlist new members. This coalition offered its members a chance to feel directly affected by and connected to the issue across a wide variety of social locations and personal experiences. "The prison" signified both a bricks-and-mortar institution and a diverse set of antagonisms. It could be an overly malleable concept, taken up for cynical or narcissistic as well as reactionary aims. But to the extent that it was anchored in prisoner demands through grassroots organizing and direct action, through an escalating sense of "we," a critique of the prison enabled a political opposition to confinement and a cultural language of expanded freedom. A belief in universal confinement, a belief that "America is the prison," as Malcolm X and then the Black Panther Party and Republic of New Afrika put it, popularized a Black Power analysis. It created the conditions under which diverse movements could challenge the criminal justice system based on their negative experiences with police, prisons, and other forms of state repression. The drive for an ever-expanding coalition of people and issues allowed organizers to break the divisions that the prison works so hard to instill: by identity and geography, by walls and gates.

Direct action unites these modalities of care, chronicle, and coalition. The most successful and enduring forms of organizing freedom from violence have been found in direct confrontation with the state. During the civil rights era and perhaps again today, activist prisoners demonstrated that confinement would not sap their energy or their intellect. Through a series of dramatic encounters—in courtrooms and prison cells, in the pages of books and letters—prisoners displayed a collective initiative, political sophistication, and global imagination. They showed that it is possible to enact radical visions and social structures even—or especially—in situations where state power was at its most abusive and restrictive. From solitary confinement, George Jackson and Angela Davis made the world aware of the prison's racist violence. Ruchell Magee, the San Quentin 6, and other prisoners in solitary confinement (as well as in the general population) showed that the prison was deeply entwined with the afterlife of slavery.

In the connections they made between people they knew well and those they never met, between other prisoners and outside supporters, prisoners expressed an auspicious transformative potential that still has the power to recalibrate notions of race and gender in ways that might undermine bedrock structures of state violence. Through such challenges to the U.S. state, prison organizers learn to develop their own modes of governance. To succeed, they must create an affirmative freedom from violence as well as an opposition to the dominant form of freedom with violence. And to the extent that they succeed in any element of their work, campaigns and initiatives that reduce and supplant the life and scope of the carceral state remain the most urgent, life-affirming political task imaginable.

Captivity and nationality lie at the heart of race in the United States. They form a dialectic found in terms of both how the U.S. state racializes certain populations and how such populations respond to and make sense of their conditions. Captivity continues to animate black social life. From poverty and unemployment to mass incarceration and health discrimination, from educational inequity and police violence to diverse forms of disenfranchisement, blackness in the United States remains a marker of premature death, of the "poor-butchered half-lives" of which George Jackson spoke in 1971.[22]

Yet the fact that black prisoners have, time and again, emerged as spokespeople for and theorists of a different kind of freedom shows that nothing can be taken for granted and that the tragedy of American imprisonment— like the greater tragedy of racial state violence of which it is a part—is neither preordained nor permanent. That knowledge provides a potent and poignant glimpse of freedom, the contingent and courageous struggle for freedom from violence, that always haunts systems of captivity. It is an expansive, reparative, and transformative freedom. It is a future-oriented freedom with deep roots and sprouting seeds to be nurtured. It is a freedom hopeful that the world can be defined by something greater than captivity, something more meaningful than nationality.

Notes

ABBREVIATIONS

The following abbreviations are used throughout the notes.

ADLDF   Angela Davis Legal Defense Fund, Schomburg Center for Research in
Black Culture, New York Public Library, New York

AS   *Arm the Spirit*

BB   *Berkeley Barb*

BL   Bancroft Library, University of California at Berkeley

ECP   Eldridge Cleaver Papers, Bancroft Library, University of California at Berkeley

FA   Freedom Archives, San Francisco

GL   Green Library, Stanford University, Palo Alto, Calif.

HPNFP   Huey P. Newton Foundation Papers, Green Library, Stanford University,
Palo Alto, Calif.

IJ   *Independent Journal* (San Rafael)

JMP   Jessica Mitford Papers, Series III: A Kind and Usual Punishment Files,
Harry Ransom Center, University of Texas at Austin

KFAP   Kendra and Franklin Alexander Papers, Southern California Library,
Los Angeles

LAT   *Los Angeles Times*

MCLIR   Meiklejohn Civil Liberties Institute Records, Bancroft Library, University of
California at Berkeley

MS   *Midnight Special*

NLC   New Left Collection, 1964–2004, Hoover Institute, Stanford University,
Palo Alto, Calif.

NLGC   National Lawyers Guild Collection, Bancroft Library, University of
California at Berkeley

NYT   *New York Times*

PPSB   Papers Relating to the Publication of *Soledad Brother*, Bancroft Library,
University of California at Berkeley

RRSP   Raúl R. Salinas Papers, Green Library, Stanford University, Palo Alto, Calif.

SC   Schomburg Center for Research in Black Culture, New York Public Library,
New York

SFC   *San Francisco Chronicle*

SPC   Social Protest Collection, Bancroft Library, University of California
at Berkeley

SR   *Sun Reporter* (San Francisco)

TL   Tamiment Library, New York University, New York

1. Ronald Berkman, *Opening the Gates*, 64; Frank Browning, "Organizing behind Bars," in Atkins and Glick, *Prisons*, 132–39. The full manifesto is reprinted in Ronald Berkman, *Opening the Gates*, 183–86, and Angela Y. Davis et al., *If They Come in the Morning*, 65–74. The version in *If They Come in the Morning* lists twenty-nine demands; Berkman lists thirty-one yet redacts two demands concerning freedom for "condemned prisoners, avowed revolutionaries, and prisoners of war" as well as for certain "celebrated and prominent political prisoners." Those two demands, 16 and 19, appear in Davis et al., *If They Come in the Morning*, 72.

2. Quoted in Davis et al., *If They Come in the Morning*, 74.

3. Katsiaficas, *Imagination*; Prashad, *Darker Nations*.

4. David Johnson, interview.

5. Reprinted in Joy James, *New Abolitionists*, 303–10. The title bridged the Folsom demands, titled an "Anti-Oppression Platform," with the Republic of New Afrika's "Anti-Depression Platform."

6. Dayan, *Law Is a White Dog*; Rodríguez, *Forced Passages*; Cacho, *Social Death*.

7. There is, as far as I know, no global comparative history of imprisonment and its relationship to either colonial regimes or social movements, though Harlow takes up this question in regard to literature in *Barred*. For other interdisciplinary examples of different national studies that address this subject, see Feldman, *Formations of Violence*; Buntman, *Robben Island*.

8. Whitman, *Harsh Justice*.

9. Caleb Smith, *Prison and the American Imagination*; Walter Johnson, *River of Dark Dreams*.

10. Henry Bibb and Fountain Hughes quoted in Camp, *Closer to Freedom*, 13.

11. Dayan, *Law Is a White Dog*; Angela Y. Davis, *Are Prisons Obsolete?*

12. For overviews, see Blackmon, *Slavery by Another Name*; Muhammad, *Condemnation of Blackness*.

13. Du Bois, *Souls of Black Folk*, 16; Du Bois, *Black Reconstruction*, 12, 701. For the carceral experiences of enslavement, see Paton, *No Bond*; Angela Y. Davis, "From the Prison of Slavery to the Slavery of Prison," in *Angela Y. Davis Reader*, 74–95; O'Donovan, "Universities of Social and Political Change."

14. Kunzel, *Criminal Intimacy*.

15. Foucault, "Intellectuals and Power," 210; Lubiano, "Black Ladies," 352.

16. Beth Ritchie argues in *Arrested Justice* that such metaphors are explicitly suited for black women's engagements with domestic violence and state violence.

17. Angela Y. Davis, "Political Prisoners, Prisons, and Black Liberation," in *Angela Y. Davis Reader*, 47.

18. Baker, "Critical Memory."

19. Kelley, *Freedom Dreams*; Moten, "Uplift and Criminality"; Harney and Moten, *Undercommons*; Wagner, *Disturbing the Peace*.

20. Larry Weiss, interview.

21. Hahn, *Nation under Our Feet*, 7.

22. Rodríguez, "'Social Truth'"; Ruth Wilson Gilmore, *Golden Gulag*; Cacho, *Social Death*.

23. "San Quentin 6: David Johnson . . . a Letter," *The Conspiracy*, June 1972, 6, NLGC, Oversized Box 8.

24. Lubiano, "Black Nationalism."

25. Higginbotham, *Righteous Discontent*; Gaines, *Uplifting the Race*; Summers, *Manliness and Its Discontents*; Joy James, *Transcending the Talented Tenth*.

26. See Rebecca N. Hill, *Men, Mobs, and Law*, especially 265–314.

27. Attica Brothers, "The Five Demands," quoted in Wicker, *Time to Die*, 401.

28. Rebecca N. Hill, *Men, Mobs, and Law*, 20.

29. Ibid.; Raiford, "Photography."

30. One of the first scholarly histories of prison protest, which is still widely cited, is Cummins, *Rise and Fall*. Cummins conducted valuable research but remains troublesomely antagonistic to prison activism. He sees the prison movement as a violence-obsessed phenomenon premised on naive white fascination with dangerous black criminal men. Such a one-sided view separates prison organizing from other social movements of the time period and plays into a range of problematic assumptions about black criminality and antiracist mobilization. It is also historically insufficient, for he ignores the centrality of print culture to later prison radicalism and neglects its connection to other social movements at the time and outside of California. My work is indebted to a growing, interdisciplinary body of scholarship studying prison radicalism. In addition to works already cited, see Lee Bernstein, *America Is the Prison*; Bissonette, *When the Prisoners*; Burton-Rose, "War behind Walls"; Chase, "Civil Rights"; Chase, "'Slaves of the State' Revolt"; Chard, "SCAR'd Times"; Chard, "Rallying for Repression"; Gómez, "Resisting Living Death"; Irwin, *Prisons in Turmoil*; Jacobs, "Prisoners' Rights Movement"; Rodríguez, *Forced Passages*; Hames-Garcia, *Fugitive Thought*; Samuels, "Improvising on Reality"; Larry E. Sullivan, *Prison Reform Movement*; Thompson, "Blinded"; Joy James, *States of Confinement*; Joy James, *Imprisoned Intellectuals*; Joy James, *New Abolitionists*; Joy James, *Warfare*.

31. My analysis here differs from several scholars who argue for the South's central role in explaining the rise of the carceral state generally and mass incarceration in particular. Robert Perkinson argues that Texas is the worst purveyor of imprisonment in the country and claims that the nation's reliance on incarceration can be explained through Texas history. While his is the strongest such claim, others argue for a distinctly Southern view of carceral expansion. The popularity of describing mass incarceration as a new form of Jim Crow would seem to provide a colloquial extension of this claim to the South's explanatory power. Others locate the rise of the carceral state either in the penitentiary model of the colonial era or, for reasons that will be made clear later in this chapter and book, see it as a product of California and the particularities of Sunbelt power. Current scholarship on the carceral state seeks to trace its emergence through one of three prominent pathways: the plantation, the penitentiary, and the political economy of post-1968 global capitalism, especially in Sunbelt states of the South and West. I remain eclectic in my own analysis of its creation. Regional explanations contribute a great deal to our understanding of many key dynamics of the carceral state but they cannot explain its power in toto. For Southern and Sunbelt emphases, see Perkinson, *Texas Tough*; Blackmon, *Slavery by Another Name*; Chase, "Civil Rights" (though Chase pursues a Sunbelt argument rather

than the Texas exceptionalism that Perkinson demonstrates in his otherwise excellent book). Alexander, *New Jim Crow*, popularized a metaphor of the southern racial order as an explanatory tool for understanding contemporary mass incarceration. McLennan, *Crisis of Imprisonment*, is perhaps the best recent exploration of the penitentiary system as origin of contemporary U.S. prison politics. Ruth Wilson Gilmore, *Golden Gulag*, is the best example of the claim that California led the country into prison expansion. For a literary attempt to synthesize the penitentiary and the plantation, see Caleb Smith, *Prison and the American Imagination*. For historical studies, see Christianson, *With Liberty for Some*; Lawrence M. Friedman, *Crime and Punishment*.

32. Periodizing the Black Power movement, in space and in time and in relation to the civil rights movement, has preoccupied scholars in what has become known as "new Black Power studies." Of particular concern has been seeing Black Power in dialogic and dialectic relation to the civil rights movement rather than the aberration that several earlier scholars (and others) described. Some, including Jacqueline Dowd Hall and Nikhil Pal Singh, see Black Power as a subset of a "long civil rights movement," a view rejected by Sundiata K. Cha-Jua and Clarence Lang for blurring temporal, spatial, and strategic distinctions between civil rights and Black Power; to them, Black Power was a deliberate break from the civil rights movement. An emerging synthesis in the literature, as exemplified in works by Donna Murch and Jeanne Theoharis, among many others, suggests that Black Power was a break from the civil rights movement made by individuals and organizations who, in various ways, could trace their origins to and through the civil rights movement. See, for example, Joseph, *Waiting 'til the Midnight Hour*; Jacqueline Dowd Hall, "Long Civil Rights Movement"; Singh, *Black Is a Country*; O'Dell, *Climbin' Jacob's Ladder*; Murch, *Living for the City*; Theoharis, *Rebellious Life*; Cha-Jua and Lang, "'Long Movement' as Vampire."

33. George L. Jackson, *Blood in My Eye*, 7.

34. See Ruth Wilson Gilmore, *Golden Gulag*; Dayan, *Law Is a White Dog*; Kunzel, *Criminal Intimacy*; Shoatz, *Maroon*; Garland, *Culture of Control*.

35. More generally on the afterlife of slavery, see Sexton, "People-of-Color Blindness"; Hartman, *Lose Your Mother*.

36. I am deeply indebted to scholars of California history and politics, most especially Ruth Wilson Gilmore, *Golden Gulag*; HoSang, *Racial Propositions*; Murch, *Living for the City*; Widener, *Black Arts West*. However, as stated above, I am not interested in pursuing a regionalist explanation for the rise and expansion of the carceral state. I see California as a historically significant and historiographically useful staging ground in which to examine larger national dynamics of prison expansion and prison organizing. Regions have their own character, of course, and I do not mean to suggest that California is interchangeable with Maine, North Carolina, or elsewhere. Nor do I wish to elide the fact that a few select states—California chief among them—expanded their prison system at much faster rates than others. I maintain, however, that the carceral state is the result of a convergence of factors that transcend particular states. Part of what I hope to draw our attention to by referring to captivity as a national problem is the way in which carceral control, from policing and surveillance to confinement and execution, is at the core of the American racial state.

37. Widener, *Black Arts West*, 57.

38. For Oakland migration, see Murch, *Living for the City*; the statistics cited in the text appear on p. 16. The notion of a "southern diaspora" comes from Gregory, *Southern Diaspora*. For more on black migration and the remaking of California politics, see also Widener, *Black Arts West*; Keith Collins, *Black Los Angeles*; George, *No Crystal Stair*; Horne, *Fire This Time*; Wilkerson, *Warmth of Other Suns*. For the racial politics of Los Angeles, see Mike Davis, *City of Quartz*; Horne, *Fire This Time*, especially 3–43; Sides, *L.A. City Limits*; Avila, *Popular Culture*; Gaye Theresa Johnson, *Spaces of Conflict*; Laslett, *Sunshine Was Never Enough*; Escobar, "Dialectics of Repression"; Pulido, *Black, Brown, Yellow, and Left*; Flamming, *Bound for Freedom*.

39. Quoted in HoSang, *Racial Propositions*, 1. See also HoSang, "Race and the Mythology."

40. Ruth Wilson Gilmore, *Golden Gulag*, 7.

41. Ibid. More generally, see National Research Council, *Growth of Incarceration*; Gottschalk, *Prison*; Pew Center, "One in 100"; Thompson, "Why Mass Incarceration Matters"; Erica Goode, "Incarceration Rates for Blacks Have Fallen Sharply, Report Shows," *NYT*, February 27, 2013, A12.

CHAPTER ONE

1. Mills, *This Little Light*, 61; Lee, *For Freedom's Sake*.

2. Quoted in Lee, *For Freedom's Sake*, 89.

3. Wagner, *Disturbing the Peace*.

4. There is a growing literature on southern prisons from the end of the Civil War through World War II, with particular emphasis on convict leasing. See Blackmon, *Slavery by Another Name*; Blue, *Doing Time*; Chase, "Civil Rights"; Curtin, *Black Prisoners*; LeFlouria, "Convict Women"; Sarah Haley, "'Like I Was a Man'"; Lichtenstein, *Twice the Work*; Mancini, *One Dies*; Oshinsky, *"Worse Than Slavery"*; Perkinson, *Texas Tough*. For the connection between slave patrols and policing, see Hadden, *Slave Patrols*. Some of these scholars, Perkinson in particular, provide a regional explanation of mass incarceration, arguing that the U.S. carceral state has its origins in a southern (or, in Perkinson's case, specifically Texan) system of confinement. While I lean toward Caleb Smith's meditation on the prison as a combination of both the plantation and the penitentiary—a combination that blended the brutal biological racism of the South with the managerial scientific racism of the North—I am less interested here in the regional roots of mass incarceration than I am in the regional specificities of prison protest as an extension of and contribution to the national and transnational black freedom struggle. See Caleb Smith, *Prison and the American Imagination*, especially 40–50, 141–71.

5. Blackmon, *Slavery by Another Name*, 375.

6. Gregory, *Southern Diaspora*.

7. Murakawa, "Origins," 237, 236.

8. Pascoe, *What Comes Naturally*; McGuire, *At the Dark End*.

9. Murakawa, "Origins," 243.

10. For Alabama and Mississippi, see Woodruff, *American Congo*; Hamlin, *Crossroads at Clarksdale*; Hasan Kwame Jeffries, *Bloody Lowndes*; McWhorter, *Carry Me Home*. On police power, see Dubber, *Police Power*; Wagner, *Disturbing the Peace*.

11. See the explications in Dayan, *Law Is a White Dog*; Dayan, *Story of Cruel and Unusual*; Angela Y. Davis, *Are Prisons Obsolete?*

12. My argument here builds on Vesla Weaver's claims that law and order served as a grander strategy of political realignment—a "frontlash" counterinsurgency instead of a "backlash" reaction. See Weaver, "Frontlash." See also Murakawa, "Electing to Punish." See also Schrader, "Local Policing."

13. For a useful but unsatisfying exception to this absence of historiography, see Colley, *Ain't Scared of Your Jail*. See also Barkan, *Protesters on Trial*; Zinn, *SNCC*.

14. Quoted in Theoharis, *Rebellious Life*, 71.

15. Quoted in Giddings, *When and Where I Enter*, 279.

16. Colley, *Ain't Scared of Your Jail*, 75.

17. Carmichael with Thelwell, *Ready for Revolution*, 307.

18. For more on these cases, see Law, "Sick of the Abuse"; Thuma, "'Not a Wedge.'"

19. Recounting the civil rights movement's emphasis on direct action and voluntary arrest undoubtedly skews toward a regional and national telling rather than a fine-tuned local history of the movement. The movement's strategy of filling the jails required people, and those people came from across the country: they were the rank-and-file churchwomen who were the movement's backbone, the preachers who fancied themselves leaders of the movement, high school and college students from the North and South, and others. In addition to the logistical reality that no one city or town had enough people willing to submit to jail for (potentially) long periods of time to make the strategy effective, the issue of publicity was also relevant. It was far more newsworthy and far less typical to have swarms of activists descend on an area and its jails. This macrofocus, however, does not suggest that "local people" were removed from this strategy. Indeed, by lore and by experience, they were often already acquainted with the local jail or prison. Local residents routinely joined with activists from across the region and throughout the country in their efforts to fill the jails. For all the tensions between local and national, between the sought-after celebrities and the unknown organizers, civil rights activists bonded through a shared engagement with the criminal justice system and a shared understanding that the American prison symbolized a larger system of white supremacy. For the synthesis of local and national organizers in this direct action strategy, see Arsenault, *Freedom Riders*; Dittmer, *Local People*; Charles Payne, *Light of Freedom*.

20. Rodríguez, *Forced Passages*.

21. Hasan Kwame Jeffries, *Bloody Lowndes*, 8.

22. Among the women who found themselves facing persecution as part of this Red Scare/race scare era were Ethel Rosenberg, a Jewish communist in New York who was executed in 1953 along with her husband, Julius, and Rose Lee Ingram, a black sharecropper in Georgia who was incarcerated with her two sons for killing a man who tried to sexually assault her in 1947. Ingram and her sons were freed in 1959. For an excellent analysis of the defense campaign as discourse and political orientation, with particular attention to the racial and gender dynamics of such efforts, see Rebecca N. Hill, *Men, Mobs, and Law*.

23. For more on these cases, see Carter, *Scottsboro*; Glenda Elizabeth Gilmore, *Defying Dixie*; Gore, *Radicalism*; Heard, *Eyes of Willie McGee*; Kelley, *Hammer and Hoe*; McDuffie, *Sojourning*; Mitford, *Fine Old Conflict*.

24. See, for example, Glenda Elizabeth Gilmore, *Defying Dixie*; Klarman, *From Jim Crow to Civil Rights*; Patricia Sullivan, *Lift Every Voice*.

25. Baker, "Critical Memory," 18–19.

26. The list of civil rights memoirs and biographies is long, but many of them treat the jail experience as a central and pivotal point in the narrative. For a partial sampling, see Carmichael with Thelwell, *Ready for Revolution*; Farmer, *Lay Bare the Heart*; James Forman, *Making of Black Revolutionaries*; Henry and Curry, *Aaron Henry*; John Lewis with D'Orso, *Walking with the Wind*; Fleming, *Soon We Will Not Cry*; Mullins, *Diane Nash*; Theoharis, *Rebellious Life*; Manis, *Fire*; Andrew Young, *Easy Burden*.

27. Perkinson, "'Hell Exploded'"; Lomax, *Land Where the Blues Began*. This process was not without its complications, as the interventions of folklorists—especially the Lomax team—naturalized a connection between race and crime; see Wagner, *Disturbing the Peace*, 185–237.

28. Garrow, *Bearing the Cross*, 15–16.

29. McGuire, *At the Dark End*, 100.

30. Branch, *Parting the Waters*, 174; Theoharis, *Rebellious Life*, 110.

31. Garrow, *Bearing the Cross*, 65. For similar descriptions, see McGuire, *At the Dark End*; Branch, *Parting the Waters*. More generally on the movement's embrace of imprisonment as part of its political development, see Zinn, *SNCC*; Halberstam, *Children*. The photographic iconicity of the movement—its photogenic quality—can be seen in other mug shots of arrested demonstrators. See, for example, Etheridge, *Breach of Peace*.

32. Rustin quoted in Arsenault, *Freedom Riders*, 64. See also the description in Theoharis, *Rebellious Life*, 72–77.

33. For descriptions of this arrest, see, among others, Garrow, *Bearing the Cross*, 55–56; Branch, *Parting the Waters*, 160–62. For a longer history of the antilynch mob, see Rebecca N. Hill, *Men, Mobs, and Law*.

34. Arsenault, *Freedom Riders*, 68; Branch, *Parting the Waters*, 176–77, 183.

35. Garrow, *Bearing the Cross*, 228.

36. Vaught, "Narrow Cells," 118–20.

37. Historians have identified the coexistence of Gandhian pacifism with armed self-defense among southern civil rights activists throughout the 1950s and 1960s, owing in part to a long regional history of gun ownership and a high percentage of military veterans. For overviews, see Tyson, *Radio Free Dixie*; Lance Hill, *Deacons for Defense*; Strain, *Pure Fire*; Umoja, *We Will Shoot Back*; Wendt, *Spirit and the Shotgun*.

38. As Slate notes in *Colored Cosmopolitanism*, 203, "Many movement participants were drawn less to Gandhian nonviolence (*ahimsa*, or non-harm) than to Gandhian nonviolent civil disobedience (satyagraha)."

39. Carson, *In Struggle*, 11. See also Chafe, *Civilities and Civil Rights*.

40. Laurie B. Green, *Battling the Plantation Mentality*.

41. Quoted in Staudenmaier, *Truth and Revolution*, 86.

42. Garrow, *Bearing the Cross*, 143.

43. Southern Regional Council, *The Delta Prisons*, quoted in Oshinsky, *"Worse Than Slavery,"* ix.

44. Chase, "'Slaves of the State' Revolt."

45. Quoted in Arsenault, *Freedom Riders*, 300, 334.

46. Giddings, *When and Where I Enter*, 279.

47. In a step in this direction, Joy James anthologizes King's letter in *Imprisoned Intellectuals*.

48. For more on the letter, see Bass, *Blessed Are the Peacemakers*; Branch, *Parting the Waters*, 737–46.

49. King, *Why We Can't Wait*, 73.

50. Ibid., 16.

51. Ibid., 30.

52. John Lewis with D'Orso, *Walking with the Wind*, 107.

53. Quoted in Branch, *Parting the Waters*, 770. On Birmingham, see Branch, *Parting the Waters*, 708–802; McWhorter, *Carry Me Home*.

54. Branch, *Parting the Waters*, 756–78. For more on freedom songs in the movement, see Sanger, *"When the Spirit Says Sing"*; Carawan and Carawan, *Sing for Freedom*. For more expansive considerations of freedom songs, see Redmond, *Anthem*; Feldstein, *How It Feels*.

55. Quoted in Colley, *Ain't Scared of Your Jail*, 71.

56. Michael Simmons, interview. Simmons was, by that point, a part of SNCC's Atlanta Project. For more, see Grady-Willis, *Challenging U.S. Apartheid*.

57. Quoted in Colley, *Ain't Scared of Your Jail*, 48.

58. See, for example, Kosek, *Acts of Conscience*; Tracy, *Direct Action*; Bennett, *Radical Pacifism*; Cornell, *"For a World"*; Cornell, *Oppose*. For more on Gandhi's influence on a longer arc of black activism, see Slate, *Colored Cosmopolitanism*; Kapur, *Raising Up a Prophet*.

59. Carmichael with Thelwell, *Ready for Revolution*, 204. Scholars have identified a more abiding political rather than tactical or philosophical connection between the southern civil rights movement and the Indian struggle for independence. See Slate, *Colored Cosmopolitanism*; David L. Lewis, *King*. Slate notes that earlier generations of black activists took more inspiration from Gandhi as a strong, determined anticolonial leader than as an apostle of nonviolence.

60. Branch, *Parting the Waters*, 550–53.

61. Carmichael with Thelwell, *Ready for Revolution*, 210; the strike is described on 206–11. See also Arsenault, *Freedom Riders*, 304–81.

62. Colley, *Ain't Scared of Your Jail*, 50. Later, however, Colley makes the untenable claim that "white male civil rights workers generally faced the greatest danger in going to jail" (101).

63. Ibid., 93–94. See also McGuire, *At the Dark End*.

64. Cagin and Dray, *We Are Not Afraid*.

65. French journalist Régis Debray first wrote of the foco theory in *Revolution in the Revolution?* Elements of its approach can be heard in Guevara, *Che Guevara Speaks*. For one of many critiques, see Saldaña-Portillo, *Revolutionary Imagination*.

66. See, for example, Crespino, *In Search*; Jason Morgan Ward, *Defending White Democracy*; Lassiter, *Silent Majority*; Sokol, *There Goes My Everything*. Although they exclude black journalists and others from their study, Roberts and Klibanoff, *The Race Beat*, note the critical role played by white southern racial moderates at several regional newspapers, among them the *Atlanta Journal-Constitution*.

67. Arsenault, *Freedom Riders*, 364; Branch, *Parting the Waters*, 726; O'Dell, *Climbin' Jacob's Ladder*, 145–59.

68. Hasan Kwame Jeffries, *Bloody Lowndes*, 44.

69. Branch, *Parting the Waters*, 242–43; Garrow, *Bearing the Cross*, 108–9.

70. Arsenault, *Freedom Riders*, 257.

71. For more on events in Albany, see Arsenault, *Freedom Riders*, 468–76; Branch, *Parting the Waters*, 524–62; Garrow, *Bearing the Cross*, 173–230.

72. Sargent, *Civil Rights Revolution*, 63; Vaught, "Narrow Cells," 133.

73. Quoted in Roberts and Klibanoff, *Race Beat*, 399. Within an earlier generation of civil rights scholarship, Carmichael's widely quoted speech has been typically described as the origin of Black Power as well as of the division of the civil rights coalition.

CHAPTER TWO

1. Willie Sundiata Tate, interview. Unless otherwise noted, the rest of this section comes from my interview with him.

2. It is difficult to track the extent of violence in prisons, as many incidents are not reported or documented. Further, the reputations of different institutions are best grasped through those who have experienced it. I rely therefore on oral history testimony not only to document the extent of the violence at DVI but also to understand the reputations of that and other facilities. Several people I interviewed used the phrase "gladiator school," suggesting that it was a common understanding for people incarcerated there.

3. Among an impressive and growing body of literature, see Goldstein, *Poverty in Common*; Katznelson, *Fear Itself*; Mantler, *Power to the Poor*; Nelson, *Body and Soul*; Sugrue, *Sweet Land*.

4. The phrase "carceral landscape" comes from Walter Johnson, *River of Dark Dreams*, 209–43. Johnson uses it to describe nineteenth-century chattel slavery.

5. Katz, *Why Don't American Cities Burn?*; Sugrue, *Origins*; Ruth Wilson Gilmore, *Golden Gulag*; Wacquant, *Punishing the Poor*.

6. Banfield, *Unheavenly City*; Clark, *Youth in Revolt*; Clark, *Dark Ghetto*.

7. Lenin, *Nationalism*. For elaborations within a Black Power context, see Cruse, *Crisis*; Cruse, *Rebellion or Revolution?*; Carmichael and Hamilton, *Black Power*.

8. James Baldwin, "A Report from Occupied Territory," *The Nation*, July 11, 1966, available at http://www.thenation.com/article/159618/report-occupied-territory; Frank Van Riper, "'Our Ghettoes Are Concentration Camps,'" *New York Sunday News*, December 29, 1968, 4–6; "Harlem Activist: Kenneth Bancroft Clark," *NYT*, June 15, 1964, 32.

9. Robert Blauner, "Internal Colonialism and Ghetto Revolt," in *Still the Big News*, 64–81 (originally published in *Social Problems* in 1969); Barrera, Muñoz, and Ornelas, "Barrio." For an overview, see Pinderhughes, "Toward a New Theory."

10. Quoted in Theoharis, *Rebellious Life*, 176.

11. Sugrue, *Sweet Land*, 327–32. More generally, see Tullis, "Vietnam at Home"; Rodríguez, "Terms of Engagement"; Wagner, *Disturbing the Peace*; Rebecca N. Hill, *Men, Mobs, and Law*.

12. Murch, *Living for the City*, 63–64.

13. Muhammad, *Condemnation of Blackness*; Jacobson, *Whiteness*; Tucker, *Science and Politics*.

14. Wacquant, "New 'Peculiar Institution'"; Satter, *Family Properties*; Chronopoulos, *Spatial Regulation*; Hicks, *Talk with You*; Kali Gross, *Colored Amazons*; Bookspan, *Germ*; Geoff D. Ward, *Black Child Savers*. For earlier efforts at the racialization of unruly, specifically immigrant, populations through policing political and sexual expression, see James Green, *Death in the Haymarket*; Shah, *Stranger Intimacy*.

15. For more on confinement and counterinsurgency, see Khalili, *Time in the Shadows* (which draws on Foucault, *Security, Territory, Population*); Donner, *Protectors of Privilege*; Schrader, "Local Policing"; Siegel, "Cold War Connections." See also Flamm, *Law and Order*; Weaver, "Frontlash." Many black women in particular protested the punitive gaze of case workers policing their sexual relationships and determining whether women deserved to receive benefits. See Chappell, *War on Welfare*; Kornbluh, *Welfare Rights*; Nadasen, *Welfare Warriors*.

16. Audley "Queen Mother" Moore, interview by Naison.

17. Losier, " . . . 'For Strictly Religious Reason[s]'" and "Prison House"; Christianson, *With Liberty for Some*, 250–58; Acoli, "Updated History," 143–44.

18. C. L. R. James, "Black People in the Urban Areas of the U.S.," in *C. L. R. James Reader*, 378.

19. Gregory, *Southern Diaspora*. True to Gregory's thesis, this southern diaspora could be found not just among the black prisoners but also, as my interviews with Ericka Huggins and Bato Talamantez anecdotally confirmed, among the white police officers and white prisoners.

20. Murch, *Living for the City*, 15.

21. Essien-Udom, *Black Nationalism*; Evanzz, *Messenger*; Gardell, *In the Name*; Marable, *Malcolm X*.

22. Ronald Berkman, *Opening the Gates*, 51–52.

23. Losier, " . . . 'For Strictly Religious Reason[s],'" 28–29.

24. Ronald Berkman, *Opening the Gates*, 51.

25. Horne, *Fire This Time*, 122–26; Marable, *Malcolm X*, 205–9; Eldridge Cleaver, *Soul on Ice*; Tibbs, *From Black Power*, 3–25.

26. Ronald Berkman, *Opening the Gates*, 50–70; Tibbs, *From Black Power*, 15–21.

27. Quoted in Tibbs, *From Black Power*, 19.

28. Quoted in Losier, " . . . 'For Strictly Religious Reason[s],'" 19.

29. Gottschalk, *Prison*, 175.

30. Jacobs, *Stateville*, 52–70; Losier, "'If You Are Black'"; Christopher E. Smith, "Black Muslims"; Cummins, *Rise and Fall*, 63–92; Pallas and Barber, "From Riot to Revolution."

31. This chronology builds on Marable, *Malcolm X*, 70–99; Marable and Felber, *Portable Malcolm X Reader*, 34–70.

32. Malcolm X, *End of White World Supremacy*.

33. Malcolm X, *Autobiography*, quoted in Ronald Berkman, *Opening the Gates*, 51.

34. An audio recording of one such speech, "Black Nationalism Can Set Us Free," is available at http://www.marxists.org/reference/archive/malcolm-x/we-have-no-freedom.mp3.

35. See Malcolm X, *Malcolm X*, 23–54. For a critique of Malcolm's house-slave/field-slave metaphor and its long-ranging implications, see Reed, *Stirrings*.

36. Eldridge Cleaver, *Soul on Ice*, 58.

37. Eldridge Cleaver, "Prisons: The Muslims' Decline," in *Ramparts* and Browning, *Prison Life*, 10–103; Eldridge Cleaver, *Soul on Ice*, 50–63; John Clutchette to author, December 19, 2012.

38. For more on Chessman, see Hamm, *Rebel and a Cause*; Cummins, *Rise and Fall*, 33–62.

39. This trope can also be found in another contemporary autobiography, Claude Brown's *Manchild in the Promised Land*. The site of Brown's transformation, however, is not prison but a reformatory school, which he likens to prison, including through several escape attempts (some of them successful). See Rolston, "Conversion"; Douglas Edward Taylor, "Hustlers, Nationalists, and Revolutionaries"; Vaught, "Narrow Cells."

40. Ashanti Alston, interview; Sugrue and Goodman, "Plainfield Burning." More generally, see Sugrue, *Sweet Land*; Horne, *Fire This Time*; Thompson, *Whose Detroit?*; Mumford, *Newark*.

41. Quoted in James T. Patterson, *Grand Expectations*, 666. For more on Watts, see Horne, *Fire This Time*.

42. Murakawa, "Origins," 245.

43. Theoharis, *Rebellious Life*, 195; Tullis, "Vietnam at Home."

44. Dulaney, *Black Police*; Pihos, "Black Police."

45. Theoharis, *Rebellious Life*, 177. In 1971, Detroit police established an undercover unit called Stop the Robberies, Enjoy Safe Streets (STRESS); during the unit's first ten months of existence, its officers killed ten people (nine of them black) and arrested more than fourteen hundred (Thompson, *Whose Detroit?*, 81–102, 145–58).

46. Flamm, *Law and Order*, 53.

47. *Iron Fist and the Velvet Glove*, 81–86; Weaver, "Frontlash."

48. D'Arcus, "Protest, Scale, and Publicity."

49. Black, *Richard M. Nixon*, 537.

50. Katz, *Why Don't American Cities Burn?*

51. Sugrue, *Sweet Land*, 347–48.

52. Ahmad, *We Will Return*; Kelley, *Freedom Dreams*, 60–109; Kelley, "Stormy Weather"; Kelley and Esch, "Black Like Mao."

53. Murch, *Living for the City*.

54. Ronald "Elder" Freeman, interview; Hakim Ali, interview. See also Ahmad, *We Will Return*; Shoatz, *Maroon*.

55. Murch, *Living for the City*. See also Joseph, *Waiting 'til the Midnight Hour*, 207; Hasan Kwame Jeffries, *Bloody Lowndes*; Ahmad, *We Will Return*; Murch, "Campus and the Street."

56. Bloom and Martin, *Black against Empire*, 70–71.

57. Black Panther platform and program, March 19, 1972, HPNFP, Series 2, Box 4, GL; Ashanti Alston, interview.

58. Genet, *Prisoner of Love*, 246. For scholarly analyses of this claim, see Singh, "Black Panthers"; Austin, *Up against the Wall*; Lazerow and Williams, *In Search*; Yohuru Williams and Lazerow, *Liberated Territory*.

59. Genet, *Prisoner of Love*, 99. Genet's ambivalent relation to the political uses of spectacle shares something with those who castigate Black Power or other expressions of radicalism through spectacular acts. For example, Reed (*Stirrings*, 72) argues that Black Power was little more than a media event, and Gitlin (*Whole World Is Watching*) challenges the white New Left for courting media attention, which then led activists to embrace grander and more foolish tactics. Payne (*Light of Freedom*) presents the ostensible "spectacle" of Black Power in direct contrast to the "organizing tradition" of the civil rights movement. Genet, however, remained more loyal to the Panthers, seeing such spectacles as necessary if inevitably limited—more, he believed, by the forces of racism and state violence than by media routines. Indeed, he argued that "the Panthers were heading for either madness, metamorphosis of the black community, death or prison. All those options happened, but the metamorphosis was by far the most important, and that is why the Panthers can be said to have overcome through poetry" (*Prisoner of Love*, 100).

60. Jean Genet, "May Day Speech," in *Declared Enemy*, 39.

61. Newton was driving with a friend in his girlfriend's car when police stopped him, perhaps because the car was one of many whose license plate number was a "known Panther vehicle" and because the car had unpaid parking tickets. Newton's arrest and trial are a mainstay of Panther histories; see Bloom and Martin, *Black against Empire*, 101–5; Joseph, *Waiting 'til the Midnight Hour*, 205–40; Jane A. Rhodes, *Framing*, 116–33, 152–80. For the antiwar movement generally, see Foley, *Confronting the War Machine*. My interview with Karen Wald was illustrative on the connections between Stop the Draft Week organizers and the Oakland Black Panther Party.

62. This discussion of Newton's arrest and the campaign for his freedom builds on Joseph, *Waiting 'til the Midnight Hour*, 205–40.

63. Rebecca N. Hill, *Men, Mobs, and Law*, 2, 3.

64. Joseph, *Waiting 'til the Midnight Hour*, 212; Richardson, *Bomb in Every Issue*, 68–74; Austin, *Up against the Wall*, 72–74; Bloom and Martin, *Black against Empire*, 74–79; Tibbs, *From Black Power*, 75–98.

65. Cleaver remains one of the most controversial of the major Panther leaders. Several former members of the Oakland branch of the party attribute the split in the organization to Cleaver's aggression and desire for violent revenge. They allege that he used his experience in prison to bolster his leadership, with disastrous results. Given his subsequent embrace of Christianity and the Republican Party, some observers have questioned the sincerity of his commitment to radicalism. In *Living for the City*, Donna Murch comes to similar conclusions based on her extensive interviews with Oakland Black Panthers. Others see Cleaver as a charismatic spokesperson for a larger current of insurrectionary politics, arguing that the split in the party resulted from a battle of two equally ego-driven men, Newton and Cleaver. Further, the differences in the party extended beyond individual leaders, even though certain people epitomized these differences at key moments. For the experience of individual Panthers, see Hilliard and Cole, *This Side of Glory*; Newton, *Revolutionary Suicide*; Assata Shakur, *Assata*; Kathleen Cleaver's introduction to Eldridge Cleaver, *Target Zero*. For scholarly accounts of Cleaver's complexity within the party, see Austin, *Up against the Wall*; Bloom and Martin, *Black against Empire*; Jane A. Rhodes, *Framing*.

66. James Forman, *Making of Black Revolutionaries*, 526. See also Matthews, "'No One Ever Asks'"; LeBlanc-Ernest, "'Most Qualified Person.'"

67. Eldridge Cleaver, introduction to *Genius of Huey P. Newton*.

68. Eldridge Cleaver, "Affidavit #1, I Am 33 Years Old," in *Eldridge Cleaver*, 8.

69. Edward P. Morgan, "Media Culture."

70. See Eldridge Cleaver, *Soul on Ice*, 3–17, 60–63, 97–111.

71. Rainwater and Yancy, *Moynihan Report*. See also James T. Patterson, *Freedom*.

72. Eldridge Cleaver, *Soul on Ice*, 201.

73. Ibid., 59.

74. Joseph, *Waiting 'til the Midnight Hour*, 212.

75. Quoted in Bloom and Martin, *Black against Empire*, 137. More generally, see Jane A. Rhodes, *Framing*.

76. This perspective saturated the efforts to defend Newton. See, for example, American Whites for the Defense of Huey P. Newton, "Who Is Huey P. Newton?," ca. 1969, and Black Panther Ministry of Information, *Bulletin*, nos. 1 and 2, both in NLC, Box 56, Folder: Black Panther Party.

77. See, for example, Newton's essays in Foner, *Black Panthers Speak*, 39–75.

78. The mandate is reprinted in Major, *Panther*, 294–95.

79. The quotations are from Scheer, introduction to Eldridge Cleaver, *Eldridge Cleaver*, xxxi. For more on Newsreel, see Cynthia A. Young, *Soul Power*, 145–83.

80. Jane A. Rhodes, *Framing*, 152. This statement likely referred not only to his incarceration but to his public battle with Reagan over whether Cleaver would be allowed to teach an experimental sociology course at the University of California at Berkeley.

81. Scheer, introduction. FBI documents show that the bureau was, in fact, afraid of the two men's popularity and of how much their philosophies of Black Power resonated with others. The claim had additional weight with Cleaver, given that the California parole board had repeatedly threatened to return him to prison on a parole violation should he continue to speak publicly on behalf of the Black Panther Party. Cleaver described having to choose between playing dead or going back to prison. See Eldridge Cleaver, "Affidavit #1," 7.

82. Eldridge Cleaver, "The Land Question and Black Liberation," in *Eldridge Cleaver*, 67. For a compelling analysis of how this "projection of sovereignty" marked the Panthers as an organization, see Singh, *Black Is a Country*, 174–211. See also Lake, "Arm(ing) of the Vanguard."

83. For more on the Panther community programs, including a gendered analysis of them, see especially Murch, *Living for the City*; Bloom and Martin, *Black against Empire*; Nelson, *Body and Soul*; Alkebulan, *Survival Pending Revolution*; Robyn Ceanne Spencer, "Engendering"; Huggins and LeBlanc-Ernest, "Revolutionary Women"; Ericka Huggins, interview by Thompson. My own interviews with former Panthers, including Ashanti Alston and Ericka Huggins, were also instrumental.

84. My interviews with two former Los Angeles Panthers, Ronald "Elder" Freeman and Ericka Huggins, were instrumental on this point, as were Bloom and Martin, *Black against Empire*; Widener, *Black Arts West*.

85. Abu-Jamal, *We Want Freedom*; Churchill and Vander Wall, *Agents of Repression*; Churchill and Vander Wall, *COINTELPRO Papers*; Cunningham, *There's Something*

Happening Here; Schultz and Schultz, *It Did Happen Here*; Donner, *Protectors of Privilege*. I thank Trevor Griffey for many enlightening conversations on the topic as well as his prodigious work navigating the archives of state secrets.

86. The Garvey-inspired title is one measure of the ways the book reflected the more heavily nationalist tenor of black politics in New York City. For more on the city's history of black radicalism, see Biondi, *To Stand and Fight*.

87. Ronald "Elder" Freeman, interview; Umoja, "Repression Breeds Resistance," 6–7; Bloom and Martin, *Black against Empire*, 144–46; Judson L. Jeffries and Foley, "To Live and Die."

88. Ronald "Elder" Freeman, interview; Ericka Huggins, interview; Ericka Huggins, interview by Thompson; Judson L. Jeffries and Foley, "To Live and Die."

89. Haas, *Assassination*; *Murder of Fred Hampton*; Jakobi Williams, *From the Bullet*; Churchill and Vander Wall, *Agents of Repression* and *COINTELPRO Papers*.

90. See Angela Y. Davis, *Autobiography*; Elaine Brown, *Taste of Power*; Bloom and Martin, *Black against Empire*, 216–25.

91. Theoharis, *Rebellious Life*, 223–24; Berger, "'Malcolm X Doctrine.'"

92. Biondi, *Black Revolution*; Bradley, *Harlem vs. Columbia University*.

93. See Heins, *Strictly Ghetto Property*. Los Siete were represented by Black Panther attorney Charles Garry. The case, along with that of Newton and later George Jackson, was a touchstone of Bay Area prison radicalism in 1969–70.

94. Hoffman in *Chicago 10*. See also Hoffman, *Autobiography*; Raskin, *For the Hell of It*.

95. Richardson, *Bomb in Every Issue*, 168.

96. See Seale, *Seize the Time*. Dave Dellinger, the oldest and least theatrical of the Chicago 8 defendants, was the only one who tried to place his body between Seale and the bailiffs after the judge ordered Seale gagged. The other defendants protested but did not physically intervene; Dellinger was, of course, unsuccessful in stopping the bailiffs from carrying out the judge's order.

97. For more on the New Haven case, see Yohuru Williams, *Black Politics*. The primary variation to this drawing is one of Seale bound but not gagged, strapped into an electric chair. Both versions appeared in several left-wing publications and flyers used in the campaign for his release.

98. Eldridge Cleaver, "Affidavit #1," 9.

99. Hampton in *Murder of Fred Hampton*.

100. Black Student Revolution Conference, May 15, 1970, press release, Harlem Black Panther Party Papers, Folder 21, SC.

101. The demands are printed in *National Strike Information Center Newsletter* 8 (May 12, 1970): 1. The number of strikes adhering to the demands appears in 12 (May 22, 1970): 2–4. That issue also included two and a half pages of material about the Panthers to bolster the solidarity dimension of the strike. Both issues can be found in Harlem Black Panther Party Papers, Folder 22. The strike demands were formulated in New Haven, where Seale, Ericka Huggins, and seven other Black Panthers were then facing trial. More generally on the student strike, see Katsiaficas, *Imagination*, 117–74.

102. Newton, *To Die*, 220.

103. Yoruba, "Huey's Out to Stay!," *Palante* 2:9 (August 15, 1970): 10.

104. On the transformations in U.S. urban political economy, see Beauregard, *Voices of Decline*; Massey and Denton, *American Apartheid*; Wilhelm, *Who Needs the Negro?*; Garland, *Culture of Control*; Katz, *Why Don't American Cities Burn?*; Sugrue, *Origins*; Wacquant, *Punishing the Poor*. I thank Robin Kelley for bringing Wilhelm's book to my attention.

105. Fanon, *Wretched of the Earth*, 103–4. See also Booker, "Lumpenization"; Douglas Edward Taylor, "Hustlers, Nationalists, and Revolutionaries."

106. See Rossinow, *Politics of Authenticity*; Moten, *In the Break*.

107. These include Assata Shakur, Nehanda Abiodun, Willie Lee Brent, Eldridge Cleaver, and Lorenzo Komboa Ervin, among others. Puerto Rican nationalist Guillermo Morales also fled to Cuba after escaping from prison in 1979. For more on the radical international imagination, see Wu, *Radicals*. Regarding Cuba, see Latner, "Irresistible Revolution."

108. Bloom and Martin, *Black against Empire*, 2–4. For personal anecdotes from antiwar activists who were involved in these missions, see Dellinger, *From Yale to Jail*, 237–56, 402–7; Hayden, *Reunion*, 220–41. See also Friedland, *Lift Up Your Voice*.

109. Boggs, *Racism*, 39–50.

110. *Black Panther*, November 1, 1969, Harlem Black Panther Party Papers, Folder 1.

111. Zayd Shakur, "America Is the Prison," 274.

112. Prison Solidarity Committee, *From Soledad to San Quentin* (San Francisco, ca. 1972), 3, Anthony Platt, Private Collection.

113. Soledad Brothers Defense Fund and Soledad House, "The Soledad Brothers" (flyer), ca. 1970, NLC, Box 41, Folder: Soledad Brothers.

114. Scheer, introduction to Eldridge Cleaver, *Eldridge Cleaver*, xxix.

115. This quotation serves as the epigraph to Lockwood, *Conversation*.

116. Eldridge Cleaver, "Playboy Interview," in *Eldridge Cleaver*, 148–49.

117. For more on the Panther split, see Murch, *Living for the City*; Self, *American Babylon*; Joseph, *Waiting 'til the Midnight Hour*; Charles E. Jones, *Black Panther Party Reconsidered*; Kathleen Cleaver and Katsiaficas, *Liberation, Imagination, and the Black Panther Party*; Yohuru Williams and Lazerow, *Liberated Territory*; Judson L. Jeffries, *Comrades*. For partisan accounts, see Elaine Brown, *Taste of Power*; Hilliard and Cole, *This Side of Glory*; Assata Shakur, *Assata*; Bukhari, *War Before*; Newton, *Revolutionary Suicide*; Eldridge Cleaver, *Target Zero*. My interviews with former party members have also been helpful in understanding its impact.

118. Cummins, *Rise and Fall*, 116–17. Cummins quotes several people, including both prison officials and former prisoners, who said *The Outlaw* garnered little respect or trust inside.

119. *The Outlaw*, reprinted in *BB* 6:4 (January 26–February 1, 1968): 8–9, JMP, Box 44, Folder 1.

120. James A. Schreiber, "San Quentin Cons to Strike," *BB* 6:4 (January 26–February 1, 1968): 1.

121. Ibid.; Cummins, *Rise and Fall*, 118.

122. James A. Schreiber, "San Quentin Cons to Strike," *BB* 6:4 (January 26–February 1, 1968): 8.

123. James A. Schreiber, "Barb Scribe Zaps 'Big Red,'" *BB* 6:7 (February 16–22, 1968): 1.

124. Cummins, *Rise and Fall*, 117–18; "San Q Rocks—Freemen Back Cons as Prison Seethes," *BB* 6:6 (February 9–15, 1968): 1.

125. Cummins, *Rise and Fall*, viii.

126. *The Outlaw*, July 1, 1968, 1, JMP, Box 44, Folder 1. In the 1970s, the California Prisoners Union called its newspaper *The Outlaw* in partial tribute to the crude San Quentin mimeograph. This subsequent iteration of *The Outlaw* also preached inter-racial unity against the prison regime, specifically in regard to its efforts to organize unions of prison laborers to press for redress.

127. James W. L. Park, "'Power to the People,'" December 1968 speech, 2, JMP, Box 36, Folder 2, 7–9. Three years later, Park still pointed to the underground press to "see how the techniques of the militant radicals are now being used against the prison system." As evidence, he pointed to rock bands playing concerts at San Quentin's gate. See Kenneth Lamott, "The San Quentin Story: The Prisons Are Getting a Tougher Class of Convicts," *NYT Magazine*, May 2, 1971, 83.

128. Park, "'Power to the People,'" December 1968 speech, 2, JMP, Box 36, Folder 2, 2.

129. Ibid., 3.

130. Ibid., 6–7.

131. For more on the Alcatraz occupation, see Strange and Loo, "Holding the Rock"; Paul Chaat Smith and Warrior, *Like a Hurricane*; Troy R. Johnson, *American Indian Occupation*.

132. Paul Chaat Smith and Warrior, *Like a Hurricane*, 71.

133. Ibid., 24, 34. For a general overview of the occupation, its demographics, and its downfall, see sources cited in note 131.

134. Support for Alcatraz Indians, flyer, SPC, Reel 23.

135. Rafter, *Shots in the Mirror*.

136. Streissguth, *Johnny Cash*, 41. Musicians often played prison shows in the 1950s and 1960s. While imprisoned in Leavenworth, Raúl Salinas wrote for the prison newspaper about some of the concerts that occurred there. See Salinas and Mendoza, *raúlrsalinas*, 54–60, and files in RRSP.

137. For more on Catonsville, see Berrigan, *Catonsville Nine*. For the Columbia unrest, see Avorn, *Up against the Ivy Wall*; Bradley, *Harlem vs. Columbia University*.

138. Hayes, "Man of Sorrow." Cash's attempt to connect himself to the prisoners was mitigated by the corporate structures that turned his concert into a commercial product. Appealing to prevailing stereotypes of prisoners as violence-crazed men, Columbia Records added applause in the postproduction editing to what became one of Cash's most famous lines, "I shot a man in Reno just to watch him die." However, radio station officials thought that the line was too violent in the context of Robert Kennedy's and Martin Luther King Jr.'s assassinations and edited it out before broadcasting the song (Streissguth, *Johnny Cash*, 89, 137–38). More generally on the album's success, see Tom Dearmore, "First Angry Man of Country Music," *NYT*, September 21, 1969, 32.

139. In the liner notes to the 2000 edition of the album, Cash writes that he gave the cameras the finger because they crowded him on stage (Johnny Cash, "The Bird," in *At San Quentin*, liner notes, 8).

140. Streissguth, *Johnny Cash*, 156–57. *At Folsom* remains a more respected album, however, and ultimately sold more than six million copies (Streissguth, *Johnny Cash*, 160). It also anchors the 2006 biopic of Cash, *Walk the Line*.

141. Mitford, *Kind and Usual Punishment*, 226–27.

142. Streissguth, *Johnny Cash*, 162–64.

143. Quoted in ibid., 42.

144. Quoted in ibid., 20.

145. Gottschalk, *Prison*, 178–79.

CHAPTER THREE

1. "Soledad Brother Party: Champagne Flows Outside Quentin," *IJ*, October 16, 1970, 21.

2. George L. Jackson, *Soledad Brother*, 33, 25.

3. Ibid., 14.

4. Ibid., 146.

5. Gottschalk, *Prison*, 178–79. These numbers are echoed in Useem and Kimball, *States of Siege*, 18. It is likely, however, that these are low estimates in part because of the difficulty of defining what constitutes a "riot" and officials' ability to limit public access to facilities and thereby to control at some level what news gets out. Prisoners certainly engaged in far more acts of collective action, both violent and peaceful, in that period and throughout the 1970s. My conversations with Dan Chard, a historian of Maine's prison movement, have been instrumental in helping me rethink the official record on prison riots.

6. George L. Jackson, *Soledad Brother*, 26.

7. George L. Jackson, *Blood in My Eye*, 42; George Jackson to *NYT*, November 16, 1970 (draft), PPSB, Carton 1, Folder 22.

8. HoSang, "Race and the Mythology."

9. John Clutchette notes that the martial arts were especially useful, since guards used pick and axe handles to beat prisoners on the knees, elbows, and arms; knowing how to block such attacks or even disarm the attacker could prevent serious injury or death (John Clutchette to author, December 22, 2012). This biographical portrait draws largely from my interviews with Stephen Bingham, John Clutchette, David Johnson, Kiilu Nyasha, Luis Bato Talamantez, Willie Sundiata Tate, Karen Wald, and Larry Weiss.

10. Rebecca N. Hill, *Men, Mobs, and Law*, 112–13.

11. Ibid., 311.

12. This account builds on many sources, including my interviews with several people who knew Jackson (cited in note 9 above) as well as the autobiographical sketch he provides in *Soledad Brother* and several published sources: Jessica Mitford, "A Talk with George Jackson," *NYT Book Review*, June 13, 1971, 30–35; Begel, "Interview," 179; Lester Jackson, "Dialogue"; Yee, *Melancholy History*; Durden-Smith, *Who Killed George Jackson?*

13. Angela Davis, "18 page letter," n.d., Angela Davis Papers, MCLIR, Carton 39, Folder: Letters to George Jackson.

14. Prison Action Project, *Freedom*, in author's files, courtesy of Tony Platt. Indeterminate sentencing and parole were notable features of the twentieth-century rehabilitative school of penology; they went in tandem with calling prisons "training facilities." See Lawrence M. Friedman, *Crime and Punishment*, 304–8. More generally, see Simon, *Poor Discipline*.

15. Chávez-García, *States of Delinquency*; Janssen, "When the 'Jungle' Met the Forest."

16. I thank Bato Talamantez for explaining the structure of the AC over several interviews and discussions. Other details come from my interviews with David Johnson and Willie Sundiata Tate.

17. Yee, *Melancholy History*; Blue, *Doing Time*; Bookspan, *Germ*.

18. Yee, *Melancholy History*, 126; "George Lester Jackson (Deceased)," November 16, 1971, FBI memo, Jonathan Peter Jackson, Federal Bureau of Investigation file 157-20544. See also James Carr, *Bad*; William F. Buckley Jr., "The Real Line on George Jackson," *Washington Star*, September 22, 1971, A12. Jackson was not always pursuing weapons, however. Tate recalled finding shotgun shells in a police car brought into the body and fender shop at San Quentin. He "sent word to George to see if he wanted them," but Jackson demurred.

19. Willie Sundiata Tate, interview; John Clutchette to author, December 19, 2012; "George Jackson: Teacher & Organizer—Interview with Jimmy Carr," in *War behind the Walls*, September 1971, 3. *War behind the Walls* was a single issue of prison-related news, printed by Red Family and People's Press in San Francisco; it is archived in Prison Newspapers, DOC001, FA.

20. Quoted in *The San Quentin Six*, ca. 1974, 8, RRSP, Box 7, Folder 12.

21. Karen Wald, interview.

22. Eric Schlosser reports that "the number of inmates in California had declined by more than a fourth, despite the state's growing population" between 1963 and 1972 ("The Prison-Industrial Complex," *The Atlantic*, December 1998, http://www.theatlantic.com/magazine/archive/1998/12/the-prison-industrial-complex/304669/).

23. Heiner, "Foucault," 331. For Pratt's involvement with Jackson, see "Interview with Geronimo," *Babylon*, ca. 1971, 12, ECP, Oversize Box 2, Folder 6: Black Panther Party.

24. The best overview of this incident can be found in Yee, *Melancholy History*, 29–68. For the lawsuit by the families of Edwards, Miller, and Nolen, see Zohrabi, "Resistance and Repression."

25. Yee, *Melancholy History*, 70.

26. Durden-Smith, *Who Killed George Jackson?* In his confessional memoir *The Dragon Has Come*, Armstrong claims that Jackson confessed to the killing.

27. Armstrong, *Dragon Has Come*, xii; Cummins, *Rise and Fall*, 165; Soledad Brothers Defense Committee, "Soledad Brothers" (pamphlet), Soledad Brothers Defense Committee Vertical File, TL.

28. Yee, *Melancholy History*, 83–84; John Clutchette to author, December 19, 2012.

29. Cummins, *Rise and Fall*, 180–82; Prison Solidarity Committee, *From Soledad to San Quentin* (San Francisco, ca. 1972), 5, Anthony Platt, Private Collection.

30. Robin Bernstein, *Racial Innocence*.

31. John Clutchette to author, December 22, 2012.

32. Fay Stender, introduction to Pell, *Maximum Security*; John Clutchette to author, December 22, 2012. My interviews with Lincoln Bergman, Stephen Bingham, Karen Wald, and Larry Weiss were also helpful in providing a portrait of Stender.

33. KPFA programs that regularly covered prison issues during the 1970s included *Real Dragons* and *Freedom Is a Constant Struggle*, the hosts and correspondents of which frequently interviewed or covered a wide variety of prisoner struggles. My conversations with two KPFA journalists during those years, Lincoln Bergman and Claude Marks, as well as the prodigious archives of prison-related material held by both Pacifica Radio and the FA confirm this point.

34. "Soledad Brothers Defense Committee," Southern California Library, L. A., 20th Cent. Organizational File, Box 38, Folder 9: Soledad Brothers Defense Committee.

35. Yee, *Melancholy History*, 133–41; Black Caucus Report, "Treatment of Prisoners at California Training Facility at Soledad Central," July 23, 1970, JMP, Box 49, Folder 3. The report was authored by Dymally and Miller after their visit. Dymally's office also compiled news articles about prison conditions into a packet, "Prisons—A California Crisis," March 22, 1971, JMP, Box 55, Folder 6.

36. For a longer arc history of this phenomenon, see Rebecca N. Hill, *Men, Mobs, and Law*.

37. Jessica Mitford to Benjamin Spock, May 21, 1970, JMP, Box 48, Folder 9.

38. John Clutchette to author, December 24, 2012; Bettina Aptheker, interview.

39. Angela Y. Davis, *Autobiography*, 150–279.

40. Jack V. Fox, "A Collision with UC Regents," *San Francisco Examiner*, July 16, 1971, 6. Working covertly in the Communist Party, FBI informant William Divale wrote in July 1969 that the University of California was employing a communist; conservative journalist Ed Montgomery of the *San Francisco Examiner* unmasked Davis as the person in question and pursued her dismissal, as did then governor Ronald Reagan. Aware of this controversy as well as Davis's prison activism, Ruchell Magee wrote to Davis via her lawyer, claiming to have details of a high-level conspiracy against her (Ruchell Magee to John McTernan, July 3, 1970, MCLIR, Carton 37, Folder: Section VI, Doc. 3, Items Turned Over in Discovery, People v. Angela Y. Davis, 404–504). This collection also includes seven folders of hate letters that Davis received during this time period.

41. Angela Davis to George Jackson, June 10, 1970, MCLIR, Carton 39, Folder: Letters to George Jackson.

42. My argument here builds on Rebecca N. Hill, *Men, Mobs, and Law*, especially 265–314.

43. Kunzel, *Criminal Intimacy*, 193. For a sampling of the ways prison informed a variety of movements of the 1970s, see the essays in Berger, *Hidden 1970s*.

44. Wacquant, *Punishing the Poor*, 117; Western and Pettit, "Incarceration." California figures cited in Rebecca N. Hill, *Men, Mobs, and Law*, 267; Ruth Wilson Gilmore, *Golden Gulag*, 91.

45. Ruth Wilson Gilmore, *Golden Gulag*; see also the U.S. Supreme Court ruling in *Brown v. Plata*, case no. 09-1233, May 2011, available at http://www.law.cornell.edu/supct/html/09-1233.ZO.html. The court ruled that California prisons were so overcrowded as to constitute cruel and unusual punishment, especially regarding the large number of people in prison suffering mental or physical problems that were exacerbated by conditions inside. The court ruled that California needed to reduce its prison

population by 46,000 people, more than one-quarter of the 156,000 prisoners it then held, within two years. The state has appealed the decision and proposed a variety of alternatives to decarceration—including an expansion of the jail system that would merely shift rather than shrink the number of people in prison.

46. Father Earl A. Neil was rector of St. Augustine's Episcopal Church in Oakland and an active supporter of the Black Panthers. He officiated at the funerals of both Jonathan and George Jackson. See "George Jackson Funeral," audio file PM 067, FA.

47. Wacquant, "Deadly Symbiosis"; Wacquant, "Class, Race, and Hyperincarceration."

48. See Bantam Books and Coward-McCann, press release announcing publication of *Soledad Brother*, September 2, 1970, and Fay Stender to Jessica Mitford, June 23, 1970, both in JMP, Box 48, Folder 9. For Newton's and Stender's involvement, see Rosenbaum, "Whither Thou Goest," 86–88, 92, 174–76.

49. Karen Wald, interview.

50. George L. Jackson, *Soledad Brother*, 332.

51. See White, *Genet*, 496–598; Genet, *Declared Enemy*, 49–70, 81–90; Laroche, *Last Genet*; Kaplan, *Dreaming in French*, 189–92.

52. Genet, *Declared Enemy*, 91.

53. George L. Jackson, *Soledad Brother*, 335.

54. Ibid., 336–37.

55. Sundiata Acoli, interview.

56. George L. Jackson, *Soledad Brother*, 204.

57. Jonathan Jackson, postscript Angela Davis to George Jackson, June 22, 1970, MCLIR, Carton 39, Folder: Letters to George Jackson.

58. George L. Jackson, *Soledad Brother*, 6.

59. Ibid., 28.

60. Ibid., 208.

61. George Jackson to Jessica Mitford, March 4, 1971, JMP, Box 48, Folder 9. In a June 2, 1971, letter to Gregory Armstrong, Jackson expresses a similar sentiment: "At this stage, I think I have more confidence in people than you tho I care much less for any individual life" (PPSB, Carton 1, Folder 37).

62. George Jackson to Gregory Armstrong, September 20, 1970, PPSB, Carton 1, Folder 38.

63. George L. Jackson, *Soledad Brother*, 234.

64. For more on black memory, see David Scott, "On the Archaeologies."

65. George L. Jackson, *Soledad Brother*, 4.

66. Ibid., 174, 283, 298–99.

67. Ibid., 110.

68. Jackson's father apparently agreed; see Lester Jackson, "Dialogue." Joy James suggests that the title for Jackson's posthumous volume, *Blood in My Eye*, also came from Georgia (introduction to *Warfare*, 15).

69. See, for example, the books he requested (*Soledad Brother*, 294) and the list of books seized from his cell after his death; comments by several of his friends and associates verify his broad range of reading topics. See N. R. Snellgrove, "Books Taken from Cell of George Jackson," September 3, 1971, www2.pslweb.org/site/DocServer/George_Jackson_s_books.pdf?docID=3661.

70. Michael Simmons, interview; H. Bruce Franklin, interview.

71. James Carr, *Bad*, 123–24.

72. George L. Jackson, *Soledad Brother*, 269.

73. Suzannah Lessard, "Beyond Cleaver," *Washington Monthly*, November 1970, 63.

74. George L. Jackson, *Soledad Brother*, 266.

75. Jessica Mitford, "A Talk with George Jackson," *NYT Book Review*, June 13, 1971, 33.

76. George L. Jackson, *Soledad Brother*, 222; Ellison, *Invisible Man*, 275; Du Bois *Souls*.

77. Rolston, "Conversion."

78. For Jackson's objections to the arrangement of the book, see the sources cited in notes 98 and 99 below.

79. George L. Jackson, *Soledad Brother*, 16.

80. Jessica Mitford, "A Talk with George Jackson," *NYT Book Review*, June 13, 1971, 31.

81. Cummins, *Rise and Fall*, 86. More generally, see Cummins, *Rise and Fall*, 4–5, 24–32; Sweeney, *Reading*.

82. A review of *Soledad Brother* in the *NYT* describes Cleaver rather than Jackson as "the greatest writer of us all" because Cleaver confronts his "criminal disposition" whereas Jackson evades it. The reviewer notes that Jackson's letters demand attention not because they are compelling but because they are disturbing (Christopher Lehmann-Haupt, "Books of the Times: 'From Dachau, with Love,'" *NYT*, November 20, 1970, 39).

83. Cummins, *Rise and Fall*, viii.

84. Jessica Mitford, "A Talk with George Jackson," *NYT Book Review*, June 13, 1971, 34.

85. L. H. Fudge, State of California Memorandum, Subject: In-Service Training Recommendations, November 4, 1970, JMP, Box 44, Folder 4.

86. L. S. Nelson, California State Prison, Subject: Inmate Activity Programs, March 22, 1971, JMP, Box 44, Folder 4.

87. "Selected Books of the Year in Nonfiction," *NYT*, December 6, 1970, National United Committee to Free Angela Davis, Box 6, Folder 1, SC.

88. Suzannah Lessard, "Beyond Cleaver," *Washington Monthly*, November 1970, 63.

89. American Library Association, press release, January 20, 1971, PPSB, Carton 2, Folder 22.

90. Colin McGlashan, "Slender Bullets," *New Statesman*, March 26, 1971, 30; A. Sivenandan, "Ghettos of the Mind," *New Society*, April 1, 1971, 54; advertisement in *The Bookseller*, January 30, 1971, 282, PPSB, Carton 1, Folder 22.

91. Jessica Mitford, "Kind and Usual Punishment in California," *Atlantic Monthly*, March 1971, 52.

92. Tony Platt, cited in notes by Jessica Mitford, JMP, Box 36, Folder 2.

93. These include leftists Daniel Berrigan and Rosenberg codefendant Morton Sobell; poets Etheridge Knight, Miguel Piñero, and Raúl R. Salinas; and Jack Henry Abbott as well as anthologies such as Pell, *Maximum Security*, and a slew of pamphlets about various prisoners. For overviews, see Franklin, *Prison Writing*; Franklin, *Victim as Criminal*; Lee Bernstein, *America Is the Prison*. For examples of Black Power on television, see Acham, *Revolution Televised*.

94. Armstrong, *Dragon Has Come*, 170.

95. Julius Lester, "Black Rage to Live: *Soledad Brother*," *NYT Book Review*, November 22, 1970, 293.

96. Gregory Armstrong to William DuBois, November 17, 1970, and Gregory Armstrong to Frances Brown, both in PPSB, Carton 1, Folder 22.

97. George Jackson to *NYT*, November 16, 1970 (draft), PPSB, Carton 1, Folder 22.

98. Fay Stender to Greg Armstrong, n.d., PPSB, Carton 1, Folder 47; Fay Stender to Frances Jackson, November 2, 1970, JMP, Box 48, Folder 9; "About Soledad Defense . . . ," *BB*, August 13–19, 1971, 3; George Jackson, "Top Secret Legal Manifesto," January 11, 1971, HPNFP, Series 2, Box 4, Folder 16; Pat Gallyot, "George Jackson: A Beautiful Black Warrior," *SR*, August 28, 1971, 2; Jessica Mitford, "A Talk with George Jackson," *NYT Book Review*, June 13, 1971, 30–35; Yee, *Melancholy History*, 117–56; Durden-Smith, *Who Killed George Jackson?*, 113–14, 158–59, 203–4.

99. George Jackson to Gregory Armstrong, September 20, 1970, PPSB, Carton 1, Folder 38.

100. Quoted in Yee, *Melancholy History*, 170.

101. Quoted in Associated Press, "Marin Kidnap Youth's Story," *SFC*, August 14, 1970, 1.

102. Bill X. Jennings to author, January 10, 2014; Kiilu Nyasha interview; Angela Y. Davis, *Autobiography*; George L. Jackson, *Blood in My Eye*.

103. Major, *Justice*, 12–13; *Oakland Tribune*, August 17, 1970, in Jonathan Peter Jackson, Federal Bureau of Investigation file 157-20544, Folder 3.

104. In an *Esquire* article, journalist Ron Rosenbaum intimates that Magee rather than McClain may have been responsible for the attack ("Whither Thou Goest," 176). Either way, McClain maintained and was trying to prove his innocence when Jonathan Jackson entered the room.

105. Cummins, *Rise and Fall*, 180–82; Prison Solidarity Committee, *From Soledad to San Quentin* (San Francisco, ca. 1972), 5, Anthony Platt, Private Collection; Major, *Justice*, 88; "1970," 15, ADLDF, Box 6, Folder 3; Alexandra Close, "The Trial of Ruchell Magee," 5, JMP, Box 49, Folder 6. Other prisoners involved in the Billingslea effort included Jeffrey Khatari Gaulden (later of the Black Guerrilla Family), David Johnson, Luis Bato Talamantez, and Willie Sundiata Tate (all later of the San Quentin 6 case). See "The San Quentin Six" (flyer), San Quentin Six Defense Fund Vertical File, TL.

106. Alexandra Close, "The Trial of Ruchell Magee," 4, JMP, Box 49, Folder 6.

107. Ruchell Magee Defense Committee, *By Any Means Necessary* (newspaper), ECP, Carton 4, Folder 21. See also Major, *Justice*, 77–122; Aptheker, *Intimate Politics*, 239–48.

108. This description draws from multiple accounts, including coverage in the *IJ* and the *SFC*; Yee, *Melancholy History*, 157–73; Liberatore, *Road to Hell*, 81–92; and the transcripts of the Angela Davis trial found in the Angela Davis Papers, Boxes 2 and 3, GL, and the MCLIR Subseries 2.5. Thomas maintained that he killed all the men inside the van, and he did seize a pistol from the men. But the San Quentin guards killed the three men and paralyzed Thomas when they opened fire on the vehicle. Haley's face was torn off as a result of a blast from the shotgun that the prisoners taped around his head when they took him hostage, though he was also shot in the chest from outside the van. See Angela Davis trial transcript, 2858–2938.

109. Earl Caldwell, "Courthouse Shootout Linked with Radical Movement and Killing of Black Inmates," *NYT*, August 24, 1970, 40; Angela Y. Davis, "An Appeal," in Angela Y. Davis et al., *If They Come in the Morning*, 148.

110. Bantam Books and Coward-McCann, press release announcing publication of *Soledad Brother*, September 2, 1970, JMP, Box 48, Folder 9. See also the back cover and inside front cover of the original paperback version of the book.

111. George L. Jackson, *Soledad Brother*, 329.

112. Ibid.; Tim Findley, "A Brother's Doubts on Plot," *SFC*, August 15, 1970, 3; George Jackson to Jessica Mitford, March 4, 1971, JMP, Box 48, Folder 9. Huey Newton echoed Jackson's description of his brother and William Christmas; see "Jonathan Jackson Funeral," audio file PM 008, FA.

113. Reid-Pharr, *Once You Go Black*, 121–45.

114. Liberatore, *Road to Hell*, 93–97; Durden-Smith, *Who Killed George Jackson?*, 127–57; Danny Meyers, "Marin Shootout: Was It a Set-Up?," *SR*, July 5, 1975, 6; Paul Avery, Jim Brewer, and Rick Carroll, "Marin Shootout—New Disclosures," *SFC*, June 23, 1975, 1. My interviews with several people in or close to the Oakland and Berkeley Black Panther chapters during this time period confirmed that Newton had backed out of the plan to support Jonathan Jackson.

115. Yoruba, "Huey's Out to Stay!," *Palante* 2:9 (August 15, 1970): 10.

116. Angela Davis to George Jackson, June 22, 1970, Angela Davis Papers, MCLIR, Carton 39, Folder: Letters to George Jackson. Not everyone agreed with proclaiming prisoners leaders of a coming revolution. Two prisoners objected to this approach in an article published in the *Guild Practitioner*, JMP, Box 36, Folder 2: "The view from behind bars is this: If the free (relatively speaking) people look to us as the vanguard of the movement, what does this say about the condition of the movement?"

117. Davis, her associates in the Che-Lumumba Club, and some of the younger communist militants described August 7 as a prisoners' revolt akin to a slave rebellion (which is not to say that they necessarily endorsed it, as Magee and his supporters did). The Communist Party leadership, however, viewed August 7 as the desperate act of a foolhardy youth. It was caused by the system's cruelty, stressed party chair Henry Winston, but it was a disastrous and misguided move by Jonathan Jackson. Some party members feared a McCarthyist reprise and wanted to distance or even expel Davis. See Winston, *Meaning*; Aptheker, *Intimate Politics*, 245. See also the Soledad Brothers Defense Committee, memorandum, October 14, 1970, Soledad Brothers Defense Committee Vertical File, TL.

118. The first song appeared on a KPFA program about the Soledad Brothers, in "Interviews with Soledad Brothers," audio file PM 058, FA. The lyrics for "Jonathan" can be found in HPNFP, Series 2, Box 41, Folder 2.

119. Quoted in "How the Panthers See It," *IJ*, August 13, 1970, 4.

120. Quoted in Bloom and Martin, *Black against Empire*, 370.

121. "Angela Davis on FBI List," *IJ*, August, 19, 1970, 1.

122. Mann, *Comrade George*, 42.

123. Prisoner Solidarity Committee, *Prisoners Call Out: Freedom* (New York City, 1971), 39, in Prisoner Solidarity Committee Vertical File, TL.

124. Major, *Justice*, 122. Magee also argued that yesterday's sword was today's gun and appealed to a warrior Jesus found in the bible (Matthew chapter 10, verse 34): "I come not to send peace but the sword," in *By Any Means Necessary* (newspaper, ca. 1971), 2, ECP, Carton 4, Folder 21: Black Panther Party Ruchell Magee Defense Committee.

125. Sol Stern, "The Campaign to Free Angela Davis and Ruchell Magee," *NYT Magazine*, June 27, 1971, http://www.nytimes.com/books/98/03/08/home/davis-campaign.html; "Jonathan Jackson Memorial," audio file PM 008, FA.

126. Jonathan Jackson Memorial Service program, PPSB, Box 1, Folder 47; "George Jackson Funeral," audio files PM 067, 068, FA; "Jonathan Jackson Memorial," audio file PM 008, FA.

127. Quoted in Cummins, *Rise and Fall*, 185.

128. The series, an attempt to contextualize the greater visibility prisons had by that time garnered, featured reporters taking temporary jobs as prison guards to describe routines in prison. The stories can be found in JMP, Box 44, Folder 1.

129. Mary Leydecker, "Magee Resists Judge in Quentin Appearance; Shouts 'This Is Not a Court,'" *IJ*, September 10, 1970, 1.

130. "Stop the San Quentin Railroad" (flyer), August 1970, SPC, Reel 20.

131. Mary Leydecker, "Court Hearings: A First at San Quentin," *IJ*, August 23, 1970, 1.

132. UPI, "Guns Puzzle Mother of Slain Youth," *IJ*, August, 12, 1970, 1.

133. Mary Leydecker, "Court Hearings: A First at San Quentin," *IJ*, August 23, 1970, 1.

134. Yee, *Melancholy History*, 35; Stender, "Violence and Lawlessness," 222. See also the timeline printed in the British journal *Soledad Brothers News*, May 1972, 12–13, 18–19, Soledad Brothers Vertical File, FA. Immediate physical violence was the most common weapon at the guards' disposal, but other strategies were used. In one chilling episode, Soledad guards tried to frame a prison psychologist for a 1971 murder after he was fired for refusing to let the administration look at a prisoner's file. Officials claimed that Dr. Frank Rundle identified too much with the prisoners in his care and tried to get one of them to collaborate in framing him. See Rundle, "Roots"; Don Jelenik, "The Soledad Frame Up," *San Francisco Bay Guardian*, June 22, 1972, 1, 4–7; Yee, *Melancholy History*, 175–86.

135. "Prison Struggle, 1970–71" in *War behind the Walls*, September 1971, 14. See also Chard, "Rallying for Repression"; Thuma, "'Not a Wedge'"; Bissonette, *When the Prisoners*; Useem and Kimball, *States of Siege*.

136. George L. Jackson, *Soledad Brother*, 222.

137. George Jackson to unknown, August 11, 1971, PPSB, Carton 1, Folder 38.

138. George Jackson, "Top Secret Legal Manifesto," January 11, 1971, 6, HPNFP, Series 2, Box 4, Folder 16.

139. John Clutchette to author, December 22, 2012.

140. Karen Wald, interview.

141. Larry Weiss, interview; "Soledad Brothers Legal Defense Committee" memo, in author's files, courtesy of Larry Weiss; *O. C. Allen et al., v. Evelle J. Younger et al.*, no. C-71 69. The seven men were O. C. Allen, Alfred Dunn, Jimmy James, Jesse Phillips, James Wagner, Walter Joe Watson, and Roosevelt Williams. The prosecution ultimately dropped the charges against four of the men, and the remaining three were acquitted in 1972. The suit brought by Jackson, Talamantez, and the Soledad 7 was dismissed in March 1971.

142. George Jackson, interview.

143. Larry Weiss, interview.

144. See Huey Newton, "Hidden Traitor, Renegade Scab: Eldridge Cleaver," HPNFP, Series 2, Box 42, Folder 1; San Quentin Black Panther Party, "Tell It Like It Is!," HPNFP, Box 42, Folder 2; Kiilu Nyasha, interview. See also Hilliard and Cole, *This Side of Glory*, 295–96, 335, 379–80.

145. See George Jackson will, March 11, 1971, HPNFP, Series 2, Box 45, Folder 6.

146. See FBI report, "Burial Service of George Lester Jackson," September 2, 1971, Jonathan Peter Jackson, Federal Bureau of Investigation file 157-20544; Grenada TV documentary, FA.

147. Steve Weissman, "Occupy This: Crazy Tom the FBI Provocateur," *Reader Supported News*, November 27, 2011, http://readersupportednews.org/opinion2/275-42 /8619-occupy-this-crazy-tom-the-fbi-provocateur. See also Citizens Research and Investigation Committee and Tackwood, *Glass House Tapes*; Durden-Smith, *Who Killed George Jackson?*; Yee, *Melancholy History*. Bennett was killed on suspicion of being a police informant, though others claimed that it was because he was having an affair with the wife of a leading Panther. Durden-Smith claims that both Carr and Bennett were police informants.

148. See Betsy Carr, afterword to James Carr, *Bad*, 198–225; Durden-Smith, *Who Killed George Jackson?*, 122–25; Fanya Carter, "Former Bodyguard to Newton Killed at San Jose Home," *Oakland Post*, April 13, 1972, 1; Jerry Cohen, "Theft of Angela Davis Funds Linked to Slaying in San Jose," *LAT*, April 8, 1972, 1. Carr was alleged to have stolen money from the Angela Davis defense committee.

149. For more on the "pants pocket letter," see Yee, *Melancholy History*, 250–53; Durden-Smith, *Who Killed George Jackson?*, 99–101; and the district attorney's closing statements in *People of the State of California v. Stephen Mitchell Bingham*, case no. 4094, June 9, 1986, 3374–79.

150. Mancino's affidavit quoted in Yee, *Melancholy History*, 255–56.

151. Pinell's affidavit is included in George Jackson FBI File, 44-HQ-47984. See also *The San Quentin Six* (pamphlet), ca. 1973, 10, RRSP, Box 7, Folder 12.

152. Jo Durden-Smith, "Who Killed George Jackson?: The Difference between Deaths," *Village Voice*, September 30, 1971, 15, 22.

153. Larry Weiss, interview.

154. Tad Szulc, "George Jackson Radicalizes the Brothers in Soledad and San Quentin," *NYT*, August 1, 1971, SM10, 16. Jackson's friend Karen Wald, who had arranged the interview with Szulc and was present during it, remembered that Jackson was bothered by Szulc and wanted to get a rise out of him (Karen Wald, interview).

155. Cummins, *Rise and Fall*, 209.

156. John Clutchette to author, January 17, 2013.

157. N. R. Snellgrove, "Books Taken from Cell of George Jackson," September 3, 1971, www2.pslweb.org/site/DocServer/George_Jackson_s_books.pdf?docID=3661. I thank scholar Gregory Thomas for finding and making public this document, which lists ninety-nine books.

158. Hugo A. Pinell, "Disciplinary Report," included as part of his Cumulative Case Summary, Mark Merin, Private Collection, *Spain v. Procunier* Files; Luis Bato

Talamantez and Sue Martinez, "The Epic Trial of the San Quentin Six," *Sedition*, March 1976, 11; "The San Quentin Six" (flyer), San Quentin Six Defense Fund Vertical File, TL; Luis Bato Talamantez, interview; Larry Weiss, interview.

159. Gibson and Justice were accused of killing officer Leo Davis as he stood guard over Herman Johnson, a prisoner who had been hospitalized after an attack by other prisoners. Johnson had testified for the prosecution in the Soledad 7 case. While that case garnered a lot of attention and ended in victory for the defendants, Gibson and Justice were ultimately sentenced to life in prison for the death of Davis. See Cummins, *Rise and Fall*, 185; "Dare to Struggle, Dare to Win," *The Anvil* 1:1 (April 1973): 3; Fred Lowe, "Two Black Men Accused of Murder in Prison Get Help," *Los Angeles Free Press*, December 29, 1972, 5.

160. Willie Sundiata Tate interview; Luis Bato Talamantez interview; David Johnson interview.

161. Anderson is a mysterious character in this case. Bingham and Anderson had never met before, and she provided the tape recorder that Bingham brought into the prison. Further, he only brought the recorder in at the guard's suggestion after Anderson was denied access. Anderson disappeared after Jackson's death: she was never listed as a person of interest or questioned in the case, much less indicted as a defendant alongside Bingham and the others. Conservative journalist Ed Montgomery interviewed her in the mid-1970s in Texas: at that time, she distanced herself from Jackson and the Black Power movement more generally, but she never testified at either of the trials stemming from the case. It is not known whether, as some allege, she was a police informant or what accounts for the government's lack of interest in her role in the events of the day. For a larger but no more conclusive set of speculations about her, see Durden-Smith, *Who Killed George Jackson?*, 41–84.

162. My account of Bingham's visit comes from several sources: Stephen Bingham, interview; the closing statements of *People of the State of California v. Stephen Mitchell Bingham*, case no. 4094, June 1986, 3265–3737; "Time Chart, San Quentin Six, August 21, 1971," KFAP, Folder: San Quentin, 1971–72.

163. Several published sources on the case, including Liberatore's *Road to Hell* and Tibbs's *From Black Power*, echo the government's version of the case: during his visit with Bingham, Jackson removed a gun, a wig, and some ammunition that had been hidden in Anderson's tape recorder, perhaps without Bingham's knowledge, and then used the gun to take over the AC. The KRON-TV documentary on the case, *Day of the Gun*, also takes this perspective. Subsequent trials, however, called into question or disproved key elements of this story but offered no satisfactory alternative explanation. Other sources, including Yee's *Melancholy History* and Durden-Smith's *Who Killed George Jackson?*, describe the government's case and criticize its weaknesses and contradictions but fail to provide a substantive counternarrative. Still others, including Rodríguez's *Forced Passages* and the *Prisons on Fire* documentary as well as a myriad of articles by Jackson's friends and supporters in a variety of left-wing magazines, insist that Jackson was set up and murdered by the state though they do not provide evidence of their own to *definitively* support this claim. See, for example, *San Quentin to Attica: The Sound before the Fury* (New York: National Lawyers Guild, ca. 1972), RRSP, Box 8, Folder 3.

164. Yee, *Melancholy History*, 216; Stephen Bingham, interview and trial transcripts.

165. I review Jackson's plans and the prison system's disgust for him elsewhere in the text. However, it is worth commenting on the suddenness of the AC takeover. Jackson did not believe in spontaneous action, telling one supporter that there "is no such thing as a spontaneous revolution, there will be no spontaneous uprising and sudden seizure of power by the people" (Pat Gallyot, "George Jackson: A Beautiful Black Warrior," *SR*, August 28, 1971, 2). If he planned to escape, it certainly was not to have taken place on August 21, 1971.

166. Luis Bato Talamantez, interview.

167. David Johnson, interview; Talamantez quoted in *Prisons on Fire* audio documentary (San Francisco: Freedom Archives, 2002). My telling of these events is indebted to my interviews with three people who were in the AC that day—David Johnson, Luis Bato Talamantez, and Willie Sundiata Tate—as well as my interviews with Nyati Bolt, then a prisoner at San Quentin but not in the AC, and Stephen Bingham. For published sources, see especially Cummins, *Rise and Fall*, 209–10; Durden-Smith, *Who Killed George Jackson?*; Liberatore, *Road to Hell*, 136–58; Yee, *Melancholy History*, 201–58.

168. Several prisoners who were there that day, however, allege that Jackson was shot more than twice, including perhaps once at close range. Yee recounts their doubts in *Melancholy History*; several of my interviewees expressed similar views.

CHAPTER FOUR

1. Unless otherwise noted, the material in this section comes from my interviews with Luis Bato Talamantez and Larry Weiss and from the *Spain v. Procunier* files provided to me by Mark Merin.

2. The "eerie quiet" quotation is from John Clutchette to author, November 2, 2013.

3. Willie Sundiata Tate, interview.

4. David Johnson to author, December 24, 2013; Luis Bato Talamantez to author, December 24, 2013.

5. Rubiaco's comment is recorded in Yee, *Melancholy History*, 227. It reflects the state of war that governed California's prison system not just on that day but in those years. Johnson recalls that Rubiaco had been involved in the death of a black prisoner, William A. Powell, during a cell extraction at Soledad Prison in 1969. Powell's death is described in Yee, *Melancholy History*, 32–33.

6. Luis Bato Talamantez, interview.

7. David Johnson, interview.

8. This description, supported by other published accounts of the day, draws largely from my interviews with John Clutchette, David Johnson, Luis Bato Talamantez, and Willie Sundiata Tate.

9. "Time Chart, San Quentin Six, August 21, 1971," KFAP, Folder: San Quentin, 1971–72; Andrews, *Black Power*, 166; Cummins, *Rise and Fall*, 225; Luis Bato Talamantez, interview; David Johnson, interview. The song demonstrates the counter-insurgent aims of policing: the goal was not just restraint but changing the mental and psychological makeup of the insurgent population. This impromptu song

suggests that the guards wished to instill docility in prisoners, to use the death of Jackson to highlight the impossibility of any social or political change in prison.

10. Mann, *Comrade George*, 132–44.

11. George Jackson People's Free Medical Research Health Clinic and Don Williams, "Facts about Black Genocide, Sickle Cell Anemia, and Glucose-6 Phosphate Dehydrogenase Deficiency," HPNFP, Series 2, Box 17, Folder 17; Black Panther Party Quiz, 1973, HPNFP, Series 2, Box 4, Folder 3; George Jackson Prisoner Contact Program flyer, HPNFP, Series 2, Box 10, Folder 11. Other Panther chapters as well as organizations such as the Young Lords also named their counterinstitutions after martyred prisoners. See Bloom and Martin, *Black against Empire*, 189. More generally, see Nelson, *Body and Soul*.

12. Vincent Brown, *Reaper's Garden*, 4.

13. Rodríguez, "Forced Passages."

14. Many historians associate the term "social death" with Orlando Patterson's influential but flawed 1982 study, *Slavery and Social Death*. They reject his usage of the term for the ways it forecloses the agency of those said to be socially dead as well as the abstract and totalizing (and for some ahistoric) power he attributes to social norms. That Patterson's subsequent work has been so neoconservative only adds to the disagreement. However, my use of the phrase draws from alternate literature—specifically, from scholars working in critical legal and ethnic studies. These scholars ground their usage of "social death" in studies of law and concrete modes of political-economic violence that render people without access to rights or other mechanisms for grievance and redress. To them, and for my purposes here, social death is a *productive* way to make sense of abjection and subjection by the state. In other words, I am interested in the subjectivities that form amid the limitations of the law. In so doing, I am following the lead of imprisoned intellectuals, who often write of death. My thinking on social death is especially indebted to Cacho, *Social Death*; Dayan, *Law Is a White Dog*; Smallwood, *Saltwater Slavery*; Vincent Brown, "Social Death and Political Life"; Rodríguez, "(Non)Scenes of Captivity"; Gordon, "Methodologies"; as well as conversations with Chandan Reddy.

15. Ruth Wilson Gilmore, "Forgotten Places." See also Marilyn Buck's introduction to Rossi, *State of Exile*.

16. John L. Jackson Jr., *Racial Paranoia*, 7.

17. "George Jackson Funeral," audio file PM 067, FA.

18. "Huey Newton on George Jackson," audio file PM 065, FA. See also "Huey Newton, eulogy for George Jackson," audio file PM 068, FA; "Huey Newton on George Jackson," audio file PM 092, FA.

19. "Revolutionary Memorial Service for George Jackson," ECP, Box 4, Folder 20: BPP–George Jackson.

20. "Outbursts Mark Burial of Jackson in Illinois," *LAT*, August 30, 1971, 17.

21. Guevara, *Che Guevara Speaks*, 159.

22. Cummins, *Rise and Fall*, 224–27.

23. Major, *Justice*, 307–8; George Jackson Tribunal flyer, July 14, 1975, Mark Merin, Private Collection, *Spain v. Procunier* Files.

24. The affidavit is reprinted in *San Quentin to Attica: The Sound before the Fury* (New York: National Lawyers Guild, ca. 1972), RRSP, Box 8, Folder 3.

25. Philip Hager and Daryl Lembke, "Newsmen Touring San Quentin Discount Maltreatment Claims," *LAT*, August 28, 1971, A1. See also "Deaths at San Quentin," audio file PM 025, FA.

26. For more on organizing at Attica prior to the rebellion, see Thompson, "Black Activism," *Blood in the Water*, "All across the Nation," "Blinded," and "Empire State Disgrace." Attica prisoners had been working to improve their conditions for quite some time before Jackson's death.

27. Tom Wicker quoted in *The Struggle Inside* conference booklet, n.p., Anthony Platt, Private Collection.

28. Rockefeller had the full support of President Richard Nixon; see Sam Roberts, "Rockefeller on the Attica Raid, from Boastful to Subdued," *NYT*, September 12, 2011. Audio file excerpts of their conversation can be heard at http://www.nytimes .com/2011/09/13/nyregion/rockefeller-initially-boasted-to-nixon-about-attica-raid .html?pagewanted=all&_r=0.

29. For more on the retaking of Attica and its implications, see Wicker, *Time to Die*; *Attica*; *San Quentin to Attica: The Sound before the Fury* (New York: National Lawyers Guild, ca. 1972), RRSP, Box 8, Folder 3; and the Thompson articles cited in note 26 above.

30. The attempted cover-up of Attica is described by the special prosecutor hired to investigate the rebellion and its aftermath in Bell, *Turkey Shoot*. The fact that government officials first said that prisoners had castrated the hostages suggests that part of the dramatic violence the state used in retaking Attica was intended to restore its masculine authority. It suggests, in other words, that the prison functions to shore up the state's patriarchal authority and that reinforcing its rule needed to restore the gendered balance of power. At least it suggests that masculinity was the symbolic terrain on which prison functioned. Further, the extreme shock-and-awe violence New York officials displayed in retaking Attica provides a needed corrective to those who insist that the spectacle of left-wing radicalism destroyed the social movements of the era. (Such ideas especially characterized earlier generations of scholarship on the 1960s, including Cummins, *Rise and Fall*; Gitlin, *Whole World Is Watching*; and Charles Payne's otherwise stellar history of the civil rights movement, *I've Got the Light*.) The government's response at Attica, among other such incidents, demonstrated that however much some leftist radicals speculated about the power of spectacle, the state always had a much stronger belief in as well as capacity for spectacular violence as a form of power.

31. Quoted in Franklin, *Victim as Criminal*, 235.

32. McKay, *Harlem Shadows*, 53.

33. Leon X. Bates, "George, in the Tradition of Malcolm," *Black Pride* 28 (May 18, 1972): 7, 14, RRSP, Box 6, Folder 30.

34. *San Quentin to Attica: The Sound before the Fury* (New York: National Lawyers Guild, ca. 1972), 14, RRSP, Box 8, Folder 3.

35. Statement quoted in Foucault, von Bülow, and Defert, "Masked Assassination," 152.

36. Angela Y. Davis, *Autobiography*, 317.

37. Gregory Armstrong in George L. Jackson, *Blood in My Eye*, xix.

38. Rebecca N. Hill, *Men, Mobs, and Law*, 17.

39. For examples of prisoners in anticolonial or antiracist movements around the world, see Buntman, *Robben Island*; Feldman, *Formations of Violence*; Harlow, *Barred*; Khalili, *Heroes and Martyrs*.

40. Weather Underground, "George Jackson: San Francisco, August 30, 1971," in Dohrn, Ayers, and Jones, *Sing a Battle Song*, 175.

41. Quoted in Mann, *Comrade George*, 135.

42. Ed Mead, interview; Mark Cook, interview; Burton-Rose, *Guerrilla USA*; Burton-Rose, *Creating a Movement*. Mead was a founding member of the brigade; Cook was a Black Panther who had organized a prison chapter and joined the brigade. For the George Jackson Brigade at San Quentin, see "From the George Jackson Brigade," *Babylon* 1:4 (January 15, 1972): 9, NLC, Box 49, Folder: RPCN.

43. "George Jackson/Communiqués Post George Jackson Assassination," audio file PM 013, FA.

44. Tim Findley, "'Guerrilla' Group Claims Oakland Copter Attack," *SFC*, October 10, 1973, 3; Tim Findley, "New Note from 'Guerrilla' Group," *SFC*, October 12, 1973, 6; Nancy Dooley, "New Questions in Oakland Copter Crash," *SFC*, December 9, 1973, 5; Bill Friedmann, "SQ Six Silent on Aug 7 Band," *BB*, October 12–18, 1973, 3. The communiqués were reprinted in *BB*, October 12–18, 1973, 3.

45. For more on the Symbionese Liberation Army, see Les Payne and Findley with Craven, *Life and Death*; Cummings, "End of an Era"; Burton-Rose, *Guerrilla USA*. Begun as a Chicano organizing group, Venceremos became a multiracial organization involved in prison work. In 1972, several of its members were involved in a badly botched prison escape led by Ronald Beatty, a Chino prisoner who subsequently cooperated with authorities against his onetime comrades. See Cummins, *Rise and Fall*, 147; H. Bruce Franklin, interview. For how these dynamics played out in Maine and New York, respectively, see Chard, "Rallying for Repression"; Fortner, "Carceral State."

46. In 2012, journalist Seth Rosenfeld revealed in *Subversives* that Richard Aoki, an Asian American radical and member of the Black Panther Party, was an FBI informant. Aoki had no known connection to Jackson or the prison movement, and Rosenfeld's style of breaking the news was sensationalistic. Still, the fact that such a high-profile party member was an FBI informant and that his actions remained secret for forty years is startling. It points to how much we have yet to learn about law enforcement infiltration and disruption of leftist organizations during those years. Questions certainly remain about the role of informants and provocateurs in the case of Jackson—Who brought him and Johnny Spain the supposedly explosive vials of liquid? Who asked Stephen Bingham to accompany Vanita Anderson, and who was she really working for? What were the intricacies of the ostensible guerrilla training ground in the Santa Cruz Mountains?

47. Brothers and Black Panthers Landon and Randy Williams were Vietnam veterans involved in the party's military capacity. Landon purchased the gun in March 1969 and was arrested in June of that year, when he was charged with participating in the grisly murder of a Black Panther in New Haven (charges on which he and other defendants were acquitted). Prior to his arrest, Landon had given the gun to Randy, who was arrested in April 1970. See Durden-Smith, *Who Killed George Jackson?*, 89, 109–10, 167; Yee, *Melancholy History*, 244–45; Yohuru Williams, *Black Politics*.

48. Quoted in Rebecca N. Hill, *Men, Mobs, and Law*, 266.

49. Quoted in George L. Jackson, *Soledad Brother*, x.

50. "Coincidence . . . or Genocide," *Up against the Bench* (newsletter of the Chicago chapter of the National Lawyers Guild) 1:5 (September 1972): 4–5, NLGC, Carton 57, Folder: Chapter Newsletter—Chicago, BL. More generally, see Rodríguez, *Forced Passages*; Nelson, *Body and Soul*, 133.

51. Quoted in Mann, *Comrade George*, 144.

52. Ossie Davis, preface to William L. Patterson, *We Charge Genocide*, v. I thank David Stein for bringing this reprint to my attention.

53. Willhelm, *Who Needs the Negro?*, 257. The literature on race and neoliberalism is vast. See, for example, Ruth Wilson Gilmore, *Golden Gulag*; Wacquant, *Punishing the Poor*; Melamed, *Represent and Destroy*; Singh, "Racial Formation."

54. Diawara, *In Search*, 100. Postcolonial theorist Ania Loomba said that learning about Jackson and Davis as a teenager in India was also part of her initial thinking regarding race and gender (introduction to Angela Davis keynote lecture at the Critical Refusals conference, University of Pennsylvania, October 28, 2011, author's notes).

55. Diawara, *In Search*, 103–4.

56. Walter Rodney, "George Jackson: Black Revolutionary," November 1971 http://www.historyisaweapon.com/defcon1/rodneyjackson.html.

57. Rebecca N. Hill, *Men, Mobs, and Law*, 296. For more on the influence of the American prison movement on French society, especially through Davis, see Kaplan, *Dreaming in French*, 177–221.

58. See Heiner, "Foucault." See also Foucault, "Michel Foucault on Attica." For more on GIP, see Bourg, *From Revolution to Ethics*, 45–103, especially 79–95; Derrida, *Negotiations*, 41–45, 125–29.

59. Foucault's conclusions in *Discipline and Punish*, including both racial and historical blind spots, have been widely criticized; see Joy James, *Resisting State Violence*, 24–43; Angela Y. Davis, "Racialized Punishment and Prison Abolition," in *Angela Y. Davis Reader*, 96–107; Heiner, "Foucault."

60. Heiner, "Foucault."

61. Foucault, von Bülow, and Defert, "Masked Assassination," 155. Genet's introduction is reprinted in *Declared Enemy*, 91–97.

62. Foucault, von Bülow, and Defert, "Masked Assassination," 142, 149.

63. Durden-Smith, *Who Killed George Jackson?*, 68–96; "Pistol and Wig Experiment," *SFC*, August 28, 1971, 1; Philip Hager, "Jackson Was Killed by Bullet in Back, New Report Indicates," *LAT*, September 22, 1971, 1; Yee, *Melancholy History*, 236.

64. Foucault, von Bülow, and Defert, "Masked Assassination," 147.

65. See, for example, Yee's otherwise excellent book, *The Melancholy History of Soledad Prison*, which presented and then challenged the state's theory of what happened on August 21. Even while acknowledging the sequence of events as "the state's case," Yee supports that perspective with the depth of his detail—narrating the last words and actions of the guards as they bled to death. Such journalism exemplifies what communications scholar James Carey later described as American journalism's excessive, obsessive attention to *how* but its inability to answer *why* ("Dark Continent").

66. Ruchell Magee poster, ca. November 1972, Anthony Platt, Private Collection.

67. "A Brother of the 3rd World," "Be Aware of the Publicity Tricks," *Black Pride*, June 1972, 7–8, RRSP, Box 6, Folder 30.

68. Omi and Winant, "Racial Formation Rules," 324.

69. *MS* 3:12 (December 1973): 15.

70. Quoted in Michael Spencer, "Tear Down the Walls," 3, JMP, Box 56, Folder 1. See also Bruce Jackson, "Prison."

71. Black Mothers United for Action, "Open Letter to Black Officials: Where Is Ruchell Magee?," August 1971, ADLDF, Box 2, Folder 7. See also Friends of San Quentin Adjustment Center, *Letters to Mother from Prison* (San Francisco, ca. 1972), Anthony Platt, Private Collection.

72. "Who Is Ruchell Magee? Cinque," 2, ADLDF, Box 2, Folder 7.

73. George Jackson to unnamed, August 11, 1971, PPSB, Carton 1, Folder 38.

74. George L. Jackson, *Blood in My Eye*, 10.

75. Ibid., 109.

76. Ibid., 29.

77. Ibid., 23, 47, 50.

78. "George Jackson interview," audio file PM 021, FA.

79. Saleem Holbrook to author, July 18, 2013. More generally, see Graham, *Cities under Siege*; Wacquant, *Punishing the Poor*; Tonry, *Punishing Race*; Thompson, "Why Mass Incarceration Matters."

80. George L. Jackson, *Soledad Brother*, 329.

81. Quoted in Gregory Armstrong, preface to George L. Jackson, *Blood in My Eye*, xvi. This text was republished approvingly in several leftist venues, suggesting that obsession was an appropriate response to incarceration. See, for example, Friends of Soledad, "Marin: August 7th" (flyer), JMP, Box 49, Folder 1.

82. George L. Jackson, *Blood in My Eye*, 19.

83. Ibid., 42.

84. For overviews, see Heiner, "Foucault"; Cusset, *French Theory*; Ross, *May '68*; Klimke, *Other Alliance*; Hale, *Nation of Outsiders*; Katsiaficas, *Imagination*.

85. Williamson, *Rough Guide*, 83.

86. Dylan, *Lyrics*, 273. The other major political song that Dylan wrote during that period was also about a black prisoner. "Hurricane," first released on the 1975 album *Desire*, put to music the lengthy travails of black boxer Rubin "Hurricane" Carter, who many believed had been framed by police for a triple murder at a New Jersey bar. The song was far more popular than "George Jackson"—it adopted the traditions of protest songs (challenging the injustice of someone wrongly accused and around whom a campaign had been launched) at a time when protest songs were far less common and provided a more musically intricate and sophisticated song. I thank Richard Iton for pushing my aesthetic assessment of these songs.

87. See Gil Scott-Heron, "H2o Gate Blues" (1973), included on *The Mind of Gil Scott Heron* (1978); Gil Scott-Heron, "Pardon Our Analysis (We Beg Your Pardon)" (1975), included on the Midnight Band's *The First Minute of a New Day* (1975).

88. Steel Pulse also included a reggae-style cover of Dylan's song about Jackson on its 2004 album, *African Holocaust*.

89. John Lennon and Yoko Ono/Plastic Ono Band, *Sometime in New York City*. The album features several protest songs, including "Attica State," about the response to the prison uprising, and a song about the failing educational system, "Born in a Prison."

90. Spillers, "Mama's Baby"; Weheliye, "Pornotropes."

91. Rolling Stones, *Exile on Main Street*.

92. Robinson, "Blaxploitation"; Dunn, *"Baad Bitches"*; Wallace, *Black Macho*. One film, *Brothers*, offered a thinly veiled presentation of the George Jackson–Angela Davis story. It was a sympathetic, simplistic tale. The film received mixed reviews in the black press and was largely unnoticed in the mainstream. It was too tame by the standards of blaxploitation films and too hackneyed in comparison to other contemporary movies. For reviews, see "'Brothers,' a Powerful Motion Picture," *SR*, April 14, 1977, 41; Margaret Tarter, "The Movie 'Brothers' a Watered-Down Love Tale," *Bay State Banner*, June 9, 1977, 18; "Theatrical News: 'Brothers' Flick Zooms to No. 25 in First Week," *Tri-State Defender*, April 23, 1977, 7.

93. Fay Stender, introduction to Pell, *Maximum Security*, 13.

94. Quoted in "Entrevista Sobre el Caso de Humberto Pagan," *Palante* 1:24 (March 1–15, 1972): 12. The interview originally appeared in *La Hora*.

95. Mel Watkins, "The Last Word: The Late George Jackson," *NYT*, September 19, 1971, BR55.

96. Pat Halloran and Free Our Sisters Collective, "Free Our Sisters!," *The Anvil* 1:3 (August–September 1971): 7, ECP, Carton 4, Folder 33.

97. Thomas E. Gaddis, introduction to Trupin, *In Prison*, xvii.

98. Ronald Reagan, "We Will All Become Prisoners," *NYT*, October 7, 1971, 47. See also AP, "Nobody Cares about Guards, San Quentin Widow Laments," *LAT*, August 25, 1971, A1.

99. William F. Buckley Jr., "The Real Line on George Jackson," *Washington Star*, September 22, 1971, A12.

100. Rosenbaum, "Whither Thou Goest," 77, 79.

101. For more of a textual analysis of these various books, see Berger, "We Are the Revolutionaries," 197–208. Horowitz's article is discussed in Pell, *We Used to Own*, 190–91. Collier and Horowitz included a larger critical analysis of Stender and the prison movement in their book *Destructive Generation*, 25–66.

102. Irwin, *Felon*; Irwin, *Prisons in Turmoil*. For a discussion of the intellectual history of the prison in those years, see Kunzel, *Criminal Intimacy*, 149–90.

103. Katz, *Undeserving Poor*; Katz, *Underclass Debate*; Reed, *Stirrings*, especially 479–96.

104. Larry Weiss, interview. See also Hartman, *Scenes of Subjection*, 4

105. David Johnson, interview.

106. My notion of care work builds on several sources, including Federici, *Revolution*; Gould, *Moving Politics*.

107. Rebecca N. Hill, *Men, Mobs, and Law*.

108. "San Quentin 6 Indicted," *The Guardian*, November 3, 1971, special insert on George Jackson's death, 4, Anthony Platt, Private Collection.

109. Ruchell Magee to Robert Treuhaft and Jessica Mitford, March 5, 1971, JMP, Box 48, Folder 9.

110. Author's interviews with Kalima Aswad, Shujaa Graham, Phyllis Prentice, Mark Merin, Fred Hiestand, and Luis Bato Talamantez were helpful on this point. See also Pell, *We Used to Own*, 161–92.

111. Shujaa Graham, interview; Phyllis Prentice, interview.

112. See Graham and Allen Defense Committee materials, "Justice for Graham and Allen" pamphlet and "Prison Murder Conspiracy" flyer, Coalition against Police Abuse Papers, Box 17, Folder 25: Political Prisoners, Southern California Library, Los Angeles. Because of his association with the Black Guerrilla Family, however, Graham remained a police target after his release. Police raided his house and intimidated his neighbors, ultimately sending him back to prison for four months in 1983. He remains an anti-death-penalty activist (Shujaa Graham, interview).

113. Shujaa Graham, interview.

114. *The Struggle Inside* (conference booklet), n.p., Anthony Platt, Private Collection.

115. "The Struggle Inside: Prison Action Conference" (flyer), Anthony Platt, Private Collection.

116. See, for example, Roger Boberg, Jaan Laaman, Richard Williams, and John Yancey, "Prisoners in Revolution: Response to the Weather Underground," letter from the New Hampshire State Prison, February 11, 1975, and Prairie Fire Organizing Committee Prison Project, "Why Do Prison Work?," January 1976, both in San Francisco PFOC FBI File, 100-77975.

117. David Stein, "Spectre"; Shank, "Looking Back." Tony Platt has written several articles about the Berkeley critical criminology school, many of them published in *Social Justice* (most recently "Legacies"), with others in such venues as Oppenheimer, Murray, and Levine, *Radical Sociologists*. In addition to the *Crime and Social Justice* journal, the short-lived radical Berkeley School of Criminology was responsible for two impressive anthologies of the era: *The Iron Fist and the Velvet Glove: An Analysis of the U.S. Police* (1975) and *Punishment and Penal Discipline: Essays on the Prison and The Prisoners' Movement* (1980). Both volumes were collectively authored, sharing an analytical as well as logistical similarity with what was perhaps the most enduring critical text of the era dedicated to the study of policing and state power in late capitalism, Stuart Hall et al., *Policing the Crisis* (1978). Other key figures in this intellectual renaissance of critical criminology include Erik Olin Wright and Gary Marx in the United States and Stanley Cohen and Jock Young in England.

118. *Harriet Tubman Prison Movement* pamphlet, ca. 1973, Anthony Platt, Private Collection. Such imagery was not limited to prison radicalism; in Boston, for example, the black feminist-socialist Combahee River Collective named itself after an 1863 escape of 750 slaves from South Carolina under Tubman's leadership. The collective became one of the most well-known radical black feminist organizations. With its 1977 political statement, the group provided an influential articulation of an intersectional approach to oppression of race, class, gender, and sexuality. And a Chicago-based successor to Students for a Democratic Society called itself the Sojourner Truth Organization.

119. Dorsey Nunn, interview.

120. Ashanti Alston, interview. For prisoner literacy, see Sweeney, *Reading*.

121. Hakim Ali, interview; Rodríguez, *Forced Passages*, 75–112.

122. Ashanti Alston, interview.

123. For books by imprisoned authors in the 1970s, see Bruchac and Witherup, *Words*; Atkins and Glick, *Prisons*; Pell, *Maximum Security*; Leinwand, *Prisons*; Norfolk Prison Brothers, *Who Took the Weight?*; Ramparts and Browning, *Prison Life*; Knight et al., *Black Voices from Prison*. Knight became a well-known poet and voice of prison dissent. For a critique of this overreliance on personal narratives, see Joan Scott, "Evidence of Experience."

124. See Thuma, "'Not a Wedge'"; Díaz-Cotto, *Gender*; Kunzel, *Criminal Intimacy*.

125. Kalima Aswad, interview. See also Ruchell Magee to Robert Treuhaft and Jessica Mitford, March 5, 1971, JMP, Box 48, Folder 9.

126. Shujaa Graham, interview; Dorsey Nunn, interview.

127. For more on Maoism's influence on the leftist movements of this period, see Kelley and Esch, "Black Like Mao"; Elbaum, *Revolution*; Fields, *Trotskyism*; Frazier, "Thunder."

128. Dorsey Nunn, interview.

129. Hakim Ali, interview.

130. Prison Action Project, *Freedom*, 25, in author's files, courtesy of Tony Platt.

CHAPTER FIVE

1. Donald B. Thackrey, "May Hear MaGee [*sic*] on 'Forced Slave' Rap," *Chicago Defender*, June 30, 1971, 4; "New Motions Filed in Miss Davis Case," *NYT*, June 29, 1971, 75.

2. This sketch of Magee comes from Major, *Justice*, 77–122; Sol Stern, "The Campaign to Free Angela Davis and Ruchell Magee," *NYT Magazine*, June 27, 1971, http://www .nytimes.com/books/98/03/08/home/davis-campaign.html; Black Mothers United for Action, "Who Is Ruchell Magee? Cinque" (flyer), ca. 1971, ADLDF, Box 2, Folder 7; Cummins, *Rise and Fall*, 180–82; Prison Solidarity Committee, *From Soledad to San Quentin* (San Francisco, ca. 1972), 5, Anthony Platt, Private Collection; Alexandra Close, "The Trial of Ruchell Magee," 5, JMP, Box 49, Folder 6. More generally on the phenomenon of prisoners who become self-taught legal mavens, see Abu-Jamal, *Jailhouse Lawyers*.

3. Nelson quoted in *People of the State of California v. Stephen Mitchell Bingham*, case no. 4094, June 19, 1986, 3655.

4. Soledad Brothers Defense Fund, *Soledad Brothers* pamphlet, ca. 1970, 7, NLC, Box 57, Folder: Black Power.

5. For studies of colonial prisons, see Paton, *No Bond*; O'Donovan, "Universities of Social and Political Change"; McLennan, "Crisis of Imprisonment."

6. Shujaa Graham, interview.

7. Hartman, *Scenes of Subjection*, 65.

8. Angela Y. Davis, "From the Prison of Slavery to the Slavery of Prison," in *Angela Y. Davis Reader*, 74–95.

9. For earlier notions of the organizing against prison slavery, see Blue, *Doing Time*; Curtin, *Black Prisoners*; Lichtenstein, *Twice the Work*; Perkinson, *Texas Tough*; Chase, "Civil Rights."

10. Angela Y. Davis, *Autobiography*, 250.

11. See Roediger, *Wages*, 65–87.

12. For the incapacitation of slavery, see Camp, *Closer to Freedom*; Walter Johnson, *Soul by Soul*; Walter Johnson, *River of Dark Dreams*; Smallwood, *Saltwater Slavery*. For the incapacitation of prison, see Ruth Wilson Gilmore, *Golden Gulag*.

13. My thinking here has been shaped by several sources, including Rodríguez, "'Social Truth'" and *Forced Passages*; Rediker, *Slave Ship*.

14. Interest in slavery as both history and allegory was resurrected during the 1970s in the United States. Marxist-influenced labor historians John Blassingame, Eugene Genovese, Herbert Gutman, Lawrence Levine, Nathan Huggins, Leon Litwack, and others produced a new scholarship on slavery that, in Hahn's summary, "showed growing and increasingly sophisticated interest in what slaves 'did' under slavery, and in how they shaped the institution and hastened its eventual demise." At the same time, radicals used slave resistance—especially Frederick Douglass's classic speech, "What to the Slave Is the Fourth of July?"—to challenge the racism that accompanied the American Bicentennial. Most dramatically, Alex Haley's *Roots* offered a massive, multimedia depiction of slavery. The book, which quickly became a best seller, traced seven generations of Haley's family, from eighteenth-century Gambia to twentieth-century America. The much-anticipated book appeared in 1976, although portions of it had first appeared in the *Reader's Digest* in 1974. On January 23–30, 1977, ABC broadcast a twelve-hour miniseries based on the book. The program "scored higher ratings than any previous entertainment program in history; its finale is still the third-most-watched (one hundred million viewers) program in television history; it averaged eighty million viewers during its initial network run; some 250 colleges planned courses around the series; the seven episodes that followed the opener earned the top seven spots in the ratings for their week; and 85 percent of all homes with televisions watched all or part of the miniseries" (Lester D. Friedman, "Introduction: Movies and the 1970s," in Lester D. Friedman, *American Cinema*, 19). *Roots* placed slavery at the center of American political culture, even if, as several scholars have noted, the most salient impact of the *Roots* phenomenon was not so much racial justice as a newfound interest in white ethnicity, multiracial American nationalism, and normative family values. See Hahn, *Political Worlds*, 108. See also Zaretsky, *No Direction Home*, 155–56; Jacobson, *Roots Too*.

15. Dennis Hevesi, "Huey Newton Symbolized the Rising Black Anger of a Generation," *NYT*, August 23, 1989, B7; John Kifner, "Eldridge Cleaver, Black Panther Who Became GOP Conservative, Is Dead at 62," *NYT*, May 2, 1998, B8.

16. Yee, *Melancholy History*, 130–31.

17. Andrews, *Black Power*; *The San Quentin Six* (pamphlet), ca. 1974, 6–7, RRSP, Box 7, Folder 12. As the title of Andrews's book makes clear, Spain's mixed-race background has been particularly tantalizing to journalistic observers. In *American Saturday*, his true-crime book about the day Jackson was killed, Clark Howard writes that Spain's background made him an "alien" consumed with anger.

18. George L. Jackson, *Soledad Brother*, 233.

19. George L. Jackson, *Blood in My Eye*, 10. For a critique, see Reid-Pharr, *Once You Go Black*, 127–28.

20. Soledad Brothers Defense Committee, *Soledad Brothers* pamphlet, ca. 1970, 6, Anthony Platt private collection.

21. Georgia Jackson quoted in "Unknown Racist Trial in Far Off Salinas," *People's World*, March 28, 1970, 1.

22. George L. Jackson, *Soledad Brother*, 210.

23. Fleeta Drumgo quoted in "Interviews with the Soledad Brothers," audio file PM 058, FA.

24. Students for a Democratic Society, "Tape on Ruchell Magee" (flyer), ca. 1972, NLC, Box 56, Folder: Black Panther Party.

25. See Akinshiju, "The Blkprisoner: Criminal or Political Prisoner[?]," *Black Pride*, March 23, 1972, 3, JMP, Box 56, Folder 3. On the broader usage of this argument in black nationalist politics, see Stuckey, *Slave Culture*.

26. See Newton, "Black Panthers." Newton describes the Panthers' goal as freeing all of humanity from slavery. Prisoner unionists also often described all prisoners as slaves of the state, though with little racial analysis.

27. Major notes, however, that black journalists and spectators abandoned this form of resistance when the verdict in Davis's trial was ready. Then, he writes, "we were up front" (*Justice*, 290).

28. For more on working-class militancy of the 1970s, see Brenner, Brenner, and Winslow, *Rebel Rank and File*; Cowie, *Stayin' Alive*; Thompson, *Whose Detroit?*; Georgakas and Surkin, *Detroit*; MacLean, *Freedom*; Staudenmaier, *Truth and Revolution*.

29. John Irwin and Willie Holder, "History of the Prisoners' Union," *The Outlaw* 2:1 (January–February 1973): 1. The "Folsom Prisoners Manifesto of Demands and Anti-Oppression Platform" is reprinted in Angela Y. Davis et al., *If They Come in the Morning*, 65–74.

30. See, for example, Emanuel Perlmutter, "Prisoners Union Formed Upstate," *NYT*, February 28, 1972, 1; Everett R. Hulles, "Convicts Seek to Form a National Union," *NYT*, September 26, 1971, 74.

31. Bissonette, *When the Prisoners*; Ed Mead, interview; Mark Cook, interview.

32. See "Goals of the Prisoners' Union," ca. 1972, United Prisoners Union Vertical File, FA.

33. In states without a union tradition rivaling California's, prisoner unionism did not produce the same cleavages or the same racial tensions among different groups of prison organizers. For the union model in other states, see Chase, "'Slaves of the State' Revolt"; Tibbs, *From Black Power*; Ronald Berkman, *Opening the Gates*; Irwin, *Prisons in Turmoil*; Burton-Rose, "War behind Walls."

34. Willie Holder, "To Persons Interested in Prisoner Organizations," March 7, 1973, JMP, Box 40, Folder 3.

35. Cummins, *Rise and Fall*, 255. Danish photographer Jacob Holdt provides a different, more sympathetic depiction of Jackson on his website, http://www .american-pictures.com/roots/chapter-67.htm.

36. "United Prisoners Union Bill of Rights," United Prisoners Union Vertical File, FA.

37. Such expressions were common features of Prisoners Union publications. See, for example, *The Anvil*, newspaper of the California Prisoners Union, and *The Outlaw*, newspaper of the Prisoners Union.

38. "Goals of the Prisoners' Union," United Prisoners Union Vertical File, FA.

39. Angela Y. Davis, "Racialized Punishment and Prison Abolition," in *Angela Y. Davis Reader*, 98–100.

40. See Painter, "Soul Murder."

41. Wilderson, "Prison Slave," 28.

42. Hahn, *Nation under Our Feet*, 3.

43. See Rodríguez, *Forced Passages*; Hartman, *Scenes of Subjection*.

44. Akinshiju, "The Blkprisoner: Criminal or Political Prisoner[?]," *Black Pride*, March 23, 1972, 3, JMP, Box 56, Folder 3.

45. *Voices from Inside: 7 Interviews with Attica Prisoners*, April 1972, 38, Voices from Inside vertical file, TL.

46. George L. Jackson, *Blood in My Eye*, 7.

47. In a similar if more theoretical way than Jackson, Foucault troubled the possibilities of prison "reform" or "alternatives." See, for example, Foucault, "Alternatives"; Foucault, *Power/Knowledge*, 1–55. For a seminal account of early abolitionist thought in Norway, see Mathiesen, *Politics*. For a critique of its ignorance of race, see Angela Y. Davis, "Racialized Punishment and Prison Abolition," in *Angela Y. Davis Reader*, 96–107.

48. Knopp and Reigier, *Instead of Prisons*.

49. Murton and Hyams, *Accomplices*; Bruce Jackson, "Our Prisons Are Criminal," *NYT*, September 22, 1968, 258; Ronald L. Goldfarb, "Why Don't We Tear Down Our Prisons," *Look*, July 27, 1971, 45–47; Robert Martinson, "The Paradox of Prison Reform," *New Republic*, four-part series on April 1 (23–25), 8 (13–14), 15 (17–18), and 29 (21–23), 1972; Sommer, *End of Imprisonment*; Dodge, *Nation without Prisons*. For more recent scholarly accounts, see Thompson, "Blinded"; Samuels, "Improvising on Reality."

50. Bissonette, *When the Prisoners*; American Friends Service Committee, *Struggle*.

51. Badillo and Haynes, *Bill of No Rights*, 171.

52. Goodell, *Political Prisoners*, 12–13. A high-profile Establishment critic of the Vietnam War, Goodell was appointed in 1968 to take over Robert Kennedy's senatorial seat but earned the enmity of Richard Nixon and lost to Nixon-backed conservative James Buckley in 1970. Goodell's book focused on "civil disobedients and victims of repression" (that is, people arrested for their political beliefs or associations). He sidestepped the radical critique of legality, looking instead only at the law's misapplication. A collection of almost uniformly negative or lackluster reviews of the book and correspondence relating to it can be found in the Charles Goodell Papers, Manuscripts, New York Public Library, New York. The element most consistently noted was Goodell's dedication of the book to "my friend Richard Nixon—May he do more than listen."

53. Quoted in Perkinson, *Texas Tough*, 3.

54. Wacquant, *Punishing the Poor*, 113.

55. Mitford, *Kind and Usual Punishment*, 274–325. Waskow's initial proposal celebrated the civil disobedience of white, primarily antiwar youth as the natural base for a campaign to abolish jails. In private correspondence, Mitford challenged Waskow by pointing out first that prisons incarcerated more people than jails (and that an ethically honest abolitionism would need to remove both institutions) and second that black radicalism lay at the root of prison radicalism more than did "white intellectuals [and] civil disobedients." The revised version of his proposal appeared in the *Saturday Review*, January 8,

1972, 20–21. Mitford still called it a false expression of abolitionism since it continued to rely on confining people. Likewise, Mitford called Clark's take on abolition "shallow and erroneous" (Jessica Mitford to Arthur Waskow, July 20, 21, 1971, JMP, Box 40, Folder 2).

56. On suburbs, see Sugrue, *Origins*; Lassiter, *Silent Majority*; Self, *American Babylon*; Freund, *Colored Property*. On conservatism, see Weaver, "Frontlash"; Teles, *Rise*; Thompson, "Why Mass Incarceration Matters"; Wilson, *Thinking about Crime*; Van Den Haag, *Punishing Criminals*. On urban transformation and policing, see Wacquant, *Prisons of Poverty*; Fortner, "Carceral State." Fortner rightly points to tensions within black communities over politics, crime, and safety—some of which lent support to law-and-order campaigns—but he overstates the role that black communities played in the creation and sustenance of mass incarceration.

57. George L. Jackson, *Blood in My Eye*, 118.

58. John Clutchette, "On Prison Reform," in Angela Y. Davis et al., *If They Come in the Morning*, 154.

59. Jordan, "Prison Reform," 786.

60. Rosenbaum, "Whither Thou Goest," 86–88, 92, 174–76.

61. While no one, himself included, disputes that Magee immediately joined the raid, his precise role in it has been described in dramatically different terms. Yee, quoting two witnesses from the courthouse, writes that Magee "spoke gently" and was the most restrained, convincing his associates not to take a couple and their young baby hostage (*Melancholy History*, 159). Other accounts, including witness testimony in court, attribute this restraint to James McClain (*Frame Up*, March 31, 1972, 4, MCLIR, Carton 37, Folder: Section XII, Docs. 30–36, Public Relations).

62. See Major, *Justice*; Sol Stern, "The Campaign to Free Angela Davis and Ruchell Magee," *NYT Magazine*, June 27, 1971, http://www.nytimes.com/books/98/03/08/home/davis-campaign.html. In a letter to Huey Newton from jail, Davis complained that the media were denying that she supported Magee (Angela Davis to Huey Newton, April 3, 1971, HPNFP, Series 2, Box 41, Folder 15, GL).

63. Major, *Justice*, 84–85.

64. *By Any Means Necessary* (newspaper), ca. 1970, ECP, Carton 4, Folder 21.

65. Untitled pamphlet for Ruchell Magee, ca. November 1972, Anthony Platt, Private Collection.

66. Ibid.

67. Students for a Democratic Society, "Tape on Ruchell Magee" (flyer), ca. 1972, NLC, Box 56, Folder: Black Panther Party.

68. The Supreme Court's ruling in the *Amistad* case upheld that slaves were property of their owners and that where slavery was legal, rebellion against it was not. It found the rebellion justified on a purely technical matter: the Africans aboard the *Amistad* ship were not legally enslaved because the Atlantic slave trade had been abolished, so they had the right to rebel against their captors. While significant, it was in fact a limited victory on legal rather than moral grounds. See Howard Jones, *Mutiny*, 188–94; Rediker, *Amistad Rebellion*, 186–237 passim.

69. Cinque (Ruchell Magee), *The Barbarian Conspirators* (pamphlet), ca. 1972, 7, Ruchell Magee Vertical File, TL; Ruchell Magee, "Letter to Angela Y. Davis," in Angela Y. Davis et al., *If They Come in the Morning*, 177.

70. Major, *Justice*, 77–122; Cinque (Ruchell Magee), *The Barbarian Conspirators* (pamphlet), ca. 1972, 9, Ruchell Magee Vertical File, TL. Davis's lead attorney, Howard Moore, was one of the attorneys who argued for the state-first strategy in 1967–68 in the South, and Moore represented Julian Bond in his effort to be seated in the Georgia legislature after winning election in 1965.

71. Nicholas von Hoffman, "Ruchell Magee: Unforgotten Man," *Washington Post*, May 14, 1971, B1. See also Nicholas von Hoffman, "'A Slave May Do Anything,'" *Washington Post*, May 17, 1971, B1; Nicholas Von Hoffman, "Magee and the Law Factory," *SFC*, May 23, 1971, 2.

72. The Metropolitan Applied Research Center files at the Schomburg Center for Research in Black Culture at the New York Public Library contain hundreds of articles about Clark's involvement in a variety of racial issues, primarily relating to education and housing inequity. In addition to his publications on schools and ghettoes, Clark edited a book of interviews (that he conducted) with Martin Luther King Jr., Malcolm X, and James Baldwin. See Clark, *King, Malcolm, Baldwin*. More generally, see Matlin, *On the Corner*.

73. "Magee Escape Bid Analyzed in Trial," *NYT*, February 28, 1973, 12; "Dr. Kenneth B. Clark Testifies for Ruchell Magee" (press release), March 1, 1973, Ruchell Magee National Defense Committee Vertical File, TL.

74. Eldridge Cleaver, "The Land Question and Black Liberation," in *Eldridge Cleaver*, 67.

75. For more on Garvey, see Grant, *Negro*, especially 349–412; Judith Stein, *World*.

76. See "Notes to and from the Press," n.d., and Ruchell Magee, "Wake Up Oppressed People (Open Address to the President)" by the San Francisco Venceremos Study Group (San Francisco, 1972), both in NLC, Box 58, Folder: Ruchell Magee.

77. *San Francisco Examiner*, June 15, 1972, 7.

78. Ruchell Magee, "San Quentin Communique," *MS* 2:7 (September 1972): 13.

79. Thomas Siporin, "Nobody May Represent This Man," *People's Justice* 5:1 (January 1973): 13.

80. Major, *Justice*, 291.

81. Alexandra Close, "The Trial of Ruchell Magee," 3, JMP, Box 49, Folder 6.

82. See Black Mothers United for Action, press statement, July 30, 1071 [sic], NLC, Box 58, Folder: Ruchell Magee.

83. Angela Y. Davis, "Notes for Arguments in Court on the Issue of Self-Representation," in Angela Y. Davis et al., *If They Come in the Morning*, 252.

84. "Angela Davis Talks about Her Future and Her Freedom," *Jet*, July 27, 1972, 57; Margaret Burnham, "Ruchell and Angela Want to Represent Themselves," in Angela Y. Davis et al., *If They Come in the Morning*, 222.

85. Sol Stern, "The Campaign to Free Angela Davis and Ruchell Magee," *NYT*, June 27, 1971, http://www.nytimes.com/books/98/03/08/home/davis-campaign.html.

86. Such vacillations between the common and the exceptional have characterized the popular visibility of black women since at least the nineteenth century. The response to the Davis trial played out the script developed through Sojourner Truth, an illiterate escaped slave turned itinerant preacher and suffragist in the second half of the nineteenth century. Truth, like Davis a century later, was the subject of various

and cross-cutting representations that sought to make her a symbol of resistant black womanhood, a person whose accomplishments surpassed and were surprising in light of her origins. The various descriptions of both women owed as much to the chronicler as to the subject herself. See Painter, *Sojourner Truth*. I thank Nancy Hewitt for helping me make this connection between Davis and Truth.

87. See Winston, *Meaning*; Aptheker, *Intimate Politics*, 245.

88. Aptheker, *Morning Breaks*; Bettina Aptheker, interview; McDuffie, *Sojourning*, 193–94.

89. Major, *Justice*, 138; *Frame Up*, February 4, 1972, 1, ADLDF, Box 5, Folder 3.

90. James Baldwin, "An Open Letter to My Sister, Angela Y. Davis," in Angela Y. Davis et al., *If They Come in the Morning*, 19.

91. Aptheker, *Intimate Politics*, 246. Aptheker made her remarks in a speech that was reprinted in the leftist newsweekly *National Guardian* in October 1970.

92. Associated Press, "Angela Davis Extradited to CA," *Sarasota Journal*, December 22, 1970, 1.

93. Ruchell Magee to Robert Treuhaft and Jessica Mitford, March 5, 1971, JMP, Box 48, Folder 9.

94. Joe Walker, "Angela Davis: What's on Her Mind?," *Muhammad Speaks*, January 1, 1971, reprinted as a pamphlet by the Committee to Free Angela Davis, JMP, Box 49, Folder 6.

95. Quoted in *Her Fight Is Our Fight* (Palo Alto Angela Davis Defense Committee newsletter) 1 (March 1972): 2. See also Diane and Gary Laison, "Angela Davis 'Prosecuted Like Fugitive Slave,'" *Philadelphia Tribune*, August 14, 1971, 5.

96. Cynthia A. Young, *Soul Power*, 187.

97. After making similarly prejudicial comments about Charles Manson and the My Lai massacre in Vietnam, Nixon conceded that he had overstepped his bounds. See "Nixon Says He Erred on Defendants," *LAT*, December 11, 1970, A17; "President Admits Error in Commenting on Three Cases," *Modesto (Calif.) Bee*, December 11, 1970, 35; John Abt, "On the Defense of Angela Davis," speech at the Unitarian Church in Los Angeles, November 22, 1970, SPC, Reel 21.

98. *Free Angela* (newsletter) 23 (1971): 1–2, SPC, Reel 21.

99. The Presbyterian Church established its Emergency Fund for Legal Aid in 1968 to provide financial assistance to political activists; it had previously given money to the NAACP and to the Panther 21 defense. Some members of the church were rankled by such a hefty donation to a figure as controversial as Davis. The church undertook an independent investigation into why the donation was made, resulting in a church-wide conversation about race, justice, imprisonment, and the church's responsibility. "Why Angela Davis," *Monday Morning*, July 1971, 7, ADLDF, Box 3, Folder 9. The Reverend Charles R. Ehrhardt of Phoenix said that Davis was literally a beloved angel: etymologically, he claimed, "Davis" means "beloved," and "Angela" means "angel" (*The Presbyter* 24:7 [July 1971]: 1, ADLDF, Box 3, Folder 9). Several documents relating to the church discussion, including its independent investigation, can be found in ADLDF, Box 3, Folder 9.

100. Quoted in Milwaukee Committee to Free Angela Davis, *Free Angela Davis*, ca. 1970, in Angela Y. Davis Vertical File, TL.

101. Dean Paul E. Miller, *Washington Sunday Star*, February 14, 1971; Milwaukee Committee to Free Angela Davis, *Free Angela Davis*, ca. 1970, in Angela Y. Davis Vertical File, TL; National United Committee to Free Angela Davis, press release, March 10, 1972, ADLDF, Box 5, Folder 3; Sol Stern, "The Campaign to Free Angela Davis and Ruchell Magee," *NYT*, June 27, 1971, http://www.nytimes.com/books/98/03/08/home/davis-campaign.html; Major, *Justice*, 105; Aptheker, *Intimate Politics*, 250.

102. For a sampling, see Linda Charlton, "FBI Seizes Angela Davis in Motel Here," *NYT*, October 14, 1970, 1; "Personality: The Fugitive," *Time*, August 31, 1970, http://content.time.com/time/magazine/article/0,9171,876780,00.html; "Can California Convict Angela Davis?: Long, Costly Battle Ahead," *Baltimore Afro-American*, October 24, 1970, 1–2; *Angela Davis—Like It Is* (Folkways, 1971), in Angela Davis Vertical File, FA.

103. Aptheker, *Intimate Politics*, 271.

104. Major, *Justice*, 231–32.

105. Angela Y. Davis, "Afro Images," in *Angela Y. Davis Reader*, 276.

106. Ibid., 275.

107. The letters can be found in MCLIR, Carton 39, Folder: Angela Davis Papers, Letters to George Jackson. I have been unable to locate Jackson's note to Davis that, along with a verbal message delivered to her by a mutual friend, caused her such frustration in the final series of letters.

108. The sexual ideology of enslavement allowed white slave owners to sexually assault black women without fear that such violations would be labeled or prosecuted as rape. Rape, as a criminal act of unwanted sexual contact that violated a person's sense of self, could not apply to those deemed less than human. Bondage defined black sexuality as lascivious, illegitimate yet available. Consent did not apply. For more, see Hartman, *Scenes of Subjection*, 80–110.

109. See the summaries presented in Aptheker, *Morning Breaks*; Major, *Justice*; Timothy, *Jury Woman*. Timothy was the forewoman of the jury in the Davis trial and became a friend of Davis and to Bettina Aptheker.

110. Angela Y. Davis, "Reflections on the Black Woman's Role in the Community of Slaves," in *Angela Y. Davis Reader*, 126.

111. Ibid., 116.

112. Weinbaum, "Gendering," 450.

113. Angela Y. Davis, "Reflections on the Black Woman's Role," 111–12.

114. Angela Y. Davis, introduction in Douglass, *Narrative*, 28.

115. Leo Branton, closing statement, June 1, 1972, 7024 court transcript XLIX, Angela Davis Papers, Box 3, Envelope: June 1, 1972, 6972–7142, GL.

116. Ibid., 7015, 7012–13, 7053.

117. Ibid., 7081.

118. Carolyn Anspacher, "Angela Trial Review," *SFC*, June 8, 1972, 3; Rick Carroll, "No Juror Cast a Ballot of Guilt," *SFC*, June 5, 1972, 2; Associated Press, "How Jury Found Angela Innocent," *Stockton Record*, June 5, 1972, 1, in Angela Davis Papers, Box 4, Folder 22, GL.

119. UPI, "Reagan Says Davis Trial Vindicates U.S. Justice," *LAT*, June 6, 1972, A23.

120. "Angela Davis' Fair Trial," *LAT*, June 6, 1972, E10. The Davis jury was often described as all-white, but one of the jurors was Chicano and identified as such. Still,

because the editorial and most other media, including information from Davis's defense team and supporters, described the jury as all-white, I offer this quotation in its original context.

121. UPI, "Reagan Says Davis Trial Vindicates U.S. Justice," *LAT*, June 6, 1972, A23.

122. Louis Claiborne, "Angela Davis, Farewell," *Intellectual Digest*, October 1972, 16 (originally printed in *Spectator*, June 17, 1972).

123. See, for example, Kevin Leary, "The Joy Outside the Court," *SFC*, June 5, 1972, 3; International Art Manifesto for the Legal Defense of Political Prisoners to Angela Davis, August 20, 1972, JMP, Box 49, Folder 7.

124. "Jury Acquits Angela Davis on All 3 Counts," *Globe*, undated clipping, Angela Davis Papers, Box 4, Folder 11, GL.

125. For more on the Little case, see Angela Y. Davis, "JoAnne Little," in *Angela Davis Reader*, 149–60; Fergus, *Liberalism*, 132–65; Law, "Sick of the Abuse"; McGuire, *At the Dark End*, 202–28; Thuma, "'Not a Wedge.'"

126. No history of the NAARPR has yet been published. Its work can be gleaned from the group's papers, some of which are housed at the SC.

127. *Real Dragons* (KPFA), February 10, 1973, audio file, RD 030, FA.

128. Quoted in "Magee," *MS* 3:6 (June 1973): 23.

129. UPI, "Mistrial Declared for Ruchell Magee; Jury Split 11 to 1," *LAT*, April 3, 1973, 3; *MS* 3:6 (June 1973): 23; Aptheker, *Intimate Politics*, 288–91.

130. Associated Press, "Ruchell Magee Pleads Guilty to Kidnapping," *LAT*, May 11, 1974, 15; UPI, "Magee Asks Judge to Withdraw Plea," *NYT*, May 14, 1974, 20.

131. Evelle J. Younger to Lynn S. Carman, August 22, 1973, 1, Mark Merin, Private Collection, *Spain v. Procunier* Files.

132. Wald, "San Quentin Six Case," 171; Major, *Justice*, 124–25. My interviews with members of the San Quentin 6 case, their attorneys, and activist Kiilu Nyasha, as well as conversations with Claude Marks and Felix Shafer, were also helpful in describing the political background of the San Quentin 6, as were the programs housed in the Prison Movement audio files, FA.

133. Quoted in National Lawyers Guild, *San Quentin to Attica: The Sound before the Fury*, 12, RRSP, Box 8, Folder 3. More generally, see James R. Bendat, "The San Quentin Six Trial: Do Chains Have a Place?," *LAT*, May 22, 1975, E7; *The San Quentin Six* pamphlet; Wald, "San Quentin Six Case"; "Justice for the San Quentin Six" (flyer) and San Quentin Six Defense Committee, press release, May 2, 1974, both in SPC, Reel 20.

134. San Quentin Six Defense Committee, "San Quentin Six Case: Whose Peers?," ca. 1971, Pamphlet Collection, Southern California Library, Los Angeles.

135. National Research Council, *Growth of Incarceration*, 33; Bosworth, *Explaining U.S. Imprisonment*; Gilmore, *Golden Gulag*; Harcourt, *Illusion*; Wacquant, *Punishing the Poor*.

136. Davidson, *Chicano Prisoners*; Joan W. Moore and Garcia, *Homeboys*; Díaz-Cotto, *Gender*.

137. For examples of the San Quentin 6 in Latino media, see "Noticias de la Pinta," *La Raza* 1:8 (1975): 32–41. The case was regularly covered in a series of leftist publications, including *Sedition*, a San Jose radical paper; *The Conspiracy*, a publication of the National Lawyers Guild; *The Guardian*, a national leftist weekly; and the Bay Area's black newspaper, the *Sun Reporter*.

138. San Quentin Six Defense Committee, fundraising appeal letter, April 1973, JMP, Box 49, Folder 7.

139. Wald, "San Quentin Six Case"; Luis Bato Talamantez, interview; Larry Weiss, interview; Willie Sundiata Tate, interview. For Acosta's political background and involvement, see Haney-López, *Racism on Trial*. Acosta was not well liked on the defense team. Talamantez and Weiss described him as disorganized and disrespectful: they recall that he treated women involved with the case inappropriately (in at least one instance he groped a woman's breast) and tried to bill the court for thousands of dollars in legal fees for work he did not do. According to them, after being fired, Acosta vandalized and burglarized Weiss's legal office.

140. Luis Bato Talamantez, interview; Larry Weiss, interview; Mark Merin, interview; Fred Hiestand, interview.

141. "Johnny Spain Appeals 1976 San Quentin Six Conviction," *Black Panther*, May 20, 1978, 3; James R. Bendat, "The San Quentin Six Trial: Do Chains Have a Place?," *LAT*, May 22, 1975, 7; Wald, "San Quentin Six Case," 169; Tate quoted in Alice Yarish, "What It's Like to Be Free and One of the San Quentin Six," *San Francisco Examiner and Chronicle*, July 13, 1975.

142. Cummins, *Rise and Fall*, 259–60; Bill Monning, "San Quentin Six: 'Justice' Shackled," *The Conspiracy*, May 1975, 3, 13, NLGC, Oversized Box 7.

143. San Francisco Special Agent in Charge to FBI Director, July 1, 1976, HPNFP, Series 2, Box 42, Folder 14; Wald, "San Quentin Six Case"; *The San Quentin Six* pamphlet, ca. 1974, RRSP, Box 7, Folder 12. See also the radio coverage of the case on the program *Nothing Is More Precious Than*, which originally aired on the Pacifica network and is housed at the FA.

144. Friends of the San Quentin Adjustment Center, "Attend the Hearing of the San Quentin Six" (flyer), SPC, Reel 20. See also *The San Quentin Six* pamphlet, ca. 1974, RRSP, Box 7, Folder 12.

145. For examples of news coverage of the case, see James R. Bendat, "The San Quentin Six Trial: Do Chains Have a Place?," *LAT*, May 22, 1975, 7; Wald, "San Quentin Six Case."

146. Prison Law Collective, "Adjustment Center Challenge by SQ6," *The Conspiracy*, April 1974, 13.

147. Luis Bato Talamantez, interview; Larry Weiss, interview; *Spain v. Procunier* opening brief, no. 76-1095, and appellants brief, both in author's files, courtesy of Mark Merin.

148. Joel Kirschenbaum and Jae Scharlin, "Indictment Quashed!: The San Quentin Six," *The Conspiracy*, February 1974, 5. Zimbardo planned a two-week experiment in which college students were randomly assigned to be either prisoners or guards. However, he called off the experiment after six days because the guards became "sadistic" and the prisoners "showed signs of extreme stress." Zimbardo maintains a website about the experiment at http://www.prisonexp.org/.

149. Yee, *Melancholy History*, 255–56; Eve Pell, "San Quentin Six: Pinell Describes August 21st," *The Conspiracy*, March 1976, 3.

150. Citizens Research and Investigation Committee and Tackwood, *Glass House Tapes*. Other books published at this time dealing with prisons and state violence

include Atkins and Glick, *Prisons*; Ramparts and Browning, *Prison Life*; Trupin, *In Prison*; Halperin et al., *Lawless State*; Sheehan et al., *Pentagon Papers*; Irwin, *Felon*; Wright, *Politics of Punishment*; *Iron Fist and the Velvet Glove*.

151. For more on Tackwood, see Durden-Smith, *Who Killed George Jackson?*, 126–62; Citizens Research and Investigation Committee and Tackwood, *Glass House Tapes*.

152. Wald, "San Quentin Six Case," 172. In postverdict interviews with members of the San Quentin 6 legal team, several jurors said that they were not sure how much of Tackwood's testimony was believable. Transcripts of undated interviews in author's files, courtesy of Larry Weiss. See also Tackwood's testimony in *People v. S. Bingham et al.*, HPNFP, Series 2, Box 33. My knowledge of the differences within the defense about Tackwood comes from my interviews with David Johnson, Luis Bato Talamantez, and Larry Weiss.

153. *The San Quentin Six* pamphlet, ca. 1974, RRSP, Box 7, Folder 12; Alfonso Zirpoli quoted in Aptheker, *Morning Breaks*, 296–97.

154. "Post-Trial Memorandum" and Richard H. Fine, "Medical Report: Hugo Pinnell," April 17, 1974, both in Mark Merin, Private Collection; Thomas O. Hilliard (National Association of Black Psychologists), "Psychological Evaluation of Adjustment Center Environment at San Quentin Prison," July 8, 1974, in author's files, courtesy of Luis Bato Talamantez. I am grateful to Talamantez, Merin, and Hiestand for sharing their recollections and their files with me.

155. See Andrews, *Black Power*, 175–232; Cummins, *Rise and Fall*, 262. See also *The San Quentin Six*, ca. 1974, 16, RRSP, Box 7, Folder 12.

156. Press release, October 4, [1972?], National Alliance against Racist and Political Repression Papers, Box 3, SC; "Who Are the San Quentin Six?," ca. 1975, KFAP, Folder: San Quentin 1971–72. After the acquittal, Talamantez spent time with family outside of California before returning to the state to continue his writing and antiprison activism. As chapter 6 describes in more detail, Drumgo had a difficult time adjusting to postprison life and was shot to death in 1979.

157. Wald, "San Quentin Six Case." For more on Spain, see Andrews, *Black Power*.

158. Quoted in Gottschalk, *Prison*, 175.

159. Thompson, "Black Activism," 24. More generally on the use of lawsuits as part of a prisoner rights movement, see Chase, "Civil Rights." See also Jacobs, "Prisoners' Rights Movement."

CHAPTER SIX

1. Kalima Aswad, interview; Aswad, "Questions"; Aswad, "Coincidences." Unless otherwise noted, the rest of this section comes from my interview with him as well as these unpublished articles, in author's private collection.

2. Hakim Ali, interview.

3. Kalima Aswad, interview; Jalil Muntaqim to author, July 14, 2011; Hakim Ali, interview. For more on black Islam in the 1970s and beyond, see Simmons, "From Muslims"; Simmons, "African American Islam"; Sherman A. Jackson, "Preliminary Reflections"; McCloud, *African American Islam*; Turner, *Islam*; Curtis, "African-American Islamization"; Curtis, *Islam*, 107–28. My conversations with Zoharah

Simmons, Jalil Muntaqim, John Jackson, Laura McTighe, and Josh Dubler, among others, have also helped me think about black radicals turning to Islam in the 1970s.

4. Keve, *McNeil Century*, 250–55; Mitford, *Kind and Usual Punishment*.

5. This argument is made most strongly in Cummins's *Rise and Fall*, though the influence of this declensionist narrative can be found elsewhere. For other attempts to historicize prisoner print culture, see Chard, "SCAR'd Times"; Thuma, "Not a Wedge"; Winn, "We Are All Prisoners."

6. My argument here builds on Murch, *Living for the City*, in which she asserts that political education was central to the rise and ongoing impact of the Black Panther Party. This robust defense of knowledge was a centerpiece of social movements in this era and perhaps of social movements generally. See also Freire, *Pedagogy*; Eyerman and Jamison, *Social Movements*. Tracing prisoners' knowledge acquisition and production as a legacy that continued in (and beyond) the late 1970s shows the inadequacy and inaccuracy of Cummins's claim (in *Rise and Fall*) that the prison movement destroyed itself in a violent rage after George Jackson's death.

7. See Anderson, *Imagined Communities*; Chatterjee, *Nation and Its Fragments*.

8. Thuma, "Within and against the 'Prison/Psychiatric State.'"

9. Thuma, "'Not a Wedge'"; Law, "Sick of the Abuse"; McGuire, *At the Dark End*, 246–78; Fergus, *Liberalism*, 132–65.

10. Ed Mead, interview; Kunzel, *Criminal Intimacy*, 191–224; Burton-Rose, *Guerrilla USA*; Burton-Rose, *Creating a Movement*.

11. On the original Communist Party position, see Glenda Elizabeth Gilmore, *Defying Dixie*; Kelley, *Hammer and Hoe*; Solomon, *Cry*; Biondi, *To Stand and Fight*. For more on the communist parties of the 1970s, see Elbaum, *Revolution*.

12. See Obadele, *War in America*.

13. For more on Moore, see McDuffie, *Sojourning*; McDuffie, "'I Wanted a Communist Philosophy'"; Ahmad, *We Will Return*, 7–13; Sugrue, *Sweet Land*, 272–73, 434–35; Naison, *Communists*, 136, 215; Audley "Queen Mother" Moore, interview by Prego.

14. Tyson, *Radio Free Dixie*; Cynthia A. Young, *Soul Power*, 18–52; Ahmad, *We Will Return*; Kelley and Esch, "Black Like Mao."

15. For the Black Arts movement, see Widener, *Black Arts West*; Lisa Gail Collins and Crawford, *New Thoughts*; Smethurst, *Black Arts Movement*; Woodard, *Nation within a Nation*.

16. The group initially used the standard English spelling. See Acoli, "Updated History," 138. Because the RNA still exists and because people still define themselves as New Afrikans, I have opted to use this spelling throughout, except in quotations. The RNA was not the first to spell Afrika with a "k." Other black organizations in the United States in the 1960s and 1970s did so, for the same reasons. These include the Los Angeles free jazz performance troupe the Pan-Afrikan Arkestra and Amiri Baraka's Congress of Afrikan People. Conversations with Daniel Widener, Robin Kelley, and Rebecca Hill were helpful in my thinking on this point.

17. New Afrikan Prisoners Organization, "We Still Charge Genocide," August 31, 1977, in New Afrikan Prisoners Organization Vertical File, FA.

18. Atiba, "Afrikan P.O.W.'s," 12.

19. For the Congress of Afrikan People, see Woodard, *Nation within a Nation*; Frazier, "Congress." For SNCC members' evolution to Pan-Africanism, see Carmichael, *Stokely Speaks*; Carmichael with Thelwell, *Ready for Revolution*; Berger and Meyer, "Pan-Africanization"; Wilkins, "'Line of Steel.'" For the African Liberation Support Committee, see Cedric Johnson, *Revolutionaries*, 131–72.

20. For scholarly accounts of the RNA, see Onaci, "Self-Determination"; Berger, "'Malcolm X Doctrine'"; Berger with Dunbar-Ortiz, "'Struggle Is for Land!'"; Cunnigen, "Republic of New Africa." For an interesting insider history of the group and its relation to other efforts at New Afrikan politics, see Chokwe Lumumba, *The Roots of the New Afrikan Independence Movement*, in author's files, courtesy of Matt Meyer.

21. See ji Jaga, "Every Nation," 75. For a more contemporary corollary, see Sanyika Shakur, *Monster*.

22. See, for example, "Black On Vanguard," *MS* 3:11 (November 1973): 15. The group claimed chapters in Ohio, North Carolina, South Carolina, and Wisconsin. As with adopting Swahili or Arabic names, such action-oriented articulations of black collectivity were common to late 1960s expressions of radicalism. In particular, as Scot Brown shows, southern California's US organization chose its name "as a dual reference to the organization and the community its members pledged to serve: *us Blacks as opposed to 'them' Whites*" (*Fighting for Us*, 38).

23. Black On Vanguards, Ohio and North Carolina, "I Have Seen America," *MS* 3:2 (February 1973): 8; letter in support of Assata and Sundiata, *MS* 3:10 (October 1973): 15.

24. For the raid, see Umoja, *We Will Shoot Back*, 201–7, The assault on the RNA headquarters used hardware first bought to police the civil rights movement; see Jack O'Dell's "The July Rebellions and the 'Military State,'" originally published in 1967 in *Freedomways* and reprinted in O'Dell, *Climbin' Jacob's Ladder*, 145–59.

25. *Black Pride*, JMP, Box 56, Folder 3. See also Gómez, "Resisting Living Death." Obadele also describes his prison organizing in *Free the Land!*, 246–82.

26. Obadele, *Foundations*, 73–106.

27. See, for example, the New Afrikan Creed, in Obadele, *Foundations*, 153; Obadele, *War in America*, iii.

28. New Afrikan Prisoners Organization, "We Still Charge Genocide," August 31, 1977, New Afrikan Prisoners Organization Vertical File, FA.

29. Roxanne Brown, "Stateville Inmate Describes His Lengthy 'Ordeal by Trial,'" *Chicago Defender*, December 23, 1978; "Overthrow the Frame-Up: Sayles/Dee Fact Sheet," ca. 1982, in author's files, courtesy of Nancy Kurshan and Steve Whiteman.

30. Bradley Abdul Greene to author, January 8, 2010; Lorenzo Ervin, "Build a Mass Prison Movement," *MS* 5:12 (October 1977): 10–11. See also African National Prison Organization Solidarity Committee Vertical File, TL. Greene remembers that NAPO members also became part of the BLA and had relationships with several gangs, including the Vice Lords and the Black Gangster Disciples.

31. Atiba, "SPO Discussion Paper No. 1," December 1976, 15, in author's files, courtesy of Nancy Kurshan and Steve Whitman. See also "An Introduction to the Words of James Yaki Sayles," in Sayles, *Meditations*, 3–40.

32. See, for example, *San Quentin News*, JMP, Box 44, Folder 2; *The Echo* (Huntsville, Texas), RRSP, Box 26, Folder 15; James C. Scott, *Domination*, especially 136–82. For

more on *Aztlán*, see Gómez, "'Nuestras Vidas Corren Casi Paralelas.'" Copies of the paper are available in RRSP, Series 3, Box 7.

33. Dorsey Nunn, interview.

34. See McMillian, *Smoking Typewriters*.

35. Harcourt, *Illusion*; Harvey, *Brief History*.

36. See Self, *American Babylon*; McGirr, *Suburban Warriors*. On Nixon and Reagan, see Perlstein, *Nixonland*; Schulman and Zelizer, *Rightward Bound*; McCartin, *Collision Course*.

37. Ruth Wilson Gilmore, *Golden Gulag*; Parenti, *Lockdown America*; Bryan, *This Soldier*.

38. Baum, *Smoke and Mirrors*; Alexander, *New Jim Crow*; Western, *Punishment*; Frydl, *War on Drugs*; Provine, *Unequal under Law*; Tonry, *Punishing Race*. On Rockefeller, see Kramer and Roberts, *"I Never Wanted"*; Seigel, "Cold War Connections."

39. Gómez, "Resisting Living Death," 59.

40. Nixon told his chief of staff, H. R. Haldeman, "You have to face the fact that the *whole* problem is really the blacks. The key is to devise a system that recognizes this while not appearing to. Problem with overall welfare plan is that it forces poor whites into the same position as blacks. Feels we have to get rid of the veil of hypocrisy and guilt and face reality" (*Haldeman Diaries*, 53). This passage is often quoted as if to suggest Nixon was speaking about the war on drugs; thanks to David Stein for the full quotation in its proper context. Recently uncovered recordings of Nixon and Rockefeller following the retaking of Attica prison confirm the depths of this line of thinking about the war on crime for both men (Sam Roberts, "Rockefeller on the Attica Raid, from Boastful to Subdued," *NYT*, September 12, 2011, A24). For the intervention of conservative public intellectuals in the mid-1970s, see Wilson, *Thinking about Crime*; Van Den Haag, *Punishing Criminals*. Recent urban histories have documented the crucial role of suburban politics in fueling the New Right; see, for example, Sugrue, *Origins*; Freund, *Colored Property*; McGirr, *Suburban Warriors*; Kruse, *White Flight*; Thompson, *Whose Detroit?*; Self, *American Babylon*. The rapid growth of the suburbs not only depleted the urban tax base but made it more difficult for black urban neighborhoods to interact with many of the institutions shaping their lives. See Katz, *Why Don't American Cities Burn?*

41. Osman, *Invention of Brownstone Brooklyn*; Wacquant, *Punishing the Poor*; Mike Davis, *City of Quartz*; Fortner, "Carceral State."

42. For more on the Statewide Correctional Alliance for Reform, see Chard, "SCAR'd Times." For more on *NEPA News*, see Bissonette, *When the Prisoners*. I am grateful to Victor Wallis and to Nancy Kurshan and Steve Whitman for sharing their copies of *The Real Deal* and *CPSB Newsletter*, respectively, with me. See also Mark Cook, interview; Winn, "'We Are All Prisoners.'" In his memoir, former Black Panther Marshall Eddie Conway describes starting a newspaper in a Maryland prison (*Marshall Law*, 98–101).

43. "Black Movies and Twentieth Century Slaves," *MS* 3:10 (October 1973): 17.

44. See issues of *Black Pride* in JMP, Box 56, Folder 3, and RRSP, Series 3, Box 6, Folder 30.

45. See *Black Pride*, March 30, 1972, 5–6.

46. "News Briefs," *Black Pride*, March 23, 1972, 2; A Brother of the 3rd World, "Be Aware of the Publicity Tricks," *Black Pride*, June 1972, 7. The column "Revolution in

Sound" by A. B. Spellman appeared in several issues and concerned jazz deemed of political and racial relevance. Articles about Davis and the RNA appeared in multiple 1972 issues of the journal.

47. See, for example, Akinshiju, "Akinshiju Raps on Malik's 'Message to the Grassroots,'" *Black Pride*, May 18, 1972, 4–5, 15, and Leon X. Bates, "George, in the Tradition of Malcolm," *Black Pride*, May 18, 1972, 7, 14, both in RRSP, Series 3, Box 6, Folder 30.

48. Eldridge Cleaver, *Soul on Ice*, especially 3–17, 205–10.

49. "One Struggle," *Black Pride*, April 6, 1972, 6, and Richard Nicholson, "Angela," *Black Pride*, April 6, 1972, 7, both in JMP, Box 56, Folder 3.

50. Hassan Siku Sabiku, "Reflections," *Black Pride*, March 23, 1972, 11, and "Review," *Black Pride*, March 23, 1972, 9, 16, both in JMP, Box 56, Folder 3.

51. Russell Neufeld, interview.

52. Ibid.; Phyllis Prentice, interview.

53. Russell Neufeld, interview.

54. See Berger, "'We Are the Revolutionaries,'" 330–439.

55. Russell Neufeld, interview.

56. *MS* 2:7 (September 1972): 1.

57. "Only the Blues Is Authorized," *MS* 3:8 (August 1973): 15.

58. "Tribute to George Jackson," *MS* 3:9 (September 1973): 9.

59. Jacobs, "Race Relations," 11. For examples of the increasingly rhetorical components of the newspaper (a product of the prison movement at the time), see National Committee for the Defense of Political Prisoners, "A Luta Continua!!," *MS* 5:5 (August–September 1975): 1–3; Benjamin Murdock, "The Midnight Special at the Crossroads: A Progressive Perpsect [*sic*]," *MS* 5:7 (December 1975–January 1976): 25; Sandino, "Strategy and Tactics: On Armed Struggle," *MS* 5:8 (June–July 1976): 8.

60. See "Midnight Benefit," *MS* 5:4 (July–August 1975): 1. See also Lorenzo Komboa Ervin, "Building a Mass Prison Movement," *MS* 7:12 (October 1977): 10–11.

61. Major, *Justice*, 307–8. For the Marion lawsuit, see Gómez, "Resisting Living Death"; Mitford, *Kind and Usual Punishment*, 134, 136, 198–99; files in RRSP and JMP. Scott-Heron's plea to the United Nations appears in the song "Who'll Pay Reparations on My Soul?," which is featured on the 1970 album, *Small Talk at 125th and Lenox*.

62. William L. Patterson, *We Charge Genocide*, vii.

63. For more on the Pattersons and the International Labor Defense, see McDuffie, *Sojourning*; Horne, *Communist Front?*; Horne, *Black Revolutionary*; William L. Patterson, *Man Who Cried*.

64. Acoli, *Sunviews*, 9, 11.

65. Kunzel, *Criminal Intimacy*, 166; Losier, "Prison House." Kunzel notes that the prison was almost half black in 1953, already well disproportionate to the population.

66. Quoted in "RNA Asks United Nations Help for 'Prisoners of War,'" *Philadelphia Tribune*, October 17, 1978, 4. The article notes that Amnesty International considered Obadele to be in prison on charges that were "purely political."

67. The petition is annotated and described in Hinds, *Illusions of Justice*; Jalil Muntaqim to author, July 10, 2013.

68. Muntaqim, "Political Prisoner's Journey," http://www.freejalil.com/life.html.

69. This biography of Muntaqim and the petition is culled from Muntaqim, "Political Prisoner's Journey"; Jalil Muntaqim to author, July 14, 2011; Fujino, *Heartbeat*, 203–4. See also Cummins, *Rise and Fall*, 255; Jacob Holdt, http://www.american-pictures.com/roots/chapter-67.htm.

70. Jalil Muntaqim to author, July 10, 2013. A brief statement relating to the petition is filed as document E/CN.4/Sub. 2/NGO/75 and can be viewed online at http://www.un.org/en/ga/search/view_doc.asp?symbol=E/CN.4/sub.%202/NGO/75. See also Muntaqim, *We Are Our Own Liberators*, 49, 271–73.

71. Acoli, *Sunviews*, 23–28. My knowledge here also comes from interviews with several participants, some of whom asked to remain anonymous on this point. For more on African People's Socialist Party, see Tani and Sera, *False Nationalism*, 163–229. For more on PFOC, see Berger, *Outlaws of America*, 201–2, 225–44; Block, *Arm the Spirit*.

72. Muntaqim, "Political Prisoner's Journey," http://www.freejalil.com/life.html.

73. Kaufman and Kaufman, *Presidency*, 126, 184; "Vance Says He's Chastised Young," *LAT*, July 13, 1978, B2; "Political Prisoners in U.S., Young Says," *NYT*, July 13, 1978, A3. The *NYT* printed other excerpts from Young's interview, in which he said the Soviet system was far more repressive, both for the number of people it incarcerated and for the reasons it did so. Young resigned on August 15, 1979.

74. Sundiata Acoli to author, January 30, 2010; Acoli, *Sunviews*, 4–42; "Revitalizing the Movement: Blacks Seek Unity over Prison Issue," *SR*, September 28, 1978, 3, African National Prison Organization Solidarity Committee Vertical File, TL. While ostensibly a coalitional effort, ANPO was ultimately a project of the African People's Socialist Party, an organization that had limited working relationships with other organizations in a climate of fracturing within the Black Left.

75. Acoli, *Sunviews*, 39.

76. For more on the BLA, see Muntaqim, *On the BLA*. This article originally appeared anonymously in *AS* 9 (October–November 1980): 6–7, 20; an abridged version appears in Joy James, *Imprisoned Intellectuals*, 107–13. See also Black Liberation Army Coordinating Committee, *Message*; Umoja, "Repression Breeds Resistance"; Umoja, "Black Liberation Army"; English, *Savage City*.

77. Ashanti Alston, interview; Bukhari, *War Before*. Alston was one of the participants in an April 1974 Tombs escape attempt. Members of the BLA went back to the Tombs four months later and tried to use an acetylene torch to break through the walls of the visiting room and free their comrades. The torch ran out of fuel within inches of breaking through, and the BLA members fled, though they were arrested a few weeks later.

78. Bukhari, *War Before*; Shoatz, *Maroon*; Assata Shakur, *Assata*; Evelyn Williams, *Inadmissible Evidence*; Castellucci, *Big Dance*. In addition, my conversations or interviews with Bradley Abdul Greene, Jalil Muntaqim, Herman Bell, Ashanti Alston, and Sundiata Acoli have been helpful in understanding the BLA's efforts at this time.

79. Black Liberation Army Coordinating Committee, *Study Guide*, 138.

80. Ibid., 137.

81. Ashanti Alston, interview.

82. Kalima Aswad, interview; Jalil Muntaqim to author, July 14, 2011; *Voices from within San Quentin* 1 and 2 (1977), in author's files, courtesy of Kalima Aswad.

83. See "Message from the Editors," *AS* 3 (May 1979): 2; George Jackson quoted on the front page of every *AS* issue, Arm the Spirit Vertical File, FA.

84. Starr, "'Hit Them Harder'"; Berger, "'We Are the Revolutionaries'"; Umoja, "Black Liberation Army"; Fernandez, *Prisoners*; Fernandez, *Macheteros*; Torres and Velázquez, *Puerto Rican Movement*; González-Cruz, "Puerto Rican Revolutionary Nationalism." In *AS*, see "Que Viva Puerto Rico!," *AS* 3 (May 1979): 10–11.

85. Morales tied together bedsheets and went out a window. He fled to Mexico, where police arrested him after a 1983 shootout that left three people dead. The Mexican government nevertheless refused to extradite him to the United States. He was freed in 1988 and took up residence as an exile in Cuba. See "William Is Free!," *AS* 4 (August 1979): 4; Selwyn Raab, "A Maimed Terrorist Flees Cell at Bellevue," *NYT*, May 22, 1979, A1; Judith Cummings, "Morales Fled U.S., Phone Caller Tells FBI," *NYT*, May 26, 1979, 23; Robert D. McFadden, "Fugitive Puerto Rican Terrorist Arrested in Mexico," *NYT*, May 28, 1983, 1; Robert D. McFadden, "Extradition of Terrorist from Mexico to Be Sought," *NYT*, May 29, 1983, 36; Associated Press, "Move to Extradite Morales Is Pressed," *NYT*, June 1, 1983, B3; Elaine Sciolino, "U.S. Recalls Mexico Envoy over Militant's Release," *NYT*, June 29, 1988, A3.

86. National Committee to Free the Puerto Rican Prisoners of War, "Long Live the Heroic FALN! Free the Eleven!," *AS* 7 (May–July 1980): 4–5; "Free All Puerto Rican Prisoners of War," *AS* 8 (August–September 1980): 4–5; "Puerto Rican Prisoners of War Respond to Sedition Charges," *AS* 11 (April–May 1981): 4–5, 9; "Grand Jury Resisters Arrested," *AS* 14 (Fall 1982): 5, 22. Issues published after April 1980 featured at least one and often multiple articles about the Puerto Rican independence movement and its most militant sectors. Some articles were written by the eleven arrested FALN members and concerned their legal standing; the paper also printed interviews with Juan Antonio Corretjer, a renowned poet, member of the Nationalist Party in the 1920s and 1930s, and the founder and head of the Puerto Rican Socialist League. Corretjer became something of a spokesman for the FALN on the island.

87. Nonrecognition of the court was a strategy used to varying degrees in subsequent FALN trials, trials involving the Macheteros (another clandestine Puerto Rican group), and trials involving the Black Liberation Army and its allies. For an overview of this "prisoner of war" approach in the 1980s, see Berger, *Outlaws of America*, 245–64; Berger, *Struggle Within*; Mutulu Shakur et al., "Genocide"; Buck, "Struggle." Many of the alleged FALN members were among the Puerto Rican independentistas freed by presidential commutation in 1999.

88. See for example, "BLA under Attack," *AS* 4 (August 1979): 8; "Close Marion Control Unit," *AS* 4 (August 1979): 15; Marian Reid, "The Situation of African Women in Maryland Prisons," *AS* 5 (November 1979): 3; "Free Leonard Peltier and All Native American POWs," *AS* 5 (November 1979): 4; "Bobby Garcia Murdered in Prison" *AS* 11 (April–May 1981): 7; "Our Human Natural Resources Are Being Destroyed," *AS* 11 (April–May 1981): 8.

89. Atiba Shanna, "War for the Cities, Part III," *The Fuse* 8 (April 1978): 4. The articles originally appeared, unsigned, in the January–February, March, and April 1978 editions of *The Fuse*. They are reprinted in their entirety in the anthology of Shanna's collected works, Sayles, *Meditations*, 43–57. From prison, Shanna retained his concern

with the city, especially black Chicago; in 1988, Shanna wrote a "fact sheet" about police raids on Chicago public housing projects that organizers printed and distributed
there. The fact sheet is reprinted in Sayles, *Meditations*, 95–100.

90. NAPO-Pontiac, "A Look at Pontiac Koncentration Kamp," *The Fuse* 6 (January–
February 1978): 5, Coalition against Police Abuse Papers, Box 17, Folder 25: Political
Prisoners, Southern California Library, Los Angeles.

91. Haas, *Assassination*, 330–34; Lydersen, "Pontiac Brothers"; Tony Sapochetti, "30
Years Later: Memories of Illinois' Worst Prison Riot," Pantagraph.com, July 28, 2008,
http://www.pantagraph.com/news/years-later-memories-of-illinois-worst-prison-riot/
article_632ea54a-f02d-5e39-9d98-b8f3b6fad2bd.html; Pontiac Brothers Support Coalition, "Ill. Prisoners Face Death," *The Guardian*, June 4, 1979; Lumumba, *Pontiac Case*. I
am grateful to Nancy Kurshan and Steve Whitman for sharing their files on the Pontiac case, including many documents from the Pontiac Prisoners Support Coalition.

92. Bradley Abdul Greene to author, January 8, 2010.

93. Pontiac Prisoners Support Coalition, "Pontiac Prison Rebellion: A Case for the
Church Response," in author's files, courtesy of Nancy Kurshan and Steve Whitman; Ly-
dersen, "Pontiac Brothers"; Bruce Shapiro, "Pontiac Brothers," *The Nation*, May 30, 1981,
653; Michael Anderson, "Charges Dismissed against Last Pontiac 6," *Chicago Sun-Times*,
June 2, 1981, 3; "Pontiac Decision Painful but Necessary," *Chicago Sun-Times* editorial,
June 4, 1981.

94. As scholars are only beginning to unpack, the 1970s witnessed a variety of political transitions. An initial wave of scholarship suggested that the period saw only one
conservative ascendance. More recent texts have explored the era as a time of great
contingency that included a range of dynamic grassroots movements. For more, see
Berger, *Hidden 1970s*; Brenner, Brenner, and Winslow, *Rebel Rank and File*; Foley, *Front
Porch Politics*; Zaretsky, *No Direction Home*.

95. Atiba, "Prison Movement Discussion Paper No. 1," 16.

96. Duggan, *Twilight of Equality?*

97. Thompson, "Black Activism," 9–10.

98. Prison Law Collective, "Lock Downs Set Ups," *The Conspiracy*, December 1974,
4, NLGC, Oversized Box 7; Useem and Kimball, *States of Siege*, 81–84; Perkinson, *Texas
Tough*; Perkinson, "Shackled Justice."

99. "Defend the August 8th Brigade," and "Communiqué No. 1," *Breakthrough* 2:2
(Fall 1978): 14–15; "New Klan Offensive," *MS* 5:12 (October 1977): 3. August 8 was the
date of a strike at the prison in Naponoch. A lawsuit about Klan presence among
prison guards reached the Supreme Court.

100. In 1974, California officials instituted an unprecedented seven-month lockdown at San Quentin, Folsom, and DVI. See Cummins, *Rise and Fall*, 232.

101. "Saturday, August 24: George Jackson Day of Unity," *SR*, August 24, 1974, 6;
Peter Magnani, "Demonstrators Protest Attacks on Black Prisoners," *SR*, August 25,
1977, 3; "Black Prisoners Call for San Quentin Demo," *SR*, July 27, 1978, 11.

102. Interview by author with anonymous member of the August 21 Coalition. For
more on the Peoples Temple, see Rebecca Moore, Pinn, and Sawyer, *Peoples Temple*.

103. Spieler, *Taking Aim*, 126–28; Willie Sundiata Tate, interview; Karen Wald,
interview.

104. Cummins, *Rise and Fall*, 246; Collier and Horowitz, *Destructive Generation*, 21–66. Stender's condition was frequently discussed in the Bay Area National Lawyers Guild newspaper, *The Conspiracy*, copies of which are available in NLGC. Edward Brooks was arrested for Stender's shooting. Brooks had served three and a half years at San Quentin and was identified as a member of the BGF. In 1980, he was sentenced to serve seventeen years in prison for murder, burglary, and two counts of robbery. Collier and Horowitz, *Destructive Generation*, 56–63; Russell, "Fay Stender," http://www.ontheissuesmagazine.com/1991spring/Russell_spring1991.php.

105. See Aptheker, *Morning Breaks*, 287; Fleeta Drumgo funeral program, KFAP, Folder: Davis, Angela. My interviews with several people close to Drumgo confirmed Drumgo's postprison difficulties.

106. Shujaa Graham, interview; Friends of San Quentin Adjustment Center, *Letters to Mother from Prison*, ca. 1972, Anthony Platt, Private Collection; "Says Skin Search Clears Him of Stabbing Guard," *Jet*, March 25, 1976, 22–23; "Four-Day Railroad: Jeffrey Gaulden Convicted in Sacramento," *Committee for Prisoner Humanity and Justice* 2:1, 5. Some observers speculate that Gaulden was deliberately killed as part of an internal feud within the BGF.

107. Shujaa Graham, interview.

108. Willie Sundiata Tate, interview. In an interview, James Carr said he and Jackson had formed a gang, called the Capone Gang, which others say later changed its name to the Wolf Pack and ultimately became the Black Guerrilla Family. Jackson's prison comrades Sundiata Tate and David Johnson dispute such claims, arguing instead that Jackson's social networks were more fluid and informal and that a larger grouping of prisoners self-consciously initiated the Black Guerrilla Family as a political project in 1970. See "George Jackson: Teacher & Organizer—Interview with Jimmy Carr," in *War behind the Walls*, September 1971, 3.

109. David Johnson, interview; Ronald "Elder" Freeman, interview. In interviews, for example, several people spoke of the BGF and "the prison movement" as interchangeable entities in these years. Given its prison seclusion and clandestine function, the BGF has left a short paper trail. More scholarship on the group is needed.

110. Quoted in Cummins, *Rise and Fall*, 137; Dorsey Nunn, interview.

111. For an overly sympathetic look at the gang based partly on oral histories with some members, see Barganier, "Fanon's Children." Much of what exists is in the form of often-sensationalistic memoirs: Sanyika Shakur, *Monster*; Stanley Tookie Williams, *Blue Rage*; Simpson with Pearlman, *Inside the Crips*. See also Hagedorn, *Gangs*.

112. Mike Davis, *City of Quartz*, 298.

113. The phrase "organized abandonment" comes from Harvey, *Limits*, 397. It is taken up in greater detail by Ruth Wilson Gilmore, *Golden Gulag*, "Fatal Couplings," and "Globalisation."

114. See Acoli, "Updated History"; "Black August Statement," *AS* 9 (October–November 1980): 12, 18; Dahariki (Hugo A. Pinell), "Black Prisoners: A Call for Unity," *AS* 10 (December 1980–January 1981): 10–13, 19–22.

115. See, for example, Kiilu Nyasha, "Black August 2009: A Story of African Freedom Fighters," *San Francisco BayView*, August 3, 2009, http://www.sfbayview.com/2009/black-august-2009-a-story-of-african-freedom-fighters; Gabriel Gonzalez,

"Black August: Resist!," *Burning Spear*, July 31, 2006, http://uhurunews.com/story?resource_name=black-august-resist; Malcolm X Grassroots Movement, "Black August 2008: Resisting Imperialist Intimidation, Terror, and Displacement from the Gulf Coast to the Continent," *Malcolm X Grassroots Movement Newsletter*, Spring 2008, http://mxgm.org/black-august-2008-resisting-imperialist-intimidation/.

116. *Black August* was also the title of a 2006 independent film about George Jackson based on Gregory Armstrong's book, *The Dragon Has Come*.

117. See "The Oath," 2, included in February 12, 1974, FBI memo to U.S. Secret Service, included in files on Black Guerrilla Family, available on FBI online reading room, http://vault.fbi.gov/black-guerilla-family.

118. Parenti, "Satellites of Sorrow." More generally, see Haney-López, "Post-Racial Racism"; Espiritu, "(E)Racing Youth"; Bargainer, "Fanon's Children"; Wallace-Wells, "Plot from Solitary." I do not mean to suggest that "gangs," unsanctioned organizations that engage in highly predatory behavior while providing some measure of mutual aid to members, do not exist or are unproblematic. Rather, I wish to mark the ways in which targeting gangs emerged as a policing strategy alongside an official embrace of color blindness. A genealogy of policing might very well go from the political repression of Red Squads and COINTELPRO during the Cold War to the antigang units in the age of mass incarceration.

119. Kunzel, *Criminal Intimacy*, 169.

120. See files available via the FBI's electronic reading room, http://vault.fbi.gov/black-guerilla-family. This large range of potential members suggests that the FBI had limited intelligence on the BGF at this time.

121. SAC San Francisco to Director, FBI, July 30, 1979, http://vault.fbi.gov/black-guerilla-family/black-guerilla-family-part-2-of-3/view.

122. Shujaa Graham, interview.

123. Cummins, *Rise and Fall*, 249–50.

124. "Prison Demonstration Marks 'Black August,'" *SR*, August 23, 1979, 5; "Black August Month: Big Demo at San Quentin," *SR*, August 20, 1979, 3.

125. Black August Committee Afrikan Community, Max-B, San Quentin, "Black August 1980," *AS* 8 (August–September 1980): 3.

126. See "Build Black August Month" and "Message from the Editors," both in *AS* 4 (August 1979): 1–2.

127. The full statement is available in the July 30, 1979, FBI report on the Black Guerrilla Family, 3, http://vault.fbi.gov/black-guerilla-family/black-guerilla-family-part-2-of-3/view. See also Black August flyers, Prairie Fire Organizing Committee Vertical File, FA.

128. Untitled flyer, August 25, 1979, Prairie Fire Organizing Committee Vertical File, FA.

129. Fanon, *Wretched of the Earth*, 170.

130. Crozier, Huntington, and Watanuki, *Crisis*; Ruth Wilson Gilmore, "Globalisation"; Gottschalk, *Prison*.

131. Wagmiller, "Male Nonemployment," 100, quoted in Cacho, *Social Death*, 120.

132. Ruth Wilson Gilmore, *Golden Gulag*, 91, 111.

133. Widener, *Black Arts West*, 263; Iton, *In Search*.

1. For historical attempts to grapple with this contradiction, see Edmund Morgan, *American Slavery*; Hixson, *American Settler Colonialism*.

2. Reddy, *Freedom*, 37. See also Melamed, *Represent and Destroy*; Nguyen, *Gift*.

3. Reddy, *Freedom*, 20.

4. See Reddy, *Freedom*; Melamed, *Represent and Destroy*; Nguyen, *Gift*; Harvey, *Brief History*; Ruth Wilson Gilmore, "Globalisation"; Cacho, *Social Death*; Prashad, *Poorer Nations*; Goldberg, *Threat*; HoSang, *Racial Propositions*; Schmidt Camacho, "Ciudadana X"; Gordon, "Methodologies."

5. Ruth Wilson Gilmore, "Fatal Couplings"; Robin D. G. Kelley, "The U.S. v. Trayvon Martin: How the System Worked," *Huffington Post*, July 15, 2013, http://www.huffingtonpost.com/robin-d-g-kelley/nra-stand-your-ground-trayvon-martin_b_3599843.html; Malcolm X Grassroots Movement, *Operation Ghetto Storm: 2012 Annual Report on the Extrajudicial Killing of 313 Black People*, April 8, 2013, http://mxgm.org/wp-content/uploads/2013/04/Operation-Ghetto-Storm.pdf.

6. Bosworth, *Explaining U.S. Imprisonment*; Gottschalk, *Prison*; Western, *Punishment*.

7. Berger, "Two Prisoners"; Bauer, "Solitary." Association with Jackson seems to be the main reason that Hugo Pinell, incarcerated consistently since the 1960s, and John Clutchette, released in 1972 but arrested and sent back to prison in 1980, were in solitary confinement as late as 2013. Until January 2014, Pinell was in Pelican Bay State Prison, a prison within a prison and perhaps the most isolating form of solitary confinement in the world. In July 2011, he was one of hundreds of Pelican Bay prisoners who participated in a hunger strike to protest long-term solitary confinement. Until late 2013, Clutchette was in the "Security Housing Unit" of California's state prison at Corcoran. He remains incarcerated at Vacaville. Ruchell Magee and Kalima Aswad, both in their seventies, are among the other participants of California's 1970s prison movement who remain incarcerated after more than forty years. They join dozens of other veterans of the black freedom struggle who are incarcerated as political prisoners. For a list of their names and addresses, see www.thejerichomovement.com.

8. Fanon, *Wretched of the Earth*, especially 27–84. Several former members of the Weather Underground, for example, describe their initial preparations for going underground—during which time they engaged in a series of bombastic and ill-fated physical confrontations and protest marches—as "psyching themselves up" for violence. See Berger, *Outlaws of America*; Varon, *Bringing the War Home*.

9. From the left, see the Invisible Committee, *The Coming Insurrection*. For analyses of right-wing antistatist violence in the form of reactionary political Islam, see Mamdani, *Good Muslim*; Retort, *Afflicted Powers*.

10. My thinking about "against and beyond" comes from years of conversations with Andy Cornell and Chris Dixon, among others. For elaborations, see Cornell, *Oppose*; Dixon, "Building" and *Another Politics*. For speculations on freedom from violence in the context of women's lives in the U.S.-Mexico border wars, see Schmidt Camacho, "Ciudadana X."

11. Robinson, *Black Marxism*, 168.

12. The poem is printed on the first page of the 2001 edition of her memoir, Assata Shakur, *Assata*.

13. New Afrikan nationalism is a prominent feature of prisoner writings and uprisings in the early twenty-first century. For examples, see Rashid Johnson, *Defying the Tomb*; Sanyika Shakur, *Stand Up*; and articles published in the San Francisco *Bay Guardian* by Pelican Bay prisoners Mutope Duguma, Kijana Tashiri Askari, Michael Zaharibu Dorrough, and J. Heshima Denham, among others. Working through a multiracial collective, Pelican Bay prisoners organized successive hunger strikes in the California state prison system between 2011 and 2013. At the height of the strike, more than 30,000 prisoners refused food in protest of California's routine use of long-term solitary confinement. For more, including the five demands that motivated these hunger strikes, see www.prisonerhungerstrikesolidarity.wordpress.com; Dayan, "Barbarous Confinement," *NYT*, July 18, 2011, A19.

14. This phrase serves as the title of the concluding essay to Abendroth's book of poetry, *Exclosures*, 61.

15. Emily Abendroth to author, December 2, 2013.

16. See, for example, Rodgers, *Age of Fracture*.

17. After his release from prison in the early 1980s, Republic of New Afrika cofounder Imari Obadele became a leading figure in the reparations movement, cofounding the National Coalition of Blacks for Reparations in America. More generally, see Biondi, "Rise."

18. On hip-hop, see Murray Forman and Neal, *That's the Joint!*; Kitwana, *Why White Kids*. On AIDS, see Kunzel, *Criminal Intimacy*, 225–37; Shabazz, "Mapping"; Schuster, "Sentenced."

19. In 2005, CR reprinted the 1976 abolitionist primer by Knopp and Reigier, *Instead of Prisons*. The group also published its own text of abolitionist theory and strategy, CR10 Publications Collective, *Abolition Now!*

20. For an overview of early twenty-first-century work against prisons, see Berger, "Social Movements."

21. For examples of activist attempts to address interpersonal harm outside the criminal justice system, see *Color of Violence*; Ritchie, *Arrested Justice*; Chen, Dulani, and Piepzna-Samarasinha, *Revolution*; Sudbury, "Maroon Abolitionists."

22. Jackson, *Blood in My Eye*, xviii.

Bibliography

ARCHIVAL AND MANUSCRIPT COLLECTIONS

Bancroft Library, University of California at Berkeley
    Eldridge Cleaver Papers
    Meiklejohn Civil Liberties Institute Records
    National Lawyers Guild Collection
    Papers Relating to the Publication of *Soledad Brother*
    Social Protest Collection
Freedom Archives, San Francisco, Calif.
    Freedom Is a Constant Struggle Audio Collection
    Nothing Is More Precious Than Audio Collection
    Prison Movement Audio Collection
    Real Dragons Audio Collection
    Vertical Files
        Arm the Spirit
        Black Liberation Army
        Black Panther Party
        Angela Davis
        New Afrikan Prisoners Organization
        Political Prisoners
        Prairie Fire Organizing Committee
        Prisons
        Puerto Rico
        Seize the Time
        Soledad Brothers
        Symbionese Liberation Army
        United Prisoners Union
        Underground Press
Green Library, Stanford University, Palo Alto, Calif.
    Angela Davis Papers
    Huey P. Newton Foundation Papers
    Raúl R. Salinas Papers
Harry Ransom Center, University of Texas at Austin
    Jessica Mitford Papers, Series III: A Kind and Usual Punishment Files
Hoover Institute, Stanford University, Palo Alto, Calif.
    New Left Collection, 1964–2004
Library of Congress, Washington, D.C.
    National Association for the Advancement of Colored People Records, 1842–1999

Marin County Civic Center, Marin, Calif.
  California History Special Collections, Crime and Criminals
Moorland-Spingarn Research Center, Howard University, Washington, D.C.
  Civil Rights Documentation Project, Vertical File Collection, Manuscript Division
New York Public Library, New York
  Manuscripts
    Charles Goodell Papers
  Schomburg Center for Research in Black Culture
    Angela Davis Legal Defense Fund
    Kenneth B. Clark Papers
    Harlem Black Panther Party Papers
    Metropolitan Applied Research Center
    National Alliance against Racist and Political Repression Papers
    National United Committee to Free Angela Davis
Southern California Library, Los Angeles
  Kendra and Franklin Alexander Papers
  Coalition against Police Abuse Papers
  La Raza Collection
  Pamphlet Collection
Tamiment Library, New York University, New York
  Midnight Special
  National Lawyers Guild
  Oral History of the American Left: Radical Histories Collection
  Pamphlet Collection
  Tear Down the Walls
  Vertical Files
    African National Prison Organization Solidarity Committee
    African People's Socialist Party
    Angela Y. Davis
    Friends of San Quentin
    Friends of Soledad
    Fuerzas Armadas de Liberación Nacional
    International Committee to Defend Eldridge Cleaver
    Ruchell Magee
    Ruchell Magee National Defense Committee
    National Alliance against Racist and Political Repression
    Prisoner Solidarity Committee
    San Quentin Six Defense Fund
    Bobby Seale Brigade
    Soledad Brothers Defense Committee
Private Collections
  Stephen Bingham (*People v. Bingham* files), San Rafael, Calif.
  Interference Archive, Brooklyn, N.Y.
  Nancy Kurshan and Steve Whitman, Chicago
  Mark Merin (*Spain v. Procunier* files), Sacramento, Calif.

Matt Meyer and Meg Starr, Brooklyn, N.Y.
Judith Mirkinson and Robert Roth, San Francisco
Anthony Platt, Berkeley, California
Puerto Rican Cultural Center, Chicago
Michael Staudenmaier, Chicago
Luis Bato Talamantez, San Francisco
Larry Weiss, Denver

GOVERNMENT DOCUMENTS

Federal Bureau of Investigation, Washington, D.C.
  Black Guerrilla Family, File 157-31288
  Marilyn Buck, File 100-10334
  George Jackson, File 44-HQ-50522
  Jonathan Peter Jackson, File 157-20544
  San Francisco Prairie Fire Organizing Committee, File 100-77975

INTERVIEWS (CONDUCTED IN PERSON BY AUTHOR, UNLESS OTHERWISE NOTED)

Sundiata Acoli, telephone interview, October 31, 2012
Hakim Ali, Philadelphia, July 16, 2012
Ashanti Alston, Philadelphia, April 14, 2012
Bettina Aptheker, telephone interview, October 7, 2011
Kalima Aswad, Vacaville, Calif., October 24, 2008
Lincoln Bergman, telephone interview, June 25, 2013
Stephen Bingham, San Rafael, Calif., April 14, 2013
Nyati Bolt, Vallejo, Calif., December 15, 2012
John Clutchette, letters to the author, December 19, 22, 24, 2012
Mark Cook, Seattle, November 14, 2012
Angela Davis, Seattle, October 17, 2013
H. Bruce Franklin, telephone interview, May 23, 2012
Ronald "Elder" Freeman, Oakland, Calif., April 10, 2013
William Goldsby, Philadelphia, July 5, 2012
Shujaa Graham, Takoma Park, Md., August 3, 2012
Bradley Abdul Greene, e-mail interview, January 8, 2010
Fred Hiestand, Sacramento, Calif., April 16, 2012
Ericka Huggins, Oakland, Calif., April 12, 2013
Ericka Huggins, interview by Fiona Thompson, fall 2007, Regional Oral History
  Office, Bancroft Library, University of California at Berkeley
George Jackson, interview by Max Bloom, July 28, 1971, PM 211A, Freedom Archives,
  San Francisco
David Johnson, Fairfield, Calif., April 12, 16, 2013
Ruchell Magee, interview by Luis Bato Talamantez, Corcoran, Calif., April 13, 2002
Ed Mead, Seattle, November 14, 2012

Mark Merin, Sacramento, Calif., April 16, 2012

Audley "Queen Mother" Moore, interview by Mark Naison, 1972, Oral History of the American Left: Radical Histories Collection, Tamiment Library, New York University, New York

Audley "Queen Mother" Moore, interview by Ruth Prego, December 23, 1981, Oral History of the American Left: Radical Histories Collection, Tamiment Library, New York University, New York

Jalil Muntaqim, letters to the author, July 14, 2011, July 10, 2013

Russell Neufeld, New York, August 25, 2011

Dorsey Nunn, telephone interview, November 21, 2011

Kiilu Nyasha, San Francisco, October 22, 2009

Phyllis Prentice, Takoma Park, Md., August 3, 2012

Michael Simmons, Philadelphia, April 12, 2012

Luis Bato Talamantez, Vallejo, Calif., December 15, 2012; Oakland, Calif., December 17, 2012; San Francisco, Calif., April 13, 2013

Willie Sundiata Tate, San Leandro, Calif., December 18, 2012

Karen Wald, San Jose, Calif., April 15, 2013

Larry Weiss, telephone interview, March 25, 2013

NEWSPAPERS AND PERIODICALS

Anvil	Oakland Tribune
Arm the Spirit	Outlaw
Aztlán	Palante
Babylon	People's Justice
Berkeley Barb	People's World
Berkeley Tribe	Philadelphia Tribune
Black Panther	Ramparts
Black Pride	Real Deal
The Conspiracy	Rebeldia
Free Angela	Right On
Freedom News	Sacramento Bee
The Fuse	San Francisco Chronicle and Examiner
Grand Jury Campaign	San Jose Mercury News
Guardian	San Rafael Independent Journal
Liberated Guardian	Seize the Time
Libertad	Soledad Brothers News
Los Angeles Times	Sun Reporter
Midnight Special	Time
Movement	Up against the Bench
Newsweek	Urgent Tasks
New York Times	Viva wa Watu
Notes from an Afrikan P.O.W. Journal	Washington Post

Abendroth, Emily. *Exclosures*. Boise, Idaho: Ahsahta Press, 2014.

Abu-Jamal, Mumia. *Jailhouse Lawyers: Prisoners Defending Prisoners v. the U.S.A.* San Francisco: City Lights, 2009.

———. *We Want Freedom: A Life in the Black Panther Party*. Cambridge, Mass.: South End, 2004.

Abu-Lughod, Janet L. *Race, Space, and Riots in Chicago, New York, and Los Angeles*. Oxford: Oxford University Press, 2007.

Acham, Christine. *Revolution Televised: Prime Time and the Struggle for Black Power*. Minneapolis: University of Minnesota Press, 2004.

Acoli, Sundiata. *Sunviews*. Newark: Creative Images, 1983.

———. "An Updated History of the New Afrikan Prison Struggle (Abridged)." In Joy James, ed., *Imprisoned Intellectuals: America's Political Prisoners Write on Life, Liberation, and Rebellion* (135–64). Lanham, Md.: Rowman and Littlefield, 2003.

Agamben, Giorgio. *Homo Sacer: Sovereign Power and Bare Life*. Stanford: Stanford University Press, 1995.

———. *State of Exception*. Chicago: University of Chicago Press, 2005.

Ahmad, Muhammad. *We Will Return in the Whirlwind: Black Radical Organizations, 1960–1975*. Chicago: Kerr, 2007.

Alexander, Michelle. *The New Jim Crow: Mass Incarceration in the Age of Colorblindness*. New York: New Press, 2010.

Alkebulan, Paul. *Survival Pending Revolution: The History of the Black Panther Party*. Tuscaloosa: University of Alabama Press, 2007.

American Friends Service Committee. *Struggle for Justice: A Report on Crime and Punishment in America*. New York: Hill and Wang, 1971.

Anderson, Benedict. *Imagined Communities: Reflections on the Origin and Spread of Nationalism*. London: Verso, 1991.

Andrews, Lori. *Black Power, White Blood: The Life and Times of Johnny Spain*. New York: Pantheon, 1996.

Aptheker, Bettina. *Intimate Politics: How I Grew Up Red, Fought for Free Speech, and Became a Feminist Rebel*. Emeryville, Calif.: Seal, 2006.

———. *The Morning Breaks: The Trial of Angela Davis*. Ithaca: Cornell University Press, 1997 (1975).

Armstrong, Gregory. *The Dragon Has Come*. New York: Harper and Row, 1974.

Arsenault, Raymond. *Freedom Riders: 1961 and the Struggle for Racial Justice*. New York: Oxford University Press, 2006.

Atiba. "Afrikan P.O.W.s and the United Nations." In *Notes from an Afrikan P.O.W. Journal: Book One* (12). Chicago: Spear and Shield, 1977. http://slideshare.net/rbgstreetscholar1/cr-book-onenotes-from-an-afrikan-pow-journal.

———. "Prison Movement Discussion Paper No. 1: Contributions toward the National Prisoners Movement." In *Notes from an Afrikan P.O.W. Journal: Book One* (13–16). Chicago: Spear and Shield, 1977. http://slideshare.net/rbgstreetscholar1/cr-book-onenotes-from-an-afrikan-pow-journal.

Atkins, Burton M., and Henry R. Glick, ed. *Prisons, Protest, and Politics*. Englewood Cliffs, N.J.: Prentice-Hall, 1972.

Attica: The Official Report of the New York State Special Commission. New York: Bantam, 1972.

Austin, Curtis. *Up against the Wall: Violence in the Making and Unmaking of the Black Panther Party*. Fayetteville: University of Arkansas Press, 2006.

Avila, Eric. *Popular Culture in the Age of White Flight: Fear and Fantasy in Suburban Los Angeles*. Berkeley: University of California Press, 2004.

Avorn, Jerry L. *Up against the Ivy Wall: A History of the Columbia Crisis*. New York: Atheneum, 1968.

Badillo, Herman, and Milton Haynes. *A Bill of No Rights: Attica and the American Prison System*. New York: Overbridge and Lazard, 1972.

Bailey, Beth, and David Farber, eds. *America in the 1970s*. Lawrence: University Press of Kansas, 2004.

Baker, Houston. "Critical Memory and the Black Public Sphere." In The Black Public Sphere Collective, ed., *The Black Public Sphere: A Public Culture Book* (5–38). Chicago: University of Chicago Press, 1995.

Baldwin, James. *The Cross of Redemption: Uncollected Writings*. New York: Vintage, 2010.

———. *The Evidence of Things Not Seen*. New York: Holt, 1995 (1985).

———. *The Fire Next Time*. New York: Vintage International, 1963.

———. *No Name in the Street*. New York: Dell, 1972.

Banfield, Edward C. *Unheavenly City: The Nature and Future of Our Urban Crisis*. New York: Little, Brown, 1970.

Barkan, Steven E. *Protesters on Trial: Criminal Justice in the Southern Civil Rights and Vietnam Antiwar Movements*. New Brunswick: Rutgers University Press, 1985.

Barrera, Mario, Carlos Muñoz, and Charles Ornelas. "The Barrio as an Internal Colony." *Urban Affairs Annual Review* 6 (1972): 465–98.

Bass, S. Jonathan. *Blessed Are the Peacemakers: Martin Luther King, Jr., Eight White Religious Leaders, and the "Letter from a Birmingham Jail."* Baton Rouge: Louisiana State University Press, 2001.

Bauer, Shane. "Solitary in Iran Nearly Broke Me. Then I went Inside America's Prisons." *Mother Jones*, November–December 2012. http://www.motherjones.com/politics/2012/10/solitary-confinement-shane-bauer.

Baum, Dan. *Smoke and Mirrors: The War on Drugs and the Politics of Failure*. Boston: Back Bay, 1996.

Beauregard, Robert. *Voices of Decline: The Postwar Fate of U.S. Cities*. New York: Routledge, 2003.

Begel, Debby. "An Interview with Willie Tate." In Tony Platt and Paul Takagi, eds., *Punishment and Penal Discipline: Essays on the Prison and the Prisoners' Movement* (176–83). San Francisco: Crime and Social Justice Associates, 1980.

Bell, Malcolm. *The Turkey Shoot: Tracking the Attica Cover-Up*. New York: Grove, 1985.

Bennett, Scott H. *Radical Pacifism: The War Resisters League and Gandhian Nonviolence in America, 1915–1963*. Syracuse: Syracuse University Press, 2003.

Berger, Dan, ed. *The Hidden 1970s: Histories of Radicalism*. New Brunswick: Rutgers University Press, 2010.

————. "Carceral Migrations: Black Power and Slavery in 1970s California Prison Radicalism." In Moon-ho Jung, ed., *The Rising Tide of Color: Race, State Violence, and Radical Movements across the Pacific* (213–36). Seattle: University of Washington Press, 2014.

————. "'The Malcolm X Doctrine': The Republic of New Afrika and National Liberation on U.S. Soil." In Karen Dubinsky, Catherine Krull, Susan Lord, Sean Mills, and Scott Rutherford, eds., *New World Coming: The Sixties and the Shaping of Global Consciousness* (46–55). Toronto: Between the Lines, 2009.

————. *Outlaws of America: The Weather Underground and the Politics of Solidarity*. Oakland, Calif.: AK Press, 2006.

————. "Regarding the Imprisonment of Others: Prison Abuse Photographs and Social Change." *International Journal of Communication* 1 (2007): 210–37.

————. "Social Movements and Mass Incarceration: What Is to Be Done?" *Souls* 15:1 (2013): 3–18.

————. *The Struggle Within: Prisons, Political Prisoners, and Mass Movements in the United States*. Oakland, Calif.: PM Press, 2014.

————. "Two Prisoners Named Williams." *The Nation*, December 14, 2005. http://www .thenation.com/article/two-prisoners-named-willams.

Berger, Dan, with Roxanne Dunbar-Ortiz. "'The Struggle Is for Land!': Race, Territory and National Liberation." In Dan Berger, ed., *The Hidden 1970s: Histories of Radicalism* (57–76). New Brunswick: Rutgers University Press, 2010.

Berger, Dan, and Matt Meyer. "The Pan-Africanization of Black Power: True History, Coalition-Building, and the All-African People's Revolutionary Party—An Interview with Bob Brown." In Elizabeth Betita Martinez, Mandy Carter, and Matt Meyer, eds., *We Have Not Been Moved: Resisting Racism and Militarism in Twenty-First Century America* (137–47). Oakland, Calif.: PM Press, 2012.

Berkman, Alexander. *Prison Memoirs of an Anarchist*. New York: Schocken, 1970.

Berkman, Ronald. *Opening the Gates: The Rise of the Prisoners' Movement*. Lexington, Mass.: Lexington Books, 1979.

Bernstein, Lee. "The Age of Jackson: George Jackson and the Culture of American Prisons in the 1970s." *Journal of American Culture* 30:3 (2007): 310–23.

————. *America Is the Prison: Arts and Politics in Prison in the 1970s*. Chapel Hill: University of North Carolina Press, 2010.

Bernstein, Robin. *Racial Innocence: Performing American Childhood and Race from Slavery to Civil Rights*. New York: New York University Press, 2011.

Berrigan, Daniel. *The Catonsville Nine*. New York: Fordham University Press, 2004.

Biondi, Martha. *The Black Revolution on Campus*. Berkeley: University of California Press, 2012.

————. "The Rise of the Reparations Movement." *Radical History Review* 87 (Fall 2003): 5–18.

————. *To Stand and Fight: The Struggle for Civil Rights in Postwar New York City*. Cambridge: Harvard University Press, 2003.

Bissonette, Jamie. *When the Prisoners Ran Walpole: A True Story in the Movement for Prison Abolition*. Cambridge, Mass.: South End, 2008.

Black, Conrad. *Richard M. Nixon: A Life in Full*. New York: PublicAffairs, 2007.

Black Liberation Army Coordinating Committee. *Message to the Black Movement: A Political Statement from the Black Underground.* Chicago: Autonomous Zone, 1997 (ca. 1975).

———. *Study Guide.* N.p., ca. 1977.

Blackmon, Douglas. *Slavery by Another Name: The Re-Enslavement of Black Americans from the Civil War to World War II.* New York: Doubleday, 2008.

Blauner, Robert. *Still the Big News: Racial Oppression in America.* Philadelphia: Temple University Press, 2001.

Block, Diana. *Arm the Spirit: A Woman's Journey Underground and Back.* Oakland, Calif.: AK Press, 2009.

Bloom, Joshua, and Waldo E. Martin Jr. *Black against Empire: The History and Politics of the Black Panther Party.* Berkeley: University of California Press.

Blue, Ethan. *Doing Time in the Depression: Everyday Life in Texas and California Prisons.* New York: New York University Press, 2012.

Boggs, James. *Racism and the Class Struggle: Further Pages from a Black Worker's Notebook.* New York: Monthly Review Press, 1970.

Booker, Chris. "Lumpenization: A Critical Error of the Black Panther Party." In Charles E. Jones, ed., *The Black Panther Party Reconsidered* (337–62). Baltimore: Black Classics, 1998.

Bookspan, Shelley. *A Germ of Goodness: The California Prison System, 1851–1944.* Lincoln: University of Nebraska Press, 1991.

Bosworth, Mary. *Explaining U.S. Imprisonment.* Thousand Oaks, Calif.: Sage, 2010.

Bourg, Julian. *From Revolution to Ethics: May 1968 and Contemporary French Thought.* Montreal: McGill-Queen's University Press, 2007.

Bradley, Stefan M. *Harlem vs. Columbia University: Black Student Power in the Late 1960s.* Urbana: University of Illinois Press, 2009.

Branch, Taylor. *Parting the Waters: America in the King Years, 1954–1963.* New York: Simon and Schuster, 1988.

Brenner, Aaron, Robert Brenner, and Cal Winslow, ed. *Rebel Rank and File: Labor Militancy and Revolt from Below during the Long 1970s.* New York: Verso, 2010.

Brown, Claude. *Manchild in the Promised Land.* New York: Simon and Schuster, 1965.

Brown, Elaine. *A Taste of Power: A Black Woman's Story.* New York: Pantheon, 1992.

Brown, Scot. *Fighting for Us: Maulana Karenga, the U.S. Organization, and Black Cultural Nationalism.* New York: New York University Press, 2003.

Brown, Vincent. *The Reaper's Garden: Death and Power in the World of Atlantic Slavery.* Cambridge: Harvard University Press, 2008.

———. "Social Death and Political Life in the Study of Slavery." *American Historical Review* 114:5 (2009): 1231–49.

Bruchac, Joseph, and William Witherup, eds. *Words from the House of the Dead: Prison Writings from Soledad.* New York: Greenfield Review, 1971.

Brundage, W. Fitzhugh. *The Southern Past: A Clash of Race and Memory.* Cambridge: Belknap Press of Harvard University Press, 2005.

Bryan, John. *This Soldier Still at War.* New York: Harcourt, Brace, Jovanovich, 1975.

Buck, Marilyn. "The Struggle for Status under International Law: U.S. Political Prisoners and the Political Offense Exception to Extradition." In Joy James, ed.,

Imprisoned Intellectuals: America's Political Prisoners Write on Life, Liberation, and Rebellion (201–15). Lanham, Md.: Rowman and Littlefield, 2003.

Bukhari, Safiya. *The War Before*. New York: Feminist Press, 2010.

Buntman, Fran Lisa. *Robben Island and Prisoner Resistance to Apartheid*. Cambridge: Cambridge University Press, 2003.

Burton-Rose, Daniel. "The Anti-Exploits of Men against Sexism, 1977–78." In Donald F. Sabo, Terry A. Kupers, and Willie London, eds., *Prison Masculinities* (224–29). Philadelphia: Temple University Press, 2001.

———. *Creating a Movement with Teeth: A Documentary History of the George Jackson Brigade*. Oakland, Calif.: PM Press, 2010.

———. *Guerrilla USA: The George Jackson Brigade and the Anticapitalist Underground in the 1970s*. Berkeley: University of California Press, 2010.

Cacho, Lisa Marie. *Social Death: Racialized Rightlessness and the Criminalization of the Unprotected*. New York: New York University Press, 2012.

Cagin, Seth, and Philip Dray. *We Are Not Afraid: The Story of Goodman, Schwerner, and Chaney, and the Civil Rights Campaign for Mississippi*. New York: Nation, 2006.

Camp, Stephanie M. H. *Closer to Freedom: Enslaved Women and Everyday Resistance in the Plantation South*. Chapel Hill: University of North Carolina Press, 2004.

Carawan, Guy, and Candie Carawan, eds. *Sing for Freedom: The Story of the Civil Rights Movement through Its Songs*. Montgomery, Ala.: New South, 2007.

Carey, James. "The Dark Continent of American Journalism." In Robert Manoff and Michael Schudson, eds., *Reading the News* (146–96). New York: Pantheon, 1986.

Carmichael, Stokely. *Stokely Speaks: From Black Power to Pan-Africanism*. Chicago: Hill Books, 2007 (1971).

Carmichael, Stokely, and Charles V. Hamilton. *Black Power: The Politics of Liberation*. New York: Vintage, 1967.

Carmichael, Stokely, with Ekwueme Michael Thelwell. *Ready for Revolution: The Life and Struggles of Stokely Carmichael (Kwame Toure)*. New York: Scribner, 2003.

Carr, James. *Bad: The Autobiography of James Carr*. Edinburgh: AK, 2002 (1975).

Carson, Clayborne. *In Struggle: SNCC and the Black Awakening of the 1960s*. Cambridge: Harvard University Press, 1995 (1981).

Carter, Dan T. *Scottsboro: A Tragedy of the American South*. Baton Rouge: Louisiana State University Press, 1979 (1969).

Castellucci, John. *The Big Dance: The Untold Story of Kathy Boudin and the Terrorist Family That Committed the Brink's Robbery Murders*. New York: Dodd, Mead, 1986.

Chafe, William H. *Civilities and Civil Rights: Greensboro, North Carolina, and the Black Struggle for Freedom*. New York: Oxford University Press, 1981.

Cha-Jua, Sundiata K., and Clarence Lang. "The 'Long Movement' as Vampire: Temporal and Spatial Fallacies in Recent Black Freedom Studies." *Journal of African American History* 92:2 (2007): 265–88.

Chappell, Marisa. *The War on Welfare: Family, Poverty, and Politics in Modern America*. Philadelphia: University of Pennsylvania Press, 2010.

Chard, Daniel S. "Rallying for Repression: Police Terror, 'Law-and-Order' Politics, and the Decline of Maine's Prisoners' Rights Movement." *The Sixties* 5:1 (2012): 47–73.

Chase, Robert T. "'Slaves of the State' Revolt: Southern Prison Labor and a Prison-Made Civil Rights Movement." In Robert Zeiger, ed., *Life and Labor in the New, New South* (177–213). Gainesville: University Press of Florida, 2012.

Chatterjee, Partha. *The Nation and Its Fragments: Colonial and Postcolonial Histories.* Princeton: Princeton University Press, 1993.

Chávez-García, Miroslava. *States of Delinquency: Race and Science in the Making of California's Juvenile Justice System.* Berkeley: University of California Press, 2012.

Chen, Ching-In, Jai Dulani, and Leah Lakshmi Piepzna-Samarasinha, eds. *Revolution Starts at Home: Confronting Intimate Violence within Activist Communities.* Brooklyn, N.Y.: South End, 2011.

Chevigny, Bell Gale, ed. *Doing Time: Twenty-Five Years of Prison Writing.* New York: Arcade, 1999.

Christianson, Scott. *With Liberty for Some: Five Hundred Years of Imprisonment in America.* Boston: Northeastern University Press, 1998.

Chronopoulos, Themis. *Spatial Regulation in New York City: From Urban Renewal to Zero Tolerance.* New York: Routledge, 2011.

Church Committee. *Intelligence Activities and the Rights of Americans: 1976 U.S. Senate Report on Illegal Wiretaps and Domestic Spying by the FBI, CIA, and NSA.* St. Petersburg, Fla.: Red and Black, 2008.

Churchill, Ward, and Jim Vander Wall. *Agents of Repression: The FBI's Secret Wars against the Black Panther Party and the American Indian Movement.* Boston: South End, 1988.

———. *The COINTELPRO Papers: Documents from the FBI's Secret Wars against Dissent in the United States.* Boston: South End, 1990.

Citizens Research and Investigation Committee and Louis E. Tackwood. *The Glass House Tapes.* New York: Avon, 1973.

Clark, Kenneth B. *Dark Ghetto: Dilemmas of Social Power.* New York: Harper and Row, 1965.

———. *King, Malcolm, Baldwin: Three Interviews.* Middletown, Conn.: Wesleyan University Press, 1985 (1963).

———. *Youth in Revolt.* New York: Haryou, 1964.

Clark, Ramsey. *Crime in America: Observations on Its Nature, Causes, Prevention, and Control.* New York: Simon and Schuster, 1970.

Cleaver, Eldridge. *Eldridge Cleaver: Post-Prison Writings and Speeches.* Ed. Robert Scheer. New York: Ramparts/Vintage, 1969.

———. *Soul on Ice.* New York: Dell, 1968.

———. *Target Zero.* New York: Palgrave Macmillan, 2006.

Cleaver, Kathleen, and George Katsiaficas, eds. *Liberation, Imagination, and the Black Panther Party: A New Look at the Panthers and Their Legacy.* New York: Routledge, 2001.

Cohen, Cathy J. *The Boundaries of Blackness: AIDS and the Breakdown of Black Politics.* Chicago: University of Chicago Press, 1999.

Colley, Zoe A. *Ain't Scared of Your Jail: Arrest, Imprisonment, and the Civil Rights Movement.* Gainesville: University Press of Florida, 2013.

Collier, Peter, and David Horowitz. *Destructive Generation: Second Thoughts about the Sixties.* New York: Summit, 1989.

Collins, Keith. *Black Los Angeles: The Maturing of the Ghetto, 1940–1950.* Saratoga, Calif.: Century Twenty One, 1980.

Collins, Lisa Gail, and Margo Natalie Crawford, eds. *New Thoughts on the Black Arts Movement.* New Brunswick: Rutgers University Press, 2006.

The Color of Violence: The Incite! Anthology. Cambridge, Mass.: South End, 2006.

Committee in Solidarity with Puerto Rican Independence. *Toward People's War for Independence and Socialism in Puerto Rico: In Defense of Armed Struggle.* [Chicago]: Committee in Solidarity with Puerto Rican Independence, 1979.

Conway, Marshall Eddie. *Marshall Law: The Life and Times of a Baltimore Black Panther.* Oakland, Calif.: AK Press, 2011.

Cornell, Andrew Ryan. *Oppose and Propose: Lessons from the Movement for a New Society.* Oakland, Calif.: AK Press, 2010.

Countryman, Matthew J. *Up South: Civil Rights and Black Power in Philadelphia.* Philadelphia: University of Pennsylvania Press, 2006.

Cowie, Jefferson. *Stayin' Alive: The 1970s and the Last Days of the Working Class.* New York: New Press, 2010.

CR10 Publications Collective. *Abolition Now!: Ten Years of Strategy and Struggle against the Prison Industrial Complex.* Oakland, Calif.: AK, 2008.

Crespino, Joseph. *In Search of Another Country: Mississippi and the Conservative Counterrevolution.* Princeton: Princeton University Press, 2007.

Crozier, Michel, Samuel P. Huntington, and Joji Watanuki. *The Crisis of Democracy.* New York: New York University Press, 1975.

Cruse, Harold. *The Crisis of the Negro Intellectual.* New York: New York Review of Books, 1967.

———. *Rebellion or Revolution?* New York: Morrow, 1968.

Cummins, Eric. *The Rise and Fall of California's Radical Prison Movement.* Stanford: Stanford University Press, 1994.

Cunnigen, Donald. "The Republic of New Africa in Mississippi." In Judson L. Jeffries, ed., *Black Power in the Belly of the Beast* (93–115). Urbana: University of Illinois Press, 2006.

Cunningham, David. *There's Something Happening Here: The New Left, the Klan, and FBI Counterintelligence.* Berkeley: University of California Press, 2004.

Curtin, Mary Ellen. *Black Prisoners and Their World, Alabama, 1865–1900.* Charlottesville: University Press of Virginia, 2000.

Curtis, Edward E., IV. "African-American Islamization Reconsidered: Black History Narratives and Muslim Identity." *Journal of the American Academy of Religion* 73:3 (2005): 659–84.

———. *Islam in Black America: Identity, Liberation, and Difference in African-American Islamic Thought.* Albany: State University of New York Press, 2002.

Cusset, François. *French Theory: How Foucault, Derrida, Deleuze, & Co. Transformed the Intellectual Life of the United States.* Minneapolis: University of Minnesota Press, 2008.

D'Arcus, Bruce. *Boundaries of Dissent: Protest and State Power in the Media Age.* New York: Routledge, 2006.

———. "Protest, Scale, and Publicity: The FBI and the H. Rap Brown Act." *Antipode* 35:4 (2003): 718–41.

Davidson, R. Theodore. *Chicano Prisoners: The Key to San Quentin*. New York: Holt, Rinehart, and Winston, 1974.

Davis, Angela Y. *The Angela Y. Davis Reader*. Ed. Joy James. Malden, Mass.: Blackwell, 1998.

———. *Are Prisons Obsolete?* New York: Seven Stories, 2003.

———. *An Autobiography*. New York: International, 1988 (1974).

Davis, Angela Y., et al. *If They Come in the Morning: Voices of Resistance*. New York: Signet, 1971.

Davis, Mike. *City of Quartz: Excavating the Future in Los Angeles*. London: Verso, 2006 (1990).

Dayan, Colin. *The Law Is a White Dog: How Legal Rituals Make and Unmake Persons*. Princeton: Princeton University Press, 2011.

———. *The Story of Cruel and Unusual*. Boston: MIT Press, 2007.

Debord, Guy. *Society of the Spectacle*. London: Rebel, 2006.

Debray, Régis. *Revolution in the Revolution?* New York: Grove, 1967.

Dellinger, David. *From Yale to Jail: The Life Story of a Moral Dissenter*. Marion, S.D.: Rose Hill, 1993.

Derrida, Jacques. *Negotiations: Interventions and Interviews, 1971–2001*. Ed. and trans. Elizabeth Rottenberg. Stanford: Stanford University Press, 2002.

Deutsch, Michael E. "The Improper Use of the Federal Grand Jury: An Instrument for the Internment of Political Activists." *Journal of Criminal Law and Criminology* 75:4 (1984): 1159–96.

Diamond, Andrew J. *Mean Streets: Chicago Youths and the Everyday Struggle for Empowerment in the Multiracial City, 1908–1969*. Berkeley: University of California Press, 2009.

Diawara, Manthia. *In Search of Africa*. Cambridge: Harvard University Press, 1998.

Díaz-Cotto, Juanita. *Gender, Ethnicity, and the State: Latina and Latino Prison Politics*. Albany: State University of New York Press, 1996.

Dittmer, John. *Local People: The Struggle for Civil Rights in Mississippi*. Urbana: University of Illinois Press, 1994.

Dixon, Chris. *Another Politics: Talking across Today's Transformative Movements*. Berkeley: University of California Press, 2014.

———. "Building Another Politics: The Contemporary Anti-Authoritarian Current in the U.S. and Canada." *Anarchist Studies* 20:1 (2012): 32–60.

Dodge, C. R., ed. *A Nation without Prisons: Alternatives to Incarceration*. Lexington, Mass.: Lexington Books, 1975.

Dohrn, Bernardine, Bill Ayers, Jeff Jones, and the Weather Underground. *Sing a Battle Song: The Revolutionary Poetry, Statements, and Communiqués of the Weather Underground, 1970–1974*. New York: Seven Stories, 2006.

Donner, Frank. *Protectors of Privilege: Red Squads and Political Repression in Urban America*. Berkeley: University of California Press, 1991.

Douglass, Frederick. *Narrative of the Life of Frederick Douglass*. Ed. Angela Y. Davis. San Francisco: City Lights, 2010.

Dubber, Markus Dirk. *The Police Power: Patriarchy and the Foundations of American Government*. New York: Columbia University Press, 2005.

Du Bois, W. E. B. *Black Reconstruction in America*. New York: Harcourt, Brace, 1935.

———. *The Souls of Black Folk*. New York: Dover, 1994 (1903).

Duggan, Lisa. *The Twilight of Equality?: Neoliberalism, Cultural Politics, and the Attack on Democracy*. Boston: Beacon, 2004.

Dulaney, W. Marvin. *Black Police in America*. Bloomington: Indiana University Press, 1996.

Dunn, Stephane. *"Baad Bitches" and Sassy Supermamas: Black Power Action Films*. Urbana: University of Illinois Press, 2008.

Durden-Smith, Jo. *Who Killed George Jackson?: Fantasies, Paranoia, and the Revolution*. New York: Knopf, 1976.

Dylan, Bob. *Lyrics, 1962–2001*. London: Simon and Schuster, 2004.

Edelman, Murray. *Constructing the Political Spectacle*. Chicago: University of Chicago Press, 1988.

———. *The Symbolic Uses of Politics*. Urbana: University of Illinois Press, 1985.

Edy, Jill A. *Troubled Pasts: News and the Collective Memory of Social Unrest*. Philadelphia: Temple University Press, 2006.

Elbaum, Max. *Revolution in the Air: Sixties Radicals Turn to Lenin, Mao, and Che*. New York: Verso, 2002.

Ellison, Ralph. *Invisible Man*. New York: Vintage International, 1995 (1952).

English, T. J. *Savage City: Race, Murder, and a Generation on the Edge*. New York: Morrow, 2011.

Escobar, Edward. "The Dialectics of Repression: The Los Angeles Police Department and the Chicano Movement, 1968–1971." *Journal of American History* 79:4 (1993): 1483–1514.

Espiritu, Nicholas. "(E)Racing Youth: The Racialized Construction of California's Proposition 21 and the Development of Alternate Contestations." *Cleveland State Law Review* 52:1 (2004): 189–209.

Essien-Udom, E. U. *Black Nationalism: A Search for an Identity in America*. Chicago: University of Chicago Press, 1962.

Etheridge, Eric. *Breach of Peace: Portraits of the 1961 Mississippi Freedom Riders*. New York: Atlas, 2008.

Evanzz, Karl. *The Messenger: The Rise and Fall of Elijah Muhammad*. New York: Pantheon, 2001.

Eyerman, Ron, and Andrew Jamison. *Social Movements: A Cognitive Approach*. University Park: Pennsylvania State University Press, 1991.

Fanon, Frantz. *The Wretched of the Earth*. New York: Grove, 1966.

Farmer, James. *Lay Bare the Heart: An Autobiography of the Civil Rights Movement*. New York: Arbor House, 1985.

Favor, J. Martin. *Authentic Blackness: The Folk in the New Negro Renaissance*. Durham: Duke University Press, 1999.

Federici, Silvia. *Revolution at Point Zero: Housework, Reproduction, and Feminist Struggle*. Oakland, Calif.: PM Press, 2012.

Feldman, Allen. *Formations of Violence: The Narrative of the Body and Political Terror in Northern Ireland*. Chicago: University of Chicago Press, 1991.

———. "Political Terror and the Technologies of Memory: Excuse, Sacrifice, Commodification, and Actuarial Moralities." *Radical History Review* 85 (Winter 2003): 58–73.

———. "Violence and Vision: The Prosthetics and Aesthetics of Terror." *Public Culture* 10:1 (1997): 24–60.

Feldstein, Ruth. *How It Feels to Be Free: Black Women Entertainers and the Civil Rights Movement*. New York: Oxford University Press, 2013.

Fergus, Devin. *Liberalism, Black Power, and the Making of American Politics, 1965–1980*. Athens: University of Georgia Press, 2009.

Ferguson, Roderick A. *Aberrations in Black: Toward a Queer of Color Critique*. Minneapolis: University of Minnesota Press, 2003.

Fernandez, Ronald L. *Los Macheteros: The Wells Fargo Robbery and the Violent Struggle for Puerto Rican Independence*. New York: Prentice Hall, 1987.

———. *Prisoners of Colonialism: The Struggle for Justice in Puerto Rico*. Monroe, Maine: Common Courage, 1994.

Fields, A. Belden. *Trotskyism and Maoism: Theory and Practice in France and the United States*. New York: Autonomedia, 1988.

Flamm, Michael W. *Law and Order: Street Crime, Civil Unrest, and the Crisis of Liberalism in the 1960s*. New York: Columbia University Press, 2005.

Flamming, Douglas. *Bound for Freedom: Black Los Angeles in Jim Crow America*. Berkeley: University of California Press, 2005.

Fleming, Cynthia Griggs. *Soon We Will Not Cry: The Liberation of Ruby Doris Smith Robinson*. Lanham, Md.: Rowman and Littlefield, 2000.

Foley, Michael S. *Confronting the War Machine: Draft Resistance during the Vietnam War*. Chapel Hill: University of North Carolina Press, 2003.

———. *Front Porch Politics: The Forgotten Heyday of American Activism in the 1970s and 1980s*. New York: Hill and Wang, 2013.

Foner, Philip S., ed. *The Black Panthers Speak*. New York: Da Capo, 2002 (1970).

Forman, James. *The Making of Black Revolutionaries*. Seattle: University of Washington Press, 1997 (1972).

Forman, Murray, and Mark Anthony Neal, eds. *That's the Joint!: Hip Hop Studies Reader*. 2nd ed. New York: Routledge, 2012.

Fortner, Michael Javen. "The Carceral State and the Crucible of Black Politics: An Urban History of the Rockefeller Drug Laws." *Studies in American Political Development* 27:1 (2013): 14–35.

Foucault, Michel. "Alternatives to the Prison: Dissemination or Decline of Social Control?" *Theory, Culture, and Society* 26:6 (2009): 12–24.

———. *Discipline and Punish: The Birth of the Prison*. New York: Vintage, 1995 (1977).

———. "Intellectuals and Power: A Conversation between Michel Foucault and Gilles Deleuze." In Donald F. Bouchard, ed., *Language, Counter-Memory, Practice: Selected Essays and Interviews by Michel Foucault* (205–17). Ithaca: Cornell University Press, 1977.

———. "Michel Foucault on Attica: An Interview." *Telos* 19 (Spring 1974): 154–61.

———. *Power/Knowledge: Selected Interviews and Other Writings, 1972–1977*. Ed. Colin Gordon. New York: Pantheon, 1980.

———. *Security, Territory, Population: Lectures at the College de France, 1977–1978*. New York: Palgrave, 2007.

———. *"Society Must Be Defended": Lectures at the College de France, 1975–1976*. New York: Picador, 2003.

Foucault, Michel, Catharine von Bülow, and Daniel Defert. "The Masked Assas- sination." In Joy James, ed., *Warfare in the American Homeland: Policing and Prison in a Penal Democracy* (140–59). Durham: Duke University Press, 2007.

Franklin, H. Bruce, ed. *Prison Writing in Twentieth-Century America*. New York: Penguin, 1998.

———. *The Victim as Criminal and Artist: Literature from the American Prison*. New York: Oxford University Press, 1978.

Frazier, Robeson Taj P. "The Congress of African People: Baraka, Brother Mao, and the Year of '74." *Souls* 8:3 (2006): 142–59.

———. "Thunder in the East: China, Exiled Crusaders, and the Unevenness of Black Internationalism." *American Quarterly* 63:4 (2011): 929–53.

Freire, Paulo. *Pedagogy of the Oppressed*. New York: Continuum, 1970.

Freund, David M. P. *Colored Property: State Policy and White Racial Politics in Suburban America*. Chicago: University of Chicago Press, 2008.

Friedland, Michael B. *Lift Up Your Voice Like a Trumpet: White Clergy and the Civil Rights and Antiwar Movements, 1954–1973*. Chapel Hill: University of North Carolina Press, 1998.

Friedman, Lawrence M. *Crime and Punishment in American History*. New York: Basic Books, 1993.

Friedman, Lester D., ed. *American Cinema in the 1970s: Themes and Variations*. New Brunswick: Rutgers University Press, 2007.

Frydl, Kathleen J. *The War on Drugs in America, 1940–1973*. New York: Cambridge University Press, 2013.

Fujino, Diane C. *Heartbeat of Struggle: The Revolutionary Life of Yuri Kochiyama*. Minneapolis: University of Minnesota Press, 2005.

Gaines, Kevin. *Uplifting the Race: Black Leadership, Politics, and Culture in the Twentieth Century*. Chapel Hill: University of North Carolina Press, 1996.

Gardell, Mattias. *In the Name of Elijah Muhammad: Louis Farrakhan and the Nation of Islam*. Durham: Duke University Press, 1996.

Garland, David. *The Culture of Control: Crime and Social Order in Contemporary Society*. Chicago: University of Chicago Press, 2001.

Garrow, David J. *Bearing the Cross: Martin Luther King, Jr., and the Southern Christian Leadership Conference*. New York: Quill, 1986.

Genet, Jean. *The Declared Enemy: Texts and Interviews*. Ed. Albert Dichy. Trans. Jeff Fort. Stanford: Stanford University Press, 2004.

———. *Prisoner of Love*. New York: New York Review of Books, 2003 (1986).

Georgakas, Dan, and Marvin Surkin. *Detroit, I Do Mind Dying: A Study in Urban Revolu- tion*. Boston: South End, 1998.

George, Lynell. *No Crystal Stair: African Americans in the City of Angels*. London: Verso, 1992.

Giddings, Paula. *When and Where I Enter: The Impact of Black Women on Race and Sex in America*. New York: Morrow, 1984.

Gilmore, Glenda Elizabeth. *Defying Dixie: The Radical Roots of Civil Rights, 1919–1950*. New York: Norton, 2008.

Gilmore, Ruth Wilson. "Fatal Couplings of Power and Difference: Notes on Racism and Geography." *Professional Geographer* 54:1 (2002): 15–24.

——. "Forgotten Places and the Seeds of Grassroots Planning." In Charles R. Hale, ed., *Engaging Contradictions: Theory, Politics, and Methods of Activist Scholarship* (31–61). Berkeley: University of California Press, 2008.

——. "Globalisation and U.S. Prison Growth: From Military Keynesianism to Post-Keynesian Militarism." *Race and Class* 40:2–3 (1998–99): 171–88.

——. *Golden Gulag: Prisons, Surplus, Crisis, and Opposition in Globalizing California*. Berkeley: University of California Press, 2007.

Gitlin, Todd. *The Whole World Is Watching: The Mass Media in the Making and Unmaking of the New Left*. Berkeley: University of California Press, 1980.

Goldberg, David Theo. *The Racial State*. Malden, Mass.: Blackwell, 2002.

——. *The Threat of Race: Reflections on Racial Neoliberalism*. Malden, Mass.: Wiley-Blackwell, 2009.

Goldstein, Alyosha. *Poverty in Common: The Politics of Community Action during the American Century*. Durham: Duke University Press, 2012.

Gómez, Alan Eladio. "'Nuestras Vidas Corren Casi Paralelas': Chicanos, Independentistas, and the Prison Rebellions in Leavenworth, 1969–1972." In Suzanne Oboler, ed., *Behind Bars: Latino/as and Prison in the United States* (67–98). New York: Palgrave Macmillan, 2009.

——. "Resisting Living Death at Marion Federal Penitentiary, 1972." *Radical History Review* 96 (Fall 2006): 58–86.

Goodell, Charles. *Political Prisoners in America*. New York: Random House, 1973.

Gordon, Avery. "Methodologies of Imprisonment." *PMLA* 123:3 (2008): 651–57.

Gore, Dayo F. *Radicalism at the Crossroads: African American Women Activists in the Cold War*. New York: New York University Press, 2011.

Gore, Dayo F., Jeanne Theoharis, and Komozi Woodard, eds. *Want to Start a Revolution?: Radical Women in the Black Freedom Struggle*. New York: New York University Press, 2009.

Gottschalk, Marie. *The Prison and the Gallows: The Politics of Mass Incarceration in America*. Cambridge: Cambridge University Press, 2006.

Gould, Deborah. *Moving Politics: Emotion and ACT UP's Fight against AIDS*. Chicago: University of Chicago Press, 2008.

Grady-Willis, Winston A. *Challenging U.S. Apartheid: Atlanta and Black Struggles for Human Rights, 1960–1977*. Durham: Duke University Press, 2006.

Graham, Stephen. *Cities under Siege: The New Military Urbanism*. London: Verso, 2010.

Grant, Colin. *Negro with a Hat: The Rise and Fall of Marcus Garvey*. Oxford: Oxford University Press, 2008.

Green, James. *Death in the Haymarket*. New York: Pantheon, 2006.

Green, Laurie B. *Battling the Plantation Mentality: Memphis and the Black Freedom Struggle*. Chapel Hill: University of North Carolina Press, 2007.

Greenberg, David F., and Fay Stender. "The Prison as a Lawless Agency." *Buffalo Law Review* 21:3 (1971–72): 799–838.

Gregory, James N. *The Southern Diaspora: How the Great Migrations of Black and White Transformed America*. Chapel Hill: University of North Carolina Press, 2005.

Griswold, H. Jack, Edward Tromanhauser, Art Powers, and Mike Misenheimer. *An Eye for an Eye: Four Inmates on the Crime of American Prisons Today*. Holt, Rinehart, and Winston, 1970.

Gross, Ariela J. *What Blood Won't Tell: A History of Race on Trial in America*. Cambridge: Harvard University Press, 2008.

Gross, Kali. *Colored Amazons: Crime, Violence, and Black Women in the City of Brotherly Love*. Durham: Duke University Press, 2006.

Guevara, Che. *Che Guevara Speaks: Selected Speeches and Writings*. Ed. George Lavan. New York: Pathfinder, 1987 (1967).

Haas, Jeffrey. *The Assassination of Fred Hampton: How the FBI and Chicago Police Murdered a Black Panther*. Chicago: Hill, 2010.

Hadden, Sally. *Slave Patrols: Law and Violence in Virginia and the Carolinas*. Cambridge: Harvard University Press, 2001.

Hagedorn, John M., ed., *Gangs in the Global City: Alternatives to Traditional Criminology*. Urbana: University of Illinois Press, 2007.

Hahn, Steven. *A Nation under Our Feet: Black Political Struggles in the Rural South from Slavery to the Great Migration*. Cambridge: Belknap Press of Harvard University Press, 2003.

———. *The Political Worlds of Slavery and Freedom*. Cambridge: Harvard University Press, 2009.

Halberstam, David. *The Children*. New York: Random House, 1998.

Haldeman, H. R. *The Haldeman Diaries: Inside the Nixon White House*. New York: Putnam's, 1994.

Hale, Grace Elizabeth. *A Nation of Outsiders: How the White Middle Class Fell in Love with Rebellion in Postwar America*. New York: Oxford University Press, 2011.

Haley, Alex. *Roots: The Saga of an American Family*. New York: Dell, 1976.

Haley, Sarah. "'Like I Was a Man': Chain Gangs, Gender, and the Domestic Carceral Sphere in Jim Crow." *Signs* 39:1 (2013): 53–77.

Hall, Jacquelyn Dowd. "The Long Civil Rights Movement and the Political Uses of the Past." *Journal of American History* 91:4 (2005): 1233–63.

Hall, Stuart, Chas Crichter, Tony Jefferson, John Clarke, and Brian Roberts. *Policing the Crisis: Mugging, the State, and Law and Order*. London: Macmillan, 1978.

Halperin, Morton H., Jerry J. Berman, Robert L. Borosage, and Christine M. Marwick. *The Lawless State: The Crimes of the U.S. Intelligence Agencies*. New York: Penguin, 1976.

Hames-Garcia, Michael. *Fugitive Thought: Prison Movements, Race, and the Meaning of Justice*. Minneapolis: University of Minnesota Press, 2004.

Hamlin, Francoise N. *Crossroads at Clarksdale: The Black Freedom Struggle in the Mississippi Delta after World War II*. Chapel Hill: University of North Carolina Press, 2012.

Hamm, Theodore. *Rebel and a Cause: Caryl Chessman and the Politics of the Death Penalty in Postwar California, 1948–1974*. Berkeley: University of California Press, 2001.

Hanchard, Michael. *Party/Politics: Horizons in Black Political Thought*. Oxford: Oxford University Press, 2006.

Haney-López, Ian F. "Post-Racial Racism: Racial Stratification and Mass Incarceration in the Age of Obama." *California Law Review* 98:3 (2010): 1023–74.

———. *Racism on Trial: The Chicano Battle for Justice*. Cambridge: Belknap Press of Harvard University Press, 2003.

Harcourt, Bernard E. *The Illusion of Free Markets: Punishment and the Myth of Natural Order*. Cambridge: Harvard University Press, 2011.

Harlow, Barbara. *Barred: Women, Writing, and Political Detention*. Hanover, N.H.: University Press of New England, 1992.

Harney, Stefano, and Fred Moten. *The Undercommons: Fugitive Planning and Black Study*. Oakland, Calif.: AK, 2013.

Hartman, Saidiya V. *Lose Your Mother: A Journey along the Atlantic Slave Route*. New York: Farrar, Straus, and Giroux, 2007.

———. *Scenes of Subjection: Terror, Slavery, and Self-Making in Nineteenth-Century America*. Oxford: Oxford University Press, 1997.

Harvey, David. *A Brief History of Neoliberalism*. Oxford: Oxford University Press, 2005.

———. *The Condition of Postmodernity*. Malden, Mass.: Blackwell, 1990.

———. *The Limits to Capital*. London: Verso, 2006 (1982).

Hayden, Tom. *Reunion: A Memoir*. New York: Random House, 1988.

Hayes, John. "Man of Sorrow at Folsom." *Radical History Review* 98 (Spring 2007): 119–35.

Heard, Alex. *The Eyes of Willie McGee: A Tragedy of Race, Sex, and Secrets in the Jim Crow South*. New York: Harper Collins, 2010.

Heath, G. Louis, ed. *Off the Pigs!: The History and Literature of the Black Panther Party*. Metuchen, N.J.: Scarecrow, 1976.

Heiner, Brady Thomas. "Foucault and the Black Panthers." *City* 11:3 (2007): 313–56.

Heins, Marjorie. *Strictly Ghetto Property: The Story of Los Siete de la Raza*. San Francisco: Ramparts, 1972.

Henry, Aaron, and Constance Curry. *Aaron Henry: The Fire Ever Burning*. Jackson: University Press of Mississippi, 2000.

Hicks, Cheryl D. *Talk with You Like a Woman: African American Women, Justice, and Reform in New York, 1890–1935*. Chapel Hill: University of North Carolina Press, 2010.

Higginbotham, Evelyn Brooks. *Righteous Discontent: The Women's Movement in the Black Baptist Church, 1880–1920*. Cambridge: Harvard University Press, 1993.

Hill, Lance. *The Deacons for Defense: Armed Resistance and the Civil Rights Movement*. Chapel Hill: University of North Carolina Press, 2004.

Hill, Rebecca N. "'The Common Enemy Is the Boss and the Inmate': Police and Prison Guard Unions in New York in the 1970s–1980s." *Labor* 8:3 (2011): 65–96.

———. *Men, Mobs, and Law: Anti-Lynching and Labor Defense in U.S. Radical History*. Durham: Duke University Press, 2009.

Hilliard, David, ed. *The Black Panther: Intercommunal News Service, 1967–1980*. New York: Atria, 2007.

Hilliard, David, and Lewis Cole. *This Side of Glory: The Autobiography of David Hilliard and the Story of the Black Panther Party*. Boston: Back Bay, 1993.

Hinds, Lennox S. *Illusions of Justice: Human Rights Violations in the United States*. Iowa City: University of Iowa School of Social Work, 1978.

Hixson, Walter L. *American Settler Colonialism: A History*. New York: Palgrave Macmillan, 2013.

Hoffman, Abbie. *The Autobiography of Abbie Hoffman*. New York: Four Walls Eight Windows, 2000.

Hogan, Wesley C. *Many Minds, One Heart: SNCC's Dream for a New America*. Chapel Hill: University of North Carolina Press, 2007.

Holt, Thomas C. *The Problem of Race in the Twenty-First Century*. Cambridge: Harvard University Press, 2000.

Horne, Gerald. *Black Revolutionary: William Patterson and the Globalization of the African American Freedom Struggle*. Urbana: University of Illinois Press, 2013.

——. *Communist Front?: The Civil Rights Congress, 1946–1956*. Rutherford, N.J.: Fairleigh Dickinson University Press, 1988.

——. *Fire This Time: The Watts Uprising and the 1960s*. New York: Da Capo, 1997.

HoSang, Daniel. "Race and the Mythology of California's Lost Paradise." *Boom* 1:1 (2011): 36–49.

——. *Racial Propositions: Ballot Initiatives and the Making of Postwar California*. Berkeley: University of California Press, 2010.

Howard, Clark. *American Saturday*. New York: Marek, 1981.

Huggins, Ericka, and Angela D. LeBlanc-Ernest. "Revolutionary Women, Revolutionary Education: The Black Panther Party's Oakland Community School." In Dayo F. Gore, Jeanne Theoharis, and Komozi Woodard, eds., *Want to Start a Revolution?: Radical Women in the Black Freedom Struggle* (161–84). New York: New York University Press, 2009.

Invisible Committee. *The Coming Insurrection*. Los Angeles: Semiotexte, 2009.

The Iron Fist and the Velvet Glove: An Analysis of the U.S. Police. Berkeley: Center for Research on Criminal Justice, 1975.

Irwin, John. *The Felon*. Englewood Cliffs, N.J.: Prentice-Hall, 1970.

——. *Prisons in Turmoil*. Boston: Little, Brown, 1980.

Iton, Richard. *In Search of the Black Fantastic: Politics and Popular Culture in the Post–Civil Rights Era*. Oxford: Oxford University Press, 2008.

Jackson, Bruce. "Prison: The New Academy." *The Nation*, December 6, 1971, 584–89.

Jackson, George L. *Blood in My Eye*. Baltimore: Black Classics, 1990 (1972).

——. *Soledad Brother: The Prison Letters of George Jackson*. Chicago: Hill, 1994 (1970).

Jackson, John L., Jr. *Racial Paranoia: The Unintended Consequences of Political Correctness*. New York: Basic Books, 2008.

——. *Real Black: Adventures in Racial Sincerity*. Chicago: University of Chicago, 2005.

Jackson, Lester. "A Dialogue with My Soledad Son." *Ebony*, November 1971, 72–82.

Jackson, Sherman A. "Preliminary Reflections on Islam and Black Religion." In Zahid H. Bukhari, Sulayman S. Nyang, Mumtaz Ahmad, and John L. Esposito, eds., *Muslims' Place in the American Public Square* (201–21). Walnut Creek, Calif.: AltaMira, 2004.

Jacobs, James B. "The Prisoners' Rights Movement and Its Impacts, 1960–1980." *Crime and Justice* 2 (1980): 429–70.

——. "Race Relations and the Prisoner Subculture." *Crime and Justice* 1 (1979): 1–27.

——. *Stateville: The Penitentiary in Mass Society*. Chicago: University of Chicago Press, 1977.

Jacobson, Matthew Frye. *Roots Too: White Ethnic Revival in Post–Civil Rights America*. Cambridge: Harvard University Press, 2006.

———. *Whiteness of a Different Color: European Immigrants and the Politics of Race.* Cambridge: Harvard University Press, 1998.

James, C. L. R. *The C. L. R. James Reader.* Ed. and intro. Anna Grimshaw. Oxford: Blackwell, 1992.

James, Joy, ed. *Imprisoned Intellectuals: America's Political Prisoners Write on Life, Liberation, and Rebellion.* Lanham, Md.: Rowman and Littlefield, 2003.

———, ed. *The New Abolitionists: (Neo)Slave Narratives and Contemporary Prison Writings.* Albany: State University of New York Press, 2005.

———. *Resisting State Violence: Radicalism, Gender, and Race in U.S. Culture.* Minneapolis: University of Minnesota Press, 1996.

———, ed. *States of Confinement: Policing, Detention, and Prisons.* New York: Palgrave, 2002.

———. *Transcending the Talented Tenth: Black Leaders and American Intellectuals.* New York: Routledge, 1997.

———, ed. *Warfare in the American Homeland: Policing and Prison in a Penal Democracy.* Durham: Duke University Press, 2007.

Janssen, Volker. "From the Inside Out: Therapeutic Penology and Political Liberalism in Postwar California." *Osiris* 22:1 (2007): 116–34.

———. "When the 'Jungle' Met the Forest: Public Work, Civil Defense, and Prison Camps in Postwar California." *Journal of American History* 96:3 (2009): 702–26.

Jeffries, Hasan Kwame. *Bloody Lowndes: Civil Rights and Black Power in Alabama's Black Belt.* New York: New York University Press, 2009.

Jeffries, Judson L., ed. *Black Power in the Belly of the Beast.* Urbana: University of Illinois Press, 2006.

———. *Comrades: A Local History of the Black Panther Party.* Bloomington: Indiana University Press, 2007.

Jeffries, Judson L., and Malcolm Foley. "To Live and Die in L.A." In Judson L. Jeffries, ed., *Comrades: A Local History of the Black Panther Party* (255–90). Bloomington: Indiana University Press, 2007.

ji Jaga, Geronimo. "Every Nation Struggling to Be Free Has a Right to Struggle, a Duty to Struggle." In Kathleen Cleaver and George Katsiaficas, eds., *Liberation, Imagination, and the Black Panther Party: A New Look at the Panthers and Their Legacy* (71–77). New York: Routledge, 2001.

Johnson, Cedric. *Revolutionaries to Race Leaders: Black Power and the Making of African American Politics.* Minneapolis: University of Minnesota Press, 2007.

Johnson, Gaye Theresa. *Spaces of Conflict, Sounds of Solidarity: Music, Race, and Spatial Entitlement in Los Angeles.* Berkeley: University of California Press, 2013.

Johnson, Kevin Rashid. *Defying the Tomb: Selected Prison Writings and Art.* Montreal: Kersplebedeb, 2010.

Johnson, Troy R. *The American Indian Occupation of Alcatraz Island: Red Power and Self-Determination.* Urbana: University of Illinois Press, 1996.

Johnson, Walter. *River of Dark Dreams: Slavery and Empire in the Cotton Kingdom.* Cambridge: Belknap Press of Harvard University Press, 2013.

———. *Soul by Soul: Life inside the Antebellum Slave Market.* Cambridge: Harvard University Press, 1999.

Johnston, Norman. *Forms of Constraint: A History of Prison Architecture*. Urbana: University of Illinois Press, 2000.

Jones, Charles E., ed. *The Black Panther Party Reconsidered*. Baltimore: Black Classics, 1998.

Jones, Howard. *Mutiny on the Amistad*. Oxford: Oxford University Press, 1997.

Jordan, Samuel. "Prison Reform: In Whose Interest?" *Criminal Law Bulletin* 7:9 (1971): 779–87.

Joseph, Peniel E. *Waiting 'til the Midnight Hour: A Narrative History of Black Power in America*. New York: Holt, 2006.

Kaplan, Alice. *Dreaming in French: The Paris Years of Jacqueline Bouvier Kennedy, Susan Sontag, and Angela Davis*. Chicago: University of Chicago Press, 2012.

Kapur, Sudarshan. *Raising Up a Prophet: The African American Encounter with Gandhi*. Boston: Beacon, 1992.

Katsiaficas, George. *The Imagination of the New Left: A Global Analysis of 1968*. Boston: South End, 1987.

Katz, Michael B., ed. *The Underclass Debate: Views from History*. Princeton: Princeton University Press, 1992.

———. *The Undeserving Poor: America's Enduring Confrontation with Poverty*. New York: Oxford University Press, 2013.

———. *Why Don't American Cities Burn?* Philadelphia: University of Pennsylvania Press, 2012.

Katznelson, Ira. *Fear Itself: The New Deal and the Origins of Our Time*. New York: Norton, 2013.

Kaufman, Burton I., and Scott Kaufman. *The Presidency of James Earl Carter*. Lawrence: University Press of Kansas, 2006.

Kelley, Robin D. G. *Freedom Dreams: The Black Radical Imagination*. Boston: Beacon, 2002.

———. *Hammer and Hoe: Alabama Communists during the Great Depression*. Chapel Hill: University of North Carolina Press, 1990.

———. *Race Rebels: Culture, Politics, and the Black Working Class*. New York: Free Press, 1994.

———. "Stormy Weather: Reconstructing Black (Inter)Nationalism in the Cold War Era." In Eddie S. Glaude Jr., ed., *Is It Nation Time?: Contemporary Essays on Black Power and Black Nationalism* (67–90). Chicago: University of Chicago Press, 2001.

Kelley, Robin D. G., and Betsy Esch. "Black Like Mao: Red China and Black Revolution." In Fred Ho and Bill V. Mullen, eds., *Afro-Asia: Revolutionary Political and Cultural Connections between African Americans and Asian Americans* (97–154). Durham: Duke University Press, 2008.

Keve, Paul W. *The McNeil Century: The Life and Times of an Island Prison*. Chicago: Burnham, 1994.

Khalili, Laleh. *Heroes and Martyrs of Palestine: The Politics of National Commemoration*. Cambridge: Cambridge University Press, 2007.

———. *Time in the Shadows: Confinement in Counterinsurgencies*. Stanford: Stanford University Press, 2012.

King, Martin Luther, Jr. *Why We Can't Wait*. New York: New American Library, 2000 (1964).

Kitwana, Bakari. *Why White Kids Love Hip Hop: Wiggers, Wannabes, and the New Reality of Race in America*. New York: Basic Books, 2005.

Klarman, Michael. *From Jim Crow to Civil Rights: The Supreme Court and the Struggle for Racial Equality*. New York: Oxford University Press, 2004.

Klimke, Martin. *The Other Alliance: Student Protest in West Germany and the United States in the Global Sixties*. Princeton: Princeton University Press, 2010.

Knabb, Ken, ed. *Situationist International Anthology*. Berkeley, Calif.: Bureau of Public Secrets, 2006.

Knight, Etheridge, and Other Inmates of Indiana State Prison. *Black Voices from Prison*. New York: Pathfinder, 1970.

Knopp, Fay, and Jon Reigier. *Instead of Prisons: A Handbook for Abolitionists*. Syracuse: Prison Research Education and Action Project, 1976.

Kornbluh, Felicia. *The Battle for Welfare Rights: Politics and Poverty in Modern America*. Philadelphia: University of Pennsylvania Press, 2007.

Kornfeld, Phyllis. *Cellblock Visions: Prison Art in America*. Princeton: Princeton University Press, 1997.

Kosek, Joseph Kip. *Acts of Conscience: Christian Nonviolence and Modern American Democracy*. New York: Columbia University Press, 2009.

Kramer, Michael S., and Sam Roberts. *"I Never Wanted to Be Vice-President of Anything": An Investigative Biography of Nelson Rockefeller*. New York: Basic Books, 1976.

Kruse, Kevin. *White Flight: Atlanta and the Making of Modern Conservatism*. Princeton: Princeton University Press, 2005.

Kunzel, Regina. *Criminal Intimacy: Prison and the Uneven History of Modern American Sexuality*. Chicago: University of Chicago Press, 2008.

———. "Lessons in Being Gay: Queer Encounters in Gay and Lesbian Prison Activism." *Radical History Review* 100 (Winter 2008): 11–37.

Lake, Tim. "The Arm(ing) of the Vanguard, Signify(ing), and Performing the Revolution: The Black Panther Party and Pedagogical Strategies for Interpreting a Revolutionary Life." In Jama Lazerow and Yohuru Williams, eds., *In Search of the Black Panther Party: New Perspectives on a Revolutionary Movement* (306–23). Durham: Duke University Press, 2006.

Laroche, Hadrien. *The Last Genet: A Writer in Revolt*. Vancouver: Arsenal Pulp, 2010.

Lasch, Christopher. *The Culture of Narcissism: American Life in an Age of Diminishing Expectations*. New York: Norton, 1979.

Laslett, John H. M. *Sunshine Was Never Enough: Los Angeles Workers, 1880–2010*. Berkeley: University of California Press, 2012.

Lassiter, Matthew D. *The Silent Majority: Suburban Politics in the Sunbelt South*. Princeton: Princeton University Press, 2006.

Law, Victoria. "Sick of the Abuse: Feminist Responses to Sexual Assault, Battering, and Self-Defense." In Dan Berger, ed., *The Hidden 1970s: Histories of Radicalism* (39–56). New Brunswick: Rutgers University Press, 2010.

———. *Resistance behind Bars: The Struggles of Incarcerated Women*. Oakland, Calif.: PM, 2012.

Lazerow, Jama, and Yohuru Williams, eds. *In Search of the Black Panther Party: New Perspectives on a Revolutionary Movement*. Durham: Duke University Press, 2006.

LeBlanc-Ernest, Angela D. "'The Most Qualified Person to Handle the Job': Black Panther Party Women, 1966–1982." In Charles E. Jones, ed., *The Black Panther Party Reconsidered* (305–35). Baltimore: Black Classics, 1998.

Lee, Chana Kai. *For Freedom's Sake: The Life of Fannie Lou Hamer*. Urbana: University of Illinois Press, 1999.

Leinwand, Gerald, ed. *Prisons*. New York: Pocket, 1972.

Lenin, Vladimir I. *Nationalism*. Chippendale, Australia: Resistance, 2002.

Lewis, David L. *King: A Biography*. 2nd ed. Urbana: University of Illinois Press, 1978.

Lewis, John, with Michael D'Orso. *Walking with the Wind: A Memoir of the Movement*. New York: Simon and Schuster, 1998.

Liberatore, Paul. *The Road to Hell: The True Story of George Jackson, Stephen Bingham, and the San Quentin Massacre*. New York: Atlantic Monthly Press, 1996.

Lichtenstein, Alex. *Twice the Work of Free Labor: The Political Economy of Convict Labor in the New South*. London: Verso, 1996.

Lockwood, Lee. *Conversation with Eldridge Cleaver*. New York: Dell, 1970.

Lomax, Alan. *The Land Where the Blues Began*. New York: New Press, 2002.

Losier, Toussaint. ". . . 'For Strictly Religious Reason[s]': Cooper v. Pate and the Origins of the Prisoners' Rights Movement." *Souls* 15:1–2 (2013): 19–38.

Lubiano, Wahneema. "Black Ladies, Welfare Queens, and State Minstrels: Ideological War by Narrative Means." In Toni Morrison, ed., *Race-ing Justice, En-gender-ing Power: Essays on Anita Hill, Clarence Thomas, and the Construction of Social Reality* (323–63). New York: Pantheon, 1992.

———. "Black Nationalism and Black Common Sense: Policing Ourselves and Others." In Wahneema Lubiano, ed., *The House That Race Built* (232–52). New York: Vintage, 1998.

Lumumba, Chokwe. *The Pontiac Case and the Black Liberation Struggle*. Chicago: John Brown Anti-Klan Committee, 1981.

———. *The Roots of the New Afrikan Independence Movement*. Jackson, Miss.: New Afrikan, 1991.

Lydersen, Kari. "The Pontiac Brothers." N.d. http://www.karilydersen.com/index .php?module=pagemaster&PAGE_user_op=view_page&PAGE_id=21.

MacLean, Nancy. *Freedom Is Not Enough: The Opening of the American Workplace*. Cambridge: Harvard University Press, 2006.

Major, Reginald. *Justice in the Round: The Trial of Angela Davis*. New York: Third Press, 1973.

———. *A Panther Is a Black Cat*. Baltimore: Black Classics, 2006 (1971).

Malcolm X. *The Autobiography of Malcolm X (As Told to Alex Haley)*. New York: Ballantine, 1965.

———. *The End of White World Supremacy: Four Speeches*. New York: Arcade, 1989.

———. *Malcolm X: The Last Speeches*. Ed. Bruce Perry. New York: Pathfinder, 1989.

Mamdani, Mahmood. *Good Muslim, Bad Muslim: America, the Cold War, and the Roots of Terror*. New York: Pantheon, 2005.

Mancini, Matthew. *One Dies, Get Another: Convict Leasing in the American South, 1866–1928*. Columbia: University of South Carolina Press, 1996.

Manis, Andrew M. *A Fire You Can't Put Out: The Civil Rights Life of Birmingham's Reverend Fred Shuttlesworth*. Tuscaloosa: University of Alabama Press, 2001.

Mann, Eric. *Comrade George: An Investigation into the Life, Political Thought, and Assassination of George Jackson*. New York: Perennial, 1974.

Mantler, Gordon K. *Power to the Poor: Black-Brown Coalition and the Fight for Economic Justice, 1960–1974*. Chapel Hill: University of North Carolina Press, 2013.

Marable, Manning. *Malcolm X: A Life of Reinvention*. New York: Viking, 2011.

Marable, Manning, and Garrett Felber, eds. *The Portable Malcolm X Reader*. New York: Penguin, 2013.

Massey, Douglas S., and Nancy A. Denton. *American Apartheid: Segregation and the Making of the Underclass*. Cambridge: Harvard University Press, 1993.

Mathiesen, Thomas. *The Politics of Abolition*. New York: Wiley, 1974.

Matlin, Daniel T. *On the Corner: African American Intellectuals and the Urban Crisis*. Cambridge: Harvard University Press, 2013.

Matthews, Tracye. "'No One Ever Asks What a Man's Role in the Revolution Is': Gender and the Politics of the Black Panther Party, 1966–1971." In Charles E. Jones, ed., *The Black Panther Party Reconsidered* (267–304). Baltimore: Black Classics, 1998.

McCartin, Joseph A. *Collision Course: Ronald Reagan, the Air Traffic Controllers, and the Strike That Changed America*. New York: Oxford University Press, 2011.

McCloud, Aminah B. *African American Islam*. New York: Routledge, 1995.

McDuffie, Erik S. "'I Wanted a Communist Philosophy, but I Wanted Us to Have a Chance to Organize Our People': The Diasporic Radicalism of Queen Mother Audley Moore and the Origins of Black Power." *African and Black Diaspora* 3:2 (2010): 181–95.

———. *Sojourning for Freedom: Black Women, American Communism, and the Making of Black Left Feminism*. Durham: Duke University Press, 2011.

McGirr, Lisa. *Suburban Warriors: The Origins of the New American Right*. Princeton: Princeton University Press, 2001.

McGraw, Peggy, and William McGraw, *Assignment: Prison Riots*. New York: Holt, 1954.

McGuire, Danielle L. *At the Dark End of the Street*. New York: Knopf, 2010.

McKay, Claude. *Harlem Shadows*. New York: Harcourt, Brace, 1922.

McLennan, Rebecca M. *The Crisis of Imprisonment: Protest, Politics, and the Making of the American Penal State, 1776–1941*. Cambridge: Cambridge University Press, 2008.

McMillian, John C. *Smoking Typewriters: The Sixties Underground Press and the Rise of Alternative Media in America*. New York: Oxford University Press, 2011.

McWhorter, Diane. *Carry Me Home: Birmingham, Alabama, the Climactic Battle of the Civil Rights Revolution*. New York: Simon and Schuster, 2001.

Melamed, Jodi. *Represent and Destroy: Rationalizing Violence in the New Racial Capitalism*. Minneapolis: University of Minnesota Press, 2011.

Melendez, Miguel. *We Took the Streets: Fighting for Latino Rights with the Young Lords*. New York: St. Martin's, 2003.

Melville, Sam. *Letters from Attica*. New York: Morrow, 1972.

Meyer, Matt, ed. *Let Freedom Ring: A Collection of Documents from the Movements to Free U.S. Political Prisoners*. Montreal: Kersplebedeb; Oakland, Calif.: PM, 2008.

Mies, Maria. *Patriarchy and Accumulation on a World Scale: Women in the International Division of Labour*. London: Zed, 1986.

Mills, Kay. *This Little Light of Mine: The Life Story of Fannie Lou Hamer.* New York: Plume, 1993.

Mitford, Jessica. *Fine Old Conflict.* New York: Vintage, 1978.

——. *Kind and Usual Punishment: The Prison Business.* New York: Knopf, 1973.

——. *Poison Penmanship: The Gentle Art of Muckraking.* New York: Knopf, 1979.

Moore, Joan W., and Robert Garcia. *Homeboys: Gangs, Drugs, and Prison in the Barrios of Los Angeles.* Philadelphia: Temple University Press, 1978.

Moore, Rebecca, Anthony B. Pinn, and Mary R. Sawyer. *Peoples Temple and Black Religion in America.* Bloomington: Indiana University Press, 2004.

Moraga, Cherríe, and Gloria Anzaldúa, eds. *This Bridge Called My Back: Writings by Radical Women of Color.* 2nd ed. New York: Kitchen Table, 1983.

Morgan, Edmund. *American Slavery, American Freedom.* New York: Norton, 2003 (1975).

Morgan, Edward P. "Media Culture and the Public Memory of the Black Panther Party." In Jama Lazerow and Yohuru Williams, eds., *In Search of the Black Panther Party: New Perspectives on a Revolutionary Movement* (324–73). Durham: Duke University Press, 2006.

Morley, David, and Kuan-Hsing Chen, eds. *Stuart Hall: Critical Dialogues in Cultural Studies.* London: Routledge, 1996.

Morris, Aldon. *The Origins of the Civil Rights Movement: Black Communities Organizing for Change.* New York: Free Press, 1986.

Moten, Fred. "The Case of Blackness." *Criticism* 50:2 (2008): 177–218.

——. *In the Break: The Aesthetics of the Black Radical Tradition.* Minneapolis: University of Minnesota Press, 2003.

——. "Uplift and Criminality." In Susan Gillman and Alys Eve Weibaum, eds., *Next to the Color Line: Gender, Sexuality, and W. E. B. Du Bois* (317–49). Minneapolis: University of Minnesota Press, 2007.

Muhammad, Khalil Gibran. *The Condemnation of Blackness: Race, Crime, and the Making of Modern Urban America.* Cambridge: Harvard University Press, 2009.

Mullins, Lisa. *Diane Nash: The Fire of the Civil Rights Movement.* Miami: Barnhardt and Ashe, 2007.

Mumford, Kevin. *Newark: A History of Race, Rights, and Riots in America.* New York: New York University Press, 2008.

Muntaqim, Jalil. *On the BLA.* Paterson, N.J.: Anarchist Black Cross Federation, 1997 (1979).

——. "A Political Prisoner's Journey in the U.S. Prison System." 2005. http://www.freejalil.com/life.html.

——. *We Are Our Own Liberators.* Montreal: Guillen, Arm the Spirit, and Anarchist Black Cross Federation, 2002.

Murakawa, Naomi. "The Origins of the Carceral Crisis: Racial Order as 'Law and Order' in Postwar American Politics." In Joseph Lowndes, Julie Novkov, and Dorian T. Warren, eds., *Race and American Political Development* (234–55). New York: Routledge, 2008.

Murch, Donna. "The Campus and the Street: Race, Migration, and the Origins of the Black Panther Party in Oakland, Calif." *Souls* 9:4 (2007): 333–45.

————. *Living for the City: Migration, Education, and the Rise of the Black Panther Party in Oakland, California.* Chapel Hill: University of North Carolina Press, 2010.

Murton, Tom, and Joe Hyams. *Accomplices to the Crime: The Arkansas Prison Scandal.* New York: Grove, 1969.

Nadasen, Premilla. *Welfare Warriors: The Welfare Rights Movement in the United States.* New York: Routledge, 2004.

Naison, Mark. *Communists in Harlem during the Great Depression.* Urbana: University of Illinois Press, 2005.

National Committee to Free Puerto Rican Prisoners of War. *Can't Jail the Spirit: Political Prisoners in the U.S.: A Collection of Biographies.* 4th ed. Chicago: Committee to End the Marion Lockdown, 1998.

National Research Council. *The Growth of Incarceration in the United States: Exploring Causes and Consequences.* Washington, D.C.: National Academies Press, 2014.

Nelson, Alondra. *Body and Soul: The Black Panther Party and the Fight against Medical Discrimination.* Minneapolis: University of Minnesota Press, 2011.

Network of Black Organizers. *Black Prison Movements USA.* Trenton: Africa World, 1995.

Newton, Huey P. "The Black Panthers." *Ebony,* August 1969, 106–12.

————. *The Genius of Huey P. Newton.* Intro. Eldridge Cleaver. San Francisco: Black Panther Ministry of Information, 1970.

————. *To Die for the People.* New York: Writers and Readers, 1999 (1972).

————. *Revolutionary Suicide.* New York: Harcourt, Brace, Jovanovich, 1973.

Nguyen, Mimi Thi. *The Gift of Freedom: War, Debt, and Other Refugee Passages.* Durham: Duke University Press, 2012.

Norfolk Prison Brothers. *Who Took the Weight?: Black Voices from Norfolk Prison.* Boston: Little, Brown, 1972.

Nyangoni, Betty W. *Angela Davis: A Resource Curriculum Guide on Angela Davis and Other Victims of Political Repression.* Washington, D.C.: Social Science Department at Howard University, 1972.

Obadele, Imari. *Foundations of the Black Nation.* Detroit: House of Songhay, 1975.

————. *Free the Land!* Washington, D.C.: House of Songhay, 1984.

————. *War in America: The Malcolm X Doctrine.* Chicago: Ujamaa, 1977 (1968).

O'Dell, Jack. *Climbin' Jacob's Ladder: The Black Freedom Movement Writings of Jack O'Dell.* Ed. and intro. Nikhil Pal Singh. Berkeley: University of California Press, 2010.

O'Donovan, Susan Eva. "Universities of Social and Political Change: Slaves in Jail in Antebellum America." In Michele Lise Tartar and Richard Bell, eds., *Buried Lives: Incarcerated in Early America* (124–46). Athens: University of Georgia Press, 2012.

Ogbar, Jeffrey O. G. *Black Power: Radical Politics and African American Identity.* Baltimore: Johns Hopkins University Press, 2004.

Olson, Joel. *The Abolition of White Democracy.* Minneapolis: University of Minnesota Press, 2004.

Omi, Michael, and Howard Winant. *Racial Formation in the United States: From the 1960s to the 1980s.* New York: Routledge, 1986.

————. "Racial Formation Rules: Continuity, Instability, and Change." In Daniel Martinez HoSang, Oneka LaBennett, and Laura Pulido, eds., *Racial Formation in the Twenty-First Century* (302–30). New York: Routledge, 2012.

Oppenheimer, Martin, Martin J. Murray, and Rhonda F. Levine, eds. *Radical Sociologists and the Movement: Experiences, Lessons, and Legacies.* Philadelphia: Temple University Press, 1991.

Oshinsky, David M. *Worse Than Slavery: Parchman Farm and the Ordeal of Jim Crow Justice.* New York: Free Press, 1997.

Osman, Suleiman. *The Making of Brownstone Brooklyn: Gentrification and the Search for Authenticity in Postwar New York City.* New York: Oxford University Press, 2011.

Painter, Nell Irvin. *Sojourner Truth: A Life, a Symbol.* New York: Norton, 1996.

———. "Soul Murder and Slavery: Toward a Fully Loaded Cost Accounting." In Linda K. Kerber, Alice Kessler Harris, and Kathryn Kish Sklar, eds. *U.S. History as Women's History: New Feminist Essays* (125–46). Chapel Hill: University of North Carolina Press, 1995.

Pallas, John, and Bob Barber. "From Riot to Revolution." In Tony Platt and Paul Takagi, eds., *Punishment and Penal Discipline: Essays on the Prison and the Prisoners' Movement* (146–55). San Francisco: Crime and Social Justice Associates, 1980.

Parenti, Christian. *Lockdown America: Police and Prisons in the Age of Crisis.* London: Verso, 1999.

———. "Satellites of Sorrow: Los Angeles, Prison, and Circuits of Social Control." In Deepak Narang Sawhney, ed., *Unmasking L.A.: Third Worlds and the City* (47–65). New York: Palgrave, 2002.

Pascoe, Peggy. *What Comes Naturally: Miscegenation Law and the Making of Race in America.* New York: Oxford University Press, 2009.

Paton, Diana. *No Bond but the Law: Punishment, Race, and Gender in Jamaican State Formation.* Durham: Duke University Press, 2004.

Patterson, James T. *Freedom Is Not Enough: The Moynihan Report and America's Struggle over Black Family Life from LBJ to Obama.* New York: Basic Books, 2010.

———. *Grand Expectations: The United States, 1945–1974.* New York: Oxford University Press, 1996.

Patterson, Orlando. *Slavery and Social Death: A Comparative Study.* Cambridge: Harvard University Press, 1982.

Patterson, William L. *The Man Who Cried Genocide: An Autobiography.* New York: International, 1971.

———. *We Charge Genocide.* New York: International, 1970 (1951).

Payne, Charles. *I've Got the Light of Freedom: The Organizing Tradition and the Mississippi Freedom Struggle.* Berkeley: University of California Press, 1995.

Payne, Les, and Tim Findley, with Carolyn Craven. *The Life and Death of the SLA.* New York: Ballantine, 1976.

Pell, Eve, ed. *Maximum Security: Letters from Prison.* New York: Dutton, 1972.

———. *We Used to Own the Bronx: Memoirs of a Former Debutante.* Albany: State University of New York Press, 2009.

Perkinson, Robert. "'Hell Exploded': Prisoner Music and Memoir and the Fall of Convict Leasing in Texas." *Prison Journal* 89:1 (2009): 54–69.

———. "Shackled Justice: Florence Federal Penitentiary and the New Politics of Punishment." *Social Justice* 21:3 (1994): 117–32.

———. *Texas Tough: The Rise of America's Prison Empire.* New York: Metropolitan, 2010.

Perlstein, Rick. *Nixonland: The Rise of a President and the Fracturing of America.* New York: Scribner, 2008.

Pew Center on the States. "One in 100: Behind Bars in America 2008." February 28, 2008. http://www.pewtrusts.org/en/research-and-analysis/reports/0001/01/01/one-in-100.

Pinderhughes, Charles. "Toward a New Theory of Internal Colonialism." *Socialism and Democracy* 25:1 (2011): 235–56.

Platt, Tony. "Legacies of Radical Criminology in the United States." *Social Justice* 39:2/3 (2014): 1–5.

Platt, Tony, and Paul Takagi, eds., *Punishment and Penal Discipline: Essays on the Prison and the Prisoners' Movement.* San Francisco: Crime and Social Justice Associates, 1980.

Prashad, Vijay. *The Darker Nations: A People's History of the Third World.* New York: New Press, 2007.

———. *The Poorer Nations: A Possible History of the Global South.* London: Verso, 2012.

Prison Action Project. *Freedom on Our Terms: The Case against the Adult Authority.* Oakland, Calif.: Prison Action Project, [ca. 1971].

Provine, Doris Marie. *Unequal under Law: Race in the War on Drugs.* Chicago: University of Chicago Press, 2007.

Pulido, Laura. *Black, Brown, Yellow, and Left: Radical Activism in Los Angeles.* Berkeley: University of California Press, 2006.

Rafter, Nicole Hahn. *Shots in the Mirror: Crime Films and Society.* Oxford: Oxford University Press, 2006.

Raiford, Leigh. "Photography and the Practices of Critical Black Memory." *History and Theory* 48:4 (2009): 112–29.

Rainwater, Lee, and William Yancy. *The Moynihan Report and the Politics of Controversy.* Cambridge: MIT Press, 1967.

Ramparts and Frank Browning, eds. *Prison Life: A Study of the Explosive Conditions in America's Prisons.* New York: Harper Colophon, 1972.

Ransby, Barbara. *Ella Baker and the Black Freedom Movement: A Radical Democratic Vision.* Chapel Hill: University of North Carolina Press, 2003.

Raskin, Jonah. *For the Hell of It: The Life and Times of Abbie Hoffman.* Berkeley: University of California Press, 1996.

Reddy, Chandan. *Freedom with Violence: Race, Sexuality, and the U.S. State.* Durham: Duke University Press, 2011.

Rediker, Marcus. *The Amistad Rebellion: An Atlantic Odyssey of Slavery and Freedom.* New York: Viking, 2012.

———. *The Slave Ship: A Human History.* New York: Penguin, 2007.

Redmond, Shana. *Anthem: Social Movements and the Sound of Solidarity in the African Diaspora.* New York: New York University Press, 2013.

Reed, Adolph, Jr. *Stirrings in the Jug: Black Politics in the Post-Segregation Era.* Minneapolis: University of Minnesota Press, 1999.

Reid-Pharr, Robert. *Once You Go Black: Choice, Desire, and the Black American Intellectual.* New York: New York University Press, 2007.

Retort. *Afflicted Powers: Capital and Spectacle in a New Age of War.* London: Verso, 2005.

Rhodes, Jane A. *Framing the Black Panthers: The Spectacular Rise of a Black Power Icon*. New York: New Press, 2007.

Rhodes, Lorna A. *Total Confinement: Madness and Reason in the Maximum Security Prison*. Berkeley: University of California Press, 2004.

Richardson, Peter. *A Bomb in Every Issue: How the Short, Unruly Life of Ramparts Magazine Changed America*. New York: New Press, 2009.

Ritchie, Beth. *Arrested Justice: Black Women, Violence, and America's Prison Nation*. New York: New York University Press, 2012.

Roberts, Gene, and Hank Klibanoff. *The Race Beat: The Press, the Civil Rights Struggle, and the Awakening of a Nation*. New York: Knopf, 2006.

Robinson, Cedric J. *Black Marxism: The Making of the Black Radical Tradition*. Chapel Hill: University of North Carolina Press, 1983.

———. "Blaxploitation and the Misrepresentation of Liberation." *Race and Class* 40:1 (1998): 1–12.

Rodgers, Daniel T. *Age of Fracture*. Cambridge: Belknap Press of Harvard University Press, 2011.

Rodríguez, Dylan. "Forced Passages." In Joy James, ed., *Warfare in the American Homeland: Policing and Prison in a Penal Democracy* (35–57). Durham: Duke University Press, 2007.

———. *Forced Passages: Imprisoned Radical Intellectuals and the U.S. Prison Regime*. Minneapolis: University of Minnesota Press, 2006.

———. "(Non)Scenes of Captivity: The Common Sense of Punishment and Death." *Radical History Review* 96 (Fall 2006): 9–32.

———. "'Social Truth' and Imprisoned Radical Intellectuals." *Social Justice* 30:2 (2003): 66–80.

———. "The Terms of Engagement: Warfare, White Locality, and Abolition." *Critical Sociology* 36:1 (2010): 151–73.

Roediger, David. *The Wages of Whiteness: Race and the Making of the American Working Class*. London: Verso, 1991.

Rolston, Simon. "Conversion and the Story of the American Prison." *Critical Survey* 23:3 (2011): 103–18.

Rosenbaum, Ron. "Whither Thou Goest." *Esquire*, July 1972, 77–91, 174–87.

Rosenblatt, Elihu, ed. *Criminal Injustice: Confronting the Prison Crisis*. Boston: South End, 1996.

Rosenfeld, Seth. *Subversives: The FBI's War on Student Radicals and Reagan's Rise to Power*. New York: Farrar, Straus, and Giroux, 2012.

Ross, Kristin. *May '68 and Its Afterlives*. Chicago: University of Chicago Press, 2004.

Rossi, Cristina Perri. *State of Exile*. San Francisco: City Lights, 2008.

Rossinow, Doug. *The Politics of Authenticity: Liberalism, Christianity, and the New Left in America*. New York: Columbia University Press, 1998.

Rundle, Frank. "The Roots of Violence at Soledad." In Erik Olin Wright, *The Politics of Punishment: A Critical Analysis of Prisons in America* (163–72). New York: Harper and Row, 1973.

Russell, Diana. "Fay Stender and the Politics of Murder." *On the Issues*, Spring 1991. http://www.ontheissuesmagazine.com/1991spring/Russell_spring1991.php.

Saldaña-Portillo, María Josefina. *The Revolutionary Imagination in the Americas and the Age of Development*. Durham: Duke University Press, 2003.

Salinas, Raúl R., and Louis G. Mendoza. *raúlrsalinas and the Jail Machine: My Weapon Is My Pen: Selected Writings by Raúl Salinas*. Austin: University of Texas Press, 2006.

Samuels, Liz. "Improvising on Reality: The Roots of Prison Abolition." In Dan Berger, ed., *The Hidden 1970s: Histories of Radicalism* (21–38). New Brunswick: Rutgers University Press, 2010.

Sanger, Kerran L. *"When the Spirit Says Sing": The Role of Freedom Songs in the Civil Rights Movement*. New York: Garland, 1995.

Sargent, Frederic O. *The Civil Rights Revolution: Events and Leaders, 1955–1968*. Jefferson, N.C.: McFarland, 2004.

Sassen, Saskia. *Territory, Authority, Rights: From Medieval to Global Assemblages*. Princeton: Princeton University Press, 2006.

Satter, Beryl. *Family Properties: Race, Real Estate, and the Exploitation of Black Urban America*. New York: Metropolitan, 2009.

Sayles, James Yaki. *Meditations on Frantz Fanon's Wretched of the Earth: New Afrikan Revolutionary Writings*. Montreal: Kersplebedeb; Chicago: Spear and Shield, 2010.

Schmidt Camacho, Alicia. "Ciudadana X: Gender Violence and the Denationalization of Women's Rights in Ciudad Juárez, Mexico." *New Centennial Review* 5:1 (2005): 255–92.

Schulman, Bruce J., and Julian E. Zelizer, eds. *Rightward Bound: Making America Conservative in the 1970s*. Cambridge: Harvard University Press, 2008.

Schultz, Bud, and Ruth Schultz, eds. *It Did Happen Here: Recollections of Political Repression in America*. Berkeley: University of California Press, 1989.

Schultz, John. *The Chicago Conspiracy Trial*. Chicago: University of Chicago Press, 2009.

Schuster, Heather W. "Sentenced to Life: AIDS, Activism, and Prison." *Journal of Medical Humanities* 19:213 (1998): 235–54.

Scott, David. "On the Archaeologies of Black Memory." *Small Axe* 12:2 (2008): v–xvi.

Scott, James C. *Domination and the Arts of Resistance: Hidden Transcripts*. New Haven: Yale University Press, 1990.

Scott, Joan. "The Evidence of Experience." *Critical Inquiry* 17:4 (1991): 773–97.

Seale, Bobby. *Seize the Time: The Story of the Black Panther Party and Huey P. Newton*. Baltimore: Black Classics, 1991 (1970).

Self, Robert O. *American Babylon: Race and the Struggle for Postwar Oakland*. Princeton: Princeton University Press, 2003.

Sexton, Jared. *Amalgamation Schemes: Antiblackness and the Critique of Multiracialism*. Minneapolis: University of Minnesota Press, 2008.

———. "People-of-Color Blindness: Notes on the Afterlife of Slavery." *Social Text* 28:2 (2010): 31–56.

Shabazz, Rashad. "Mapping Black Bodies for Disease: Prisons, Migration, and the Politics of HIV/AIDS." In Jenna M. Loyd, Matt Mitchelson, and Andrew Burridge, eds., *Beyond Walls and Cages: Prisons, Borders, and Global Crisis* (287–300). Athens: University of Georgia Press, 2012.

Shah, Nayan. *Stranger Intimacy: Contesting Race, Sexuality, and the Law in the North American West*. Berkeley: University of California Press, 2011.

Shakur, Assata. *Assata: An Autobiography*. Chicago: Hill, 1987.

Shakur, Mutulu, Anthony X. Bradshaw, Malik Dinguswa, Terry Long, Mark Cook, Adolfo Matos, and James Haskins. "Genocide against the Black Nation in the U.S. Penal System." In Joy James, ed., *Imprisoned Intellectuals: America's Political Prisoners Write on Life, Liberation, and Rebellion* (190–97). Lanham, Md.: Rowman and Littlefield, 2003.

Shakur, Sanyika (aka Monster Kody Scott). *Monster: The Autobiography of an L.A. Gang Member*. New York: Atlantic Monthly, 1993.

———. *Stand Up, Struggle Forward: New Afrikan Revolutionary Writings on Nation, Class, and Patriarchy*. Montreal: Kersplebedeb, 2013.

Shakur, Zayd. "America Is the Prison." In G. Louis Heath, ed., *Off the Pigs!: The History and Literature of the Black Panther Party* (247–80). Metuchen, N.J.: Scarecrow, 1976.

Shames, Stephen. *The Black Panthers*. New York: Aperture, 2006.

Shank, Gregory. "Looking Back: Radical Criminology and Social Movements." *Social Justice* 26:2 (1999): 114–34.

Sheehan, Neil, Hedrick Smith, E. W. Kenworthy, and Fox Butterfield. *The Pentagon Papers*. New York: Bantam, 1971.

Shoatz, Russell Maroon. *Maroon the Implacable: The Collected Writings of Russell Maroon Shoatz*. Oakland, Calif.: PM Press, 2013.

Sides, Josh. *L.A. City Limits: African American Los Angeles from the Great Depression to the Present*. Berkeley: University of California, 2006.

Simmons, Gwendolyn Zoharah. "African American Islam as an Expression of Converts' Religious Faith and Nationalist Dreams and Ambitions." In Karin van Nieuwkerk, ed., *Women Embracing Islam: Gender and Conversion in the West* (172–91). Austin: University of Texas Press, 2006.

———. "From Muslims in America to American Muslims." *Journal of Islamic Law and Culture* 10:3 (2008): 254–80.

Simon, Jonathan. *Governing through Crime: How the War on Crime Transformed American Democracy and Created a Culture a Fear*. Oxford: Oxford University Press, 2007.

———. *Poor Discipline: Parole and the Social Control of the Underclass, 1890–1990*. Chicago: University of Chicago Press, 1993.

Simpson, Coltman, with Ann Pearlman. *Inside the Crips: Life inside L.A.'s Most Notorious Gang*. New York: St. Martin's, 2006.

Singh, Nikhil Pal. *Black Is a Country: Race and the Unfinished Struggle for Democracy*. Cambridge: Harvard University Press, 2003.

———. "The Black Panthers and the 'Undeveloped Country' of the Left." In Charles E. Jones, ed., *The Black Panther Party Reconsidered* (57–105). Baltimore: Black Classics, 1998.

———. "Racial Formation in an Age of Permanent War." In Daniel Martinez HoSang, Oneka LaBennett, and Laura Pulido, eds., *Racial Formation in the Twenty-First Century* (276–301). Berkeley: University of California Press, 2012.

Slate, Nico. *Colored Cosmopolitanism: The Shared Struggle for Freedom in the United States and India*. Cambridge: Harvard University Press, 2012.

Smallwood, Stephanie. *Saltwater Slavery: A Middle Passage from Africa to the American Diaspora*. Cambridge: Harvard University Press, 2007.

Smethurst, James Edward. *The Black Arts Movement: Literary Nationalism in the 1960s and 1970s*. Chapel Hill: University of North Carolina Press, 2005.

Smith, Caleb. *The Prison and the American Imagination*. New Haven: Yale University Press, 2009.

Smith, Christopher E. "Black Muslims and the Development of Prisoners' Rights." *Journal of Black Studies* 24:2 (1993): 131–46.

Smith, Paul Chaat, and Robert Allen Warrior. *Like a Hurricane: The Indian Movement from Alcatraz to Wounded Knee*. New York: New Press, 1996.

Sokol, Jason. *There Goes My Everything: White Southerners in the Age of Civil Rights*. New York: Knopf, 2007.

Solomon, Mark. *The Cry Was Unity: Communists and African Americans, 1917–1936*. Jackson: University Press of Mississippi, 1998.

Sommer, Robert. *The End of Imprisonment*. New York: Oxford University Press, 1976.

Spencer, Michael. "Tear Down the Walls." *Synergy* (1971): 3–7.

Spencer, Robyn Ceanne. "Engendering the Black Freedom Struggle: Revolutionary Black Womanhood and the Black Panther Party in the Bay Area, California." *Journal of Women's History* 20:1 (2008): 90–113.

Spieler, Geri. *Taking Aim at the President: The Remarkable Story of the Woman Who Shot at Gerald Ford*. New York: Palgrave Macmillan, 2008.

Spillers, Hortense J. "The Idea of Black Culture." *CR: The New Centennial Review* 6:3 (2006): 7–28.

———. "Mama's Baby, Papa's Maybe: An American Grammar Book." *Diacritics* 17:2 (1987): 65–81.

Springer, Kimberly. *Living for the Revolution: Black Feminist Organizations, 1968–1980*. Durham: Duke University Press, 2005.

Starr, Meg. "'Hit Them Harder': Leadership, Solidarity, and the Puerto Rican Independence Movement." In Dan Berger, ed., *The Hidden 1970s: Histories of Radicalism* (135–54). New Brunswick: Rutgers University Press, 2010.

Staudenmaier, Mike. *Truth and Revolution: A History of the Sojourner Truth Organization, 1969–1986*. Oakland, Calif.: AK Press, 2012.

Stein, David. "A Spectre Is Haunting Law and Society: Revisiting Radical Criminology at UC Berkeley." *Social Justice* 40, nos. 1-2 (2014): 72–84.

Stein, Judith. *The World of Marcus Garvey: Race and Class in Modern Society*. Baton Rouge: Louisiana State University Press, 1991.

Steiniger, Klaus. *Free Angela Davis: Hero of the Other America*. N.p.: National Council of the National Front of the German Democratic Republic, Peace Council of the German Democratic Republic, and GDR Committee for Human Rights, 1972.

Stender, Fay. "Violence and Lawlessness at Soledad Prison." In Erik Olin Wright, *The Politics of Punishment: A Critical Analysis of Prisons in America* (222–33). New York: Harper and Row, 1973.

Stephens, Michelle Ann. *Black Empire: The Masculine Global Imaginary of Caribbean Intellectuals in the United States, 1914–1962*. Durham: Duke University Press, 2005.

Strain, Christopher B. *Pure Fire: Self-Defense as Activism in the Civil Rights Era*. Athens: University of Georgia Press, 2005.

Strange, Carolyn, and Tina Loo. "Holding the Rock: The 'Indianization' of Alcatraz Island, 1969–1999." In Van Gosse and Richard Moser, eds., *The World the Sixties Made: Politics and Culture in Recent America* (219–41). Philadelphia: Temple University Press, 2003.

Streissguth, Michael. *Johnny Cash at Folsom Prison: The Making of a Masterpiece*. New York: Da Capo, 2004.

Stuckey, Sterling. *Slave Culture: Nationalist Theory and the Foundations of Black America*. New York: Oxford University Press, 1987.

Sudbury, Julia, ed. *Global Lockdown: Race, Gender, and the Prison-Industrial Complex*. New York: Routledge, 2005.

———. "Maroon Abolitionists: Black Gender-Oppressed Activists in the Anti-Prison Movement in the U.S. and Canada." *Medians* 9:1 (2009): 1–29.

Sugrue, Thomas J. *The Origins of the Urban Crisis: Race and Inequality in Postwar Detroit*. Princeton: Princeton University Press, 1996.

———. *Sweet Land of Liberty: The Forgotten Struggle for Civil Rights in the North*. New York: Random House, 2008.

Sugrue, Thomas J., and Andrew M. Goodman. "Plainfield Burning: Black Rebellion in the Suburban North." *Journal of Urban History* 33:4 (2007): 568–601.

Sullivan, Larry E. *The Prison Reform Movement: Forlorn Hope*. Boston: Twayne, 1990.

Sullivan, Patricia. *Lift Every Voice: The NAACP and the Making of the Civil Rights Movement*. New York: New Press, 2009.

Summers, Martin. *Manliness and Its Discontents: The Black Middle Class and the Transformation of Masculinity, 1900–1930*. Chapel Hill: University North Carolina Press, 2004.

Sweeney, Megan. *Reading Is My Window: Books and the Art of Reading in Women's Prisons*. Chapel Hill: University of North Carolina Press, 2010.

Tani, E., and Kae Sera. *False Nationalism, False Internationalism: Class Contradictions in the Armed Struggle*. N.p.: Seeds beneath the Snow, 1985.

Teles, Steven M. *The Rise of the Conservative Legal Movement: The Battle for Control of the Law*. Princeton: Princeton University Press, 2008.

Theoharis, Jeanne. *The Rebellious Life of Mrs. Rosa Parks*. Boston: Beacon, 2013.

Thomas, Deborah A. *Exceptional Violence: Embodied Citizenship in Transnational Jamaica*. Durham: Duke University Press, 2011.

Thompson, Heather Ann. "All across the Nation: Urban Black Activism, North and South, 1965–1975." In Kenneth L. Kusmer and Joe W. Trotter, eds., *African American Urban History since World War II* (181–202). Chicago: University of Chicago Press, 2009.

———. "Blinded by a 'Barbaric' South: Prison Horrors, Inmate Abuse, and the Ironic History of American Penal Reform." In Matthew D. Lassiter and Joseph Crespino, eds., *The Myth of Southern Exceptionalism* (74–95). Oxford: Oxford University Press, 2010.

———. *Blood in the Water: The Attica Uprising of 1971 and Its Legacy*. New York: Pantheon, forthcoming.

———. "Empire State Disgrace: The Dark, Secret History of the Attica Prison Tragedy." *Salon*, May 25, 2014. http://www.salon.com/2014/05/25/empire_state_disgrace_the_dark_secret_history_of_the_attica_prison_tragedy/?utm_source=twitter&utm_medium=socialflow.

———. *Whose Detroit?: Politics, Labor, and Race in a Modern American City*. Ithaca: Cornell University Press, 2002.

———. "Why Mass Incarceration Matters: Rethinking Decline, Crisis, and Transformation in Postwar American History." *Journal of American History* 97:3 (2010): 703–34.

Thuma, Emily. "Within and against the 'Prison/Psychiatric State': Coalition Politics and Opposition to Institutional Violence in the Feminist 1970s." *Feminist Formations* (forthcoming).

Tibbs, Donald F. *From Black Power to Prison Power: The Making of Jones v. North Carolina Prisoners' Labor Union*. New York: Palgrave Macmillan, 2012.

Timothy, Mary. *Jury Woman*. San Francisco: Glide and Emty, 1975.

Tonry, Michael. *Punishing Race: The Continuing American Dilemma.* New York: Oxford University Press, 2011.

Torres, Andrés, and José E. Velázquez, eds. *The Puerto Rican Movement: Voices from the Diaspora*. Philadelphia: Temple University Press, 1998.

Tracy, James. *Direct Action: Radical Pacifism from the Union Eight to the Chicago Seven*. Chicago: University of Chicago Press, 1996.

Trupin, James E., ed. *In Prison*. New York: Mentor, 1975.

Tucker, William H. *The Science and Politics of Racial Research*. Urbana: University of Illinois Press, 1994.

Turner, Richard B. *Islam in the African American Experience*. Bloomington: Indiana University Press, 1997.

Tyson, Timothy B. *Radio Free Dixie: Robert F. Williams and the Roots of Black Power*. Chapel Hill: University of North Carolina Press, 1999.

Umoja, Akinyele Omowale. "The Black Liberation Army and the Radical Legacy of the Black Panther Party." In Judson L. Jeffries, ed., *Black Power in the Belly of the Beast* (224–51). Urbana: University of Illinois Press, 2006.

———. "Repression Breeds Resistance: The Black Liberation Army and the Radical Legacy of the Black Panther Party." In Kathleen Cleaver and George Katsiaficas, eds., *Liberation, Imagination, and the Black Panther Party* (3–19). New York: Routledge, 2001.

———. *We Will Shoot Back: Armed Resistance in the Mississippi Freedom Movement*. New York: New York University Press, 2013.

Useem, Bert, and Peter Kimball. *States of Siege: U.S. Prison Riots, 1971–1986*. Oxford: Oxford University Press, 1991.

Van Den Haag, Ernest. *Punishing Criminals: Concerning a Very Old and Painful Question*. New York: Basic Books, 1975.

Varon, Jeremy. *Bringing the War Home: The Weather Underground, the Red Army Faction, and Revolutionary Violence in the Sixties and Seventies*. Berkeley: University of California Press, 2004.

Vigil, Ernesto B. *The Crusade for Justice: Chicano Militancy and the Government's War on Dissent*. Madison: University of Wisconsin Press, 1999.

Wacquant, Loïc. "Class, Race, and Hyperincarceration in Revanchist America." *Daedalus* 139:3 (2010): 74–90.

———. "Deadly Symbiosis: When Ghetto and Prison Meet and Mesh." *Punishment and Society* 3:1 (2001): 95–134.

———. "The New 'Peculiar Institution': On the Prison as Surrogate Ghetto." *Theoretical Criminology* 4:3 (2000): 377–89.

———. *Prisons of Poverty*. Minneapolis: University of Minnesota Press, 2009.

———. *Punishing the Poor: The Neoliberal Government of Social Insecurity*. Durham: Duke University Press, 2009.

Wagmiller, Robert L. "Male Nonemployment in White, Black, Hispanic, and Multiethnic Urban Neighborhoods, 1970–2000." *Urban Affairs Review* 44:1 (2008): 85–125.

Wagner, Bryan. *Disturbing the Peace: Black Culture and the Police Power after Slavery*. Cambridge: Harvard University Press, 2009.

Wald, Karen. "The San Quentin Six Case: Perspective and Analysis." In Tony Platt and Paul Takagi, eds., *Punishment and Penal Discipline: Essays on the Prison and the Prisoners' Movement*, 165–75. San Francisco: Crime and Social Justice Associates, 1980.

Wallace, Michele. *Black Macho and the Myth of the Superwoman*. London: Verso, 1999 (1978).

Wallace-Wells, Benjamin. "The Plot from Solitary." *New York*, February 26, 2014, http://nymag.com/news/features/solitary-secure-housing-units-2014-2/.

Ward, Geoff D. *Black Child Savers: Racial Democracy and Juvenile Justice*. Chicago: University of Chicago Press, 2012.

Ward, Jason Morgan. *Defending White Democracy: The Making of a Segregationist Movement and the Remaking of Racial Politics, 1936–1965*. Chapel Hill: University of North Carolina Press, 2011.

Weaver, Vesla. "Frontlash: Race and the Development of Punitive Crime Policy." *Studies in American Political Development* 21:2 (2007): 230–65.

Weheliye, Alexander G. "Pornotropes." *Journal of Visual Culture* 7:1 (2008): 65–81.

Weinbaum, Alys Eve. "Gendering the General Strike: W. E. B. Du Bois's Black Reconstruction and Black Feminism's 'Propaganda of History.'" *South Atlantic Quarterly* 112:3 (2013): 437–63.

Wendt, Simon. *The Spirit and the Shotgun: Armed Resistance and the Struggle for Civil Rights*. Gainesville: University Press of Florida, 2007.

Western, Bruce. *Punishment and Inequality in America*. New York: Sage, 2007.

Western, Bruce, and Becky Pettit. "Incarceration and Social Inequality." *Daedalus* 139:3 (2010): 8–19.

White, Edmund. *Genet: A Biography*. New York: Knopf, 1993.

Whitman, James Q. *Harsh Justice: Criminal Punishment and the Widening Divide between America and Europe*. New York: Oxford University Press, 2003.

Wicker, Tom. *A Time to Die*. New York: Ballantine, 1975.

Widener, Daniel. *Black Arts West: Culture and Struggle in Postwar Los Angeles*. Durham: Duke University Press, 2010.

Wiener, Jon, ed. *Conspiracy in the Streets: The Extraordinary Trial of the Chicago Eight*. New York: New Press, 2006.

Wilderson, Frank B., III. "The Prison Slave as Hegemony's (Silent) Scandal." In Joy James, ed., *Warfare in the American Homeland: Policing and Prison in a Penal Democracy* (25–34). Durham: Duke University Press, 2007.

Willhelm, Sidney M. *Who Needs the Negro?* Cambridge, Mass.: Schenkman, 1970.

Wilkerson, Isabel. *The Warmth of Other Suns: The Epic Story of America's Great Migration.* New York: Random House, 2010.

Wilkins, Fanon Che. "'A Line of Steel': The Organization of the Sixth Pan-African Congress and the Struggle for International Black Power, 1969–1974." In Dan Berger, ed., *The Hidden 1970s: Histories of Radicalism* (97–114). New Brunswick: Rutgers University Press, 2010.

Williams, Evelyn. *Inadmissible Evidence.* Chicago: Hill, 1993.

Williams, Jakobi. *From the Bullet to the Ballot: The Illinois Chapter of the Black Panther Party and Racial Coalition Politics in Chicago.* Chapel Hill: University of North Carolina Press, 2013.

Williams, Stanley Tookie. *Blue Rage, Black Redemption: A Memoir.* New York: Touchstone, 2004.

Williams, Yohuru. *Black Politics, White Power: Civil Rights, Black Power, and the Black Panthers in New Haven.* Malden, Mass.: Blackwell, 2008.

Williams, Yohuru, and Jama Lazerow, eds. *Liberated Territory: Untold Local Perspectives on the Black Panther Party.* Durham: Duke University Press, 2008.

Williamson, Nigel. *The Rough Guide to Bob Dylan: The Man, the Music, the Myth.* 2nd ed. London: Rough Guides, 2006.

Wilson, James Q. *Thinking about Crime.* New York: Vintage, 1983 (1975).

Winant, Howard. *The New Politics of Race: Globalism, Difference, Justice.* Minneapolis: University of Minnesota Press, 2004.

Winn, Maisha. "'We Are All Prisoners': Privileging Prison Voices in Black Print Culture." *Journal of African American History* 95:3–4 (2010): 392–416.

Winston, Henry. *The Meaning of San Rafael.* New York: New Outlook, 1971.

Woodard, Komozi. *A Nation within a Nation: Amiri Baraka (LeRoi Jones) and Black Power Politics.* Chapel Hill: University of North Carolina Press, 1999.

Woodruff, Nan Elizabeth. *American Congo: The African American Freedom Struggle in the Delta.* Cambridge: Harvard University Press, 2003.

Wright, Erik Olin. *The Politics of Punishment: A Critical Analysis of Prisons in America.* New York: Harper and Row, 1973.

Wu, Judy Tzu-Chun. *Radicals on the Road: Internationalism, Orientalism, and Feminism during the Vietnam Era.* Ithaca: Cornell University Press, 2013.

Yee, Min S. *The Melancholy History of Soledad Prison: In Which a Utopian Scheme Turns Bedlam.* New York: Harper's Magazine Press, 1973.

Young, Andrew. *An Easy Burden: The Civil Rights Movement and the Transformation of America.* New York: Harper Collins, 1996.

Young, Cynthia A. *Soul Power: Culture, Radicalism, and the Making of a U.S. Third World Left.* Durham: Duke University Press, 2006.

Zaretsky, Natasha. *No Direction Home: The American Family and the Fear of National Decline, 1968–1980.* Chapel Hill: University of North Carolina Press, 2007.

Zinn, Howard. *SNCC: The New Abolitionists.* Westport, Conn.: Greenwood, 1965.

Zohrabi, Azadeh. "Resistance and Repression: The Black Guerrilla Family in Context." *Hastings Race and Poverty Law Journal* 9:1 (2012): 167–90.

DISSERTATIONS, THESES, AND UNPUBLISHED SOURCES

Aswad, Kalima. "Coincidences." Unpublished manuscript, in author's files.

———. "Questions Raised about Political Prisoners and My 'Politicization' Which Came during My Days on Death Row." Unpublished manuscript, in author's files.

Barganier, George Percy. "Fanon's Children: The Black Panther Party and the Rise of the Crips and Bloods in Los Angeles." Ph.D. diss., University of California at Berkeley, 2011.

Berger, Dan. "'We Are the Revolutionaries': Visibility, Protest, and Racial Formation in 1970s Prison Radicalism." Ph.D. diss., University of Pennsylvania, 2010.

Burton-Rose, Daniel. "War behind Walls: Work Strikes and Prisoner Self-Organization in U.S. Prisons, 1967–1976." Bachelor's thesis, Oberlin College, 1998.

Chard, Daniel S. "SCAR'd Times: Maine's Prisoners' Rights Movement, 1971–1976." Master's thesis, University of Massachusetts at Amherst, 2011.

Chase, Robert T. "Civil Rights on the Cell Block: Race, Reform, and Violence in Texas Prisons and the Nation, 1945–1990." Ph.D. diss., University of Maryland at College Park, 2009.

Cornell, Andrew Ryan. "'For a World without Oppressors': U.S. Anarchism from the Palmer Raids to the Sixties." Ph.D. diss., New York University, 2011.

Corrigan, Lisa Marie. "Reimagining Black Power: Prison Manifestos and the Strategies of Regeneration in the Rewriting of Black Identity, 1969–2002." Ph.D. diss., University of Maryland at College Park, 2006.

Cummings, Gregory Garth. "The End of an Era: The Symbionese Liberation Army and the Fall of the New Left." Ph.D. diss., University of California at Riverside, 2010.

Fernández, Johanna L. del C. "Radicals in the Late 1960s: A History of the Young Lords Party in New York City, 1969–1974." Ph.D. diss., Columbia University, 2004.

González-Cruz, Michael. "Puerto Rican Revolutionary Nationalism (1956–2005): Immigration, Armed Struggle, Political Prisoners, and Prisoners of War." Ph.D. diss., State University of New York at Binghamton, 2005.

Gossett, Che. "Silhouettes of Defiance: The Memorialization of Historical Sites of Queer and Transgender Resistance in an Age of Neoliberal Inclusivity." Unpublished manuscript. Used with permission of the author.

Janssen, Volker. "Convict Labor, Civic Welfare: Rehabilitation in California's Prisons, 1941–1971." Ph.D. diss., University of California at San Diego, 2005.

Latner, Teishan Aaron. "Irresistible Revolution: Cuba and American Radicalism, 1968–1992." Ph.D. diss., University of California at Irvine, 2013.

LeFlouria, Talitha. "Convict Women and Their Quest for Humanity: Examining Patterns of Race, Class, and Gender in Georgia's Convict Lease and Chain Gang Systems, 1865–1917." Ph.D. diss., Howard University, 2009.

Losier, Toussaint. "'If You Are Black, You Were Born in Jail': The Nation of Islam, Stateville Penitentiary, and the Rise of Racialized Incarceration, 1953–1967." Paper presented at the American Studies Association conference, 2009.

———. "Prison House of Nations: Police Violence and Mass Incarceration in the Long Course of Black Insurgency in Illinois, 1953–1987." Ph.D. diss., University of Chicago, 2014.

McCarty, Heather Jane. "From Con-Boss to Gang Lord: The Transformation of Social Relations in California Prisons, 1943–1983." Ph.D. diss., University of California at Berkeley, 2004.

Murakawa, Naomi. "Electing to Punish: Congress, Race, and the American Criminal Justice State." Ph.D. diss., Yale University, 2005.

Onaci, Edward. "Self-Determination Means Determining Self: Lifestyle Politics and the Republic of New Afrika, 1968–1989." Ph.D. diss., University of Illinois at Urbana-Champaign, 2013.

Pihos, Peter C. "Black Police and Black Power in 1970s Chicago." http://avery.cofc .edu/wp-content/uploads/2012/08/Peter-Pihos-Black-Police-and-Black-Power-ARC-Conference-Paper.pdf.

Schrader, Stuart. "Local Policing Meets Global Counterinsurgency: The 1964 Riots and the Transnational Frontlash." Paper presented at the American Studies Association conference, 2013.

Seigel, Micol. "Cold War Connections: Attica, Latin America, and U.S. Prison Growth." Paper presented at the American Studies Association conference, 2011.

Taylor, Douglas Edward. "Hustlers, Nationalists, and Revolutionaries: African American Prison Narratives of the 1960s and 1970s." Ph.D. diss., University of North Carolina at Chapel Hill, 2002.

Thompson, Heather Ann. "Black Activism behind Bars: Toward a Rewriting of the American Civil Rights Movement." Unpublished manuscript. Used with permission of the author.

Thuma, Emily. "'Not a Wedge, but a Bridge': Prisons, Feminist Activism, and the Politics of Gendered Violence, 1968–1987." Ph.D. diss., New York University, 2011.

Tullis, Tracy. "A Vietnam at Home: Policing the Ghettos in the Counterinsurgency Era." Ph.D. diss., New York University, 1999.

Vaught, Seneca. "Narrow Cells and Lost Keys: The Impact of Jails and Prisons on Black Protest, 1940–1972." Ph.D. diss., Bowling Green State University, 2006.

RECORDS, FILMS, AND VIDEOS

Angela Davis—Like It Is. Folkways, 1971.

Brothers. Written by Edward and Mildred Lewis. Directed by Arthur Barron. Warner Bros. Pictures, 1977.

Cash, Johnny. *At Folsom Prison*. Columbia, 1968.

———. *At San Quentin*. Sony BMG, 1969.

Chicago 10. Written and Directed by Brett Morgen. Paramount Home Entertainment, 2008.

The Day of the Gun. Directed by Ken Swartz. KRON-TV, 2003.

Dylan, Bob. *Desire*. Columbia, 1976.

Lennon, John, and Yoko Ono/Plastic Ono Band. *Sometime in New York City*. Capitol, 2005 (1972).

Midnight Band. *The First Minute of a New Day*. Arista, 1975.

The Murder of Fred Hampton. Directed by Howard Alk. Chicago Film Group, 1971.

Rolling Stones. *Exile on Main Street*. Virgin, 1994 (1972).

Scott-Heron, Gil. *The Mind of Gil Scott-Heron*. Arista, 1978.

———. *Small Talk at 125th and Lenox*. Flying Dutchman/RCA, 1970.

Steel Pulse. *African Holocaust*. RAS, 2004.

———. *Tribute to the Martyrs*. Mango Records, 1979.

Acknowledgments

I was sitting in a grimy doughnut shop near downtown San Francisco, reading a yellowing and long-forgotten 1971 affidavit from a prisoner that someone had chased down for me while cockroaches scurried across the table, and next to me an employee chastised a would-be patron for falling asleep, when I realized that I truly and completely loved my life. I have many people to thank for that, not least among them the many people over many years who have taught me about race, prison, politics, and the world.

My first debt is to all those who shared their stories and their files with me. Within that list, I extend special thanks to Bato Talamantez, David Johnson, Sundi Tate, and Shujaa Graham for recounting especially harrowing histories over several conversations. I offer them and everyone else I interviewed my deepest thanks. Thanks also to the friends and friends of friends—in Illinois, New York, Texas, Washington, D.C., and especially California—who fed or housed me during my various research trips. My deepest appreciation to the various librarians and archivists at both professional and independent collections who facilitated my access to a variety of documents, recordings, and photographs.

As the preface makes clear, the ideas and conversations presented here build on fifteen years of critical engagement with imprisonment. For teaching me about so much more than prison, I owe special gratitude to Sundiata Acoli, Herman Bell, Diana Block, Susie Day, David Gilbert, Naomi Jaffe, Ray Luc Levasseur, Claude Marks, Rob McBride, Jalil Muntaqim, Laura Whitehorn, and Donna Willmott. I developed and worked through my ideas across a variety of collective settings. Special thanks go to those involved in the Critical Prison Studies Caucus of the American Studies Association, Critical Resistance, the Jericho Movement, the National Boricua Human Rights Network, Resistance in Brooklyn, and, above all, Decarcerate PA and the Wild Poppies Collective.

Barbie Zelizer, John Jackson, Barbara Savage, and Michael Delli Carpini supervised my dissertation at the University of Pennsylvania with aplomb. I hope they recognize their lasting intellectual imprint on my work. Marie Gottschalk, Steven Hahn, Rebecca Hill, and Nikhil Singh read and commented on a rough first draft of this project with an eye toward the book it needed to become. Their discerning feedback and inspired support made a huge difference. I thank John Jackson for suggesting and then facilitating the manuscript workshop that enabled such scholarly exchange, as well as for the model of scholarly praxis he continues to provide. Likewise, Dana Barnett, Chris Dixon, Karl Kersplebedeb, Layne Mullett, Sarah Small, and Laura Whitehorn slogged their way through that initial version, I suspect as much out of friendship as of interest, and I thank them for that and much else.

Many people read and commented on various aspects of the manuscript as it wound its way from idea to finished product: Luther Adams, David Allen, Christian Anderson, Raymond Arsenault, Kathleen Belew, Stephen Berrey, Rob Chase, Jasmine Cobb, Cheryl

Cooke, Johanna Crane, Jane Dailey, Chris Dixon, Michael Flamm, Trevor Griffey, Gillian Harkins, Nancy Hewitt, Joy James, Moon-Ho Jung, Kari Lerum, Ania Loomba, Khalil Muhammad, Chandan Reddy, Dylan Rodríguez, Riley Snorton, Whit Strub, Deborah Thomas, Heather Ann Thompson, and Emily Thuma. I thank those who read drafts of different chapters but are sadly not here to see the finished project. Stephanie M. H. Camp was a comrade and colleague from day one. Richard Iton gave excellent feedback on a conference paper that sketched the main argument of this project many years before the book took shape. When he was healthy, Felix Shafer asked me to "keep [his] name out of it"; after some discussion, he agreed that I could mention him in the acknowledgments. I thank him for his guidance and insight at several key moments in the gestation of this project. Their loss is heavy, their memory a blessing.

I thank colleagues in several settings where I presented this work. I got especially rich feedback from the Rutgers Center on Historical Analysis 2011–2012 cohort (special thanks to coordinators Donna Murch and Deborah Gray White for inviting me to be an associate fellow), the University of Pennsylvania's Race and Empire Reading Group in 2012 (special thanks to Ania Loomba for inviting me to the group and to David Eng for facilitating it), and the University of Washington at Bothell's Critical Legal and Prison Studies research group in 2013 for the opportunity to collectively workshop different chapters. Thanks also to the audience members and copanelists at the various conferences at which I presented sections of this work.

Conversations with and support from several others also shaped my thinking about many of the ideas presented here. Among a long list of friends, comrades, and colleagues, my deepest thanks go to Hakim Ali, Brian Behnken, Lincoln Bergman, Lee Bernstein, Lindsey Beutin, Martha Biondi, Rose Braz, Bo Brown, Beth Castle, Daniel S. Chard, Matthew Countryman, Thomas Dichter, Joshua Dubler, Roxanne Dunbar-Ortiz, Sofiyah Elijah, Nava EtShalom, Jeff Frank, Diane Fujino, Craig Gilmore, Ruth Wilson Gilmore, William Goldsby, Alan Gomez, Che Gossett, Sarah Haley, Emily Hobson, Drew Christopher Joy, Robin D. G. Kelley, Scott Kurashige, Vikki Law, Bob Lederer, Sonia Lee, Luce Lincoln, Toussaint Losier, Jenna Loyd, Gordon Mantler, Sharon Martinas, Daniel McGowan, Geoff McNamara, Laura McTighe, Matt Meyer, Anoop Mirpuri, Alejandro Molina, Sarah Morris, Louise Newman, Moira O'Keeffe, Dave Onion, Yasmeen Perez, Laura Pulido, Barbara Ransby, Irit Reinheimer, Dave Roediger, Joshua Kahn Russell, J. Sakai, Luis Sanabria, Micol Seigel, Danielle Sered, Michael Simmons, Zoharah Simmons, Andrea Smith, Louisa Solomon, Dean Spade, Meg Starr, Mike Staudenmaier, Jan Susler, James Tracy, Lokman Tsui, Jeremy Varon, Stephen Ward, Daniel Widener, Craig Steven Wilder, Ari Wohlfeiler, and Natasha Zaretsky. Their insights and support fill the nooks and crannies of this project in so many ways.

Emily Abendroth, Dana Barnett, Rachel Herzing, Saleem Holbrook, and Daniel Martinez HoSang read penultimate drafts of the whole manuscript with careful eyes and pens at the ready. The project is far better as a result of their insights. Norwood Andrews and Donna Murch proved insightful and engaging interlocutors for the University of North Carolina Press. Their comments greatly improved the book, and I especially appreciate their combination of speed and depth in reviewing the manuscript. I am delighted to have this book appear in the Justice, Power, and Politics series and so thankful for the chance to work with Heather Thompson and Rhonda Williams. I thank Heather in particular for having coffee with an anonymous graduate student so many years ago and for all her encouragement ever since.

At the University of North Carolina Press, I was delighted to begin this project with David Perry and complete it with Brandon Proia. David offered a supportive welcome, while Brandon's enthusiasm, vision, and steady support made this a far better project. Mark Simpson-Vos was always a great sounding board, and the entire team at the press was a delight to work with from start to finish. Thanks to Ellen Goldlust for copyediting the manuscript and to Laurie Prendergast for providing another wonderful index.

I thank those institutions that funded aspects of the research, especially the Mellon Dissertation Fellowship of the Council on Library and Information Resources, the University of Pennsylvania's Annenberg School for Communication, and the University of Washington. A grant from the University of Washington Royalty Research Fund allowed me to include many of the images here; a grant from the School of Interdisciplinary Arts and Sciences paid for a weekend getaway to San Juan island to finish the manuscript. Beth Blum, Sha Grogan-Brown, and especially Penny Miller transcribed numerous interviews; Alexandra White helped me square away some of the photo permissions; and first D. Chou and then Jen Rice kept me in good enough physical shape to maintain my work regimen.

I had the good sense to write much of this book in Philadelphia and the good fortune to complete it in Seattle. There are too many people to thank in both places and beyond, but I need to mention at least some of them. Many people make the School of Interdisciplinary Arts and Sciences at the University of Washington at Bothell such a special place. A short list includes Christian Anderson, Lauren Berliner, Bruce Burgett, S. Charusheela, Johanna Crane, Karam Dana, Colin Danby, Sarah Dowling, Ben Gardner, Susan Harewood, Ron Krabill, Kari Lerum, Yolanda Padilla, Janelle Silva, Wadiya Udell, Camille Walsh, and Linda Watts. At the Seattle campus, Gillian Harkins, Moon-Ho Jung, and Chandan Reddy have been especially gracious and welcoming, as was Stephanie Camp prior to her death. Thanks also to the larger crew of Seattleites—among them Angélica Chazaro, Eva Dale, the Flaxhammer family, Trevor Griffey, Alex Guy, Briana Herman-Brand, the Hanson Stansbury family, Jessie Kindig, Mijo Lee, Andrea Marcos, Shon Meckfessel, Tamara Meyers, Dean Spade, Laila Suidan, Emily Thuma, Becka (and Harriet) Tilsen, and Scott Winn—for making two out-of-place East Coasters feel at home in a strange, beautiful new city.

Thanks as well to my families, both the one I was born into and the ones I've made through friendship, love, and shared commitments. The Berger, Barnett, Friedman, and Mozer families have not always understood what I do or why I do it, but they've loved me all the same. I thank my parents, Alan and Naomi, for raising me with words such as "genocide" and "liberation," even if they do not like all the places such vocabulary took me. I thank my nieces and nephews—Eliana and Jackson Berger, Daniel and Annie Mozer—for providing much laughter and joy along the way. The rest of the clan is pretty good too.

Many people keep me thinking, keep me laughing, and keep me whole. Riley Snorton's intellectual breadth and support always amaze me. Suzy Subways is an indefatigable editor and steadfast friend. Josh MacPhee is a great artist and a constant source of inspiration. Walidah Imarisha has been a true friend over many years and many miles.

Same, too, for Molly McClure, always there across a series of changing latitudes. David Stein has been a much-needed resource for theory, history, humor, and television—sometimes simultaneously. Bench Ansfield has been a trusted custodian of the heart, among much else. Mendal Polish is a consummate community builder and always a favorite cousin; I thank her and Nova McGiffert for the refuge they offered at Shabbat dinners. Chris Dixon is an unfailing source of thoughtfulness, intentionality, and insight. I hope I have half the insight, impact, and all-around skill that B. Loewe has; I am grateful for his steadfastness in all things. Likewise, gabriel sayegh is doing the real work in the world, with the full-bodied laughter to make it matter, and he's nice enough to let me tag along. Andy Cornell's wit, wisdom, and musical taste shape everything I do, and I am so glad we are in it together. Claire, Matthew, and Leo made me an honorary member of the Lyons McGuire family, to my eternal delight. Though it is a tragedy that we never lived in Philadelphia at the same time, I am delighted that Sha Grogan-Brown and Matt Kavanaugh took our place there and continue to make it a city we can call home.

I was too distracted by all David Gilbert showed me about friendship and lifelong commitment to realize that he was also teaching me about the political horizons of imprisonment. Claude Marks and Diana Block are trusted keepers and makers of history. Donna Willmott and Rob McBride have long provided a home away from home, full of good food and natural beauty as well as their treasured company. Laura Whitehorn continued to pay for dinner even after the joke ended, and now that I have said so publicly she must keep doing it; Susie Day never fails to raise a smile and sometimes an eyebrow. The two of them together are unstoppable forces of good in the world.

Over many meals, meetings, road trips, games of Marxist scrabble, and other adventures filled with puns and political synergy, Layne Mullett and Sarah Small have been steady inspirations and consistent companions. Emily Abendroth's brilliance and laugh greatly improved the life of the collective. Dana Barnett took a big leap of faith moving across the country for my job. I am grateful for her faith in me and in us, and I thank her for many other leaps of faith over our years together. She had to live with this project more literally than anyone else, had to put up with my pleas for solitude amid the allure of exploring new and familiar places. I hope these pages properly record my love and appreciation.

Over the years, I have been struck by the many ways people work together to imagine worlds of endless beauty when surrounded by such relentless violence. This book is dedicated to three such giants of the heart, spirit, and intellect who are gone far too soon. In dedicating this book to Marilyn Buck, Dara Greenwald, and Stephanie Camp, I want to remember three amazing and amazingly creative women. I also want to remember, each and every day, the loving communities of care that their lives as much as their respective illnesses and untimely deaths brought together. And so the dedication is both to them individually and to the larger collectivities they anchored: for Marilyn, for Dara, for Stephanie, for the worlds they created and called into being.

Index

radical black feminism, 314 (n. 118); sexual violence and, 25, 30, 42, 113, 206. *See also* Davis, Angela Y.

Blaxploitation films, 163, 164–65, 239–40, 313 (n. 92)

Blood in My Eye (Jackson), 14, 134, 141, 158–61, 173, 189, 210, 300 (n. 68), 312 (n. 81)

Boggs, Grace Lee, 231

Boggs, James, 82, 231

Bolt, Nyati Bo, 307 (n. 167)

Bond, Julian, 106, 320 (n. 70)

Boone, John, 190

Bottom, Anthony. *See* Muntaqim, Jalil

Bower, Veronza, xi, xii

Branton, Leo, 201, 202, 204, 210–11

Breckenridge, Charles, 137, 140

Brent, Willie Lee, 295 (n. 107)

Broderick, Henry, 218

Brooks, Edward, 333 (n. 104)

Brothers (1977), 313 (n. 92)

Brown, Bo, 274

Brown, Claude, 291 (n. 39)

Brown, Elaine, 126, 224

Brown, H. Rap (now Jamil Al-Amin), 63, 69, 134, 231

Brown, Herman, 50

Brown, James, 162

Brown, John, 210

Brown v. Plata, 299 (n. 45)

Buck, Marilyn, xii, 380

Buckley, James, 318 (n. 52)

Buckley, William F., Jr., 165, 166

Bukhari, Safiya, 203, 249, 274

Burke, Kathleen, 247

Burnham, Margaret, 201

Burning Spear (publication), 247

Burns, Haywood, 202

Cabral, Amilcar, 43

California: Black Caucus of the California Legislature, 105, 106, 299 (n. 35); decline in prison population, 298 (n. 22); demographic changes within, 16–17; prison expansion and, 16–17, 109, 283 (n. 31), 284 (n. 36), 299 (n. 45); rehabilitative penology and, 97–98, 116, 237; role in prison movement, 16–17; southern diasporic migration to, 16–17, 55–56; Sunbelt power and, 283 (n. 31)

California Institute for Women in Chino, 227

California Prisoners Union, 296 (n. 126), 317 (n. 37). *See also* United Prisoners Union (UPU)

California prison system: Adult Authority (parole board), 97–98; California Youth Authority, 49, 64, 97, 101; indeterminate sentencing, 97–98, 131, 175–76, 237, 266, 298 (n. 14); in-prison trials and, 128–29; liberal prison governance, 98; overcrowding within, 299 (n. 45); prison casualties, 129, 178, 214, 259; rates of imprisonment, 17, 109; Soledad Correctional Facility, 50, 98–99, 307 (n. 5). *See also* Folsom State Prison; Prisons; San Quentin State Prison

Captive nation, 4–6, 9, 15, 21–24, 25, 174, 185–86, 193, 208–9, 226, 267

Carceral state, 10–13, 18, 30, 32, 56, 75, 78, 172, 237, 255, 275

Care work, 168, 276–77, 313 (n. 106)

Carmichael, Stokely, 25, 47–48, 69

Carr, James Jimmy, 50, 132, 133, 166, 305 (n. 147), 305 (n. 149), 333 (n. 108)

Carriger, Little Ray, 135

Carrow, Robert, 216

Carson, Clayborne, 33

Carter, Alprentice Bunchy, 75, 76–77, 107

Carter, Rubin Hurricane, 312 (n. 86)

Cash, Johnny, 88–89, 90, 296 (nn. 136, 138, 139), 297 (n. 140)

Castro, Fidel, 245, 251

Causey, Clarence, 102

Cha-Jua, Sundiata K., 284 (n. 32)

Chard, Dan, 297 (n. 5)

Chase, Robert T., 283 (n. 31), 317 (n. 33), 325 (n. 159)

Hall, Stuart, 314 (n. 117)
Halloran, Pat, 164
Hamer, Fannie Lou, 20–21, 26, 27–28, 41, 42, 48
Hammer, Joan, 132
Hampton, Fred, 75, 76–77, 79, 80, 198
Harlow, Barbara, 282 (n. 7)
Harpers Ferry Raid (1859), 210
Harriet Tubman Prison Movement, 171
Harris, Albert, 208, 211
Harris, Billie Buzzard, 102, 246
Hartman, Saidiya, 180
Hayden, Tom, 106, 127, 128
Health Revolutionary Unity Movement, 204, 242
Hearst, Patty, 237
Henry, Aaron, 36
Henry, Milton, 231
Henry, Richard, 231
Hetland, Gary, 135
Hewitt, Nancy, 320 (n. 86)
Hiestand, Fred, 221, 314 (n. 110), 325 (n. 154)
Hill, Rebecca N., 10, 68, 96, 154, 326 (n. 16)
Hoffman, Julius, 79, 199
Hoffman, Nicholas von, 197
Holder, Willie, 186. See also California Prisoners Union; United Prisoners Union (UPU)
Holdt, Jacob, 317 (n. 35)
Horowitz, David, 166, 313 (n. 101)
Horton, Miles, 43
Howard, Clark, 166, 316 (n. 17)
Huggins, Ericka, 67, 76, 290 (n. 19), 293 (nn. 83, 84)
Huggins, John, 75–77, 107
Hunger strikes, 41, 42, 141, 148, 272, 335 (n. 7), 336 (n. 13)
Huntington, Samuel, 266
Hutton, Bobby, 74

Iced Pig (prison publication), 236
If They Come in the Morning (Davis et al.), 204, 282 (n. 1)
"If We Must Die" (McKay), 149
"I Have Seen America" (poem), 233

Incarceration: convict leasing system, 12, 21–23, 35, 53, 55; as extension of enslavement, 14, 111–12; gendered southern racism and, 42, 55–56; hypercriminalization and, 29–30; penitentiary system, 283 (n. 31), 285 (n. 4); prison as transformative experience, 291 (n. 39); prison reform, 16, 89, 187–88, 191–92, 235–36; sex-segregated institutions, 6; slavery of confinement, 14, 181, 188, 316 (n. 12); surveillance and, 10, 18, 53, 59, 79, 86–87, 118, 154–55, 184, 204, 218, 237, 269, 284 (n. 36). See also Prison pedagogy; Prisons
Incite! Women of Color against Violence, 274
Indians of All Tribes, 87–88
Infiltration/informants: death of BPP activists and, 77, 107, 133, 138; Detroit STRESS unit, 291 (n. 45); FBI informants, 108, 299 (n. 40); George Jackson death and, 138, 305 (n. 147); police informants, 132–33, 152, 305 (n. 147); Spook Who Sat by the Door (Greenlee), 235; Tackwood as informant, 220–21, 325 (n. 152)
Ingram, Rose Lee, 286 (n. 22)
Inside-outside organizing: coalition building and, 277–78; family members and, 106, 131, 147, 168, 171, 175, 278; gatherings and conferences, 170–71; intimate relationships and, 169; media and, 85–87, 226; music and, 85–86; nationalism and, 226–27; popular education and, 126, 161–64, 307 (n. 9), 312 (nn. 86, 87, 88), 313 (n. 89), 313 (n. 92); print culture and, 85–87, 226; prison publications and, 170, 235–37; prison visits, 171; racial consciousness and, 169, 278; racial nationalism and, 169
Instead of Prisons (Knopp and Reiger), 189, 336 (n. 19)
Internal colonialism, 25, 52, 220, 324 (n. 148)

International movements, 3–4, 43, 154–55, 156–57, 295 (n. 107), 310 (n. 39)

Interracial relations: antiracist organizing, 50; black/Latino associations, 139; interracial alliances and, 236; interracial unity, 296 (n. 126); intimate relationships and, 169; miscegenation law repeals, 62; rightlessness, 7–8, 179

Invisibility, 6, 94, 143, 157, 168, 243, 271. *See also* Media visibility; State violence

Invisible Man (Ellison), 115

Iron Fist and the Velvet Glove (CRCJ), 166–67, 170, 314 (n. 117)

Islam, 56–61, 69, 76, 111, 245, 252, 325 (n. 3)

Iton, Richard, 312 (n. 86)

I've Got the Light of Freedom (Payne), 292 (n. 59), 309 (n. 30)

Jackson, Bruce, 190

Jackson, George Lester: biography of, 97; AC takeover, 133–38, 306 (nn. 161, 163), 307 (nn. 165, 167, 168); August 7 rebellion and, 124–25; BGF and, 259–60, 333 (n. 108); black prison radicalism and, 13–14, 91–93; *Blood in My Eye*, 14, 134, 141, 158–61, 173, 189, 210, 300 (n. 68), 312 (n. 81); BPP membership, 101–2; civil lawsuit by, 131, 304 (n. 141); Clutchette and, 270, 335 (n. 7); death of, xi, 96, 133, 141–42, 146–47, 152–53, 155, 156, 306 (n. 163), 307 (n. 168); emotional sensibility of, 112, 114, 155; escape plans of, 133–34, 136–37, 145; film/fictionalized portrayals of, 166, 298 (n. 26), 334 (n. 116); funeral of, 144–47, 300 (n. 46); gender politics of, 113–14, 240–41; Genet and, 110–11, 154, 155; impact on international struggles, 153–55; imprisonment of, 91–92, 97; indeterminate sentencing and, 97, 131, 165; as inspiration, 13, 148, 150–52; as intellectual, 92, 95–96, 109, 118, 119, 150; Jonathan Jackson and, 111, 160–61; Lester on, 119–20; literary expression of, 91–93; masculinity and, 96, 150, 162;

media visibility and, 140–41, 155; memorialization of, 141, 150, 257–59; on mental enslavement, 91, 94, 112; military strategy theory of, 129–32, 158–61; Newton and, 101, 119, 132, 145; pants pocket letter, 133, 305 (n. 149); parole requests, 99, 111; patriarchy and, 112; Pinell and, 131, 133, 335 (n. 7); political consciousness evolution, 91, 92–93, 99–102; prison guard responses to his death, 141, 307 (n. 9); prisons as schools, 94; reading list of, 115, 300 (n. 69); sentencing/imprisonment of, 98–102; slave politics and, 14, 130–31, 152, 183–84; Soledad Brothers case, 102–9, 131; solitary confinement, 116; on spontaneous action, 307 (n. 165); Stender and, 101, 104–6, 109–11, 119–20, 130–31, 164, 184, 258; threats against, 133; weapons and, 298 (n. 18); will and testament of, 131–32. See also *Soledad Brother* (Jackson)

Jackson, Georgia, 97, 114, 145, 146, 183, 244

Jackson, Jesse, 206

Jackson, John, 144, 325 (n. 3)

Jackson, Jonathan Peter: ADJ (After the Death of Jonathan Jackson), xi, 125; August 7 rebellion, 93, 122–29, 302 (n. 104), 303 (n. 117); Black August and, 258; Davis and, 108, 121, 193; death of, xi, 93, 121, 123; emotional discipline of, 300 (n. 61); funeral of, 127–28, 300 (n. 46); George Jackson and, 121, 160–61; as inspiration, 126–27; Newton on, 127, 303 (nn. 112, 114); symbolism of violence and, 160–61

Jackson, Penny, 132, 133

Jackson, Wilbert Popeye, 187, 258, 276–77

Jacobs, James, 243

James, C. L. R., 55

James, Jimmy, 304 (n. 141)

James, Joy, 288 (n. 47), 300 (n. 68)

Jeffries, Hasan, 27, 45

Jericho Amnesty Movement, 274

Lomax, Alan, 287 (n. 27)

Look for Me in the Whirlwind (prison publication), 248

Loomba, Ania, 311 (n. 54)

Lopez, Luis, 134, 140

López Rivera, Oscar, xii

Los Siete de la Raza, 78, 294 (n. 93)

Lynching, 11, 27, 31–32, 92, 181, 287 (n. 33)

Lynn, John, 137

Macheteros, Los, 331 (n. 87)

Madhubuti, Haki, 235

Magee, Ruchell Cinque: early incarcerations of, 192–93; August 7 rebellion trial, 14, 177–79, 192–201, 212–14, 302 (n. 104), 303 (n. 117), 319 (n. 61); continued imprisonment of, 335 (n. 7); Davis and, 122, 177, 178, 193–94, 299 (n. 40), 319 (n. 62); George Jackson funeral, 145; on guerrilla warfare, 303 (n. 124); in-prison trials and, 128–29; IQ test lawsuit, 199–200; Jonathan Jackson and, 127; legal self-representation, 178–79, 192–95, 197–201, 213–14; masculinity and, 195–96, 201; public support of, 168–69, 195–96, 201; renaming as Cinque, 196–97; San Quentin 6 and, 214; on slave politics, 177–79, 182–83, 184, 194–99; Vencer-emos Study Group, 199

Mailer, Norman, 69

Major, Reginald, 185, 194–95, 200, 317 (n. 27)

Malcolm X Grassroots Movement, 274

Malcolm X Liberation University, 232

Manchild in the Promised Land (Brown), 291 (n. 39)

Mancino, Allan, 133, 135, 141

"Manifesto of Demands and Anti-Depression Platform" (Attica Brothers), 3, 282 (n. 5)

Manson, Charles, 246–47

Marion (United States Penitentiary), 238, 240, 244

Marks, Claude, xii, 299 (n. 33), 323 (n. 132), 377, 380

Marx, Gary, 314 (n. 117)

Marxism, 11, 81–82, 94–95, 100–101, 112, 174, 180, 187, 225, 244, 250, 260, 315 (n. 127)

Masculinity: black matriarch thesis, 71, 113, 209–10; Cleaver on, 70–72; hypermasculinity, 71, 125, 163, 175–76, 195–96, 201; Men against Sexism, 227–28; Newton and, 125; prisoner organizing and, 10–11, 61, 73, 96, 126, 133, 150, 162, 175, 195–96, 201

Matthews, John, 121

McClain, James, 122–24, 178, 258–59, 302 (n. 104), 319 (n. 61); Black August and, 258–59

McCray, Kenneth, 137, 140

McGee, Willie, 27

MCI Walpole, 185–86, 190

McKay, Claude, 149

McLennan, Rebecca M., 283 (n. 31)

McTighe, Laura, 325 (n. 3)

Mead, Ed, 227–28, 310 (n. 42)

Media visibility: access to prison conditions, 128; Attica uprising and, 149; collusion with prison systems, 155; George Jackson death and, 140–41, 155; invisibility, 6, 94, 143, 157, 168, 243, 271; journalism reliance on the state, 156–57; spectacular politics and, 30, 34–35, 48, 149, 292 (n. 59); underground press, 84, 86–87, 296 (n. 127); visibility as organizing strategy, 6, 94

Melancholy History of Soledad Prison (Yee), 298 (n. 24), 306 (n. 163), 307 (n. 168), 311 (n. 65), 319 (n. 61)

Memory: Black Solidarity Day protest, 257; memorialization, 14, 141, 143, 144, 149, 176, 261–62; prison in public, 176, 261–62, 275–76; slavery and, 112, 143, 204. *See also* Black August

Meredith, James, 47

Merin, Mark, 221, 325 (n. 154)

Midnight Special (prison publication), 15, 169, 229, 236–37, 239–40, 241–44

Miller, Alvin Jug, 102, 298 (n. 24)

Prisoners Union, 186, 187, 317 (n. 37)

Prison Law Project, 101, 105, 131

Prison movements: impact on social movements, 299 (n. 43), 311 (n. 57); inaccurate claims of its demise, 326 (n. 6); internationalism of, 243–44; military strategy theory of, 129–32; prisoners as revolutionary leadership, 303 (n. 116)

Prison narratives: authentic heroes, 31–32, 96, 119–20, 162; authenticity, 144, 161–62, 167; metaphoric prisoners, 164–65; outlaw antihero tropes, 31–32, 88–89; patriarchal power, 70–72, 164; personal conversion in, 117–18; prison life and, 61; prisoners as dangerous threats, 165–67; as reflection of broader social conditions, 61, 166. See also *Autobiography of Malcolm X*; *Soledad Brother* (Jackson); *Soul on Ice* (Cleaver);

Prison pedagogy: Black August, 15, 229, 257–59, 261–67, 274; collectivism, 168; creativity of, 167–68, 274–75; gangs and, 107, 216, 223, 255, 257, 260–61, 270; gatherings and conferences, 170–71, 274; genocide framework, 153, 158, 232, 244–45, 247; interracial relations, 134; knowledge production, 143–44, 172, 234–35, 245, 272; literacy, 171–72, 171–75, 226, 236; literacy as a, 171–75, 226, 236; media critiques, 157–58; mobilization opportunities and, 23–24, 34, 92, 144, 215–16; print culture and, 226, 236–44, 326 (n. 5); prisoner solidarity, 2, 24, 40, 68, 99–100, 120, 134, 183, 200, 202, 257; relationship building, 168–70; self-education, 157, 171–72, 315 (n. 2); sex segregation, 6, 10, 95, 113, 167, 210; study groups, 39, 50, 58, 64, 100, 143, 172, 175, 199, 234, 245, 272; visibility strategy, 6, 94–95

Prison publications: bibliotherapy and, 116–17, 235–36; black womanhood within, 240–41; gender within, 240–41;

inside-outside organizing and, 170, 235–37; nationalist publications, 225–26, 236–37; New Afrikan nationalism and, 336 (n. 13)

Prison radicalism: black freedom struggles and, 2–11; critical slave politics and, 177–85; freedom and, 2–11, 18–19, 275–78; histories of, 283 (n. 30); impact of, 93–94, 283 (n. 30); self-governance and, 185–92, 255–60. *See also* Blackness; Freedom

Prison reform, 16, 89, 187–88, 191–92, 235–36

Prison Research Education and Action Project, 189, 336 (n. 19)

Prisons: cities as carceral space, 52–54; as classification system, xiv, 5–6, 12, 157, 167; decline in prison population, 298 (n. 22); as gendered space, 6, 210; increase in prisoners, 258, 266–67; journalism and, 128, 225–26, 304 (n. 128); as living archive, xiii; media access to prisoners, 133–34; as metaphor, 6, 52–53, 282 (n. 16); overcrowding, 299 (n. 45); in popular films, 88; prisoner critiques of, 157; prison expansion, 283 (n. 31); prison reform, 16, 89, 187–88, 191–92, 235–36; questioning of the state, 155–57; racial make-up of, 329 (n. 65); rates of imprisonment, 109; as redemption, 110–11; as regime, 18, 26, 40, 54, 86, 115. 245, 252; as regulator of social order, 22; role of Islam in, 56–61, 69, 76, 111, 245, 252; as schools of liberation, 7, 90; slave politics and, 178–85; solitary confinement, 14, 18, 85, 98, 100, 116, 137, 170, 220–21, 270, 274, 335 (n. 7), 336 (n. 13); southern prisons, 21–23, 285 (n. 4); as a state of war, 155; surveillance and, 10, 18, 53, 59, 79, 86–87, 118, 154–55, 184, 204, 218, 237, 269, 284 (n. 36); underground press, 84, 86 87, 296 (n. 127). *See also* California prison system; Incarceration

Rodney, Walter, 154
Rodriguez, Alicia, xii
Rodríguez, Dylan, 306 (n. 163)
Rodriguez, Lucy, xii
Rolling Stones, the, 163
Roots (Haley), 181–82, 316 (n. 14)
Rosenbaum, Ron, 165–66, 302 (n. 104)
Rosenfeld, Seth, 309 (n. 46)
Rubiaco, Urbano, Jr., 137, 140, 307 (n. 5)
Ruchell Magee Defense Committee,
195–96
Rundle, Frank, 304 (n. 134)
Rustin, Bayard, 31, 43

Sadaukai, Owusu, 232
Salinas, Raúl R., 296 (n. 136), 301 (n. 93)
San Quentin 6 case, 14–15, 147–48,
214–22, 324 (n. 139), 325 (n. 152). *See
also* Drumgo, Fleeta; Johnson, David;
Pinell, Hugo Yogi; Spain, John Larry;
Talamentez, Luis Bato; Tate, Willie
Sundiata Sundi
San Quentin State Prison: Adjustment
Center takeover, 133–38, 306 (nn. 161,
163), 307 (nn. 165, 167, 168); Adjust-
ment Center (AC), 98–99; forced
high-security prison tour of, 50; *Out-
law* (prison publication), 84–85, 86,
236, 295 (n. 118), 296 (n. 126); prison-
based courtrooms, 128–29
Sarte, Jean-Paul, 110, 134, 154
Satcher, Earl, 258
Sayles, James (Owusu Yaki Yakubu;
known earlier as Atiba Shanna), 232,
235, 253–54, 256, 331 (n. 89)
Scheer, Robert, 74, 83
Schlosser, Eric, 298 (n. 22)
Scott-Heron, Gil, 162, 244, 312 (n. 87), 329
(n. 61)
Scottsboro Boys campaign, 27, 230,
244–45, 255
Seale, Bobby, 64, 67, 70, 75, 79, 80, 199,
294 (n. 96)
Seize the Time (Seale), 75, 236–37
Self-determination, 15, 79, 99, 234, 267

Sellers, Clyde, 45
Sexual politics: black matriarch thesis, 71,
113, 209–10; hypersexuality, 165–66;
sexual violence, 25, 30, 42, 113, 173, 206,
286 (n. 22); slave politics and, 208–9,
322 (n. 108). *See also* Gender
Shabazz, Betty, 231
Shakur, Assata, 24, 203, 248, 250, 252, 272,
295 (n. 107)
Shakur, Zayd, 83, 248
Shanna, Atiba (born James Sayles; later
known as Owusu Yaki Yakubu), 232,
235, 253–54, 256, 331 (n. 89)
Shepard, Moses, 213
Shepp, Archie, 162
Sherley, Glen, 89
Sherrod, Charles, 40
Shoatz, Russell Maroon, xii, 249–50
Silent protests, 264
Simmons, Michael, 39
Simmons, Steve Kumasi, 2, 3
Simmons, Zoharah, 325 (n. 3)
Simone, Nina, 144–45, 206
Singh, Nikhil Pal, 284 (n. 32), 293 (n. 82)
Siporin, Thomas, 200
Sixth Pan-African Congress, 232
Slate, Nico, 287 (n. 38), 288 (n. 59)
Slausons gang, 76
Slavery: *Amistad* rebellion, 196–97, 319
(n. 68); black matriarch thesis and, 71,
113, 209–10; black womanhood and,
314 (n. 118), 320 (n. 86); carceral experiences of, 282 (n. 13), 289 (n. 4); chattel
bondage/prison bondage, 5, 15–16,
180, 187–88; convict leasing system,
12, 21–23, 35, 53, 55; hypermasculinity of, 195–96, 201; incapacitation,
14, 181, 316 (n. 12); legal self-defense
and, 194–95; Marxist-influenced
labor historians on, 188, 316 (n. 14);
nationalism as resistance to slavery,
9, 14–15, 183–85, 230–35; New Afrikan
politics and, 231–35; prison abolition, 189–92; prison as metaphor for,
178–85; prisoners as captive workers,

185–92; prisoner-slaves, 188–90; prisoner unions and, 185–89; *Roots* (Haley), 181–82, 316 (n. 14); sexual ideologies of, 208–9, 322 (n. 108); slave patrols, 285 (n. 4); slave resistance, 60, 171, 181–82, 185, 197, 316 (n. 14); slavery of confinement, 14, 181, 316 (n. 12); southern diaspora and, 182–83. *See also* Captive nation; Davis, Angela Y.; Magee, Ruchell Cinque

Smith, Caleb, 283 (n. 31), 285 (n. 4)

Smith, Ruby Doris, 40

Sobell, Morton, 301 (n. 93)

Social death, 153, 168, 171, 179, 308 (n. 14)

Sojourner Truth Organization, 254, 255, 314 (n. 118)

Soledad 7, 131, 304 (n. 141), 306 (n. 159)

Soledad Brother (Jackson): overview of, 91–96, 109–20; as black protest literature, 117–18; comparisons to Cleaver, 301 (n. 82); critical responses to, 116–20; Genet and, 110–11, 154, 155; George Jackson's critiques of, 115, 120; literary structure of, 111; marketing campaign of, 93, 110, 119–20; prisoner responses to, 118–19; prison official response to, 116–17; reviews of, 117–19, 301 (n. 82); slave politics in, 91, 183–84; Stender and, 109–11, 119–20. *See also* Jackson, George Lester

Soledad Brothers case, 102–9, 120, 129–31, 164, 193, 211, 304 (n. 141). *See also* Clutchette, John; Drumgo, Fleeta; Jackson, George Lester; Stender, Fay

Soledad Brothers Defense Committee (SBDC), 105–6, 120, 128–29, 164, 193, 304 (n. 141)

Soledad Correctional Facility, 50, 98–99, 307 (n. 5)

Solidarity, 2, 24, 40, 68, 99–100, 120, 134, 183, 200, 202, 257. *See also* Black August

Solitary confinement, 14, 18, 85, 98, 100, 116, 137, 170, 220–21, 270, 274, 335 (n. 7), 336 (n. 13)

Soul on Ice (Cleaver), 70–72, 109, 116, 117–18

Souls of Black Folk (Du Bois), 5

Southern Christian Leadership Conference (SCLC), 8, 24, 26, 34–35, 77

Southern diaspora politics: carceral state and, 45–46, 283 (n. 31); civil rights movement and, 12; convict leasing systems, 12, 21–23; jailhouse experiences, 22–23, 27–30, 35–46, 287 (n. 26), 287 (n. 31); Jim Crow and, 12, 17, 55–56, 283 (n. 31); mass incarceration, 17, 55–56, 283 (n. 31); Montgomery Bus Boycott, 24–25, 31–33; northern urban Black Power movement and, 12–13, 16, 183; politics of respectability and, 9–10, 12, 25, 30; prison communities, 17, 55–56, 283 (n. 31), 290 (n. 19); prisoners rights movement and, 35–46; RNA and, 230; slave politics and, 12, 182–83; spectacular strategies, 286 (n. 19), 287 (n. 31); voluntary arrest, 286 (n. 19), 287 (nn. 26, 31)

Spain, John Larry, 134, 137–38, 140, 182, 214, 215, 216, 309 (n. 46), 316 (n. 17)

Special Weapons and Tactics police units (SWAT), 63, 237, 261

Spectacular politics: Black Power and, 18, 66–67, 292 (n. 59), 309 (n. 30); civil rights movement and, 25–26, 34–35; international law and, 1, 153, 226, 228, 244–46, 275, 329 (n. 61); media and, 30, 34–35, 48, 149, 292 (n. 59); as organizing strategy, 18, 87–88, 273, 292 (n. 59); the panopticon and, 154–55; political uses of, 66–67, 292 (n. 59); spectacles of freedom, 25–26; spectacular violence, 13, 18, 22–23, 25–26, 66–67, 126, 149, 151, 159–60, 237–38, 309 (n. 30); state violence as, 159, 167–68, 237–38, 309 (n. 30); surveillance and, 154–55; symbolic political violence and, 158–61; trials as spectacular political theater, 78–79

Spellman, A. B., 328 (n. 46)

Spook Who Sat by the Door, The (Greenlee), 235

Weinbaum, Alys, 209

Weinglass, Leonard, 106

Weiss, Larry, 131, 167, 324 (n. 139), 325
  (n. 152)

Wells, Warren, 50

West, James, 21

"We Still Charge Genocide" (1977), 245

We Will Return in the Whirlwind (Ahmad),
  75

Whitehorn, Laura, xii, 377, 380

White supremacy: northern criminal justice system and, 52–55, 62;
  slave politics and, 179, 183, 234, 245;
  southern criminal justice system and,
  22–23, 25–26, 28–30, 55–56

Whitman, Steve, 328 (n. 42), 332 (n. 91)

Who Killed George Jackson? (Durden-
  Smith), 166, 305 (n. 147), 306 (nn. 161,
  163)

Whole World Is Watching (Gitlin), 292
  (n. 59), 309 (n. 30)

Why We Can't Wait (King), 37–38

Wicker, Tom, 148

Widener, Daniel, 16, 326 (n. 16)

Wilderson, Frank, 188

Wilkins, Roy, 35

Willhelm, Sidney, 153

Williams, Cecil, Reverend, 106, 107

Williams, Inez, 168, 259

Williams, Landon, 310 (n. 47)

Williams, Louis Randy, 152

Williams, Randy, 310 (n. 47)

Williams, Robert F., 33, 231

Williams, Roosevelt, 304 (n. 141)

Willmott, Donna, xii, 377, 380

Wilmington 10 case, 212

Wilson, James Q., 238

Winston, Henry, 303 (n. 117)

With My Mind Set on Freedom (Davis), 205

Women. *See* Black womanhood; Gender

Woods, Dessie, 203, 227

Wright, Ellen, 110

Wright, Erik Olin, 314 (n. 117)

X, Booker, 58

X, Malcolm: biography of, 58–61; anti-
  imperialism, 59–60; assassination
  of, 50, 150, 152–53; *Autobiography of
  Malcolm X*, 60–61, 117–18, 119, 174; BPP
  and, 65, 66, 69, 72, 231; Davis/King/X
  image anecdote, 224; impact on prison
  nationalism, 59–61, 234; on imprisonment, 12, 48, 49, 51, 59–60, 68, 118, 291
  (n. 35); literary impact of, 117–18, 119,
  174, 236; Moore and, 230–31; NOI and,
  59–60, 61, 65, 225, 232. *See also* Nation
  of Islam (NOI)

Yakubu, Owusu Yaki (born James Sayles;
  known earlier as Atiba Shanna), 232,
  235, 253–54, 256, 331 (n. 89)

Yee, Min S., 99, 102, 306 (n. 163), 307
  (n. 168), 311 (n. 65), 319 (n. 61)

Young, Andrew, 248, 330 (n. 73)

Young, Jock, 314 (n. 117)

Young Lords, 80–81, 125, 148, 242, 308
  (n. 11)

Zimbardo, Philip, 220, 324 (n. 148)

Zirpoli, Alfonso, 221, 224